MANAGEMENT

A Global, Innovative, and Entrepreneurial Perspective

Heinz Weihrich | Mark V. Cannice | Harold Koontz

中国财经出版传媒集团
经济科学出版社
Economic Science Press
·北京·

McGraw Hill

图书在版编目（CIP）数据

管理学：全球化、创新与创业视角：第 15 版 = Management：A Global，Innovative，and Entrepreneurial Perspective，15e：英文 /（美）海因茨·韦里克（Heinz Weihrich），（美）马克·V. 坎尼斯（Mark V. Cannice），（美）哈罗德·孔茨（Harold Koontz）著 . -- 北京：经济科学出版社，2025. 4. -- ISBN 978-7-5218-6933-0

Ⅰ . C93

中国国家版本馆 CIP 数据核字第 2025DG9690 号

责任编辑：孙丽丽　纪小小
责任校对：易　超　徐　昕
责任印制：范　艳

Management

A Global，Innovative，and Entrepreneurial Perspective
Heinz Weihrich　　Mark V. Cannice　　Harold Koontz
经济科学出版社出版、发行　新华书店经销
社址：北京市海淀区阜成路甲 28 号　邮编：100142
总编部电话：010-88191217　发行部电话：010-88191522
网址：www.esp.com.cn
电子邮箱：esp@esp.com.cn
天猫网店：经济科学出版社旗舰店
网址：http：//jjkxcbs.tmall.com
固安华明印业有限公司印装
787×1092　16 开　38.5 印张　760000 字
2025 年 4 月第 1 版　2025 年 4 月第 1 次印刷
ISBN 978-7-5218-6933-0　定价：156.00 元
（图书出现印装问题，本社负责调换。电话：010-88191545）
（版权所有　侵权必究　打击盗版　举报热线：010-88191661
QQ：2242791300　营销中心电话：010-88191537
电子邮箱：dbts@esp.com.cn）

Management

A Global, Innovative, and Entrepreneurial Perspective

Fifteenth Edition

Heinz Weihrich
University of San Francisco

Mark V. Cannice
University of San Francisco

Harold Koontz
University of California
Los Angeles

McGraw Hill Education (India) Private Limited

Heinz Weihrich, Mark V. Cannice, Harold Koontz

Management: A Global, Innovative, and Entrepreneurial Perspective, 15e

ISBN-13: 978-81-942446-0-8

Copyright © 2020 by McGraw Hill Education (India) Private Limited.

All Rights reserved. No part of this publication may be reproduced or transmitted in any form or by any means, electronic or mechanical, including without limitation photocopying, recording, taping, or any database, information or retrieval system, without the prior written permission of the publisher.

This authorized English Abridgement is published by Economic Science Press in arrangement with McGraw-Hill Education (Singapore) Pte. Ltd. This edition is authorized for sale in the People's Republic of China only, excluding Hong Kong, Macao SAR and Taiwan.

Copyright © 2025 by McGraw-Hill Education (Singapore) Pte. Ltd

版权所有。未经出版人事先书面许可，对本出版物的任何部分不得以任何方式或途径复制或传播，包括但不限于复印、录制、录音，或通过任何数据库、信息或可检索的系统。

此英文影印删减版本经授权仅限在中华人民共和国境内（不包括香港特别行政区、澳门特别行政区和台湾）销售。

版权©2020由麦格劳—希尔教育（新加坡）有限公司所有

本书封面贴有McGraw Hill 公司防伪标签，无标签者不得销售。

北京市版权局著作权合同登记号：01-2025-1493

About the Authors

Heinz Weihrich, Ph.D is Professor Emeritus of Global Management and Behavioral Science with the University of San Francisco (USF). He received his doctorate from the University of California at Los Angeles (UCLA) and an honorable doctorate from San Martin University in Peru. He was a visiting scholar at the University of California in Berkeley, the Harvard Business School, and the KAIST Business School in Seoul. His fields of work are management, international management, and behavioral science. Professor Weihrich has taught at Arizona State University, UCLA, and in countries such as Austria, China (Beijing, Shanghai, Hong Kong and Taiwan), Egypt, France, Germany, Jamaica, Kuwait, Malaysia, Mexico, Singapore, South Korea, Switzerland, and Thailand. He has also been a faculty member at the Graduate School of Business in Zurich, Switzerland and at the China European International Business School (CEIBS) in Shanghai, China. He is a visiting professor at Peking University in Beijing, the East China University of Science and Technology (ECUST) in Shanghai, and the University of Applied Science in Ludwigshafen, Germany.

He has authored more than 90 books, including its various editions and translations, and is the coauthor of the classic *Management: A Global Perspective*, formerly coauthored by the late Harold Koontz and the late Cyril O'Donnell (translated into 16 languages in its various editions), *Management: A Global and Entrepreneurial Perspective*, and *Essentials of Management* (also in several language editions). The book *Management* has been the best seller around the world for many years and has been the best seller in the Spanish-language edition for more than 25 years. Another book, *Management Excellence—Productivity Through MBO*, discusses a goal-driven, success-oriented management system. The book has been translated into Chinese, German, Greek, Italian, Japanese, and Spanish. Over 140 of his articles have been published in the United States and overseas in several languages in journals such as *Human Resource Planning*, *Journal of Systems Management*, *Management International Review*, *Long Range Planning*, *The Academy of Management Executive*, and the *European Business Review* ("Analyzing the Competitive Advantages and Disadvantages of Germany with the TOWS Matrix—an Alternative to Porter's Model" was selected as the most outstanding paper in 1999). His current research interests are in improving the global competitiveness of enterprises and nations, strategic management, managerial excellence, and career strategy.

In addition to pursuing his academic interests, Dr. Weihrich has been active in management consulting as well as in management and organizational development in the United States, Europe, Africa, and Asia. His consulting, business, and teaching experiences include working with companies such as Eastman Kodak, Volkswagen, Hughes Aircraft, ABB (Switzerland), Mercedes-Benz, China Resources Co., Guangdong Enterprises (China), and the Institute Pembangunan Keusahawanan (Malaysia). He has given many speeches on global management topics in the United States, Europe, Asia, Mexico, and Peru. He has been elected as a Fellow of the International Academy of Management, the highest honor conferred by the international management movement. For more biographical information on this author, see *International Businessmen's Who's Who*, *Men of Achievement*, *Dictionary of International Biography*, *International Leaders in Achievement*, *Who's Who in California*, *Who's Who in American Education*, *Marquis' Who's Who in the West*, *Who's Who in America*, *Who's Who in the World*, *Five Thousand Personalities of the World*, and his website at http://www.usfca.edu/facstaff/weihrichh/

Mark V. Cannice, Ph.D is Department Chair and Professor of Entrepreneurship and Innovation with the University of San Francisco (USF) School of Management and the founder of the USF Entrepreneurship Program (recognized among the nation's leading entrepreneurship programs, with Forbes ranking USF a top 20 entrepreneurial research university in 2015 and U.S. News ranking the USF undergraduate and graduate entrepreneurship programs among the top 20 in the nation in 2017 and 2018). He has been recognized by the USF School of Management for outstanding research, teaching, service, and student advocacy and support. Dr. Cannice publishes a quarterly report on Silicon Valley Venture Capitalist confidence, which is carried globally on Bloomberg Professional Services in 170 countries (Bloomberg ticker symbol: SVVCCI) and has been referenced in the *Economist*, *Wall Street Journal*, *New York Times*, *BusinessWeek*, CNBC, National Public Radio, and many other media. He published a similar quarterly report for China Venture Capitalist confidence (Bloomberg ticker symbol: CVCCI). Professor Cannice has published in leading academic and professional journals (e.g., *Management International Review*, *Journal of High Technology Management Research*, *Venture Capital: An International Journal of Entrepreneurial Finance*, *Thunderbird International Business Review*, *Journal of Small Business and Entrepreneurship*, *Journal of Private Equity*, *Entrepreneur Magazine*, etc.) and is the coauthor of *Management: A Global and Entrepreneurial Perspective*, 14th edition (2016) (published and distributed by McGraw-Hill in four languages). Dr. Cannice has advised governments and universities from Asia, Europe, and Latin America on entrepreneurial education and has been a Visiting Professor with the University of Paris 2 (Pantheon-Assas), and a Visiting Associate Professor with the Hong Kong University of Science and Technology and Peking University. He founded his own company, Pacific Business Development, Inc., an international trading firm. He also served nine years as a Naval Flight Officer in the U.S. Navy—most notably as a Patrol Plane Mission Commander, leading a 12-member aircrew in military operations throughout the

Pacific—and was promoted to Commander in the U.S. Naval Reserves. He holds a Ph.D. and M.S. from Indiana University Kelley School of Business, an MBA from USF, and a B.S. from the United States Naval Academy *(Annapolis)*.

Harold Koontz, Ph.D was active as a business and government executive, university professor, company board chairman and director, management consultant, lecturer to the top management of organizations worldwide, and an author. From 1950 he was Professor of Management and from 1962 Mead Johnson Professor of Management at the University of California at Los Angeles; from 1978 to 1982 he was World Chancellor at the International Academy of Management. He was the author or coauthor of 19 books and 90 journal articles, including this book, which was originally called *Principles of Management*. His *Board of Directors and Effective Management* was given the Academy of Management Book Award in 1968. After his doctorate at Yale, Dr. Koontz served as Assistant to the Trustees of the New Haven Railroad, Chief of the Traffic Branch of the War Production Board, Assistant to the Vice-President of the Association of American Railroads, Assistant to the President of Trans World Airlines, and Director of Sales for Convair. He acted as management consultant for, among others, Hughes Tool Company, Hughes Aircraft Company, Purex Corporation, KLM Royal Dutch Airlines, Metropolitan Life Insurance Company, Occidental Petroleum Corporation, and General Telephone Company. Professor Koontz's honors include election as a Fellow of the American Academy of Management and the International Academy of Management and a term of service as president of the former. He received the Mead Johnson Award in 1962 and the Society for Advancement of Management Taylor Key Award in 1974 and is listed in *Who's Who in America*, *Who's Who in Finance and Industry*, and *Who's Who in the World*. He passed away in 1984.

In memory of Harold Koontz
A pioneer in management education
who
"untangled the management theory jungle"
by organizing managerial knowledge
according to the management functions,
the framework used in
today's popular textbooks.

To my wife Ursula
Heinz Weihrich

To my family, colleagues, and students
Mark Cannice

Preface

The objective of the 15th edition of this book is to prepare men and women for exciting, challenging, and rewarding managerial careers.

For many years, previous editions of this book have been global best sellers. The Latin American editions have been best sellers in the Spanish-speaking world for more than a decade. This book has had an international orientation long before it became fashionable to be so. The 15th edition builds on that tradition, but it not only adds much new information pertinent to the 21st century, it also includes the very important topics of entrepreneurship and innovation. The entrepreneurial and innovative viewpoints are integrated throughout the book.

Each chapter in this edition has been updated with recent managerial applications, new management insights, and professional activities. For example, interviews with Silicon Valley executives, entrepreneurs, and investors have been included to bring current professional expertise to students. Importantly, this edition also focuses on the professional development and network of its readers, providing exercises that encourage students to use professional networking sites like LinkedIn to enhance their professional profile and network.

As the title *Management: A Global, Innovative, and Entrepreneurial Perspective* indicates, the book takes an international view of managing. At the same time, we realize that it is the entrepreneurial spirit and innovative capability that drives much organizational and personal success. Through our research, travels, and teaching in many countries, we have learned from students, managers, and professors and listened to their challenges. Consequently, they have responded by using this book, which has been translated into 16 languages. The international perspective is essential because national barriers are crumbling and new alliances among companies and peoples are being formed. In this edition, as in previous ones, we have drawn from our business experiences and integrated theory with practice. We also now highlight the Silicon Valley innovative and entrepreneurial perspective in this text. Through our experience of working with many leaders in the business eco-system of Silicon Valley, we strive to include an innovative and entrepreneurial perspective to the practice of management not found in other management texts. Beyond the discussion of managerial issues in the Americas, attention is given to topics in the European Union and Asia, regions that are sometimes neglected in other management textbooks.

WHO WILL BENEFIT FROM THIS BOOK?

All persons who work in organizations and entrepreneurs will benefit from learning about contemporary managing. They include students in colleges and universities—who will one day join organizations—aspiring managers, managers who want to become more effective, other professionals who want to understand the organization in which they work, and entrepreneurs who need to learn how to plan new businesses and communicate their competitive edge to investors. This book is for people in all kinds of organizations, such as governments, health-care providers, educational institutions, and other not-for-profit enterprises.

The managerial functions are essentially the same for first-line supervisors, middle managers, and top executives. To be sure, there are considerable variations in the environment, scope of authority, and types of problems in the various positions. Yet all managers undertake the same basic functions to obtain results by establishing an environment for effective and efficient performance of individuals working together in groups.

ORGANIZATION OF THE BOOK

As in previous editions, managerial knowledge is classified according to the functions of planning, organizing, staffing, leading, and controlling. A systems model, used throughout the book, integrates these functions into a system; it also links the enterprise with its environment. The suggested open systems view is even more important now than in the past, as the external environment has become more challenging through internationalization and more open to communication over the Internet.

Part 1 covers the basics of global management theory and practice; it also introduces the systems model that serves as the framework of this book. To provide the perspective of the book, Part 1 includes chapters on management and its relations to the external environment, social responsibility, and ethics. Moreover, to emphasize the international orientation, it also includes a chapter on global, comparative, and quality management. Parts 2 through 6 discuss the managerial functions of planning, organizing, staffing, leading, and controlling. The relevant principles, or guides, for each function are summarized in Appendix A at the end of the book.

The innovative, entrepreneurial, and international perspectives of managing are emphasized upon in each of the part's closing section. Specifically, the closings for Parts 1 to 6 have an international and entrepreneurial focus section that gives special attention to important issues such as China as a new economic power and the entrepreneurial environment of Silicon Valley. To exemplify the global competitiveness of automobile companies, a global car industry case is presented in each part closing, and to assist new entrepreneurs, we include a business plan outline in the format expected by business professionals in Silicon Valley.

REVISION WORK IN THIS EDITION

While material that was well received over the years has been retained, much new information has been added. For example, this edition builds on the strong characteristics of previous editions, such as breadth, depth, the use of examples, and cases; at the same time, many modern ideas, techniques, and features have been added, especially those providing an Asian perspective of managing. And while the last two editions have included a strong entrepreneurial perspective, we have added a comprehensive discussion of innovation along with numerous innovative perspectives for management to this edition. As innovation provides key competitive advantages for firms, we provided special and comprehensive attention on this element of management in this new edition. And the discussion and application of entrepreneurship is carried on and deepened throughout the book.

In revising this book, we have responded to three major influences. One is the valuable feedback from teachers, scholars, and students in the United States and abroad who have used past editions of this book at various levels of academic and practical management education in a wide variety of universities and enterprises. Another major influence to which we have responded is the great volume of research, new ideas, and advanced techniques, especially those being applied to management from the behavioral, social, and physical sciences as well as information technology. The final influence on the new edition has come from innovative executives, entrepreneurs, venture capitalists, and attorneys who generously shared their experiences.

The emphasis is on managerial practice based on sound theory. Although not all changes can be mentioned here, certain revision work should be pointed out. All chapters have been updated with current international, innovative, and entrepreneurial perspectives on management.

While the whole book has been updated, the following examples illustrate new features in this edition:

- Interviews with leading Silicon Valley executives, entrepreneurs, and investors
- Professional Application Exercises that help each reader develop and grow a professional profile and network with LinkedIn.
- Developing a white paper
- Writing a business plan
- Creating a business case
- Silicon Valley perspectives and cases
- Updated management theoretical perspectives
- And, importantly, the removal of outdated information to help ensure time spent reading is as productive as possible

Part 1 (Chapters 1 to 3) now includes a discussion on management during the global financial crisis and the pursuit of energy independence as well as cases on China and the EU. Part 2 (Chapters 4 to 6) presents new cases on management in India as well as numerous interviews and insights from Silicon Valley. The various issues of organizing are considered in Part 3 (Chapters 7 to 10) focusing on topics such as the "boundaryless" organization as practiced by General Electric along with new insights into the management of intellectual property for competitive advantage.

Staffing issues are examined in Part 4 (Chapters 11 to 13) with the identification of the "best companies to work for" as well as the "most admired companies" based on research by Fortune magazine along with a discussion of human resource management in India and Silicon Valley. The managerial function of leading is discussed in Part 5 (Chapters 14 to 17). Focus on Tata and Cisco has been included along with a perspective on the impact of proper corporate communications. Part 6 (Chapters 18 to 20) deals with the managerial function of controlling and includes new perspectives on managing for operational efficiency and effectiveness as well as new theoretical content on the balanced scorecard approach and value chain activities.

Two appendixes are present at the end. Appendix A summarizes the principles, or guides, for the managerial functions of planning, organizing, staffing, leading, and controlling. The principles allow students and managers to check whether organizational problems can be traced to the violation of managerial principles. Appendix B is even more specific, identifying specific areas critical for the success of managers and organizations. The Management Excellence Survey can be used for managerial and organizational development. The purpose of both appendixes is to facilitate the integration of theory with practice.

LEARNING AIDS

To aid learning, each chapter is organized. It begins with the objectives that are to be accomplished after reading the chapter. The text in the left margins gives an overview of the key points in the chapter. It also aids in reviewing key concepts. Included in the margins as well are websites to refer readers for further information related to the organization or topic under discussion. The use of international, innovative, and entrepreneurial perspectives illustrates the concepts, principles, and theories presented. Each chapter concludes with a summary and a list of key ideas and concepts for review. To relate these ideas and concepts to the "real" world, exercises and action steps are suggested. Readers are encouraged to make use of the World Wide Web by conducting Internet research. A case with questions ends each chapter.

What makes this book different from many other management textbooks is the addition of the closing section in each of the six parts. Each of the closings contains an international focus discussion with a challenging topic, a current entrepreneurial discussion, and a global car industry case. These closings, together with the discussion of international management issues throughout the book, give the book a truly global perspective of management theory and practice.

ACKNOWLEDGMENTS

The late Dr. Harold Koontz is sorely missed. At a memorial session at an Academy of Management meeting, Professor Ronald Greenwood stated that Howdy Koontz was many years ahead of his time. Indeed, his inspiration and guidance popularized the classification of management knowledge according to managerial functions, a framework now used around the world. He will never be forgotten for his contributions to management, preserved in his numerous articles and his many books, which have been continuously updated.

Professor Koontz and we are indebted to so many persons contributing to the various editions that a complete acknowledgment would be encyclopedic. Many scholars, writers, and managers are acknowledged through references in the text. Many managers with whom we have served in business, government, educational, and other enterprises have contributed by word and example. Thousands of managers in all kinds of enterprises in various countries have honored us over the years by allowing us to test our ideas in executive training classes and lectures. Especially helpful were the many executives around the world who generously shared their international experiences. For example, the managers in executive programs in Switzerland, Kuwait, Malaysia, Thailand, and China provided us with opportunities to learn about their cultures and their managerial practices. Specifically, the students and executives at the China Europe International Business School (CEIBS) in Shanghai, Peking University in Beijing, Hong Kong University of Science and Technology, and Chulalongkorn University in Bangkok provided valuable insights into managerial practices in their countries. Moreover, to those executives with whom we have been privileged to work as directors, consultants, or teachers, we are grateful for the opportunity to gain the clinical practice of managing.

Many colleagues, scholars, managers, and students have contributed their ideas and suggestions to this book. The late Professor Keith Davis of Arizona State University was particularly generous with his time. Weihrich's mentors at the University of California, Los Angeles, especially Professor George S. Steiner, have done much to stimulate the interest in the development of the TOWS Matrix for strategic planning. Professors Peter F. Drucker, George S. Odiorne, and Gene Seyna, to whom Weihrich's book *Management Excellence: Productivity through MBO* has been dedicated, have sharpened the thinking about goal-driven management systems and managerial productivity. In previous editions, special appreciation was expressed to those who contributed in many important ways. While they are not named here, their contributions have been important for this edition too. We thank the many executives, venture capitalists, entrepreneurs, and attorneys who generously provided their insightful perspectives to make this book more vital and valuable to its readers.

We would like to thank the many adopters and contributors to the best-selling Spanish-language editions of *Management: A Global, Innovative, and Entrepreneurial Perspective* and the many people at McGraw-Hill Interamericana who were involved in publishing previous editions. They have contributed greatly to make the book a bestseller in the Spanish-speaking world.

For this edition we would like to express our appreciation to all the people at McGraw-Hill India for their interest in and contribution to our book.

Finally, we thank our wives Ursula and Gay for their continuing support.

HEINZ WEIHRICH
MARK CANNICE

List of Figures

Chapter 1

Figure 1.1	Time spent in carrying out managerial functions	7
Figure 1.2	Skills and management levels	8
Figure 1.3	Approaches to management	19
Figure 1.4	The management process, or operational, approach	23
Figure 1.5	Input–output model	24
Figure 1.6	Systems approach to management	25

Chapter 2

Figure 2.1	The organization and its external environment	39

Chapter 3

Figure 3.1	Forms of international business	67
Figure 3.2	The Baldrige award criteria framework: dynamic relationships	89
Figure 3.3	The European Foundation for Quality Management model for business excellence	91
Figure C1.1	TOWS Matrix for the competitive situation of China	98

Chapter 4

Figure 4.1	Close relationship of planning and controlling	109
Figure 4.2	Steps in planning	114
Figure 4.3	Relationship of objectives and the organizational hierarchy	119
Figure 4.4	Systems approach to management by objectives	124

Chapter 5

Figure 5.1	Strategic planning process model	133
Figure 5.2	TOWS Matrix for strategy formulation	139
Figure 5.3	Dynamics of the TOWS Matrix	140
Figure 5.4	Business portfolio matrix	142

Chapter 6

Figure 6.1	Bases for selecting from among alternative courses of action	158
Figure 6.2	The nature of problems and decision making in the organization	160
Figure C2.1	TOWS Matrix—A conceptual model	171
Figure C2.2	TOWS Matrix for India	172
Figure C2.3	TOWS Matrix for Chrysler Corporation before the merger	182
Figure C2.4	TOWS Matrix for Daimler-Benz before the merger	183
Figure C2.5	TOWS Matrix for Daimler-Chrysler after the merger	184

Chapter 7

Figure 7.1	Formal and informal organizations	192
Figure 7.2	Organization structures with narrow and wide spans	194
Figure 7.3	Management by processes	202
Figure 7.4	The organizing process	203

Chapter 8

Figure 8.1	A functional organization grouping (in a manufacturing company)	214
Figure 8.2	A territorial, or geographic, organization grouping (in a manufacturing company)	216
Figure 8.3	Customer departmentation (in a large bank)	217
Figure 8.4	A product organization grouping (in a manufacturing company)	218
Figure 8.5	Matrix organization (in engineering)	220
Figure 8.6	Typical SBU organization (in a large industrial chemical company)	222

Chapter 9

Figure 9.1	Centralization and decentralization as tendencies	234

Chapter 10

Figure 10.1	Formal and informal or informational organizations	251

Chapter 11

Figure 11.1	Systems approach to staffing	272
Figure 11.2	Manager inventory chart	274
Figure 11.3	Personnel actions based on manager supply and demand within the enterprise	275
Figure 11.4	Systems approach to selection. Variables marked with broken lines are staffing and other activities that are discussed in other chapters	282

Chapter 12

Figure 12.1	The appraisal process	305
Figure 12.2	Formulation of a career strategy	314

Chapter 13

Figure 13.1	Manager development process and training	326
Figure 13.2	Analysis of training needs	327
Figure 13.3	Moving an organizational equilibrium	337
Figure 13.4	A model of the organization development process	340

Chapter 14

Figure 14.1	Maslow's hierarchy of needs	365
Figure 14.2	Comparison of Maslow's and Herzberg's theories of motivation	367
Figure 14.3	Porter and Lawler's motivation model	369
Figure 14.4	Equity theory	370
Figure 14.5	Objective or goal setting for motivation	371

Chapter 15

Figure 15.1	The flow of influence with three leadership styles	390
Figure 15.2	Managerial grid	392
Figure 15.3	Continuum of manager–nonmanager behavior	394
Figure 15.4	Fiedler's model of leadership	398
Figure 15.5	Path–goal approach to leadership effectiveness	399

Chapter 16

Figure 16.1	Increased complexity of relationships through increase in group size	414
Figure 16.2	Which comparison line is the same length as the standard line?	416

Chapter 17

Figure 17.1	The purpose and function of communication	427
Figure 17.2	A communication process model	428
Figure 17.3	Information flow in an organization	431

Chapter 18

Figure 18.1	Feedback loop of management control	468
Figure 18.2	Comparison of simple feedback and feedforward systems	471
Figure 18.3	System of inputs for feedforward inventory control	472

Chapter 19

Figure 19.1	Transition from a Gantt chart to PERT	490
Figure 19.2	PERT flowchart	492
Figure 19.3	Matrix for e-commerce	503

Chapter 20

Figure 20.1	Operations management system	515
Figure 20.2	Inventory control model	520
Figure C6.1	The future of global management matrix	535
Figure C6.2	Illustration of milestones and financing to achieve rapid growth and liquidity	540

List of Tables

Chapter 1
Table 1.1	The emergence of management thought	14

Chapter 2
Table 2.1	Arguments for and against social involvement of business	46
Table 2.2	Ethical and unethical use of power	55

Chapter 3
Table 3.1	Managing domestic and international enterprises	65
Table 3.2	Five dimensions of behavior	75

Chapter 4
Table 4.1	Examples of nonverifiable and verifiable objectives	121
Table 4.2	Checklist of manager objectives	122

Chapter 7
Table 7.1	Factors influencing the span of management	196

Chapter 9
Table 9.1	Advantages and limitations of decentralization	238

Chapter 10
Table 10.1	Illustrations of organization culture and management practice	255
Table C3.1	Comparison of business entities	264
Table C3.2	Intellectual property overview	265

Chapter 11
Table 11.1	Major U.S. federal laws governing equal employment opportunity	277

Chapter 12
Table 12.1	Sample questions for appraising managers as managers	308

Chapter 19

Table 19.1	An example of the balanced scorecard approach for operationalizing strategic objectives strategic objective: Be perceived as leading-edge technology firm that delights it customers with innovative products and consistently posts increasing earnings	494

Chapter 20

Table 20.1	Examples of operations systems	515
Table 20.2	Mass production versus lean production managerial practices	525
Table 20.3	Sample value chain activities and managerial actions for a computer manufacturer	528

List of Perspectives

Global Perspectives

Who Manages Best in 2008, the Year of the Global Financial Crisis?	9
The Wisdom of Peter Drucker	17
Apple + Foxconn = iFactory in China	43
Social Responsiveness at Infosys	45
Philanthropy in the Silicon Valley and Around the World is Expanding According to Laura Arrillaga-Andreessen	48
Deng Xiaoping Who Changed China from the Planned Economy Toward a Market Economy	49
Scandals and Corporate Governance	50
Moving Toward a Global Ethics View?	51
Code of Ethics for Government Service	52
Truth in Advertising Regulations Differs in Various Countries	56
Who Will be Leading the Way to Cheap Cars?	67
Multinational Challenges and Opportunities in India for Companies like Wipro	70
Thailand's Competitive Advantage: Pickup Trucks	74
Is There a European Management Model?	77
The Globalization of Chinese Enterprises	81
A Comparison of China and India	83
Is China Losing Its Competitive Advantage?	83
General Motors (GM) Expansion in India	84
Evaluating Alternative Courses for the Indian Automakers to Mitigate the Environmental Impact	116
Value- and Policy-Driven Samsung Strives for Global Recognition	132
Decisions, Decisions, Decisions	154
IBM's Louis Gerstner as Decision Maker	161
Post-it Note Pads	200
Reengineering and Lean Production at Starbucks	201
Organizing the Chrysler Fiat Strategy	219
Organizational Challenges at the TATA Conglomerate	223
GE's Decentralization Under the Leadership of Jeff Immelt	235
Transformational Leadership of Mother Teresa	256
Wipro's Development Center in Atlanta	278

Managing Human Resources at Wal-Mart	280
Where Do Chinese Companies Recruit?	288
HRM in India and Other Countries	293
Creating an Environment that People Enjoy	294
How About a Twitter Performance Evaluation?	307
What is Your Career Path?	316
Career Planning in the New Economy	318
India's Leadership Needs	326
Cisco's Talent Development in India and Elsewhere	335
Wal-Mart's Global Learning	342
Disillusioned Middle Managers	361
The Other Side of the Coin	374
Executive Pay for Performance	375
Corporate Governance	410
What People Say about Committees	413
Pressure Toward Conformity: How Would You Respond?	416
Cross-Cultural Barriers	429
Transformational Communication by American Presidents	432
Country Differences in Explicit and Implicit Communication	438
The Multilingual CEO	438
Special Considerations in Controlling International Companies	464
Examples of Feedback Systems	468
Will China Assume the Role of India in IT Outsourcing?	495
UPS: From Time Management to Information Technology (IT)	497
Volkswagen's High Operating Costs — Should VW Refocus Its Strategy?	518
Quality Circles in Japan	523
Merging the Production Systems of Daimler and Chrysler: A Mission Possible?	526

Innovative Perspectives

The World's Most Innovative Companies	30
The Third Wave: The Knowledge Age	42
The Greening of GM	43
Google's Mission	110
Google's Ten Points	112
Facebook and Monetizing Mobile	124
Apple's Strategy for Innovation	134
Zipcar	142
Nissan's Leaf—The First Mass-Produced Electric Car	146
Boeing's Decision to Go Digital in Developing the 777	160
To Risk or Not to Risk—That Is the Question for Tesla	162
Innovation in India: Microfinancing	164
Learning Innovation from Emerging Countries	164
How 3M Fosters Innovation	165

Reed Hastings, CEO of NETFLIX—From Peace Corps to Netflix	199
Intel Capital	215
Empowerment at Zappos	232
Pandora	252
The Third Wave: The Knowledge Age	253
Pay for Performance at Lincoln Electric	312
How to Lead the Generation Xers?	313
Managing Human Resources at PriceWaterhouseCoopers in China	328
Innovation Education in the United States and Europe	330
How to Get into the Business School of Your Choice	331
Thinking about the Future at Singularity University	332
Making Management Education Relevant	336
Successful Teamwork	341
Interview with Dr. Kern Peng, Project Manager with Intel Corporation	360
Can the Khan Academy Change Education and Motivate Students?	364
QWL in Action	376
Jim Sinegal, Costco's CEO—A Leader with Heart or Smart?	385
Leading in Innovation: Interview with Kern Peng at Intel Corporation	391
Interview with Mr. Reginald Chatman, Senior Manager of Corporate Quality Solutions, Cisco Systems, on Managing Work Teams	419
Communicating with Portfolio Firms of a Venture Capital Company: An Interview with Elton Sherwin, Senior Managing Director at Ridgewood Capital	431
Communicating with White Papers	434
Learning from Newscasters	444
Planning and Control in Engineering	489
Cisco's Approach to "Convergence"	499
Apple's iPhone a Truly Global Product and the New iPhone 5 Introduction	500
GE's Transformation from Products to Services	513
How an Information System Facilitates Operations	519
GE's Contribution to India's Outsourcing Boom	522
Managing Quality for Success	524

Innovation Perspectives

The Digital Impact on GE	72
International Innovation and Entrepreneurship in Silicon Valley	78
The Autonomous Vehicle	115
Was Disneyland Paris Built on the Wrong Assumptions?	162
Post-it Note Pads	224
Trouble at Apple!—The Early Days	247
The Impact of Technologies on Human Resource Management	285
Self-motivation	362

UPS: From Time Management to Information Technology (IT)	436
The Digital Impact on GE	504

International Perspectives

Forbes Asia Ranks Asia's Top 50 Firms in 2018	10
The Battle of the Titans: Boeing vs. Airbus	137
Looking for a Company to Work For? Try Infosys	276

Entrepreneurial Perspectives

Silicon Valley Immersion	11
The Fastest-Growing Companies	12
Social Entrepreneurship in Action	45
Interview with David Epstein, CEO of Sol Voltaics, on Social Responsibility in Entrepreneurial Management	48
Ethics and Trust for the Entrepreneur and Investor	57
Interview with Bryant Tong, Venture Capitalist Partner with Nth Power, on Cultural Differences and Entrepreneurial Management	68
Venture Capital in China	81
Writing a Business Plan for a New Venture	117
Interview with Bryant Tong, Managing Director with Nth Power	123
Interview with Jon B. Fisher, Cofounder of Bharosa, an Oracle Corporation Company	135
Buying Skype, eBay's Mistake?	144
Interview with Jeb Miller, Venture Capitalist Partner with JAFCO Ventures, on the Investment Decision Process	157
What Is in Your Future?	198
Linkedin's Organizational Chart for its IPO S-1 Filing	250
What Do You Do After you Retire or Get Fired?	283
How to Staff an Entrepreneurial Firm?	289
Interview with Shomit Ghose, Venture Capitalist Partner with Onset Ventures, on Evaluating Managers of Venture-Backed Portfolio Firms	306
How to Manage Entrepreneurial Managers	365
Steve Job's Entrepreneurial Leadership	387
Leadership at the Chinese Haier Group and Volkswagen	401
Accepting Negative Feedback	430
Interview with Lori Teranishi, Co-Principal, IQPR, on Developing an Effective Enterprise Communication Strategy	440
In New Ventures Cash Is King	487
Google Brings Quality Measures to the Advertising Industry	514

Leadership Perspectives

Marisa Bellisario Leading Italian ITALTEL	225
Brain Drain at BMW	273

Leadership on the New York Hudson River	386
Ratan N. Tata: Leadership at the TATA Group	388
Leading by Example—Pope Francis	395
Lack of Upward Communication Can Be Disastrous	433
Can a Person Fearful of Public Speaking Become the Head of the Largest Publicly Owned Corporation?	435

Visual

CHAPTER 2

Management and Society: The External Environment, Social Responsibility, and Ethics

Learning Objectives

After studying this chapter, you should be able to:

LO 1 Describe the nature of the pluralistic society and selected environments
LO 2 Understand the impact of the technological and innovative environments
LO 3 Explain the social responsibility of managers and the arguments for and against the social involvement of business
LO 4 Understand the nature and importance of ethics in managing and ways to institutionalize ethics and raise ethical standards
LO 5 Recognize that some ethical standards vary in different societies
LO 6 Realize that trust is the basis for human interaction
LO 7 Update your LinkedIn profile

Learning Objectives

Each chapter begins with learning objectives which outline what each chapter aims at achieving and what the reader should know on its completion.

PART 1 The Basis of Management Theory and Practice

www.apple.com
www.microsoft.com
www.oracle.com

Here are some managers you are familiar with: Tim Cook of Apple, Satya Nadella of Microsoft, and Larry Ellison of Oracle. The president of the United States and the prime minister of India are also managers. Beyond top-level managers, middle-level managers and first-line supervisors also make important contributions to the goal of their organizations.

An **organization** is defined as a group of people working together to create a surplus. In business organizations, this surplus is profit. In nonprofit organizations, such as charitable organizations, it may be the satisfaction of needs or providing additional services. Universities also create a surplus through the generation and dissemination of knowledge as well as providing service to the community and society.

The Functions of Management

Five managerial functions around which managerial knowledge is organized in this book: planning, organizing, staffing, leading, controlling.

Many scholars and managers have found that the analysis of management is facilitated by a useful and clear organization of knowledge. In studying management, therefore, it is helpful to break it down into five managerial functions—planning, organizing, staffing, leading, and controlling—around which the knowledge that underlies those functions can be organized. Thus, the concepts, principles, theories, and techniques of management are grouped into these five functions in this book.

This framework has been used and tested for many years. Although there are different ways of organizing managerial knowledge, most textbooks and authors today have adopted this or a similar framework even after experimenting at times with alternative ways of structuring knowledge.

External elements that affect operation include: economic, technological, social, ecological, political, and ethical factors.

Although the emphasis in this book is on managers' tasks that pertain to designing an internal environment for performance within an organization, it must never be overlooked that managers must operate in the external environment of an enterprise as well. Clearly, managers cannot perform their tasks well unless they have an understanding of, and are responsive to, the many elements of the external environment—economic, technological, social, ecological, political, and ethical factors—that affect their areas of operation. Moreover, many organizations now operate in different countries. Therefore, this book takes a global perspective of managing.

Margin Notes

These notes in the text margins give an overview of the key points in the chapter. They also aid in reviewing key concepts. Also included in the margins are websites for readers to refer to for further information related to the organization or the topic under discussion.

Walkthrough

TABLE 3.2 Five Dimensions of Behavior

Individualism	*Collectivism*
People focus on their own interests and the people close to them. Tasks more important than relationships.	Emphasis on the group, with group support expected. Relationships more important than task orientation.
Large power distance	*Small power distance*
Society accepts unequal distribution of power. Respect for authority. Emphasis on titles and ranks. Subordinates expect to be told what to do. Centralization emphasized.	Society less accepting of power. Employees more open to the idea of dialogue with their superior. Less emphasis on authority, titles, and ranks. Inequality minimized. Decentralization emphasized.
Uncertainty tolerance	*Uncertainty avoidance*
People accept uncertainty and are open to risk taking. Willing to take risks.	Afraid of ambiguity and uncertainty. Structure and formal rules preferred.
Masculinity*	*Femininity*
Aggressive and assertive behavior. Emphasis on material things, success, and money.	Relationship oriented. Quality of life favored. Concern for the welfare of others; caring. Emphasis on modesty.

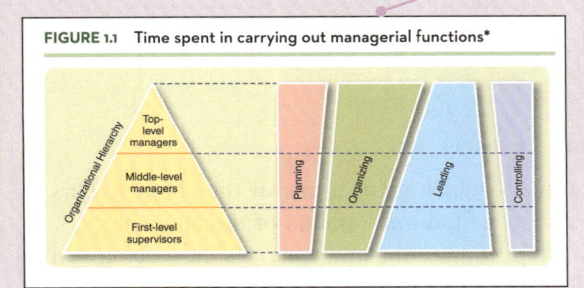

Tables and Figures

The tables give details pertaining to the concepts discussed in the chapter, while the figures illustrate these concepts.

FIGURE 1.1 Time spent in carrying out managerial functions*

Boxed Items

Boxes containing global, innovative, and entrepreneurial perspectives illustrate the concepts, principles, and theories presented in each chapter.

Moving Toward a Global Ethics View?[23]

Throughout the financial crisis, it became clear that the financial architecture reflects a largely outdated postwar model primarily dominated by rich nations of the developed countries. Countries such as India and China still lag on the margins along with other emerging countries. There is evidence that a decisive factor that provoked such a large financial meltdown has been the sub-prime crisis in the United States. The crisis might be a reminder that a financial structure that represents in a more appropriate way the globalized world may be better equipped to create a stable financial and economic environment on a global and a local level.

In handling the crisis, it is also evident that countries like China and India proved much more resilient to overcome difficulties and hardships in comparison with their Western counterparts. Applying the principle of justice in the area of a more and more globalized financial and economic market means therefore to finally recognize that new dominant economic players such as India and China should be given their well-deserved position within a new financial architecture.

The macroeconomic implications of ethics need also to be analyzed in the way countries like China are becoming more and more involved in Africa. Are the business activities truly beneficial and in the vital interest of the people, or is beneath just another neocolonial style reemerging which abuses natural resources, discriminative hiring, unsafe working conditions, and other issues.

A further element that makes ethics a must is the growing impact of consumer associations in developing countries that closely monitor how a product is produced. In addition the ethical and unethical behavior of state and business leaders are under much more scrutiny.

GLOBAL PERSPECTIVE

The Impact of Technologies on Human Resource Management[14]

We live in a time when many activities formerly performed by people are now being done by technology. For example, many of the flights are now guided by the autopilot instead by a person, and passengers themselves do the check-in at many airports now instead by an airline person behind the desk. On the telephone, it is often very difficult to talk to a real person, but instead one talks to voice-recognizing machines. What are the effects of these developments on human resources? An extensive study by McKinsey suggests that many of the jobs will be redefined rather than eliminated. The McKinsey study identified 2,000 work activities. Some 45% of them could be automated with already existing technology. Advances in artificial intelligence cloud probably increase this percentage.

It has been estimated that fewer than 5% of the occupations can be completely automated. But many more occupations can be partially automated. It is clear that many job definitions will need to be changed. Not only the labor-saving costs will be reduced but also the persons in the highest-paid jobs will be aided by technology. For example, lawyers already use text-mining technology to scan thousands of documents, tasks that were performed previously by a clerk. It is estimated that more than 20% of the CEO's time could be automated by technologies that already exist today. Clearly, technology greatly impacts on human resource management.

INNOVATION PERSPECTIVE

Silicon Valley Immersion[2]

Silicon Valley remains the primary destination for those with ambition to develop a high-growth venture. For example, Mark Zuckerberg, the co-founder and CEO of Facebook, realized early on that while he developed Facebook at Harvard University he would need to move to Silicon Valley to take advantage of its eco-system that supported high-growth entrepreneurship. The Silicon Valley eco-system features venture capital to finance high-growth ventures, legal expertise to guide these ventures, and technological and human capital to develop creative new ventures.

Entrepreneurs, firms, universities, and governments from around the world also recognize the value of the Silicon Valley eco-system and desire to learn from it and leverage it to promote successful entrepreneurship and innovation. Groups from around the world visit Silicon Valley to do just that. Programs like the Silicon Valley Immersion Program at the University of San Francisco host groups from Latin America, Asia, and Europe and introduce them to the unique Silicon Valley entrepreneurial eco-system through lectures by local experts, visits to cutting-edge firms, and networking events with local entrepreneurs and investors. Groups from Portugal, Mexico, Argentina, Peru, Chile, China, and elsewhere have come to the University of San Francisco to live and learn in the Silicon Valley eco-system and increase their own capacity to entrepreneurship and innovativeness, the Silicon Valley way. https://www.usfca.edu/management/executive-education/silicon-valley-immersion-program

ENTREPRENEURIAL PERSPECTIVE

Visual

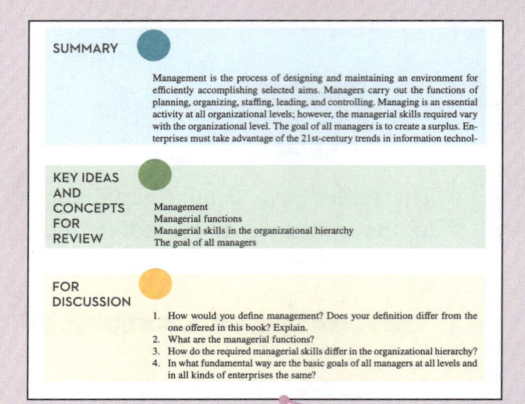

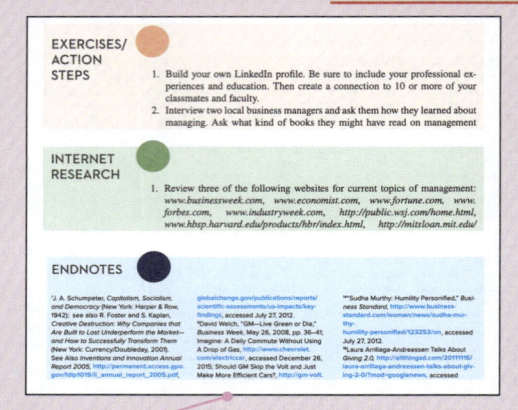

Chapter-end Features

Summary: Each chapter concludes with a summary which gives a gist of the chapter. This will be helpful for the reader to have a quick review of the main points of the chapter.

Key Ideas and Concepts for Review: A list of important terms and concepts has been given at the end of each chapter. This will help readers recapitulate what all has been dealt with in the different topics covered.

For Discussion: These are questions which encourage readers to think about and discuss the topics taught in the chapter.

Exercises/Action Steps: These exercises encourage readers to relate the ideas and concepts given in the chapter to the real world.

Internet Research: This part lists out addresses of some websites which will be useful to readers for further knowledge – both broader and in-depth.

Endnotes: A comprehensive list of material for further reading is provided at the end of each chapter, which will help the readers in upgrading their knowledge.

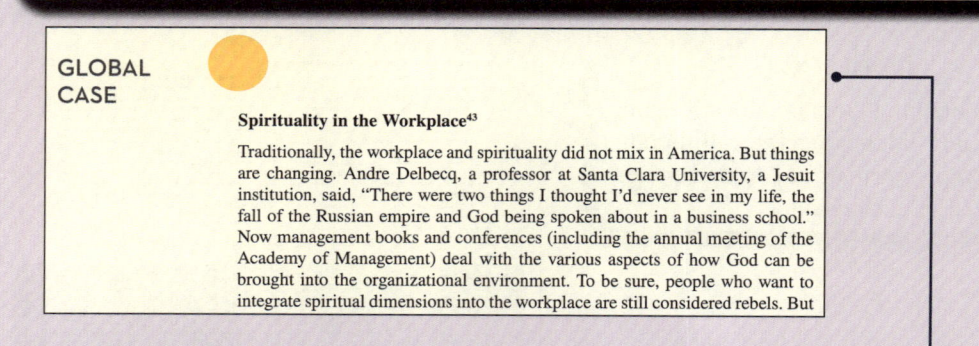

Case

Each chapter ends with a case with questions. This case exemplifies the concepts discussed in the chapter, and its questions help in initiating discussion on the topic.

Walkthrough

PART 1 CLOSING

The Basis of Global and Entrepreneurial Management

The closing part first focuses on the global environment. We will illustrate the international environment by the rising economic power of China (referring to the People's Republic of China in this book). The unique aspects of the entrepreneurial environment in the Silicon Valley near San Francisco in California will then be analyzed. Finally, the discussion will conclude with the global car industry case.

GLOBAL FOCUS: CHINA—THE NEW ECONOMIC GIANT[58]

During the past 25 years, China has been transformed from a Marxist system to an entrepreneurial force. It has been a breathtaking transformation since the country opened its doors. Its continual hyper-growth of 9 to 10 percent annually was achieved without excessive inflation. With this growth rate and a population of about one-fifth of the world's total, China attracts significant amounts of foreign investment.

The revolutionary economic development, spearheaded first by the late Deng Xiaoping (who, by the way, was not an economist) and continued by the then President Jiang Zemin, was accompanied by rising expectations. It was only in 1992 that the goal of the market economy (although a socialistic one) was declared.

In his path-setting speech to the 15th Party Congress on September 12, 1997, Mr. Jiang announced some sweeping changes. His plan was to convert most of the 305,000 state-owned companies to shareholding firms that would be exposed to international competition. Although the issue of ownership was only vaguely mentioned, some companies declared bankruptcy. At that time, state-owned companies still produced about 40 percent of industrial output; but they used most of the available capital, thus constraining more productive, flexible, privately owned firms. Still, the 1,000 largest firms remained under the control of the government; however, most of them would have to compete in the marketplace. Thus, Mr. Jiang had to deal with the industry dinosaurs on which 100 million workers depended for their

Part Closing

The entrepreneurial and international perspectives of managing are emphasized upon in each of the part's closing section. Each of the closings contains an international focus discussion with a challenging topic, a current entrepreneurial discussion, and a global car industry case.

APPENDIX A

Summary of Major Principles or Guides for the Managerial Functions of Planning, Organizing, Staffing, Leading, and Controlling

APPENDIX B

Management Excellence Survey

INTRODUCTION

Broadly speaking, the objectives of management education are (1) to increase managerial knowledge, (2) to improve skills in the analysis of cases and in conducting research, (3) to examine one's attitudes

Appendix

Two appendices are given at the end. Appendix A summarizes the principles, or guides, for the managerial functions of planning, organizing, staffing, leading, and controlling. These principles allow students and managers to check whether organizational problems can be traced to the violation of managerial principles. Appendix B identifies specific areas critical for the success of managers and organizations. The Management Excellence Survey can be used for managerial and organizational development. The purpose of both appendices is to facilitate the integration of theory with practice.

Subject Index

Achievement needs, 372–373, 420
Achievement-oriented leadership, 399
Action plans, 132, 317
Affiliation, or acceptance, needs, 363–376
Alliances (of companies), 66, 136, 139–140
Alliances (of countries), 72–73
Alternatives:
  determination of, 116
  development of, 155
  evaluation of, 153, 155
  identification of, 153
  planning &, 125, 152
  selection from, 152, 158
Amazon.Com, 241–242
Appraisal:
  approaches to, 302–307
  criteria, 301–302
  kinds of, 303–307
  of performance as manager, 302, 307–309, 315
  team approach to, 309–310
  against verifiable objectives, 302–307, 305–307
Apprenticeship system, 347
Aptitude tests, 291

  power vs., 231
  relationships, 248
  responsibility &, 16, 232
  sharing of, 412
  splintered, 412
  teams &, 284
  see also Centralization; Decentralization; Recentralization
Autocratic leaders, 389–390

B2B transactions, 503
B2C transactions, 503
Behavior modification (motivation approach), 371
Benchmarking, 341, 467
Best practices, 341, 345
Biological needs, 366
Board of directors, 120, 410, 412
Body language *see* Nonverbal communication
Boundaryless organizations, 224
"Bounded" rationality, 154
Brainstorming, 164
Bribery, 55–56

Subject Index

A one-level comprehensive subject index will aid the readers in locating the entries in the text accurately and easily.

Brief Contents

About the Authors — v
Preface — xi
List of Figures — xvii
List of Tables — xxi
List of Perspectives — xxiii

PART 1 The Basis of Management Theory and Practice

1. Management: Science, Theory, and Practice — 4
2. Management and Society: The External Environment, Social Responsibility, and Ethics — 38
3. Global, Comparative, and Quality Management — 64

PART 1 CLOSING The Basis of Global and Entrepreneurial Management — 96

PART 2 Planning

4. Essentials of Planning and Managing by Objectives — 108
5. Strategies, Policies, and Planning Premises — 130
6. Decision Making — 152

PART 2 CLOSING Global and Entrepreneurial Planning — 170

PART 3 Organizing

7. The Nature of Organizing, Entrepreneuring, and Reengineering — 190
8. Organization Structure: Departmentation — 212
9. Line/Staff Authority, Empowerment, and Decentralization — 230
10. Effective Organizing and Organization Culture — 244

PART 3 CLOSING Global and Entrepreneurial Organizing — 262

PART 4 Staffing

11. Human Resource Management and Selection	270
12. Performance Appraisal and Career Strategy	300
13. Managing Change through Manager and Organization Development	324
PART 4 CLOSING Global and Entrepreneurial Staffing	347

PART 5 Leading

14. Human Factors and Motivation	358
15. Leadership	384
16. Committees, Teams, and Group Decision Making	408
17. Communication	426
PART 5 CLOSING Global and Entrepreneurial Leading	450

PART 6 Controlling

18. The System and Process of Controlling	462
19. Control Techniques and Information Technology	486
20. Productivity, Operations Management, and Total Quality Management	510
PART 6 CLOSING Global Controlling and Challenges and Entrepreneurial Controlling	534
Appendix A: Summary of Major Principles or Guides for the Managerial Functions of Planning, Organizing, Staffing, Leading, and Controlling	544
Appendix B: Management Excellence Survey	554
Subject Index	562

Contents

About the Authors   v
Preface   xi
List of Figures   xvii
List of Tables   xxi
List of Perspectives   xxiii

PART 1   The Basis of Management Theory and Practice

1. Management: Science, Theory, and Practice   4
   Definition of Management: Its Nature and Purpose   5
   Managing: Science or Art?   13
   The Evolution of Management Thought   13
   History of Selected Managerial Innovations   17
   Patterns of Management Analysis: A Management Theory Jungle?   18
   The Systems Approach to the Management Process   23
   The Functions of Managers   27
   Three Management Perspectives: Global, Innovative, and Entrepreneurial   30
   The Systems Model of Management and the Organization of This Book   31
   Summary   32
   Key Ideas and Concepts for Review   33
   For Discussion   33
   Exercises/Action Steps   34
   Internet Research   35
   Innovation Case   35
   Endnotes   36

2. Management and Society: The External Environment, Social Responsibility, and Ethics   38
   Operating in a Pluralistic Society   40
   The Technological and Innovative Environments   40
   The Ecological Environment   42
   The Social Responsibility of Managers   43
   Ethics in Managing: An Integrative Approach   50

Ethical Theories *51*
Trust as the Basis for Change Management *56*
The Digital Revolution Affects the Technological, Economical, Ecological, Social, and Ethical Environments *57*
Summary 58
Key Ideas and Concepts for Review 59
For Discussion 59
Exercises/Action Steps 60
Online Research 60
Global Case 61
Endnotes 62

3. **Global, Comparative, and Quality Management** 64
International Management and Multinational Corporations *65*
Country Alliances and Economic Blocs *72*
International Management: Cultural and Country Differences *75*
Porter's Competitive Advantage of Nations *84*
Global Innovation Indexes *84*
Gaining a Global Competitive Advantage through Quality Management *86*
Summary 92
Key Ideas and Concepts for Review 92
For Discussion 93
Exercises/Action Steps 94
Internet Research 94
Global Case 94

PART 1 CLOSING The Basis of Global and Entrepreneurial Management 96
Endnotes 103

PART 2 Planning

4. **Essentials of Planning and Managing by Objectives** 108
Types of Plans *110*
Steps in Planning *113*
Objectives *118*
Evolving Concepts in Management by Objectives *123*
Summary 126
Key Ideas and Concepts for Review 126
For Discussion 127
Exercise/Action Steps 128
Online Research 128
Global Case 128
Endnotes 129

5. **Strategies, Policies, and Planning Premises** 130
The Nature and Purpose of Strategies and Policies *131*
The Strategic Planning Process *132*

The TOWS Matrix: A Modern Tool for Analysis of the Situation   *138*
Blue Ocean Strategy: In Pursuit of Opportunities in an Uncontested Market   *140*
The Portfolio Matrix: A Tool for Allocating Resources   *142*
Major Kinds of Strategies and Policies   *143*
Hierarchy of Company Strategies   *144*
Porter's Industry Analysis and Generic Competitive Strategies   *144*
Premising and Forecasting   *145*
Summary   147
Key Ideas and Concepts for Review   148
For Discussion   149
Exercises/Action Steps   149
Online Research   150
Endnotes   150

6. **Decision Making**   152
   The Importance and Limitations of Rational Decision Making   *153*
   Development of Alternatives and the Limiting Factor   *155*
   Heuristics in Decision Making   *155*
   Evaluation of Alternatives   *156*
   Selecting an Alternative: Three Approaches   *158*
   Programmed and Nonprogrammed Decisions   *160*
   Decision Making under Certainty, Uncertainty, and Risk   *161*
   Creativity and Innovation   *163*
   Summary   167
   Key Ideas and Concepts for Review   167
   For Discussion   168
   Exercise/Action Steps   168
   Online Research   169
   International Case   169

PART 2 CLOSING   **Global and Entrepreneurial Planning**   170
   Endnotes   186

PART 3   Organizing

7. **The Nature of Organizing, Entrepreneuring, and Reengineering**   190
   Formal and Informal Organization   *192*
   Organizational Division: The Department   *193*
   Organizational Levels and the Span of Management   *193*
   An Organizational Environment for Entrepreneuring and Intrapreneuring   *196*
   Reengineering the Organization   *200*
   The Structure and Process of Organizing   *202*
   Basic Questions for Effective Organizing   *204*
   Summary   204
   Key Ideas and Concepts for Review   205
   For Discussion   205
   Exercises/Action Steps   205

Innovation Case 206
Internet Research 210
Endnotes 210

8. **Organization Structure: Departmentation**   212
   Departmentation by Enterprise Function *213*
   Departmentation by Territory or Geography *215*
   Departmentation by Customer Group *217*
   Departmentation by Product *217*
   Matrix Organization *219*
   Strategic Business Units *221*
   Organization Structures for the Global Environment *222*
   The Virtual Organization *223*
   The Boundaryless Organization *224*
   Choosing the Pattern of Departmentation *225*
   Summary 226
   Key Ideas and Concepts For Review 226
   For Discussion 227
   Exercises/Action Steps 227
   Internet Research 227
   Global Case 228
   Endnotes 229

9. **Line/Staff Authority, Empowerment, and Decentralization**   230
   Authority and Power *231*
   Empowerment *232*
   Line/Staff Concepts and Functional Authority *233*
   Decentralization of Authority *233*
   Delegation of Authority *235*
   The Art of Delegation *235*
   Recentralization of Authority and Balance as the Key to Decentralization *238*
   Summary 239
   Key Ideas and Concepts For Review 239
   For Discussion 240
   Exercises/Action Steps 240
   Internet Research 241
   Innovation Case 241
   Endnotes 242

10. **Effective Organizing and Organization Culture**   244
    Avoiding Mistakes in Organizing by Planning *245*
    Avoiding Organizational Inflexibility *246*
    Making Staff Work Effective *247*
    Avoiding Conflict by Clarification *249*
    Ensuring Understanding of Organizing *252*
    Promoting an Appropriate Organization Culture *254*
    Summary 257

Key Ideas and Concepts for Review   258
For Discussion   258
Exercise/Action Steps   259
Internet Research   259
Global Car Company Case   259

PART 3 CLOSING   Global and Entrepreneurial Organizing   262
Endnotes   267

PART 4   Staffing

11. Human Resource Management and Selection   270
Definition of Staffing   271
The Systems Approach to Human Resource Management: An Overview of the Staffing Function   272
Situational Factors Affecting Staffing   276
Selection: Matching the Person with the Job   281
The Systems Approach to Selection: An Overview   281
Position Requirements and Job Design   283
Skills and Personal Characteristics Needed in Managers   286
Matching Qualifications with Position Requirements   287
Selection Process, Techniques, and Instruments   289
Orienting and Socializing New Employees   293
Managing Human Resources While Moving Toward 2020   294
Summary   295
Key Ideas and Concepts for Review   296
For Discussion   297
Exercises/Action Steps   297
Internet Research   297
Global Case   298
Endnotes   299

12. Performance Appraisal and Career Strategy   300
Choosing Appraisal Criteria   301
Appraising Managers against Verifiable Objectives   302
Appraising Managers as Managers: A Suggested Program   307
A Team Evaluation Approach   309
Application of Performance Review Software   310
Rewards and Stress of Managing   311
Formulating the Career Strategy   313
Summary   319
Key Ideas and Concepts For Review   320
For Discussion   320
Exercises/Action Steps   321
Internet Research   321
Global Case   321
Endnotes   322

13. Managing Change through Manager and Organization Development — 324
Manager Development Process and Training *325*
Approaches to Manager Development: On-the-Job Training *328*
Approaches to Manager Development: Internal and External Training *330*
Evaluation and Relevance of Training Programs *335*
Managing Change *336*
Organizational Conflict *338*
Organization Development *339*
The Learning Organization *341*
Summary 342
Key Ideas and Concepts for Review 343
For Discussion 343
Exercises/Action Steps 344
Internet Research 344
Global Case 344

PART 4 CLOSING   Global and Entrepreneurial Staffing — 347
Endnotes 354

PART 5   Leading
---

14. Human Factors and Motivation — 358
Human Factors in Managing *359*
Motivation *361*
An Early Behavioral Model: McGregor's Theory X and Theory Y *362*
Maslow's Hierarchy of Needs Theory *364*
Alderfer's ERG Theory *366*
Herzberg's Motivation–Hygiene Theory *366*
The Expectancy Theory of Motivation *367*
Equity Theory *369*
Goal Setting Theory of Motivation *370*
Skinner's Reinforcement Theory *371*
McClelland's Needs Theory of Motivation *372*
Special Motivational Techniques *373*
Job Enrichment *377*
A Systems and Contingency Approach to Motivation *378*
Summary 379
Key Ideas and Concepts for Review 380
For Discussion 380
Exercises/Action Steps 381
Internet Research 381
Innovative Perspective 381
Endnotes 383

15. Leadership — 384
Defining Leadership *385*
Ingredients of Leadership *386*

Trait Approaches to Leadership *388*
Charismatic Leadership Approach *389*
Leadership Behavior and Styles *389*
Situational, or Contingency, Approaches to Leadership *395*
Transactional and Transformational Leadership *400*
Other Leadership Theories and Approaches *402*
Summary 402
Key Ideas and Concepts for Review 403
For Discussion 403
Exercises/Action Steps 404
Internet Research 404
Innovation Case 404
Endnotes 407

16. Committees, Teams, and Group Decision Making — 408
The Nature of Committees and Groups *409*
Reasons for Using Committees and Groups *411*
Disadvantages and Misuse of Committees *413*
Successful Operation of Committees and Groups *413*
Additional Group Concepts *415*
Teams *418*
Conflict in Committees, Groups, and Teams *419*
Summary 420
Key Ideas and Concepts for Review 421
For Discussion 421
Exercises/Action Steps 422
Internet Research 422
Global Case 422
Endnotes 424

17. Communication — 426
The Purpose of Communication *427*
The Communication Process *428*
Communication in the Organization *430*
Barriers and Breakdowns in Communication *436*
Toward Effective Communication *440*
Electronic Media in Communication *444*
Summary 446
Key Ideas and Concepts for Review 446
For Discussion 447
Exercises/Action Steps 447
Internet Research 448
Global Case 448

PART 5 CLOSING Global and Entrepreneurial Leading — 450
Endnotes 458

PART 6 Controlling

18. The System and Process of Controlling — 462
  The Basic Control Process *463*
  Business Analytics *464*
  Critical Control Points, Standards, and Benchmarking *465*
  Control as a Feedback System *467*
  Real-Time Information and Control *469*
  Feedforward, or Preventive, Control *470*
  Control of Overall Performance *473*
  Profit and Loss Control *474*
  Control through Return on Investment *474*
  Management Audits and Accounting Firms *475*
  The Balanced Scorecard *475*
  Bureaucratic and Clan Control *476*
  Requirements for Effective Controls *476*
  Summary 479
  Key Ideas and Concepts for Review 480
  For Discussion 480
  Exercises/Action Steps 481
  Internet Research 481
  Global Case 481
  Endnotes 485

19. Control Techniques and Information Technology — 486
  The Budget as a Control Device *487*
  Traditional Nonbudgetary Control Devices *488*
  Time–Event Network Analyses *489*
  The Balanced Scorecard *493*
  Information Technology *494*
  Opportunities and Challenges Created by Information Technology *497*
  The Digital Economy, E-Commerce, and M-Commerce *502*
  Summary 505
  Key Ideas and Concepts for Review 506
  For Discussion 507
  Exercises/Action Steps 507
  Innovation Case 508
  Endnotes 509

20. Productivity, Operations Management, and Total Quality Management — 510
  Productivity Problems and Measurement *511*
  Production and Operations Management: Manufacturing and Service *512*
  Quality Measurement in the Information Age *513*

The Operations Management System *514*
Tools and Techniques for Improving Productivity *519*
Supply Chain and Value Chain Management *527*
Summary 529
Key Ideas and Concepts for Review 530
For Discussion 530
Exercises/Action Steps 531
Internet Research 531
Global Car Industry Case 532

PART 6 CLOSING Global Controlling and Challenges and Entrepreneurial Controlling 534
    Endnotes 542

Appendix A: **Summary of Major Principles or Guides for the Managerial Functions of Planning, Organizing, Staffing, Leading, and Controlling** 544

Appendix B: **Management Excellence Survey** 554

Subject Index 562

Management

A Global, Innovative, and
Entrepreneurial Perspective

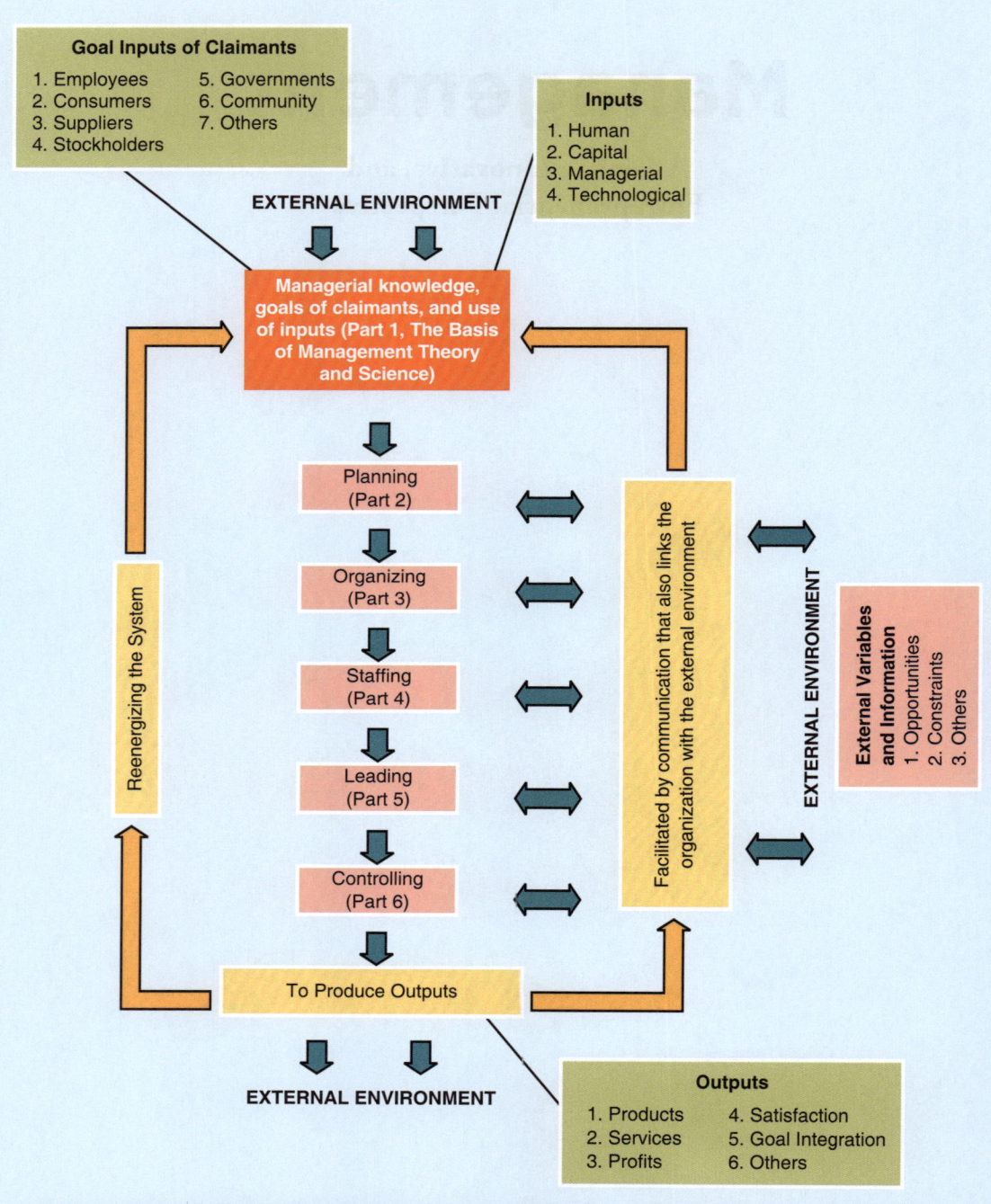

Goal Inputs of Claimants
1. Employees
2. Consumers
3. Suppliers
4. Stockholders
5. Governments
6. Community
7. Others

Inputs
1. Human
2. Capital
3. Managerial
4. Technological

EXTERNAL ENVIRONMENT

Managerial knowledge, goals of claimants, and use of inputs (Part 1, The Basis of Management Theory and Science)

- Planning (Part 2)
- Organizing (Part 3)
- Staffing (Part 4)
- Leading (Part 5)
- Controlling (Part 6)

Reenergizing the System

Facilitated by communication that also links the organization with the external environment

EXTERNAL ENVIRONMENT

External Variables and Information
1. Opportunities
2. Constraints
3. Others

To Produce Outputs

EXTERNAL ENVIRONMENT

Outputs
1. Products
2. Services
3. Profits
4. Satisfaction
5. Goal Integration
6. Others

SYSTEMS APPROACH TO MANAGEMENT: THE BASIS OF GLOBAL MANAGEMENT THEORY AND PRACTICE

PART 1

The Basis of Management Theory and Practice

Chapter 1: Management: Science, Theory, and Practice
Chapter 2: Management and Society: The External Environment, Social Responsibility, and Ethics
Chapter 3: Global, Comparative, and Quality Management
Part 1 Closing: The Basis of Global and Entrepreneurial Management

CHAPTER 1

Management: Science, Theory, and Practice

Learning Objectives

After studying this chapter, you should be able to:

LO 1   Explain the nature and purpose of management

LO 2   Understand that management, as used in this book, applies to all kinds of organizations and to managers at all organizational levels

LO 3   Recognize that the aim of all managers is to create a surplus

LO 4   Identify the trends in technology and globalization that impact the practice of management

LO 5   Explain the concepts of productivity, effectiveness, and efficiency

LO 6   Describe the evolution of management and some foundational and recent contributions to management thought

LO 7   Describe the various approaches to management, their contributions, as well as their limitations

LO 8   Realize that managing requires a systems approach and that practice must always take into account situations and contingencies

LO 9   Define the managerial functions of planning, organizing, staffing, leading, and controlling

LO 10 Understand how this book is organized

LO 11 Identify a successful manager's career path that you may wish to emulate

LO 12 Identify a relevant management software that you may be expected to use in your career

LO 13 Build initial LinkedIn Profile: www.LinkedIn.com

One of the most important human activities is managing. Ever since people began forming groups to accomplish aims they could not achieve as individuals, managing has been essential to ensure the coordination of individual efforts. As society has come to rely increasingly on group effort, and as many organized groups have become very large, the tasks of managers have been gaining importance. The purpose of this book is to promote excellence among all persons in organizations, especially among managers, aspiring managers, and other professionals.*

DEFINITION OF MANAGEMENT: ITS NATURE AND PURPOSE

Management is the process of designing and maintaining an environment in which individuals, working together in groups, efficiently accomplish selected aims. However, this basic definition needs to be expanded:

- As managers, people carry out the managerial functions of planning, organizing, staffing, leading, and controlling
- Management applies to any kind of organization
- It applies to managers at all organizational levels
- The ultimate aim of all managers is the same: to create a surplus
- Managing is concerned with productivity, which implies effectiveness and efficiency

Management
The process of designing and maintaining an environment in which individuals, working together in groups, efficiently accomplish selected aims.

---

* At times, the term non manager is used in reference to persons who have no subordinates. Thus, non managers include professionals who may have a high status in organizations.

Here are some managers you are familiar with: Tim Cook of Apple, Satya Nadella of Microsoft, and Larry Ellison of Oracle. The president of the United States and the prime minister of India are also managers. Beyond top-level managers, middle-level managers and first-line supervisors also make important contributions to the goal of their organizations.

www.apple.com
www.microsoft.com
www.oracle.com

An **organization** is defined as a group of people working together to create a surplus. In business organizations, this surplus is profit. In nonprofit organizations, such as charitable organizations, it may be the satisfaction of needs or providing additional services. Universities also create a surplus through the generation and dissemination of knowledge as well as providing service to the community and society.

The Functions of Management

Many scholars and managers have found that the analysis of management is facilitated by a useful and clear organization of knowledge. In studying management, therefore, it is helpful to break it down into five managerial functions—planning, organizing, staffing, leading, and controlling—around which the knowledge that underlies those functions can be organized. Thus, the concepts, principles, theories, and techniques of management are grouped into these five functions in this book.

Five managerial functions around which managerial knowledge is organized in this book: planning, organizing, staffing, leading, controlling.

This framework has been used and tested for many years. Although there are different ways of organizing managerial knowledge, most textbooks and authors today have adopted this or a similar framework even after experimenting at times with alternative ways of structuring knowledge.

Although the emphasis in this book is on managers' tasks that pertain to designing an internal environment for performance within an organization, it must never be overlooked that managers must operate in the external environment of an enterprise as well. Clearly, managers cannot perform their tasks well unless they have an understanding of, and are responsive to, the many elements of the external environment—economic, technological, social, ecological, political, and ethical factors—that affect their areas of operation. Moreover, many organizations now operate in different countries. Therefore, this book takes a global perspective of managing.

External elements that affect operation include: economic, technological, social, ecological, political, and ethical factors.

Management as Element of any Organization

Managers are charged with the responsibility of taking actions that will enable individuals to make their best contributions to group objectives. Management, thus, applies to small and large organizations, to profit and not-for-profit enterprises, to manufacturing as well as service industries. The term **enterprise** refers to a business, government agency, hospital, university, or other types of organizations, because almost everything said in this book refers to business as well as non-business organizations. Effective management is the concern of the corporation president, the hospital administrator, the government first-line supervisor, the Boy Scout leader, the church bishop, the baseball manager, and the university president.

Enterprise A business, government agency, hospital, university, and other types of organizations.

Managerial Functions at Different Organizational Levels

In this book, no basic distinction is made between managers, executives, administrators, and supervisors. To be sure, a given situation may differ considerably between various levels in an organization or between various types of enterprises. Similarly, the scope of authority held may vary and the types of problems dealt with may be considerably different. Furthermore, the person in a managerial role may be directing people in the sales, engineering, or finance department. But the fact remains that, as managers, all obtain results by establishing an environment for effective group endeavor.

All managers carry out managerial functions. However, the time spent for each function may differ. Figure 1.1 shows an approximation of the relative time spent for each function. Thus, top-level managers spend more time on planning and organizing than do lower-level managers. Leading, on the other hand, takes a great deal of time for first-line supervisors. The difference in time spent on controlling varies only slightly for managers at various levels.

> All managers carry out managerial functions, but the time spent for each function may differ.

FIGURE 1.1 Time spent in carrying out managerial functions*

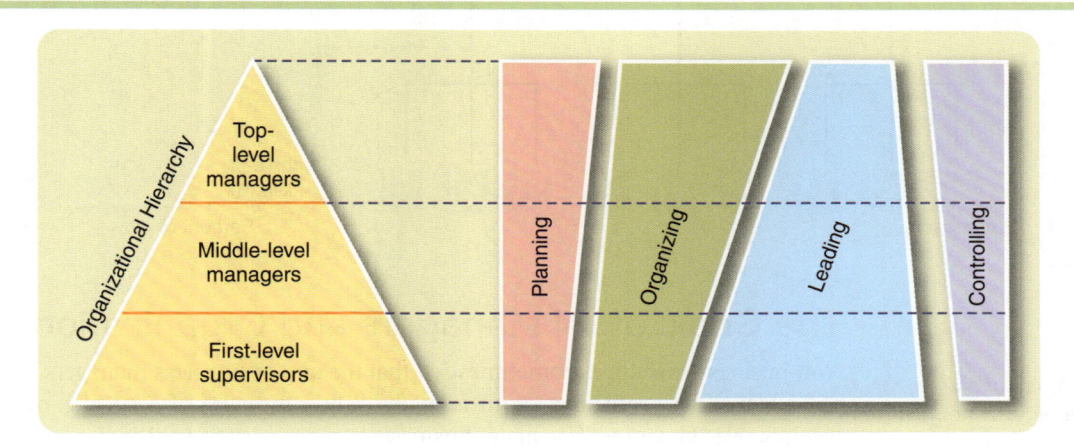

Managerial Skills and the Organizational Hierarchy

Robert L. Katz identified three kinds of skills for administrators—technical, human, and conceptual.[1] To these may be added a fourth—the ability to design solutions.

The relative importance of these skills may differ at various levels in the organizational hierarchy. As shown in Figure 1.2, *technical skills* are of the greatest importance at the supervisory level, and *human skills* are helpful in the frequent

> Four skills required of administrators: technical, human, conceptual, and design skills.

---

* Partly based on and adapted from Thomas A. Mahoney, Thomas H. Jerdee, and Stephen J. Carroll, "The Job(s) of Management," Industrial Relations (February 1965), pp. 97–110.

interactions with subordinates. *Conceptual and design skills*, on the other hand, are usually not critical for lower-level supervisors. At the middle management level, the need for technical skills decreases, human skills are still essential, while conceptual skills gain in importance. At the top management level, conceptual and design abilities and human skills are especially valuable, but there is relatively little need for technical abilities. It is assumed, especially in large companies, that chief executive officers (CEOs) can utilize the technical abilities of their subordinates. In smaller firms, however, technical experience may still be quite important.

FIGURE 1.2 Skills and management levels

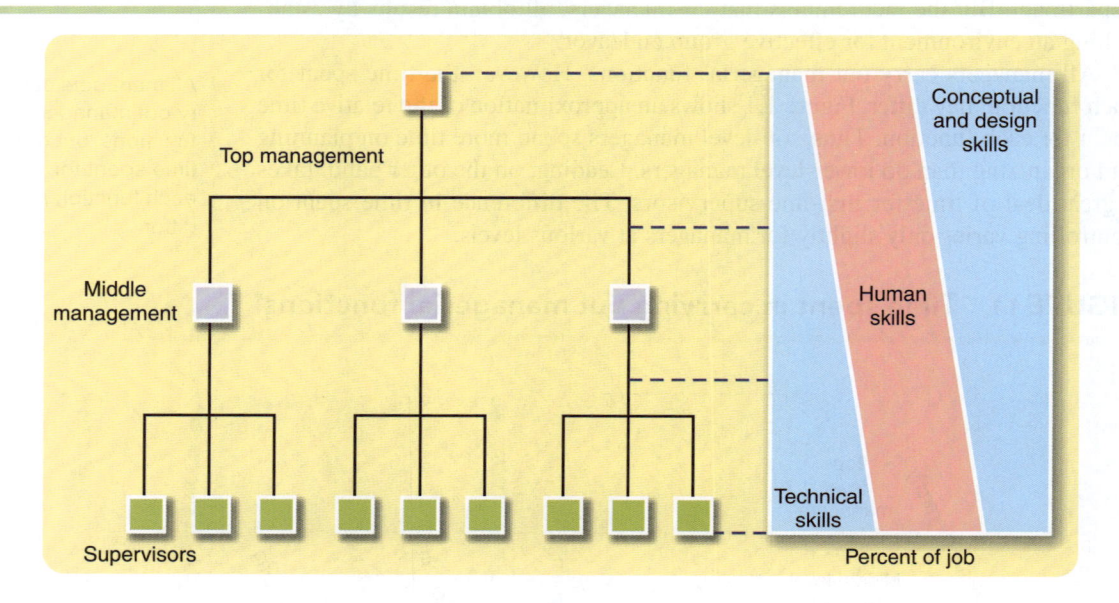

The Goals of All Managers and Organizations

> The aim of all managers should be to create a surplus by establishing an environment in which people can accomplish group goals with the least amount of time, money, materials, and personal dissatisfaction.

Non-business executives sometimes say that the aim of business managers is simple—to make a profit. But profit is really only a measure of a surplus of sales receipts over expenses. For many businesses, an important goal is the long-term increase in the value of their common stock. Michael Porter at Harvard is critical about the emphasis of shareholder value when he wrote that "we lost sight of profitability as the goal and substituted shareholder value measured by stock price."[2] This, Porter suggests, has destroyed many enterprises. In a very real sense, in all kinds of organizations, whether business or non-business, the logical and publicly desirable aim of all managers should be a *surplus*. Thus, managers must establish an environment in which people can accomplish group goals with the least amount of time, money, materials, and personal dissatisfaction or in which they can achieve as much as possible of a desired goal with available resources. In a non-business enterprise such as a police department, as well as in units of a business that are not responsible for total business profits (such as an accounting department), managers still have goals and should strive to accomplish them with the minimum of resources or to accomplish as much as possible with available resources.

GLOBAL PERSPECTIVE

Who Manages Best in 2008, the Year of the Global Financial Crisis?[3]

The year 2008 was a year of economic crises around the world. Who manages best during such times? *Business Week* identified twelve executives who performed well during very difficult times. Here are some examples and what one can learn from them:

Jim Sinegal, the CEO of Costco, did not raise prices despite rising costs. This helped the company to gain market share. The members-only retail chain retained 87 percent of their members by providing a sense of value during uncertain economic times.

Frank Blake, the CEO at Home Depot, simplified his company and increased morale among its employees. He thinks that people should feel comfortable in speaking their minds. He also visited Jack Welch, the former GE CEO, yearly, for advice.

Mark Hurd, the CEO at Hewlett Packard, was successful by keeping his eyes on cost, improving efficiency, and focusing on innovation. He got rid of businesses that were not No. 1 or No. 2 in their field. This is similar to Jack Welch's early strategy at GE.

David Axelrod, main strategist of the Obama campaign, helped Obama to the presidency of the United States of America. He helped to communicate Obama's vision of change. He recruited effective people who worked well together with good conflict resolution. He viewed himself as the messenger for Barack Obama.

Satoru Iwata, CEO of Nintendo in Tokyo, doubled the sales of the successful Wii. Consumers spent money on this innovative product despite hard economic times. He plans to continue with redefining games, music, camera, and even health management features.

Takeo Fukui, CEO of Honda in Tokyo, continued to focus on fuel-efficient small cars and continues his efforts on innovation and research. His managerial approach is influenced by the classic American book by Dale Carnegie with the title "How to Stop Worrying and Start Living."

Peter Loscher, CEO of Siemens in Munich, did a good job of restructuring the company while at the same time dealing with the corruption and foreign bribery charges. His advice: "Listen, and then make clear decisions."

Jeroen Van Der Veer, CEO of Royal Dutch Shell in the Netherlands, is guided by the philosophy of: Eliminate, Simplify, Standardize, and Automate.[4]

While the global financial and economic crisis persisted throughout 2009, those managers who were able to adjust to the rising economic challenges through effective planning and organizing were able to lead their firms successfully through the worst of the Great Recession.

Characteristics of Excellent and Most Admired Companies

In the United States, profitability is an important measure of company excellence. At times, however, other criteria are also used that frequently coincide with financial performance. In their book *In Search of Excellence*, Thomas Peters and Robert Waterman identified 43 companies that they regarded as excellent.[5] In choosing the firms, they considered factors such as growth of assets and equity, average return on total capital, and similar measures. They also asked industry experts about the innovativeness of the companies.

The authors identified eight characteristics of excellent enterprises. Specifically, these firms

1. were oriented toward action
2. learned about the needs of their customers
3. promoted managerial autonomy and entrepreneurship
4. achieved productivity by paying close attention to the needs of their people
5. were driven by a company philosophy often based on the values of their leaders
6. focused on the business they knew best
7. had a simple organization structure with a lean staff
8. were centralized as well as decentralized, depending on appropriateness

Two years after *In Search of Excellence* was published, *Business Week* took a second look at the companies that Peters and Waterman had considered excellent.[6] The magazine's survey revealed that at least 14 of the 43 companies did not measure up very well to several of the eight characteristics of excellence.

Nine companies showed a great decline in earnings. While Peters and Waterman have been criticized in several respects (e.g., their methods of collecting and interpreting the data, such as extensive use of anecdotes and quotations from leaders in the field rather than using more scientific research sources), the performance review of the firms indicated that success may be only transitory and that it demands continuing hard work to adapt to the changes in the environment.[7]

INTERNATIONAL PERSPECTIVE

Forbes Asia Ranks Asia's Top 50 Firms in 2018[8]

The top firms included Anta Sports Products (China) that reached $10 billion Yuan in annual sales, Ashok Leyland (India) which is the second largest maker of commercial vehicles, Netmarble (South Korea) which is the nation's largest mobile gaming firm, and Outsourcing Inc (Japan), and TVS Motors (India) which is the nation's largest maker of mopeds. High growth to a global size requires thoughtful management on key activities throughout the life of the organization.

To be successful in the 21st century, companies must take advantage of information technology—especially the Internet—globalization, and entrepreneurship.

Advances in Technologies, Trends in Globalization, and a Focus on Innovation and Entrepreneurship for Adapting to Changes in the 21st Century

To succeed and survive in the 21st century, companies must leverage advances in technology, trends in globalization, and manage entrepreneurially.

Technology[9]

Technology, especially information technology (IT), has a pervasive impact on both organizations and individuals. The Internet makes possible rapid and efficient communications and commerce among individuals and organizations around the world. Access to the Internet, though it varies among countries, continues to grow and provide for new opportunities that require effective management to be fully realized.

Mobile commerce, social media, the increasing use of externally hosted IT infrastructure (e.g., The Cloud), and the analysis of these growing sources of data (analytics) are growing trends and are creating opportunities for new organizational forms that require new management capabilities. These and other technology trends are so important that they will be further discussed in Chapter 19.

Globalization[10]

The second major trend is globalization. Most major corporations have an international presence. The World Trade Organization (WTO), an umbrella organization, was established in 1995 to govern international trade. Despite street protests at WTO meetings, globalization continues. The gains from globalization not only benefit Western corporations but also result in higher incomes for people in rapidly developing countries. For example, the globalization of firms from India and China[11] has created a new group of competitive multinational corporations which bring the benefits of innovation to the countries they operate in and bring innovative practices back to their homelands. Clearly, managers must develop an international perspective. Chapter 3 will address several global issues in detail. In addition, international topics are discussed in the international perspectives shown throughout the book.

Innovation and Entrepreneurship

An increasing focus on innovation and entrepreneurship as a national and organizational imperative has become more and more evident. Entrepreneurship and innovation are seen by governments as a means to increase employment, productivity, and prosperity among their populations, while organizations—large and small—find that entrepreneurial innovation and expansion into new customer segments are essential to their success and survival in increasingly competitive markets.

Innovation is focused on enhancing products and services and commercializing them while entrepreneurship is a process that is centered in the notion of identifying market opportunities and unmet needs. It is building solutions that meet these needs and bring value to customers. Entrepreneurs build organizations that provide products that alleviate people's pain (e.g., pharmaceutical companies) or provide the means for people to enhance their own lives through sophisticated telecommunications (e.g., information technology companies) while creating economic surplus. Venkatramen (1997) asserted that "Entrepreneurship as a scholarly field seeks to understand how opportunities to bring into existence 'future' goods and services are discovered, created and exploited, by whom and with what consequence."[12]

From the entrepreneurial and innovative epicenter of Silicon Valley to emerging entrepreneurial centers around the world, new venture creation and innovation are the driving forces of progress for mankind. We highlight these entrepreneurial trends and their correspondence with a wide range of management challenges throughout each chapter.

Silicon Valley Immersion[13]

Silicon Valley remains the primary destination for those with ambition to develop a high-growth venture. For example, Mark Zuckerberg, the co-founder and CEO of Facebook, realized early on that while he developed Facebook at Harvard University he would need to move to Silicon Valley to take advantage of its eco-system that supported high-growth entrepreneurship. The Silicon Valley eco-system features venture capital to finance high-growth ventures, legal expertise to guide these ventures, and technological and human capital to develop creative new ventures.

Entrepreneurs, firms, universities, and governments from around the world also recognize the value of the Silicon Valley eco-system and desire to learn from it and leverage it to promote successful entrepreneurship and innovation. Groups from around the world visit Silicon Valley to do just that. Programs like the Silicon Valley Immersion Program at the University of San Francisco host groups from Latin America, Asia, and Europe and introduce them to the unique Silicon Valley entrepreneurial eco-system through lectures by local experts, visits to cutting-edge firms, and networking events with local entrepreneurs and investors. Groups from Portugal, Mexico, Argentina, Peru, Chile, China, and elsewhere have come to the University of San Francisco to live and learn in the Silicon Valley eco-system and increase their own capacity to entrepreneurship and innovativeness, the Silicon Valley way. https://www.usfca.edu/management/executive-education/silicon-valley-immersion-program.

ENTREPRENEURIAL PERSPECTIVE

Productivity, Effectiveness, and Efficiency

Another way to view the aim of managers is that they must raise productivity. After World War II, the United States became the world leader in productivity. But in the late 1960s, productivity growth began to decelerate. Today, the urgent need for productivity improvement is recognized around the world by governments, industry, and universities. The Organisation for Economic Cooperation and Development (OECD) measures productivity across nations. As of 2017, the OECD found that Luxembourg is the most productive country as measured by gross domestic product (GDP) per person. Ireland,

Norway, Switzerland, and the United States make up the next four most productive countries.[14]

Definition of Productivity

Successful companies create a surplus through productive operations. Although there is no complete agreement on the true meaning of **productivity**, let us define it as the output–input ratio within a time period with due consideration for quality. It can be expressed as follows:

$$\text{Productivity} = \frac{\text{Outputs}}{\text{Inputs}} \text{ (within a time period, quality considered)}$$

> **Productivity**
> The output–input ratio within a time period with due consideration for quality.

The formula indicates that productivity can be improved by (1) increasing outputs with the same inputs, (2) decreasing inputs but maintaining the same outputs, or (3) increasing outputs and decreasing inputs to change the ratio favorably. Companies use several kinds of inputs, such as labor, materials, and capital. Total-factor productivity combines various inputs to arrive at a composite input. In the past, productivity improvement programs were mostly aimed at the worker level. Yet, as Peter F. Drucker, one of the most prolific writers in management, observed, "The greatest opportunity for increasing productivity is surely to be found in knowledge work itself, and especially in management."[15]

Definitions of Effectiveness and Efficiency

Productivity implies effectiveness and efficiency in individual and organizational performance. **Effectiveness** is the achievement of objectives. **Efficiency** is the achievement of the ends with the least amount of resources. Effectiveness alone is not sufficient unless a firm is also efficient in meeting its objectives. For example, an organization may achieve its goal through an inefficient method that would result in higher costs and a noncompetitive product or service. Similarly, an enterprise may be very efficient in achieving suboptimal goals and miss the market entirely. Therefore, a high-performing company must be both effective and efficient. Managers cannot know whether they are productive unless they first know their goals and those of the organization, a topic that will be discussed in Chapter 4.

> **Effectiveness**
> The achievement of objectives.
>
> **Efficiency**
> The achievement of the ends with the least amount of resources.

ENTREPRENEURIAL PERSPECTIVE

The Fastest-Growing Companies[16]

Managing entrepreneurially may lead to a rapid increase in sales. *Fortune* Magazine published its list of the 100 fastest growing companies in 2015. *Fortune* ranked those firms that were listed on a U.S. exchange based on revenue growth, profit growth, and total return over the preceding three years. We list here *Fortune's* top ten fastest growing companies.[17] If rapid growth is an indicator of successful entrepreneurial management, then these companies fit the bill.

1. Lannett (Pharmaceuticals)
2. Natural Health Trends (Household and personal care)
3. Federated National Holding (Insurance)
4. Centene (Insurance and managed care)
5. Noah Holdings (Financial Services)
6. Acadia Healthcare (Healthcare)
7. Qihoo 360 Technology (Internet Services)
8. Wisdomtree Investments (Financial Services)
9. Gilead Sciences (Pharmaceuticals)
10. Facebook (Internet Services)

MANAGING: SCIENCE OR ART?[18]

Managing, like all other practices—whether medicine, music composition, engineering, accountancy, or even baseball—is an art. It is know-how. It is doing things in light of the realities of a situation. Yet managers can work better by using the organized knowledge about management. It is this knowledge that constitutes a science. Thus, managing as practice is an *art*; the organized knowledge underlying the practice may be referred to as a *science*. In this context, science and art are not mutually exclusive; they are complementary.

> **Managing** as practice is an art; the organized knowledge underlying the practice is a science.

As science improves, so should art, as has happened in the physical and biological sciences. To be sure, the science underlying managing is fairly crude and inexact because the many variables that managers deal with are extremely complex. Nevertheless, such management knowledge can certainly improve managerial practice. Physicians without the advantage of science would be little more than witch doctors. Executives who attempt to manage without management science must trust luck, intuition, or do what they did in the past.

In managing, as in any other field, unless practitioners are to learn by trial and error (and it has been said that managers' errors are their subordinates' trials), there is no place they can turn to for meaningful guidance other than the accumulated knowledge underlying their practice.

THE EVOLUTION OF MANAGEMENT THOUGHT[19]

Many different contributions of writers and practitioners have resulted in different approaches to management, and these make up a "management theory jungle." Later in this chapter, you will learn about the different patterns of management analysis and what can be done to untangle the jungle. Table 1.1 summarizes the major contributions of management writers and practitioners.[20] We will highlight Frederick Taylor's scientific management, Henri Fayol's modern operational management theory, and Elton Mayo and F. J. Roethlisberger's Hawthorne studies.

Frederick Taylor and Scientific Management[21]

Frederick Winslow Taylor gave up going to college and started out as an apprentice pattern maker and machinist in 1875, joined the Midvale Steel Company in Philadelphia as a machinist in 1878, and rose to the position of chief engineer after earning a degree in engineering through evening study. He invented high-speed steel-cutting tools and spent most of his life as a consulting engineer. Taylor is generally acknowledged as the father of scientific management. Probably no other person has had a greater impact on the early development of management. His experiences as an apprentice, a common laborer, a foreman, a master mechanic, and then the chief engineer of a steel company gave Taylor ample opportunity to know first-hand the problems and attitudes of workers and to see the great possibilities for improving the quality of management.

TABLE 1.1 The emergence of management thought

Name and year of major work	Major contribution to management
Scientific management	
Frederick W. Taylor *Shop Management* (1903) *Principles of Scientific Management* (1911) *Testimony before the Special House Committee* (1912)	Acknowledged as the father of scientific management. His primary concern was to raise productivity through greater efficiency in production and increased pay for workers, by applying the scientific method. His principles emphasize using science, creating group harmony and cooperation, achieving maximum output, and developing workers.
Henry L. Gantt (1901)	Called for scientific selection of workers and "harmonious cooperation" between labor and management. Developed the Gantt chart (Chapter 19). Stressed the need for training.
Frank and Lillian Gilbreth (1900)	Frank is known primarily for his time and motion studies. Lillian, an industrial psychologist, focused on the human aspects of work and the understanding of workers' personalities and needs.
Modern operational management theory	
Henri Fayol *Administration Industrielle et Générale* (1916)	Referred to as the father of modern management theory. Divided industrial activities into six groups: technical, commercial, financial, security, accounting, and managerial. Recognized the need for teaching management. Formulated 14 principles of management, such as authority and responsibility, unity of command, scalar chain, and esprit de corps.
Behavioral sciences	
Hugo Münsterberg (1912)	Application of psychology to industry and management.
Walter Dill Scott (1910, 1911)	Application of psychology to advertising, marketing, and personnel.
Behavioral sciences	
Max Weber (translations 1946, 1947)	Theory of bureaucracy.
Vilfredo Pareto (books 1896–1917)	Referred to as the father of the social systems approach to organization and management.
Elton Mayo and F. J. Roethlisberger (1933)	Famous studies at the Hawthorne plant of the Western Electric Company on the influence of social attitudes and relationships of work groups on performance.
Systems theory	
Chester Barnard *The Functions of the Executive* (1938)	The task of managers is to maintain a system of cooperative effort in a formal organization. Suggested a comprehensive social systems approach to managing.

Name and year of major work	Major contribution to management
Modern management thought	
Many authors are discussed in this book. Major contributors include Chris Argyris, Robert R. Blake, C. West Churchman, Ernest Dale, Keith Davis, Mary Parker Follett, Frederick Herzberg, G. C. Homans, Harold Koontz, Rensis Likert, Douglas McGregor, Abraham H. Maslow, Lyman W. Porter, Herbert Simon, George A. Steiner, Lyndall Urwick, Norbert Wiener, and Joan Woodward.	
Peter F. Drucker (1974)	Very prolific writer on many general management topics.
W. Edwards Deming (after World War II)	Introduced quality control in Japan.
Laurence Peter (1969)	Observed that eventually people get promoted to a level where they are incompetent.
William Ouchi (1981)	Discussed selected Japanese managerial practices adapted in the U.S. environment.
Thomas Peters and Robert Waterman (1982)	Identified characteristics of companies they considered excellent.
C.K. Prahalad and Gary Hamel (1990)	Introduced the view of the "core competency of the corporation" that envisions the firm as a portfolio of core competencies rather than a collection of business units to better enable managers to identify and employ the firm's competitive advantage.
Birger Wernerfelt (1985) Jay Barney (1991)	Introduced the "resource-based view of the firm" which helps managers identify sustainable competitive advantage by determining which of its resources are valuable, rare, hard to copy, and hard to substitute for.
Clayton Christensen (1997)	Introduced Disruptive Innovation as a method by which firms can develop new products and processes.
Henry Chesbrough (2003)	Introduced Open Innovation Model as a method by which firms can incorporate multiple sources of creativity and innovation to develop new products and processes.

Source: Some information in this table is based on Claude S. George, Jr., *The History of Management Thought* (Englewood Cliffs, NJ: Prentice Hall, 1972).

Taylor's famous work *Principles of Scientific Management* was published in 1911. The fundamental principles that Taylor saw underlying the scientific approach to management are as follows:

- Replacing rules of thumb with science (organized knowledge).
- Obtaining harmony, rather than discord in group action.
- Achieving cooperation of human beings, rather than chaotic individualism.
- Working for maximum output, rather than restricted output.
- Developing all workers to the fullest extent possible for their own and their company's highest prosperity.

You will notice that these basic precepts of Taylor are not far from the fundamental beliefs of the modern manager.

Henri Fayol, the Father of Modern Management Theory[22]

Perhaps the real father of modern management theory is the French industrialist Henri Fayol. He recognized a widespread need for principles and management teaching. Consequently, he identified 14 such principles, noting that those are flexible, not absolute, and must be usable regardless of changing conditions. Let us look at some of these principles:

- *Authority and responsibility*. Fayol suggests that authority and responsibility are related, with the latter arising from the former. He sees authority as a combination of official factors, deriving from the manager's position, and personal factors, "compounded of intelligence, experience, moral worth, past service, etc."
- *Unity of command*. Employees should receive orders from one superior only.
- *Scalar chain*. Fayol thinks of this as a "chain of superiors" from the highest to the lowest ranks, which, while not to be departed from needlessly, should be short-circuited when following it scrupulously would be detrimental.
- *Esprit de corps*. This is the principle that "in union there is strength," as well as an extension of the principle of unity of command, emphasizing the need for teamwork and the importance of communication in obtaining it.

Fayol regarded the elements of management as the functions of planning, organizing, commanding, coordinating, and controlling.

Elton Mayo and F. J. Roethlisberger and the Hawthorne Studies

Elton Mayo, F. J. Roethlisberger, and others undertook the famous experiments at the Hawthorne plant of the Western Electric Company between 1927 and 1932.[23] Earlier, from 1924 to 1927, the National Research Council made a study in collaboration with Western Electric to determine the effect of illumination and other conditions on workers and their productivity. Finding that productivity improved when illumination was either increased or decreased for a test group, the researchers were about to declare the whole experiment a failure. However, Mayo of Harvard saw in it something unusual and, with Roethlisberger and others, continued the research.

What Mayo and his colleagues found, partly on the basis of the earlier thinking of Vilfredo Pareto, was to have a dramatic effect on management thought. Changing illumination for the test group, modifying rest periods, shortening workdays, and varying incentive pay systems did not seem to explain changes in productivity. Mayo and his researchers then came to the conclusion that other factors were responsible. They found, in general, that the improvement in productivity was due to such social factors as morale, satisfactory interrelationships between members of a work group (a sense of belonging), and effective management—a kind of managing that takes into account human behavior, especially group behavior, and serves it through such interpersonal skills as motivating, counseling, leading, and communicating. This phenomenon, arising basically from people being "noticed," has been named the Hawthorne effect.

Recent Contributors to Management Thought

Among the contributors to management thought are public administrators, business managers, and behavioral scientists, whose important works are discussed throughout this book. We will mention only a few here.

Peter F. Drucker has written on a variety of general management topics. Keith Davis helped us understand the informal organization. The late W. Edwards Deming[24] and Joseph M. Juran,[25] two Americans, did much to improve the quality of Japanese products. The late Laurence Peter suggested that eventually people get promoted to a level where they are incompetent and no further promotion is possible. Unfortunately, this may result in organizations with incompetent people. William Ouchi, who wrote the best-selling book *Theory Z*, showed how selected Japanese management practices may be adapted in the United States. Finally, Thomas Peters and Robert Waterman discussed characteristics of excellent companies. Most of these works are discussed in greater detail in other parts of this book.

The Wisdom of Peter Drucker[26]

The late Peter Drucker was one of the most influential management thinkers. During his 60-year career, he wrote 39 books and consulted with executives of major companies. However, his interests were not restricted to managerial insights, but extended to Japanese art and European history. Yet, his focus was on making workers more productive. He popularized Management by Objectives in his classic book *The Practice of Management* in which he emphasized the importance of having a clear purpose and the setting of verifiable objectives. This means that objectives are verifiable if at the end of the period one can see whether the objective has been achieved.

Drucker consulted with CEOs of major companies such as Jack Welch, the former CEO of General Electric (GE) who is considered by many as the most effective executive manager of a large complex organization. Drucker's questioning may have led to Welch's axiom which suggested that if one of GE's business units is not No. 1 or No. 2 in its industry (or has a good chance to become so) it should be discarded. Drucker's effectiveness was in raising important questions. One top manager asked why he should pay Drucker's consulting fees if the CEO was to answer all the questions. However, Drucker's questioning approach often led to identifying the direction the company should go. Andrew Grove, the former CEO at Intel was impressed by Drucker's discussion of the multiple roles of the CEO, namely that of presenting the firm to the public, the role of the strategist, and that of the operational manager. Moreover, Drucker suggested that a manager should not be promoted on his or her potential, but on performance.

In 1943 he studied the organizational structure of GM which resulted in the book *The Concept of the Corporation*. His view was that "it takes people capable of joint performance, to make their strengths effective and weaknesses irrelevant."

Drucker had a deep concern not only for making workers more productive, but that employees are the organization's most valuable assets and that decision making should be pushed down in the organization to the lowest levels in the hierarchy (i.e., delegation). Some other nuggets of his managerial philosophy are that at the center of the organization are human beings—not machines or buildings. He also suggested that managers do the same in the United States, Germany, Japan, China, but **how** they do it may be different.

Organizational learning, training, and development need to be done at all levels of the organization. It is a continuing effort. Profitability is not the purpose but a necessity in organizations. Marketing starts with the customer and his or her values and needs. He asked questions such as: Where do the customers live and what do they want to buy? Simple? Yes, but it is powerful for an effective strategy.

Long before it was generally recognized, Drucker popularized the notion of the "knowledge worker" and the special considerations for managing him or her. But management is not only for profit-oriented enterprises, but also for churches, labor unions, youth groups, and hospitals, a view that is emphasized in this book.

GLOBAL PERSPECTIVE

HISTORY OF SELECTED MANAGERIAL INNOVATIONS[27]

Innovation is critical to organizational success. History, however, has shown that over the years, innovative ideas have come and gone. Here are some of them (the dates are approximate):

1910: Henry Ford with the Model T used the assembly line production to increase the output.
1920: Alfred Sloan at General Motors set the stage for the modern organization by using the divisional organization structure, letting the divisions operate as separate companies.

1931: Proctor & Gamble introduced brand management for soaps so that individual managers were held responsible for the success or failure of the brand.
1943: Lockheed's Skunk Works organization was able to build a new fighter plane in a very short time using small groups with minor interruptions from the parent company.
1950s: Toyota innovated ways to improve efficiencies without letting workers go; this led to the quality control concept in 1961.
1967: The idea was to assume different alternative events and plan for them. Shell used the idea to cope with the 1970s oil crisis.
1973: The DuPont Company used the 360-Degree Review process to give managers feedback from other managers, peers, and subordinates.
1987: Motorola used the Six Sigma process to improve efficiency and to reduce defects. General Electric was an early adopter of this approach.
1989: IBM managed Kodak's data processing. During the 1990s the approach was used to move work to other countries.
1990: Reengineering involved radically rethinking organizational processes. This might result in layoffs, although Michael Hammer who popularized the approach says that this was not the primary purpose of reengineering.
2000s: Companies are working with other firms and customers to come up with new, innovative ideas. Proctor & Gamble, for example, hopes that half their innovations come from outsiders.
2012: An increasing focus on hosting organizational technology externally (The Cloud), mobile computing, and leveraging social media to interact more effectively with customers helps to shape organizational strategy and directly impacts the way leaders manage their companies.

Innovative approaches are also at times pursued in search for the solution to managerial problems. Some of these approaches, indeed, may serve as tools for making the organization more effective (e.g., data analytics). However, success will only result from a systematic approach to management using innovations as tools.

2016: Increasing convergence of health care technologies and information technology to help people better manage their own health (e.g., FitBit, Apple Watch) as well as methods to help health care providers better deliver services.

PATTERNS OF MANAGEMENT ANALYSIS: A MANAGEMENT THEORY JUNGLE?

Although academic writers and theorists contributed notably little to the study of management until the early 1950s (previous writings having come largely from practitioners), the past several decades have seen a veritable deluge of writing from the academic halls. The variety of approaches to management analysis, the amount of research, and the great number of differing views have resulted in much confusion as to what management is, what management theory and science are, and how managerial events should be analyzed. As a matter of fact, Harold Koontz many years ago called this situation "the management theory jungle."[28] Since that time, the vegetation in this jungle has changed somewhat—new approaches have developed and older approaches have taken on some new meanings with some new words attached, but the developments of management science and theory still have the characteristics of a jungle.

The various approaches to management analysis are summarized in Figure 1.3, where they are grouped into 14 categories. The characteristics, contributions, and limitations of each approach are shown in the figure. We will focus here on the managerial roles approach and the management process (or operational) approach.

FIGURE 1.3 Approaches to management

EMPIRICAL, OR CASE, APPROACH*

Studies experience through cases. Identifies successes and failures.

Situations are all different. No attempt to identify principles. Limited value for developing management theory.

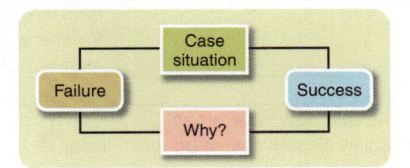

MANAGERIAL ROLES APPROACH

Original study consisted of observations of five chief executives. On the basis of this study, ten managerial roles were identified and grouped into interpersonal, informational, and decision roles.

Original sample was very small. Some activities are not managerial. Many activities are evidence of planning, organizing, staffing, leading, and controlling. Some important managerial activities are left out (e.g., appraising managers).

CONTINGENCY, OR SITUATIONAL, APPROACH

Managerial practice depends on circumstances (i.e., a contingency or a situation). Contingency theory recognizes the influence of given solutions on organizational behavior patterns.

Managers have long realized that there is no one best way to do things. Difficult to determine all relevant contingency factors and to show their relationships. Can be very complex.

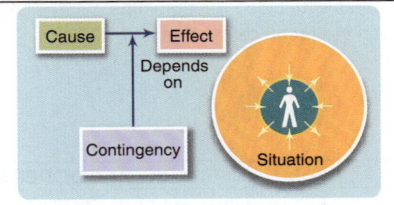

MATHEMATICAL, OR "MANAGEMENT SCIENCE," APPROACH

Sees managing as mathematical processes, concepts, symbols, and models. Looks at management as a purely logical process, expressed in mathematical symbols and relationships.

Preoccupation with mathematical models. Many aspects in managing cannot be modeled. Mathematics is a useful tool, but hardly a school or an approach to management.

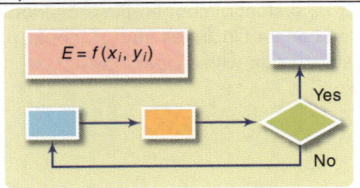

$E = f(x_i, y_i)$

DECISION THEORY APPROACH

Focuses on the making of decisions, persons or groups making decisions, and the decision-making process. Some theorists use decision-making as a springboard to study all enterprise activities. The boundaries of study are no longer clearly defined.

There is more to managing than making decisions. The focus is at the same time too narrow and too wide.

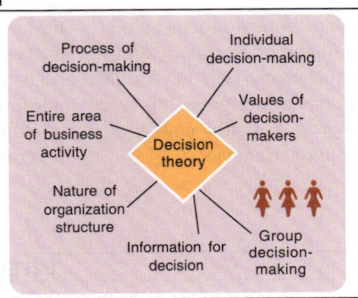

---

* Larry E. Greiner, Arvind Bhambri, and Thomas G. Cummings, "Searching for a Strategy to Teach Strategy," *Academy of Management – Learning & Education*, December 2003, pp. 402–419.

REENGINEERING APPROACH

Concerned with fundamental rethinking, process analysis, radical redesign, and dramatic results.	Neglects external environment. Possibly ignores customers' needs. Neglects human needs. Ignores total management system, unlike the management process, or operational, approach.	Input → Transformation → Output (Operations)

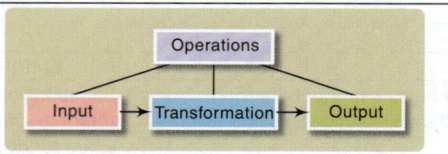

SYSTEMS APPROACH

Systems concepts have broad applicability. Systems have boundaries, but they also interact with the external environment; that means organizations are open systems. Recognizes the importance of studying interrelatedness of planning, organizing, and controlling in an organization as well as in the many subsystems.	Can hardly be considered a new approach to management, as claimed by some proponents of this approach.	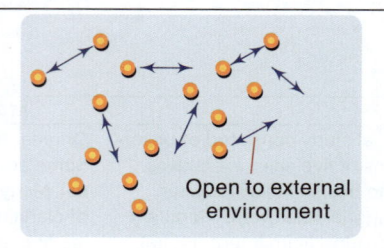 Open to external environment

SOCIOTECHNICAL SYSTEMS APPROACH

Technical system has a great effect on social system (personal attitudes, group behavior). Focuses on production, office operations, and other areas with close relationships between the technical system and people.	Emphasizes only blue-collar and lower-level office work. Ignores much of other managerial knowledge.	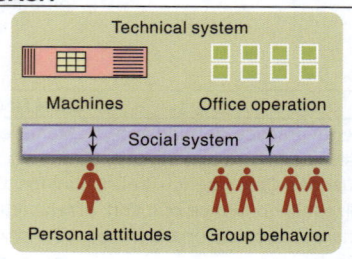 Technical system: Machines, Office operation. Social system: Personal attitudes, Group behavior.

COOPERATIVE SOCIAL SYSTEMS APPROACH

Concerned with both interpersonal and group behavioral aspects leading to a system of cooperation. Expanded concept includes any cooperative group with a clear purpose.	Too broad a field for the study of management. At the same time, it overlooks many managerial concepts, principles, and techniques.	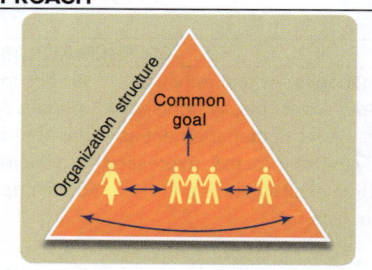 Organization structure, Common goal

GROUP BEHAVIOR APPROACH

Emphasizes behavior of people in groups. Based on sociology and social psychology. Primarily studies group behavior patterns. The study of large groups is often called organizational behavior.	Often not integrated with management concepts, principles, theory, and techniques. Need for closer integration with organizational structure design, staffing, planning, and controlling.	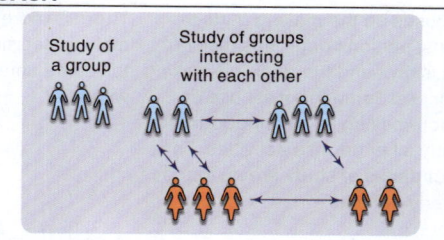 Study of a group; Study of groups interacting with each other

INTERPERSONAL BEHAVIOR APPROACH

Focuses on interpersonal behavior, human relations, leadership, and motivation. Based on individual psychology.	Ignores planning, organizing, and controlling. Psychological training is not enough for becoming an effective manager.	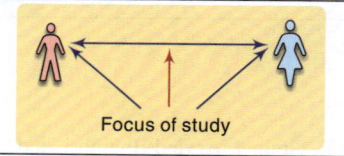 Focus of study

MCKINSEY'S 7-S FRAMEWORK

The seven S's are (1) strategy, (2) structure, (3) systems, (4) style, (5) staff, (6) shared values, and (7) skills.

Although this experienced consulting firm uses a framework similar to that found useful by Koontz and colleagues since 1955 and confirms its practicality, the terms used are not precise and topics are not discussed in depth.

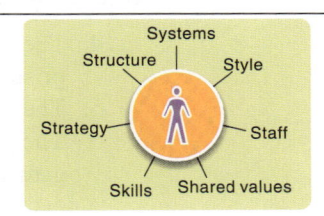

TOTAL QUALITY MANAGEMENT APPROACH

Focuses on providing dependable, satisfying products and services (Deming) or products or services that are fit for use (Juran), as well as conforming to quality requirements (Crosby). The general concepts are continuous improvement, attention to details, teamwork, and quality education.

No complete agreement on what total quality management is.

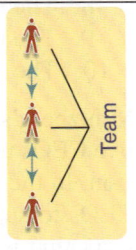

Focus:
Customer needs:
Quality Products and Services
Concern for quality and cost

MANAGEMENT PROCESS, OR OPERATIONAL, APPROACH

Draws together concepts, principles, techniques, and knowledge from other fields and managerial approaches. The attempt is to develop science and theory with practical application. Distinguishes between managerial and nonmanagerial knowledge. Develops a classification system built around the managerial functions of planning, organizing, staffing, leading, and controlling.

Does not, as some authors do, identify representing or coordination as a separate function. Coordination, for example, is the essence of managership and is the purpose of managing.

The Managerial Roles Approach

One widely discussed approach to management theory is the managerial roles approach, popularized by Henry Mintzberg of McGill University.[29] Essentially, his approach is to observe what managers actually do and from such observations come to conclusions as to what managerial activities (or roles) are. Although many researchers have studied the actual work of managers—from CEOs to line supervisors—Mintzberg has given this approach higher visibility.

After systematically studying the activities of five CEOs in a variety of organizations, Mintzberg came to the conclusion that executives do not perform the classical managerial functions of planning, organizing, commanding, coordinating, and controlling. Instead, they engage in a variety of other activities. From his research and the research of others who had studied what managers actually did, Mintzberg concluded that managers really fill a series of ten roles:

Interpersonal Roles

1. The figurehead role (performing ceremonial and social duties as the organization's representative)
2. The leader role
3. The liaison role (particularly with outsiders)

Informational Roles

4. The recipient role (receiving information about the operation of an enterprise)
5. The disseminator role (passing information to subordinates)
6. The spokesperson role (transmitting information to those outside the organization)

Decision Roles

7. The entrepreneurial role
8. The disturbance handler role
9. The resource allocator role
10. The negotiator role (dealing with various persons and groups of persons)

Mintzberg's approach has also been criticized. In the first place, the sample of five CEOs used in his research is far too small to support so sweeping a conclusion. In the second place, in analyzing the actual activities of managers—from CEOs to supervisors—any researcher must realize that all managers do some work that is not purely managerial; one would expect even presidents of large companies to spend some of their time in public and stockholder relations, in fund-raising, and perhaps in dealer relations, marketing, and so on. In the third place, many of the activities Mintzberg found are in fact evidence of planning, organizing, staffing, leading, and controlling. For example, what is resource allocation but planning? The entrepreneurial role is certainly an element of planning. And the interpersonal roles are mainly instances of leading. In addition, the informational roles can be fitted into a number of functional areas.

Nevertheless, looking at what managers really do can have considerable value. In analyzing activities, an effective manager might wish to ascertain how activities and techniques fall into the various fields of knowledge reflected by the basic functions of managers. However, the roles Mintzberg identified appear to be incomplete. Where does one find such unquestionably important managerial activities as structuring an organization, selecting and appraising managers, and determining major strategies? Omissions such as these make one wonder whether the executives in his sample were really effective managers. They certainly raise a serious question as to whether the managerial roles approach, at least as put forth here, is an adequate one on which to base a practical, operational theory of management.

The Management Process, or Operational, Approach

> The **management process,** or **operational, approach** draws together the pertinent knowledge of management by relating it to the managerial job.

The process, or operational, approach to management theory and science draws together the pertinent knowledge of management by relating it to the managerial job—what managers do. Like other operational sciences, it tries to integrate the concepts, principles, and techniques that underlie the task of managing.

This approach recognizes that there is a central core of knowledge about managing that is pertinent only to the field of management. Such matters as line and staff, departmentation, managerial appraisal, and various managerial control techniques involve concepts and theories found only in situations involving managers. In addition, this approach draws on and absorbs knowledge from other fields, including systems theory, quality and reengineering concepts, decision theory, theories of motivation and leadership, individual and group behavior, social systems, and cooperation and communications, as well as the application of mathematical analyses and concepts.

The nature of this approach can be seen in Figure 1.4. As this diagram shows, the management process, or operational, school recognizes the existence of a central core of science and theory peculiar to managing and also draws important contributions from various other schools and approaches. In addition, the management process theorist is interested not in all the important knowledge in these various fields but only in that which is deemed most useful and relevant to managing.

FIGURE 1.4 The management process, or operational, approach

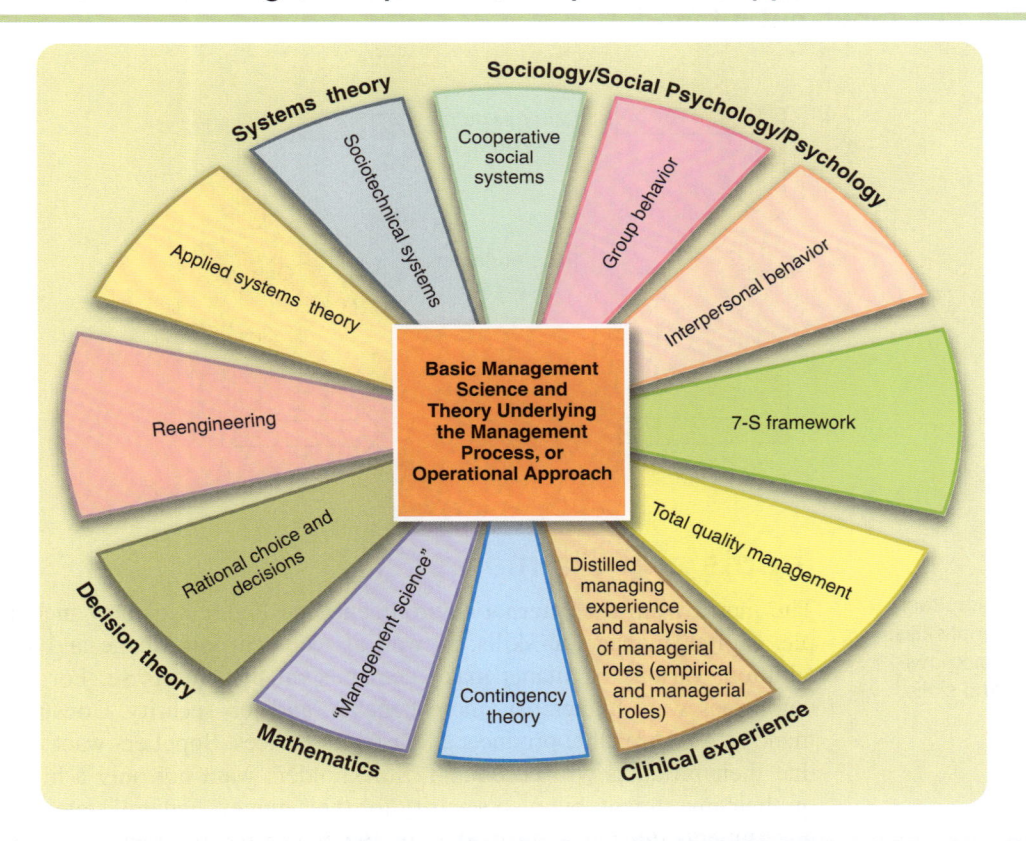

THE SYSTEMS APPROACH TO THE MANAGEMENT PROCESS

An organized enterprise does not, of course, exist in a vacuum. Rather, it is dependent on its external environment; it is a part of larger systems, such as the industry to which it belongs, the economic system, and society. Thus, the enterprise receives inputs, transforms them, and exports the outputs to the environment, as shown by the very basic model in Figure 1.5. However, this simple model needs to be expanded and developed into a model of process, or operational, management that indicates how the various inputs are transformed through the managerial functions of planning, organizing, staffing, leading, and controlling, as shown in Figure 1.6. When Peter Senge, the author of *The Fifth Discipline: The Art and Practice of the Learning Organization*, was asked what is the most important issue faced by domestic and international businesses today, he said, "I would say the system of management."[30] This book is about the systems approach to the management process. Not only is the concern about the internal functioning of the enterprise, but it must include the interactions between the enterprise and its external environment.

FIGURE 1.5 Input-output model

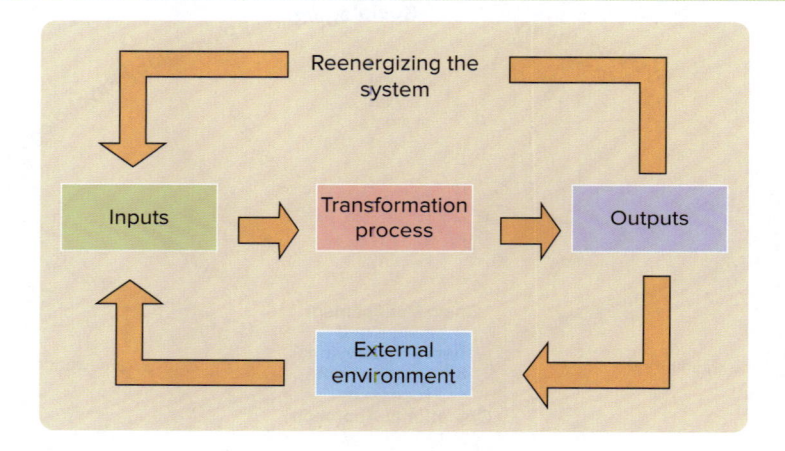

Inputs
People, capital, managerial skills, technical knowledge, and skills.

Inputs and Claimants*

The inputs from the external environment (see Figure 1.6) may include people, capital, managerial skills, as well as technical knowledge and skills. In addition, various claimants make demands on the enterprise. For example, employees want higher pay, more benefits, and job security. Consumers demand safe and reliable products at reasonable prices. Suppliers want assurance that their products will be bought. Stockholders want not only a high return on their investment, but also security for their money. Federal, state, and local governments depend on taxes paid by the enterprise, but they also expect the enterprise to comply with their laws. Similarly, the community demands that enterprises be "good citizens," providing the maximum number of jobs with a minimum of pollution. Other claimants to the enterprise may include financial institutions and labor unions; even competitors have a legitimate claim for fair play. It is clear that many of these claims are incongruent, and it is the manager's job to integrate the legitimate objectives of the claimants. This may need to be done through compromises, trade-offs, and denial of the manager's own ego.

*Claimants may also be called stakeholders.

FIGURE 1.6 Systems approach to management

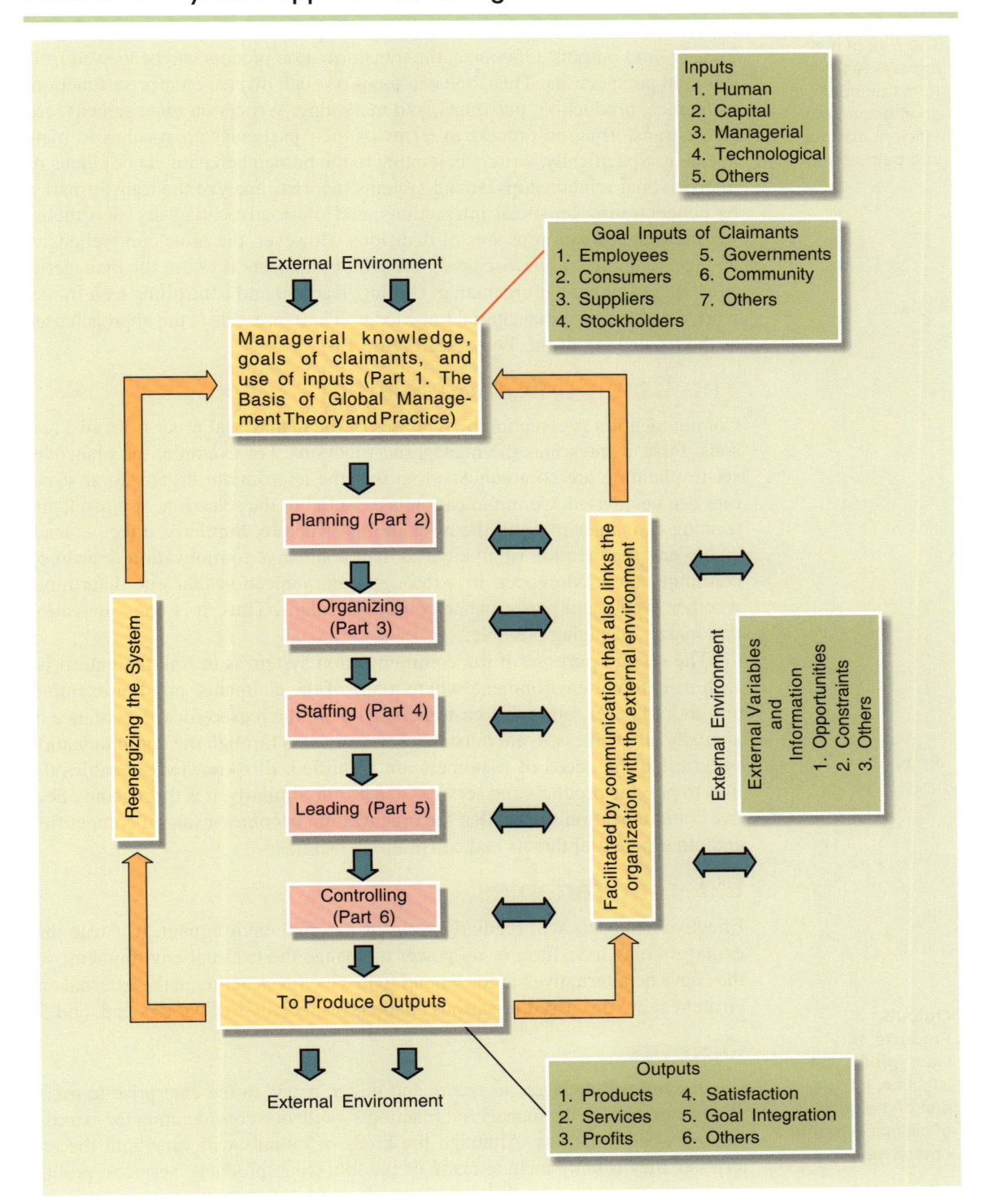

Inputs
1. Human
2. Capital
3. Managerial
4. Technological
5. Others

Goal Inputs of Claimants
1. Employees
2. Consumers
3. Suppliers
4. Stockholders
5. Governments
6. Community
7. Others

External Environment

Managerial knowledge, goals of claimants, and use of inputs (Part 1. The Basis of Global Management Theory and Practice)

- Planning (Part 2)
- Organizing (Part 3)
- Staffing (Part 4)
- Leading (Part 5)
- Controlling (Part 6)

Facilitated by communication that also links the organization with the external environment

External Environment
External Variables and Information
1. Opportunities
2. Constraints
3. Others

Reenergizing the System

To Produce Outputs

External Environment

Outputs
1. Products
2. Services
3. Profits
4. Satisfaction
5. Goal Integration
6. Others

The Managerial Transformation Process

> The task of managers is to transform the inputs, in an effective and efficient manner, into outputs.

It is the task of managers to transform the inputs, in an effective and efficient manner, into outputs. Of course, the transformation process can be viewed from different perspectives. Thus, one can focus on such diverse enterprise functions as finance, production, personnel, and marketing. Writers on management look at the transformation process in terms of their particular approaches to management. Specifically, writers belonging to the human behavior school focus on interpersonal relationships, social systems theorists analyze the transformation by concentrating on social interactions, and those advocating decision theory see the transformation as sets of decisions. However, the most comprehensive and useful approach for discussing the job of managers is to use the managerial functions of planning, organizing, staffing, leading, and controlling as a framework for organizing managerial knowledge. Therefore, this is the approach used as the framework of this book (see Figure 1.6).

The Communication System

Communication is essential to all phases of the managerial process for two reasons. First, it integrates the managerial functions. For example, the objectives set in planning are communicated so that the appropriate organization structure can be devised. Communication is essential in the selection, appraisal, and training of managers to fill the roles in this structure. Similarly, effective leadership and the creation of an environment conducive to motivation depend on communication. Moreover, it is through communication that one determines whether events and performance conform to plans. Thus, it is communication that makes managing possible.

The second purpose of the communication system is to link the enterprise with its external environment, where many of the claimants* are. For example, one should never forget that customers, who are the reason for the existence of virtually all businesses, are outside a company. It is through the communication system that the needs of customers are identified; this knowledge enables the firm to provide products and services at a profit. Similarly, it is through an effective communication system that the organization becomes aware of competition and other potential threats and constraining factors.

External Variables

Effective managers will regularly scan the external environment. It is true that managers may have little or no power to change the external environment, yet they have no alternative but to respond to it. The forces acting in the external environment are discussed in various chapters, especially in Chapters 2, 3, and 5.

Outputs

> **Outputs**
> Products, services, profits, satisfaction, integration of the goals of claimants to the enterprise.

It is the task of managers to secure and utilize inputs to the enterprise to transform them through the managerial functions—with due consideration for external variables—into outputs. Although the kinds of outputs will vary with the enterprise, they usually include many of the following: products, services, profits, satisfaction, and integration of the goals of various claimants to the enterprise. Most of these outputs require no elaboration, and only the last two will be discussed.

The organization must indeed provide many "satisfactions" if it hopes to retain and illicit contributions from its members. It must contribute to the satisfaction not only of basic material needs (e.g., employees' needs to earn money for food and shelter or to have job security) but also of the needs for affiliation, acceptance, esteem, and perhaps even self-actualization so that one can realize one's potential at the workplace.

Another output is goal integration. As noted earlier, the different claimants to the enterprise have very divergent—and often directly opposing—objectives. It is the task of managers to resolve conflicts and integrate these aims.

Reenergizing the System

Finally, it is important to note that, in the systems model of the management process, some of the outputs become inputs again. Thus, the satisfaction and new knowledge or skills of employees become important human inputs. Similarly, profits, the surplus of income over costs, are reinvested in cash and capital goods, such as machinery, equipment, buildings, and inventory. You will see shortly that the model shown in Figure 1.6 will serve as a framework in this book for organizing managerial knowledge. But, let us first look closer at the managerial functions.

THE FUNCTIONS OF MANAGERS

The functions of managers provide a useful structure for organizing management knowledge (see the central part of Figure 1.6). There have been no new ideas, research findings, or techniques that cannot readily be placed in the classifications of planning, organizing, staffing, leading, and controlling.

Planning

Planning involves selecting missions and objectives as well as the actions to achieve them; it requires decision making, that is, choosing future courses of action from among alternatives. As Chapter 4 will show, there are various types of plans, ranging from overall purposes and objectives to the most detailed actions to be taken, such as ordering a special stainless steel bolt for an instrument or hiring and training workers for an assembly line. No real plan exists until a decision—a commitment of human or material resources—has been made. Before a decision is made, all that exists is a planning study, an analysis, or a proposal; there is no real plan. The various aspects of planning are discussed in Part 2 of this book.

> **Planning**
> Selecting missions and objectives as well as the actions to achieve them, which requires decision making.

Organizing

People working together in groups to achieve some goal must have roles to play, much like the parts actors fill in a drama, whether these roles are the ones they develop themselves, are accidental or haphazard, or are defined and structured by someone who wants to make sure that they contribute in a specific way to group effort. The concept of a role implies that what people do has a definite purpose or objective; they know how their job objective fits into the group effort, and they have the necessary authority, tools, and information to accomplish the task. This can be seen in as simple a group effort as setting up camp on a fishing expedition. Everyone could do anything he or she wants to do, but activity would almost certainly be more effective and certain tasks would be less likely to be left undone if one or two persons were given the job of gathering firewood, some the assignment of getting water, others the task of starting a fire, yet others the job of cooking, and so on.

Organizing, then, is that part of managing which involves establishing an intentional structure of roles for people to fill in an organization. It is intentional in the sense of making sure that all the tasks necessary to accomplish goals are assigned and, it is hoped, assigned to people who can do them best.

The purpose of an organization structure is to help create an environment for human performance. It is then a management tool and not an end in and of itself. Although the structure must define the tasks to be done, the roles so established must also be designed in light of the abilities and motivations of the people available.

Designing an effective organization structure is not an easy managerial task. Many problems are encountered in making structures fit situations, including both defining the kinds of jobs that must be done and finding the people to do them. These problems and the essential theories, principles, and techniques of handling them are the subjects of Part 3.

> **Organizing**
> Establishing an intentional structure of roles for people to fill in an organization.

Staffing

Staffing involves filling, and keeping filled, the positions in the organization structure. This is done by identifying workforce requirements; inventorying the people available; and recruiting, selecting, placing, promoting, appraising, planning the careers of, compensating, and training or otherwise developing both candidates and current jobholders so that tasks are accomplished effectively and efficiently. This subject is dealt with in Part 4.

> **Staffing**
> Filling, and keeping filled, the positions in the organization structure.

Leading

Leading is influencing people so that they will contribute to organizational and group goals; it has to do predominantly with the interpersonal aspect of managing. All managers would agree that their most important problems arise from people—their desires and attitudes as well as their behavior as individuals and in groups—and that effective managers also need to be effective leaders. Since leadership implies followership and people tend to follow those who offer means of satisfying their own needs, wishes, and desires, it is understandable that leading involves motivation, leadership styles and approaches, and communication. The essentials of these subjects are dealt with in Part 5.

> **Leading**
> Influencing people so that they will contribute to organizational and group goals.

Controlling

Controlling is measuring and correcting individual and organizational performance to ensure that events conform to plans. It involves measuring performance against goals and plans, showing where deviations from standards exist, and helping to correct deviations from standards. In short, controlling facilitates the accomplishment of plans. Although planning must precede controlling,

> **Controlling**
> Measuring and correcting individual and organizational performance to ensure that events conform to plans.

plans are not self-achieving. Plans guide managers in the use of resources to accomplish specific goals; then activities are checked to determine whether they conform to the plans.

Control activities generally relate to the measurement of achievement. Some means of controlling, like the budget for expenses, inspection records, and the record of labor-hours lost, are generally familiar. Each of these measures indicates whether plans are working out or not. If deviations persist, corrective action must be taken. Of course, corrective actions must be made by people in the organization. But what is corrected? Nothing can be done about reducing scrap, for example, or buying according to specifications, or handling sales returns unless one knows who is responsible for these functions. Ensuring that events conform to plans means locating the persons who are responsible for results that differ from planned action and then taking the necessary steps to improve performance. Thus, outcomes are controlled by controlling what people do. This subject is treated in Part 6.

Coordination, the Essence of Management

Some authorities consider coordination to be a separate function of the manager. It seems more accurate, however, to regard it as the essence of management for achieving harmony among individual efforts toward the accomplishment of group goals. Each of the managerial functions is an exercise contributing to coordination.

Even in the case of a church or a fraternal organization, individuals often interpret similar interests in different ways, and their efforts toward mutual goals do not automatically mesh with the efforts of others. It, thus, becomes the central task of the manager to reconcile differences in approach, timing, effort, or interest and to harmonize individual goals to contribute to organizational goals.

Managers or Leaders—That Is the Question

While some scholars make a distinction between managers and leaders (with managers often depicted less favorably), we suggest that good managers certainly need to be competent leaders. We also maintain that good leaders must be able to direct, oversee, and occasionally carry out effectively the managerial functions of planning, organizing, staffing, controlling, and, of course, leading. Fred Luthans, in his chapter, "Great Leaders: An Evidence-Based Approach," uses the term *leaders* and *managers* interchangeably. Specifically, he argues "this chapter on leadership styles, activities, and skills is also on management styles, activities, and skills,"[31] contending that managing and leading are closely intertwined. This book, therefore, is about management with special attention given to the leadership aspects of managing.

Leadership
Influence, that is, the art or process of influencing people so that they will strive willingly and enthusiastically toward the achievement of group goals

THREE MANAGEMENT PERSPECTIVES: GLOBAL, INNOVATIVE, AND ENTREPRENEURIAL

In previous editions of this book, we viewed management from the global perspective. With the increasing demands in the global competitive environment, we have added the innovative and entrepreneurial perspectives in this book. Many management issues have global, innovative, and entrepreneurial dimensions. Therefore, the managerial perspectives throughout the text can be discussed from several viewpoints.

The Global Perspective

This edition continues the tradition of viewing management from a global perspective, which requires an understanding of the social, political, legal, and environmental forces across national and regional boundaries that influence managing. Managers must develop their knowledge, attitude, and skills necessary to operate in the international environment. Managers need to understand not only the forces in the developed countries, but also those in emerging and developing countries. Because the economies of China and India play vital roles in the world economy, this book will illustrate many management issues in those nations.

The Innovative Perspective

> **Innovation**
> The enhancement, adaptation, or commercialization of new products, services, or processes.

Innovation is one of the most important elements in improving governments and businesses. It is the driver for succeeding in today's competitive environment. Indeed, innovation often means the difference between the success and failure of an organization. Innovation is important for enterprises (business and non-business alike) as well as societies. There is no complete agreement on the term "innovation." We define **innovation** as *the enhancement, adaptation, or commercialization of new products, services, or processes.*

INNOVATIVE PERSPECTIVE

The World's Most Innovative Companies[32]

The Fast Company magazine identified and ranked the world's 50 most innovative companies. Perhaps of little surprise, the four top-ranked companies are Apple, Facebook, Google, and Amazon. Other highly ranked enterprises are Square, the credit card reader for the iPhone and Android. Twitter ranks next. Also highly ranked is the Occupy Movement that is challenging financial, political, and social institutions. The Southern New Hampshire University, which transformed an old college, ranked twelfth. Tesla Motors known for electric cars and its introduction of the new Model S family sedan ranked thirteenth. The German technology conglomerate Siemens is also an innovative giant known for producing components for electric cars and for demonstrating the hybrid electric plane. Many of the readers of this text may store their files in the DropBox which is profitable despite the competition from Apple and Google.

Starbucks overcame a challenging period from 2007 to 2010 and has introduced innovations such as its "Jobs for U.S.A." program and its lighter roast called "Blonde." Starbuck's more recent focus is on health and wellness issues. With the current high health care costs, Narayana Hrudayalaya Hospitals in India make a major contribution by providing medical care for the poor. Dr. Devi Shetty's response to Mother Teresa's request for help changed not only his life, but also the low-cost–high-quality specialty care approach in India and Africa.

The mind map outlines some of the major innovative companies that were identified by the Fast Company. While most are located in the United States, companies in other countries are also noted for their contribution to innovation. This mind map only gives an overview of some innovative companies, but some of the listed ones will be discussed later in this book.

FIGURE 1.7

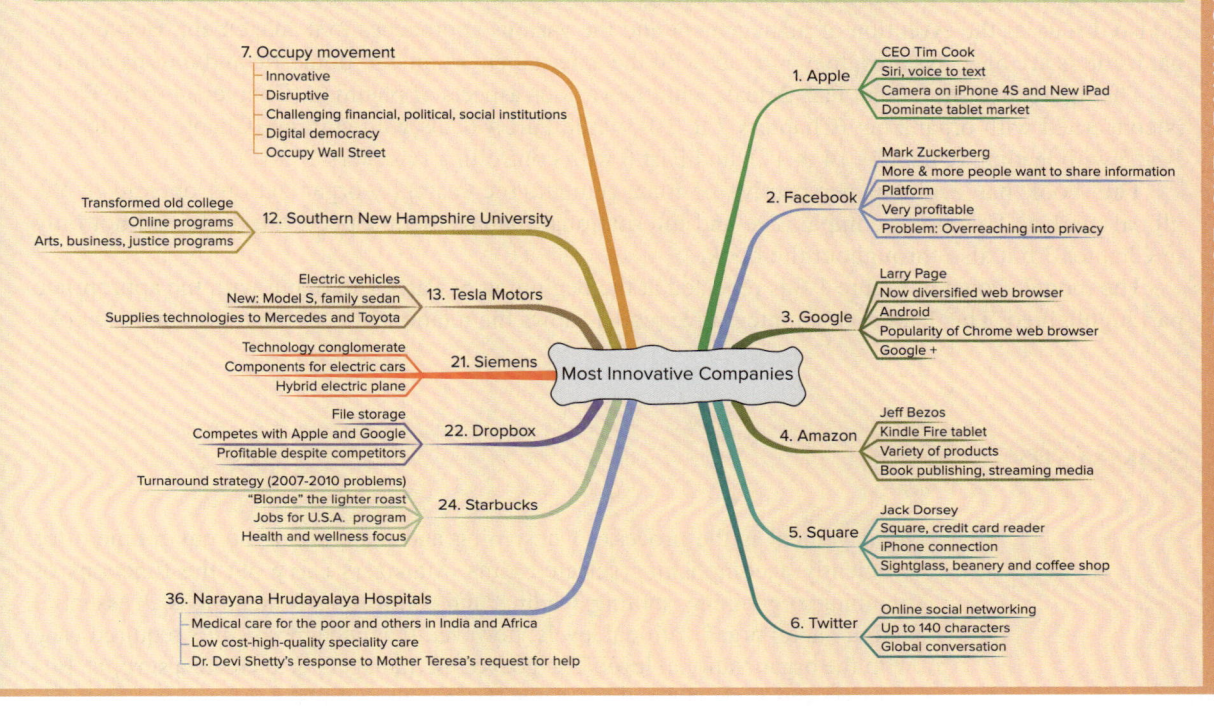

Most Innovative Companies

- 1. Apple
  - CEO Tim Cook
  - Siri, voice to text
  - Camera on iPhone 4S and New iPad
  - Dominate tablet market
- 2. Facebook
  - Mark Zuckerberg
  - More & more people want to share information
  - Platform
  - Very profitable
  - Problem: Overreaching into privacy
- 3. Google
  - Larry Page
  - Now diversified web browser
  - Android
  - Popularity of Chrome web browser
  - Google +
- 4. Amazon
  - Jeff Bezos
  - Kindle Fire tablet
  - Variety of products
  - Book publishing, streaming media
- 5. Square
  - Jack Dorsey
  - Square, credit card reader
  - iPhone connection
  - Sightglass, beanery and coffee shop
- 6. Twitter
  - Online social networking
  - Up to 140 characters
  - Global conversation
- 7. Occupy movement
  - Innovative
  - Disruptive
  - Challenging financial, political, social institutions
  - Digital democracy
  - Occupy Wall Street
- 12. Southern New Hampshire University
  - Transformed old college
  - Online programs
  - Arts, business, justice programs
- 13. Tesla Motors
  - Electric vehicles
  - New: Model S, family sedan
  - Supplies technologies to Mercedes and Toyota
- 21. Siemens
  - Technology conglomerate
  - Components for electric cars
  - Hybrid electric plane
- 22. Dropbox
  - File storage
  - Competes with Apple and Google
  - Profitable despite competitors
- 24. Starbucks
  - Turnaround strategy (2007-2010 problems)
  - "Blonde" the lighter roast
  - Jobs for U.S.A. program
  - Health and wellness focus
- 36. Narayana Hrudayalaya Hospitals
  - Medical care for the poor and others in India and Africa
  - Low cost-high-quality speciality care
  - Dr. Devi Shetty's response to Mother Teresa's request for help

INNOVATIVE PERSPECTIVE

The Entrepreneurial Perspective

If innovation is about improving products and processes, entrepreneurship is about creating these products and processes and organizations in the first place. In fact, while innovation has a bent toward enhancement of goods and services, entrepreneurship is more of an organizational variable where the entrepreneur creates the organization and the innovator helps develop or improve the product that the organization intends to sell. Innovators may find a home in a large organization while entrepreneurs are typically most satisfied when they can create their own organization. Simply put, entrepreneurs make things and organizations and innovators make those things better or more efficient. We define entrepreneurship as the act of creating an organization which would not exist without you. It is seizing upon an opportunity to solve a problem or provide a desired service which results in a sustainable surplus cash flow.

> **Entrepreneurship** is the act of creating an organization that would not otherwise exist. It is seizing upon an opportunity to solve a problem or provide a desired service which results in a sustainable surplus cash flow.

THE SYSTEMS MODEL OF MANAGEMENT AND THE ORGANIZATION OF THIS BOOK

The model of the systems approach to management is also the foundation for organizing managerial knowledge. Note that in Figure 1.6 the numbers shown in the model correspond to the parts of this book. Part 1 covers the basis of management and the interactions between the organization and its environment. This part cuts across all managerial functions. It deals with basic managerial knowledge, such as theory, science, and practice. It also discusses the evolution of management and the various approaches to management. Because organizations are open systems, they interact with the external environment: domestic and international.

The figure also shows that Part 2 deals with the various aspects of planning (Chapters 4 to 6). Part 3 is concerned with organizing (Chapters 7 to 10), while Part 4 deals with staffing (Chapters 11 to 13), Part 5 with leading (Chapters 14 to 17), and Part 6 with controlling (chapters 18 to 20).

This book has a global perspective of management. Increasingly, organizations operate in the global market. Therefore, comparative and international management aspects are discussed not only in Chapter 3 but also throughout the book.

The model shown in Figure 1.6 is repeated at the beginning of Parts 2 to 6, but with the appropriate part highlighted. This feature of an integrative model shows the relationships of the topics in this book.

SUMMARY

Management is the process of designing and maintaining an environment for efficiently accomplishing selected aims. Managers carry out the functions of planning, organizing, staffing, leading, and controlling. Managing is an essential activity at all organizational levels; however, the managerial skills required vary with the organizational level. The goal of all managers is to create a surplus. Enterprises must take advantage of the 21st-century trends in information technology, globalization, and entrepreneurship. They must also focus on productivity, that is, to achieve a favorable output–input ratio within a specific time period with due consideration for quality. Productivity implies effectiveness (achieving of objectives) and efficiency (using the least amount of resources). Managing as a practice is an art; organized knowledge about management is a science.

Many writers and practitioners have contributed to the development of management thought. The major contributors and their works are shown in Table 1.1. Many theories about management have been proposed, and each contributes something to our knowledge of what managers do. The characteristics and contributions as well as the limitations of the various approaches to management are summarized in Figure 1.3. The management process (or operational) approach draws from other theories of management and integrates them into a total system of managing.

The organization is an open system that operates within and interacts with the environment. The systems approach to management includes inputs from the external environment and from claimants, the transformation process, the communication system, external factors, outputs, and a way to reenergize the system. The transformation process consists of the managerial functions, which also provide the framework for organizing knowledge in this book. Throughout the book, international and entrepreneurial aspects of managing are emphasized.

KEY IDEAS AND CONCEPTS FOR REVIEW

Management
Managerial functions
Managerial skills in the organizational hierarchy
The goal of all managers
Characteristics of excellent and most admired companies
Three major trends: Advances in technology, globalization, and entrepreneurship
Productivity, effectiveness, and efficiency
Managing: science or art?
Major contributors to management thought
Contributors to scientific management
Fayol's operational management theory
Mayo and Roethlisberger
Recent contributors to management thought
Management theory jungle
Managerial roles approach
Management process, or operational, approach
Systems approach to the management process
Five managerial functions
Entrepreneurship and innovation defined
Open and disruptive innovation

FOR DISCUSSION

1. How would you define management? Does your definition differ from the one offered in this book? Explain.
2. What are the managerial functions?
3. How do the required managerial skills differ in the organizational hierarchy?
4. In what fundamental way are the basic goals of all managers at all levels and in all kinds of enterprises the same?
5. What are the characteristics of excellent companies (according to Peters and Waterman)? Do the companies you know have these characteristics?
6. How do advances in technologies, globalization, and entrepreneurship affect businesses?
7. What are the differences between productivity, effectiveness, and efficiency?
8. Is managing a science or an art? Could the same explanation apply to engineering or accounting?
9. Why has Frederick Taylor been called the father of scientific management and Henri Fayol the father of modern management theory?

10. In the Systems Approach to Management (Figure 1.6), identify the inputs from the external environment, show how they are transformed through the management functions to produce the outputs to the external environment. Why is the communication with the external environment important? LO7
11. Describe the relationship of Figure 1.6 and the organization of this book.

EXERCISES/ACTION STEPS

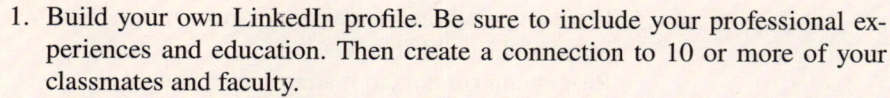

1. Build your own LinkedIn profile. Be sure to include your professional experiences and education. Then create a connection to 10 or more of your classmates and faculty.
2. Interview two local business managers and ask them how they learned about managing. Ask what kind of books they might have read on management (e.g., textbooks or popular books). Here are examples of management books: Gary Hamel and C. K. Prahalad, *Competing for the Future*; Michael Hammer and James Champy, *Reengineering the Corporation*; Charles Handy, *The Age of Paradox*; John P. Kotter, *The New Rules: How to Succeed in Today's Post-Corporate World*; Peter M. Senge, *The Fifth Discipline*; W. Chan Kim and Renee Mauborgne, *Blue Ocean Strategy*. Probe to what extent these books have helped them to manage. You may also find it interesting to read one of the best-selling books on management and mention it in the class discussion.
3. Interview two public administrators and ask them how their job differs from that of business managers. How do they know how well their department, agency, or organization is performing since profit is probably not one of their criteria for measuring effectiveness and efficiency? Do they consider management an art or a science?
4. Interview two entrepreneurs and ask them about their approach to managing. How does their approach differ from those of managers of commercial or public organizations?
5. Identify and discuss two major examples of corporate innovation (product or service). Have these innovations been successful? What have them meant for the company and its customers?
6. Identify a management software package that you may be expected to use in your career and describe its use to the class.
7. Identify a manager whose career you might like to emulate and be able to describe her/his career path to the class.

INTERNET RESEARCH

1. Review three of the following websites for current topics of management: www.businessweek.com, www.economist.com, www.fortune.com, www.forbes.com, www.industryweek.com, http://public.wsj.com/home.html, www.hbsp.harvard.edu/products/hbr/index.html, http://mitsloan.mit.edu/smr/index.html. If you are interested in Indian issues, see http://www.businessworld.in
2. Read the cover stories of *Business Week, Fortune, Entrepreneur* Magazine, and *The Economist* on the web (www.businessweek.com, www.fortune.com, www.entrepreneur.com, www.economist.com) and identify any section in this book that relates to these stories.

INNOVATION CASE

The Most Innovative Companies in the World[33]

The FastCompany publication identified some 50 companies in the world that are known for innovation, ranging from Google to Philips.

Google Illustration
Google is probably best known for Google Search, the most widely used search engine on the World Wide Web. But there are many more recent and lesser-known innovations. Google Glass is a wearable computer with a display that is worn like a pair of eyeglasses. It displays information similar to the smartphone and can communicate with the Internet. Then there is the autonomous car or self-driving car which drove 500,000 miles without an accident. The project involves some ten cars from Toyota, Audi, and Lexus. Chrome OS uses a Linux-based operating system to work especially with Web applications. This operating system is used for low-cost computers by Acer, Asus, Samsung, and other companies. YouTube is a mobile-friendly program that allows individuals to upload content on the video-sharing website. Street View allows a panoramic view in Google Maps and Google Earth. The viewer can see, for example, many streets and buildings in cities around the world. There are many other Google innovations, some of them you may have been using such as Gmail, Calendar; Google Maps, Picasa, Google Images, Google News, Google Drive, and others. To better manage the disparate businesses in Google, it recently reorganized under an umbrella holding company named Alphabet, in order to allow greater focus for each of its innovative divisions. Find some of them on the Web.

Questions:

1. Select any company shown in the mindmap Figure 1.7 and discuss the impact of the innovation as well as some limitations.
2. Select two innovations by Google, including some not listed in the mindmap, and discuss the potential impact locally or globally.
3. Predict what the next Google (Alphabet Company) will be.

ENDNOTES

1. Robert L. Katz, "Skills of an Effective Administrator," *Harvard Business Review*, January–February 1955, pp. 33–42; Robert L. Katz, "Retrospective Commentary," *Harvard Business Review*, September–October 1974, pp. 101–102.
2. Nicholas Argyres and Anita M. McGahan, "An Interview with Michael Porter," *Academy of Management Executive*, May 2002, p. 47.
3. "The Best Managers," *Business Week*, January 19, 2009, pp. 40–41.
4. Note that this approach is similar to concepts as discussed in the book *Blue Ocean Strategy* by W. Chan Kim and Renee Mauborgne which will be discussed later in this book.
5. Thomas J. Peters and Robert H. Waterman, Jr., *In Search of Excellence* (New York: Harper & Row, 1982); for an 2014 interview see Tom Peters on leading the 21st-century organization, interview by Suzanne Heywood, Aaron De Smet and Allen Webb, McKinsey Quarterly, September 2014, http://www.mckinsey.com/insights/organization/tom_peters_on_leading_the_21st_century_organization?cid=mckq50-eml-alt-mip-mck-oth-1410, accessed January 2, 2016.
6. "Who's Excellent Now?" *Business Week*, November 5, 1984, pp. 76–88. See also Michael A. Hitt and R. Duane Ireland, "Peters and Waterman Revisited: The Unending Quest for Excellence," *Academy of Management Executive*, May 1987, pp. 91–98.
7. Peters and Waterman, *In Search of Excellence*. For excellent discussions with the authors conducted by William C. Bogner some 20 years after the publication of their book (as well as their other books), see the February 2002 issue of *Academy of Management Executive* for "Introduction: A Bright Signal in a Dark Time," pp. 38–39; "Tom Peters on the Real World of Business," pp. 40–44; and "Robert H. Waterman, Jr., on Being Smart and Lucky," pp. 45–50. There are also two valuable commentaries on *In Search of Excellence* in the same issue of the journal: Les Misik, "The Attributes of Excellence: The Importance of Doing," pp. 51–52; John W. Newstrom, "In Search of Excellence: Its Importance and Effects," *Academy of Management Executive*, February 2002, pp. 53–56.
8. https://www.forbes.com/sites/forbesasia/2018/09/05/asias-fab-50-2018-newcomers-breaking-into-the-ranks-of-asias-top-companies/#358c-141d6efc, accessed February 25, 2019.
9. See for example the Technology Quarterly in *The Economist*, December 2, 2006 that discusses, for example, trends in the impact of technology on society, computing, robotics, communications, electronics, news media, innovation, biometrics and security, transportation, and other areas; see also *Business Week* Online at http://www.businessweek.com/ebiz, accessed January 5, 2009. http://search-mobilecomputing.techtarget.com/sDefinition/0,,sid40_gci214590,00.html, accessed January 2, 2016 and; Technology & Operations Management, http://www.hbs.edu/units/tom, accessed January 2, 2016.
10. See *The Economist*, September 23, 2000 issue, which covers "The Case for Globalization"; but there are also arguments against globalization "The Case Against Globalization, http://www.washingtonpost.com/wp-dyn/content/article/2008/02/14/AR2008021402674.html, accessed December 9, 2009. See also Alan M. Rugman and Richard M. Hodgetts, *International Business: A Strategic Management Approach* (Harlow: Pearson Education, 2000); John J. Wild, Kenneth L. Wild, and Jerry C.Y. Han, *International Business: The Challenges of Globalization, 4th Ed.* (Upper Saddle River, NJ, 2008); Ricky W. Griffin and Michael W. Pustay, *International Business, 5th Ed.* (Upper Saddle River, NJ, 2007).
11. X. Yang and C. Stoltenberg, "Growth of Made-in-China Multinationals: An Institutional and Historical Perspective", in Globalization of Chinese Enterprises, eds. *Alon and McIntyre* (Palgrave, 2008), pp. 61–76; X. Yang, Y. Jiang, R. Kang, and Y. Ke, "A Comparative Analysis of Internationalization of Chinese and Japanese Firms", *Asia Pacific Journal of Management*, 2009, 26 (1): 141–162; J. Duanmu and Y. Guney, "A Panel Data Analysis of Locational Determinants of Chinese and India Outward Foreign Direct Investment", *Journal of Asia Business Studies*, 2009, 3 (2): 1–15.
12. S. Venkataraman, "The Distinctive Domain of Entrepreneurship Research", in J. Katz, ed. *Advances in Entrepreneurship, Firm Emergence and Growth* (Greenwich, CT: JAI Press, 1997), pp. 119–138.
13. Silicon Valley Immersion Program, https://www.usfca.edu/management/corporate/Silicon_Valley_Immersion_Programs/, accessed July 25, 2015.
14. https://stats.oecd.org/Index.aspx?DataSetCode=PDB_LV, access February 26, 2019.
15. Peter F. Drucker, *Management: Tasks, Responsibilities, Practices* (New York: Harper & Row, 1973), p. 69. See also Tim R. V. Davis, "Information Technology and White-Collar Productivity," *Academy of Management Executive*, February 1991, pp. 55–67; Peter Drucker, "The Next Society," *The Economist*, November 3,

2001, Insert pp. 3–20; "The Drucker Institute," www.peter-drucker.com, accessed January 5, 2009.
16. *Fortune* Magazine, http://fortune.com/100-fastest-growing-companies/, accessed November 2015.
17. We indicate each firm's name and its industry.
18. W. H. Weiss, "The Science and Art of Managing," in Fred H. Maidment, ed. *Annual Editions—Management* (New York: McGraw-Hill, 2009), pp. 16–18.
19. For a critical view of management theory see Philip Delves Broughton, "Bogus Theories, Bad for Business," *The Wall Street Journal,* August 5, 2009 and http://online.wsj.com/article_email/SB10001424052970204313604574329183846704634-IMyQjAxMDA5MDAwOTEwNDkyWj.html, accessed January 2, 2016.
20. Table 1-1 shows some of the earlier contributors to management thought, from Henry Gantt to Chester Barnard. For more information on their contributions, see "Lilian Moller Gilbreth," www.sdsc.edu/ScienceWomen/gilbreth.html, accessed January 2, 2016, and www.lib.uwo.ca/business/barnard.html, accessed March 30, 2007.
21. For further discussion of Frederick Taylor, see: Modern History Sourcebook: Frederick W. Taylor: The Principles of Scientific Management, 1911, www.fordham.edu/halsall/mod/1911taylor.html, accessed December 9, 2009; www.cohums.ohio-state.edu/history/courses/hist563/fwt5-29.htm, accessed January 5, 2009.
22. Henri Fayol, *General and Industrial Management* (New York: Pitman, 1949); http://sol.brunel.ac.uk/~jarvis/bola/competence/fayol.html, accessed October 5, 2002. See also Henri Fayol, "Planning", in Fred H. Maidment, ed. *Annual Editions—Management* (New York: McGraw-Hill, 2009), pp. 26–29.
23. For a full description of these experiments, see Elton Mayo, *The Human Problems of an Industrial Civilization* (New York: Macmillan, 1933), Chaps. 3–5; F. J. Roethlisberger and W. J. Dickson, *Management and the Worker* (Cambridge, MA: Harvard University Press, 1939). See also www.thoemmes.com/encyclopedia/mayo.htm, accessed October 5, 2002.
24. See "The W. Edwards Deming Institute," www.deming.org, accessed December 9, 2009.
25. For Juran's biography, see www.juran.com/drjuran/bio_jmj.html, accessed December 9, 2009.
26. Scott Thurm and Joann S. Lublin, "Peter Drucker's Legacy Includes Simple Advice: It's All About People," *The Wall Street Journal*, November 14, 2005 and James Flanigan and Thomas S. Mulligan, "Drucker Regarded as Father of Modern Management," *Los Angeles Times* in *The Contra Costa Times*, November 12, 2005; Peter Drucker, *Management—Revised Edition* (New York: Harper Collins, 2008).
27. Jena McGregor, "There is No More Normal", *Business Week*, March 23, 2009, pp. 30–34, see also Strategic Innovation by Booz, Allen, Hamilton one of the of the oldest management consulting firm at http://boozallen-wp-aws03.siteworx.com/consulting/strategic-innovation, accessed November 2, 2015.
28. Harold Koontz, "The Management Theory Jungle," *Journal of the Academy of Management*, December 1961, pp. 174–188. See also his "Making Sense of Management Theory," *Harvard Business Review*, July–August 1962, p. 24ff.; "The Management Theory Jungle Revisited," *Academy of Management Review*, April 1980, pp. 175–187. Much of this material has been drawn from these articles. See *also "Management Theory Jungle,"* http://maaw.info/ArticleSummaries/ArtSumKoontz61.htm, accessed January 2, 2016 and "The Management Theory Jungle Revisited," http://www.jstor.org/pss/257427, accessed January 2, 2016
29. Especially Mintzberg's "The Manager's Job: Folklore and Fact," *Harvard Business Review*, July–August 1975, pp. 49–61, and his *The Nature of Managerial Work* (New York: Harper & Row, 1973).
30. "Peter Senge and the Learning Organization", www.infed.org/thinkers/senge.htm, accessed January 5, 2009.
31. See Fred Luthans, *Organizational Behavior: An Evidence-Based Approach*, 12th Edition (New York: McGraw-Hill, Irwin, 2011), pp. 445 and 446.
32. The World's 50 Most Innovative Companies," Fast Company, March 2012; also http://www.fastcompany.com/most-innovative-companies/2011/, accessed April 3, 2012. For the listings by Forbes magazine, see http://innovatorsdna.com/forbes-50-most-innovative-companies-2011/, accessed April 3, 2012; for the World's Most Admired Companies see http://money.cnn.com/magazines/fortune/mostadmired/2011/best_worst/best1.ht, accessed April 4, 2012. The World's Most Innovative Companies rated by Business Week, http://www.businessweek.com/magazine/content/06_17/b3981401.htm, accessed April 4, 2012.
33. "The World's Most Innovative Companies," FastCompany, March 2014, pp. 75–148; www.google.com, accessed February 21, 2014; "Chrome," http://www.google.com/intl/en/chrome/devices/#foreveryone-promo-family, accessed February 21, 2014; "Unique Identification Authority of India," http://uidai.gov.in/, accessed January 14, 2016.

CHAPTER 2

Management and Society: The External Environment, Social Responsibility, and Ethics

Learning Objectives

After studying this chapter, you should be able to:

LO 1   Describe the nature of the pluralistic society and selected environments

LO 2   Understand the impact of the technological and innovative environments

LO 3   Explain the social responsibility of managers and the arguments for and against the social involvement of business

LO 4   Understand the nature and importance of ethics in managing and ways to institutionalize ethics and raise ethical standards

LO 5   Recognize that some ethical standards vary in different societies

LO 6   Realize that trust is the basis for human interaction

LO 7   Update your LinkedIn profile

Every time managers plan, they take into account the needs and desires of members of society outside the organization, as well as the needs for material and human resources, technology, and other requirements in the external environment. They do likewise to some degree with almost every other kind of managerial activity.

All managers, whether they operate in a business, a government agency, a church, a charitable foundation, or a university, must, in varying degrees, take into account the elements and forces of their external environment. While they may be able to do little or nothing to change these forces, they have no alternative but to respond to them. They must identify, evaluate, and react to the forces outside the enterprise that may affect its operation. The impact of the external environment on the organization is illustrated in Figure 2.1. The constraining influences of external factors on the enterprise are even more crucial in international management (a fact to be discussed in Chapter 3).

This chapter deals with the impact of the external environment on the organization—with a focus on the technological and ecological environment—and the relationships between business and the society in which it operates. First, the focus is on the nature of the pluralistic society. Then the discussion expands to the topics of social responsibility and ethical behavior.

FIGURE 2.1 The organization and its external environment

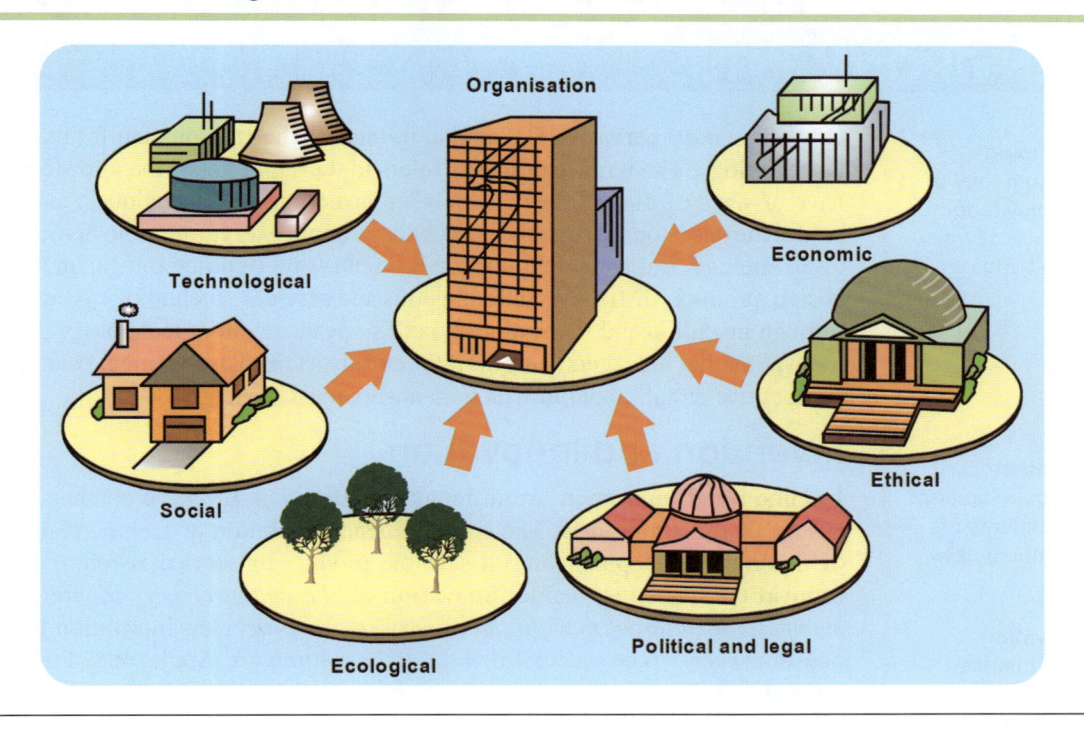

OPERATING IN A PLURALISTIC SOCIETY

Pluralistic society
A society where many organized groups represent various interests.

Managers operate in a **pluralistic society**, in which many organized groups represent various interests. Each group has an impact on other groups, but no one group exerts an inordinate amount of power. Many groups exert some power over business. As explained in Chapter 1, there are many stakeholders or claimants on the organization, and they have divergent goals. It is the task of the manager to integrate their aims.

Working within a pluralistic society has several implications for business. First, various groups, such as environmental groups, keep business power in balance. Second, business interests can be expressed by joining groups such as the Chamber of Commerce. Third, business can participate in projects with other responsible groups for the purpose of bettering society; an example is working toward the renewal of inner cities. Fourth, in a pluralistic society, there can be conflict as well as agreement among groups. Finally, in such a society, one group is quite aware of what other groups are doing.

THE TECHNOLOGICAL AND INNOVATIVE ENVIRONMENTS[1]

Technology
The sum total of the knowledge we have of ways to do things.

One of the most pervasive factors that influences the environment for managers is technology. The term **technology** refers to the sum total of the knowledge we have of ways of doing things. It includes inventions and techniques, and it includes the vast store of organized knowledge about everything from aerodynamics to zoology. But its main influence is on our ways of doing things, on how we design, produce, distribute, and sell goods and services. Technology is advanced through invention and innovation. It is this advancement of technology through innovation that managers must monitor closely as this advancement changes the competitive environment in which managers must operate.

Invention and Innovation

Invention
The development or discovery of something new.

Innovation
The enhancement, adaptation or commercialization of new products, services, or processes.

Invention and innovation are different. **Invention** is the development or discovery of something new. The enhancement, adaptation or commercialization of this new development into a saleable product or service is referred to as **innovation**. Thus, we define **innovation** as *the enhancement, adaptation, or commercialization of new products, services, or processes*. Innovation is not a one-time event; to be successful, it has to be *continuous*. Apple, one of the most innovative companies, started with the computer, continued with the iPod, the iPhone, and the iWatch. Similarly, Amazon started with books, continued with the Amazon Reader, and now offers the Amazon Fire that could be a low-cost alternative to the iPad. In the past, television viewers in the United States essentially had to choose from three networks, ABC, CBS, and NBC. Now they can choose from many cable or satellite providers or "over the top" channels offered directly over the Internet.

Product, Service, and Process Innovation

One can distinguish between *product innovation* as illustrated by Apple's, iPod, and *service innovation* such as Apple's iTunes, and *process innovation* such as producing goods or services in a more efficient or effective manner.

Incremental and Breakthrough/Disruptive/Radical Innovation

By **incremental innovation** we mean the use of existing knowledge, making changes or continuous improvements of existing products or services. In other parts of the book we point out that the Japanese are known for the *kaizen* approach which is a continuous effort to make products, services, and processes better, more effective, and efficient by reducing cost or improving quality. Companies, such as Google, may have been breakthrough innovators but then may continue with incremental innovation by introducing new products or services that are not necessarily radical. Other established enterprises may not want to radically change the existing organization or power structure and may opt for incremental innovation. Clayton Christensen refers to these incremental innovations as "sustaining technologies" in his book, *The Innovator's Dilemma*.

One incremental innovation approach involves *continuous improvement* by using *Six Sigma* that aims at reducing defects, improving quality, and consequently increasing consumer satisfaction. In statistical terms, Six Sigma means a failure rate of 3.4 parts per million. The Six Sigma approach involves the following steps: First, *define* the issue by, for example, listening to customer complaints; second, *measure* the process; third, *analyze* the data, by for example, identifying the cause-and-effect of a problem; fourth, *improve* the situation by, for example, conducting a brainstorming session; and fifth, *control* through, for example, statistical process control or documenting a process.[2]

Disruptive or breakthrough innovations are new and radical and may use new methods, materials, products, or services that serve new markets. Tesla's growing line of electric cars and Apple's iPhone are recent examples. The introduction of the low-cost Swatch in the 1990s disrupted the expensive "watch-as-jewelry" market. Ford's Model T mass-produced car is another illustration of break through innovation from earlier times and digital imaging disrupted the film-based photography market. Innovation can be risky. Michael Treacy reported in the *Harvard Business Review* that breakthrough innovation is risky and may be less effective than incremental innovation.[3] Clayton Christensen argued that disruptive technologies might lead to new value propositions that were not earlier accessible.[4]

The discussion in this chapter highlights some of the innovation issues. More detailed discussions of innovation will follow and is mentioned throughout this book.

> **Incremental innovation** The application of technology to adapt, enhance, or commercialize existing products, services, or processes.

> **Disruptive or breakthrough innovations** apply technology to develop and commercialize new categories of products, services, or processes that serve new market segments.

INNOVATIVE PERSPECTIVE

The Third Wave: The Knowledge Age[5]

The first-wave economy was based on land and farm labor. The second wave centered on machines and large industries. The third-wave economy is the knowledge age, which encompasses data, images, symbols, culture, ideology, values, and information. Being at the frontiers of the new technologies, society must rethink the way it structures itself and how it strikes a balance between freedom and restrictions (e.g., how to manage or control the massive amount of information available on the Internet). Cyberspace is a bioelectronic environment that exists wherever one can find telephone and coaxial cables, fiber-optic lines, or electromagnetic waves. It requires a rethinking of centralization versus decentralization, organizational hierarchy versus empowerment, and vertical versus horizontal organization structures, just to mention a few.

What is next? The need for creative ways to fashion knowledge to develop coveted products and services may lead to a differentiation of successful firms that leverage the creativity of their employees versus those that simply assign tasks to their employees. It is likely that this creative age is already upon us. Managers must be able to inspire and apply the creative abilities of the employees they intend to lead.

THE ECOLOGICAL ENVIRONMENT

Managers must take into account the ecological factors in their decision-making. By **ecology** we mean the relationship of people and other living things with their environment, such as soil, water, and air. Land, water, and air pollution is of great concern to all people. Land may be polluted by industrial waste such as packaging. Water pollution may be caused, for example, by hazardous waste and sewage. Air pollution can be caused by a variety of sources, such as acid rain, vehicle exhaust fumes, and carcinogens from manufacturing processes.

A variety of legislation has been passed dealing with solid waste, water, and air pollution. Managers must be keenly aware of these laws and regulations and must incorporate ecological concerns into their decision making.

In order to protect the environment, European countries developed the ISO 14001 standard to assure that company policies address a variety of public concerns, including pollution prevention and compliance with relevant laws and regulations. Since the adoption of ISO 14001 in 1996, some 10,000 companies had registered by the year 2000. Although the standard had a slow start in the United States, it received a boost when Ford Motor Company certified all its facilities around the world as conforming to ISO 14001.[6] Other companies such as General Motors, IBM, and Xerox followed. The standard was valuable to Ford for reducing water consumption, disposed paint sludge, and disposable packing materials.

More recently, ecological concerns have focused on climate change and global warming. Global warming refers to the increase in temperature of the Earth's atmosphere and oceans that is believed to be caused by the human creation of excess carbon dioxide. The increase in temperature may lead to rising sea levels and an increase in extreme weather.[7] Managers must now consider how their products and production processes impact the earth's climate over the long term and seek ways to minimize any negative consequence of their firms' activities.

INNOVATIVE PERSPECTIVE

The Greening of GM[8]

"Green and fuel-efficient" are the key words for success in the car market. General Motors (GM) is late, perhaps too late, in this game. Toyota started working on hybrids in the mid-1990s.

Chairman Richard Wagoner Jr. with a finance background seemed to have seen the light around 2005. Oil prices got out of control, global warming became an increasing concern, and fuel economy requirements all driving GM toward change. Actually, GM worked on an experimental electric car, the EV1, several years earlier. This idea was killed and superseded the profitable gas-guzzling SUVs.

In the middle of 2000 it became clear, go green or die. GM opted for the former with a revolutionary electric car: the Chevrolet Volt. The goal is to go green, go 40 miles by electric power before the gasoline engine kicks in, and get some 100 miles per gallon. All this is to be achieved by 2010. Will it work? That is the big question because of a variety of factors. It is costly and may increase the cost by $10,000 per vehicle; it is risky because it is based on new unproven technology; it is questionable whether the lithium batteries will be available for mass production; it is also not clear if the customers will buy a $39,000 to $45,000 car because other alternatives may be available.

Most rival car companies are prepared to offer fuel-efficient, low-carbon cars. Toyota already has several hybrids on the market, with the Prius being the most prominent one. Honda bets its future on fuel-efficient clean diesel engines. Nissan, using the Toyota hybrid technology, will be another competitor. However, eventually, Nissan may opt for an approach similar to GM. In Europe, BMW and Mercedes also invested in hydro cars. Mercedes produced diesel cars since the mid-1930s and finally was able to make them clean.

With all that competition, can financially stretched GM invest greatly into a risky technology with an uncertain prospect for success? What other choices does GM really have? These are some of the consideration the chairman and CEO has to consider. The strategy is at a critical point.

www.gm.com

THE SOCIAL RESPONSIBILITY OF MANAGERS

In the early 1900s, the mission of business firms was exclusively economic. Today, partly owing to the interdependencies of the many groups in our society, the social involvement of business has increased. As pointed out in the model of the systems approach to management in Chapter 1, there are many stakeholders or claimants to the organization. There is indeed a question as to what the social responsibility of business really is. Moreover, the question of social responsibility, originally associated with businesses, is now being posed with increasing frequency in regard to governments, universities, nonprofit foundations, charitable organizations, and even churches. Thus, we are talking about the social responsibility and social responsiveness of all organizations, although the focus of this discussion is on business. Society, awakened and vocal with respect to the urgency of social problems, is asking managers, particularly those at the top, what they are doing to discharge their social responsibilities and why they are not doing more.

GLOBAL PERSPECTIVE

Apple + Foxconn = iFactory in China[9]

Apple, known for its very successful iPhone and iPad, sources parts and assembly for these products from the Foxconn Company in China. Apple has been criticized for the poor working conditions in its partner supply-chain company, Foxconn, although that company also produces parts for other well-known firms such as Samsung, HP, and Dell. An ABC television reporter recently had the opportunity to visit what may be called the iFactory at Foxconn in China where many Apple products are produced. Several questions and issues may be raised about the relationships of Apple with its suppliers.

GLOBAL PERSPECTIVE

- One question may be "To what extent is Apple responsible for the working conditions at its suppliers as they are separate companies?"
- The publicity of several suicides at Foxconn put Apple in a negative light. Subsequently, Foxconn arranged for a survey to address the problems. The common complaints were low pay, high cost of canteen food, the pace of work along with other issues. Moreover, the company provided for counseling services. The company also joined the labor council that engages labor and management in discussions. This may even lead eventually to a unionized work force.
- Although the rate of pay at Foxconn is higher than at other firms in the area, the rates are very much lower than in Western countries where Apple products are sold.
- Specifically, the labor costs in China are the third highest in Asian emerging counties.
- President Obama raised the very important question why the high-tech products could not be produced in the United States with a very high unemployment rate (the official rate in mid-2012 is 8.2 percent, but later dropped to 7.9 percent at election time in November 2012). There are many reasons, besides the lower labor costs, for differences in various countries. Some include the different economic environments, the work environments, ethical considerations, laws, social habits, and housing.

Partly in response to the bad publicity, Foxconn doubled the starting salaries from 900 ($143) to 1,800 Yuan per month, still very low by Western standards. Companies such as HP and Dell, firms that are financially weaker than Apple, contend that the increased cost will result in higher prices for consumers in Western countries. While Apple may absorb the higher labor costs, other less financially secure companies plan to pass the costs to the consumers through higher prices. But some suggest to those firms: "Try innovation instead of complaining!"

www.foxconn.com
www.apple.com.

Social Responsibility and Social Responsiveness

Corporate social responsibility
The serious consideration of the impact of the company's actions on society.

Social responsiveness
The ability of a corporation to relate its operations and policies to the social environment in ways that are mutually beneficial to the company and to society.

The concept of social responsibility is not new. Although the idea was already considered in the early part of the 20th century, it received a major impetus with the 2009 book *Strategic Management and Business Policy* by By C Appa Rao, B Parvathiswara Rao, K Sivaramakrishna, who suggested that businesses should consider the social implications of their decisions.[10] As might be expected, there is no complete agreement on the definition. In a survey of 439 executives, 68 percent of the managers who responded agreed with the following definition: **corporate social responsibility** is "seriously considering the impact of the company's actions on society."[11]

A concept that is newer, but very similar to social responsibility, is **social responsiveness**, which in simple terms means "the ability of a corporation to relate its operations and policies to the social environment in ways that are mutually beneficial to the company and to society."[12] Both definitions focus on corporations, but these concepts should be expanded to include enterprises other than businesses and to encompass relationships within an enterprise. The main difference between social responsibility and social responsiveness is that the latter implies actions and the "how" of enterprise responses. In this discussion, the terms will be used interchangeably.

GLOBAL PERSPECTIVE

Social Responsiveness at Infosys

Sudha Murthy, the wife of the founder and former chairman and CEO of Infosys, Narayana Murthy, is known for her philanthropic work through the Infosys Foundation. For example, she initiated a move to provide all government schools in Karnataka with library facilities and computers. She also teaches computer science and is a fiction writer. For her social work, she received the Raja-Lakshmi Award. She was also the first woman engineer at Telco, which is now Tata Motors.[13]

In the meantime, more Indian women have taken on key managerial positions in the workplace.

As we define entrepreneurship as the process of creating an organization with the aim at addressing a market need and earning economic surplus, we distinguish social entrepreneurship as that activity which addresses societal needs with less focus on the associated goal of pursuing financial benefit for the entrepreneur.

> **Social Entrepreneurship**
> The process of developing an organization to address a societal need with less focus on the associated goal of creating economic benefit for the entrepreneur.

ENTREPRENEURIAL PERSPECTIVE

Social Entrepreneurship in Action

Social entrepreneurship can take many forms and organizational structures. In fact, many say that most entrepreneurial endeavors contain a social component as by their nature they create value, at least some of which is transmitted to consumers of the venture's endeavors. Still, some enterprises' clear social impact focus should be recognized for their contribution to improving the human condition. For example, Just Business was launched to incubate social enterprises as a response to human trafficking. This incubator invests in enterprises that have a clear social impact focus and may also generate profit for investors. For example, Just Business incubates Not for Sale, which fights modern-day slavery through business creation and supply chain evaluation. We interviewed the founder of Not for Sale, Dr. David Batstone, to learn more about social entrepreneurship in action.

1. What inspired you to found Not for Sale and Just Business?

   Batstone: "I started Not For Sale in order to address the crisis of human trafficking. In 2005–2006 I undertook an investigation journey around the world that gave me a deep appreciation of the extent of the problem, and the mechanisms that allow the trade to thrive. For some inexplicable reason, I opened up my heart but shut down my brain. I had been a venture capitalist in the tech industry in California, and knew how to deploy capital and talent to scale valuable enterprises. But when it came to a social issue like human trafficking, I turned to funding models that relied almost wholly on charity, even though they are simply not sustainable. Beginning in 2011, I decided to experiment in creating new business models. Just Business is a venture fund that invests in for-profit enterprises that simultaneously delivers tangible and measurable social and/or environmental impact. In most cases the company shares revenue with Not For Sale or some other non-profit organization. Just as importantly, the companies that Just Business incubates or accelerates deliver social and environmental benefits in the implementation of its business process."

2. What have been the most satisfying outcomes of these ventures?

   Batstone: "One of the most inspiring companies we initiated and incubated out of Just Business is REBBL, an herbal organic beverage. While many companies look for a 'cause' to which they can align and deliver philanthropic help, REBBL is a 'cause' that created a company. Based on our yearning to create a stable economic platform in the Amazonia region of Peru, we explored a product that could create jobs in the way that it sourced its ingredients. REBBL stands for 'roots, extracts, bark, berry, leaves' — and our initial ingredient was uno de gate, or 'cats claw', which is legendary for its health benefits and grows prolifically in the Amazon. REBBL now sells in every state in the USA, in quality supermarkets like Sprouts and Whole Foods. The impact sourcing of ingredients continues to be a central component of the company. The business is building significant equity value for its venture investors, and helps Not For Sale tell its story through the marketing of the products."

3. How does the Just Business business model differ from traditional venture capital firms.
Batstone: "Just Business distinguishes itself from other venture capital firms by our selection criteria for investment. We apply the same rigor of due diligence that any other venture investor would consider. We only invest in companies that demonstrate a promising value proposition that can scale, and will bring a health return back to investors. But we undergo equal due diligence to the social and/or environmental impact. If it cannot demonstrate the latter, even though we determine it to be a promising business, we will pass on the enterprise. On the other hand, if it demonstrates great capacity for social or environmental impact, but does not have a business model that promises investors a return, we will encourage that enterprise to pursue a non-profit charter."

4. What advice would you give to prospective social entrepreneurs?
Batstone: "My advice to prospective social entrepreneurs is to make small bets. Test what might work. Then keep scaling the test. Social impact investing is a pioneer field. There is no roadmap, so limit your risk exposure and scale on what works. It may be wise for an aspiring, new social entrepreneur to ride alongside a fund or an enterprise that is in the throes of the practice. The landmines that one might encounter are unique to the field, so having a sense of the landscape will prove valuable."

5. Any other topics you may want to mention?
Batstone: "The world of social entrepreneurship is expanding to the non-profit sector itself. Traditional charity is slowly diminishing, and non-profits need to think more creatively about the elaboration of their mission. Not For Sale, for example, does not simply rely on Just Business to be its donor revenue source. Not For Sale has innovated its own products and services that fulfill its mission to inoculate vulnerable populations to exploitation and trafficking. For instance, Not For Sale has its own private label coffee in Europe (over 800 stores) and its own beer label, Not For Sale Ale. In Amsterdam Not For Sale runs a very successful restaurant, and many of the staff come out of commercial sex industry in the Red Light District."

Arguments for and Against Business Involvement in Social Actions

Although there are arguments for business involvement in social activities, there are also arguments against it, as shown in Table 2.1.

TABLE 2.1 Arguments for and against social involvement of business

Arguments For Social Involvement of Business
1. Public needs have changed, leading to changed expectations. Business, it is suggested, received its charter from society and consequently has to respond to the needs of society.
2. The creation of a better social environment benefits both society and business. Society gains through better neighborhoods and employment opportunities; business benefits from a better community, since the community is the source of its workforce and the consumer of its products and services.

Arguments For Social Involvement of Business

3. Social involvement discourages government regulation and intervention. The result is greater freedom and more flexibility in decision making for business.

4. Business has a great deal of power that, it is reasoned, should be accompanied by an equal amount of responsibility.

5. Modern society is an interdependent system, and the internal activities of the enterprise have an impact on the external environment.

6. Social involvement may be in the interests of stockholders.

7. Problems can become profits. Items that may once have been considered waste (e.g., empty soft-drink cans) can be profitably used again.

8. Social involvement creates a favorable public image. As a result, the firm may attract customers, employees, and investors.

9. Business should try to solve the problems that other institutions have not been able to solve. After all, business has a history of coming up with novel ideas.

10. Business has the resources. Specifically, business should use the talents of its managers and specialists, as well as its capital resources, to solve some of society's problems.

11. It is better to prevent social problems through business involvement than to cure them. It may be easier to help the hard-core unemployed than to cope with social unrest.

Arguments Against Social Involvement of Business

1. The primary task of business is to maximize profit by focusing strictly on economic activities. Social involvement could reduce economic efficiency.

2. In the final analysis, society must pay for the social involvement of business through higher prices. Social involvement would create excessive costs for business, which cannot commit its resources to social action.

3. Social involvement can create a weakened international balance-of-payment situation. The cost of social programs, the reasoning goes, would have to be added to the price of the product. Thus, socially involved companies selling in international markets would be at a disadvantage when competing with companies from other countries that do not have these social costs to bear.

4. Business has enough power, and additional social involvement would further increase its power and influence.

5. Businesspeople lack the social skills to deal with the problems of society. Their training and experience are with economic matters, and their skills may not be pertinent to social problems.

6. There is a lack of accountability of business to society. Unless accountability can be established, business should not get involved.

7. There is no full support for involvement in social actions. Consequently, disagreements among groups with different viewpoints will cause friction.

Based on a variety of sources, including William C. Frederick, Keith Davis, and James E. Post, *Business and Society*, 6th ed. (New York: McGraw-Hill, 1988), Chap. 2; Robert D. Hay and Edmund Gr. Gray, "Introduction to Social Responsibility" in Marc D. Street and Vera L. Street, *Taking Sides: Classing Views in Management*, 3rd ed. Marc D. Street and Vera L. Street, Edit. (New York: McGraw-Hill, 2010). p. 4.

GLOBAL PERSPECTIVE

Philanthropy in the Silicon Valley and Around the World is Expanding According to Laura Arrillaga-Andreessen[14]

Laura Arrillaga-Andreessen, the wife of Marc Andreessen, the Netscape Creator,[15] lives in the heart of Silicon Valley near San Francisco. She is surrounded by technology gurus who may have influenced her book *Giving 2.0: Transform Your Giving and Our World*[16] in which she discusses the importance of giving: giving time, sharing experience and skills, giving money, or helping people to access networks. Giving may be a $1 donation, or giving your time by volunteering for a cause about which you are passionate. This means first of all identifying your goal(s) of giving and then developing a strategy for sharing to satisfy not only local or national needs, but global causes. This may include, for example, giving to those people affected by the 2010 floods in Pakistan, the 2004 Asian tsunami, the 2010 earthquake in Haiti, or the more recent 2011 earthquake in Japan that caused the tsunami and nuclear reactor damages.

Laura quotes Winston Churchill who said: "We make a living by what we get; we make a life by what we give."

Giving is universal, but to be effective and efficient, it should be strategic, which means that giving should be to where it does the most good. This requires reflecting about who you are, what your passion is, and then thinking strategically how you can contribute your time, your money, or your skills. For example, if you work in the human resource department in your company, you probably have interviewing skills; you could share your expertise with an unemployed, job-seeking person by teaching effective interviewing skills, resume-writing, or helping a person in conducting Internet job searches. On a national scale, one could be involved in a program that facilitates, for example, micro-lending, that is, making small loans to low-income entrepreneurs. The repayment rates of those loans have been phenomenal. In short, strategic giving is an idea worth spreading.

Today, many businesses are involved in social actions. A good example is the Ben & Jerry ice-cream company, which contributes to the conservation of the rainforest. The company also purchases nuts from tribes in the rainforest so that they do not rely on cutting trees for survival. A decision as to whether companies should extend their social involvement requires careful examination of the arguments for and against such actions. Certainly, society's expectations are changing, and the trend seems to be toward greater social responsiveness.

ENTREPRENEURIAL PERSPECTIVE

Interview with David Epstein, CEO of Sol Voltaics, on Social Responsibility in Entrepreneurial Management[17]

David Epstein was the CEO of Sol Voltaics, a nanotechnology firm in Norway. Previously, Dave has been a new business advisor and investor who specializes in matching markets, teams, strategies, innovation, engineering, and funding resources. Dave was also a venture capitalists at Crosslink Capital where he was for seven years as a General Partner, Venture Partner, and Venture Advisor, focusing on Clean Tech, Semiconductors, Hardware, Software, and Systems. In addition to being an accomplished venture capitalist, he has deep executive operational experience in starting, managing, investing in, and helping high-tech companies grow for 30 years.

Given Dave's deep and broad experience in high-tech ventures, we asked him to reflect on the role that social responsibility or social awareness has in entrepreneurial management. Epstein asserts that social responsibility will be different for different firms. He continued, "In our case, social awareness is important if it directly impacts the company and its plans. For instance, clean energy is a major social issue that is top of mind for many. But where that plays in the evaluation of an enterprise is not in how good this is for the environment, but rather how will that social awareness affect the company and the industry. Is demand higher because of the awareness? Are there government incentives that will spur on the adoption? These again need to be quantified."

We asked Dave if social impact was a factor in the venture financing decision. He explained: "Companies are not funded because it feels good. It must produce an economic benefit. Investors must profit for it to be a success. This is not true for philanthropic firms since they are not looking for returns. However, the venture industry is. The founder may get into the business for socially conscience reasons, but it will only succeed if there is a favorable monetary outcome. Social programs outside of the core business should be left out until the company is self-sustaining and can afford such programs without the use of outside funding…Each investor and the investor's investors choose where and how they would like to spend their charitable allocations, and money invested in entrepreneurial ventures has already been allocated to profit-making assets. It says nothing about how philanthropic the entities actually are."

Our discussion revealed that while firms should consider social imperatives in their business model, in order for them to be a factor in financing criteria, they must also create value for the enterprise and its investors.

Reaction or Proaction?

To live within an environment and be responsive to it does not mean that managers should merely react in the face of stress. Because no enterprise can be expected to react very quickly to unforeseen developments, an enterprise must practice ways of anticipating developments through forecasts. An alert company, for example, does not wait until its product is obsolete and sales have fallen off before coming out with a new or improved product. A government agency should not wait until its regulations are obsolete and discredited before looking for another way to achieve its objectives. No enterprise should wait for problems to develop before preparing to face them. Proaction, such as aiming for energy independence, is an essential part of the planning process.

The Role of the Government

Local, regional, and national governments play an essential role in developing ecosystems for entrepreneurship and innovation. Tax policies that provide incentive for commercial investment can help to establish clusters of firms that lead to the development of industries that help ensure employment and competitiveness for regions.

There are also many instances in which social changes can be implemented only by the enactment of legislation. However, many managers in business and elsewhere have found it to their advantage to do something about pressing social problems. For example, many businesses have profited by filtering smokestack pollutants and selling or utilizing these recovered wastes. Some companies have made a profit by building low-cost apartment buildings in economically depressed areas. In other words, contributing to the solution of social problems does not always involve net expenses. But society may need the bludgeoning force of legislation to get improvements underway.

Deng Xiaoping Who Changed China from the Planned Economy Toward a Market Economy[18]

Deng Xiaoping was a statesman, diplomat, and theorist. He has been credited with leading China from a planned economy to a market-driven economy that led to China's growth after the Cultural Revolution. He encouraged foreign investment and allowed limited private investment, which resulted in China became one of the fastest growing economies today. Deng's idea of moving toward a market economy was:

"Planning and market forces are not the essential difference between socialism and capitalism. A planned economy is not the definition of socialism, because there is planning under capitalism; the market economy

GLOBAL PERSPECTIVE

happens under socialism, too. Planning and market forces are both ways of controlling economic activity."[19]

When Deng Xiaoping visited Singapore in 1978, he was impressed by the modern, technologically advanced nation that planned its economic development, built its infrastructure, and encouraged foreign investment. Deng considered Singapore's approach as the model for China, resulting in what has been called "socialism with Chinese characteristics." Combining the planning techniques with Singapore's developmental approach resulted in economic growth rates around 9 percent for several years. China began building new coal mines, modern power grids, nuclear power plants, new roads and highways, and other projects. Much of the development that can be attributed to the leadership of Deng Xiaoping.

ETHICS IN MANAGING: AN INTEGRATIVE APPROACH[20]

Ethics The discipline dealing with what is good and bad and with moral duty and obligation.

Business ethics Concerned with truth and justice in the context of commercial enterprise.

All persons, whether in business, government, university, or any other enterprise, are concerned with ethics. In *Webster's Ninth New Collegiate Dictionary*, **ethics** is defined as "the discipline dealing with what is good and bad and with moral duty and obligation." **Business ethics** is concerned with truth and justice and has a variety of aspects, such as the expectations of society, fair competition, advertising, public relations, social responsibility, consumer autonomy, and corporate behavior in the home country as well as abroad.

There are widespread misunderstandings about business ethics: Not only that ethical concepts have quite often been dismissed in management theory as "soft" factors and quite often as useless chatter, business ethics according to another prejudicial view are merely some philanthropic efforts by companies.

GLOBAL PERSPECTIVE

Scandals and Corporate Governance[21]

In July 2002, WorldCom filed the largest bankruptcy claim in U.S. history (until Lehman Brothers in 2008). While the investors of WorldCom, Global Crossing, and other telecommunication companies were suffering, top managers of many of these companies got rich. Jack Grubman of Citigroup's Salomon Smith Barney seemed to have misled "outsiders", resulting in losses and bankruptcies that could hurt not only investors but also the U.S. telecommunication industry in the global competition with firms in countries such as South Korea and Japan, which already are technologically ahead of U.S. companies in certain areas.

Corporate scandals such as those of Enron and WorldCom have shaken the confidence of investors. In response to the disclosure of alleged improprieties, the United States initiated new legislation.

Starting from August 2002, chief executive officers (CEOs) and chief financial officers (CFOs) of many of the largest U.S. companies are required to state under oath that to the best of their knowledge the latest financial reports are true. Under the Sarbanes–Oxley law, CEOs and CFOs are required to certify the correctness of the reports to regain the confidence of investors. This legislation also stipulates that subsidized personal loans to executives be banned.

Business Week suggests several ideas for the creation of the ideal corporation, which must be built on integrity, ethics, fairness, and trust.[22] The new corporate model must be more transparent for investors, suppliers, customers, and employees. Performance data need to be accurate so that investors can trust the numbers. Executive pay must be perceived as being fair. The more open corporate culture needs to emphasize accountability, and employees must feel free to report unethical and unfair practices.

The more fundamental problem stems from the fact that ethics has usually in theory and teaching not consistently been related to other management disciplines such as economics and finance. Ethical considerations have quite often been rejected as related to values and religion. Therefore, a rather isolated academic discipline assumed a kind of a fig leaf status besides simplified management theories focusing on cost cutting, profit maximization, and "efficiency".

The financial crisis between 2007 and 2009, along with numerous corporate scandals has been a powerful reminder of an economic system that lacks a necessary ethical framework. Volatility and unpredictability of the market system has been largely underestimated. Therefore, the conventional means of management education have come under fierce criticism due to their narrow-minded approach and for their apparent failure to prevent corporate scandals to happen.

GLOBAL PERSPECTIVE

Moving Toward a Global Ethics View?[23]

Throughout the financial crisis, it became clear that the financial architecture reflects a largely outdated postwar model primarily dominated by rich nations of the developed countries. Countries such as India and China still lag on the margins along with other emerging countries. There is evidence that a decisive factor that provoked such a large financial meltdown has been the sub-prime crisis in the United States. The crisis might be a reminder that a financial structure that represents in a more appropriate way the globalized world may be better equipped to create a stable financial and economic environment on a global and a local level.

In handling the crisis, it is also evident that countries like China and India proved much more resilient to overcome difficulties and hardships in comparison with their Western counterparts. Applying the principle of justice in the area of a more and more globalized financial and economic market means therefore to finally recognize that new dominant economic players such as India and China should be given their well-deserved position within a new financial architecture.

A further element that makes ethics a must is the growing impact of consumer associations in developing countries that closely monitor how a product is produced. In addition the ethical and unethical behavior of state and business leaders are under much more scrutiny.

ETHICAL THEORIES[24]

In organizations, managers compete for information, influence, and resources. The potential for conflicts in selecting the ends as well as the means to the ends is easy to understand, and the question of what criteria should guide ethical behavior becomes acute.

Three basic types of moral theories in the field of normative ethics have been developed. First, the **utilitarian theory** suggests that plans and actions should be evaluated by their consequences. The underlying idea is that plans or actions should produce the greatest good for the greatest number of people. Second, the **theory based on rights** holds that all people have basic rights. Examples are the rights to freedom of conscience, free speech, and due process. A number of those rights can be found in the Bill of Rights in the Constitution of the United States. Third, the **theory of justice** demands that decision makers be

Utilitarian theory
Plans and actions should be evaluated by their consequences.

Theory based on rights
All people have basic rights.

Theory of justice Decision makers must be guided by fairness and equity, as well as impartiality.

guided by fairness and equity, as well as impartiality.

Institutionalizing Ethics

Business ethics are increasingly addressed in seminars and at conferences.[25] Managers, especially top managers, do have a responsibility to create an organizational environment that fosters ethical decision making by institutionalizing ethics. This means applying and integrating ethical concepts with daily actions. Theodore Purcell and James Weber suggest that this can be accomplished in three ways: (1) by establishing an appropriate company policy or a code of ethics, (2) by using a formally appointed ethics committee, and (3) by teaching ethics in management development programs.[26] The most common way to institutionalize ethics is to establish a code of ethics; much less common is the use of ethics committees. Management development programs dealing with ethical issues are seldom used, although companies such as Allied Chemical, IBM, and General Electric have instituted such programs.

The publication of a code of ethics is not enough. Some companies require employees to sign the code and include ethics criteria in performance appraisal. Moreover, certain firms connect compensation and rewards to ethical behavior. Managers should also take any opportunity to encourage and publicize ethical behavior. At the same time, employees should be encouraged to report unethical practices. Most important, managers must set a good example through ethical behavior and practices.

Code Statement of policies, principles, or rules that guide behavior.

A **code** is a statement of policies, principles, or rules that guide behavior. Certainly, codes of ethics do not apply only to business enterprises; they should guide the behavior of persons in all organizations and in everyday life.

Simply stating a code of ethics is not enough to ensure compliance, and the

---

GLOBAL PERSPECTIVE

Code of Ethics for Government Service

The U.S. federal government has established the following code.[27] Any person in government service should:

1. Put loyalty to the highest moral principles and to country above loyalty to persons, party, or government department.
2. Uphold the Constitution, laws, and regulations of the United States and of all governments therein and never be a party to their evasion.
3. Give a full day's labor for a full day's pay, giving earnest effort and best thought to the performance of duties.
4. Seek to find and employ more efficient and economical ways of getting tasks accomplished.
5. Never discriminate unfairly by the dispensing of special favors or privileges to anyone, whether for remuneration or not; and never accept, for himself or herself or for family members, favors or benefits under circumstances which might be construed by reasonable persons as influencing the performance of governmental duties.
6. Make no private promises of any kind binding upon the duties of office, since a government employee has no private word that can be binding on public duty.
7. Engage in no business with the government, either directly or indirectly, which is inconsistent with the conscientious performance of governmental duties.
8. Never use any information gained confidentially in the performance of governmental duties as a means of making private profit.
9. Expose corruption wherever discovered.
10. Uphold these principles, ever conscious that public office is a public trust.

appointment of an ethics committee, consisting of internal and external directors, is considered essential for institutionalizing ethical behavior.[28] The functions of such a committee may include (1) holding regular meetings to discuss ethical issues, (2) dealing with "gray areas," (3) communicating the code to all members of the organization, (4) checking for possible violations of the code, (5) enforcing the code, (6) rewarding compliance and punishing violations, (7) reviewing and updating the code, and (8) reporting activities of the committee to the board of directors.

Factors that Raise Ethical Standards[29]

The two factors that raise ethical standards the most, according to the respondents in one study, are (1) public disclosure and publicity and (2) the increased concern of a well-informed public. These factors are followed by government regulations and by education to raise the professionalism of business managers.[30]

For ethical codes to be effective, provisions must be made for their enforcement. Unethical managers should be held responsible for their actions. This means that privileges and benefits should be withdrawn and sanctions should be applied. Although the enforcement of ethical codes may not be easy, the mere existence of such codes can increase ethical behavior by clarifying expectations. On the other hand, one should not expect ethical codes to solve all problems. In fact, they can create a false sense of security. Effective code enforcement requires demonstration of consistent ethical behavior and support from top management. Another factor that could raise ethical standards is the teaching of ethics and values in higher education institutions.

Guidelines for International Business Ethics with a Focus on China[31]

With increased business activities in China, decision makers search for guidelines. Stephan Rothlin with his book *18 Rules of International Business Ethics, Becoming a Top-Notch Player* aims to assist managers not only to be ethical but also to be successful. Although the book was written primarily for Chinese managers (the text in the book is side-by-side in English and Chinese), the concepts certainly have a wider application. The guides are discussed in four parts dealing with international business ethics, labor conditions, justice, and virtue ethics. It is clear that those guides focus on many current issues in China as well as in other countries.

Part 1 International Business Ethics

1. If you strive to understand the values of different cultures, you will find common points.
2. If you analyze the facts, you will realize that honesty and reliability benefit you.
3. If you analyze case studies from different perspectives, you will discover the benefits of fair plan.

Part 2 Labor Conditions

4. Respecting your colleagues is the smartest investment you can make.
5. To increase productivity, provide safe and healthy working conditions.
6. To inspire trust, make your performance transparent.
7. Your loyal dissent can lead your institution in the right direction.
8. Downsizing your labor force is only beneficial when you respect each stakeholder.

Part 3 Areas of Justice

9. To establish your brand name, act as a fair competitor.
10. Reduce the gap between the rich and poor by developing a new social security system.

11. If you act against discrimination, you will increase your productivity and profitability.
12. If you protect intellectual property, all stakeholders will receive their due share.
13. Ongoing changes in information technology require new forms of loyalty.
14. Your public relations strategy will only secure your reputation if it witnesses your drive for quality and excellence.
15. Your economic achievements will only stand on firm ground if you diminish corruption.
16. Long-term success urgently calls you to constantly care for the environment.

Part 4 Towards Virtue Ethics

17. To become a refined player, sharpen your discernment and cultivate good manners.
18. Care for your business by caring for society.

China's fast economic growth results in increased business activities. Business leaders search for guidelines to operate not only in their country, but compete globally. These guides may assist Chinese managers as well as those in other countries in their decision making.

Whistle-Blowing

Whistle-Blowing Making known to outside agencies unethical company practices.

Another way of encouraging ethical corporate behavior is through **whistle-blowing**, which means making known to outside agencies unethical company practices. *Black's Law Dictionary* defines a whistle-blower as "an employee who refuses to engage in and/or reports illegal or wrongful activities of his employer or fellow employees". There is even a whistle-blower website that discusses whistle-blowing issues, including legal matters and protection.[32] This whistle-blowing center is a nonprofit organization that helps enforce environmental laws and works for the accountability of business and government organizations. Its primary objective is to protect and defend persons who disclose actions harmful to the environment and public health.

As we will discuss later in this book in greater detail, Roger Boisjoly, an engineer at Morton Thiokol, the contractor for the rocket booster in the Challenger Space Shuttle, pointed out the problem with the O-rings, which became ineffective at low temperatures. His fears and concerns were largely ignored by management and eventually led to the Challenger disaster. Another example is that of Mr. Ruud, a whistle-blower who was fired from his job at the nuclear plant operator Westinghouse Hanford Company. He sued the company and was awarded by a federal judge an entitlement for lifetime front pay.[33] In America, legislation now gives greater protection to government whistle-blowers. There is some evidence that after the September 11, 2001, World Trade Center suicide attacks, more employees have come forward to disclose security issues.[34]

Ethical and Unethical Leader Behavior in Carrying Out the Managerial Functions

Leaders can have a positive or negative influence on its followers. This book emphasizes ethical leadership behavior. The following contrasts ethical and unethical use of power (see Table 2.2).

TABLE 2.2 Ethical and unethical use of power

Ethical Leadership Behavior	Unethical Leadership Behavior
Using power to serve the good of the followers	Using power to serve self-interest
Respecting followers and colleagues	Lack of respect for others
Pursuing a vision and goals through ethical means	Pursuing goals at any cost with disregard to ethical considerations
Listening to feedback and criticism from followers	Rejecting criticism from anyone
Encouraging participation	Leading in an autocratic manner
Communicating vertically (up and down) and crosswise	Communicating top-down
Creating a flexible, situation-adaptable organization structure	Having a rigid, bureaucratic organization structure
Adapting leadership style to the culture of the enterprise and the country	Leading autocratically with disregard of the culture of the enterprise and the country
Teaching and coaching followers to become ethical leaders	Not teaching or coaching followers for fear of losing power
Controlling by persuasion	Controlling by punishing
Leading by a good example	Leading by ignoring ethics and customs

Ethical leadership behaviors are required to carry out to all managerial functions, namely planning, organizing, staffing, leading, and controlling.

Differing Ethical Standards between Societies[35]

Ethical, as well as legal, standards differ, particularly between nations and societies. For example, certain nations permit privately owned companies to make monetary contributions to political parties, campaigns, and candidates (which is prohibited in the United States). In some countries, payments to government officials and other persons with political influence to ensure favorable handling of a business or other transaction are regarded not as bribes but as payments for services rendered. In some cases, payments made in order to win a contract are even looked upon as a normal and acceptable way of doing business. Consider the Quaker Oats Company, which faced a situation in which foreign officials threatened to close its operation if the demand for "payouts" was not met; or a company may find itself in a predicament where its plant manager's safety will be in jeopardy if payoffs are not made.[36]

The question facing responsible foreign business managers is: What ethical standards should they follow?[37] For example, *guanxi*, which pertains to informal relationships and exchange of favors, influences business activities in East Asia. There is no question of what to do in similar situations in the United States: executives have to refuse the suggestion of putting money in a "paper bag." But in a country where such practices are expected and are common, American executives are faced with a difficult problem. With the passage of laws by the U.S. Congress and the adoption of regulations by the Securities and Exchange Commission, not only must American firms report

www.quakeroats.com

www.sec.gov

anything that could be called a payoff, but also anything else that can be construed as a bribe is unlawful. The Foreign Corrupt Practices Act (FCPA) Antibribery Provisions state: "U.S. firms seeking to do business in foreign markets must be familiar with the FCPA. In general, the FCPA prohibits corrupt payments to foreign officials for the purpose of obtaining or keeping business."[38] Thus, the United States has attempted to export its standards for doing business to other countries, which can improve ethical standards abroad.

> **GLOBAL PERSPECTIVE**
>
> **Truth in Advertising Regulations Differs in Various Countries[39]**
>
> Advertising in China is getting tougher. Proctor & Gamble (P&G) claimed that its Pantene product makes the hair ten times stronger. Government authorities demanded proof which was difficult to show through objective studies. Consequently, P&G withdrew the advertising. In the past, advertisers in China were relatively free in making claims for their products. Yet, a 1995 Chinese law that states that statistical claims should be accurate and true, had rarely been enforced.
>
> Advertising regulations differ among countries. In the United States, for example, the Federal Trade Commission provides an oversight. Moreover, competitors also watch for and expose questionable claims of their adversaries. In most European countries, industry is guided by self-regulation as well as strong governmental regulation.

TRUST AS THE BASIS FOR CHANGE MANAGEMENT

Managers are bombarded with new managerial concepts, and old ones often are disguised by new terminology—all designed for coping with managerial change demanded by global competition, customer expectations, and the need to respond quickly to environmental changes. Although various approaches to managing change in the New Age will be discussed throughout the book, one often-overlooked concept is trust. Professor Salvatore Belardo points out that trust is at the center of communication, collaboration, and the willingness to change.[40] Traditionally, the concept of trust is equated with integrity, loyalty, caring, and keeping promises in the relationships between and among individuals. But Belardo points out that trust should go beyond individual relationships and extend to the organization through the creation of a culture of trust that transcends individual leadership. Leaders come and go; the organization continues. For example, David Packard of Hewlett-Packard left as his legacy the HP Way, a philosophy that emphasizes a code of ethics, which permeates the whole organization and continues after his death.

www.hp.com

In this book, many managerial concepts, principles, theories, and practices will be introduced for managing change in the New Age. But an enterprise is essentially a human organization, which functions well only when it is based on trust, ethical behavior, and the recognition of human dignity.

ENTREPRENEURIAL PERSPECTIVE

Ethics and Trust for the Entrepreneur and Investor

What role do ethics and trust have in entrepreneurial management? Ethics and trust are paramount in the relationship between the entrepreneur and investor and other parties central to the new enterprise. Any question of integrity from any party will typically end the relationship and often terminate the new business. In fact, when investors are asked what is the most important criterion in evaluating a new company for investment, they will usually say the management team. And that management team's integrity must be above reproach.

THE DIGITAL REVOLUTION AFFECTS THE TECHNOLOGICAL, ECONOMICAL, ECOLOGICAL, SOCIAL, AND ETHICAL ENVIRONMENTS[41]

The change from analog to digital technology affects all people in all environments, domestic and global. It impacts our daily life, the way we interact with the government and other developed, developing, and underdeveloped nations.

Let us first look at the impact on our domestic and local environment. Greater efficiency is achieved, for example, by iRobot's vacuum cleaners. Self-driving cars are tested by Google. The greater impact may be achieved by self-driving trucks in the future. Individuals have more time for leisure activities such as inexpensively listening to music and watching streamed video. Digital technology makes it possible to obtain the latest news from various sources. For example, people followed the developments in the Arab Spring revolutions in Tunisia, Egypt, and other countries. Healthcare is dramatically changed by remotely controlled tests and scans. We even now see robotic nurses and surgeries.

In the business and work environment, we can see greater efficiencies with new business opportunities. Geographic boundaries become less important in the global new digital environment. Amazon.com is selling books, music, and a variety of items in many countries. The new 3-D printing now produces not only parts of airplanes, but it also makes body parts through bioprinting. Communicating in the global environment is facilitated by language translations. Coauthors of books and articles can collaborate instantly. While these are exciting ways to operate in the digital age, there is also the concern for privacy. Amounts of private information, whether stored on a computer, in a data bank, or in the clouds may be misused and can be stolen by criminals.

New digital technologies impact on governments and international relations. Again, there is the concern of civil liberties that could be impaired by national and foreign governments. There are also security concerns for water, power, gas, and oil pipelines that are vulnerable to sabotage by criminals. Terrorist attacks, corporate espionage, and cyber-information thefts are also big concerns. Protecting the infrastructure from thieves is much more costly to corporations and society than is the cost to terrorists.

Cyberwar with automated weaponry is linked to digital technology. The Internet has been used to recruit terrorists while on the other hand, digital technology can help in detecting terrorists and their criminal activities. Drone warfare with unmanned vehicles is already in use in Pakistan and many other countries. Drones can be used for many purposes, such as traffic control. Jeff Bezos, the CEO of Amazon.com, foresees that in the future drones can be used for delivery of small packages. But this application, if at all possible, is years in the future and requires governmental approval.

Digital technology is already extensively used in developed nations, but the impact on developing countries can be dramatic as the price of the technology is continuously dropping. Education, for example, can be delivered globally as illustrated by the Khan Academy which has as its goal to provide free world-class education to anyone anywhere. Also, textbooks are increasingly replaced with iPads. Certain editions of this book are available as eBooks. While the new technology can assist in toppling a regime, as seen in Egypt for example, it could also help people through emergency help with a natural disaster such as an earthquake or a tsunami.

It is clear that the digital revolution is still in its early stage. It has great potential to benefit mankind, it can be used for the good of all, but it could also be misused.

SUMMARY

Managers operate in a complex environment. They are affected by—and to some extent influence—the environment. Managers operate in a pluralistic society in which many organized groups represent various interests.

In their decision making, managers must consider the external environment. Technology provides many benefits but also creates some problems. Increasingly, firms are considering the impact of managerial actions on the ecological environment. Many business corporations and other organizations are making serious efforts to establish an environment that is beneficial to individuals, business, and society.

Corporate social responsibility requires that organizations consider seriously the impact of their actions on society. Similarly, social responsiveness is relating corporate operations and policies to the social environment in ways that are beneficial to both the company and society. Determining the appropriate relationships between various types of organizations and society is not an easy task, and one can make arguments for and against business involvement in social activities. However, there is now a general recognition that the responsibility of business goes beyond profit maximization.

Ethics deals with what is good and bad as well as with moral duty and obligation. There are three moral theories in normative ethics: the utilitarian theory, the theory based on rights, and the theory of justice. Some authors have suggested that businesses institutionalize ethics and develop a code of ethics. There are also other factors that raise ethical standards, including whistle-blowing. Managers have to make difficult choices when the standards differ in other societies. Trust is the foundation for human relations and modern management approaches.

KEY IDEAS AND CONCEPTS FOR REVIEW

Pluralistic society
Technological environment
Invention and innovation
Incremental and breakthrough/disruptive/radical innovation
Disruptive or breakthrough innovations
Ecological environment
Corporate social responsibility
Social responsiveness
Arguments for and against social involvement of business
Government's role in enforcing ethical behavior
Ethics
Ethics in managing: an integrative approach
Utilitarian theory of ethics
Ethical theory based on rights
Ethical theory of justice
Institutionalizing ethics
Code of ethics
Factors raising ethical standards
Eighteen guides of international business ethics
Whistle-blowing
Differing ethical standards
Trust as a critical factor for change
Digital revolution

FOR DISCUSSION

1. Why is the environment external to an enterprise so important to all managers? Can any manager avoid being influenced by the external environment?
2. Identify the elements of the external environment that are likely to be the most important to each of the following: a company president, a sales manager, a production manager, a controller, and a personnel manager.
3. What are the major social responsibilities of business managers or public administrators? Have these responsibilities changed over the years? How?
4. If you were the chief executive of a large corporation, how would you institutionalize ethics in the organization?

5. What ethical codes would you recommend for your university, your class, and your family? How should these codes be enforced?
6. Give one example of a successful entrepreneur and one example of a successful social entrepreneur. What are some of the distinctive qualities of each?
7. How has the digital revolution affected you?

EXERCISES/ ACTION STEPS

1. The class should select and read an article published in a recent issue of the *Wall Street Journal*, *Business Week*, or *Fortune* that raises some ethical issues. Divide the class into groups and analyze the situation using the ethical theories discussed in this chapter.
2. Interview one business manager and one administrator in the local government and ask how they perceive their social responsibilities. Do these responsibilities relate primarily to the environment external to the organization, or do they also include internal aspects?
3. Develop an idea for a new company. Would this company be a for-profit business or a social enterprise? Why?

ONLINE RESEARCH

1. Search the Internet for "business ethics" and select two articles for class discussion.
2. Cars do pollute the air. Search the Internet for "ecology" and "cars" to find out what car makers are doing to reduce pollution.
3. Search the Internet for "knowledge age" and describe three developments that might affect you or provide opportunities for you.

GLOBAL CASE

Spirituality in the Workplace[42]

Traditionally, the workplace and spirituality did not mix in America. But things are changing. Andre Delbecq, a professor at Santa Clara University, a Jesuit institution, said, "There were two things I thought I'd never see in my life, the fall of the Russian empire and God being spoken about in a business school." Now management books and conferences (including the annual meeting of the Academy of Management) deal with the various aspects of how God can be brought into the organizational environment. To be sure, people who want to integrate spiritual dimensions into the workplace are still considered rebels. But ServiceMaster, a Fortune 500 company with some 75,000 employees, created a spiritual organization culture many years ago. Indeed, Peter Drucker, one of the most prolific writers on management, had high regard for the company that is known for its products such as Terminix, TruGreen, and Merry Maids.

When people in the United States were asked if they believe in God, some 95 percent said yes. It is in a spiritual context that businesspeople under the daily pressure of work can discuss their inner feelings. As the baby boomers, now in their 50s, are reaching the top in their corporate life, they begin to wonder what life is all about. They lived through the youth culture of the 1960s and the greed-dominated 1980s. They are now questioning the real meaning of life and the ethical dimension of work. Jose Zeilstra, an executive at PriceWaterhouseCoopers, worked around the world, practicing her Christian principles in different cultures. In the long run, integrating her personal beliefs with her work resulted in a very successful career. Academic institutions such as the University of St. Thomas, University of Denver, and Harvard Divinity School are following and studying the movement of spirituality. Other American schools such as Antioch University, University of New Haven, University of Scranton, and Santa Clara University, as well as institutions abroad such as the University of Bath in England and the Indian Center for Encouraging Excellence in India, are conducting research, conferences, or lectures on spirituality.

The cover story of *Business Week* (November 1, 1999) discussed how companies such as Taco Bell, Pizza Hut, McDonalds, and Xerox pay attention to the spiritual needs of their employees. Some companies claim an increase in productivity, decrease in turnover, and reduction in fear. A research study by the consulting firm McKinsey in Australia found that firms with spiritual programs showed reduced turnover and improved productivity. Professor Ian I. Mitroff at the University of Southern California even stated, "Spirituality could be the ultimate competitive advantage." But there is also the concern that cult members and groups with a radical perspective could use the workplace for their own aims. Still, employees in companies that integrate spirituality in their workplace count on the potential benefits of greater respect for individuals, more humane treatment of their fellow workers, and an environment with greater trust that permeates their organization.

Questions:

1. What does spirituality mean to you?
2. Could spirituality affect ethical behavior?
3. Is this topic appropriate for business?
4. What are the arguments for and against inclusion of spirituality in business?

ENDNOTES

1. J. A. Schumpeter, *Capitalism, Socialism, and Democracy* (New York: Harper & Row, 1942); see also R. Foster and S. Kaplan, *Creative Destruction: Why Companies that Are Built to Last Underperform the Market—and How to Successfully Transform Them* (New York: Currency/Doubleday, 2001). See Also *Inventions and Innovation Annual Report 2005*, http://permanent.access.gpo.gov/fdlp1019/ii_annual_report_2005.pdf, accessed December 26, 2015.
2. Steps of Six Sigma, http://www.ehow.com/way_5254907_steps-six-sigma.html, accessed December 25, 2015.
3. Ibid.
4. Michael Treacy, "Innovation As a Last Resort," *Harvard Business Review*, July 1, 2004 and on the web at http://hbr.org/2004/07/innovation-as-a-last-resort/ar/1, accessed December 26, 2015.
5. Clayton Christensen, *The Innovator's Dilemma* (Harvard Business School Press, 1997).
6. "A Magna Carta for the Knowledge Age," *New Perspectives Quarterly* (Center for the Study of Democratic Institutions), 1994; Peter Drucker, "Knowledge Is All," *The Economist*, November 3, 2001, Insert p. 4. See also Jeremy Rifkin, *The Third Industrial Revolution—How Lateral Power is Transforming Energy, the Economy, and the World* (New York: Palgrave Macmillan, 2011); Alvin and Heidi Toffler, *Revolutionary Wealth* (New York: Alfred A. Knopf, 2006).
7. Stanley Fielding, "ISO 14001 Brings Change and Delivers Profits," *Quality Digest*, November 2000, pp. 32–35.
8. "Climate Change: A Summary of the Science (Sept 2010) (PDF). Royal Society, http://royalsociety.org/WorkArea/DownloadAsset.aspx?id=4294972963; "Key Findings. On (Website): Global Climate Change Impacts in the United States", U.S. Global Change Research Program website, http://www.globalchange.gov/publications/reports/scientific-assessments/us-impacts/key-findings, accessed July 27, 2012.
9. David Welch, "GM—Live Green or Die," *Business Week*, May 26, 2008, pp. 36–41; Imagine: A Daily Commute Without Using A Drop of Gas, http://www.chevrolet.com/electriccar, accessed December 26, 2015; Should GM Skip the Volt and Just Make More Efficient Cars?, http://gm-volt.com, accessed December 26, 2015; Not as Green as it Seems by Christian Wüst, http://www.spiegel.de/international/spiegel/0,1518,448648,00.html, accessed December 26, 2015.
10. "The World's 50 Most Innovative Companies," *FastCompany*, March 2012, pp. 70–149. The 2011 Most Innovative Companies.htm, accessed February 25, 2012; ABC Television Nightly News program in February 2012 and March 29, 2012; "The Stark Reality of iPod's Chinese Factories," Mail Online, July 27, 2012, http://www.dailymail.co.uk/news/article-401234/The-stark-reality-iPods-Chinese-factories.htm, accessed December 25, 2015.
11. C Appa Rao, B Parvathiswara Rao, K Sivaramakrishna, *Strategic Management and Business Policy* (Excel Books, 2009)
12. John L. Paluszek, *Business and Society, 1976–2000* (New York: AMACOM, 1976), cited in George A. Steiner and John B. Miner, *Management Policy and Strategy*, 3rd ed. (New York: Macmillan, 1986), pp. 38–39; Richard E. Wokutch, "Corporate Social Responsibility Japanese Style," *Academy of Management Executive*, May 1990, pp. 56–74.
13. Keith Davis and William C. Frederick, *Business and Society*, 5th ed. (New York: McGraw-Hill, 1984), p. 564. See also William C. Frederick, Keith Davis, and James E. Post, *Business and Society*, 6th ed. (New York: McGraw-Hill, 1988).
14. "Sudha Murthy: Humility Personified," *Business Standard*, http://www.business-standard.com/women/news/sudha-murthy-humility-personified/123253/on, accessed July 27, 2012.
15. Laura Arrillaga-Andreessen Talks About *Giving 2.0*, http://allthingsd.com/20111115/laura-arrillaga-andreessen-talks-about-giving-2-0/?mod=-googlenews, accessed December 26, 2015; Giving 2.0, http://giving2.com, accessed November 22, 2011; Philanthropy, accessed November 22, 2011.
16. "Mark Andreessen," *Forbes*, http://www.forbes.com/pictures/ekge45eg/marc-andreessen, accessed December 26, 2015.
17. Laura Arrillaga-Andreessen, *Giving 2.0—Transform Your Giving and Our World*, book is available in a hard cover edition as well as an e-book at Amazon.com Kindle edition, http://allthingsd.com/20111115/laura-arrillaga-andreessen-talks-about-giving-2-0/?mod=-googlenews, accessed December 26, 2015.
18. Email interview updated on August 13, 2009 from original discussion in January 8, 2007 with Mr. David Epstein, Founder, Epstein Advisors, by Mark Cannice.
19. Robyn Meredith, *The Elephant and the Dragon* (New York: Norton & Company, 2008), Chapter 1. Richard Evans, *Deng Xiaoping and the Making of Modern China*, 2nd ed. (Penguin Books, 1995).
20. Cited by John Gittings in *The Changing Face of China* (Oxford: Oxford University Press, 2005).
21. The Special Issue on Ethics and Social Responsibility in *The Academy of Management Learning & Education*,

September 2006 discusses various view on ethics. This section was prepared with the assistance of Professor Stephan Rothlin and Li Xiaosong and CIBE research team. Used with permission.

22. Steven Rosenbush, Heather Timmons, Roger O. Crockett, Christopher Palmeri, and Charles Haddad, "Scandals in Corporate America," *Business Week*, August 5, 2002, pp. 34–40; "I Swear ... Oaths Are Only a Small Step in the Business of Cleaning up American Companies," *The Economist*, August 17, 2002, p. 11; "In Search of Honesty," *The Economist*, August 17, 2002, pp. 49–50; John A. Byrne, "After Enron: The Ideal Corporation," *Business Week*, August 26, 2002, pp. 68–74; "When Something Is Rotten," *The Economist*, July 27, 2002, pp. 53–54; Anthony Bianco, "The Angry Market," *Business Week*, July 29, 2002, pp. 32–33; Stephanie N. Mehta, "Is There Any Way Out of the Mess?" *Fortune*, July 22, 2002, pp. 83–86; "The Pay of Chief Executives Can Seem Ridiculous. Often, It Is," *The Economist*, July 13, 2002, p. 64; Mark Gimein, "You Bought. They Sold," *Fortune*, September 2, 2002, pp. 64–74.

23. **Byrne, "After Enron".**

24. Used with permission by Stephan Rothlin in Beijing.

25. See also Daniel J. Brass, Kenneth D. Butterfield, and Bruce C. Skaggs, "Relationships and Unethical Behavior: A Social Network Perspective," *Academy of Management Review*, January 1998, pp. 14–31.

26. Jeffrey M. Kaplan, "Business Ethics Conferences," *Business and Society Review*, Spring 1999, p. 53ff.; Francis J. Daly, "The Ethics Dynamics," ibid., p. 37ff.

27. Much of this discussion is based on James Weber, "Institutionalizing Ethics into the Corporation," *MSU Business Topics*, Spring 1981, pp. 47–52; and Theodore V. Purcell and James Weber, *Institutionalizing Corporate Ethics: A Case History* (New York: Presidents Association, Chief Executive Officers' Division of the American Management Association, 1979).

28. *Public Law 96-303*, July 3, 1980.

29. Purcell and Weber, "Institutionalizing Ethics into the Corporation."

30. See also James Weber, "Bribery: Not Only Wrong, But Costly Too?" *The Academy of Management Perspectives*, August 2007, pp. 86–87.

31. Steven N. Brenner and Earl A. Molander, "Is the Ethics of Business Changing?" *Harvard Business Review*, January–February 1977, p. 63.

32. "Google stops censoring in China," CNNMoney, March 22, 2010 http://money.cnn.com/2010/03/22/technology/google_china/index.htm, accessed December 26, 2015.

33. National Whistleblower Center, www.whistleblowers.org, accessed December 26, 2015.

34. Michelle L. Allen, "Whistle Blowing," Summer 1999, http://science.kennesaw.edu/csis/msis/stuwork/WhistleBlowing.html.

35. "Whistleblowing," *The Economist*, January 12, 2002, pp. 55–56.

36. See also Sandra Waddock, "Building New Institutional Infrastructure of Corporate Responsibility," *The Academy of Management Perspectives*, August 2008, pp. 87–108.

37. Clarence D. Walton (ed.), *The Ethics of Corporate Conduct* (Englewood Cliffs, NJ: Prentice Hall, 1977), Chap. 7.

38. Steve Lovett, Lee C. Simmons, and Raja Kali, "Guanxi versus the Market: Ethics and Efficiency," *Journal of International Business Studies*, Summer 1999, p. 231ff.

39. Foreign Corrupt Practices Act Antibribery Provisions (U.S. Department of Justice Fraud Section, Criminal Division), www.lectlaw.com/files/bur21.htm, accessed November 20, 2012.

40. Jonathan Cheng with contributions by Geoffrey A. Fowler, Ivy Zhang, and Sarah Ellison, "China Demands Concrete Proof of Ad Claims," *Wall Street Journal*, July 8, 2005.

41. Salvatore Belardo and Anthony W. Belardo, "Re-engineering Re-engineering: How an Ethical Organization Can Encourage the Generative Use of Reengineering," manuscript.

42. Eric Schmidt and Jared Cohen, *The New Digital Age—Reshaping the Future of People, Nations, and Business* (Knopf Doubleday Publishing Group, 2013 and 2014); A.D. Thibeault, An Executive Summary of Eric Schmidt and Jared Cohen's The New Digital Age—Reshaping the Future of People, Nations, and Business, http://www.amazon.com/Executive-Summary-Brynjolfsson-McAfees-Machine-ebook/dp/B00I3ME0YO/ref=sr_1_1?s=digital-text&ie=UTF8&qid=1394920454&sr=1-1, accessed March 12, 2014; Jan Puhl, "Silicon Savannah: Africa's Transformative Digital Revolution," Spiegel Only International, December 5, 2013, http://www.spiegel.de/international/world/silicon-savannah-how-mobile-phones-and-the-internet-changed-africa-a-936307.html, accessed December 25, 2015; Janet Maslin, "Formatting a World with no Secrets," The New York Times, April 25, 2013; "Digital Revolution: iPad Replace Textbooks," Arab News, March 15, 2014, http://www.arabnews.com/news/534066, accessed December 25, 2015; The Wall Street Journal's column "All Things Digital" had useful information on the digital age. Although the column has been discontinued, Walt Mossberg who reviewed and commented on digital devices, can now be viewed at http://recode.net, accessed March 15, 2014; "A free World-Class Education for Anyone Anywhere," http://www.khanacademy.org/about, accessed December 25, 2015.

43. A variety of sources were consulted, including Ian I. Mitroff and Elizabeth A. Denton, "A Study of Spirituality in the Workplace," *MIT Sloan Management Review*, Summer 1999; Michelle Conlin, "Religion in the Workplace," *Business Week*, November 1, 1999, pp. 150–158; Ian I. Mitroff and Elizabeth A. Denton, *A Spiritual Audit of Corporate America* (San Francisco: Jossey-Bass, 1999); "*Fortune* Magazine: Spirituality in the Workplace Surging," www.ezboard_com.htm, accessed December 1, 2001; Andre L. Delbecq, "Spirituality for Business Leadership: Reporting on a Pilot Course for MBAs and CEOs," *Journal of Management Inquiry*, June 2000, pp. 117–128; Andre L. Delbecq, J. Thomas, and Kathleen L. McCarthy, "*Seminar in Spirituality and Business Leadership*," http://contemplativemind.org/programs/academic/syllabi/delbecq.pdf#search=%22Andre%20L.%20Delbecq%20Spirituality%20%22, accessed December 9, 2009; Peter Vaill, "Introduction to Spirituality for Business Leadership," *Journal of Management Inquiry*, June 2000, pp. 115–116; see the 2006 Academy of Management Annual Meeting http://meeting.aomonline.org/2006/index.php?option=com_content&task=view&id=93&Itemid=98, accessed December 9, 2009; see also Robert A. Sirico, "The Pope on 'Love in Truth'" *The Wall Street Journal*, July 19, 2009 and "Caritas in Veriate". http://www.vatican.va/holy_father/benedict_xvi/encyclicals/documents/hf_ben-xvi_enc_20090629_caritas-in-veritate_en.html, accessed November 20, 2012.

CHAPTER 3

Global, Comparative, and Quality Management

Learning Objectives

After studying this chapter, you should be able to:

LO 1   Discuss the nature and purpose of international business and multinational corporations

LO 2   Understand country alliances that form trade blocs

LO 3   Appreciate cultural and country differences and their implications for managing

LO 4   Recognize the differences in managing in selected countries

LO 5   Describe the managerial practices in Japan and Theory Z

LO 6   Understand the factors that influence the competitive advantages of nations, according to Michael Porter

LO 7   Recognize the major contributions to quality management and describe the Baldrige Quality Award, ISO 9000, and the European Quality Award

The previous chapter focused on the external factors that are present, especially in the domestic environment. The constraining factors on managing are likely to be more severe for international firms. Executives operating in a foreign country need to learn a great deal about the country's educational, economic, legal, and political systems, especially its sociocultural environment.

The first section in this chapter deals with international management and the role of multinational corporations (MNCs). Then the environmental impact on managing in selected countries is examined, with special attention given to Japanese managerial practices. Finally, the competitive advantage of nations and quality management is discussed.

INTERNATIONAL MANAGEMENT AND MULTINATIONAL CORPORATIONS

The study of international management focuses on the operation of international firms in host countries. It is concerned with managerial issues related to the flow of people, goods, and money, with the ultimate aim of managing better in situations that involve crossing national boundaries.

The environmental factors that affect domestic firms usually are more critical for international corporations operating in foreign countries. As illustrated in Table 3.1, managers involved in international business are faced with many factors that are different from those of the domestically oriented firm. They have to interact with employees who have different educational and cultural backgrounds and value systems; they also must cope with different legal, political, and economic factors. These environments understandably influence the way managerial and enterprise functions are carried out.

International Management focuses on the operation of international firms in host countries.

TABLE 3.1 Managing domestic and international enterprises

Managerial function	Domestic enterprise	International enterprise (in industrialized country)
Planning		
• Scanning the environment	• National market	• Worldwide market for threats and opportunities
Organizing		
• Organization structure	• Structure for domestic	• Global structure operations
• View of authority	• Similar	• Different

Managerial function	Domestic enterprise	International enterprise (in industrialized country)
Staffing		
• Sources of managerial talent	• National labor pool	• Worldwide labor pool
• Manager orientation	• Often ethnocentric	• Geocentric
Leading		
• Leadership and motivation	• Influenced by similar culture	• Influenced by many different cultures
• Communication lines	• Relatively short	• Network with long distances
Controlling		
• Reporting system	• Similar requirements	• Many different requirements

The Nature and Purpose of International Business

International businesses engage in transactions across national boundaries.

Although business has been conducted on an international scale for a long time, international business gained greater visibility and importance because of the growth of large MNCs. **International businesses** engage in transactions across national boundaries. These transactions include the transfer of goods, services, technology, managerial knowledge, and capital to other countries.

The interaction of a firm with the host country can take many forms, as illustrated in Figure 3.1. One is the exportation of goods and services. Another is a licensing agreement for producing goods in another country. The company may also engage in management contracts for operating foreign companies. Still another form of interaction is a joint venture with a firm in the host country. One form of joint venture is the strategic alliance that is often formed in order to expand geographically (airlines do this extensively) or to expand the market for products or services. Finally, multinationals may set up wholly owned subsidiaries or branches with production facilities in the host country. Thus, in developing a global strategy, an international firm has many options.

The contact between the parent firm and the host country is affected by several factors; some are unifying, while others can cause conflicts.

Unifying Effects

Unifying influences occur when the parent company provides and shares technical and managerial know-how, thus assisting the local company in the development of human and material resources. Moreover, both partners may find it advantageous to be integrated into a global organizational structure. Whatever the interaction, organizational policies must provide for equity and result in benefits for both the parent firm and the local company. Only then can one expect a long-lasting relationship.

FIGURE 3.1 Forms of international business

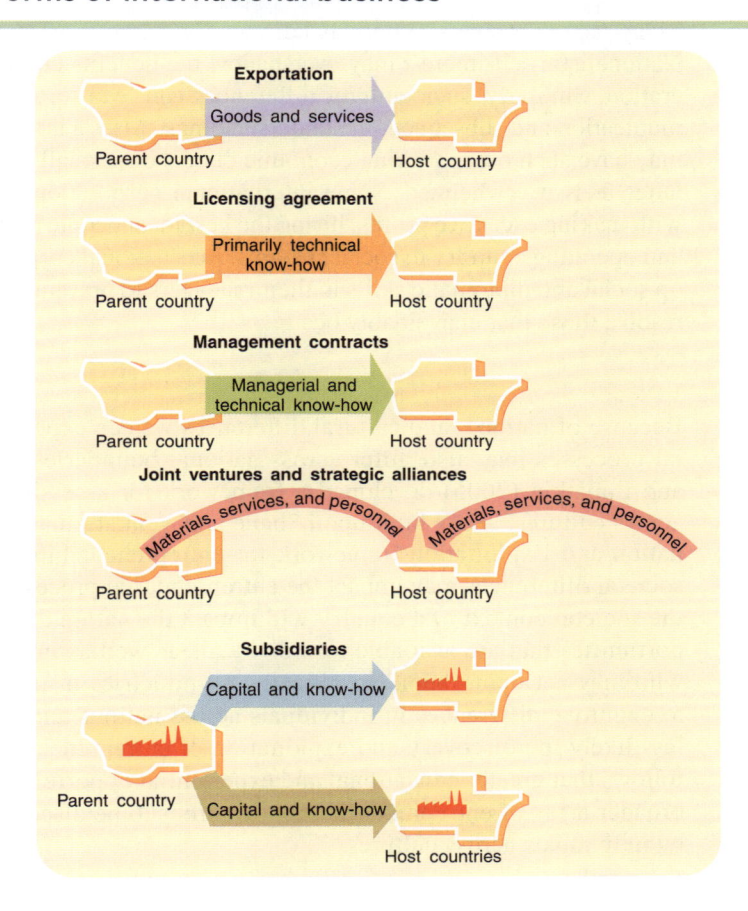

Exportation: Parent country → Goods and services → Host country

Licensing agreement: Parent country → Primarily technical know-how → Host country

Management contracts: Parent country → Managerial and technical know-how → Host country

Joint ventures and strategic alliances: Parent country ↔ Materials, services, and personnel ↔ Host country

Subsidiaries: Parent country → Capital and know-how → Host countries

GLOBAL PERSPECTIVE

Who Will be Leading the Way to Cheap Cars?[1]

With high gasoline prices and saturated markets in developed countries, carmakers focus now on emerging markets. These markets need cheap cars and manufacturers are responding. However, cars should not only be cheap, they must also be robust and reliable. Carlos Ghosn, Renault-Nissan's CEO, in the past focused on large, expensive cars. Renault plans are to build a $3,000 car with Bajaj Auto Ltd, an Indian motorbike maker. Renault has been very successful with its Logan model that sold in India for about $7,500, a car that was suited for the middle class. Renault moved to the low-cost car, produced in Romania. While the Logan has made no inroads in Western Europe, it is now produced in seven countries such as Columbia and Russia.

Chrysler together with China's Chery Automobile Co. is planning to sell cars in Europe under the Dodge name. General Motors plans operations in Argentina and Brazil and is opening engineering centers in India, South Korea, and Brazil.

Traditionally, customers in developing countries bought used European and Japanese cars. Now, African customers look for cheap cars. New cars from China are replacing used cars from developing countries. Chinese companies such as Great Wall, Chery Automobile Co., and Geely Group Ltd. are making inroads in Africa. India's TATA Motors is offering a car for less than $2,500. Western manufacturers such as French Renault and Japan's Nissan Motors Co. are working together with India's Mahindra & Mahindra Ltd. in developing a $3,000 car.

Emerging countries demand cheap cars, and global carmakers are responding to these needs using global strategies. International demand for cheap cars can help unify countries.

Potentials for Conflict

Many factors can cause conflicts between the parent firm and the host country. Nationalistic self-interest may overshadow the benefits obtained through cooperation. Similarly, sociocultural differences can lead to a breakdown in communication and subsequent misunderstandings. Also, a large multinational firm may have such overpowering economic effects on a small host country that the latter feels overwhelmed. Some international corporations have been charged with making excessive profits, hiring the best local people away from local firms and operating contrary to social customs. International corporations must develop social and diplomatic skills in their managers to prevent such conflicts and to resolve those that unavoidably occur.

Comparative Entrepreneurship Across Nations

Because of national and cultural differences we can expect that entrepreneurial processes may also differ across national boundaries. Baker, Gedajlovic, and Lubatkin (2005) developed a framework for assessing entrepreneurship across cultures.[2] They built upon Shane and Venkatarman's[3] Discovery, Evaluation and Exploitation framework for entrepreneurship to account for how societal differences may impact the entrepreneurial process. They suggest that the societal context of a country will impact the nature of entrepreneurial opportunities that are available to individuals as well as impact the individuals who may act upon them. Specifically, asymmetries in information will lead to cognitive differences in individuals across nations and thus make more or less likely the discovery and exploitation of entrepreneurial opportunities. It follows that greater educational and experiential opportunities will allow for a broader array of entrepreneurial opportunities to be discovered and exploited by individuals across cultures.

ENTREPRENEURIAL PERSPECTIVE

Interview with Bryant Tong, Venture Capitalist Partner with Nth Power, on Cultural Differences and Entrepreneurial Management[4]

Bryant Tong is a venture capitalist partner with Nth Power in San Francisco, California. Nth Power is a highly regarded venture capital (VC) firm that focuses on high-potential investments in the global energy industry. The company was founded in 1997 and has $420 million under management in four funds. The financing that Nth Power provides to its portfolio firms comes from organizations around the world. Bryant Tong joined Nth Power in 2001. Previously, Bryant was founder, president, and CEO of Pacific Venture Capital, LLC, the VC arm of the PG&E Corporation. Since joining Nth Power, he has led its investments in Accelergy Corporation, NanoGram Corporation, Microposite, Inc., and Arxx Corporation, and serves on each of these companies' boards.

We asked Bryant how cultural differences manifested themselves in his business, given the international nature of the investors in Nth Power's funds. Mr. Tong indicated that expectations and styles seemed much more subject to individual characteristics rather than cultural ones. He continued, stating that investors, regardless of cultural background, expect financial returns on their invested capital, and it is this unifying expectation that supersedes any cultural differences.

Multinational Corporations[5]

Multinational corporations have their headquarters in one country but operate in many countries.

Fortune magazine annually identifies the 500 largest global companies.

The ten largest corporations ranked by revenues in 2013 were: (1) Royal Dutch Shell, (2) Wal-Mart Stores, (3) Exxon Mobile, (4) Sinopec Group (one of China's largest oil and gas producer), (5) China National Petroleum (also one of China's biggest oil and gas producer), (6) BP, (7) State Grid (China's largest power distributor), (8) Toyota Motor, (9) Volkswagen, and (10) Total French oil company.[6]

From Ethnocentric to Geocentric Orientation[7]

In its early stages, international business was conducted with an **ethnocentric** outlook, with the orientation of the foreign operation based on that of the parent company.[8] The **polycentric** attitude, on the other hand, is based on the notion that it is best to give the foreign subsidiaries, staffed by local nationals, a great deal of managerial freedom. It is assumed that local nationals understand the local environment best. A **regiocentric** orientation favors the staffing of foreign operations on a regional basis. Thus, a European view may be composed of British, French, German, Italian, and other European influences. The modern MNC has a **geocentric** orientation. This means that the entire organization is viewed as an interdependent system operating in many countries. The relationships between headquarters and subsidiaries are collaborative, with communication flowing in both directions. Furthermore, key positions are filled by managers of different nationalities. In short, the orientation of the MNC is truly international and goes beyond a narrow nationalistic viewpoint.

Advantages of Multinationals

MNCs have several advantages over firms that have a domestic orientation. Obviously, the MNC can take advantage of business opportunities in many different countries. It can also raise money for its operations throughout the world. Moreover, it benefits by being able to establish production facilities in countries where its products can be produced most cost-effectively and efficiently. Companies with worldwide operations sometimes have better access to natural resources and materials that may not be available to domestic firms. Finally, large MNCs can recruit managers and other personnel from a worldwide labor pool.

Challenges for Multinationals

The advantages of multinational operations must be weighed against the challenges and risks associated with operating in foreign environments. One problem is the increasing nationalism in many countries. Years ago, developing countries lacked managerial, marketing, and technical skills. Consequently, they welcomed MNCs. But the situation is changing, with people in developing countries also acquiring those skills. In addition, countries have not only

---

Multinational corporations have their headquarters in one country but operate in many countries.

Ethnocentric orientation The style of the foreign operations is based on that of the parent company.

Polycentric orientation The foreign subsidiaries are given a great deal of managerial freedom.

Regiocentric orientation The foreign operations are staffed on a regional basis.

Geocentric orientation The entire organization is viewed as an interdependent system operating in many countries.

become aware of the value of their natural resources but have also become more skilled in international negotiations. Finally, MNCs must maintain good relations with the host country, a task that may prove difficult in some countries because their governments frequently change and corporations must deal with, and adapt to, these changes.

> **GLOBAL PERSPECTIVE**
>
> **Multinational Challenges and Opportunities in India for Companies like Wipro[9]**
>
> Challenges for some companies can be opportunities for others. In the late 1970s, IBM was selling obsolete and outdated machines in India. The Indian government told the company to shift to newer equipment or it would have to leave. IBM left, creating opportunities for Indian companies such as Wipro, which was a very small company in the late 1970s. But by 2006, the company grew to be a $3 billion firm by providing information technology, business process operations, and R&D services, serving customers throughout the world.
>
> Wipro, under the Stanford University-educated Chairman Azim H. Premji, took advantage of the outsourcing trend. Developed countries began to outsource manufacturing to China, while India, with a well-educated, English-speaking workforce began outsourcing services. Wipro and other Indian companies provided services such as call centers, payroll software for foreign companies, interactive training systems, and portfolio management for insurance companies. Today, India is considered to be the low-cost quality IT services provider.
>
> These high-tech companies, such as Wipro, can draw students from the highly respected Indian Institute of Technology, the Indian Institute for Management in Bangalore, and other higher education institutions. Wipro, which began as a peanut oil-producing company is now in a rapidly growing and innovative business with sophisticated R&D capabilities.

From Multinational to Global, or Transnational, Corporations

Global, or transnational, corporations view the whole world as one market.

Simply operating in different countries or the establishment of manufacturing plants in several countries is not sufficient to be competitive in the world market. The shift is toward the **global, or transnational, corporation**, which views the whole world as one market. This means, however, that a corporation also has to adapt to national and even local needs.

Domestic markets have become too small for some products. For example, developing a new drug may cost several hundred million dollars or more and may take more than ten years. To recover these costs requires selling the drug in a world market. Moreover, global companies have to keep abreast of technological developments around the world. For instance, Ford Motor Company decided in the latter half of the 1980s to become a global corporation. Previous attempts to build the "world car" (named the Escort) were not very successful. However, the use of modern communication technology, such as teleconferencing, establishes now a much closer link between Ford's headquarters and its European operations. While Ford was aiming at becoming a global corporation, it had no plants in Japan. To compensate for this void, Ford bought a 25 percent share in Mazda, which was later increased to 33.4 percent. After Ford gained a controlling interest, Henry Wallace was appointed president, the first foreigner to lead a major Japanese firm.[10] Moreover, the company has another project with

Nissan in Japan that designed the minivan built by Ford and marketed as the Villager and as the Quest that is sold by Nissan dealerships.

While many firms are aiming at becoming global, only a few have really done so. It requires developing products with the whole world in mind, especially the markets in North America, Asia, and Western Europe. Similarly, strategic decisions must take into account the whole world, but tactics must be adapted to the national and local environments. In staffing, opportunities must be opened for non-nationals to move into upper management ranks. In countries where the global corporation cannot enter, strategic alliances may need to be formed with local companies.

Research studies have shown that international expansion by new venture firms may enhance the viability of these companies.[11] This is because of the learning that will come from international expansion. That learning can then be incorporated back into the firm, which will aid the new venture in developing a sustainable competitive advantage. Thus, if resources are available, expansion into foreign markets may allow for increases in knowledge along with increases in sales and thus lead to greater success.

www.ford.com
www.mazda.com

Entrepreneurial Management in the Silicon Valley

Some say Silicon Valley is a mindset rather than a place. Perhaps this is the case, but this mindset originated in a place that we still refer to as Silicon Valley. Geographically, Silicon Valley the place is typically thought to encompass the region inclusive of (San Jose through Palo Alto) the southern end of the San Francisco Bay Area, although, practically, it has spread its physical as well as its intellectual borders to include most of the San Francisco Bay Area and beyond today. The technology prowess and influence of the Silicon Valley mindset and infrastructure have created an indelible mark on the tenor of the region.

What is the Silicon Valley mindset? Look at any of the numerous local calendars of business and technology events in the Bay Area and it becomes apparent that Silicon Valley is about confidence, vision, and hope mixed with science, engineering, and salesmanship. It is about seeing around the corner or at least convincing others that you can. It is about leadership and showmanship and brilliance.

As many would-be actors flock to Hollywood and New York City to pursue dreams of stardom, starry-eyed entrepreneurs come to Silicon Valley to build their dreams into entrepreneurial success. Silicon Valley attracts brilliance and moxy and provides the resources and expertise to mold gifted bravado into sustainable growth enterprises. Whether it is leaving Harvard to grow a social network website in Palo Alto or crossing the Atlantic or Pacific to study engineering, science, or business knowing opportunity lurks around the corner, Silicon Valley attracts the brightest and the boldest and gains with each new ambitious person. As a mindset, Silicon Valley can be learned, but the mindset can only be learned well by being in Silicon Valley the place.

INNOVATION PERSPECTIVE

The Digital Impact on GE[12]

Many big companies are now not only in the industrial sector but also in the information business. GE, General Electric, is one of them. Jeff Immelt, CEO and Chairman of GE, described the company's transition from the industrial sector to the information age responding to the digitization. This is the future of GE and many companies.

The jet engine, for example, has hundreds of sensors that transmit data continuously about the environment, the heat of the engine, fuel consumption, and so on. The digitization of the business requires many managerial decisions such as hiring the right people who have the knowledge and skills for adapting to the changes in the digital world. Consequently, GE hired data scientists who have been integrated within the GE culture. Changing the organizational culture is a difficult process realizing that the company that at one time had 70 percent of its operations inside the United States now has 70 percent of the operations outside the United States. GE not only has become more global, it also changed its focus because of the digital revolution.

COUNTRY ALLIANCES AND ECONOMIC BLOCS

At one time, countries in a region were competing against each other (and they still do). But now, countries are forming regional alliances that are competing with each other. Examples are the European Union, the North American Free Trade Agreement (NAFTA), the Association of Southeast Asian Nations (ASEAN), and Mercosur.

European Union

Europe 1992 marked the completion of the first stage of European economic ties. The European Community (EC) 1992 program caused dramatic shifts in economic power. Some saw the new program as the New Europe, while others, especially outsiders, saw it as a fortress that could provide serious challenges to other countries, including the United States. In order to compete effectively, North American and Asian countries prepared for the New Europe by forming NAFTA and ASEAN.

www.siemens.com

The European Commission worked on some 300 legislative actions for removing trade barriers and creating an internal market. The new measures were intended to increase market opportunities, escalate competition within the EC, and boost competition from companies outside the EC. The abolition of transnational trade restrictions and the relaxation of border controls had a considerable impact on U.S. companies doing business in Europe. Moreover, strong European companies have become formidable competitors in the U.S. market, as illustrated by Siemens, the German global company.

The objective of Europe 1992 was to create a single market through the removal of trade barriers and through free movement of goods, people, service, and capital. The changes go beyond economic interests and encompass many social changes as well. Educational qualifications, for example, are also affected. The Council of Ministers submitted a directive that recognizes diplomas of higher education across national boundaries, making it easier for professionals to work in different countries. It is clear, then, that the EC is more than an economic community: it is a state of mind with political power.

The recent global financial crisis has tested the bonds of the EU as Greece, Ireland, Portugal, and Spain have struggled with fiscal deficits that strain their ability to maintain the euro as a common currency. It remains to be seen if the underlying principle and goals of a united Europe will be enough to counterweight the fiscal challenges of some of its member states.

www.europa.eu.int

The original EC 1992 (which later became the European Union) consisted of 12 member nations: Belgium, Denmark, France, Germany, Greece, Ireland, Italy, Luxembourg, the Netherlands, Portugal, Spain, and the United Kingdom. It expanded in 1995 to include Austria, Finland, and Sweden. Since then, Cyprus, the Czech Republic, Estonia, Hungary, Latvia, Lithuania, Malta, Poland, Slovakia, and Slovenia have been admitted.

North American Free Trade Agreement and Other Latin American Free Trade Blocs[13]

In 1994, NAFTA, which included agreements among the United States, Canada, and Mexico, went into effect. Since then, trade among those countries has increased greatly. The objectives of NAFTA are to eliminate trade barriers and facilitate cross-border movements of goods and services, promote fair trade, increase investment opportunities, protect intellectual property, provide for resolution of disputes, and present opportunities to improve the benefits of this agreement. The agreement covers a variety of areas, such as market access, rules governing the origin of goods, customs procedures, energy, agriculture, and measures to be taken in emergencies.

www.nafta-sec-alena.org

Other Latin American and Caribbean countries have also formed their own trade blocs. Argentina, Brazil, Bolivia, Chile, Paraguay, and Uruguay are members of the Mercosur group.[14] The European Union has extensive trade with Mercosur members, which was further strengthened by the Fifth Round of Association negotiations held in July 2001. In addition, the Caribbean and Central and South American countries consider reductions in trade barriers through the Free Trade Area of the Americas (FTAA), which some consider an extension of NAFTA.[15]

www.mercosur.org

www.ftaa-alca.org

These trade agreements, however, do not go unchallenged, as shown by the protests at World Trade Organization (WTO) meetings. Critics see them as benefiting only developed nations.

Association of Southeast Asian Nations[16]

The ten countries of Brunei Darussalam, Cambodia, Indonesia, Laos, Malaysia, Myanmar, the Philippines, Singapore, Thailand, and Vietnam formed a trading bloc that will increasingly counter NAFTA and the European Union, not only economically but also politically.

www.aseansec.org

During the ASEAN summit conference in October 2003 in Bali, the leaders discussed political security, sociocultural cooperation, and economic issues with the leaders of China, Japan, India, and South Korea. Also, ASEAN economic ministers meet frequently to discuss economic issues and strategies. The 35th such meeting was held in Phnom Penh in September 2003. The following month, ASEAN ministers held the inaugural meeting on culture and arts in Kuala Lumpur, Malaysia. The goal of the meeting was to improve cooperation among ASEAN countries, enhance understanding among their people, and promote a regional identity. More recently, the countries have also begun to cooperate each other to fight terrorism. Eventually, the ASEAN alliance could rival NAFTA and the European Union.

GLOBAL PERSPECTIVE

Thailand's Competitive Advantage: Pickup Trucks[17]

As the United States and Thailand prepared for the new trade pact, American car companies and unions and Thai bankers feared greater competition. Thailand's banking industry had been protected from foreign competition. Thailand's pickup trucks could pose formidable competition to U.S. carmakers. Thailand has already a free-trade agreement (FTA) with Japan and the United States does not want to fall behind in influence in Southeast Asia where China increasingly gains foothold in that region.

Thai pickup trucks could provide tough competition to the U.S. industry if the 25 percent tariff were removed from imported pickups. In early 2006, the tariff issue had not yet been decided. American unions were very concerned about job losses especially since Ford announced in January 2006 that during the next six years it would close some 14 plants in North America, resulting in the loss of some 34,000 jobs. Similarly, General Motors also faces the need for downsizing its labor force.

But, Ford and GM could also benefit greatly from the trade deal. Both companies produce pickup trucks in Thailand which have, however, been sold primarily in Southeast Asia, but none in the United States. It is now Thailand's aim to become "the Detroit of the East." If the FTA between Thailand and the United States proceeds as planned, the pickup truck industry could contribute to Thailand's competitive advantage.

India's Role in the World Economy

In 1947 India became independent from British rule followed by a new constitution in 1950. Geographically, India is the seventh largest country, but it ranks first in population. India has the 5th largest economy. It is estimated that by 2025 India's market will surpass the consumer market in Germany.[18] Despite the economic growth, India still has a high poverty and illiteracy level.[19] India plays an increasing role in the WTO, in the ASEAN, and in the South Asian Association for Regional Cooperation (SAARC). Its large, technically trained workforce plays an increasing role in the global services economy and has linked India tightly to free market economies around the world.

INTERNATIONAL MANAGEMENT: CULTURAL AND COUNTRY DIFFERENCES[20]

It is interesting to know some of the differences in managerial practices. A comprehensive study by Geert Hofstede provides a good framework for studying cultural differences between countries. Our discussion will focus on selected countries. It is illustrative, rather than comprehensive, and is based on generalizations. We have to bear in mind that there are, for example, great differences between the managers in any country. Furthermore, a society is not static, and changes do occur over time. For instance, the traditional authoritarian style of German managers is slowly giving way to a more participative approach.

Behaviors in Different Cultures[21]

The study by Geert Hofstede, a Dutch researcher, found that a country's culture impacts on the behavior of employees. In his initial study of more than 110,000 people, he identified four dimensions and later added a fifth. These are (1) individualism versus collectivism, (2) large versus small power distance, (3) uncertainty tolerance versus avoidance, (4) masculinity versus femininity or aggressive versus passive goal behavior, and (5) short- versus long-term orientation. The behaviors in the five dimensions are summarized in Table 3.2.

TABLE 3.2 Five dimensions of behavior

Individualism	*Collectivism*
People focus on their own interests and the people close to them. Tasks more important than relationships.	Emphasis on the group, with group support expected. Relationships more important than task orientation.
Large power distance	*Small power distance*
Society accepts unequal distribution of power. Respect for authority. Emphasis on titles and ranks. Subordinates expect to be told what to do. Centralization emphasized.	Society less accepting of power. Employees more open to the idea of dialogue with their superior. Less emphasis on authority, titles, and ranks. Inequality minimized. Decentralization emphasized.
Uncertainty tolerance	*Uncertainty avoidance*
People accept uncertainty and are open to risk taking. Willing to take risks.	Afraid of ambiguity and uncertainty. Structure and formal rules preferred.
Masculinity*	*Femininity*
Aggressive and assertive behavior. Emphasis on material things, success, and money.	Relationship oriented. Quality of life favored. Concern for the welfare of others; caring. Emphasis on modesty.
Long-term orientation	*Short-term orientation*
Characterized by hard work and perseverance. Savings driven.	Less emphasis on hard work and perseverance. Consumption driven.

*Some authors prefer to use the terms *quantity versus quality of life* or *aggressive versus passive goal orientation* instead of *masculinity versus femininity*, the terms Hofstede used originally.

The results of Hofstede's research showed that, for example, individualism prevailed in the United States, Australia, Britain, and Canada. In contrast, collectivism prevailed in countries such as Guatemala, Ecuador, and Panama. Among the 50 countries and regions studied, India ranked 21, close to the Japanese ranking (22/23). On the other hand, Singapore and Thailand ranked between 37 and 44, indicating a tendency toward collectivism.[22] On the masculinity/femininity index, Japan, Austria, Italy, and Switzerland ranked high, while Sweden, Norway, the Netherlands, and Denmark ranked low, meaning that these countries are skewed toward feminism.[23]

These findings suggest that managers need to understand the cultural environments and their implications in order to be successful in the country in which they do business. We shall now discuss the management styles in selected countries.

France: Le Plan and the Cadre

In France, government planning on a national scale (legal–political environment factor) helps coordinate the plans of individual industries and companies (managerial function of planning). The government's aim is to utilize most effectively the country's resources and to avoid expansion in uneconomic areas. Although government planning—which is also extended to regional areas—is carried out by relatively few, but competent, people, other government departments, employers' organizations, unions, and consumers provide cooperation and assistance.

At times, the plan becomes a global strategy helping specific industries. For example, the government attempts to integrate the electronics industry into a whole so that it can overcome its weaknesses in information processing, consumer electronics, microelectronics, and automation. To implement the strategy, the government plans to support several national projects, such as speech synthesis, mini- and micro-computers, and mainframe computers. Clearly, there is a close relationship between government planning and firms, especially those that are owned and directly aided by the government.

The heavy involvement of government in economic and social activities resulted in a large civil service with some 4.5 million workers.[24] Civil servants have advantages over private-sector workers: higher pay, shorter hours, more holidays, better pension, more bonuses, almost complete job security, and other perks. In France, in contrast to other European countries, the government workforce grew some 20 percent between 1979 and 1999 so that about one in four French workers received their pay from the government. It is no surprise then that many French people would like to become civil servants, or "functionaries".

Jean-Louis Barsoux and Peter Lawrence noted not only the close relationship between government and industry but also the impact of the elite universities, the *Grandes Écoles*, on forming the French managerial mind, which is considered essential for managing in both government and business organizations.[25] These schools supply the *cadre*, the managerial elite. Moreover, the schools' connections are vital for managerial success. What is valued in these managers is analytical ability, independence, and proficiency in synthesizing facts. While written communication is considered very important, oral communication is deemphasized. These managers exhibit intellectual ability rather than action. Rationality, problem solving, and numerical analysis are important for obtaining high managerial posts in government as well as in business organizations. Indeed, it is not unusual for managers to work for both alternately.

The French managerial model also has drawbacks. It may limit managers in dealing with non-quantifiable and "non-rational" data and in responding quickly to changes in the environment, and it may not result in the selection of the best managers because school ties may be more important than performance. Although the managerial characteristics may also be limiting in terms of obtaining a global outlook, French managers, in general, are quite supportive of the European Union. They see it as an opportunity to restructure the New Europe.

Germany: Authority and Codetermination

In the past, and to a lesser extent today, the German cultural environment favored reliance on authority in directing the workforce, although it was often benevolent authoritarianism (managerial function of leading). Even today, while managers may show concern for subordinates, they also expect obedience. In 1951, a law was passed that provided for **codetermination**, which requires labor membership in the supervisory board and the executive committee of certain large corporations. Furthermore, a labor director is elected as a member of the executive committee. This position is a difficult one. Labor directors supposedly must represent the interests of the employees and, at the same time, must make managerial decisions that are in the best interest of the enterprise.

> **Codetermination** requires labor membership in the supervisory board and the executive committee of the corporation.

Selected Factors Influencing Managing in Other Western Countries

Managing in Australia is influenced by the country's moralistic stance and its emphasis on political and social values, achievement, and risk taking.

Italian managers operate in an environment of low tolerance for risks. Italians are very competitive, but at the same time they like group decision making.

Management in Austria (and Germany) is characterized by self-realization and leadership. Independence and competitiveness are valued. Tolerance for risk taking is rather low.

In Britain, job security is important, and so are resourcefulness, adaptability, and logic. Individualism is also highly valued.

GLOBAL PERSPECTIVE

Is There a European Management Model?[26]

Managers in European countries manage in different ways. Yet there are some commonalities, as interviews with top managers from European firms found:

- European managers think of themselves as being more people-oriented than American managers are.
- A great deal of negotiation takes place within European firms, such as between management and workers or unions and between headquarters and subsidiaries. The practice of codetermination in large German firms may be an illustration of such extensive negotiations. European managers perceive the American style as more top-down.
- Europeans also have developed great skills in managing international diversity. Managing across borders is achieved more through people than through structures and procedures. The ability of most European managers to speak several languages facilitates the "people approach".
- European managers operate between the extremes of short-term profit orientation (of American managers, as perceived by European managers) and the long-term growth orientation of Japanese managers.
- European managers, on the other hand, have adopted many managerial techniques from the Americans, and they also could learn from American entrepreneurship. In the global environment, with free flow of information and with MNCs operating in many countries, there may be some convergence of managerial approaches.

Korean Management

Japanese management receives a great deal of attention, partly because of the economic success of Japanese companies in the past. The Republic of Korea

(South Korea, referred to here as Korea) has also shown remarkable economic growth, but the Asian economic crisis that began in 1997 resulted in a dramatic downturn of its economy. Korean management practices are not well known. It would be incorrect to assume that Korean management is simply an extension of Japanese management. It is not, although there are some cultural and structural similarities, such as the dominance of powerful conglomerate companies. The Korean model has been characterized by the **Chaebol**, a tight collusion between government and industrial conglomerates. However, Kim Young Sam, when he was the Korean president, suggested: "We need a better balance between big and small companies. We cannot just let the Chaebol grow by taking over small businesses."[27] He even declared: "The Chaebol system, which puts the emphasis on outward expansion that burdens the people, has come to an end."[28]

Chaebol is characterized by a tight collusion between government and industrial conglomerates.

INNOVATION PERSPECTIVE

International Innovation and Entrepreneurship in Silicon Valley

We know that Silicon Valley's reputation for invention and innovation in the creation of new industries attracts entrepreneurs from around the world. That same reputation also attracts government interest from nations across the globe. As innovation is the key to increases in competitiveness and productivity and, thus, living standards of citizens from all countries, it is no surprise that many governments want to learn from participating directly in its innovative and entrepreneurial processes. For example, South Korea, through its Korean Innovation Center (KIC) in Silicon Valley, supports Korean entrepreneurial teams as they strive to develop the next generation of global enterprises. Through an integrated support system of professional and technical mentorship, access to capital, coworking space, and related services, KIC accelerates Korean companies seeking to establish themselves in Silicon Valley and the United States. KIC also supports the efforts of U.S.-based enterprises seeking to initiate or grow operations in Korea, thus providing a two-way thoroughfare for international business, innovation, and entrepreneurship.

Inhwa Korean concept of harmony.

In Japan, managers emphasize group harmony and cohesion expressed in the concept of *wa*; the Korean concept of **inhwa** also translates into harmony, but with less accent on group values. Korean organizations are quite hierarchical, with family members occupying key positions. Beyond blood relationships, the factors affecting hiring decisions often include the school attended or being from the same geographic region as the top person. The leadership style can best be described as top-down, or autocratic/paternalistic. This approach enables the firm to adjust quickly to demands in the environment by issuing commands. Lifetime employment does not prevail. Indeed, the labor turnover rates are high when compared with the low rates in Japan. Turnover is primarily attributable to resignations rather than dismissals. All in all, Korean management is different from both Japanese and American management practices.

Japanese Management and Theory Z

Japan, one of the leading industrial nations in the world, has adopted managerial practices that are quite different from those of other economically advanced countries in the Western world. The discussion here deals with two common Japanese practices: lifetime employment and consensus decision making. Then it compares and contrasts Japanese and U.S. managerial practices, including Theory Z. In the closing sections of Parts 2 to 6 of this book, other managerial practices in Japan are discussed and compared with those in the United States and China.

Lifetime Employment

Important features of Japanese management are lifelong employment for permanent employees (related to the managerial function of staffing), great concern for the individual employee, and emphasis on seniority.

Typically, employees spend their working life with a single enterprise, which in turn gives employees security and a feeling of belonging. This practice brings the culturally induced concept of **wa** (harmony) to the enterprise, resulting in employee loyalty and close identification with the aims of the company. However, it also adds to business costs because employees are kept on the payroll even when there is insufficient work. Consequently, firms are beginning to question this practice. Indeed, changes appear to be in the making, but they are slow. What is often overlooked, however, is that this permanent employment practice is used primarily by large firms. In fact, it is estimated that the job security system applies to only about one-third of the labor force.

Wa Japanese concept of harmony.

Closely related to lifelong employment is the seniority system, which provides privileges for older employees who have been with the enterprise for a long time. But there are indications that this system may be superseded by a more open approach that provides opportunities for advancement for young people. For example, the relatively new Sony Corporation has team leaders (a point is made of not calling them supervisors) who are often young women 18 or 19 years of age. There is practically no age difference between these leaders and the operators they lead.

The lifetime employment concept has worked well in Japan for a long time. However, the job security is changing as illustrated by the Sony Corporation, which plans to lay off 10,000 people worldwide, or 6 percent of the workforce in 2012.[29]

www.world.sony.com

Decision Making in Japan

The managerial practice of decision making in Japan is also considerably different from that in the United States. It is built on the concept that change and new ideas should come primarily from below. Thus, lower-level employees prepare proposals for higher-level personnel. Supervisors, rather than simply accepting or rejecting the proposals, tactfully question them, make suggestions, and encourage subordinates. If necessary, proposals are sent back to the initiator for more information. Still, in major decisions, top management retains its power.

Japanese management, then, uses decision making by consensus to deal with everyday problems. Lower-level employees initiate an idea and submit it to the next higher level, until it reaches the desk of the top executive. If the proposal is approved, it is returned to the initiator for implementation.

Theory Z

Theory Z The adaptation of selected Japanese managerial practices to the U.S. environment.

In **Theory Z**, selected Japanese managerial practices are adapted to the environment of the United States. This approach is practiced by companies such as IBM, Hewlett-Packard, and the diversified retail company, Dayton-Hudson. One of the characteristics of Type Z organization, as suggested by Professor William Ouchi, is an emphasis on the interpersonal skills needed for group interaction.[30] Yet, despite the emphasis on group decision making, responsibility remains with the individual (which is quite different from the Japanese practice, which emphasizes collective responsibility). There is also an emphasis on informal and democratic relationships based on trust. Yet the hierarchical structure remains intact, as illustrated by IBM, where not only goals, but also authority, rules, and discipline guide corporate behavior.

www.ibm.com
www.hp.com

Rise of China: Deng Xiaoping Changed China from the Planned Economy Toward a Market Economy[31]

Deng Xiaoping was a statesman, diplomat, and theorist. He has been credited with leading China from a planned economy to a market-driven economy that led to China's growth after the Cultural Revolution. He encouraged foreign investment and allowed limited private investment, which resulted in China becoming one of the fastest growing economies today. Deng's idea of moving toward a market economy was:

> Planning and market forces are not the essential difference between socialism and capitalism. A planned economy is not the definition of socialism, because there is planning under capitalism; the market economy happens under socialism, too. Planning and market forces are both ways of controlling economic activity.[32]

When Deng Xiaoping visited Singapore in 1978, he was impressed by the modern, technologically advanced nation that planned its economic development, built its infrastructure, and encouraged foreign investment. Deng considered Singapore's approach as the model for China, resulting in what has been called "socialism with Chinese characteristics". Combining the planning techniques with Singapore's developmental approach resulted in economic growth rates around 9 percent in recent years. Much of that can be attributed to the leadership of Deng Xiaoping. China began building new coalmines, modern power grids, nuclear power plants, new roads and highways, and other projects. Much of the development can be attributed to the leadership of Deng Xiaoping.

More recently, focus has risen on the increasing globalization of Chinese firms. As the Chinese economy has grown rapidly and taken on increased levels of technological sophistication, more of its firms (e.g., Haier) have been able to compete on a global stage, internationalizing their value chain and expanding to new markets.[33]

The Globalization of Chinese Enterprises

Interview with Professor Xiaohua Yang on the Globalization of Chinese Enterprises

As Chinese MNCs have taken a more global role in recent years, we spoke to an expert in the development, progression, impact, and future of this trend of international expansion. Dr. Xiaohua Yang's scholarship has centered on firms' competitive strategies in the context of international institutional environments and she is particularly interested in understanding forces driving Chinese enterprises to expand overseas and the determinants of their operation and performance abroad.

We asked Dr. Yang to discuss the development of Chinese global businesses and she offered the following[34] (based on her recent contribution to M. Pellicano, M.V. Ciasullo in *La visione strategica dell'impresa*, Giappichelli, Torino). Dr. Yang indicated that Chinese firms have invested in locations that enable them reduce the costs of their operations (Cheung 2006). Often these destinations of investment are developing economies because they possess needed natural resources. More recently Chinese firms have increased investment in OECD countries as government policies and company objectives have changed and Chinese firms seek to become global players (Sauvant 2005).[35]

As assets in the Western countries have become more affordable during the global economic meltdown, many Chinese firms have invested internationally through mergers and acquisitions. China's MNEs have also begun pursuing aggressive strategies in attaining technological capability and human capital (Yang & Stoltenberg, 2008).[36] The acquisition of companies in the United States and E.U. has enabled Chinese MNEs to diversify more quickly and cheaply than developing their own technologies, directing investment toward advanced proprietary, strategic technologies that are immobile such as distribution networks and specific branding already in place (Buckley 2007).[37] Given this recent trends in foreign expansion, we expect Chinese MNCs to play a more prominent role in the world economy.

GLOBAL PERSPECTIVE

Venture Capital in China

VC has long been the fuel for growth in technology-focused regions like Silicon Valley. VC investments have made possible the rapid rise of firms like Google and Facebook. Over the last decade, the venture industry has also developed in China.

Confidence among venture capitalists in China has generally kept pace with confidence of their counterparts in the United States. The quarterly *China Venture Capitalist Confidence Index*™ *(Bloomberg ticker symbol: CVCCI)* is based on an ongoing survey of China's Mainland and Hong Kong SAR. venture capitalists. The China VC Index measures and reports the opinions of China-based professional venture capitalists in their estimation of the high-growth venture entrepreneurial environment in China over the next 6–18 months.[38]

ENTREPRENEURIAL PERSPECTIVE

ENTREPRENEURIAL PERSPECTIVE

The China Venture Capitalist Confidence Index for the second quarter of 2012, based on a July 2012 survey of twelve China's Mainland and Hong Kong SAR. venture capitalists, *registered 2.79 on a 5-point scale* (with 5 indicating high confidence and 1 indicating low confidence).

This quarter's reading dropped by 21.63 percent from the previous quarter's number and set up a new historic low point since our index started in the second quarter of 2005.

Graph 1
Trend line of China Venture Capitalists Confidence over recent 29 quarters

The depressed global and domestic economy started to show impact on VC activities in China. Political risks and valuation risks further add to VCs' pessimism.

Will confidence among venture capitalists in China rebound? History suggests it will.

The Rise of India

India has grown by the dramatic reform beginning in 1991, which resulted in the reduction of bureaucracy. Many restrictions on imports were removed and exports were encouraged. India's business leadership contributed to that change especially in the high-tech area. One of those leaders was Narayana Murthy who by some is considered the Bill Gates of India. He and his colleagues started Infosys Consultants.

Another respected business leader was Ratan Tata who had the challenging task of modernizing Tata Steel. Mr. Tata, an architect educated in the United States, is sometimes compared with Jack Welch of General Electric.[39] More recently, he gained prominence through the 2008 introduction of the $2,500 Nano car. Indian politicians now also look at the amazing economic developments in China. Still India is far behind China, a country that learned from Singapore, in many areas, now India looks toward China. One area that needs improvement is India's infrastructure, the state of which discourages investments by foreign companies.

While China focused on manufacturing, India's strength is in the high-technology area. While Bangalore is considered India's Silicon Valley, other cities also have moved into the technology sector. In Bangalore, one can find many foreign multinationals such as Nokia, Intel, Philips, and General Electric.

While the changes in India are fairly rapid, these are slow when compared with China. Reaching consensus by the various interest groups takes time. Still, India today makes progress that could not have been imagined fifty years ago. The International perspective highlights some of the differences between China and India.

GLOBAL PERSPECTIVE

A Comparison of China and India[40]

China	India
Den Xiaoping's modernization after 1978; market-based socialism	Historic reforms began 1991
Rapid transformation	Same
Large population	Same
Development of middle class	Same
Planned and market-driven economy	Increasingly market-driven economy
Focus on infrastructure	Poor infrastructure
Fast changes	Slow consensus requiring changes
Factory advantage	Backoffice advantage
Relatively high literacy rate	Relatively low literacy rate

GLOBAL PERSPECTIVE

Is China Losing Its Competitive Advantage?[41]

For many years, China enjoyed a steady GDP of around 9 percent. Chinese manufacturers benefited from low-cost labor, a cheap currency, and minimal regulations. However, things are beginning to change with higher labor and energy costs, cancelation of preferential policies, and an appreciation of the Chinese currency. Clothing, shoe, and toy factories in the Guangdong area had to close. Other companies in the Pearl River Delta experienced similar problems. Big multinational companies also have reconsidered their investment strategies. In an environment of globalization, firms are considering leaving China and looking for opportunities in India and Vietnam. A German sportsware company is looking for opportunities in India where the costs are lower even though productivity would probably lag in India.

The Chinese manufacturing environment is changing. New laws now require firms to provide benefits such as pensions. Moreover, employees are gaining collective bargaining rights. While many of the changes have benefitted labor, middle-class families have also been affected negatively by rising housing costs and other increasing living expenses. For example, the consumer price inflation was 4.8 percent in 2007, but has risen to 5.3 percent in 2011.[42]

Because of the rising costs in the cities and the coastal regions, companies now are looking at relocating to inner China as well as opportunities in Vietnam and India.

PORTER'S COMPETITIVE ADVANTAGE OF NATIONS[43]

Besides appreciating cultural differences in management style, managers should also understand the economic situations of other countries. Michael Porter, a Harvard Business School professor, questions the economic theory of comparative advantage. He suggests four sets of factors that contribute to a nation's well-being. The first set pertains to conditions such as a nation's resources, its labor costs, and the skills and education of its people. The second factor set consists of the demand conditions of a nation, such as the market size, the way products may be advertised, and the degree of consumer sophistication. The third set of factors concerns the suppliers: a company prospers when supporting companies are located in the same area. The fourth factor set consists of the firm's strategy and structure as well as rivalry among competitors.

A favorable combination of the four sets of factors leads to competitive advantage for a nation. When only two sets are favorable, competitive advantage usually cannot be sustained. On the other hand, the availability of resources is not always necessary. Japan, for example, lacks natural resources, yet the country prospered in the past. In fact, economic hardship may stimulate economic activity and success, as illustrated by Japan and Germany after World War II. However, these two countries have consumers who demand sophisticated products of high quality. Similarly, Japanese and German companies have good relationships with their suppliers. They also benefit from good education systems and a skilled labor force. Despite cooperation among Japanese companies on certain levels, they are also fiercely competitive.

GLOBAL PERSPECTIVE

General Motors (GM) Expansion in India[44]

The automobile industry will be an important part in increasing the competitive advantage of India. Many car companies are investing in India as illustrated by General Motors. GM announced the opening of the second auto plant in India. This seems to indicate GM's strategy to expand in emerging markets. The company expects that India is going to be an important income source for the company in the coming years. Although it ranks only fifth in sales in 2008, GM invested heavily in the new plant in Talegaon near Pune, which is not far away from Mumbai. The plant is to produce the mini-car called Spark. The introduction of new cars is not sufficient, a supportive dealer and service network is required for success; therefore, GM will expand this network. In addition, the company has a technical center in Bangalore where it is employing engineers and designers. The Indian expansion, although small when compared with China, seems to indicate that GM sees India as an opportunity for its Asian expansion.

GLOBAL INNOVATION INDEXES[45]

Innovation is critically important for the economic, social, and intellectual development for countries of the world. Many attempts have been made to measure the degree of innovations of countries by developing indexes. The focus here is on the Global Innovation Index by the Boston Consulting Group and on the Global Innovation Index 2011 (INSEAD).

The Global Innovation Index by the Boston Consulting Group

The Global Innovation Index (Boston Consulting Group) is a part of a study focusing on business innovation outcomes as well as the ability of governments to support and encourage innovation. The survey consisted of more than 1,000 senior executives and in-depth interviews with 30 executives, conducted in 110 countries and 50 U.S. States and measured the "innovation friendliness" of those countries and states.[46]

The *positively* ranked countries and regions are as follows:

1. Singapore
2. Switzerland
3. South Korea
4. Iceland
5. Finland
6. Hong Kong, China
7. Ireland
8. Japan
9. United States
10. Sweden
11. The Netherlands
12. Denmark

Some *negatively* ranked countries in Latin America are:

57. Mexico
62. Costa Rica
72. Brazil
74. Columbia
92. Argentina
99. Peru

http://www.bcg.com/

http://www.insead.edu/home/

The INSEAD Global Innovation Index 2011 and Other Indexes

The *Global Innovation Index 2011* by INSEAD using different criteria showed the following highest ranking countries and regions:

1. Switzerland
2. Sweden
3. Singapore
4. Hong Kong, China
5. Finland
6. Denmark
7. United States

8. Canada
9. The Netherlands
10. United Kingdom
11. Iceland
12. Germany

In this index, some of the Latin America countries ranked as follows:

Costa Rica ranked 45th, Brazil 47th, Argentina 58th, Columbia 71st, Mexico 81st, and Peru 83rd.

The *INSEAD Global Innovation Index 2011* uses different criteria. It focuses on innovation **inputs** that include institutions, human capital and research, infrastructure, market sophistication, and business sophistication. The innovation **outputs** include scientific outputs (in respect to knowledge creation, knowledge impact, and knowledge diffusion) and creative outputs (creative intangibles and creative goods/services).

Several of the countries are ranked similarly in both the INSEAD *Global Innovation* Index and the one by *the Boston Consulting Group*. For example, the latter ranked Singapore first, while the INSEAD Innovation Index ranked it third. Keep in mind that the rankings can vary when based on different criteria and conducted at different times. Nevertheless, one can note certain innovation patterns.

Besides the two indexes mentioned here, there are other indexes on innovation such as the Oslo Manual, Bogota Manual, Innovation Capacity Index (compiled by many professors), and the Innovation Index.

GAINING A GLOBAL COMPETITIVE ADVANTAGE THROUGH QUALITY MANAGEMENT

Quality has become a strategic weapon in the global marketplace. American companies, once the acknowledged world leaders in productivity, have come under siege from firms around the globe. One reason is that many American companies became complacent and failed to see the changing needs of the global market, which increasingly demanded high-quality products. This complacency and lack of foresight enabled competitors, especially those from Japan, to use a powerful weapon to increase their market shares in the U.S. and European markets. This weapon is quality.

Before managers can revolutionize the production process, they must first revolutionize the way they think about quality. The need for a new philosophy of quality is paramount. The old philosophy of adequacy—maintaining the status quo for as long as a product turns a profit—is no longer acceptable. Now the aim of companies must be nothing short of excellence. To attain excellence, however, managers must be willing to put the needs of their customers first. They must never forget that customers are indispensable: they are the reason for which the company exists.

Traditional Quality Management Gurus[47]

Although the concern for quality may seem like a recent phenomenon, there were several quality gurus who tried to introduce their theories to American companies in the 1950s. But, U.S. managers did not listen. This, however, was the beginning to change. In fact, early quality management pioneers have now been joined by many new advocates of quality. We will briefly review the contributions of three quality champions: Deming, Juran, and Crosby. Each has taken a different approach to quality management, yet each has helped to shape its direction.

There are several interesting parallels between the career paths of the two American professors: Dr. Deming and Dr. Juran. Both men taught in the business department at New York University in the 1950s. During the post-World War II economic boom, Deming and Juran made unsuccessful attempts to persuade American managers to focus on quality. When Americans ignored their teachings, the two scholars decided to take their message to a more receptive audience—the Japanese.

Their pilgrimage to Japan could not have occurred at a more favorable time. Before the 1950s, Japan's export trade suffered because their domestic goods had a reputation for shoddy workmanship and inferior quality. Japanese-made cars, for example, were poorly designed and manufactured, unreliable, and featured unattractive styling. With such a combination of undesirable product features, it is not surprising that American consumers were uninterested in Japanese-made vehicles.

But over the last four decades, Japanese automakers have steadily increased market share in the United States by selling high-quality cars. This transformation from inferior to superior quality was, to a great extent, made possible by the teachings of Deming and Juran. They helped to revolutionize the quality of Japan's industries, and they have become the quality heroes. Partly because of their work, consumers all over the world now equate Japanese products with high quality. As a tribute to his contributions, the most coveted quality award in Japan is named in the honor of the late Dr. Deming. Today, many years after Deming and Juran showed Japanese managers how to produce quality products, they are getting some much-deserved attention from American managers.

The last of this trio of quality gurus is Phil Crosby. Unlike Deming and Juran, Crosby did not cross the Pacific to instruct the Japanese, nor did his approach originate within the university setting. Crosby was not an academic. He formulated practical ideas for improving quality while working in a variety of U.S. corporations. His hands-on style enabled him to put his ideas into action at Martin Marietta and ITT, where he worked before becoming a corporate consultant.

While all three experts—Deming, Juran, and Crosby—view quality as an imperative for survival, each of them defines quality differently. For Deming, quality meant providing customer-satisfying products and services at a low cost. It also meant a commitment to continual innovation and improvement that the Japanese call *kaizen*. For Juran, a key element in the definition of quality is a product's "fitness for use". Finally, Crosby explains quality from an engineering perspective as the conformance to precise standards and requirements. His motto is "Do it right the first time [and] achieve zero defects". All three experts consider statistics a valuable tool for measuring quality, although Deming is perhaps the best known for his commitment to statistical analysis.

www.deming.org
www.juran.com
www.philipcrosby.com

Other Quality Approaches and Awards[48]

As mentioned earlier, the Deming Award recognizes companies that have achieved superior quality in Japan. A similar award, but with a different emphasis, is the Malcolm Baldrige National Quality Award established by the U.S.

Congress in 1987. Another approach is known as ISO 9000, pioneered by the Europeans. There is also the European Quality Award given by the European Foundation for Quality Management.[49]

Malcolm Baldrige National Quality Award 1996[50]

The Malcolm Baldrige award is the highest national recognition a U.S. company can receive for business excellence. The award helps the understanding of performance requirements of excellence and competitiveness. The three categories for participation are (1) manufacturing firms, (2) service companies, and (3) small businesses. Applicants for the award are expected to share information about the company's improvement processes and the results so that this information can be used by other organizations. Each company benefits by getting feedback from the examiners.

www.quality.nist.gov

Participants in the award program must show results and improvements in a variety of areas. Specifically, the criteria are grouped into seven categories with 24 items. The assessment, however, is tailored to the requirements of key success factors of the specific company, depending on the kind of business, its size, its strategy, and its stage of development. The seven categories, illustrated in Figure 3.2, are as follows[51]:

1. The *leadership* category requires that senior executives set direction and build and maintain the leadership required for high performance. This criterion also demands leadership in creating an effective organization and management system as well as demonstrating public responsibility and corporate citizenship.
2. The *information and analysis* category examines the company's effectiveness and use of management information (financial and nonfinancial). It not only requires the analysis of company data but also includes competitive analysis and benchmarking, comparing performance with the best firms.
3. *Strategic planning* includes business planning with an emphasis on translating the plans into customer and operational requirements. Planning has to be driven by customer needs and operational improvement.
4. The category of *human resource development and management* includes criteria for all key aspects of human resources.
5. *Process management* focuses on all key work processes, including the design, introduction, production, and delivery of products and services. It also includes criteria for support services and supplier performance.
6. Organizations are result-oriented. This category looks at *results*: quality results in products and services as well as company operational and financial results; it also includes human resource and supplier performance results.
7. The final category is *customer focus and satisfaction*. Specifically, the criteria in this category require excellence in customer and market knowledge, relationships with customers, and customer satisfaction compared with that of the firm's competitors.

FIGURE 3.2 The Baldrige award criteria framework: dynamic relationships

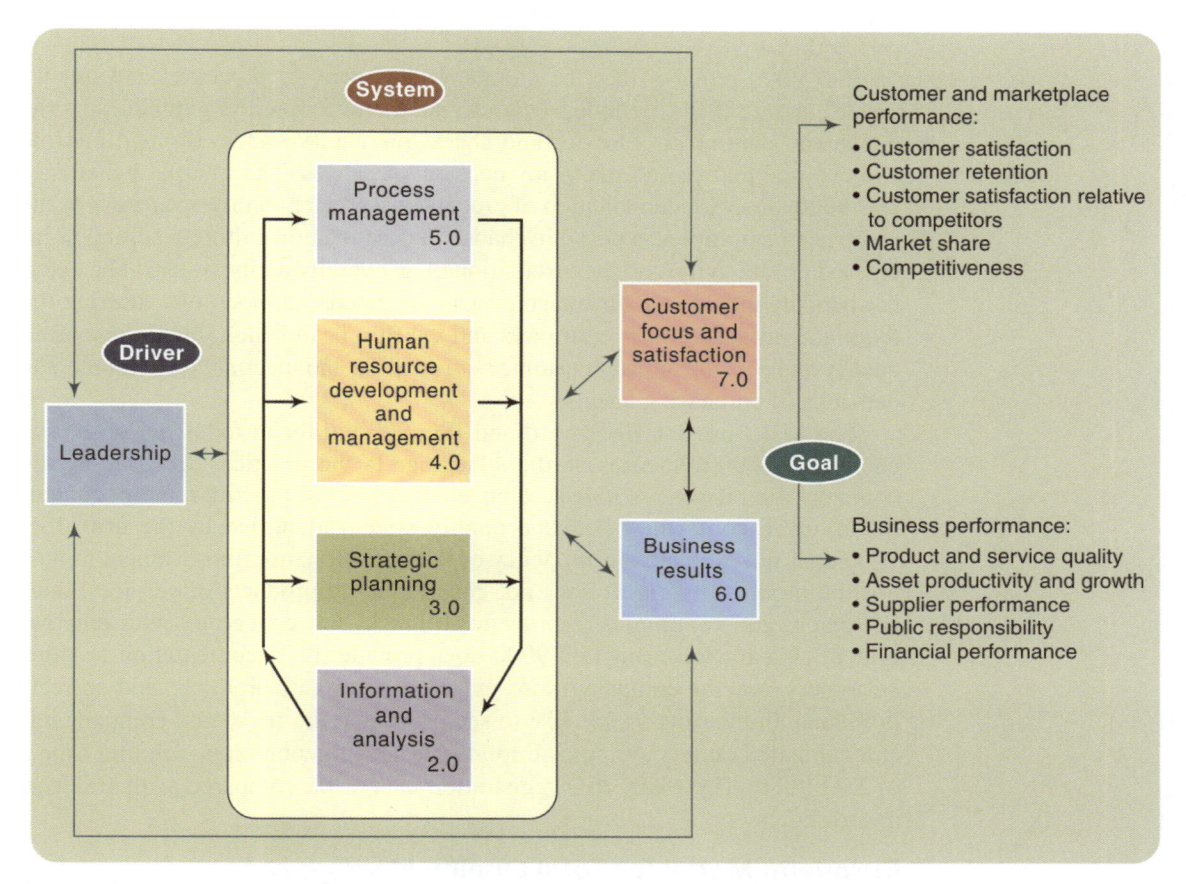

Source: U.S. Department of Commerce, "The Baldrige award criteria framework: dynamic relationships", *Malcolm Baldrige National Quality Award 1996 Award Criteria.*

The award criteria focus on business results. They are non-prescriptive, which means the requirements can be met in a variety of ways. As shown in the seven categories, the criteria are comprehensive, involving interrelated processes and results that focus on improvement and continuous learning. They also emphasize a systems approach in which all parts of the organization are aligned with each other. Moreover, the criteria serve as a diagnostic tool, pointing out the strengths and weaknesses of the company.

ISO 9000[52]

ISO 9000 has become so popular that some have termed it ISOmania. ISO, which is derived from the Greek *isos*, meaning equal, was founded in 1946 in Geneva, Switzerland. The ISO 9000 document was first published in 1987 and consists actually of five related standards numbered from 9000 to 9004 (and expanding). Although the ISO movement originated in Europe, now more than 100 countries participate in ISO, including Japan, the United States, and European Union nations. Most large companies, such as General Electric, Du Pont, British Telecom, and Philips Electronic, urge and even demand suppliers to be ISO 9000 certified.

ISO 9000 requires that the company document its processes and quality system, assure that all employees understand and follow the guidelines of the document, continually monitor and check the quality system through internal and external audits, and make any necessary changes. The internal benefits of ISO 9000 are the documentation of processes, a greater quality awareness of the company's employees, a possible change in organization culture resulting in increased productivity, and the installation of an overall quality system. The external benefits include an advantage over nonregistered competitors, meeting the requirements set forth by customers and the European Union, higher perceived quality and possible greater customer satisfaction, and meeting, for example, the demands of purchasing agents.

The Malcolm Baldrige award and ISO 9000 differ in focus, purpose, and content. ISO 9000 focuses on the adherence to the practices specified by the company. Its purpose is to assure buyers that certain practices and documentation are in conformity with the quality system identified by the firm. ISO 9000 does not evaluate the efficiency of the operation, nor improvement trends, nor the product quality. It does not ensure quality products or services, does not emphasize continuous improvement, and is not concerned with empowerment or teamwork. But ISO 9000 does provide the documentation to show customers how the company trains employees, tests its products, and corrects problems. Purchasing agents like to see proof that the registered company has a documented quality system and follows it. Documentation is a central aspect of ISO 9000. Therefore, ISO registration cannot be compared with Baldrige award scores.

European Model for Total Quality Management

Another quality program is the European Quality Award bestowed upon excellent companies by the European Foundation for Quality Management (EFQM).[53] The 1996 European model for total quality management, shown in Figure 3.3, is built on the following premise: "Customer Satisfaction, People (employee) Satisfaction, and Impact on Society are achieved through Leadership driving Policy and Strategy, People Management, Resources and Processes, leading ultimately to excellence in Business Results."[54] The percentages shown in the figure are used for assigning weights in the award.

The European total quality management model is built on the American Baldrige award but contains some new aspects, as a comparison of the two models reveals. Still, the models are very similar. For example, the "impact on society" variable in the European model is considered in the "leadership" concept of the Baldrige award as "public responsibility and corporate citizenship." Similarly, "people satisfaction" in the European model is part of "human resource development and management" in the Baldrige model. What is interesting in the European model is that the first five variables (leadership, people management, policy and strategy, resources, and processes) are called "enablers." This means that they deal with *how* an organization achieves the results. The four other criteria (people satisfaction, customer satisfaction, impact on society, and business results) are called "results" and deal with *what* an organization has achieved.

FIGURE 3.3 The European Foundation for Quality Management model for business excellence

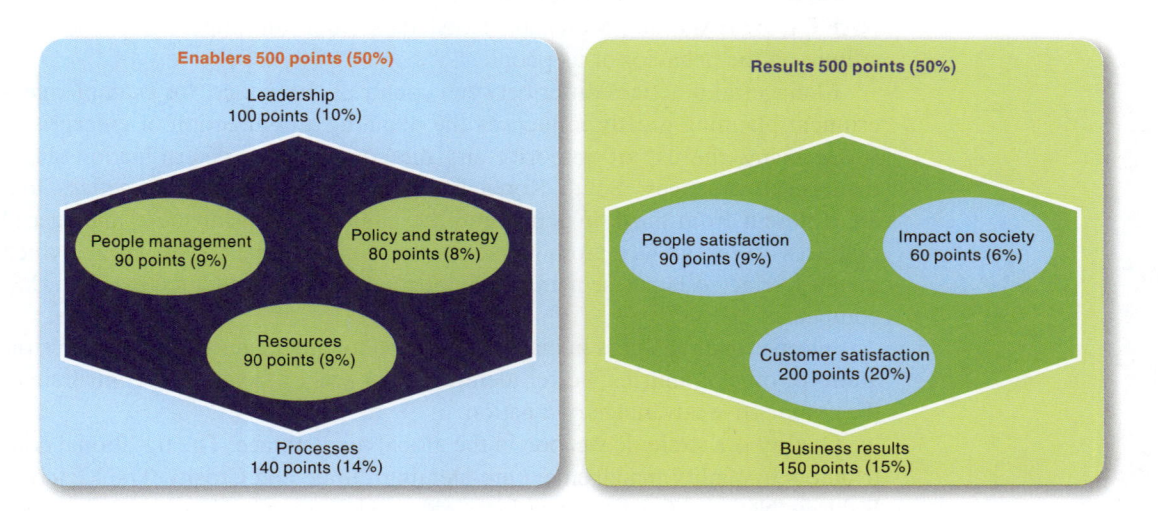

Enablers 500 points (50%)
- Leadership 100 points (10%)
- People management 90 points (9%)
- Policy and strategy 80 points (8%)
- Resources 90 points (9%)
- Processes 140 points (14%)

Results 500 points (50%)
- People satisfaction 90 points (9%)
- Impact on society 60 points (6%)
- Customer satisfaction 200 points (20%)
- Business results 150 points (15%)

Source: European Foundation for Quality Management, "*The European Foundation for Quality Management Model for Business Excellence*", Self-Assessment 1997 Guidelines for Companies.

In conclusion, then, the American Malcolm Baldrige National Quality Award model and the European model for total quality management are similar, but both are very different from ISO 9000.

SUMMARY

International businesses, which extend their operations across national boundaries, are particularly affected by the educational, sociocultural–ethical, political–legal, and economic environments of the host countries. MNCs have developed different orientations for operating in foreign countries, ranging from ethnocentric (the foreign operation's views are based on those of the parent company) to geocentric (the organization is viewed as an interdependent system operating in many countries, that is, it is truly international).

Countries are forming regional alliances, such as the European Union, NAFTA, ASEAN, and Mercosur. Hofstede studied the impact of a country's culture on the behavior of its people.

Managerial practices differ between countries. In France, for example, government planning greatly influences the planning and direction of enterprises. In Germany, the use of authority and the concept of codetermination shape managerial practices. South Korea has developed managerial practices that are different from those in Japan and the United States. Japanese managerial practices differ greatly from those in the United States. Theory Z, which involves selected Japanese managerial practices, has been adopted by some U.S. companies.

International business managers also need to understand the economic situations of other countries. Porter identified four sets of factors that contribute to the competitive advantage of a nation.

Quality is a strategic weapon in the global marketplace. The traditional contributors to quality management are Deming, Juran, and Crosby. The Malcolm Baldrige National Quality Award recognizes U.S. organizations for their excellent performance. The European quest for quality is exemplified by ISO 9000 and the European Quality Award.

KEY IDEAS AND CONCEPTS FOR REVIEW

International business
Exportation
Licensing
Management contract
Joint venture
Subsidiary
Multinational corporation
Ethnocentric orientation
Polycentric orientation

Regiocentric orientation
Geocentric orientation
Global, or transnational, corporation
Country alliance and trade bloc
Hofstede's five dimensions of behavior
Management practices in France, Germany, and South Korea
Globalization of Chinese enterprises
Venture capitalists' confidence in China
Management practices in Japan and Theory Z
Porter's competitive advantage of nations
Global innovation indexes
Contributions to quality management by Deming, Juran, and Crosby
Malcolm Baldrige National Quality Award criteria
ISO 9000
European Quality Award model

FOR DISCUSSION

What advantages do MNCs have? What challenges must they meet? Give examples.

What are the five cultural dimensions identified by Hofstede?

What are some key characteristics of French, German, Korean, and Japanese management practices?

1. What is Theory Z?
2. Do you think the managerial concepts and practices applied in the United States can be transferred to Britain, France, Germany, or any other country that you know?
3. Take any country with which you are familiar and discuss how factors in the educational environment impact on managing an enterprise.
4. Discuss how a company with a geocentric orientation may manage. Compare these practices with a company having an ethnocentric outlook.
5. Do you think that the way managerial decisions are made in Japan could work in the United States? Why or why not?
6. From the various approaches to quality management, which model do you find most useful? Why?

EXERCISES/ACTION STEPS

Interview the managers of a company that is known for excellent products or services. Ask how they achieved the high level of quality.

INTERNET RESEARCH

1. Search the Internet for Geert Hofstede and identify his articles and books. Discuss the cultural characteristics of any three countries.
2. Use the Internet to find the economic conditions of the Eastern European countries that have been admitted to the European Union. Select one country to discuss in detail.

GLOBAL CASE

Starbucks—Quality Plus Social Consciousness Sells Around the World[55]

Starbucks was started in 1971 by three academicians in Seattle. Ten years later, Howard Schultz joined the company. During his trip to Italy he realized that the coffee house can be much more than a simple place where you drink coffee. However, his ideas were not accepted by the owners of the company. Being frustrated, Howard Schultz looked for investors and eventually bought the company. From 1987 until 1992, Starbucks remained a privately held company. When the company ventured outside the Pacific Northwest, the company first experienced disappointments which were followed by mixed to moderate successes.

Howard's dream was to not only provide a friendly environment for its customers, but also to provide friendly service for its employees. This meant taking good care of its employees by providing healthcare benefits not only for its full-time employees, but also for those working 20 hours or more. Moreover, employees could also purchase stocks in the company. In all, company pay and benefits attracted motivated employees with good skills.

Starbucks' aim was "to build a company with soul". This meant that employees had to listen carefully to what customers want and meet their expectations. The customer-oriented philosophy was expressed in the mission statement which also emphasized that employees treat each other with dignity, enjoy diversity in the workplace, reflect the local community, have high standards for coffee, be a good member of the community, and be, of course, profitable.

The mission statement resulted in strategies that led not only to domestic, but also international expansion. The long-range goal was to have some 25,000 stores in various locations. To achieve this long-range aim, Starbucks designed stores with a pleasant ambiance which customers, surrounded by coffee aroma, really enjoy. Also, since 2002, the company worked with T-Mobile USA by providing Internet access in the coffee shops. Besides offering caffeinated and decaffeinated beverages, a great variety of specialty coffees as well as teas are offered. Customers can also get juices, pastries, coffee mugs, coffee-making equipment, and even CDs. Moreover, Starbucks partnered with PepsiCo and Dreyer's Grand Ice Cream and engaged in licensing agreements with Kraft Foods. Coffee is also offered at warehouse clubs, Marriott Host International, United Airlines, and even at Wells Fargo Bank. Catalog sales were tried but did not succeed and consequently were discontinued. Starbucks also invested unsuccessfully in a number of dot.com companies.

The sense of social responsibilities guided the company's actions. Not only did the firm participate in local charities to "give back" to the community in which it operates, but also applied this sense of responsibility to its purchasing practices. Most of its retail stores and hotels with which the company had licensing agreements used Fair Trade-Certified coffee.[56]

Clearly, the company has been successful despite competition from coffee makers such as Proctor & Gamble, Nestle, and Kraft General Foods. How, then, will Starbucks meet those and other challenges in the future?

Questions:

1. Why was Starbucks so successful?
2. How does Starbucks differ from other coffee houses?
3. How could the company attract non-coffee drinkers?
4. What other challenges may Starbucks encounter in the future?

PART 1 CLOSING

The Basis of Global and Entrepreneurial Management

The closing part first focuses on the global environment. We will illustrate the international environment by the rising economic power of China. The unique aspects of the entrepreneurial environment in the Silicon Valley near San Francisco in California will then be analyzed. Finally, the discussion will conclude with the global car industry case.

GLOBAL FOCUS: CHINA—THE NEW ECONOMIC GIANT[57]

During the past 25 years, China has been transformed from a Marxist system to an entrepreneurial force. It has been a breathtaking transformation since the country opened its doors. Its continual hyper-growth of 9 to 10 percent annually was achieved without excessive inflation. With this growth rate and a population of about one-fifth of the world's total, China attracts significant amounts of foreign investment.

The revolutionary economic development, spearheaded first by the late Deng Xiaoping (who, by the way, was not an economist) and continued by the then President Jiang Zemin, was accompanied by rising expectations. It was only in 1992 that the goal of the market economy (although a socialistic one) was declared.

In his path-setting speech to the 15th Party Congress on September 12, 1997, Mr. Jiang announced some sweeping changes. His plan was to convert most of the 305,000 state-owned companies to shareholding firms that would be exposed to international competition. Although the issue of ownership was only vaguely mentioned, some companies declared bankruptcy. At that time, state-owned companies still produced about 40 percent of industrial output; but they used most of the available capital, thus constraining more productive, flexible, privately owned firms. Still, the 1,000 largest firms remained under the control of the government; however, most of them would have to compete in the marketplace.

The plan was to form large corporations operating in industries such as high-tech electronics, telecommunication, and petrochemicals. China is already a major exporter of appliances, garments, and several lower-end products. To implement the ambitious plan, China has to reduce the tariffs on many goods to operate in the WTO. Shanghai and Hong Kong can become financial centers rivaling those in London, Tokyo, and New York.

However, the ambitious plans are accompanied by the risk of massive unemployment which, in turn, could result in political unrest. Therefore, if many firms close down in the transformation process, those adversely affected must be taken care of. Provisions have to be made for helping them meet housing and medical expenses as well as for pensions, benefits that were previously granted by their employers. Besides providing a social safety net, workers also need to be trained for the demands created by the market economy.

China is facing some tough questions of how to proceed. While some politicians hold on to the communist philosophy, others forge ahead with Western ideas. The country has many strengths, but it faces many challenges too. Among the strengths are the relative openness toward reform, advances in technology, reunification with Hong Kong, educational progress through partnerships with Western universities, and access to modern technology through joint ventures. Many multinational firms can also be found in oil, gas, pharmaceuticals, telecommunication, and a variety of services.

In management education, the Beijing International MBA of Peking University and China Europe International Business School offer a variety of management programs, including an Executive MBA (Master of Business Administration) degree. These schools introduce executives to management theories and practical skills necessary to integrate the Chinese economy into the global economy.

The situation is aggravated by the migration of people to the already overcrowded urban areas, which are plagued by pollution and other urban ailments. Furthermore, inconsistent government regulation could discourage foreign investment.

Outside its boundaries, China has great opportunities. It is a major force in the Pacific Rim region. It also has access to Western technology, enabling it to catch up rapidly with developed countries. The eagerness of foreign firms to enter the market enables the Chinese to negotiate favorable terms. On the other hand, China also faces considerable threats from abroad. The reduction of trade barriers may help the country as a whole, but will hurt individual firms as they will have to compete with quality products from abroad.

In all, then, China has strength not only to overcome its weaknesses but also to take advantage of its opportunities and to cope with threats. The challenges are to keep the economy growing (although at a lower rate than in the 1990s) without inflation and to deal with the social forces that may become restless during the transformation at a time of rising expectations. China also needs to provide a political and legal environment free from corruption to attract foreign investors and to become a major force in the global community.[58]

After 15 years of negotiations, China has become a member of WTO. The signing of the membership agreement with WTO on November 11, 2001, and the ratification of its membership a month later as WTO's 143rd member will certainly create opportunities and challenges (e.g., it will drastically reduce the barriers for importing agricultural products from the United States) for China as well as for President Hu Jintao, Mr. Jiang's successor.[59]

Figure C1.1 summarizes the competitive position of China showing its internal strengths and weaknesses as well as the external opportunities and threats from other countries. The figure also indicates possible Chinese strategies by combining the internal and external factors, shown as Maxi–Maxi (maximizing internal strengths to take advantage of external opportunities), Mini–Maxi (minimizing weaknesses and maximizing opportunities), Maxi–Mini (maximizing strengths and minimizing threats), and Mini–Mini (minimizing both weaknesses and threats) strategies. These alternative strategies are driven by China's culture, purpose, and objectives, shown in the first box in the figure.

FIGURE C1.1 TOWS Matrix for the competitive situation of China

Country culture, values, purpose, objectives, etc.	Internal strengths (S)	Internal weaknesses (W)
• To be a powerful member of the international community (World Trade Organization, WTO) • To move toward a market economy • To improve the living standard of its people • To unify a diverse culture • To gain political and economic power	• Aggressive government reforms • Ability to change regulations (government intervention) • Strong bargaining position with interested investors • Large domestic market • Growing strength in high-tech, wireless, and electronics products • Low labor costs and Confucian ethics (loyalty, duty, etc.) • Vast natural resources (coal, iron ore, petroleum, etc.) • High growth with low inflation • Vastly improved socioeconomic conditions in last decade (health, nutrition, lite expectancy, education) • Competitive advantage in clothing, consumer goods, fabric, toys, electrical machinery, and switch gear • Scholars educated abroad • WTO member	• Unemployment: risk of labor unrest • Regional economic development gap • Lack of trained managers • Poor legal system; lack of copyright/patent protection • Despite natural resources, insufficient energy supply • Outdated banking system • Oversupply of expensive housing and office buildings • Consumer demand dropping • Variety of dialects hinders communication • High inventory with deflationary tendencies
External opportunities (O)	**SO: Maxi-Maxi**	**WO: Mini-Maxi**
• Export light industrial goods to high-cost, high-priced markets and attract foreign investors • Technological developments demand for low-cost goods in high-priced and poor countries • Asia and Pacific Rim: traditional ties to these economies; financing from Singapore, other countries or regions • United States: eagerness to access Chinese economy allows Chinese business access to its market; improved political relations • European Union (EU): same eagerness as United States; Hong Kong's traditional tie to EU economies creates natural links for China, especially in the banking industry	• Attract investment by reducing trade barriers and introducing clear long-term policies • Continue policy of constructive engagement with the United States • Expand presence throughout Asia by bolstering large and competitive SOEs • Introduce protectionism by setting up new barriers and changing rules • Export items where China has a competitive advantage (electrical machinery, toys, footwear, apparel, power generation equipment, textiles, iron and steel)	• Improve management education by continuing to establish and promote linkages with Western universities and offering MBA at state universities • Provide a social safety net • Reform legal system and eliminate corruption; strengthen and enforce laws protecting intellectual property • Assist transition of unprofitable SOEs through absorption by larger SOEs or privatization (East German model) • Encourage foreign direct investment in the less-developed Western regions to promote growth and reduce migration into the eastern cities

External threats (T)	ST: Maxi-Mini	WT: Mini-Mini
• Asian financial crisis • Competition for exports and foreign investment due to falling labor costs and devalued currencies in other Asian countries • Hesitation of foreign investors due to Asian crisis along with political and legal uncertainties • Antidumping investigations	• Invest in high-tech industries • Lower tariffs and other barriers to free trade • Provide a stable legal system for foreign investors • Continue to move toward a market economy and reform of SOEs and reduction of government subsidies • Consider investing in emerging economies • Consider devaluing currency as a last resort	• Meet the requirements for WTO membership • Increase social reforms to reduce poverty and improve quality of life for workers

(continuation from previous page, O column): WTO membership allows China even more access to the United States, EU, and Japanese markets • Raise money from other Asian countries for restructuring • Reduce bureaucracy and introduce policies that reduce arbitrary restrictions for foreigners • Attract foreign companies that are willing to share technology

The TOWS Matrix is described in Chapter 5. The authors would like to acknowledge the assistance of Chris Capistran in conducting the research. The information is based on a forthcoming paper "An Analysis of China's Competitive Environment with the TOWS Matrix: An Alternative to Porter's Model" by Heinz Weihrich and Chunguan Ma; Michael E. Porter, *The Competitive Advantage of Nations* (New York: Free Press, 1990), p. 71; Heinz Weihrich, "The TOWS Matrix: A Tool for Situational Analysis," *Long Range Planning*, 1982, pp. 54–66; World Bank, *China Country Brief* (Washington, DC, 1998), p. 1; Dexter Roberts and Mark L. Clifford, "The Engine Is Misfiring", *Business Week*, October 1, 2001, pp. 80–81; "China Opens Up," *The Economist*, November 20, 1999, pp. 17–18; "China's Future: A Dampened Blaze," *The Economist*, March 9, 2002, pp. 4–7; "Systemic Corruption: Something Rotten in the State of China", *The Economist*, February 16, 2002, pp. 37–38; "Corruption in China: Rocking the Boat", *The Economist*, November 24, 2001; "China's Economy: East Asia's Whirlwind Hits the Middle Kingdom," *The Economist*, February 14, 1998, pp. 37–39; Roger Chen, "An Analysis of China's Economic Development Policies and Prospects," *Business Economics*, July 1998, pp. 29–34; "Chinese Companies, Silicon Valley, PRC," *The Economist*, June 27, 1998, pp. 64–65; data released by the International Data Company, January 21, 2003, by the Chinese Ministry of Information Technology, January 21, 2003, and by the Chinese Ministry of Foreign Trade and Economic Cooperation, January 23, 2003; "China in Transition," *Far Eastern Economic Review*, January 29, 1998, p. 26; Greg Mastel, *The Rise of the Chinese Economy* (Armonk, NY: M. E. Sharpe, 1997), p. 44; John Bryan Starr, *Understanding China* (New York: Hill and Wang, 1997), p. 61; U.S. Census Bureau, Foreign Trade Division, Data Dissemination Branch, www.census.gov/foreign-trade, accessed May 22, 2002; "Bush's Asian Challenge," *The Economist*, March 17, 2002, pp. 13–14; "China, America and Japan," *The Economist*, March 17, 2001, pp. 21–23; "Crashing to Earth," *The Economist*, April 7, 2002, p. 29; "China Complains to WTO," *Far Eastern Economic Review*, April 4, 2002; Catherine Gelb, "Are You Ready?" *China Business Review*, January–February 2002; www.BIMBA.edu.cn, accessed March 9, 2003; "Cars in China: Leave It to the Locals," *The Economist*, April 13, 2002, pp. 60–61.

Asian economic conditions are also linked to Europe, and one of the driving forces in the European Union is the car industry, which is illustrated by the following case.

ENTREPRENEURIAL FOCUS: SILICON VALLEY AND THE ENVIRONMENT OF ENTREPRENEURIAL MANAGEMENT

Silicon Valley has been recognized around the world as the epicenter of technology innovation and VC investment. The historical development and the resulting culture of Silicon Valley have led to the formation of an ideal entrepreneurial environment, a business creation "eco-system" as it is sometimes called. This entrepreneurial environment has led to the creation of firms that have changed the face of the world (see, e.g., Intel, Yahoo, Apple, Google, Facebook, YouTube, Twitter, and others). What factors have led to the development of this new venture creation *eco-system* in Silicon Valley? What entrepreneurial management techniques developed in the Silicon Valley can be applied to other organizations that wish to be more nimble and innovative? These questions should be considered by those wishing to learn how to manage more entrepreneurially.

Several key elements have come together in the Silicon Valley that helped make it the world standard for innovation and entrepreneurial management.[60] These factors include the historical and cultural development of the region; the resulting eco-system of related and supporting service industries; key historical Pacific Rim networks of production, talent, and resources; excellent universities focusing on scientific and business research; and, perhaps most decisively, locationally bound sources of immense funding for new businesses in the form of VC. Each of these will be discussed now.

The entrepreneurial culture of Silicon Valley has been key to its rise as the hotbed for innovation that influences the world.[61] A history of success with innovative companies (e.g., Hewlett Packard and Apple) has helped foster a culture of confidence in launching new ventures. Around this success, an eco-system of supporting industries has arisen which fosters the development of high-growth start-up firms. Prestigious legal and accounting firms in the Bay Area frequently represent tiny start-up companies that may have a big future ahead of them. In most business centers around the world, this is not the case, as large prestigious service firms tend to represent large well-established companies. This risk-taking culture of supporting a new business, that could be either the next Yahoo or a failure, helps provide the necessary infrastructure to support technology innovation and business growth. This risk-taking capacity also extends to professional managers throughout the Silicon Valley. Being part of a failed start-up company is not necessarily considered as a disadvantage for a manager's career in Silicon Valley. Rather, it can be noted as a great experiential learning that the manager can take with her to the next company.[62] Further, the use of stock option grants as a significant portion of compensation tends to encourage managers to take a risk with young start-up companies.

Pacific Rim networks of development, production, distribution, and talent allow for an integrated and efficient system of innovation and product creation. Many integrated circuit design companies establish themselves in the Silicon Valley for design, outsource the production of their chips to Malaysia or other regions, and distribute them through cooperative and competitive networks around the world. This efficient development and manufacturing infrastructure permits the development of numerous small design firms that bring different models of thought to a flexible production system. The outcomes for many of these entrepreneurial information technology firms are world class, bringing their products in record time to the market.

Other factors, such as a network of universities dedicated to research and development in engineering and science (e.g., Stanford University and University of California, Berkeley) and business entrepreneurship (such as at the University of San Francisco), provide the raw materials in technology and educated human capital that are necessary to propel local high-growth firms.

VC is perhaps the element that is most difficult to replicate elsewhere in terms of its size and availability as it tends to be bound to the location of the VC firms.[63] Silicon Valley and San Francisco Bay Area VC firms account for more than one-third of this investment.[64] Why is this important? VC finances new high-potential and high-risk businesses that banks and other traditional sources of business financing simply cannot accommodate. Silicon Valley VC firms, in particular, tend to focus on financing high-technology firms—whether these firms are focused on software, communication architecture, life science, energy, or materials. In these high-technology industries, there exists an additional product development risk. It is often questionable whether the time and financing devoted to research and development will lead to a workable product.

Additional risk of product acceptance or first to market must also be accounted for. VC firms are experienced in evaluating and financing firms that take these risks. In return for financing firms in these challenging endeavors, VC firms expect returns from firms they invest in to top 40–50 percent per year. These high returns from successful VC portfolio firms are necessary as other firms in their portfolio will fail completely and all the VC investment in them will be lost. For example, a successful investment in the next Yahoo or Google more than makes up for investments in a slate of failed firms. This ready availability of venture financing makes possible the founding of these firms in Silicon Valley, whereas they probably could not get financed in most other places around the globe.[65] Entrepreneurial managers must understand the VC process to effectively manage in this environment.

The local impact of VC is undeniable. In 2003 in California alone, 2,479,000 individuals were employed by venture-financed firms. This is approximately 3 times the VC firm employment of the next closest state of Texas.[66] VC-backed firms also tend to outperform non-VC-backed firms in terms of sales and employment growth.[67] Again, VC firms have tended to invest locally, as they take an active role in the firms they back. This historical tendency to stay local reinforces the value of a regional comparative advantage in technological innovation.[68]

The great availability of VC to firms in the Silicon Valley clearly presents opportunities to the region. Leading a VC-backed firm also takes unique management abilities. VC firms pride themselves on not only being a source of capital for their portfolio companies, but also a critical source of strategic advice, industry contacts, and intellectual capital. The managing partner of a VC firm who led the financing of a specific portfolio company also often takes a board seat on the young firm and exerts significant control on the future of the firm. The venture-backed company manager must be aware of VC rules and manage effectively in that context.

Venture Capitalists have definite opinions on the importance of the management teams of the firms they finance. In the 2006 2nd quarter report of the *Silicon Valley Venture Capitalist Confidence Index*™ (Bloomberg ticker symbol USFSVVCI), Robert Troy of Geneva Venture Capital, offered, "The stage is set for the expected maturity boom in the high-tech industry. Sophisticated entrepreneurs who have obviously learned from the mistakes of the recent past, with next paradigms in place, can better serve customers with great value added and interesting business models… The Bay Area is more than ever the high-tech Mecca thanks to an extraordinary pool of talent."[69] In the same report, Charles Beeler of El Dorado Ventures stated, "We have continued to see a number of very compelling investment opportunities led by strong early-stage management teams. These are the type of people who can turn good opportunities into great outcomes and will adjust to the market as needed in order to succeed." In fact, VC Confidence has been shown to precede public offerings of venture-backed firms, perhaps due to VC's unique informational advantage they develop from working at the intersection of public and private capital.[70] So, it is prudent for entrepreneurs and other interested parties to take note of what they expect to occur.

These regional factors of innovation and entrepreneurial advantage have not been replicated elsewhere completely to date. What successful entrepreneurial management techniques can be learned from the example of Silicon Valley? How can managers best lead and grow firms in an innovative and entrepreneurial way? Can managers outside of Silicon Valley take advantage of this eco-system of innovation and opportunity as a potential market or alliance? The following chapters provide a context for taking best advantage of the entrepreneurial power of the Silicon Valley for students of management in their own national and regional context. The spread of VC globally from Silicon Valley has unleashed a new wave of entrepreneurial opportunities for managers attuned to the environment. Networks of capital, talent, technology, and entrepreneurial passion link together thoughtful managers around the globe. An understanding of the entrepreneurial process to foster these links for the development of companies and regions is the responsibility of the managers in each organization. How to manage entrepreneurially and successfully? These are two of the key questions addressed in this text.

GLOBAL CAR INDUSTRY CASE

Will the Chinese Geely Car Be the Next Indian Nano?[71]

Probably no inexpensive car got as worldwide attention in recent years as the Indian Nano. Yet, is the Nano being threatened by Geely, a Chinese manufacturer that started in 1986 by producing refrigerators and moved to diversify into motorcycles in 1996? Perhaps not many people have heard of Geely, the biggest privately owned Chinese car company. Yet, Geely drew attention at car shows around the world (Frankfurt, Detroit). Chairman and cofounder Li Shufu likes to be viewed as the Henry Ford of China. While maintaining the chairmanship, Mr. Li gave up the CEO title to Yue Guisheng in 2006. Geely's mission statement includes references to safety, environment-friendliness, and efficiency.

In 1998, Geely started the production of automobiles; the first cars were exported in 2003. Mr. Li Shufu plans to export two-thirds of the cars to other countries. It already sells cars in Peru, Uruguay, Venezuela, Romania, Pakistan, South Africa, and Bangladesh.

Mr. Li's plan includes launching nine new cars, which are amazing by any standards. But, there is a suspicion that the cars do not meet Western standards. The Russian car crash test showed a low survival rate of the test dummy. Yet, cars are being assembled and sold from Russian assembly kits in countries such as Ukraine and Indonesia. At this time, there are rumors of negations of buying the well-known Swedish car companies Saab and Volvo.[72]

Geely illustrates that the car market is indeed global and extends beyond the nameplates of Ford, GM, Chrysler, Mercedes, BMW, Volkswagen, and others. Certainly TATA Motors with its successful Nano has to consider Geely as a potential competitor.

Questions:

1. What are the strengths and weaknesses of Nano? Please conduct Internet research and/or talk to people who own a Nano.
2. Based on your findings, what do you think is the competitive advantage of Nano in India and other countries?
3. How important is car safety to the Indian consumer?
4. What are your criteria in the purchase of a car?

ENDNOTES

1. David Gauhtier-Villars, "Ghosn Bets Big on Low-Cost Strategy," *The Wall Street Journal,* September 4, 2007; John W. Miller, "Africa's New Car Dealer: China," *The Wall Street Journal,* August 28, 2007.
2. Ted Baker, Eric Gedajlovic, and Michael Lubatkin, "A Framework for Comparing Entrepreneurship Processes Across Nations", *Journal of International Business Studies,* 2005, 36: 492–504.
3. S. Shane and S. Venkataraman, "The Promise of Entrepreneurship as a Field of Research", *Academy of Management Review,* 2000, 25(1): 217–226.
4. Email interview updated on August 17, 2009 from original discussion in January 11, 2007 with Mr. Bryant Tong, Partner, Nth Power, by Mark Cannice.
5. CNN Money, "Global 500", *Fortune,* www.money.cnn.com/magazines/fortune/global500/2011/full_list/index.html, accessed on July 31, 2012.
6. Fortune Global 500, http://money.cnn.com/magazines/fortune/global500/2013/full_list/, accessed March 15, 2014.
7. See also Tatiana Kostova and Srilata Zaheer, "Organizational Legitimacy under Conditions of Complexity: The Case of the Multinational Enterprise," *Academy of Management Review,* January 1999, pp. 64–81.
8. David A. Heenan and Howard V. Perlmutter, *Multinational Organization Development* (Reading, MA: Addison-Wesley, 1979), Chap. 2. See also George Balabanis, Adamantios Diamantopoulos, Rene Dentiste Mueller, and T. C. Melewar, "The Impact of Nationalism, Patriotism and Internationalism on Consumer Ethnocentric Tendencies (in Turkey and the Czech Republic)," *Journal of International Business Studies,* Spring 2001, p. 157.
9. Joel McCormick, "The World According to Azim Premji," *Stanford Magazine,* May–June 2006; "Q&A With Wipro's Azim Premji," *Business Week Online,* November 27, 2006; Internet http.www.wipro.com, accessed November 30, 2006.
10. Karl Schoenberger, "Has Japan Changed?" *Fortune,* August 19, 1996, pp. 72–82.
11. Shaker Zahra, Duane Ireland, and Michael Hitt, "International Expansion by New Venture Firms: International Diversity, Mode of Market Entry, Technological Learning, and Performance," *Academy of Management Journal,* 2000, 43(5): 925–950.
12. GE's Jeff Immelt on Digitizing in the Industrial Space, Interview of Jeff Immelt, interviewed by Rik Kirkland, McKinsey, http://www.mckinsey.com/insights/organization/ges_jeff_immelt_on_digitizing_in_the_industrial_space, accessed January 7, 2016.
13. NAFTA Secretariate, www.nafta-sec-alena.org, accessed November 8, 2008.
14. Mercosur, www.mercosur.org/english/default.htm, accessed November 8, 2008: There is concern that Mercosur, South America's largest trade bloc, is losing its direction and effectiveness, as discussed in "Another Blow to Mercosur," *The Economist,* March 31, 2001, pp. 33–34.
15. ASJE Global Trade Working Group, www.stopftaa.com, accessed March 1, 2002.
16. Association of Southeast Asian Nations, www.aseansec.org, accessed November 8, 2008; People's Daily Online, http://english.peopledaily.com.cn, accessed November 8, 2008.
17. James Hookway, "Big Stakes Hang Up U.S.-Thai Trade Pact," *The Wall Street Journal,* January 30, 2006.
18. Ibid.
19. India, "National Symbols of India", *Know India* (National Informatics Centre, Government of India), http://india.gov.in/knowindia/national_symbols.php, accessed July 31, 2012.
20. For a discussion of the global transfer of management knowledge see the special issue on this topic in *The Academy of Management Executive,* May 2005.
21. Geert Hofstede, *Cultures and Organizations: Software of the Mind* (New York: McGraw-Hill, 1991); *Uncommon Sense about Organizations: Cases, Studies and Field Observations* (Thousand Oaks, CA: Sage, 1994); *Culture's Consequences: Comparing Values, Behaviors, Institutions and Organizations across Nations* (Thousand Oaks, CA: Sage, 2001). See also Tilburg University's Center for Hofstede's Works, http://center.kub.nl/extra/hofstede, accessed October 1, 2006; Hofstede's study has been expanded in the Global Leadership and Organizational Behavior Effectiveness (GLOBAL) 61-nations research project. This project identified nine dimensions of national cultures. They are: (1) Avoidance of uncertainty, (2) power distance, (3) societal collectivism, (4) group collectivism, (5) egalitarianism of gender, (6) assertiveness, (7) orientation toward the future, (8) performance orientation, and (9) humane orientation. See Robert House, Mansour Javidan, Paul Hanges, and Peter Dorfman, "Understanding Cultures and Implicit Leadership Theories Across the Globe: An Introduction to Project GLOBE," *Journal of World Business,* 2002, 37: 3–10, and Mansour Javidan and Robert J. House, "Cultural Acumen for the Global Manager: Lesson from Project GLOBE," *Organizational Dynamics,* 2001, 29 (4): 289–305.
22. Hofstede, *Cultures and Organizations,* p. 53.
23. Ibid., p. 84.

24. "France: A Civil Self-Service," *The Economist*, May 1, 1999, pp. 49–50.
25. See, for example, Jean-Louis Barsoux and Peter Lawrence, "The Making of a French Manager," *Harvard Business Review*, July–August 1991, pp. 58–67.
26. Roland Calori and Bruno Dufour, "Management European Style," *Academy of Management Executive*, August 1995, pp. 61–71. See also EUROCADRES, www.etuc.org/EUROCADRES/info/2-43.cfm, accessed September 2006.
27. Interview with President Kim Young Sam, "Now It Is Our Turn to Contribute to the World," *Business Week*, July 31, 1995, p. 64. See also "Hollowing out South Korea's Corporations," *The Economist*, September 14, 1996, pp. 63–64.
28. "Nation-Builders," *The Economist*, July 10, 1999, Insert p. 6.
29. Steven Musil, "Sony Confirms 10,000 Layoffs as Part of 'One Sony' Initiative," http://news.cnet.com/8301-1023_3-57412857-93/sony-confirms-10000-layoffs-as-part-of-one-sony-initiative, accessed January 2, 2016.
30. William G. Ouchi, *Theory Z* (Reading, MA: Addison-Wesley, 1981).
31. Robyn Meredith, *The Elephant and the Dragon* (New York: Norton & Company, 2008), Chapter 1.
32. Cited by John Gittings in *The Changing Face of China* (Oxford: Oxford University Press, 2005).
33. X. Yang, Y. Lim, Y. Sakurai, and S. Seo, "Comparative Analysis of Internationalization of Chinese and Korean Firms," *Thunderbird International Business Review*, 2009, 51 (1): 37–51.
34. Based on a recent contribution to M. Pellicano, M.V. Ciasullo in *La visione strategica dell'impresa*, Giappichelli, Torino.
35. Karl Sauvant, "New Sources of FDI: The BRICs Outward FDI from Brail, Russia, India, and China," *Journal of World Investment & Trade*, 2005, 6 (5): 639–709.
36. X. Yang and C. Stoltenberg, "Growth of Made-in-China Multinationals: An Institutional and Historical Perspective," in Alon and McIntyre, eds. *Globalization of Chinese Enterprises* (Palgrave, 2008), pp. 61–76.
37. P. J. Buckley, L. J. Clegg, A. R. Cross, X. Liu, H. Voss, P. Zheng, "The Determinants of Chinese Outward Foreign Direct Investment," *Journal of International Business Studies*, 2007, 38 (4): 499–518.
38. *China Venture Capitalist Confidence Report Q2 2012*, Mark Cannice and Ling Ding. (In publishing a recurring confidence index of China-based venture capital investors, we intend to utilize the local knowledge and insight of our respondents to provide an essential perspective and an ongoing leading indicator of the dynamic Chinese entrepreneurial business environment.)
39. Meredith, *The Elephant and the Dragon*; *The 'Bird of Gold': The Rise of India's Consumer Market* (New York: McKinsey Global Institute, May 2007).
40. Robyn Meredith, op. cit.; see also see also Thomas L. Friedman, *The World is Flat* (New York: Picador and Thomas L. Friedman, 2007).
41. Dexter Roberts, "China's Factory Blues," *Business Week*, April 7, 2008, pp. 78–81.
42. http://www.bbc.co.uk/news/business-13356567, accessed January 2, 2016.
43. Michael E. Porter, *The Competitive Advantage of Nations* (New York: Free Press, 1990), especially Chap. 3; Heinz Weihrich, "Analyzing the Competitive Advantages and Disadvantages of Germany with the TOWS Matrix: An Alternative to Porter's Model," *European Business Review*, 1999, 99 (1): 9–22.
44. Erika Kinetz, "GM's Talegaon Unit to Start Production by September," *Associated Press, September 3, 2008*. http://www.thehindu.com/2008/04/17/stories/2008041756341700.htm, accessed September 3, 2008.
45. INSEAD, *The Global Innovation Index 2011*, http://www.globalinnovationindex.org/gii/, accessed April 5, 2012.
46. "U.S. Ranks #8 In Global Innovation Index," *Industry Week*, http://www.industryweek.com/articles/u-s-_ranks_8_in_global_innovation_index_18638.aspx, accessed February 16, 2012. Note that in the table, the U.S. ranks 9th.
47. See Edwards W. Deming, *Out of the Crisis*, 2nd ed. (Cambridge, MA: MIT Center for Advanced Engineering Study, 1986); J. M. Juran, *Juran on Leadership for Quality: An Executive Handbook* (New York: Free Press, 1989); Philip B. Crosby, *Quality Is Free: The Art of Making Quality Certain* (New York: McGraw-Hill, 1979) and "Criticism and Support for the Baldrige Award," *Quality Progress*, May 1991, pp. 42–43.
48. See also *Journal of Quality Management*, 1996–2003.
49. For European sources on quality approaches, see *Qualität: Garanti fuer die Zukunft* (Frankfurt: Deutsche Gesellschaft fuer Qualität e.V., undated); *DQS Deutsche Gesellschaft zur Zertifizierung von Qualitätsmanagementsystemen* (Frankfurt: DQS, 1993); Klaus J. Zink and Rolf Schildknecht, "German Companies React to TQM," *Total Quality Management*, October 1990, pp. 259–262.
50. The 1996 Regional Malcolm Baldrige Award Conference, San Francisco, June 13, 1996; *Malcolm Baldrige National Quality Award 1996 Award Criteria* (Gaithersburg, MD: U.S. Department of Commerce, Technology Administration, National Institute of Standards and Technology, undated); Richard J. Schonberger, "Is the Baldrige Award Still about Quality?" *Quality Digest*, December 2001, p. 30.
51. Malcolm Baldrige National Quality Award 1996 Award Criteria.
52. Les Landes, *Leading the Duck at Mission Control* (St. Peters, MO: Wainwright Industries, 38–219, undated); Ronald Henkoff, "The Hot New Seal of Quality," *Fortune*, June 28, 1993, pp. 116–120; Navin S. Dedhia, "The Basics of ISO 9000," *Quality Digest*, October 1995, pp. 52–54; Caroline G. Hemenway, "10 Things You Should Know about ISO 14000," *Quality Digest*, October 1995; Caroline G. Hemenway and Gregory J. Hale, "Implementing ISO 14000: Taking the First Steps," *Quality Digest*, January 1996, pp. 25–30; Gregory J. Hale and Caroline G. Hemenway, "ISO 14001 Certification: Are You Ready?" *Quality Digest*, July 1996, pp. 35–41; R. Michael Kirchner, "What's beyond ISO 9000?" *Quality Digest*, November 1996, pp. 41–45; William A. Stimson, "Internal Quality: Meeting the Challenge of ISO 9000:2000," *Quality Digest*, November 2001, pp. 39–43. (Although not related to product and service quality, ISO 14000 standards are very much in the news. These standards pertain to voluntary standards for environmental management. They were created under the direction of the International Organization for Standardization.)
53. *Total Quality Management: The European Model for Self-Appraisal, 1993* (Eindhoven, Netherlands: European Foundation for Quality Management, 1992); *Self-Assessment 1996 Guidelines for Companies* (Brussels: European Foundation for Quality Management, 1995); "The EFQM Model for Business Excellence," in *Self-Assessment 1997 Guidelines for Companies* (Brussels: European Foundation for Quality Management, 1997), p. 9.
54. *Self-Assessment 1996 Guidelines for Companies*, p. 7.
55. This case is based on a variety of sources including Howard Schultz and Dori Jones Yang, *Pour Your Heart Into It* (New York: Hyperion, 1997),

2005 Starbuck's Annual Report, www.starbucks.com, accessed February 4, 2006. See also the Annual Report, http://www.starbucks.com/aboutus/FY05_CSR_Total.pdf#-search=%22Starbucks%20Annual%20Report%22, accessed October 5, 2006.

56. Starbucks has a fight concerning Ethiopian coffee-bean trademarks; see "Starbucks vs. Ethiopia—Storm in a Coffee Cup," *The Economist*, December 2, 2006, pp. 66–67.

57. "After Deng," *The Economist*, February 22, 1997, p. 15; "Greeting the Dragon," *The Economist*, October 25, 1997, pp. 15–16; "Shanghai Volkswagen," Harvard Business School Case 9-696-092, April 23, 1996; *Multinational Companies in China* (Hong Kong: Economist Intelligence Unit, 1997); "China Learns the World's Rules," in *The World in 2001* (London: *The Economist*, 2001); World Trade Organization, www.wto.org, accessed December 8, 2009; *BBC Business News*, http://news.bbc.co.uk/hi/english/business, accessed January 14, 2002.

58. "Corruption in China: Rocking the Boat," *The Economist*, November 24, 2001, p. 40.

59. World Trade Organization, www.wto.org, accessed January 10, 2002.

60. See also Ward Winslow and John McLaughlin, *The Making of Silicon Valley: A 100 Year Renaissance* (Santa Clara Valley Historical Foundation, 1996), for a historical perspective on the development of the region.

61. See also Elton Jr. Sherwin, *The Silicon Valley Way*, 2nd ed. (Prima Lifestyles, 2000), for a discussion on the entrepreneurial culture of Silicon Valley.

62. While learning from failure is acceptable, too many failures might bring the judgment of the manager into question.

63. Venture capitalists take an active role in the portfolio companies they finance; therefore, they tend to invest primarily in firms they can easily drive to for board meetings and other occasions.

64. PricewaterhouseCoopers/National Venture Capital Association MoneyTree Report Investments by Region Q1–Q2 2006.

65. Other venture capital hubs exist in New England, New York, Texas, North Carolina, and elsewhere—but these hubs are much smaller.

66. Venture Impact 2004—*Venture Capital Benefits to the US Economy*, 2004, Global Insight, National Venture Capital Association.

67. Ibid.

68. A 2006 study in global trends in venture capital by Deloitte and Touché does indicate a gradual shift of about half of venture firms that now consider investment internationally. The main interest was in China and India.

69. Mark V. Cannice, Silicon Valley Venture Capitalists' Confidence Index Report Q2 2006, ProQuest.

70. Mark Cannice and Cathy Goldberg, "Venture Capitalists' Confidence, Asymmetric Information and Liquidity Events," *Journal of Small Business and Entrepreneurship*, 2009, 22 (2): 141–164.

71. "The Ambition of Geely," *The Economist*, August 1, 2009, p. 56; Geely, http://202.155.223.21/~geelm-hk1/en/index.html, accessed August 1, 2010.

72. Chinese Media: Volvo Bought by Geely, http://www.thetruthaboutcars.com/volvo-bought-by-geely, accessed January 2, 2016.

Goal Inputs of Claimants
1. Employees
2. Consumers
3. Suppliers
4. Stockholders
5. Governments
6. Community
7. Others

Inputs
1. Human
2. Capital
3. Managerial
4. Technological

EXTERNAL ENVIRONMENT

Managerial knowledge, goals of claimants, and use of inputs (Part 1, *The Basis of Management Theory and Science*)

- **Planning (Part 2)**
- Organizing (Part 3)
- Staffing (Part 4)
- Leading (Part 5)
- Controlling (Part 6)

To Produce Outputs

Reenergizing the System

Facilitated by communication that also links the organization with the external environment

EXTERNAL ENVIRONMENT

External Variables and Information
1. Opportunities
2. Constraints
3. Others

EXTERNAL ENVIRONMENT

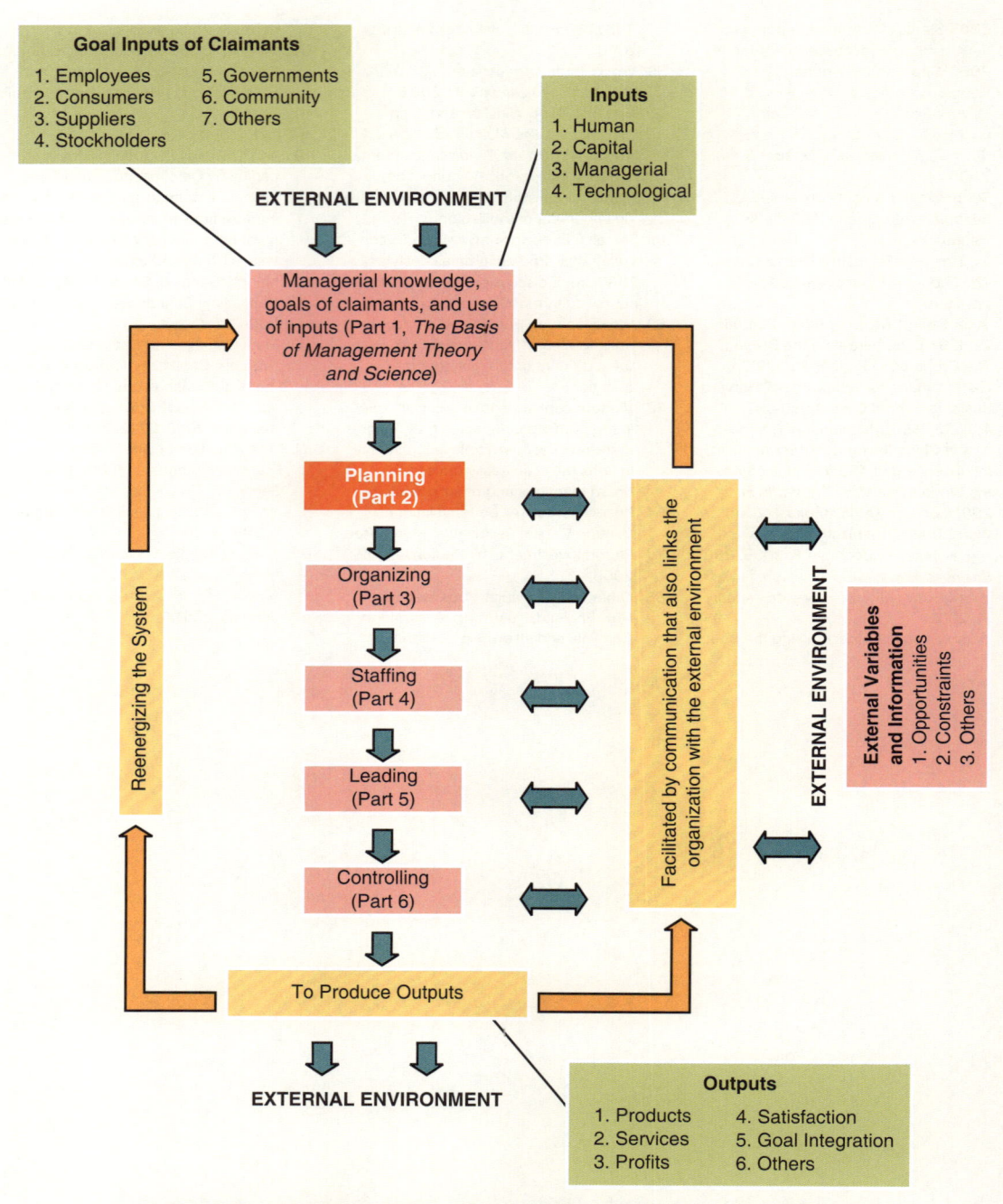

Outputs
1. Products
2. Services
3. Profits
4. Satisfaction
5. Goal Integration
6. Others

SYSTEMS APPROACH TO MANAGEMENT: PLANNING

PART 2

Planning

Chapter 4:   Essentials of Planning and Managing by Objectives
Chapter 5:   Strategies, Policies, and Planning Premises
Chapter 6:   Decision Making
Part 2 Closing: Global and Entrepreneurial Planning

CHAPTER 4

Essentials of Planning and Managing by Objectives

Learning Objectives

After studying this chapter, you should be able to:

LO 1   Understand what managerial planning is and why it is important

LO 2   Identify and analyze the various types of plans and show how they relate to each other

LO 3   Outline and discuss the logical steps in planning and see how these steps are essentially a rational approach to setting objectives and selecting the means of reaching them

LO 4   Explain the nature of objectives

LO 5   Describe how verifiable objectives can be set for different situations

LO 6   Outline the evolving concepts in management by objectives (MBO)

LO 7   Understand the model of the systems approach to MBO

LO 8   Describe the benefits of MBO

LO 9   Recognize the weaknesses of MBO and suggest ways to overcome them

You are now familiar with the basic management theory and have been introduced to the five essential managerial functions: planning, organizing, staffing, leading, and controlling. In Part 2 of this book, we shall discuss planning.

In designing an environment for the effective performance of individuals working together in a group, a manager's most essential task is to see that everyone understands the group's mission and objectives and the methods for attaining them. If group effort is to be effective, people must know what they are expected to accomplish. This is the function of planning. It is the most basic of all the managerial functions. **Planning** involves selecting missions and objectives and deciding on the actions to achieve them; it requires decision making, that is, choosing a course of action from among alternatives. Plans, thus, provide a rational approach to achieving preselected objectives. Planning also strongly implies managerial innovation, as will be discussed in Chapter 6. Planning bridges the gap from where we are to where we want to go. It is also important to point out that planning and controlling are inseparable—the Siamese twins of management (see Figure 4.1). Any attempt to control without plans is meaningless, since there is no way for people to tell whether they are going where they want to go (the result of the task of control) unless they first know where they want to go (part of the task of planning). Plans thus furnish the standards of control.

Planning Selecting missions and objectives as well as the actions to achieve them, which requires decision making, that is, choosing a course of action from among alternatives.

FIGURE 4.1 Close relationship of planning and controlling

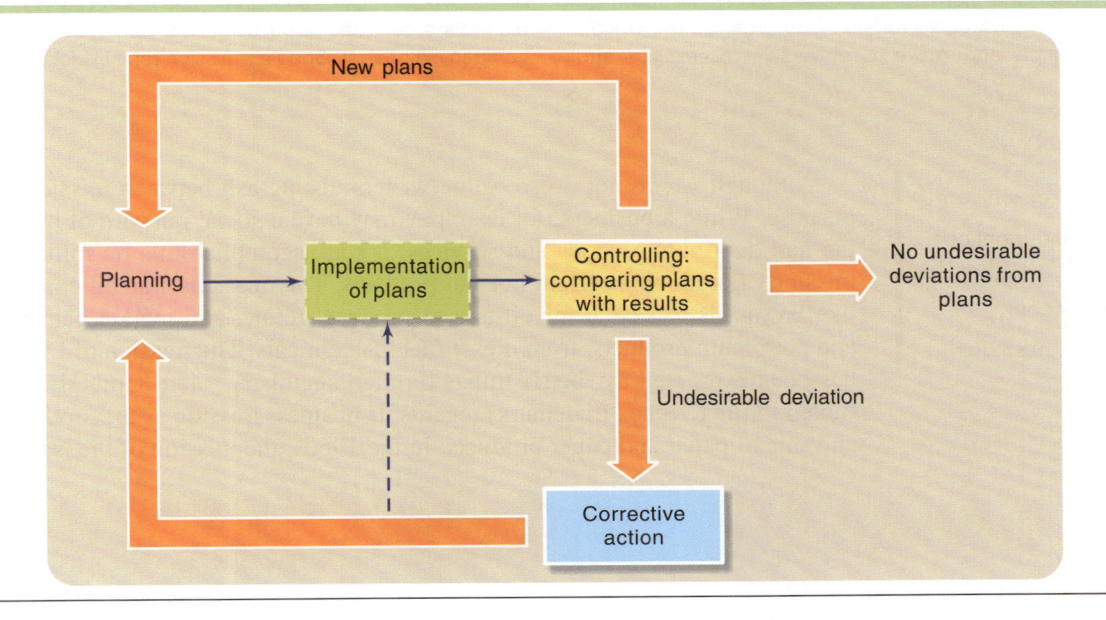

TYPES OF PLANS

Plans can be classified as (1) missions or purposes, (2) objectives or goals, (3) strategies, (4) policies, (5) procedures, (6) rules, (7) programs, and (8) budgets.

Missions or Purposes*

> **Mission or purpose**
> The basic function or tasks of an enterprise or agency or any part of it.

The **mission**, or **purpose** (the terms are often used interchangeably),[1] identifies the basic function or tasks of an enterprise or agency or any part of it. Every kind of organized operation has, or at least should have if it is to be meaningful, a mission or purpose. In every social system, enterprises have a basic function or task assigned to them by society. For example, the purpose of a business generally is the production and distribution of goods and services. The purpose of a state highway department is designing, building, and operating a system of state highways. The purpose of the courts is the interpretation of laws and their application. The purpose of a university is teaching, research, and providing services to the community.

INNOVATIVE PERSPECTIVE

Google's Mission

Google is well known as the world's leading Internet Search Engine. While its success is a function of numerous factors, its clear and focused mission has created an unambiguous direction for the company that has set in motion the steps to its global success. As listed on its website, "Google's mission is to organize the world's information and make it universally accessible and useful."[2] This simple and clear mission helps inform and contextualize all that Google does. The mission is also helpful in directing employee actions in daily duties, as each task should be in support of its mission. A clear and direct mission inspires and directs and is a necessary condition for organizational success. Now part of the holding company, Alphabet, Google's mission remains focused.

---

www.exxon.com

www.dupont.com

www.kimberly-clark.com

www.nasa.gov

Although we do not do so, some writers distinguish between mission and purpose. While a business, for example, may have a social purpose of producing and distributing goods and services, it can accomplish this by fulfilling a mission of producing certain lines of products. The mission of an oil company, like Exxon, is to search for oil and to produce, refine, and market petroleum and petroleum products, from diesel fuel to chemicals. The mission of Du Pont has been expressed as "better things through chemistry," and Kimberly-Clark (noted for its Kleenex trademark) regards its business mission as the production and sale of paper and paper products. In the 1960s, the mission of the National

---

* Often the term vision is mentioned in connection with the discussion of mission. Popular books on management discuss concepts such as goal setting, team management, and orientation toward the future, in connection with the discussion of vision.

Aeronautics Space Administration (NASA) was to get a person to the moon before the Russians. It is true that in some businesses and other enterprises, the purpose or mission often becomes fuzzy. For example, many conglomerates have regarded their mission as **synergy**,* which is accomplished through the combination of a variety of companies.

Synergy Whole is greater than its parts.

An organization's mission is also often accompanied by its vision. For example, the core mission of the University of San Francisco (USF) is to "promote learning in the Jesuit Catholic tradition." USF's vision is to "be internationally recognized as a premier Jesuit Catholic, urban university with a global perspective that educates leaders who will fashion a more humane and just world."[3] What is the vision and mission of your organization? Does it inspire?

Objectives or Goals

Objectives, or **goals** (the terms are used interchangeably in this book), are the ends toward which activity is aimed. They represent not only the end point of planning but also the end toward which organizing, staffing, leading, and controlling are aimed. The nature of objectives and management by objectives (MBOs) will be discussed in greater detail later in this chapter.

Objectives or goals The ends toward which activity is aimed.

Strategies

For years, the military used the word *strategies* to mean grand plans made in light of what it was believed an adversary might or might not do. While the term still usually has a competitive implication, managers increasingly use it to reflect broad areas of an enterprise's operation. In this book, **strategy** is defined as the determination of the basic long-term objectives of an enterprise and the adoption of courses of action and allocation of resources necessary to achieve these goals.

Strategy Determination of the basic long-term objectives of an enterprise and the adoption of courses of action and allocation of resources necessary to achieve these goals.

Policies

Policies also are plans in that they are general statements or understandings that guide or channel thinking in decision making. Not all policies are "statements"; they are often merely implied from the actions of managers. The president of a company, for example, may strictly follow—perhaps for convenience rather than as policy—the practice of promoting from within; the practice may then be interpreted as policy and carefully followed by subordinates. In fact, one of the problems of managers is to make sure that subordinates do not interpret as policy minor managerial decisions that are not intended to serve as patterns.

Policies General statements or understandings that guide or channel thinking in decision making.

---

* The concept of synergy can be expressed simply as a situation in which 2 plus 2 becomes equal to 5, or in which the whole is greater than the sum of the parts.

INNOVATIVE PERSPECTIVE

Google's Ten Points

Google further explicates its core mission with "Ten things it knows to be true".[4] These statements of truth help guide specific actions and, thus, serve as broad policies that help guide decisions and behavior in the firm. Its first statement is: "Focus on the user and all else will follow." This direct and simple statement directs efforts toward enhancing the user experience first and then allowing success in that objective to drive sales and profits in its business. Its second statement reads "It's best to do one thing really, really well." Again this philosophy for the firm also translates to other areas of firm management, from employee development to niche marketing. Focused statements of policy or management that help guide employee actions translate to organizational performance and profits.

Policies define an area within which a decision is to be made and ensure that the decision will be consistent with, and contribute to, an objective. Policies help decide issues before they become problems, make it unnecessary to analyze the same situation every time it comes up, and unify other plans, thus permitting managers to delegate authority and still maintain control over what their subordinates do.

There are many types of policies. Examples include policies of hiring only university-trained engineers, encouraging employee suggestions for improved cooperation, promoting from within, conforming strictly to a high standard of business ethics, and setting competitive prices.

Procedures

Procedures Plans that establish a required method of handling future activities.

Procedures are plans that establish a required method of handling future activities. They are chronological sequences of required actions. They are guides to action, rather than to thinking, and they detail the exact manner in which certain activities must be accomplished. For example, Case Western University outlines three steps for its appraisal process: (1) setting performance objectives, (2) performing a mid-year review of the objectives, and (3) conducting a performance discussion at the end of the period.[5] Procedures often cut across departmental lines. For example, in a manufacturing company, the procedure for handling orders may involve the sales department (for the original order), the finance department (for acknowledgment of receipt of funds and for customer credit approval), the accounting department (for recording the transaction), the production department (for the order to produce the goods or the authority to release them from stock), and the shipping department (for determination of shipping means and route).[6]

A few examples illustrate the relationship between procedures and policies. Company policy may grant employees vacations; procedures established to implement this policy will provide for scheduling vacations to avoid disruption of work, setting rates of vacation pay and methods for calculating them, maintaining records to ensure each employee of a vacation, and spelling out the means for applying for leave.

Rules

Rules spell out specific required actions or nonactions, allowing no discretion. They are usually the simplest type of plan. "No smoking" is a rule that allows no deviation from a stated course of action. The essence of a rule is that it reflects a managerial decision that a certain action must—or must not—be taken. Rules are different from policies. While policies are meant to guide decision making by marking off areas in which managers can use their discretion, rules allow no discretion in their application.

> **Rules** spell out specific required actions or nonactions, allowing no discretion.

Programs

Programs are a complex of goals, policies, procedures, rules, task assignments, steps to be taken, resources to be employed, and other elements necessary to carry out a given course of action; they are ordinarily supported by budgets. They may be as major as an airline's program to acquire a $20 billion fleet of jets or a five-year program to improve the status and quality of its thousands of flights. Or they may be as minor as a program formulated by a single supervisor to improve the morale of workers in the parts manufacturing department of a farm machinery company.

> **Program** Complex assembly of goals, policies, policies, procedures, rules, task assignments, steps to be taken, resources to be employed, and other elements necessary to carry out a given course of action.

Budgets

A **budget** is a statement of expected results expressed in numerical terms. It may be called a "quantified" plan. In fact, the financial operating budget is often called a *profit plan*. A budget may be expressed in financial terms: in terms of labor-hours, units of product, or machine-hours; or in any other numerically measurable terms. It may deal with operation, as the expense budget does; it may reflect capital outlays, as the capital expenditure budget does; or it may show cash flow, as the cash budget does. One of the most comprehensive budgets is prepared by the Office of Management and Budget of the White House.[7] The budget proposal is then presented to the Congress by the president of the United States.

Since budgets are also control devices, we reserve our principal discussion of them for Chapter 19 on control techniques. However, making a budget is clearly planning. The budget is the fundamental planning instrument in many companies. It forces a company to make in advance—whether for a week or for five years—a numerical compilation of expected cash flow, expenses and revenues, capital outlays, or labor- or machine-hour utilization. The budget is necessary for control, but it cannot serve as a sensible standard of control unless it reflects plans.

> **Budget** Statement of expected results expressed in numerical terms.

STEPS IN PLANNING

The practical steps listed below, and diagramed in Figure 4.2, are of general application. In practice, however, one must study the feasibility of possible courses of action at each stage.

FIGURE 4.2 Steps in planning

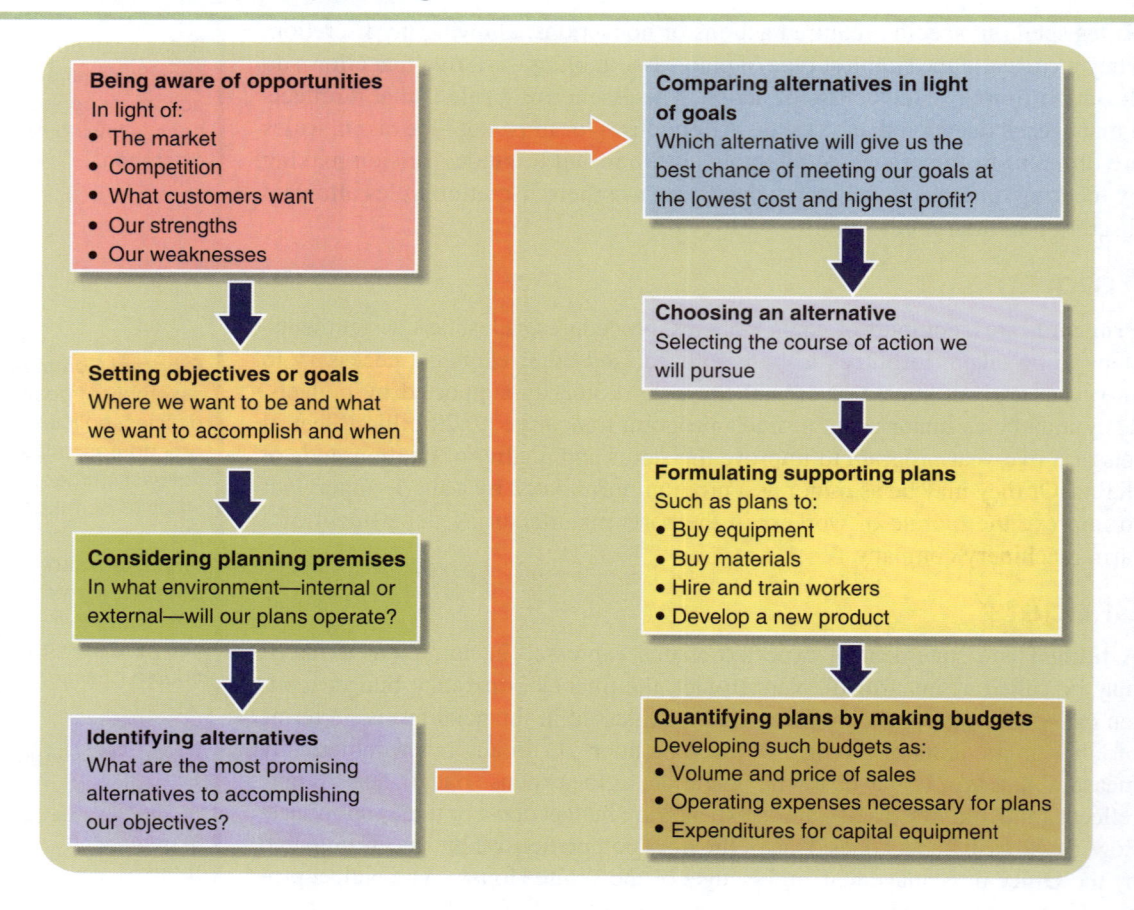

Being aware of opportunities
In light of:
- The market
- Competition
- What customers want
- Our strengths
- Our weaknesses

Setting objectives or goals
Where we want to be and what we want to accomplish and when

Considering planning premises
In what environment—internal or external—will our plans operate?

Identifying alternatives
What are the most promising alternatives to accomplishing our objectives?

Comparing alternatives in light of goals
Which alternative will give us the best chance of meeting our goals at the lowest cost and highest profit?

Choosing an alternative
Selecting the course of action we will pursue

Formulating supporting plans
Such as plans to:
- Buy equipment
- Buy materials
- Hire and train workers
- Develop a new product

Quantifying plans by making budgets
Developing such budgets as:
- Volume and price of sales
- Operating expenses necessary for plans
- Expenditures for capital equipment

1. Being Aware of Opportunities

Although it precedes actual planning and is therefore not strictly a part of the planning process, an awareness of opportunities* in the external environment as well as within the organization is the real starting point for planning. All managers should take a preliminary look at possible future opportunities and see them clearly and completely, know where their company stands in light of its strengths and weaknesses, understand what problems it has to solve and why, and know what it can expect to gain. Setting realistic objectives depends on this awareness. Planning requires a realistic diagnosis of the opportunity situation.

2. Establishing Objectives

The second step in planning is to establish objectives for the entire enterprise and then for each subordinate work unit. This is to be done for the long term as well as for the short range. Objectives specify the expected results and indicate the end points of what is to be done, where the primary emphasis is to be placed, and what is to be accomplished by the network of strategies, policies, procedures, rules, budgets, and programs.

---

* The word problems might be used instead of opportunities. However, a state of disorder or confusion and a need for a solution to achieve a given goal can more constructively be regarded as an opportunity. In fact, one very successful and astute company president does not permit his colleagues to speak of problems; they must speak only of opportunities.

Enterprise objectives give direction to the major plans, which, by reflecting these objectives, define the objective of every major department. Major departmental objectives in turn control the objectives of subordinate departments, and so on down the line. In other words, objectives form a hierarchy. The objectives of lesser departments will be more accurate if subdivision managers understand the overall enterprise objectives and the derivative goals. Managers should also have the opportunity to contribute ideas for setting their own goals and those of the enterprise.

3. Developing Premises

The next logical step in planning is to establish, circulate, and obtain agreement to utilize critical planning premises such as forecasts, applicable basic policies, and existing company plans. **Premises** are assumptions about the environment in which the plan is to be carried out. It is important for all the managers involved in the planning process to agree on the premises. In fact, the major **principle of planning premises** is: the more thoroughly individuals charged with planning understand and agree to utilize consistent planning premises, the more coordinated enterprise planning will be.

Forecasting is important in premising: What kinds of markets will there be? What volume of sales? What prices? What products? What technical developments? What costs? What wage rates? What tax rates and policies? What new plants? What policies with respect to dividends? What political or social environment? How will expansion be financed? What are the long-term trends? Forecasts should be based on careful research that uses rigorous analytical techniques.

> **Premises**
> Assumptions about the environment in which the plan is to be carried out.
>
> **Principle of planning premises**
> The more thoroughly individuals charged with planning understand and agree to utilize consistent planning premises, the more coordinated enterprise planning will be.

INNOVATION PERSPECTIVE

The Autonomous Vehicle[8]

The success of the automobile has changed our society over the last 100 years. Vehicles not only provided greater freedom, but also resulted in today's problems such as air pollution and traffic congestions, just to mention a few.

From the affordable Ford Model T to today's driverless vehicles, the car has changed greatly.* In the past, the focus was on mechanical improvements and innovations, while today's focus is on using digital innovations. Digital technology ranges from connecting cars with other cars to autonomous cars sometimes called driverless or self-driving cars.

The advantages of the autonomous car may include reduced accidents because most are caused by human error. Disabled, visually impaired, and elderly people who may not be able to drive will then be able to use the self-driving vehicle by simply putting the destination into the car computer and then enjoying the ride. Other advantages often cited are also better insurance rates because of the reduction in collision.

There are also potential disadvantages and other problematic issues with the self-driving car. For one, people may not want to give control to the car computer and question the software reliability. There is also the question of liability in case of an accident. Should the car maker be held responsible for mishaps? A new legal framework would have to be established. There are other issues: Would the car be able to adjust to bad weather, or could the sensors of the car interpret hand signals of the police?

Despite the potential difficulties, virtually all carmakers are moving ahead in exploring possible applications of the digital innovations. Mercedes, for example, is working on the autobahn pilot, Tesla Motors aims at introducing a self-driving vehicle before 2020. Similarly, Volvo is working toward a crash-free vehicle by 2020. Nissan is exploring the multilane highway innovation. Virtually all manufacturers, Audi, BMW, GM, Goggle, Mercedes, Renault, and Toyota, aim for developing a self- or partly self-driving car by 2020.

*The first motor car was developed by the Daimler Company during 1885–1886.

INNOVATION PERSPECTIVE

So what is the state of the art? The Google driverless car is often used as foreshadowing the development. Google does road testing with Audi, Lexus, the hybrid Toyota Prius, and others. The Google car uses the Lidar system which is mounted on top of the car, using the range finder, and maps the 3D environment. It has been extensively road-tested, by driving around Lake Tahoe in California and even on the San Francisco Lombard Street which is often called the most crooked street in the world. The Google entry into the car business shows that often innovations come from outside the industry, which has been illustrated already in the Tesla electric car.

The autonomous car impacts society in many different ways. The major cities in China, for example, Beijing and Shanghai, already suffer from great congestion. Additional vehicles would make it worse. There is really a question whether such a car would be able to navigate this kind of traffic. Car ownership may also be affected. Especially in cities one may question whether car ownership is necessary or be replaced by the car-sharing services instead. Reserving a car on the cellphone has become popular, especially by the millennials, the 18- to 34-year-olds. The car has changed greatly with a focus on mechanical innovations to the digital innovations. In several respects, the future of the car is already here.

4. Determining Alternative Courses

The fourth step in planning is to search for and examine alternative courses of action, especially those not immediately apparent. There is seldom a plan for which reasonable alternatives do not exist, and quite often an alternative that is not obvious proves to be the best.

The more common problem is not finding alternatives but reducing the number of alternatives so that the most promising may be analyzed. Even with mathematical techniques and the computer, there is a limit to the number of alternatives that can be thoroughly examined. The planner must usually make a preliminary examination to discover the most fruitful possibilities.

5. Evaluating Alternative Courses

After seeking out alternative courses and examining their strong and weak points, the next step is to evaluate the alternatives by weighing them in light of premises and goals. One course may appear to be the most profitable but may require a large cash outlay and have a slow payback; another may look less profitable but may involve less risk; still another may better suit the company's long-range objectives.

There are so many alternative courses in most situations and so many variables and limitations to be considered that evaluation can be exceedingly difficult. Because of these complexities, the newer methodologies and applications and analysis are discussed in Part 6 on controlling.

GLOBAL PERSPECTIVE

Evaluating Alternative Courses for the Indian Automakers to Mitigate the Environmental Impact[9]

India is well known for its motorcycles. Hindustan Motors is known for its traditional Ambassador. But with the introduction of TATA's $2,500 Nano, Indian auto industry got into the international limelight. Many car companies have entered India. For example, General Motors built its second plant in India in 2008. GM will compete with Maruti, Nano, and others. However, the car is expected to be more expensive than the advertised $2,500 Nano by TATA Motors. Volkswagen, the biggest car company in Europe, entered the preowned auto market in India. With the high gasoline prices, companies focused on fuel efficiency and at the same time developed eco-friendly engines. Toyota has been very successful with its Prius hybrid car. Honda is moving in the same direction and even luxury carmaker BMW plans to introduce later a hybrid vehicle. TATA Motors is working on an electric car and experimenting with lithium ion batteries.

But India's long-term goal is to develop hydrogen fueled automobiles. But at the outset, hybrid vehicles would have to be imported, which could run into barriers. Still, Honda Siel Cars India has already introduced its very popular Civic model with hybrid propulsion. Government policy makers wonder what alternative courses should be pursued to minimize the environmental impact of the increasing number of cars.

6. Selecting a Course

This is the point at which the plan is adopted—the real point of decision making. Occasionally, an analysis and evaluation of alternative courses will disclose that two or more are advisable, and the manager may decide to follow several courses rather than the one best course.

7. Formulating Derivative Plans

When a decision is made, planning is seldom complete, and a seventh step is indicated. Derivative plans are almost invariably required to support the basic plan.

8. Quantifying Plans by Budgeting

After decisions are made and plans are set, the final step in giving them meaning, as was indicated in the discussion on types of plans, is to quantify them by converting them into budgets. The overall budget of an enterprise represents the sum total of income and expenses, with resultant profit or surplus, and the budgets of major balance sheet items such as cash and capital expenditures. Each department or program of a business or some other enterprise can have its own budgets, usually of expenses and capital expenditures, which tie into the overall budget.

If done well, budgets become a means of adding the various plans and set important standards against which planning progress can be measured.

ENTREPRENEURIAL PERSPECTIVE

Writing a Business Plan for a New Venture

Entrepreneurs typically begin the planning process by writing a business plan for their new venture. In their business plan, entrepreneurs attempt to clearly describe the purpose of their business (what it is the business actually does), and they then identify the market opportunity or market problem they wish to solve. They describe how their product relates to the market opportunity and how they intend to sell their product, and how to finance the running of their new business. This business planning process is essential to help direct the efforts of the entrepreneur. The business plan is also essential to present to potential investors in the new business to gain their confidence and backing. A complete business plan outline is presented in the closing of Part 2 of this text that can be used as a reference for entrepreneurial managers and students.

Coordination of Short- and Long-Range Plans

Often short-range plans are made without reference to long-range plans. This is plainly a serious error. The importance of integrating the two types cannot be overemphasized, and no short-run plan should be made unless it contributes to the achievement of the relevant long-range plan. Much waste arises from decisions about immediate situations that fail to consider their effect on more remote objectives.

Responsible managers should continually review and revise immediate decisions to determine whether they contribute to long-range programs, and subordinate managers should be regularly briefed on long-range plans so that they will make decisions consistent with the company's long-range goals. Doing this is far easier than to correct inconsistencies later, especially since short-term commitments tend to lead to further commitments along the same line.

INNOVATIVE PERSPECTIVE

With the rise of enterprise software applications, many aspects of organizational planning can be automated to help achieve better integration between planning between various departments in an enterprise. For example, Enterprise Resource Planning (ERP) is a category of software applications that links information flows between various business functions (e.g., procurement, production, sales) Management students should familiarize with ERP systems that are in use in their ideal companies so that they can develop facility with those systems as they seek to join their target organization.

OBJECTIVES

An objective is **verifiable** when at the end of the period one can determine whether or not it has been achieved.

Objectives were defined earlier as the important ends toward which organizational and individual activities are directed. Since writers and practitioners make no clear distinction between the terms *goals* and *objectives*, these are used interchangeably in this book. Within the context of the discussion, it will become clear whether the objectives are long-term or short-term, broad or specific. The emphasis is on **verifiable** objectives, which means at the end of the period it should be possible to determine whether or not the objective has been achieved. The goal of every manager is to create a surplus (in business organizations, this means profit). Clear and verifiable objectives facilitate measurement of the surplus as well as the effectiveness and efficiency of managerial actions.

The Nature of Objectives

Objectives state end results, and overall objectives need to be supported by sub objectives. Thus, objectives form a hierarchy as well as a network. Moreover, organizations and managers have multiple goals that are sometimes incompatible and may lead to conflicts within the organization, within the group, and even within individuals. A manager may have to choose between short-term and long-term performance, and personal interests may have to be subordinated to organizational objectives.

Hierarchy of Objectives

As Figure 4.3 shows, objectives form a hierarchy, ranging from the broad aim to specific individual objectives. The zenith of the hierarchy is the purpose or mission, which has two dimensions. First, there is the social purpose, such as contributing to the welfare of people by providing goods and services at a reasonable price. Second, there is the mission or purpose of the business, which might be to furnish convenient, low-cost transportation for the average person. The stated mission might be to produce, market, and service automobiles. As you will notice, the distinction between purpose and mission is a fine one, and, therefore, many writers and practitioners do not differentiate between the two terms. At any rate, these aims are in turn translated into general objectives and strategies, such as designing, producing, and marketing reliable, low-cost, fuel-efficient automobiles.

FIGURE 4.3 Relationship of objectives and the organizational hierarchy

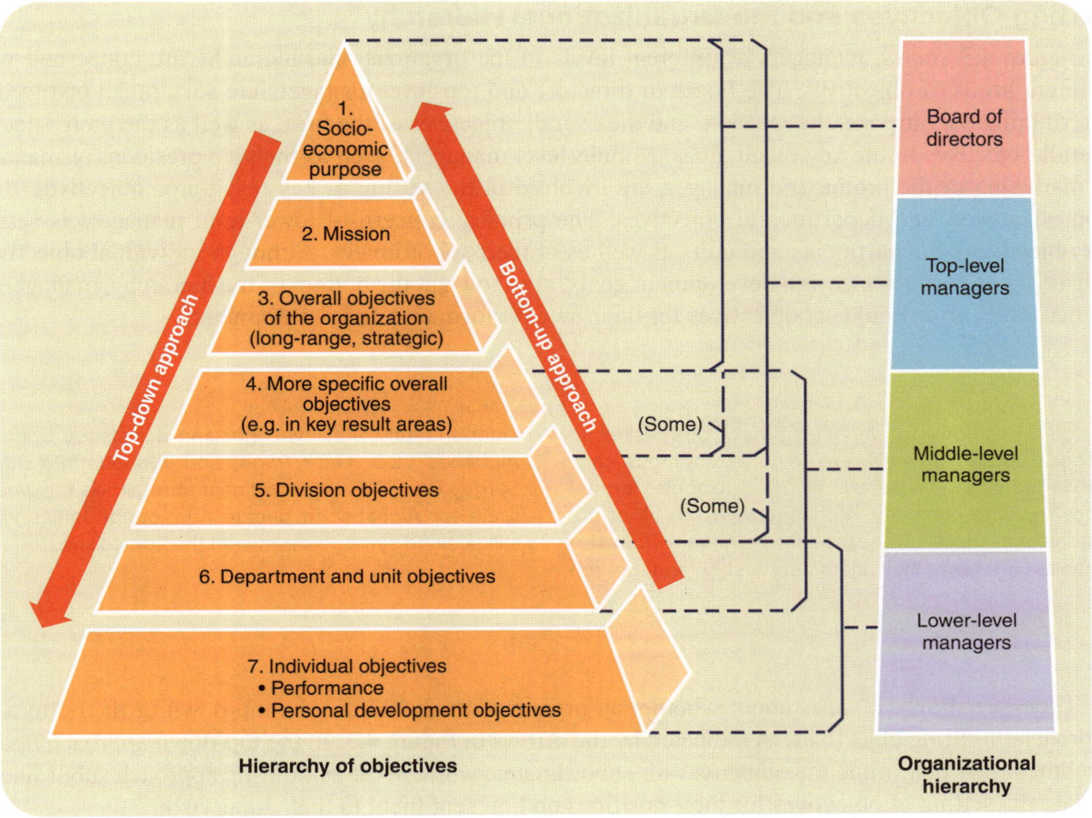

1. Socio-economic purpose
2. Mission
3. Overall objectives of the organization (long-range, strategic)
4. More specific overall objectives (e.g. in key result areas)
5. Division objectives
6. Department and unit objectives
7. Individual objectives
• Performance
• Personal development objectives
Top-down approach
Bottom-up approach
(Some)
(Some)
Board of directors
Top-level managers
Middle-level managers
Lower-level managers
Hierarchy of objectives
Organizational hierarchy

The next level of the hierarchy contains more specific objectives, such as those in the **key result areas**. These are the areas in which performance is essential for the success of the enterprise. More recent business terminology for the same concept is key performance indicator (KPI). Each company will monitor its own KPIs. These are often similar within an industry and may also be similar across industries on some measures (i.e., customer satisfaction).

> **Key result area** Area in which performance is essential for the success of the enterprise.

Although there is no complete agreement on what the key result areas of a business should be—and they may differ between enterprises—Peter F. Drucker suggests the following: market standing, innovation, productivity, physical and financial resources, profitability, manager performance and development, worker performance and attitude, and public responsibility.[10] More recently, however, two other key result areas have become of strategic importance: service and quality.

Examples of objectives for key result areas are the following: to obtain a 10 percent return on investment by the end of calendar year 2021 (profitability); to increase the number of units of product X produced by 7 percent by June 30, 2020 without raising costs or reducing the current quality level (productivity).

The objectives have to be further translated into those of divisions, departments, and units down to the lowest level of the organization.

Setting Objectives and the Organizational Hierarchy[11]

As Figure 4.3 shows, managers at different levels in the organizational hierarchy are concerned with different kinds of objectives. The board of directors and top-level managers are very much involved in determining the purpose, the mission, and the overall objectives of the firm, as well as the more specific overall objectives in the key result areas. Middle-level managers, such as the vice president or manager of marketing or the production manager, are involved in the setting of key-result-area objectives, division objectives, and departmental objectives. The primary concern of lower-level managers is setting the objectives of departments and units as well as of their subordinates. Although individual objectives, consisting of performance and development goals, are shown at the bottom of the hierarchy, managers at higher levels also should set objectives for their own performance and development.

> **INNOVATIVE PERSPECTIVE**
>
> Google is famous for launching new businesses in potential future growth areas (e.g., autonomous cars, mobile operating systems). In 2015 Google formed a new holding company, Alphabet, in which all of the current and future businesses that emanate from this organization can enjoy clear leadership and be run independently with oversight and assistance from the Alphabet CEO, Larry Page, and Alphabet President, Sergey Brin. This organizational form allows for greater scale for Alphabet to pursue new opportunities while still seeking synergies between the subsidiaries.

There are different views about whether an organization should use the top-down or the bottom-up approach in setting objectives, as indicated by the arrows in Figure 4.3. In the top-down approach upper-level managers determine the objectives for subordinates, while in the bottom-up approach subordinates initiate the setting of objectives for their positions and present them to their supervisor.

Proponents of the top-down approach suggest that the total organization needs direction through corporate objectives provided by the chief executive officer (in conjunction with the board of directors). Proponents of the bottom-up approach, on the other hand, argue that top management needs to have information from lower levels in the form of objectives. In addition, employees are likely to be highly motivated by, and committed to, goals that they initiate. Personal experience has shown that the bottom-up approach is underutilized, and that either approach alone is insufficient.

Multiplicity of Objectives

Objectives are normally multiple. For example, merely stating that a university's mission is education and research is not enough. It would be much more accurate (but still not verifiable) to list the overall objectives, which might be the following:

- Attracting highly motivated students
- Offering basic training in the liberal arts and sciences as well as a range of professional fields
- Granting postgraduate degrees to qualified candidates
- Attracting highly regarded professors
- Creating and organizing new knowledge through research
- Operating as a private school supported principally through tuition and gifts of alumni and friends

Likewise, at every level in the hierarchy of objectives, goals are likely to be multiple. Some people think that a manager cannot effectively pursue more than two to five objectives. The argument is that too many objectives tend to dilute the drive for their accomplishment. But, the limit of two to five objectives seems too arbitrary; managers might pursue more significant objectives. It would be wise to state the relative importance of each objective so that major goals receive more attention than lesser ones. At any rate, the number of objectives managers should realistically set for themselves depends on how much they will do themselves and how much they can assign to subordinates, thereby limiting their role to that of assigning, supervising, and controlling.

How to Set Objectives[12]

Without clear objectives, managing is haphazard. No individual and no group can expect to perform effectively and efficiently unless there is a clear aim. Table 4.1 illustrates some objectives and how they can be restated in a way that allows measurement.

TABLE 4.1 Examples of nonverifiable and verifiable objectives

Nonverifiable objective	Verifiable objective
1. To make a reasonable profit	1. To achieve a return on investment of 12% at the end of the current fiscal year
2. To improve communication	2. To issue a two-page monthly newsletter beginning July 1, 2020, involving not more than 40 working hours of preparation time (after the first issue)
3. To improve productivity of the production department	3. To increase production output by 5% by December 31, 2020, without additional costs while maintaining the current quality level
4. To develop better managers	4. To design and conduct a 40-hour in-house program on the "fundamentals of management," to be completed by October 1, involving not more than 200 working hours of the management development staff and with at least 90% of the 100 managers passing the exam (specified)
5. To install a computer system	5. To install a computerized control system in the production department by December 31, requiring not more than 500 working hours of systems analysis and operating with not more than 10% downtime during the first three months or 2% thereafter

Quantitative and Qualitative Objectives

To be measurable, objectives must be verifiable. This means that one must be able to answer this question: At the end of the period, how do I know if the objective has been accomplished? For example, the objective of making a reasonable profit (see Table 4.1) does not state how much profit is to be made, and what is reasonable to the subordinate may not be at all acceptable to the superior. In the case of such a disagreement, it is of course the subordinate who loses the argument. In contrast, a return on investment of 12 percent at the end of the current fiscal year can be measured; it answers these questions: how much or what or when?

At times, stating results in verifiable terms is more difficult. This is especially true when it involves the objectives for staff personnel and in government. For example, installing a computer system is an important task, but "to install a computer system" is not a verifiable goal. However, suppose the objective is "to install a computerized control system (with certain specifications) in the production department by December 31, with an expenditure of not more than 500 working hours." Then, goal accomplishment can be measured. Moreover, quality can also be specified in terms of computer downtime, such as "the system shall be operational 90 percent of the time during the first two months of operation."

Guidelines for Setting Objectives

Setting objectives is indeed a difficult task. It requires intelligent communication by management and buy-in by employees. The guidelines shown in Table 4.2 will help managers in setting their objectives.

The list of objectives should not be too long, yet it should cover the main features of the job. As this chapter has emphasized, objectives should be verifiable and should state what is to be accomplished and when. If possible, the quality desired and the projected cost of achieving the objectives should be indicated. Furthermore, objectives should present a challenge, indicate priorities, and promote personal and professional growth and development. These and other criteria for good objectives are summarized in Table 4.2. Testing objectives against the criteria shown in the checklist is a good exercise for managers and aspiring managers.

TABLE 4.2 Checklist of manager objectives

If the objectives meet the criterion, write "+" in the box on the right of the statement. If they do not, mark "–" in the box.	
1. Do the objectives cover the main features of my job?	☐
2. Is the list of objectives too long? If so, can I combine some objectives?	☐
3. Are the objectives verifiable, that is, will I know at the end of the period whether they have been achieved?	☐
4. Do the objectives indicate:	
(a) quantity (how much)?	☐
(b) quality (how well, or specific characteristics)?	☐
(c) time (when)?	☐
(d) cost (at what cost)?	☐
5. Are the objectives challenging yet reasonable?	☐
6. Are priorities assigned to the objectives (ranking, weight, etc.)?	☐
7. Does the set of objectives also include:	
(a) improvement objectives?	☐
(b) personal development objectives?	☐
8. Are the objectives coordinated with those of other managers and organizational units?	☐
Are they consistent with the objectives of my superior, my department, and the company?	☐
9. Have I communicated the objectives to all who need to be informed?	☐
10. Are the short-term objectives consistent with the long-term aims?	☐
11. Are the assumptions underlying the objectives clearly identified?	☐
12. Are the objectives expressed clearly, and are they in writing?	☐

13. Do the objectives provide for timely feedback so that I can take any necessary corrective steps? ☐
14. Are my resources and authority sufficient for achieving the objectives? ☐
15. Have I given the individuals who are expected to accomplish the objectives a chance to suggest their objectives? ☐
16. Do my employees have control over the aspects for which they are assigned responsibility? ☐

ENTREPRENEURIAL PERSPECTIVE

Interview with Bryant Tong, Managing Director with Nth Power[13]

As a venture capitalist with a leading Silicon Valley venture firm, Nth Power, Bryant Tong advises the entrepreneurs of the companies his firm finances in setting aggressive but attainable objectives or milestones. These milestones are not always related to financial targets as the firms may take many months to develop saleable products. Still, the milestones are key and verifiable, such as developing product prototypes, securing intellectual property protection for key products, filling out a management team with the best people, beginning a sales cycle with potential customers. These objectives or milestones are often linked to additional rounds of financing and so the success of the firm is very much linked toward meeting them.

EVOLVING CONCEPTS IN MANAGEMENT BY OBJECTIVES[14]

MBO is now practiced around the world. Yet, despite its wide application, it is not always clear what is meant by MBO. Some still think of it as an appraisal tool; others see it as a motivational technique; still others consider MBO a planning and control device. In other words, definitions and applications of MBO differ widely.

We define **management by objectives** as a comprehensive managerial system that integrates many key managerial activities in a systematic manner and is consciously directed toward the effective and efficient achievement of organizational and individual objectives. This view of MBO as a system of managing is not shared by all. While some still define MBO in a very narrow, limited way, we prefer to see it as a comprehensive goal-driven, success-oriented management system as shown in Figure 4.4. Besides being used for performance appraisal, as an instrument for motivating individuals, and in strategic planning, there are still other managerial subsystems that can be integrated into the MBO process. They include human resource planning and development (staffing as well as individual and organization development), career planning (building on personal strengths and overcoming weaknesses), the reward system (paying for performance), budgeting (planning and controlling), and other managerial activities important for a specific position. These various managerial activities need to be integrated into a system. In short, MBO, to be effective, must be considered a way of managing, as shown in Figure 4.4, and not an addition to the managerial job.[15]

> **Management by objectives** Comprehensive managerial system that integrates many key managerial activities in a systematic manner and is consciously directed toward the effective and efficient achievement of organizational and individual objectives.

FIGURE 4.4 Systems approach to management by objectives

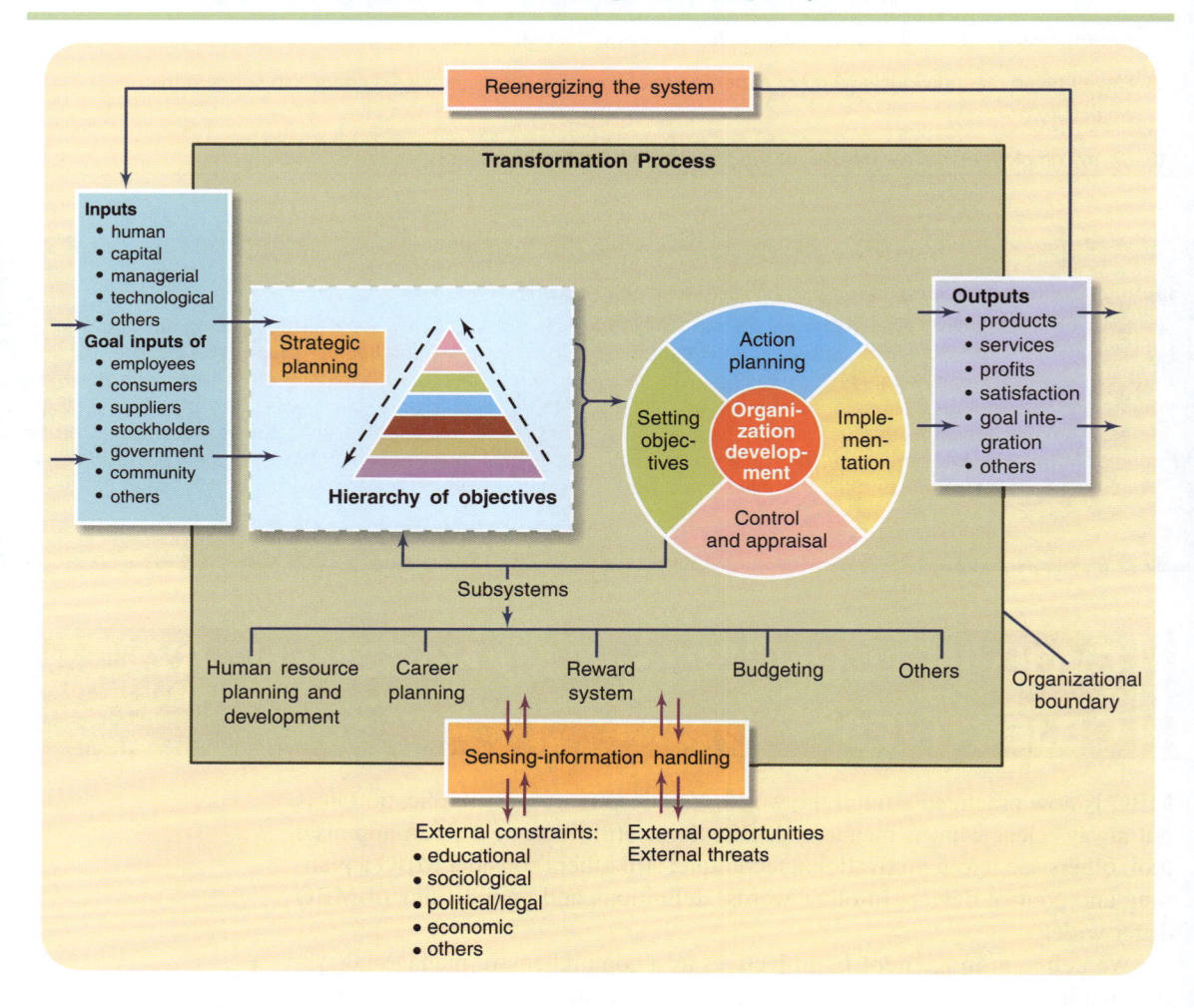

Reenergizing the system

Transformation Process

Inputs
- human
- capital
- managerial
- technological
- others

Goal inputs of
- employees
- consumers
- suppliers
- stockholders
- government
- community
- others

Strategic planning

Hierarchy of objectives

Action planning · Setting objectives · Organization development · Implementation · Control and appraisal

Outputs
- products
- services
- profits
- satisfaction
- goal integration
- others

Subsystems: Human resource planning and development · Career planning · Reward system · Budgeting · Others

Sensing-information handling

External constraints:
- educational
- sociological
- political/legal
- economic
- others

External opportunities
External threats

Organizational boundary

INNOVATIVE PERSPECTIVE

Facebook and Monetizing Mobile

Facebook, the world's leading social network, had its initial public offering in May 2012 to great fanfare. However, after months and years of anticipation, its IPO process and performance failed to meet expectations. Widely criticized for an inflated price and excessive release of shares, Facebook lost about half its market value over the ensuing months. Concerns over its ability to manage and innovate on its mobile platform were among some of the issues raised. Zuckerberg, the Facebook founder and CEO, was also criticized for his informal style and limited communication with the financial markets and media. Finally, on September 11, 2012, Zuckerberg spoke with the media and, after admitting to some strategic missteps in its mobile strategy, gave a cogent explanation of Facebook's plan to innovate upon and monetize (make significant revenue from) its mobile platform.[16] With many investors convinced and even impressed, Facebook stock recovered somewhat the following day. Clear communication of a viable plan and objectives creates value as it reduces uncertainty and enhances confidence within and outside the organization.

Benefits and Weaknesses of Management by Objectives

Although goal-oriented management is now one of the most widely practiced managerial approaches, its effectiveness is sometimes questioned. Faulty implementation is often blamed, but another reason is that MBO may be applied as a mechanistic technique focusing on selected aspects of the managerial process without integrating them into a system.

Benefits of Management by Objectives

There is considerable evidence, much of it from laboratory studies, that shows the motivational aspects of clear goals. But there are other benefits, such as the following:

- Improvement of managing through results-oriented planning
- Clarification of organizational roles and structures as well as delegation of authority according to the results expected from the people occupying the roles
- Encouragement of commitment to personal and organizational goals
- Development of effective controls that measure results and lead to corrective actions

Failures of Management by Objectives and Some Recommendations

Despite all its advantages, an MBO system has a number of weaknesses. Most are due to shortcomings in applying the MBO concepts. Failure to teach the philosophy of MBO is one of the weaknesses of certain programs. Managers must explain to subordinates what it is, how it works, why it is being done, what part it will play in appraising performance, and, above all, how participants can benefit. The philosophy is built on the concepts of self-control and self-direction.

Failure to give guidelines to goal setters is often another problem. Managers must know what the corporate goals are and how their own activities fit in with them. Managers also need planning premises and knowledge of major company policies.

There is also the difficulty of setting verifiable goals with the right degree of flexibility. Participants in MBO programs report at times that the excessive concern with economic results puts pressure on individuals that may encourage questionable behavior. To reduce the probability of resorting to unethical means to achieve results, top management must agree to reasonable objectives, clearly state behavioral expectations, and give high priority to ethical behavior, rewarding it as well as punishing unethical activities.

In addition, emphasis on short-run goals can be done at the expense of the longer-range health of the organization. Moreover, the danger of inflexibility can make managers hesitate to change objectives, even if a changed environment would require such adjustments.

Other dangers include the overuse of quantitative goals and the attempt to use numbers in areas where they are not applicable, or they may downgrade important goals that are difficult to state in terms of end results. For example, a favorable company image may be the key strength of an enterprise, yet stating this in quantitative terms is difficult. There is also the danger of forgetting that managing involves more than goal setting.

But, even with the difficulties and dangers of managing by objectives in certain situations, this system emphasizes in practice the setting of goals long known to be an essential part of planning and managing.

SUMMARY

Planning involves selecting the missions and objectives as well as the actions to achieve them. It requires decision making, which means choosing a future course of action from among alternatives. Planning and controlling are closely interrelated, although they are discussed separately in this book. There are many types of plans, such as missions or purposes, objectives or goals, strategies, policies, procedures, rules, programs, and budgets. Once an opportunity is recognized, a manager plans rationally by establishing objectives, making assumptions (premises) about the present and future environment, finding and evaluating alternative courses of action, and choosing a course to follow. Next, the manager must make supporting plans and devise a budget. These activities must be carried out with attention to the total environment. Short-range plans must, of course, be coordinated with long-range plans.

Objectives are the end points toward which activities are aimed. Objectives are verifiable if it is possible at the end of the period to determine whether they have been accomplished. Objectives form a hierarchy, starting from corporate missions or purposes going down to individual goals. Managers can best determine the number of objectives they should realistically set for themselves by analyzing the nature of the job and how much they can do themselves and how much they can delegate. In any case, managers should know the relative importance of each of their goals.

MBO has been widely used for performance appraisal and employee motivation, but it is really a system of managing. Among its benefits, MBO results in better managing, often forces managers to clarify the structure of their organizations, encourages people to commit themselves to their goals, and helps develop effective controls.

Some of its weaknesses are that managers sometimes fail to explain the philosophy of MBO (which emphasizes self-control and self-direction) to subordinates or give them guidelines for their goal setting. In addition, goals themselves are difficult to be set, tend to be short term, and may become inflexible despite changes in the environment. People, in their search for verifiability, may overemphasize quantifiable goals.

KEY IDEAS AND CONCEPTS FOR REVIEW

Planning
Mission or purpose
Objective or goal
Strategy
Policy

Procedure
Rule
Program
Budget
Planning steps
Hierarchy of objectives
Key result areas
Quantitative and qualitative objectives
Verifiability
Evolving concepts in management by objectives (MBO)
Systems approach to MBO
Benefits of MBO
Weaknesses of MBO
Recommendations for improving MBO

FOR DISCUSSION

1. "Planning is looking ahead, and control is looking back". Comment.
2. Draw up a statement of policy and devise a brief procedure that might be useful in implementing it. Are you sure your policy is not a rule?
3. Take an organization that you know and identify its purpose or mission, even if it is not formally stated by the enterprise.
4. To what extent do you believe that managers you have known in business or elsewhere have a clear understanding of their objectives? If you think they do not, how would you suggest that they go about setting their objectives?
5. Some people object to defining long-term goals because they think that knowing what will happen over a long period is impossible. Do you believe this is an intelligent position to take? Why or why not?
6. Do you think that managing by objectives could be introduced in a government agency? A university? A college fraternity or sorority?
7. What are your five most important personal objectives? Are they long- or short-range? Are the objectives verifiable?
8. In your organization, what does your superior expect from you in terms of performance? Is it stated in writing? If you wrote down your job objective and your boss wrote down what he or she expects of you, would the two be consistent?
9. How can MBO be applied to a new venture? Give an example.
10. Which company does a better job at managing by objective: Facebook or Google? Explain your position. Which company will be more successful in the next five years? Why?

EXERCISE/ACTION STEPS

In this chapter, the overall objectives of a university were identified. Develop overall objectives for your university, for your college, and for the various departments in your college. Show how these objectives are interrelated to form a network.

ONLINE RESEARCH

1. Use a search engine to look for "management by objectives" and identify how MBO is used: as a planning tool? for managerial appraisal? for motivating people? in conjunction with strategic planning? for developing managers?
2. Search the Internet for the term "budget" and discuss your findings with the class.

GLOBAL CASE

Developing Verifiable Goals

The division manager had recently heard a lecture on management by objectives. His enthusiasm, kindled at that time, grew the more he thought about it. He finally decided to introduce the concept and see what headway he could make at his next staff meeting.

He recounted the theoretical developments in this technique, cited the advantages to the division of its application, and asked his subordinates to think about adopting it. It was not as easy as everyone had thought. At the next meeting, several questions were raised. "Do you have division goals assigned by the president to you for next year?" the finance manager wanted to know.

"No, I do not," the division manager replied. "I have been waiting for the president's office to tell me what is expected, but they act as if they will do nothing about the matter."

"What is the division to do then?" the manager of production asked, rather hoping that no action would be indicated.

"I intend to list my expectations for the division," the division manager said. "There is not much mystery about them. I expect $30 million in sales; a profit on sales before taxes of 8 percent; a return on investment of 15 percent; an ongoing program in effect by June 30, with specific characteristics I will list later, to develop our own future managers; the completion of development work on our XZ model by the end of the year; and stabilization of employee turnover at 5 percent."

The staff was stunned that their superior had thought through to these verifiable objectives and stated them with such clarity and assurance. They were also surprised about his sincerity in wanting to achieve them.

"During the next month, I want each of you to translate these objectives into verifiable goals for your own functions. Naturally, they will be different for finance, marketing, production, engineering, and administration. However you state them, I will expect them to add up to the realization of the division goals."

Questions:

1. Can a division manager develop verifiable goals, or objectives, when these have not been assigned to him or her by the president? How? What kind of information or help do you believe is important for the division manager to have from headquarters?
2. Did the division manager set the goals in the best way? What would you have done?

ENDNOTES

1. A recent study found no agreement among executives of the meaning of vision. Seven factors, however, were identified in the structure and content of vision statements. They were "formulation, implementation, innovative realism, general, degree of detail, risk propensity, and profit orientation."
2. https://www.google.com/intl/en/about/, accessed September 12, 2012.
3. https://www.usfca.edu/who-we-are/reinventing-education/our-mission-and-values, accessed April 22, 2019.
4. https://www.google.com/intl/en/about/company/philosophy/, accessed September 12, 2012.
5. Case Western University, www.cwru.edu/finadmin/humres/policies/III-2a.html, accessed July 27, 2011.
6. Michael Hammer and James Champy suggest, however, that many of those steps can be combined. See their book *Reengineering the Corporation* (New York: HarperBusiness, 1993).
7. Office of Management and Budget at the White House, www.whitehouse.gov/omb, accessed January 2, 2016.
8. Semi-Autonomous Car Control Using Brain Computer, Interfaces, www. Daniel Göhring, David Latotzky, Miao Wang, Raúl RojasArtificial Intelligence GroupInstitut für InformatikFreie Universität Berlin, Germany, accessed November 18, 2015; "Ten Ways Autonomous Driving Could Redefine the Automotive World", McKinsey, June 2015 by Michele Bertoncello and Dominik Wee, http://www.mckinsey.com/insights/automotive_and_assembly/ten_ways_autonomous_driving_could_redefine_the_automotive_world, accessed November 11, 2015; Self-Driving Cars Really Will Revolutionize the Economy. Here's How, by Alex Davies http://www.slate.com/blogs/future_tense/2015/03/09/self_driving_cars_will_revolutionize_economy_mckinsey_company_report_shows.html; Autonomous Vehicle Technology, A Guide for Policymakers, by James M. Anderson, Nidhi Kalra, Karlyn D. Stanley, Paul Sorensen, Constantine Samaras, Oluwatobi A. Oluwatola, accessed November 18, 2015; Google Self-Driving Car Project, Video, https://www.google.com/selfdrivingcar/ accessed November 19, 2015.
9. "Second Car Plant from General Motors," http://www.cartradeindia.com/news/second-car-plant-from-general-motors-in-india-110332.html, accessed November 16, 2011; "Volkswagen to Enter Pre-Owned Car Business in India," http://economictimes.indiatimes.com/Volkswagen_to_enter_pre-owned_car_business_in_India/articleshow/3282378.cms, accessed November 16, 2011; "Indian Automobile Industry Gears Up for Ecofriendly vehicles; Hybrid, Electric Cars Attract Attention," http://www.tradingmarkets.com/.site/news/Stock%20News/1806966, accessed August 6, 2008.
10. Peter F. Drucker, *The Practice of Management* (New York: Harper & Brothers, 1954), p. 63. For Drucker's contributions to management, see http://drucker.cgu.edu/html/aboutdrucker/index.htm and http://drucker.cgu.edu/html/aboutdrucker/timelineh.htm, which are maintained by the Peter F. Drucker, Graduate School of Management (accessed March 30, 2002): Peter F. Drucker, *Management, Revised Edition* (New York: HarperCollins Publishers, 2008).
11. Parts of this discussion are based on Heinz Weihrich, *Management Excellence: Productivity through MBO* (New York: McGraw-Hill, 1985), Chap. 4.
12. "Planning and Goal Setting for Small Business," U.S. Small Business Administration MP-6, www.sba.gov/library/pubs/mp-6.doc; accessed July 27, 2011; Heinz Weihrich, "How to Set Goals that Work for Your Company—and Improve the Bottom Line," www.usfca.edu/fac-staff/weihrichh/docs/goals.pdf, accessed July 27, 1011.
13. Interview conducted with Bryant Tong of Nth Power on January 9, 2007 by Mark Cannice.
14. See also Heinz Weihrich, "A New Approach to MBO: Updating a Time-honored Technique," www.usfca.edu/fac-staff/weihrichh/docs/newmbo.pdf, accessed January 2, 2016.
15. Heinz Weihrich, "A Study of the Integration of Management by Objectives with Key Managerial Activities and the Relationship to Selected Effectiveness Measures," doctoral dissertation, University of California, Los Angeles, 1973; Weihrich, *Management Excellence: Productivity through MBO*; A. J. Vogl, "Drucker, of Course," *Across the Board*, November/December 2000.
16. http://topics.nytimes.com/topics/reference/timestopics/people/z/mark_e_zuckerberg/index.html, accessed September 12, 2012.

CHAPTER 5

Strategies, Policies, and Planning Premises

Learning Objectives

After studying this chapter, you should be able to:

LO 1   Explain the nature and purpose of strategies and policies

LO 2   Describe the strategic planning process

LO 3   Understand the TOWS Matrix and the business portfolio matrix

LO 4   Describe some major kinds of strategies and policies and the hierarchy of strategies

LO 5   Identify Porter's generic strategies

LO 6   Discuss the nature of premises and forecasts

LO 7   Analyze your ideal company with the strategy tools discussed.

Today, most business enterprises engage in strategic planning, although the degree of sophistication and formality varies considerably. Conceptually, strategic planning is deceptively simple: analyze the current and expected future situation, determine the direction of the firm, and develop means for achieving the mission. In reality, this is an extremely complex process that demands a systematic approach for identifying and analyzing factors external to the organization and matching them with the firm's capabilities.

Planning is done in an environment of uncertainty. No one can be sure if the external as well as the internal environment will be the same even next week, much less several years from now. Therefore, people make assumptions or forecasts about the anticipated environment. Some of the forecasts become assumptions for other plans. For example, the gross domestic product forecast becomes the assumption for sales planning, which in turn becomes the basis for production planning, and so on.

In this chapter, you will learn about the nature and purpose of strategies and policies, the strategic planning process (which identifies the critical aspects of formulating a strategy), the TOWS Matrix (a tool for systematically integrating external and internal factors), the business portfolio matrix (a tool for allocating resources), some major kinds of strategies and policies, the hierarchy of strategies, and generic strategies. Because plans are made in an environment of uncertainty, you will also learn about premising and forecasting.

THE NATURE AND PURPOSE OF STRATEGIES AND POLICIES

Strategies and policies are closely related. Both give direction, both are the framework for plans, both are the basis of operational plans, and both affect all areas of managing.

The term *strategy* (which is derived from the Greek word *strategos*, meaning "general") has been used in different ways. Authors' applications differ in at least one major aspect. Some writers focus on both the end points (mission/purpose and goals/objectives) and the means of achieving them (policies and plans). Others emphasize the means to the ends in the strategic process rather than the ends *per se*. As pointed out in Chapter 4, **strategy** refers to the determination of the mission (or the fundamental purpose) and the basic long-term objectives of an enterprise, followed by the adoption of courses of action and allocation of resources necessary to achieve these aims. Therefore, objectives are part of strategy formulation.

Policies are general statements or understandings that guide managers' thinking in decision making. They ensure that decisions fall within certain boundaries. They usually do not require action but are intended to guide managers in their commitment to the decision they ultimately make.

For example, corporate policies that emphasize diversity and equity in hiring and pay have become more widespread in recent years. These policies do not dictate decisions on individual hiring or pay decisions; they do, however, guide managers' decisions on these key issues that help the organization achieve higher performance, better morale, and broader societal benefits.

Strategy Determination of the mission or purpose and the basic long-term objectives of an enterprise, followed by the adoption of courses of action and allocation of resources necessary to achieve these aims.

Policies General statements or understandings that guide managers' thinking in decision making.

The essence of policy is discretion. Strategy, on the other hand, concerns the direction in which human and material resources will be applied in order to increase the chance of achieving selected objectives.

> **GLOBAL PERSPECTIVE**
>
> **Value- and Policy-Driven Samsung Strives for Global Recognition[1]**
>
> The Samsung Group is a large Korean conglomerate that focuses on electronics and financial services. In the past, many Korean companies encountered difficulties because they diversified into unrelated fields. In its new approach to management, Samsung tries to avoid the pitfalls of other companies. At the turn of the century, Samsung initiated a policy designed to make the company a leader in its field, competing against firms such as Sony of Japan.
>
> Samsung realizes the importance of its people and the use of the latest technologies for achieving success in the marketplace. At the same time, it is aware of the responsibility to contribute to society, not only in Korea but also worldwide.
>
> Chairman Lee Kun-Hee laid the groundwork for a new approach to management that considers defects as a crime. Quality, superior products, and excellent customer service are considered key factors for success in the very competitive environment that has been dominated by Japanese firms. With its "digital management" approach, Samsung attempts to exploit the opportunities created by the information age technologies.

To be effective, strategies and policies must be put into practice by means of plans, with increasing details until they get down to the nuts and bolts of operation. The action plans through which strategies are executed are known as *tactics*. Strategies must be supported by effective tactics.

THE STRATEGIC PLANNING PROCESS

Although specific steps in the formulation of a strategy may vary, the process can be built, at least conceptually, around the key elements shown in Figure 5.1 and elaborated in the following.

Inputs to the Organization

The various organizational inputs, including the goal inputs of the claimants, were discussed in Chapter 1 and need no elaboration.

Industry Analysis

As will be pointed out later in this chapter, Michael Porter suggests that the formulation of a strategy requires the evaluation of the attractiveness of an industry by analyzing the external environment. The focus should be on the kind of competition within an industry, the possibility of new firms entering the market, the availability of substitute products or services, and the bargaining positions of the suppliers as well as the buyers or customers.

Enterprise Profile

The enterprise profile is usually the starting point for determining where the company is and where it should go. Thus, top managers determine the enterprise's mission and clarify its geographic orientation, such as whether it should operate in selected regions, throughout the home country, or even in different countries. In addition, managers assess the competitive position of their firm.

FIGURE 5.1 Strategic planning process model

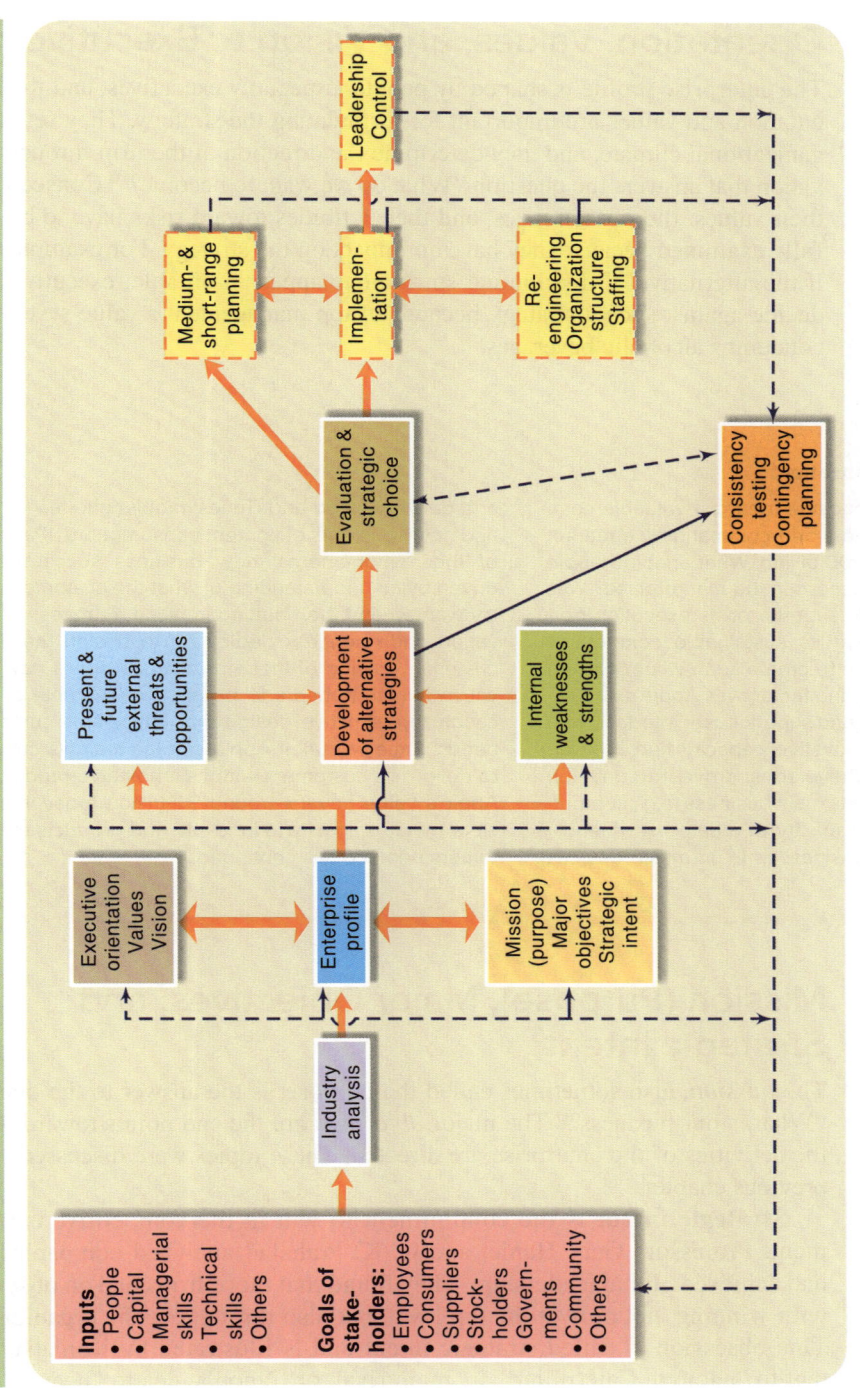

Adapted and modified from Heinz Weihrich, "The TOWS Matrix: A Tool for Situational Analysis," *Long Range Planning*, Vol. 15, no. 2 (1982), pp. 54–66.

Orientation, Values, and Vision of Executives[2]

The enterprise profile is shaped by people, especially executives, and their orientation and values are important for formulating the strategy. They set the organizational climate, and they determine the direction of the firm through their vision that answers the question "What do we want to become?"[3] Consequently, their values, their preferences, and their attitudes toward risks have to be carefully examined because they have an impact on the strategy. For example, even if the alternative of distributing spirits may appear profitable, executives may decide against such a strategy because of top management's value system that condemns alcoholic beverages.

> **INNOVATIVE PERSPECTIVE**
>
> **Apple's Strategy for Innovation[4]**
>
> In August 2012 Apple became the most valuable company in the history of the world commanding a market valuation of well over $600 billion. What enabled Apple to achieve such great success in the marketplace? Was its strategy exceptionally superior or its execution perfect? How did it achieve its sustainable competitive advantage that allowed it to create such value? One of the factors, if not the leading factor, was Apple's dedication to distinctive design and superior user interface with its products. Apple's innovative capacity tied in large part to its late founder, Steve Jobs, drove it to develop not only new products in its main business (e.g., computers) but to leverage its capacity to create user-friendly designs to enter new businesses (e.g., music devices and delivery—iPod and iTunes; mobile phones—iPhone; and new segments of content consumption—iPad). Each of these monumental new business successes was driven by an understanding of what the customer implicitly wanted and then putting in place a process of innovation and relentless dedication to design that led to customer craving of these products. Apple's new innovative iWatch appears to be another example of dedication to distinctive design that anticipates customers' needs. Time will tell if Apple can maintain its capability to delight its customers with its innovative products. As Apple's value hovers around $1 trillion today, it seems clear that its capacity to innovate and products that customers demand has continued.

Mission (Purpose), Major Objectives, and Strategic Intent[5]

Mission
Statement that answers the question "What is our business?"

Strategic intent
Commitment to win in the competitive environment.

www.caterpillar.com
www.xerox.com
www.honda.com
www.ford.com

The *mission*, also sometimes called the purpose, is the answer to the question "What is our business?" The major *objectives* are the end points toward which the activities of the enterprise are directed. These topics were discussed in the previous chapter.

Strategic intent is the commitment to win in the competitive environment. Professors Gary Hamel and C. K. Prahalad analyzed companies that had achieved global leadership.[6] They found that those firms had an obsession with winning, not only at the top level, but also throughout the organization. This obsession is called strategic intent and is illustrated by Komatsu's intent to "encircle Caterpillar", its main rival, or Canon's idea to "beat Xerox", or Honda's intent to become an automotive pioneer, "a second Ford." The authors point out that strategic intent requires personal effort and commitment. The intent statement is stable over time and focuses on the essence of winning.

ENTREPRENEURIAL PERSPECTIVE

Interview with Jon B. Fisher, Cofounder of Bharosa, an Oracle Corporation Company[7]

Jon Fisher is a serial Silicon Valley entrepreneur, founding several technology firms, the most recent of which is Bharosa. Bharosa is an enterprise security software firm that was purchased by Oracle Corporation in 2007. Mr. Fisher's take on entrepreneurism is centered on what he calls "strategic entrepreneurism". He defines strategic entrepreneurism as creating and growing a company with the aim of having it acquired by a dominant firm in the industry. In our communication, he elaborated, "Identify the companies that you believe would most benefit from acquiring your company. Of course, you can never control what another company does, but by understanding which company may acquire you and what their own needs may be, you can steer your company in their direction as an acquisition target. Then, when your company gets acquired by this larger corporation, everyone will remark on how lucky you are, not knowing that this was your goal from the beginning." Fisher's strategic entrepreneurism is his trademark approach to the strategic planning process of industry analysis, building an enterprise profile to suit the industry the firm is operating in, analyzing strategic alternatives, and making a strategic choice early in the life of an enterprise. His entrepreneurial success is linked to his strategic intent of "beginning with the end in mind."

A classic serial entrepreneur, Mr. Fisher now leads his new venture, CrowdOptic, which focuses on developing middleware software that applies AI to provide "Intelligent Live Streaming" to create actionable information for enterprise clients.[8]

Present and Future External Environment

The present and future external environment must be assessed in terms of threats and opportunities. The evaluation focuses on the competitive situation as well as on economic, social, political, legal, demographic, and geographic factors. In addition, the environment is scanned for technological developments, for products and services on the market, and for other pertinent factors in determining the competitive situation of the enterprise.

Internal Environment[9]

Similarly, the firm's internal environment should be audited and evaluated with respect to its resources and its weaknesses and strengths in research and development, production, operation, procurement, marketing, products, and services. Other internal factors that are important for formulating a strategy should be assessed, including human and financial resources, as well as the company image, organization structure and climate, planning and control system, and relations with customers.

Development of Alternative Strategies

Strategic alternatives are developed on the basis of an analysis of the external and internal environments. An organization may pursue many different kinds of strategies.[10] It may *specialize* or *concentrate*, as the Korean Hyundai did by producing lower-priced cars (in contrast to General Motors, for example, which has a complete product line ranging from inexpensive to luxury cars). Under the leadership of its chief executive, Chung Mong Koo, the company introduced the competitively priced sport utility vehicle Santa Fe, which was well received by the market.[11]

www.hyundai.com

www.gm.com

www.kmart.com
www.bordersgroupinc.com (Walden)
www.paylessdrug.com
www.toyota.com
www.nummi.com

Alternatively, a firm may *diversify*, extending the operation into new and profitable markets. Kmart Corporation formed a Specialty Retailing Group that included stores such as Walden Book Company, Builders Square, Designer Depot, and PayLess Drug Stores. Still another strategy is *international expansion* to other countries, as described in Chapter 3. Other examples of possible strategies are *joint ventures* and *strategic alliances*, which may be appropriate for some firms.[12] They are especially suitable for big undertakings in which firms have to pool their resources, as illustrated by the joint venture of General Motors and Toyota to produce small cars in California. The Fremont plant opened in 1984, but was closed in 2010.[13]

Under certain circumstances, a company may have to adopt a *liquidation* strategy by terminating an unprofitable product line or even dissolving the firm, as illustrated by the Savings and Loan Associations, or declare bankruptcy, as exemplified by the energy company Enron. But in some cases, liquidation may not be necessary, but a *retrenchment* strategy may be sufficient. In such a situation, the company may curtail its operation temporarily.

Bowman and Hurry (1993)[14] applied Options Theory[15] to strategy-making, equating resource investments by the organization to the development of options on future courses of action. By developing a portfolio of strategic options through resource investments, the firm can create value and create alternatives to "strike" various options and pursue new strategic alternatives that appear most promising. Options are most valuable when there exists high uncertainty in the future and when there is sufficient time to the expiration of the option and when the option is on a potentially large outcome. The deployment of resources to create options to make sustained progress on existing products is referred to as incremental options, while resource investments that create a path to build potential new products are referred to as flexibility options.

These are just a few examples of possible strategies. In practice, companies, especially large ones, pursue a combination of strategies.

Evaluation and Choice of Strategies[16]

The various strategies have to be carefully evaluated before the choice is made. Strategic choices must be considered in light of the risks involved in a particular decision. Some profitable opportunities may not be pursued because failure in a risky venture could result in bankruptcy of the firm. Another critical element in choosing a strategy is timing. Even the best product may fail if it is introduced to the market at an inappropriate time. Moreover, the reaction of competitors must be taken into consideration. When IBM reduced the price of its personal computer in reaction to the success of Apple's Macintosh computer, firms producing IBM-compatible computers had little choice but to reduce their prices as well. This illustrates the interconnection of the strategies of firms in the same industry.

The Battle of the Titans: Boeing vs. Airbus[17]

Many quantitative and qualitative factors had to be evaluated by Boeing and Airbus in their battle for leadership in the aircraft industry. Beginning around the year 2000 Airbus, a unit of the European Aeronautic Defense & Space Co. (EAD), was the leading aircraft maker over the American Boeing company. This may have resulted in overconfidence. The super-sized Airbus A380 was developed with the aim to overtake the Boeing 747, the 450-seat aircraft that had dominated the skies for many ears. In 2006, however, the fortunes seemed to change.

The A380 production ran into trouble, resulting in delays at a very high cost for the company. Airbus underestimated the complexity of the big aircraft with its sophisticated equipment. The installation of communication and in-flight entertainment systems caused major problems. The shortage of qualified engineers made it difficult to introduce multiple models designed to compete with Boeing. The squabbles within Airbus's management did not help the company either.

Several airlines rethought their decisions, with some airlines placing their orders with Boeing instead. Thai Airways, for example, was considering cancelling its orders of six planes. In December 2006, Lufthansa, the German airline, announced that it would buy the updated Boeing 747 jumbo jet which had dominated the jumbo jet market in the past. Singapore Airlines, an important buyer of new aircrafts, also ordered 20 Boeing 787 Dreamliners, which was well received by the customers for its comfort and efficiency. The aircraft is less expensive to operate and to maintain than the competing Airbus A330. Consequently, Airbus developed the A350 in response to Boeing's 787. However, the Dreamliner is expected to be in service four years earlier than the A350 (2008 vs. 2012).

To assist the troubled Airbus, the European Union plans to continue its support of the aircraft maker. Consequently, Boeing filed arguments with the World Trade Organization (WTO), suggesting that the subsidies paid for the development of Airbus planes were Illegal. Boeing, on the other hand, was accused of receiving state subsidies for developing new aircrafts.

As the arguments play out in the courts, Airbus and Boeing continue their battle in the marketplace.

INTERNATIONAL PERSPECTIVE

Consistency Testing and Contingency Planning

The last key aspect of the strategic planning process is testing for consistency and preparing for contingencies. During all phases of the strategic planning process, consistency testing is essential. Since the future cannot be predicted with a high degree of certainty, contingency plans need to be prepared. For example, a strategy may be prepared with the assumption that the gross domestic product may increase 3 percent annually over the next three years. A contingency plan may also be made in which the scenario includes a major recession.

Medium- and Short-Range Planning, Implementation through Organizing, Staffing, Leading, and Controlling

Although not a part of the strategic planning process (and therefore shown by broken lines in Figure 5.1), medium- and short-range planning as well as implementation of the plans must be considered during all phases of the process. Implementation of the strategy requires organizing, perhaps even reengineering the organization (Part 3 in this book); staffing, that is filling and keeping filled the positions in the organization structure (Part 4); and providing leadership through motivation and effective communication (Part 5). Controls must also be installed for monitoring performance against plans (Part 6). The importance of feedback is shown by the loops in the model. These aspects of strategy implementation are discussed later in the book.

THE TOWS MATRIX: A MODERN TOOL FOR ANALYSIS OF THE SITUATION

Today, strategy designers are aided by a number of matrices that show the relationships of critical variables, such as the Boston Consulting Group's business portfolio matrix, which will be discussed later. For many years, the SWOT analysis has been used to identify a company's strengths, weaknesses, opportunities, and threats. The TOWS Matrix has been introduced for analyzing the competitive situation of the company or even of a nation that leads to the development of four distinct sets of strategic alternatives.[18]

The TOWS Matrix has a wider scope and a different emphasis from the business portfolio matrix. The former does not replace the latter. The TOWS Matrix is a conceptual framework for a systematic analysis that facilitates matching of the external threats and opportunities with the internal weaknesses and strengths of the organization.

It is common to suggest that companies should identify their strengths and weaknesses, as well as the opportunities and threats in the external environment, but what is often overlooked is that combining these factors may require distinct strategic choices. To systematize these choices, the TOWS Matrix has been proposed, where *T* stands for threats, *O* for opportunities, *W* for weaknesses, and *S* for strengths. The TOWS model starts with the threats (*T* in TOWS) because in many situations a company undertakes strategic planning as a result of a perceived crisis, problem, or threat.

Four Alternative Strategies

Figure 5.2 presents the four alternative strategies of the TOWS Matrix.* The strategies are based on the analysis of the external environment (threats and opportunities) and the internal environment (weaknesses and strengths):

1. The *WT strategy* aims to minimize both weaknesses and threats and may be called the Mini–Mini (for "minimize–minimize") strategy. It may require that the company, for example, form a joint venture, retrench, or even liquidate.
2. The *WO strategy* attempts to minimize the weaknesses and maximize the opportunities. Thus, a firm with weaknesses in some areas may either develop those areas within the enterprise or acquire the needed competencies (such as technology or persons with needed skills) from outside in order to enable it to take advantage of opportunities in the external environment.
3. The *ST strategy* is based on using the organization's strengths to deal with threats in the environment. The aim is to maximize the former while minimizing the latter. Thus, a company may use its technological, financial, managerial, or marketing strengths to cope with the threats of a new product introduced by its competitor.
4. The *SO strategy*, which capitalizes on a company's strengths to take advantage of opportunities, is the most desirable. Indeed, it is the aim of enterprises to move from other positions in the matrix to this one. If they have weaknesses, they will strive to overcome them, making them strengths. If they face threats, they will cope with them so that they can focus on opportunities.

---

* Although the emphasis is on strategies in this discussion, similar analyses can be made for developing more detailed tactics or action plans.

FIGURE 5.2 TOWS Matrix for strategy formulation

	Internal strengths (S) e.g., strengths in management, operations, finance, marketing, R&D, engineering	**Internal weaknesses (W)** e.g., weaknesses in areas shown in the "strengths" box
External opportunities (O): (Consider risks also) e.g., current and future economic conditions, political and social changes, new products, services, and technology	**SO strategy: Maxi-Maxi** Potentially the most successful strategy, utilizing the organization's strengths to take advantage of opportunities	**WO strategy: Mini-Maxi** e.g., developmental strategy to overcome weaknesses in order to take advantage of opportunities
External threats (T): e.g., energy shortage, competition, and areas similar to those shown in the "opportunities" box above	**ST strategy: Maxi-Mini** e.g., use of strengths to cope with threats or to avoid threats	**WT strategy: Mini-Mini** e.g., retrenchment, liquidation, or joint venture to minimize both weaknesses and threats

(Top-left cell labels: Internal factors / External factors)

Time Dimension and the TOWS Matrix

So far, the factors displayed in the TOWS Matrix pertain to analysis at a particular point in time. However, external and internal environments are dynamic: some factors change over time, while others change very little. Hence, strategy designers must prepare several matrices at different points in time, as shown in Figure 5.3. Thus, one may start with a TOWS analysis of the past, continue with an analysis of the present, and, perhaps most important, focus on different time periods (T1, T2, etc.) in the future.

Application of the TOWS Merger Matrix for Mergers, Acquisitions, Joint Ventures, and Alliances

Companies around the world now use the TOWS Matrix; the matrix has also been included in several modern textbooks on strategic management.[19] The TOWS Matrix concept has been introduced for planning mergers, acquisitions, joint ventures, and alliances.[20] Whenever two partners consider joint activities, it is prudent to analyze the strengths and weaknesses for each partner as well as their opportunities and threats. Moreover, their alternative strategies *before* their association should be considered: these two TOWS Matrices provide a better understanding of the prospective partners before the actual linkage. For example, complementary strengths and weaknesses could result in a competitive advantage for both companies. On the other hand, repetition and overlap may result in duplication of efforts. After the two matrices are evaluated, a third matrix should be developed for the partnership. This is especially important for acquisitions and mergers because of the relative permanency of the resulting entity. Preparing the three TOWS Matrices can also allow potential problems to be identified in more loosely coupled partnerships such as a strategic alliance. The TOWS Merger Matrix will be illustrated by the Daimler–Chrysler merger in the closing section of Part 2.

FIGURE 5.3 Dynamics of the TOWS Matrix

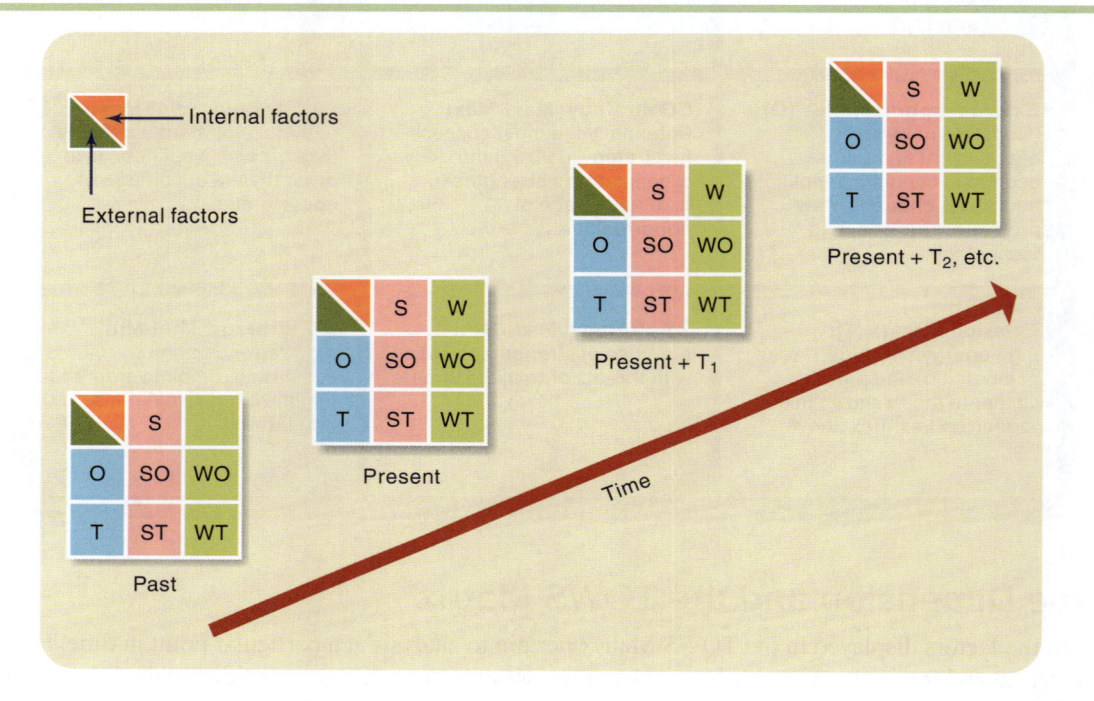

BLUE OCEAN STRATEGY: IN PURSUIT OF OPPORTUNITIES IN AN UNCONTESTED MARKET[26]

In the TOWS Matrix discussion, it was shown that companies could use their strengths and overcome their weaknesses by taking advantage of opportunities and coping with threats. It was suggested that the potentially most successful strategy is to use the enterprise's strengths and to take advantage of opportunities.

In the recently published book *Blue Ocean Strategy—How to Create Uncontested Market Space and Make the Competition Irrelevant,* the authors W. Chan Kim and Renee Mauborgne specifically suggest to focus on opportunities that explore uncontested waters (opportunities) in the "blue ocean" rather than trying to beat the competition in the existing industry, or the "red ocean" as the authors suggest. The red ocean may be illustrated by the "bloody" current competition in the automobile industry in which companies try to be a little better than their competitor by, for example, having a lower cost structure. In contrast, the blue ocean strategy may be illustrated by eBay's online auction by entering a market without competitors. Let us explore further the differences between the red and blue ocean strategies.

Traditional competitive strategies, operating in the red ocean, aimed at beating the competition in an existing market. Companies tried to be better than their competitors. Michael Porter at Harvard suggested that companies have to make a strategic choice between differentiation by offering the customers something special for which they are willing to pay a premium price, or having a lower cost structure as exemplified by Wal-Mart as discussed later in this chapter.

The blue ocean strategy, by contrast, focuses on the uncontested market by offering a product or service that is unique in a market space where there is no competitor, thus making competition irrelevant as the subtitle of the book *Blue Ocean Strategy* suggests. Rather than competing in an existing demand situation, the blue ocean strategy attempts to create and develop new demand for its products or services. Moreover, the successful company will pursue strategies that focus on differentiation and low cost as was illustrated by the introduction of the Lexus car that had differentiation features of luxury cars but at a lower price. This way, Toyota, the maker of Lexus, created value for the buyer. **Value innovation** is more than simply innovation. It is a strategy that requires that the total company is commitment of the creation of value for the customer by offering something special with relatively low cost and price.[16]

To capture the blue ocean and to make the competition irrelevant, Kim and Mauborgne introduce a diagnostic tool and framework for action called *The Strategic Canvas*. This tool identifies the important relevant factors in an industry in which companies compete. These factors vary from industry to industry. In the airline industry the factors may, for example, include the price of the airfare, the meals, the friendliness of the service, and so on. Southwest Airlines, the successful airline in America, rates low in price, meals, and connections at airport hubs. But it rates higher in service friendliness and frequency of flights than other airlines. Since Southwest had little competition on those latter criteria where it had high ratings, it pursued a blue ocean strategy.

For companies aiming for a blue ocean strategy, four actions should be considered. First, identify and eliminate those factors that may be unimportant to the buyer. Second, if elimination is not an option, consider reducing those factors. Third, raise or strengthen those factors that are unique. And fourth, create new or new and unique factors that are wanted by the buyers but are ignored by the competitors. This was what Southwest Airlines and other enterprises did in charting a blue ocean strategy.

How can the blue ocean strategy be applied in formulating a strategy based on the TOWS Matrix in Figure 5.2? The traditional red ocean strategy can be exemplified by the ST (strengths–threats) strategy whereby a company uses its strengths to cope with the threats created by the competition. Head-on competition often results in a blood bath through a red ocean strategy. In contrast, the SO (strengths–opportunities) strategy in which a company uses its strengths to take advantage of opportunities would be an illustration of a blue ocean strategy. It is true that in the TOWS Matrix analysis opportunities in general were considered while Kim and Mauborgne focus on unique opportunities that have been neglected by competitors.

There is another blue ocean strategy alternative, namely the WO strategy in which a company realizes its weakness and recognized that one way to overcome the weakness is to search for unique opportunities to overcome its weakness. Often a company with weaknesses may be in distress and then may be motivated to search intensely for opportunities that have not been exploited by its competitors, that is, adopting a blue ocean strategy.

In summary, companies adopting a blue ocean strategy may pursue both the SO as well as the SW alternative strategies shown in Figure 5.2. While it may be unavoidable to engage in the ST strategy, enterprises may be wise to first attempt to chart a blue ocean strategy to avoid the bloody confrontation resulting from the ST alternative.

INNOVATIVE PERSPECTIVE

Zipcar[22]

One example of a company with a blue ocean strategy is Zipcar, a car-sharing company founded in Cambridge, Massachusetts. The company with a new concept in the United States focuses on an uncontested market by using wireless technology at strategically placed bases in cities. The company uses a simple reservation system through which customers can view the availability of the car, which can then be reserved online. A wireless link records the time and usage. Zipcar faces some competition from "CarShare" in the United States; the big rental companies such as Hertz and Enterprise, "WeCar" in St. Louis and "I-GO" in Chicago also beginning to use a similar car-sharing concept. Firms in other countries do likewise. Therefore, to some extent, the market is contested. The untapped market for Zipcar would be the use of the sharing concept with partnering with other firms by offering, for example, boat sharing or car sharing in cities that do not have such services.

THE PORTFOLIO MATRIX: A TOOL FOR ALLOCATING RESOURCES

The Boston Consulting Group developed the business portfolio matrix.[23] Figure 5.4, a simplified version of the matrix, shows the linkages between the growth rate of the business and the relative competitive position of the firm, identified by the market share. Businesses in the "question marks" quadrant, with a weak market share and a high growth rate, usually require cash investment so that they can become "stars," the businesses in the high-growth, strongly competitive position. These kinds of businesses have opportunities for growth and profit. The "cash cows", with a strong competitive position and a low growth rate, are usually well established in the market, and such enterprises are in a position to make their products at low costs. Therefore, their products provide the cash needed for their operation. The

FIGURE 5.4 Business portfolio matrix

	Strong	Weak
High	Stars	Question marks
Low	Cash cows	Dogs

Business growth rate (vertical axis) / Relative competitive position (market share) (horizontal axis)

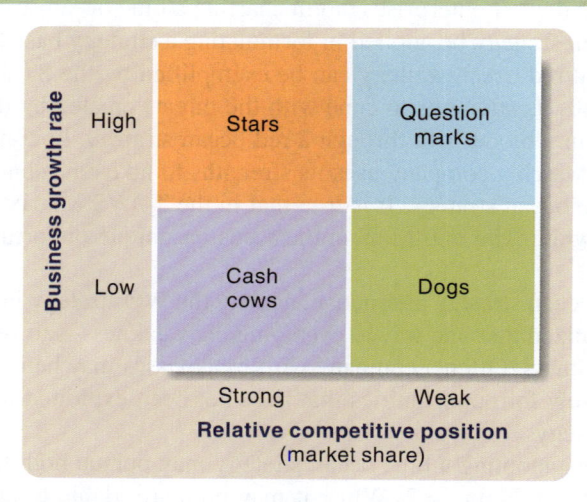

Adapted from *The Product Portfolio Matrix*, copyright © 1970, the Boston Consulting Group, Inc.

"dogs" are businesses with a low growth rate and a weak market share. These businesses are usually not profitable and generally should be disposed of.

The portfolio matrix was developed for large corporations with several divisions that are often organized around strategic business units (a topic to be discussed in Chapter 8). While portfolio analysis was popular in the 1970s, it is not without its critics, who contend that it is too simplistic. Also, the growth rate criterion has been considered insufficient for the evaluation of an industry's attractiveness. Similarly, the market share as a yardstick for estimating the competitive position may be inadequate.

www.bcg.com

MAJOR KINDS OF STRATEGIES AND POLICIES

For a business enterprise (and, with some modification, for other kinds of organizations as well), the major strategies and policies that give an overall direction to operation are likely to be in the areas of growth, finance, organization, personnel, public relations, products or services, and marketing. We will elaborate on the last two areas.

Products or Services

A business exists to furnish products or services. In a very real sense, profits are merely a measure—although an important one—of how well a company serves its customers. New products or services, more than any other single factor, determine what an enterprise is or will be.

The key questions in this area can be summarized as follows:

- What is our business?
- Who are our customers?
- What do our customers want?
- How much will our customers buy and at what price?
- Do we wish to be a product leader?
- What is our competitive advantage?
- Do we wish to develop our own new products?
- What advantages do we have in serving customer needs?
- How should we respond to existing and potential competition?
- How far can we go in serving customer needs?
- What profits can we expect?
- What basic form should our strategy take?

Marketing

Marketing strategies are designed to guide managers in getting products or services to customers and in encouraging customers to buy. Marketing strategies are closely related to product strategies; they must be interrelated and mutually supportive. As a matter of fact, Peter Drucker regards the two basic business functions as innovation (e.g., the creation of new goods or services) and marketing. A business can scarcely survive without at least one of these functions and preferably both.

The key questions that serve as guides for establishing a marketing strategy are these:

- Where are our customers, and why do they buy?
- How do our customers buy?
- How is it best for us to sell?
- Do we have something to offer that competitors do not?
- Do we wish to take legal steps to discourage competition?
- Do we need, and can we supply, supporting services?
- What are the best pricing strategy and policy for our operation?
- How can we best serve our customers?

ENTREPRENEURIAL PERSPECTIVE

Buying Skype, eBay's Mistake?[24]

The acquisition of Skype at a very high price may have been a mistake by the otherwise very successful Margaret Whitman, eBay's CEO. Skype's Internet venture was a new phenomenon in 2005. By 2007/2008 Skype was not the success envisioned. The integration with eBay's main business was not done well. Perhaps even more important was Google's entry into the market, enabling people to find buyers for their goods. Moreover, Google began providing online payment and telephone services that compete with eBay's Skype and PayPal. In 2011, Microsoft acquired Skype Communication and it became a division of Microsoft. Millions of people around the world take advantage of the free or low-cost service that is also used increasingly by teachers and schools in educational projects.

www.skype.com

HIERARCHY OF COMPANY STRATEGIES

In large, diversified companies, the overall strategy may take the form of a hierarchy. At the top of the pyramid is the *corporate-level strategy*. At this level, executives craft the overall strategy for a diversified company. Decisions are made as to the industries in which the company wants to compete. A portfolio of businesses is often selected to achieve synergies among the business units.

The second level in the hierarchy is *business strategies*, which are usually developed by the general manager of a business unit. These strategies are reviewed and approved or rejected by the chief executive. The aim of the business strategy is to gain a competitive advantage in a particular area of product line.

On the third hierarchical level, *functional strategies* (or policies) are developed. These strategies are devised for departments or other organizational units, such as finance, production, marketing, service, and personnel. The aim is to support the business and corporate strategies.

PORTER'S INDUSTRY ANALYSIS AND GENERIC COMPETITIVE STRATEGIES[25]

Professor Michael Porter suggests that strategy formulation requires an analysis of the attractiveness of an industry and the company's position within that industry. This analysis becomes the basis for formulating generic strategies.

Industry Analysis[26]

In the analysis of the industry, Porter identified five forces: (1) the competition among companies, (2) the threat of new companies entering the market, (3) the possibility of using substitute products or services, (4) the bargaining power of suppliers, and (5) the bargaining power of buyers or customers. On the basis of the industry analysis, a company may adopt generic strategies. These strategies are generic because they may be suitable on a broad level for different kinds of organizations. Any enterprise, however, may use more than one strategy.

Overall Cost Leadership Strategy

This strategic approach aims at reduction in costs, based to a great extent on experience. Thus, the emphasis may be on keeping a close watch on costs in areas such as research and development, operation, sales, and service. The objective is for a company to have a low-cost structure compared with its competitors. This strategy often requires a large relative market share and cost-efficient operation, as illustrated by the low-cost Ivory soap sold in a broad market.

Differentiation Strategy

A company following a differentiation strategy attempts to offer something unique in the industry in terms of products or services. Porsche sports cars are indeed special; so is the Caterpillar Company, which is known for its prompt service and availability of spare parts. In the broad consumer market, Dial soap is differentiated from other brands of soap by its use of deodorants.

Focused Strategy

A company adopting a focused strategy concentrates on special groups of customers, a particular product line, a specific geographic region, or other aspects that become the focal point of the firm's efforts. Rather than serving the entire market with its products or services, an enterprise may emphasize a specific segment of the market. A low-cost strategy, differentiation, or both may accomplish this. Porter illustrates the *focused low-cost strategy* with the example of La Quinta Inns, a motel chain that operates in a certain region of the United States and appeals to traveling business representatives, such as salespeople. The *focused differentiation strategy* may be exemplified by Cray Research Inc., which specializes in very powerful and sophisticated supercomputers. The differentiation allows the company to charge premium prices.

In general, a company needs to choose a generic strategy and should not "get stuck in the middle," according to Porter. A company that gets stuck in the middle needs to decide on a low-cost strategy in a broad or narrow market or offer a differentiated (i.e., unique) product or service in a broad or narrow market.

PREMISING AND FORECASTING

One of the essential and often overlooked steps in effective and coordinated planning is premising, which is the establishment of and the agreement by managers and planners to utilize consistent assumptions

Planning premises Anticipated environment in which plans are expected to operate.

critical to plans under consideration. **Planning premises** are defined as the anticipated environment in which plans are expected to operate. They include assumptions or forecasts of the future and known conditions that will affect the operation of plans.[27] Examples are prevailing policies and existing company plans that control the basic nature of supporting plans.

A distinction should be drawn between forecasts that are planning premises and forecasts that are translated into future expectancies, usually in financial terms, from actual plans developed. For example, a forecast to determine future business conditions, sales volume, or political environment furnishes premises on which to develop plans. However, a forecast of the costs or revenues from a new capital investment translates a planning program into future expectations. In the first case, the forecast is a prerequisite of planning; in the second case, the forecast is a result of planning.

At the same time, plans themselves and forecasts of their future effects often become premises for other plans. The decision by an electricity company to construct a nuclear generating plant, for example, creates conditions that give rise to premises for transmission line plans and other plans necessarily dependent on the generating plant being built.

INNOVATIVE PERSPECTIVE

Nissan's Leaf—The First Mass-Produced Electric Car[28]

When CEO Carlos Ghosn was asked to give a 30-second sales pitch for the all-electric car, he said:

"This is the only zero-emission car on the market. Other electric cars use gasoline; this one, there is not one drop. It's fun to drive, but I can't describe it. The only way you'll discover it is by getting behind the wheel. There's no vibration, no smell, no noise. This is the future—and everything else is going to look obsolete, like sending messages with pigeons."[29]

The Brazilian-born CEO Ghosn predicted that within 10 years, electric cars will have 10 percent market share while several studies suggest a much lower market share percentage. The primary targets are young people and women. Already since 2006, Nissan moved in the direction of the electric car based on the prediction of higher oil prices, the assumption of battery technology progress, and the exploding Asian market with the increased emission problem.

But Ghosn has his skeptics. The change-oriented Carlos Ghosn even had to convince the 350,000 employees of the importance of preparing for the future. The Leaf is especially targeted for the emerging markets in India, China, Russia, and Brazil. The growth in those countries will also mean growth in pollution-emitting cars, thus electric cars will help to cope with the emission problem. However, it is expected that the Leaflet will also be offered in Japan, North America, and Europe. The future will show whether Ghosn's forecasting of the future and the demand for the electric cars are correct.

http://www.nissanusa.com/

www.rand.org

Environmental Forecasting

If the future could be forecast with accuracy, planning would be relatively simple. Managers would need only to take into account their human and material resources and their opportunities and threats, compute the optimum method of reaching their objective, and proceed with a relatively high degree of certainty toward it. In practice, forecasting is much more complicated.

Values and Areas of Forecasting

Forecasting has values aside from its use. First, the making of forecasts and their review by managers compel thinking ahead, looking to the future, and providing for it. Second, preparation of the forecast may disclose areas where necessary control is lacking. Third, forecasting, especially when there is participation throughout the organization, helps unify and coordinate plans. By focusing attention on the future, it assists in bringing a singleness of purpose to planning.

The environmental areas that are frequently chosen for making forecasts include the economic, social, political/legal, and technological environments.

Forecasting with the Delphi Technique

One of the attempts to make technological forecasting more accurate and meaningful is the Delphi technique. This technique, developed by Olaf Helmer and his colleagues at the RAND Corporation, has a degree of scientific respectability and acceptance. A typical process of the Delphi technique is as follows:

1. A panel of experts on a particular problem area is selected, usually from both inside and outside the organization.
2. The experts are asked to make (anonymously, so that they will not be influenced by others) a forecast as to what they think will happen, and when, in various areas of new discoveries or developments.
3. The answers are compiled, and the composite results are fed back to the panel members.
4. With this information at hand (but still with individual anonymity), further estimates of the future are made.
5. This process may be repeated several times.
6. When a convergence of opinion begins to evolve, the results are then used as an acceptable forecast.

Note that the purpose of the successive opinions and feedback is not to force the experts to compromise but rather, by bringing additional informational inputs to bear, to make opinions more informed. It is thus hoped, and experience has verified this hope, that an informed consensus among experts will be arrived at.

SUMMARY

There are different definitions of strategy. A comprehensive one refers to the determination of the firm's mission or purpose and its basic long-term objectives, followed by the adoption of courses of action and allocation of resources necessary to achieve these aims. Policies are general statements or understandings that guide managers' thinking in decision making. Both strategies and policies give direction to plans. They provide the framework for plans and serve as a basis for the development of tactics and other managerial activities.

The strategic planning model shows how the process works. It identifies the critical elements of this process and indicates how they relate to each other.

The TOWS Matrix is a modern tool for analyzing the threats and opportunities in the external environment and their relationships to the organization's internal weaknesses and strengths. Three TOWS Matrices have to be developed for mergers, acquisitions, joint ventures, and alliances. The portfolio matrix is a tool for allocating resources, linking the business growth rate with the relative competitive position (measured by market share) of the firm.

The blue ocean strategy focuses on the market space with no serious competition. In contrast, the red ocean strategy engages competitors in a bloody fight.

Major kinds of strategies and policies need to be developed in areas such as growth, finance, organization, personnel, public relations, products or services, and marketing. Strategies form a hierarchy from the corporate level to the business level and the functional level. Porter identified three generic competitive strategies related to overall cost leadership, differentiation, and focus.

Planning premises are the anticipated environment. They include assumptions or forecasts of the future and known conditions. More recently, environmental forecasting has become important. One approach to forecasting is the Delphi technique developed by the RAND Corporation.

KEY IDEAS AND CONCEPTS FOR REVIEW

Strategy
Policy
Tactics
Key elements in the strategic planning process
TOWS Matrix by Weihrich
TOWS Merger Matrix
Blue ocean strategy
Portfolio matrix by the Boston Consulting Group
Major kinds of strategies
Hierarchy of strategies
Porter's generic strategies
Planning premises
Environmental forecasting
Delphi technique

FOR DISCUSSION

1. How can you distinguish between strategies and policies?
2. Are strategies and policies as important in a nonbusiness enterprise (such as a labor union, a government department, a hospital, or a city fire department) as they are in a business? Why and how?
3. Why are contingency plans important?
4. Choose an organization that you know and identify its strengths and weaknesses. What are its special opportunities and threats in the external environment?
5. How would you make an organizational appraisal of your college or university? What kind of "business" is the school in?
6. How can strategies be implemented effectively?
7. Identify major premises that, in your judgment, Honda Motor Company would need in order to forecast its sales of automobiles for the next two years.

EXERCISES/ ACTION STEPS

1. Read two articles that deal with strategy in magazines such as *Fortune* or *Business Week*. List the strengths and weaknesses of a company reported as well as the opportunities and threats faced by the firm.
2. Take a major decision problem facing you and outline the more critical planning premises surrounding it. How many of these are matters of knowledge and how many are matters of forecast? How many are qualitative and how many are quantitative? How many are within your control?
3. Play a game of chess with another student in the class. After the game reflect on what aspect of strategy you employed during the game. How might the strategy of chess be applied to managing a business?
4. Update your LinkedIn profile and follow three companies that you find interesting.

ONLINE RESEARCH

1. The TOWS Matrix has been used for developing alternative strategies for organizations, for analyzing the competitive advantages of nations, as well as for developing a career strategy. Search the Internet for the "TOWS Matrix" and identify the application of the matrix.
2. Search the Internet for the term "strategic intent" and compare the intents of four organizations.
3. Search the Internet for "competing for the future" and find reviews of the book by that name by Hamel and Prahalad.

ENDNOTES

1. Moon Ihlwan and Gerry Khermouch, "Samsung: No Longer Unsung," *Business Week*, August 6, 2001. See also www.samsung.com, accessed July 27, 2011.
2. For a discussion of vision, see James C. Collins and Jerry Porras, "Building Your Company's Vision", in Arthur A. Thompson, Jr., and A. J. Strickland III (eds.), *Crafting and Executing Strategy*, 12th ed. (Burr Ridge, IL: McGraw-Hill, 2001), pp. 442–456.
3. Fred R. David, "Vision versus Mission", in *Strategic Management*, 8th ed. (Upper Saddle River, NJ: Prentice Hall, 2001), p. 56.
4. CNN Tech News, http://www.cnn.com/2012/11/12/tech/innovation/apple-innovative-company/index.html (accessed November 14, 2012).
5. Gary Hamel and C. K. Prahalad, "Strategic Intent," in Arthur A. Thompson, Jr., A. J. Strickland III, and Tracy Robertson Kramer, eds. *Readings in Strategic Management*, 5th ed. (Chicago: Irwin, 1995), pp. 56–76; Gary Hamel and C. K. Prahalad, *Competing for the Future* (Boston, MA: Harvard Business School Press, 1994), pp. 141–49; Gray Hamel, *Leading the Revolution* (Boston: Harvard Business School Press, 2000); Gray Hamel, "Inside the Revolution: Take It Higher," *Fortune*, February 5, 2001, pp. 169–170.
6. The article by Hamel and Prahalad was originally published in the *Harvard Business Review* (May–June 1989) and was reprinted with certain deletions in Henry Mintzberg and James Brian Quinn, *The Strategy Process: Concepts and Cases* (Upper Saddle River, NJ: Prentice Hall, 1996), pp. 41–45.
7. E-mail interview conducted with Mr. Jon B. Fisher, Cofounder, Bharosa, by Mark Cannice on August 6–7, 2009.
8. https://www.crowdoptic.com, accessed May 1, 2019.
9. Howard Thomas, Timothy Pollock, and Philip Gorman, "Global Strategic Analyses: Frameworks and Approaches," *Academy of Management Executive*, February 1999, pp. 70–82.
10. For a detailed discussion of various types of strategies, see David, *Strategic Management*, Chap. 5.
11. Brian Bremner, "Hyundai Gets Hot," *Business Week*, December 17, 2001, pp. 84–86.
12. For a discussion of strategic alliances, see Manuel G. Serapio, Jr., and Wayne F. Cascio, "End-Games in International Alliances," *Academy of Management Executive*, February 1996, pp. 62–73; Gabor Garai, "Leveraging the Rewards of Strategic Alliances," in Arthur A. Thompson, Jr., and A. J. Strickland III, eds. *Crafting and Executing Strategy*, 12th ed. (Burr Ridge, IL: McGraw-Hill, 2001), pp. 601–606; Andrew C. Inkpen, "Learning and Knowledge Acquisition through International Strategic Alliances," *Academy of Management Executive*, November 1998, pp. 69–80.
13. New United Motor Manufacturing Inc., www.nummi.com, accessed July 27, 2011.
14. E.H. Bowman and D. Hurry, "Strategy through Options lens: An Integrated View of Resource Investments and the Incremental-Choice Process", *Academy of Management Review*, 1993, 18 (4): 760–782.
15. Fischer Black and Myron Scholes, "The Pricing of Options and Corporate Liabilities," Journal of Political Economy, May–June 1973, 81 (3): 637–654.
16. See also Gary Hamel, "Strategy as Revolution," *Harvard Business Review*, July–August 1996, pp. 69–82.
17. J. Lynn Lunsford and Daniel Michaels, "Bet on Huge Plane Trips Up Airbus," *The Wall Street Journal*, June 15, 2006; J. Lynn Lunsford and Daniel Michaels, "Boeing May Get Lift From Lufthansa," *The Wall Street Journal*, December 6, 2006, "EU Vows Continuing Airbus Support," BBC News, December 6, 2006; Daniel Michaels and J. Lynn Lunsford, "Airbus Pitch: New A350 was Worth Wait," *The Wall Street Journal*, December 4, 2006; "Airbus-A Long Haul to Recovery," *The Economist*, December 9, 2006, p. 70; Daniel Michaels, "Airbus A380 Is Set to Gain Clearance," *The Wall Street Journal*, December 12, 2006; J. Lynn Lunsford, "Boeing Flight Plan for Growth," *The Wall Street Journal,* January 5, 2007.
18. This discussion and the accompanying figures have been adapted from Heinz

Weihrich, "The TOWS Matrix: A Tool for Situational Analysis," *Long Range Planning*, 1982, 15 (2): 54–66; Weihrich, "Analyzing the Competitive Advantages and Disadvantages of Germany with the TOWS Matrix: An Alternative to Porter's Model," *European Business Review*, 1999, 99 (1): 9–22. See also http://www.usfca.edu/fac-staff/weihrichh/docs/germany.pdf, accessed July 27, 2011.

19. David, "Vision versus Mission," Chap. 6; J. David Hunger and Thomas L. Wheelen, *Essentials of Strategic Management* (Upper Saddle River, NJ: Prentice Hall, 2001), Chap. 5.

20. The TOWS Merger Matrix was presented at the Eastern Academy of Management Conference in San Jose, Costa Rica, June 17–21, 2001, and was illustrated by the Daimler–Chrysler merger.

21. W. Chan Kim and Renee Mauborgne, *Blue Ocean Strategy—How to Create Uncontested Market Space and Make the Competition Irrelevant* (Boston: Harvard Business School Press, 2005); Robert D. Hof and Michael Arndt, "How to Hit a Moving Target," *Business Week Online*, August 21, 2006; "Blue Ocean Strategy," http://knowledge.insead.edu, accessed November 8, 2008.

22. Adam Aston, "Growth Galore, But Profits Are Zip," *Business Week*, September 8, 2008.

23. Bruce D. Henderson, *The Experience Curve Revisited* (Boston: Boston Consulting Group, undated); Barry Hedly, "Strategy and the 'Business Portfolio'," *Long Range Planning*, February 1977, pp. 9–15; Bruce D. Henderson, "The Application and Misapplication of the Experience Curve," *Journal of Business Strategy*, Winter 1984; Boston Consulting Group, www.bcg.com, accessed November 9, 2008.

24. "Meg Whitman's Career at eBay Suffers An Impairment Write-Down," *Business Week*, October 6, 2007, p. 80.

25. Michael E. Porter, "How Competitive Forces Shape Strategy," *Harvard Business Review*, March–April 1979, pp. 137–145. See also his *Competitive Strategy* (New York: Free Press, 1980); *Competitive Advantage* (New York: Free Press, 1985); *The Competitive Advantage of Nations* (New York: Free Press, 1990); "The Competitive Advantage of the Inner City," *Harvard Business Review*, May–June 1995, pp. 55–71; "Strategy and the Internet," *Harvard Business Review*, March 2001, p. 63ff; Michael Porter and Nicolaj Siggelkow, "Contextuality within Activity Systems and Sustainability of Competitive Advantage," *The Academy of Management Perspectives*, May 2008, pp. 34–56. See also Carolin Decker and Thomas Mellewigt, "Thirty Years After Michael E. Porter: What Do We Know About Business Exit?" *The Academy of Management Perspective*, May 2007, pp. 41–55.

26. Fred Nickols, "Industry Analysis Ala Michael Porter: Five Forces Affecting Competitive Strategy," 2000, http://home.att.net/~nickols/five_forces.htm, accessed November 9, 2008.

27. For insights about the future, see special report by Peter Drucker, "The Next Society: A Survey of the Near Future," *The Economist*, November 3, 2001, Insert pp. 3–20.

28. Nissan Leaf, http://www.nissanusa.com/leaf-electric-car/index#/leaf-electric-car/index, accessed November 3, 2012; Carlos Ghosn, http://en.wikipedia.org/wiki/Carlos_Ghosn, accessed January 2, 2016.

29. Nissan—For Creating the Leaf, the first mass-market all-electric car, http://bx.businessweek.com/apple/view?url=http%3A%2F%2Fwww.fastcompany.com%2Fmost-innovative-companies%2F2011%2F, accessed March 1, 2012; http://bx.businessweek.com/apple/view?url=http%3A%2F%2F, assessed March 1, 2012.

CHAPTER 6

Decision Making

Learning Objectives

After studying this chapter, you should be able to:

LO 1   Analyze decision making as a rational process

LO 2   Develop alternative courses of action with consideration of the limiting factor

LO 3   Evaluate alternatives and select a course of action from among them

LO 4   Differentiate between programmed and nonprogrammed decisions

LO 5   Understand the differences between decisions made under conditions of certainty, uncertainty, and risk

LO 6   Recognize the importance of creativity and innovation in managing

Decision making is defined as the selection of a course of action from among alternatives; it is at the core of planning. A plan cannot be said to exist unless a decision—a commitment of resources, direction, or reputation—has been made. Until that point, there are only planning studies and analyses. Managers sometimes see decision making as their central job because they must constantly choose what is to be done, who is to do it, and when, where, and, occasionally even, how it will be done. Decision making is, however, only a step in planning. Even when it is done quickly and with little thought or when it influences action for only a few minutes, it is a part of planning. It is also a part of everyone's daily life. A course of action can seldom be judged alone because virtually every decision must be geared to other plans.

Decision making Selection of a course of action from among alternatives.

THE IMPORTANCE AND LIMITATIONS OF RATIONAL DECISION MAKING

In the discussion of the steps in planning in Chapter 4, decision making was considered a major part of planning. As a matter of fact, given an awareness of an opportunity and a goal, the decision-making process is really the core of planning. Thus, in this context, the process leading to making a decision might be thought of as (1) premising, (2) identifying alternatives, (3) evaluating alternatives in terms of the goal sought, and (4) choosing an alternative, that is, making a decision.

Although this chapter emphasizes the logic and techniques of choosing a course of action, the discussion will show that decision making is really one of the steps in planning.

Rationality in Decision Making

It is frequently said that effective decision making must be rational. But what is rationality? When is a person thinking or deciding rationally?

People acting or deciding rationally are attempting to reach some goal that cannot be attained without action. They must have a clear understanding of alternative courses by which a goal can be reached under existing circumstances and limitations. They also must have the information and the ability to analyze and evaluate alternatives in light of the goal sought. Finally, they must have a desire to come to the best solution by selecting the alternative that most effectively satisfies the goal achievement.

People seldom achieve complete rationality, particularly in managing.[1] In the first place, since no one can make decisions affecting the past, decisions must operate for the future, and the future almost invariably involves uncertainties. In the second place, it is difficult to recognize all the alternatives that might be followed to reach a goal; this is particularly true when decision making involves doing something that has not been done before. Moreover, in most instances, not all alternatives can be analyzed, even with the newest analytical techniques and computers available.

10-10-10 Decision Making[2]

Suzy Welch wrote a book with this eye-catching title. What does it mean? Do you make decisions that have consequences within ten minutes from now? Ten months from now? Or ten years from now? The answers to those questions may be quite different. A ten-minute decision may be necessary for action, but it may also be a decision shortly afterward to be regretted. A decision with a ten-year perspective may be quite different based on many uncertainties, but such decisions may have life-long consequences. To become a doctor or a professor requires forecasting and making many assumptions. The rewards may be great, but require many ten-month decisions on how to acquire financing, forgoing the purchase of a house, or skipping vacations with the time devoted to studying.

For managers, the 10-10-10 rule can become a valuable strategic decision-making tool such as for resource allocation. The decision may have immediate consequences, intermediate consequences (let us say in ten months or a year), or long-term consequences such as a major investment in a new product or project.

Raising the time perspective of the consequences may result in better short-term, immediate-term, and long-term personal as well as managerial decisions.

Limited, or "Bounded", Rationality

Satisfising Picking a course of action that is satisfactory or good enough under the circumstances.

A manager must settle for limited or "bounded" rationality. In other words, limitations of information, time, and certainty limit rationality, even if a manager tries earnestly to be completely rational. Since managers cannot be completely rational in practice, they sometimes allow their dislike of risk—their desire to "play it safe"—to interfere with the desire to reach the best solution under the circumstances. Herbert Simon[3] called this **satisficing**, that is, picking a course of action that is satisfactory or good enough under the circumstances. Although many managerial decisions are made with a desire to "get by" as safely as possible, most managers do attempt to make the best decisions that they can within the limits of rationality and in light of the degree and nature of the risks involved.

GLOBAL PERSPECTIVE

Decisions, Decisions, Decisions[4]

What a difference bad weather can make. When a blizzard hit the U.S. East coast, many decisions were initiated. Let's just take one airline to illustrate such a situation. At the command center at American Airlines, hundreds of domestic and international flights are tracked. Information needs to be gathered from meteorologists, the visibility has to be checked, local information has to be obtained such as whether employees will be able to come to work, how many customers are booked on the various flights, which flights need to be cancelled or rerouted. Imagine the complexity of rebooking hundreds or thousands of passengers.

The weather also can affect equipment failure. The airline is also concerned about flight delays because the Federal Aviation Administration keeps a record of flights arriving late 15 minutes or more. Flights need also be coordinated with other airlines. Certainly, decision makers are aided by computers, but many decisions have to be made by a person. Certainly customers will be affected, those on important business trips and those who planned a vacation perhaps years ago. Realizing the complexity of decisions, passengers could be more compassionate when a flight is delayed or cancelled.

DEVELOPMENT OF ALTERNATIVES AND THE LIMITING FACTOR

Assuming that we know what our goals are and agree on clear planning premises, the first step of decision making is to develop alternatives. There are almost always alternatives to any course of action; indeed, if there seems to be only one way of doing a thing, that way is probably wrong. If we can think of only one course of action, clearly we have not thought hard enough.

The ability to develop alternatives is often as important as being able to select correctly from among them. On the other hand, ingenuity, research, and common sense will often unearth so many choices that none of them can be adequately evaluated. The manager needs help in this situation, and this help, as well as assistance in choosing the best alternative, is found in the concept of the limiting or strategic factor.

A **limiting factor** is something that stands in the way of accomplishing a desired objective. Recognizing the limiting factors in a given situation makes it possible to narrow the search for alternatives to those that will overcome the limiting factors. The **principle of the limiting factor** states that, by recognizing and overcoming those factors that stand critically in the way of a goal, the best alternative course of action can be selected.

Principle of the limiting factor
By recognizing and overcoming factors that stand critically in the way of a goal, the best alternative course of action can be selected.

HEURISTICS IN DECISION MAKING

Sometimes when there seem to be too many alternatives to choose from, managers rely on their own decision rules. These decision rules are called heuristics, and they allow complex judgments to be made more simply.[5] Because of these heuristics, decisions may vary with the characteristics or biases of the decision maker. Tversky and Kahneman (1974) wrote the seminal work on individual heuristics, defining them as simplifying mechanisms for complex decisions. And Daft and Weick (1984) noted that cognitive structures are necessary to prevent decision makers from becoming paralyzed by the need to analyze extensive data.[6]

Values and cognitive biases of the organization's top managers are seen in the organization's strategies and effectiveness. Shrivastava and Lim (1984) and Stubbart and Ramaprasad (1990) focus on identifying simplifications and biases in executives' maps of their industries.[7] Simplifying heuristics may be necessary in entrepreneurial situations where there are many unknown variables. For example, venture capitalists manage uncertainty in their decision making at an unconscious level by assessing entrepreneurs through the prism of their own values. These "values" underpin their heuristics and may be revealed by the predominant metaphors that VCs employ.[8] Managers should be aware of their own heuristics, how they may bias their decisions, and attempt to compensate for them through a comprehensive decision process.

Adjusting the decision process may minimize the impact of individual heuristics and allow for more effective choices. For example, a firm's decision context is defined in terms of the comprehensiveness of its decision process and the heterogeneity of its decision team. Organizational decision models introduced by March and Simon (1958), and Cyert and March (1963), made the rational decision process the mainstay in the management literature. Janis and Mann (1977) list the following steps in this rational decision process[9]:

1. "Surveying a diversity of objectives based upon a multiplicity of values derived from the collectivity of stakeholders;
2. Generating a wide range of alternative courses of action;
3. Systematically acquiring relevant information to evaluate alternatives;
4. Objectively evaluating all relevant information;
5. Reevaluating the positive and negative consequences of alternatives initially considered as unacceptable;
6. Carefully evaluating the costs and risks of negative and positive consequences of the preferred alternative;
7. Developing detailed implementation plans and control systems for the chosen alternative, as well as contingency plans for identified risks."

The procedures delineated by Janis and Mann (1977) demonstrate the comprehensiveness of the decision-making process and may be applied to help facilitate better decision making.

EVALUATION OF ALTERNATIVES

Once appropriate alternatives have been found, the next step in planning is to evaluate them and select the one that will best contribute to the goal. This is the point of ultimate decision making, although decisions must also be made in the other steps of planning—in selecting goals, in choosing critical premises, and even in selecting alternatives.

Quantitative and Qualitative Factors

Quantitative factors Factors that can be measured in numerical terms.

Qualitative, or intangible, factors Factors that are difficult to measure numerically.

In comparing alternative plans for achieving an objective, people are likely to think exclusively of **quantitative factors**. These are factors that can be measured in numerical terms, such as time or various fixed and operating costs. No one would question the importance of this type of analysis, but the success of the venture would be endangered if intangible, or qualitative, factors were ignored. **Qualitative, or intangible, factors** are factors that are difficult to measure numerically, such as the quality of labor relations, the risk of technological change, or the international political climate. There are too many instances in which an excellent quantitative plan was destroyed by an unforeseen war, a fine marketing plan made inoperable by a long transportation strike, or a rational borrowing plan hampered by an economic recession. These illustrations point out the importance of giving attention to both quantitative and qualitative factors when comparing alternatives.

To evaluate and compare the intangible factors in a planning problem and make decisions, managers must first recognize these factors and then determine whether a reasonable quantitative measurement can be given to them. If not, they should find out as much as possible about the factors, perhaps rate them in terms of their importance, compare their probable influence on the outcome with that of the quantitative factors, and then come to a decision. This decision may give predominant weight to a single intangible.

Marginal Analysis

Evaluating alternatives may involve utilizing the technique of **marginal analysis** to compare the additional revenue and the additional cost arising from increasing output. Where the objective is to maximize profit, this goal will be reached, as elementary economics teaches, when the additional revenue and additional cost are equal. In other words, if the additional revenue of a larger quantity is greater than its additional cost, more profit can be made by producing more. However, if the additional revenue of the larger quantity is less than its additional cost, a larger profit can be made by producing less.

Marginal analysis can be used in comparing factors other than cost and revenue. For example, to find the best output of a machine, input could be varied against output until the additional input equals the additional output. This would then be the point of maximum efficiency of the machine. Or the number of subordinates reporting to a manager might conceivably be increased to the point at which additional cost savings, better communication and morale, and other factors equal additional losses in the effectiveness of control, leadership, and similar factors.

> **Marginal analysis** Comparing the additional revenue and the additional cost arising from increasing output.

Cost-Effectiveness Analysis

An improvement on, or variation of, traditional marginal analysis is cost-effectiveness, or cost–benefit, analysis. **Cost-effectiveness analysis** seeks the best ratio of benefit and cost; this means, for example, finding the least costly way of reaching an objective or getting the greatest value for a given expenditure.

> **Cost-effectiveness analysis** seeks the best ratio of benefit and cost.

ENTREPRENEURIAL PERSPECTIVE

Interview with Jeb Miller, Venture Capitalist Partner with JAFCO Ventures, on the Investment Decision Process[10]

JAFCO Ventures focuses on risk-adjusted early-stage investments in the information technology and Internet sectors. Jeb Miller joined JAFCO in 2009 as a general partner, bringing 15 years of experience working with early-stage technology companies as a venture capitalist, operating executive, and investment banker. Jeb has focused his investments in the software, Internet, and IT infrastructure sectors and is passionate about teaming with entrepreneurs to help build successful companies. Before joining JAFCO, Jeb was a principal with the US Growth Fund at The Carlyle Group, one of the world's largest private equity firms.

We asked Mr. Miller to share his perspective on the investment decision process. Specifically, we wanted to know how JAFCO Ventures decided which new businesses to finance. He indicated "The three primary considerations JAFCO Ventures factors into an investment decision are the size of the market opportunity, the unique and disruptive nature of the technology and/or business model, and the quality of the team." Mr. Miller explained that a sufficient market is a prerequisite for a successful investment as it is very difficult to generate an outsized return within a limited market. He remarked further that JAFCO Ventures spends a significant amount of time conducting due diligence on the nature of the technology as that is where they strive to select the emerging winners. He justified this effort, noting: "History has proven that the leading company in an emerging market sector generally captures the lion's share of returns within that sector."

Mr. Miller emphasized that the third component (the quality of the team) is what they, as venture capitalists, can help shape the most following an investment by helping augment the founding technical team with business and functional experts out of the networks of talent that they have worked with over the years. Jeb concluded by sharing three other investment considerations that JAFCO Ventures values. They are "...the quality of the early-stage venture capital firms with whom they co-invest, the capital efficiency of the business plan, and the strategic value of an emerging technology to the industry incumbents." From our communication, it became clear that JAFCO Ventures employs a comprehensive and rational decision process to increase the odds of picking winners and developing these new ventures to their fullest potential.

JAFCO Ventures recently decided to rebrand as Icon Ventures and focus on series B and C investments across five funds and about $760 million under management.

SELECTING AN ALTERNATIVE: THREE APPROACHES

When selecting from among alternatives, managers can use three basic approaches: (1) experience, (2) experimentation, and (3) research and analysis (Figure 6.1).

Experience

Reliance on past experience probably plays a larger part than it deserves in decision making. Experienced managers usually believe, often without realizing it, that the things they have successfully accomplished and the mistakes they have made furnish almost infallible guides to the future. This attitude is likely to be more pronounced the more experience a manager has had and the higher he or she has risen in an organization.

To some extent, experience is the best teacher. The very fact that managers have reached their position appears to justify their past decisions. Moreover, the process of thinking problems through, making decisions, and seeing programs succeed or fail does make for a degree of good judgment (at times bordering on intuition). Many people, however, do not learn from their errors, and there are managers who seem never to gain the seasoned judgment required by the modern enterprise.

Relying on past experience as a guide for future action can be dangerous. In the first place, most people do not recognize the underlying reasons for their mistakes or failures. In the second place, the lessons of experience may be entirely inapplicable to new problems. Good decisions must be evaluated against future events, while experience belongs to the past.

On the other hand, if a person carefully analyzes experience, rather than blindly following it, and if he or she distills from experience the fundamental reasons for success or failure, then experience can be useful as a basis for decision analysis. A successful program, a well-managed company, a profitable product promotion, or any other decision that turns out well may furnish useful data for such distillation.

FIGURE 6.1 Bases for selecting from among alternative courses of action

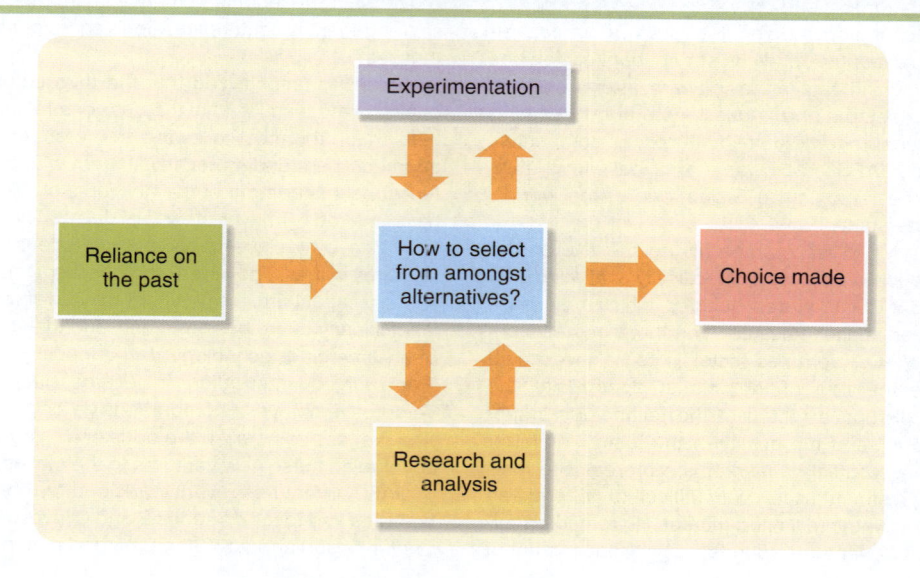

Just as scientists do not hesitate to build upon the research of others and would be foolish indeed merely to duplicate it, managers can learn much from others.

Experimentation

An obvious way to decide among alternatives is to try one of them and see what happens. Experimentation is often used in scientific inquiry. People often argue that it should be employed more often in managing and that the only way a manager can make sure some plans are right—especially in view of the intangible factors—is to try the various alternatives and see which is best.

The experimental technique is likely to be the most expensive of all techniques, especially if a program requires heavy expenditures of capital and personnel and if the firm cannot afford to vigorously attempt several alternatives. Besides, after an experiment has been tried, there may still be doubt about what it proved, since the future may not duplicate the present. This technique, therefore, should be used only after considering other alternatives.

On the other hand, there are many decisions that cannot be made until the best course of action can be ascertained by experiment. Even reflections on experience or the most careful research may not assure managers of correct decisions. This is nowhere better illustrated than in the planning of a new airplane.

An airplane manufacturer may draw from personal experience and that of other plane manufacturers and new plane users. Engineers and economists may make extensive studies of stress, vibration, fuel consumption, speed, space allocation, and other factors. But all these studies do not answer every question about the flight characteristics and economics of a successful plane; therefore, some experimentation is almost always involved in the process of selecting the right course to follow. Ordinarily, a first-production, or prototype, airplane is constructed and tested; and on the basis of these tests, production airplanes are made according to a somewhat revised design.

Experimentation is used in other ways. A firm may test a new product in a certain market before expanding its sale nationwide. Organizational techniques are often tried in a branch office or plant before being applied over an entire company. A candidate for a management job may be tested in the job during the incumbent's vacation.

Research and Analysis

One of the most effective techniques for selecting from alternatives when major decisions are involved is research and analysis. This approach means solving a problem by first comprehending it. It thus involves a search for relationships among the more critical of the variables, constraints, and premises that bear upon the goal sought. It is the pencil-and-paper (or, better, the computer-and-printout) approach to decision making.

Solving a planning problem requires breaking it into its component parts and studying the various quantitative and qualitative factors. Study and analysis is likely to be far cheaper than experimentation. The hours of time and reams of paper used for analyses usually cost much less than trying the various alternatives. In manufacturing airplanes, for example, if careful research did not precede the building and testing of the prototype airplane and its parts, the resulting costs would be enormous.

A major step in the research-and-analysis approach is to develop a model simulating the problem. Thus, architects often make models of buildings in the form of extensive blueprints or three-dimensional renditions. Engineers test models of airplane wings and missiles in a wind tunnel. But, the most useful simulation is likely to be a representation of the variables in a problem situation by mathematical terms and relationships. Conceptualizing a problem is a major step toward its solution. The physical sciences have long relied on mathematical models to do this, and it is encouraging to see this method being applied to managerial decision making.

INNOVATIVE PERSPECTIVE

Boeing's Decision to Go Digital in Developing the 777[11]

Boeing's 777 airliner may be one of the most advanced aircraft in the world. The most innovative aspect, however, is the way the airliner was built: 100 percent three-dimensional digital design using CAD/CAM technology. To go digital was a critical decision for Boeing. Using the new system, engineers could see on the screen the design and preassemble the plane's more than 3 million parts and its 132,500 uniquely engineered parts. This new approach, a paradigm shift, required completely new relationships with suppliers and customers. For example, the company requested ideas for the 777 from eight airlines. Internally, planners, engineers, and toolers worked together as a team, and they had current information on the development process. Previously, engineers and mechanics had to work on some full-scale mock-ups to see whether parts did or did not fit, and problems would result in costly reworks. More recently, Boeing has begun using an advanced, intelligent CAD (called ICAD) system that makes major changes in the design possible. Now, and in the future, emerging technologies aid decision making.

www.boeing.com

PROGRAMMED AND NONPROGRAMMED DECISIONS

Programmed decisions are used for structured or routine work.

Nonprogrammed decisions are used for unstructured, novel, and ill-defined situations of a nonrecurring nature.

A distinction can be made between programmed and nonprogrammed decisions. A **programmed decision**, as shown in Figure 6.2, is applied to structured or routine problems. Lathe operators, for instance, have specifications and rules that tell them whether the part they made is acceptable, has to be discarded, or should be reworked. Another example of a programmed decision is the reordering of standard inventory items. This kind of decision is used for routine and repetitive work; it relies primarily on previously established criteria. It is, in effect, decision making by precedent.

Nonprogrammed decisions are used for unstructured, novel, and ill-defined situations of a nonrecurring nature. Examples are the introduction of the Macintosh computer by Apple Computer or the development of the four-wheel-drive passenger car by Audi. In fact, strategic decisions, in general, are nonprogrammed decisions, since they require subjective judgments.

FIGURE 6.2 The nature of problems and decision making in the organization

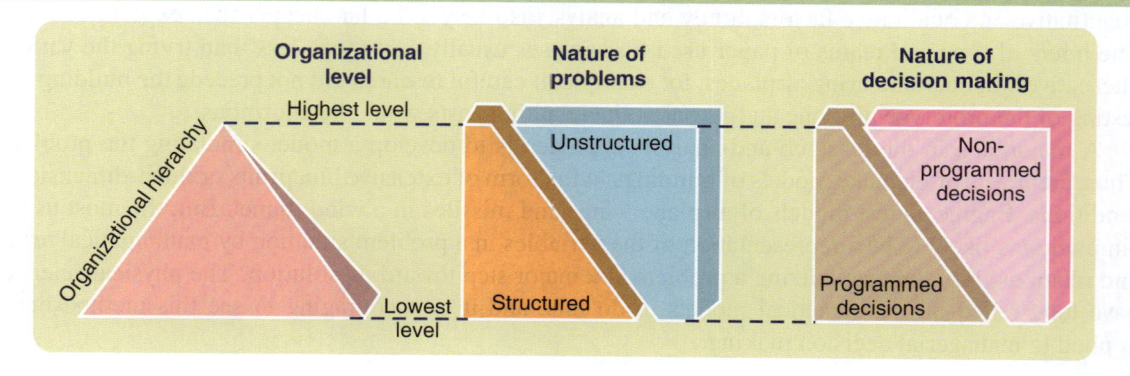

Most decisions are neither completely programmed nor completely nonprogrammed; they are a combination of both. As Figure 6.2 indicates, most nonprogrammed decisions are made by upper-level managers; this is because upper-level managers have to deal with unstructured problems. Problems at lower levels of the organization are often routine and well structured, requiring less decision discretion by managers and nonmanagers.

GLOBAL PERSPECTIVE

IBM's Louis Gerstner as Decision Maker[12]

At first, it might seem unlikely that a manager with a career at RJR Nabisco and American Express would be the person who could lead a technically oriented company like IBM out of its difficult 1993 position. Yet, this was precisely what Louis Gerstner did with two key decisions: first, he did not break up the company; and second, he focused on the service business. By 2001, its global business was the area with the fastest growth. Despite the demands on his time, he still took time for social causes, especially those related to schooling.

One of Gerstner's strategic decisions was in the server market, where Sun Microsystems had been dominant with its UNIX servers. IBM was able to lower its prices and therefore put its competitors such as Sun, Hewlett-Packard, and Compaq under extreme pressure.

Thus, as a top-level manager, Gerstner had to balance his time resources between making strategic and tactical decisions, deciding on products and services, global and domestic planning, and strategy formulation and implementation, as well as balancing his energy between organizational and socially responsible actions.

DECISION MAKING UNDER CERTAINTY, UNCERTAINTY, AND RISK

Virtually all decisions are made in an environment of at least some uncertainty. However, the degree will vary from relative certainty to great uncertainty. There are certain risks involved in making decisions.

In a situation involving certainty, people are reasonably sure about what will happen when they make a decision. The information is available and is considered to be reliable, and the cause and effect relationships are known.

In a situation of uncertainty, on the other hand, people have only a meager database, they do not know whether or not the data are reliable, and they are very unsure about whether or not the situation may change. Moreover, they cannot evaluate the interactions of the different variables. For example, a corporation that decides to expand its operation to an unfamiliar country may know little about the country's culture, laws, economic environment, and politics. The political situation may be so volatile that even experts cannot predict a possible change in government.

In a situation with risks, factual information may exist, but it may be incomplete. To improve decision making, one may estimate the objective probability of an outcome by using, for example, mathematical models. On the other hand, subjective probability, based on judgment and experience, may be used.

All intelligent decision makers dealing with uncertainty like to know the degree and nature of the risk they are taking in choosing a course of action. One of the deficiencies in using the traditional approaches of operations research for problem solving is that many of the data used in a model are merely estimates and others are based on probabilities. The ordinary practice is to have staff specialists come up with "best estimates".

INNOVATIVE PERSPECTIVE

To Risk or Not to Risk—That Is the Question for Tesla[13]

The need for energy independence directs the focus to electric cars. Tesla Motors, the California-based car company, has been in the business of designing, manufacturing, and selling electric cars for many years. The Tesla Roadster was one of the first cars using the lithium-ion battery with a driving range exceeding 200 miles. The car, it is said, will be much more energy efficient than the hybrid Prius vehicle by Toyota.

In 2010, Tesla entered the finance world through the public offering (IPO), being confident that the new sedan S Model will be successful. It is hoped that the S Model eventually will sell 20,000 cars a year. But Tesla faced many challenges, such as the 2010 weak car industry.

Also the company needs additional cash and hopes for improved battery technology that could extend the driving range. The expected competition from companies such as Nissan[14] and Toyota which is offering a plug-in hybrid.[15] General Motors, for example, developed the much-hyped Chevrolet Volt, a hybrid sedan. Moreover, Tesla does not seem to be quite clear whether it can become a high-volume car producer. Opportunities for an electric car are there, but the risk for Tesla is great. Tesla's hope is that the S Model sedan will succeed, justifying the risky decision.

www.teslamotors.com/

Virtually, every decision is based on the interaction of a number of important variables, many of which have an element of uncertainty but, perhaps, a fairly high degree of probability. Thus, the wisdom of launching a new product might depend on a number of critical variables: the cost of introducing the product, the cost of producing it, the capital investment that will be required, the price that can be set for the product, the size of the potential market, and the share of the total market that it will represent.

INNOVATION PERSPECTIVE

Was Disneyland Paris Built on the Wrong Assumptions?[16]

Assumptions are critical for making strategies; their importance can be illustrated by the decision to build Euro Disney, which was later called Disneyland Paris. The venture was planned in an uncertain environment and based on wrong assumptions. In the early days of this undertaking, from 1992 to 1994, the company lost more than $1 billion. Disney initially owned 49 percent of the venture, but its share was later reduced to 39 percent. So what went wrong? After all, the earlier move into Japan was very successful. Using the experiences with other ventures as the premises for the French Disneyland was precisely the problem. In the United States and Japan, the admission price was gradually raised after initial interest had been built. In contrast, Euro Disney started with an unsustainable entrance price of more than $40. This was very high in comparison with other theme parks. Consequently, the admission price had to be drastically reduced and then gradually increased. In 1996, the one-day adult admission was about $38. Nevertheless, the initial high price may have resulted in the loss of customers in the early years of operation.

Another flawed assumption was that people would stay on average four days in Disney's hotels. However, in 1993, the average stay was only two days. The theme park opened with about one-third of the rides found at Disney World in America. Thus, all the rides could be done in one day, requiring a shorter hotel stay.

The European tradition of having the main meal at noontime was not taken into consideration either. The available eating places were overcrowded at noon and underutilized at other times. Rather than wait, visitors left to eat outside the park. In the United States and Japan, people eat throughout the day, thus avoiding long lines in the restaurants.

The mix of merchandise purchases is also different in France from that in the United States: Europeans buy fewer high-margin items.

These few illustrations seem to indicate that Disney did not sufficiently test its premises for the Euro Disney venture. Using assumptions based on previous successes may prove to be very costly. A careful analysis of cultural habits and observations of other theme parks may have prevented making plans based on incorrect assumptions.

While Euro Disney was suffering, certain competitors prospered. Euro Park was one of them. It is a theme park smaller than Euro Disney, located in Germany close to the French and Swiss borders. While Euro Disney may not have considered the cultural differences, management at Euro Park was very familiar with European customs. In surveys, visitors were asked to rate cleanliness, price, hours, rides, special shows, and so on. The surveys indicated, for example, that French visitors like to bring their baskets with bread, cheese, and wine. So patrons are allowed to bring their own food to the park (which is not allowed at Disney). The admission price was also substantially lower than at Euro Disney. Euro Park was considering building a hotel, but management realized that this would be a risky undertaking because it is a different kind of business, requiring competencies that are different from managing a theme park.

www.disneyland-paris.com

CREATIVITY AND INNOVATION[17]

A distinction can be made between creativity and innovation. The term **creativity** usually refers to the ability and power to develop new ideas. **Innovation**, on the other hand, usually means the use of these ideas. In an organization, this can mean a new product, a new service, or a new way of doing things. Although this discussion centers on the creative process, it is implied that organizations not only generate new ideas but also translate them into practical applications.

Creativity Ability to develop new ideas that are relevant to the issue

The Creative Process

The creative process is seldom simple and linear. Instead, generally it consists of four overlapping and interacting phases: (1) unconscious scanning, (2) intuition, (3) insight, and (4) logical formulation.

The first phase, *unconscious scanning*, is difficult to explain because it is beyond consciousness. This scanning usually requires an absorption in the problem, which may be vague in the mind. Yet, managers working under time constraints often make decisions prematurely rather than dealing thoroughly with ambiguous, ill-defined problems.

The second phase, *intuition*, connects the unconscious with the conscious. This stage may involve a combination of factors that may seem contradictory at first. For example, Donaldson Brown and Alfred Sloan of General Motors conceived the idea of a decentralized division structure with centralized control, concepts that seem to contradict each other. Yet, the idea makes sense when one recognizes the underlying principles of (1) giving responsibility for the operations to the general manager of each division and (2) maintaining centralized control in headquarters over certain functions. It took the intuition of two great corporate leaders to see that these two principles could interact in the managerial process.

Intuition needs time to work. It requires that people find new combinations and integrate diverse concepts and ideas. Thus, one must think through the problem. Intuitive thinking is promoted by several techniques, such as brainstorming.

Insight, the third phase of the creative process, is mostly the result of hard work. For example, many ideas are needed in the development of a usable product, a new service, or a new process. What is interesting is that insight may come at times when the thoughts are not directly focused on the problem at hand. Moreover, new insights may last for only a few minutes, and effective managers may benefit from having paper and pencil ready to make notes of their creative ideas.

Innovation Use or commercialization of creative ideas or inventions

Four phases of the creative process: unconscious scanning, intuition, insight, and logical formulation or verification.

www.gm.com

The last phase in the creative process is *logical formulation or verification*. Insight needs to be tested through logic or experiment. This may be accomplished by continuing to work on an idea or by inviting critiques from others. Brown and Sloan's idea of decentralization, for example, needed to be tested against organizational reality.

INNOVATIVE PERSPECTIVE

Innovation in India: Microfinancing[18]

Innovation is not restricted to large companies with big research and development budgets. In India, the self-help groups (SHGs) consisting of some 12 to 15 women organize to get bank loans from large banks. While individuals would not obtain loans, the groups did. Group members discuss which project should be financed and how priorities should be set. These groups know the local environment well and can identify the needs and opportunities in the community. They also oversee how the money is used. Indeed the loan repayment rates are as high as 99.5 percent. This innovative microfinancing arrangement illustrates the decision and innovation at the lowest level.

Brainstorming[19]

Creativity can be taught. Creative thoughts are often the fruits of extensive efforts. Some techniques focus on group interactions, while others on individual actions. One of the best-known techniques for facilitating creativity was developed by Alex F. Osborn, who has been called the father of brainstorming.[20] The purpose of this approach is to improve problem solving by finding new and unusual solutions. In the brainstorming session, a multiplication of ideas is sought. The rules are as follows:

- No ideas are ever criticized.
- The more radical the ideas are, the better.
- The quantity of idea production is stressed.
- The improvement of ideas by others is encouraged.

Brainstorming, which emphasizes group thinking, was widely accepted after its introduction. However, enthusiasm was dampened by research which showed that individuals could develop better ideas working by themselves than they could working in groups. Additional research, however, showed that in some situations the group approach may work well. This may be the case when the information is distributed among various people or when a poorer group decision is more acceptable than a better individual decision that, for example, may be opposed by those who have to implement it. Also, the acceptance of new ideas is usually greater when the decision is made by the group charged with its implementation.

INNOVATIVE PERSPECTIVE

Learning Innovation from Emerging Countries[21]

Companies learned that they could profit from selling low-price products in other countries. General Electric's Healthcare Unit developed an electrocardiograph machine for doctors in China and India. Traditionally, innovations were first developed in the United States, Europe, and Japan. Now some of the innovations come from poor countries. Indeed, some U.S. companies send their innovation managers to less developed countries. Research is now conducted abroad. For example, Hewlett-Packard has a research laboratory in India. Innovation can originate in developed, developing, and even underdeveloped countries.

Limitations of Traditional Group Discussion

Although the technique of brainstorming may result in creative ideas, it would be incorrect to assume that creativity flourishes only in groups. Indeed, the usual group discussion can inhibit creativity. For example, group members may pursue an idea to the exclusion of other alternatives. Experts on a topic may not be willing to express their ideas in a group for fear of being ridiculed. Also, lower-level managers may be inhibited in expressing their views in a group with higher-level managers. Pressures to conform can discourage the expression of deviant opinions. The need for getting along with others can be stronger than the need for exploring creative but unpopular alternatives to the solution of a problem. Finally, because they need to arrive at a decision, groups may not make the effort of searching for data relevant to a decision.

INNOVATIVE PERSPECTIVE

How 3M Fosters Innovation[22]

Companies have different strategies for fostering innovation. At Johnson & Johnson, autonomous operating units are encouraged to innovate. The organization culture allows failure. At Rubbermaid, 30 percent of its sales are derived from products that are less than five years old. Hewlett-Packard encourages researchers to spend 10 percent of their time on their pet projects, and Merck allocates time and resources to its researchers for working on high-risk products with a potential for high payouts. Dow Corning and General Electric engage in joint projects with customers to develop new products. One of the masters in innovation is Minnesota Mining & Manufacturing (3M).

When one hears of 3M, one thinks of innovation. The organizational environment of 3M fosters creative thinking and a tolerance for new ideas. Although the financial performance in 1995 was not as good as before, the company met its goal of obtaining at least 30 percent of its sales from products that were less than four years old. Continual innovation is fostered by the 15 percent rule, which suggests that researchers spend 15 percent of their time on things that are not related to their main project.

The company is very decentralized. Its 8,300 researchers work in many different laboratories. This results in redundancy. In theory, the main labs and development centers should do research, while the others do the development. Often, however, it does not work this way. The company operates with few rules and does not have a strategy in the traditional sense. Instead, it is guided by two things: (1) to be very innovative and (2) to satisfy the customer in every respect. Anything that hampers innovation, such as excessive planning or intolerance for mistakes, is eliminated. On the other hand, information sharing is required. Although financial measures act as a control, the real control comes from peers, who review each other's work.

The typical innovative process at 3M works as follows: When a person in the organization has an idea for a new product, he or she forms a team consisting of individuals from the functional areas, such as the technical department, manufacturing, marketing, sales, and, at times, finance. The company also encourages customers to contribute their ideas. The team works on product design, production, and marketing. Moreover, various uses of the product are explored. Team members are rewarded for the success of the product.

Rules or guidelines are rather simple: develop a tolerance for failure; reward those who have a good product idea and who can form an effective action team to promote the product; establish close relationships with customers; share technology with others in the company; keep the project alive by allocating time or financial grants; keep the divisions small.

The future will tell whether innovation will continue to be a key success factor for 3M.

www.jnj.com
www.rubbermaid.com
www.hp.com
www.dowcorning.com
www.ge.com
www.3m.com

The Creative Manager[23]

All too often, it is assumed that most people are noncreative and have little ability to develop new ideas. This assumption, unfortunately, can be detrimental to the organization, for in the appropriate environment, virtually all people are capable of being creative, although the degree of creativity varies considerably between individuals.

Generally speaking, creative people are inquisitive and come up with many new and unusual ideas; they are seldom satisfied with the status quo. Although intelligent, they not only rely on the rational process, but also involve the emotional aspects of their personality in problem solving. They appear to be excited about solving a problem, even to the point of tenacity. Creative individuals are aware of themselves and capable of independent judgment. They object to conformity and see themselves as being different.

It is beyond question that creative people can make great contributions to an enterprise. At the same time, however, they may also cause difficulties in organizations. Change—as any manager knows—is not always popular. Moreover, change frequently has undesirable and unexpected side effects. Similarly, unusual ideas, pursued stubbornly, may frustrate others and inhibit the smooth functioning of an organization. Finally, creative individuals may be disruptive by ignoring established policies, rules, and regulations. John Kao, who teaches at Harvard Business School, suggests that creative people should have enough freedom to pursue their ideas, but not too much that they waste their time or do not find enough time to collaborate with others in working toward common goals. He suggests that managers should view themselves as jazz musicians who follow a set of scores but have enough freedom for variations.[24]

As a result, the creativity of most individuals is probably underutilized in many cases, despite the fact that unusual innovations can be of great benefit to the firm. However, individual and group techniques can be effectively used to nurture creativity, especially in the area of planning. Nonetheless, creativity is not a substitute for managerial judgment. It is the manager who must determine and weigh the risks involved in pursuing unusual ideas and translating them into innovative practices.

Invention
Development or discovery of something new.

Innovation
Enhancement, adaptation, or commercialization of new products, services, or processes.

Invention and Innovation[25]

Invention alone is not sufficient for business success—it has to be followed by innovation. **Invention** pertains to the development or discovery of something new and **innovation** is the enhancement, adaptation, or *commercialization* of new products, services, or processes. Innovation, on the other hand, is using the idea and putting it into practice. Innovation is the realization of the idea. The IBM team was instructed not to invent the computer, but bring the off-the-shelf components together resulting in the IBM PC. Thus it was innovation that resulted in the PC.[26]

SUMMARY

Decision making is the selection of a course of action from among alternatives; it is the core of planning. Managers must make choices on the basis of limited, or bounded, rationality—that is, in light of everything they can learn about a situation, which may not be everything they should know. *Satisficing* is a term sometimes used to describe picking a course of action that is satisfactory under the circumstances.

Because there are almost always alternatives—usually many—to a course of action, managers need to narrow them down to those few that deal with the limiting factors. These are the factors that stand in the way of achieving a desired objective. Alternatives are then evaluated in terms of quantitative and qualitative factors. Other techniques for evaluating alternatives include marginal analysis and cost-effectiveness analysis. Experience, experimentation, and research and analysis come into play in selecting an alternative.

Programmed and nonprogrammed decisions are different. The former are suited for structured or routine problems. These kinds of decisions are made especially by lower-level managers and nonmanagers. Nonprogrammed decisions, on the other hand, are used for unstructured and nonroutine problems and are made especially by upper-level managers.

Virtually all decisions are made in an environment of at least some uncertainty involving the interaction of a number of important variables, and there are certain risks involved in making decisions. Managers dealing with uncertainty should know the degree and nature of the risk they are taking in choosing a course of action.

Creativity, the ability and power to develop new ideas, is important for effective managing. Innovation is the use of these ideas. The creative process consists of four overlapping phases: unconscious scanning, intuition, insight, and logical formulation. A popular technique for enhancing creativity is brainstorming. Creative individuals can make a great contribution to the enterprise. At the same time, they can be disruptive by not following commonly accepted rules of behavior. Invention is the development or discovery of something new while innovation is the enhancement, adaptation, or commercialization of new products, services, or processes.

KEY IDEAS AND CONCEPTS FOR REVIEW

Decision making
Limited or bounded rationality
Satisficing
Principle of the limiting factor
Quantitative factors
Qualitative factors

Marginal analysis
Cost-effectiveness analysis
Three approaches to selecting an alternative
Programmed decisions
Nonprogrammed decisions
Decision making under certainty, uncertainty, and risk
Creativity
Invention
Innovation
Creative process
Brainstorming
Creative manager

FOR DISCUSSION

1. Why is experience often referred to not only as an expensive basis for decision making, but also as a dangerous one? How can a manager make the best use of experience?
2. In a decision problem you now know of, how and where would you apply the principle of the limiting factor? Did you apply this principle in selecting the class or section of the class you are attending? In what ways?
3. Identify five decision problems and recommend programmed or nonprogrammed decisions. If the examples are from an organizational setting, did they occur at upper or lower levels?
4. "Decision making is the primary task of the manager." Comment.
5. Think of a problem that was creatively solved. Did the solution come from group discussion or was it the result of an individual effort? Reconstruct the phases of the creative process.

EXERCISE/ ACTION STEPS

1. Your boss offers you a promotion to a position in a location that your family does not like. Make the necessary assumptions and then state how and what you would decide.
2. Ask for one recommendation from a current or former professor or supervisor for your LinkedIn profile.

ONLINE RESEARCH

1. Search the Internet for "creativity" and illustrate how creativity can be applied to decision making.
2. Find three applications of brainstorming on the Internet.

INTERNATIONAL CASE

Carrefour—Which Way to Go?[27]

Wal-Mart's biggest global competitor is the big French retailer Carrefour, a firm that has hypermarkets, big stores offering a variety of goods. It has made large investments around the globe in Latin America and China. But not all is well as competitors have taken market share in its home market, for instance. There has even been speculation of a takeover by Wal-Mart or Tesco, an English chain. Mr. Barnard has been ousted after heading the company for 12 years; he was replaced by Jose Luis Durant who is of German-Spanish descent. Although the global expansion is cited by some as success, it may be even a big mistake. It withdrew from Japan and sold 29 hypermarkets in Mexico. Carrefour also had problems competing with Tesco in Slovakia and the Czech Republic. In Germany, the company faced tough competition from Aldi and Lidle, two successful discounters. On the other hand, it bought stores in Poland, Italy, Turkey, and opened new stores in China, South Korea, and Columbia. Carrefour has become more careful in selecting markets. But the company is eager to enter the Indian market, but found out in late 2006 that Wal-Mart will do so as well.

In France, where Carrefour is well established, the company made the big mistake in its pricing policy. It probably started with the 1999 merger with Promodes, the French discount chain. Carrefour confused the French clientele by losing its low-cost image; whether the image can be changed remains to be seen. Mr. Durant, the new chief executive officer (CEO) since 2005, embarked on the new strategy by offering 15 percent new products in its hypermarkets and 10 percent in its supermarkets. Moreover, he wants to employ more staff, extend the operating hours in certain hypermarkets, cut prices, try small stores, and pushi down decision making. Mr. Durant aims to stay only in countries where Carrefour is among the top retailers.

Questions:

1. How should Mr. Durant assess the opportunities in various countries around the world?
2. Should Carrefour adopt Wal-Mart's strategy of "low prices every day?" What would be the advantage or disadvantage of such a strategy?
3. How could Carrefour differentiate itself from Wal-Mart?
4. Identify cultures in selected countries that need to be considered in order to be successful.

PART 2 CLOSING

Global and Entrepreneurial Planning

This part closing focuses on the entrepreneurial and global dimensions of planning. First, the competitive advantages and disadvantages of India are identified. Second, the entrepreneurial focus is on writing a business plan for a new venture. Finally, the global car industry case discusses the merger between the German Daimler and the American Chrysler corporations.

GLOBAL FOCUS: A TOWS ANALYSIS OF THE COMPETITIVE ADVANTAGES AND DISADVANTAGES OF INDIA*

Every nation is concerned with competing effectively in the global market. Competitiveness does not depend only on the effectiveness of individual companies, but also on the industries and the socioeconomic system of a nation. The rapidly changing environments of the free world markets dictate that nations fully use their comparative advantages to remain or become prosperous in the future. Political, economic, and business leaders must evaluate the opportunities in and threats from the external environment in order to build appropriate strategies that take advantage of their nation's and industry's strengths and shore up weaknesses. Therefore, the discussion should be viewed from the leaders of the respective country.

GAINING COMPETITIVE ADVANTAGE WITH THE TOWS MATRIX—A CONCEPTUAL MODEL

The TOWS Matrix was originally introduced by Weihrich for the formulation of company strategies.[28] Later, it was used as a conceptual framework for developing career strategies for individuals.[29] In this book, the framework will be used to analyze industries in particular, and the nation in general to identify the competitive advantage of a nation illustrated by India.

The development of a strategy, be it for a career, a company, an industry, or a nation, requires a systematic analysis of the weaknesses (W) and strengths (S) of the respective system (the nation in our

---

* Based on "Analyzing the Competitive Advantages and Disadvantages of India with the Tows Matrix—An Alternative to Porter's Model by Heinz Weihrich and Chunguang Ma", presented at the Eastern Academy of Management Conference "Global Economy XIII" in Rio de Janeiro, June 21–25, 2009.

discussion), which, in turn, operates within a larger external environment that poses not only threats (T), but also provides opportunities (O) to the system. These four factors are illustrated in the TOWS Matrix in Figure C2.1.

These four factors will become the basis for four distinct strategies. The most favorable situation occurs when a nation uses its strengths (S) to take advantage of opportunities (O) outside that nation. This is called an S-O (or maxi-maxi) strategy in our model because the nation exploits opportunities using its strengths. But in a globally competitive market, the nation also faces threats, which, in turn, may be overcome by its strengths. Such a situation is deemed as S-T (or maxi-mini) strategy because the aim is to maximize strengths by minimizing the threats (see Figure C2.1).

Every nation also possesses weaknesses that must be overcome in order to take advantage of external opportunities. Such a W-O (or mini-maxi) strategy is often a developmental plan that attempts to convert a nation's weaknesses into strengths. The least favorable situation in the TOWS Matrix occurs when a nation faces external threats in light of its weaknesses, which may make it difficult for the nation to operate and compete in the global market. This strategy, shown as W-T (or mini-mini) in the Matrix, aims at minimizing both the internal weaknesses and the external threats.

The conceptual TOWS Matrix will be used for the country analysis of India and for specific analyses of selected industries to illustrate the practical application of the Matrix.

FIGURE C2.1 TOWS Matrix—A conceptual model

Country Culture, Values, Purpose, Objectives, etc.	Internal Strengths [S] e.g. cultural norms, education system, political system, natural resources, transportation system, infrastructure, technological innovation, managerial practices	Internal Weaknesses [W] e.g. weaknesses in areas shown in the box of "internal strengths"
External Opportunities [O] e.g. European Community, North America, South America, Eastern Europe, Pacific Rim & Asia	SO: Maxi-Maxi Potentially the most successful strategy, utilizing the nation's strengths to take advantage of opportunities in the global market	WO: Mini-Maxi e.g. a developmental strategy to overcome the weaknesses in order to take advantage of opportunities
External Threats [T] e.g. from companies or whole industries from areas shown in the "external opportunities" box	ST: Maxi-Mini e.g. use of strengths to copy with the threats in the world	WT: Mini-Mini e.g. invite foreign investments and make it attractive to those firms or industries

ANALYSIS OF THE COMPETITIVE SITUATION OF INDIA

The conceptual model for analyzing the competitive advantages and disadvantages were introduced in Figure C2.1. This part discusses specific strategies that India and its industries can pursue in light of their inherent strengths and weaknesses and of the opportunities and threats in the macro-environment. The TOWS Matrix, shown in Figure C2.2, illustrates the competitive situation of India.

India's Internal Environment: Its Strengths and Weaknesses[30]

Geographically, India is the seventh largest country in the world. It is estimated that by 2025 India's market will surpass the consumer market in Germany.[31] The prevailing religion is Hindu, followed by Muslims, and a much smaller percentage of Christians, Sikhs, and Buddhists. The English language is used in business and administration. About 65 percent of the population is literate. Despite the economic growth, India still has a high poverty rate.[32]

In 1947 India became independent from the British rule, followed by a new Constitution in 1950. India plays an increasing role in the World Trade Organization (WTO); it is also a member in the Association of Southeast Asian Nations (ASEAN) and the South Asian Association for Regional Cooperation (SAARC). In order to analyze the competitive advantages and disadvantages, we will now use the TOWS Matrix shown in Figure C2.2.

FIGURE C2.2   TOWS Matrix for India[33]

Country Culture, Values, Purpose, Objectives, etc.	Internal Strengths [S]	Internal Weaknesses [W]
Emphasis on pluralism and syncretism, i.e. attempting to reconcile different beliefs, traditions and culture. Globalization is seen as an opportunity to economic growth, modernize by using technology, reduce poverty, improve the quality of life. Inferred: To become a major global player and power within a democratic context	• Economic growth about 9% and above • Stable democratic government promoting increased privatization • Low labor cost • Young labor force • Low cost producer of steel • Auto component industries, trucks, and buses • Pharmaceuticals and chemicals • English widely spoken • Educated workforce • Medical tourism • IT, software back office services • Hi-tech office park (e.g. Bangalore, Hyderabad, and others) • Good higher education system (e.g. IIT) • Outsourcing capabilities • Growth of the middle class (almost 30%) • Textile sector (silk, cotton, yarn, fabrics) • Various natural resources and agricultural products • Various industries	• Energy dependent (high oil prices) • Poor roads, terrible traffic • Crowded airports • Poor mass transit • Infrastructure (e.g. bridges) • Power blackouts • Horrendous traffic • Energy dependent • Pollution • Business judicial system; long time in resolving business disputes • Inflation • General education, low graduation rate • Low investment in R&D • How to employ rural people with low literacy • Government bureaucracy and corruption

External Opportunities [O]	SO: Maxi-Maxi	WO: Mini-Maxi
• Globalization provides opportunity for outsourcing (e.g. legal and tax profession) • R&D in India by foreign companies • Attractive for high-tech companies • Attractive for pharmaceutical firms • Growing investments from the U.S. • Export opportunities for engineering goods, petroleum products, textile, gems & jewelry • Increasing need for IT products and services • Business process outsourcing • Increased tourism, including medical tourism	• Provide outsourcing services • Continue government policy of pro-growth, pro-reform, open the market to competition • Attract new industries • Promotion of knowledge process outsourcing (e.g. analysis of X-ray pictures, risk management, accounting) • Develop key industries such as biotechnology, pharmaceuticals, IT, textiles • Promote tourism (e.g. Thailand)	• Policies that promote the infrastructure such as building roads, bridges, airports (the new airport in Bangalore was opened in 2008) • Develop global energy policy • Invest in solar and hydrogen energy • Improve judicial process to solve disputes quickly • Allow foreign universities to participate and invest (joint ventures) • Encourage company training (e.g. apprenticeship training in Germany) • Install controls to fight corruption • Improve compulsory elementary education
External Threats [T]	**ST: Maxi-Mini**	**WT: Mini-Mini**
• World resource shortage • High price of oil • Agricultural subsidies in America and Europe • US government lobbying against outsourcing to protect US jobs • Competition from China, Philippines, Malaysia, Vietnam • Cheap labor in other countries • Intellectual resources lured away by other countries	• Negotiate with America and Europe to reduce agricultural subsidies • Develop solar and wind power • Negotiate with western countries for the reduction of farm subsidies in their countries • Improve productivity to compete with low-cost countries • Provide incentives to retain human resources	• Provide China with software and get manufacturing technology in return • Get surplus of rural people employed in manufacturing • Incentives for industry to employ surplus people in agriculture • Promote solar energy policies

India's Internal Strengths

India's progress has been called an economic miracle. While during the past several years India has seen a phenomenal growth, the future also looks promising. The highly respected McKinsey Global Institute anticipates a growth rate of 6 to 9 percent from 2005 to 2025. In anticipation of the consumer potential, McKinsey conducted a major study on the rise of India's consumer market and the development of a strong middle class.[34]

India has the second largest workforce with young, highly educated people, most with a good command over the English language, which is very beneficial in the global market. Several universities have an excellent reputation (e.g., the prestigious Indian Institute of Technology). The industry sectors include companies in automobiles, transportation equipment, pharmaceuticals, chemicals, consumer electronics, food processing, petroleum, cement, mining, steel, technological services, and many firms that are outsourcing their services such as back office services; the film industry, known as Bollywood, is also a strength. Some of the greatest strengths are in the development of software. Indeed, the major exports are software, engineering goods, textiles, and jewelry. Perhaps less known, but gaining in importance, is medical tourism.[35] Americans with a medical condition who cannot afford the high medical costs at home may opt for medical services in India.

Natural resources include coal, iron ore, titanium, bauxite, diamonds, natural gas, petroleum, lime stone, and other resources. Agricultural products include rice, wheat, cotton, jute, potatoes, oilseed, and sugarcane.

Although India's greatest strength is in the information technology area, there are also other companies worth noting. Among the top ten Indian companies, a variety of industries are represented, including firms such as Reliance Industries Ltd., Oil & Natural Gas Corporation, the State Bank of India, and well-known firms such as Tata Steel, Tata Consultancy Services, and Tata Motors.[36] Let us focus on some examples.

India has been known for its car parts industry. But, now cars are also assembled in even greater numbers. Indeed, many foreign car manufacturers have entered the market. The recently introduced US$2,500 "Nano" car by Tata Motors got a great deal of attention by potential car buyers in India and other countries.

While these examples are showing the developments in India, the greatest change occurred in the technology sector. Some major high-tech companies are located in what is called "Cyber City." In Pune, for example, there is a gated community that includes not only offices, but also apartments next to the factories; this eliminates the need for commuting through the crowded old city.[37] Companies such as Infosys and Wipro have their modern facilities in Bangalore and so have multinationals such as Philips, Intel, Nokia, and General Electric.

Although the bureaucratic government reacts slowly, entrepreneurs such as Narayana Murthy, who is considered by some as the Bill Gates of India, initiated great changes in India. He and his coworkers started the very successful Infosys Consultants firm. Similarly, Ratan Tata took Tata Steel, which was far behind in technology, and turned it around. He is sometimes compared with Jack Welch, the former CEO at General Electric.

India's Internal Weaknesses

While India has much strength, especially its remarkable growth rate of about 9 percent over several years, the country also has many weaknesses that must be addressed. The country must import most of its energy which is especially critical in a sky-high oil market. One of the biggest problems is the poor infrastructure. Mass transit is almost nonexistent and probably could be described as "mess transit" with a high level of pollution. Therefore, Infosys, the very successful technology firm, has invested in buses, minivans, and taxies to transport its employees to the airport.[38] In the meantime, new airports around the country are under construction.

Other factors that hinder India to achieve its potential are the frequent power blackouts, the business judicial system, the cumbersome bureaucracy, and corruption. Many foreign firms can describe horror stories of their experiences. Yet, multinational corporations are investing heavily in India despite the chaotic situation.

While India has a number of excellent universities, the general education with a low graduation rate is a weakness and so is the problem of employing rural people with a low literacy rate.

India is accountable to the parliament as well as the population and the free press. Reaching consensus among the parties, often, delays reforms and change. There is a general complaint about governmental bureaucracy and corruption.

External (Geographic) Opportunities and Threats for India

Opportunities for India can be found in various geographic regions: the European Union, North America, Eastern Europe (including the former Soviet Republics), the Pacific Rim, and Asia. India has many trading partners in the Unites States, in countries of the European Union, as well as China. The major exports are software, engineering, and textiles.

External Opportunities

With the increased globalization, many outsourcing opportunities exist. For many years Indian companies have provided customer call centers. More recently, the legal and tax professions have used the Indian services. In general, business process outsourcing is an attractive opportunity. Also, increasingly foreign companies conduct their research and development activities in India. The educated labor force makes investments in high-tech and pharmaceuticals very attractive to foreign firms. In general, the global environment provides export opportunities for engineering goods, petroleum products, textiles, gems, and jewelry. The increased use of information technology, a distinct strength of India, provides Indian firms with opportunities to offer those products and services globally. Moreover, increased tourism makes India very attractive. As illustrated by Thailand, tourism can become an important part of the economy. With the demand for cars, Indian automobiles are selling well in South Africa, Spain, and Italy.

Threats from the External Environment

While various regions of the world do provide opportunities, they also pose threats to India. The worldwide resource shortages as well as the high oil prices pose serious threats for India. The agricultural subsidies provided by the governments in Europe and America make it difficult for Indian farmers to compete. Lobbying in the US government aims at protecting jobs in America which, in turn, may reduce the outsourcing of services to India. While India gained competitive advantage by low labor costs, other countries, such as Vietnam, compete in this area as well. One of the concerns of foreign companies is the protection of intellectual properties. Unless more stringent property laws are initiated, foreign firms may be discouraged to share their expertise. Attractive job offers from abroad may lure highly qualified professionals to accept those offers.

Four Sets of Strategies for India

In light of India's internal strengths and weaknesses and the opportunities and threats from other countries, four sets of distinct strategies should be considered.

Strengths–Opportunities (SO) Strategies (Maxi-Maxi)

The potentially most successful strategy for India is using its internal strengths to take advantage of external opportunities outside the country. This set of alternative strategies is shown in the Matrix, Figure C2.2, as SO or maxi-maxi strategy; this means maximizing the internal strengths to take advantage of external opportunities. Figure C2.2 illustrates some SO strategies. For example, companies should be encouraged and supported by policies that facilitate outsourcing services. Moreover, the government should continue the pro-growth and pro-reform policies as well as open the market to competition in order to attract new industries such as biotechnology, pharmaceuticals, and information technology. The textile industry may also benefit from advancement in new technologies from other countries. Knowledge-based outsourcing such as analyzing X-ray pictures and risk management accounting may also benefit the industry as well as the country. Tourism may attract the increasingly affluent people in developing countries.

Weaknesses–Opportunities (WO) Strategies (Mini-Maxi)

A country also has internal weaknesses which it should aim to overcome in order to take advantage of external opportunities; this means minimizing the weaknesses to maximize the opportunities. These alternatives are illustrated in the WO or Mini-Maxi strategy shown in the Matrix in Figure C2.2. With the poor roads and the chaotic traffic situation, the government should promote the building of a stronger infrastructure by building roads, bridges, and airports. Some efforts are underway as shown by the opening of the new Bangalore airport in 2008. With the energy dependency, a global energy policy needs to be developed. This could mean investments in solar and hydrogen energy.

In order to attract foreign investment, the judicial process needs to be improved so that disputes are resolved quickly and fairly. It may also be advantageous to allow foreign universities to participate in joint ventures. For developing skills, companies may be encouraged to initiate internal training such as illustrated by the German apprenticeship system.[39] Siemens India, for example, may learn from the parent company in Germany and adopt the apprentice model to the Indian environment. It should be noted that Siemens India has a strong foothold in the country and was ranked first in the *Business Week* 50 of Asian countries.[12] The apprentice program could also help to employ rural people with low literacy. One important strategy would be the installation of controls to fight corruption which, in turn, would encourage investments by foreign corporations. Education is critical for moving a country into the twenty-first century. While India has a few very good universities, the country would greatly benefit from improved compulsory elementary education.

Strengths–Threats (ST) Strategies (Maxi-Mini)

India has much internal strength that can be used to cope with external threats through the ST strategy by maximizing the country's strengths and to minimize its threats. One such strategy would be to develop renewable energy, such as solar or wind power, and to reduce the dependency on oil. Another approach would be to negotiate with American and European governments to reduce their agricultural subsidies. To be competitive, India needs to cope with the low-cost competition from China, the Philippines, Malaysia, and Vietnam by emphasizing productivity. While these countries may pose a threat, they may also become opportunities for trade. Finally, the companies as well as government policy should aim for keeping intellectual human resources in the country and discourage people seeking employment abroad. Since China, for example, is a serious threat, especially in manufacturing, one strategy would be to cooperate with China by exporting software while importing manufactured goods and technologies.

Weaknesses–Threats (WT) Strategies (Mini-Mini)

The WT strategy that tries to minimize both India's weaknesses and threats to the country is often the most difficult alternative. One such alternative would be to use the surplus of rural people and get them employed in manufacturing. Government may also provide incentives for employing people for building roads, bridges, and airports. To deal with the world's natural resource shortage, solar energy policies may be promoted.

Country Culture, Values, Purpose, and Objectives

These are a few alternatives the government, with the help of industry, could pursue. Clearly, alternative strategies are intertwined. In reality, a combination of strategies would be required. But, whatever strategies may be selected, they have to be congruent with India's culture, values, and national purpose as shown in the upper left part of the Matrix in Figure C2.2. For example, India needs to recognize pluralism and syncretism that means attempting to reconcile different cultures, beliefs, and traditions. India should not be seen as an island, rather as an important part of the global environment that provides opportunities for growth. That may require forward-looking leadership that uses technology to modernize and improve the quality of life of its citizens and to reduce poverty. Thoughtful attention should be given to the nation's aim of becoming a global player operating within a democratic context.

Concluding Comments about the Competitive Situation of India and Other Countries

The TOWS Matrix approach generates various alternatives for gaining a competitive advantage for a nation. These alternatives can assist policy makers in the systematic analysis of internal and external factors and in combining them to achieve a synergistic effect. Although we illustrated the practical application of the TOWS Matrix for India, other countries may also benefit from generating strategies for maintaining or gaining competitive advantages in the global market.[40]

ENTREPRENEURIAL FOCUS: WRITING A BUSINESS PLAN FOR AN ENTREPRENEURIAL VENTURE

As discussed in Part 2, the planning process is the first step toward effective management. It involves developing a vision and mission for the organization as well as setting objectives and goals. In the entrepreneurial context, planning is normally associated with writing a business plan for a new venture. Business plans are used by entrepreneurs as the planning mechanism to help them launch and grow their new firms. These are also used by entrepreneurs to help raise funds from professional investors, such as venture capitalists or banks. While many resources for business plan writing may be found online,[41] the following describes what most investors and entrepreneurs expect in the Silicon Valley.[42]

Specifically, business plans can range up to 40 pages and more, but with time limitations of executives and investors, most professionals want to see a relatively brief document that cuts to the essence of the business concept. The entrepreneur will normally first complete a full business plan that details numerous milestones, operational plans, and financial forecasts. However, the presentation and persuasion of potential investors and partners normally rely on a brief document or presentation.

The following details the essential elements of a business plan proposal that have been developed based on close interactions with Silicon Valley venture capitalist and executives.[43] The basic outline is provided first, followed by more detail on each section.

Business Plan Proposal Format

A business plan can take many forms. This proposed format outlines the essential parts of the proposal:

1. Company name and brief description. (Explaining the business concept clearly and persuasively is essential!)
2. Opportunity or problem in the market to be addressed.
3. How does the product/service address the problem or opportunity?
4. Who are the current and potential competitors, and what is the company's competitive advantage?
5. Description of the target market in terms of its demographic attributes (e.g., gender, income level, age) and its size.
6. Marketing strategy to reach target market and an estimate of the projected market penetration over the first five years.
7. Business model and strategic milestones.
8. Summary of projected revenue and profit based on the penetration of target market, the market size growth, and estimated expenses for years 1 to 5.

9. Management team description and their relevant experience.
10. Amount of money needed from investors, and for what purpose.
11. Current state of the firm (e.g., product development stage, patents, contracts, current sales, profit level, equity/debt raised so far).

Naturally, entrepreneurs and investors in different industries or at different stages of their business will emphasize some elements of this proposal format more or less. However, discussions with dozens of investors and entrepreneurs indicate that these are the essential elements that professional investors look for in a business plan proposal. The following provides more details for each section:

1. Company name and brief description
   Explaining the business concept clearly, concisely, and persuasively is the key! Again, time is the most precious resource of busy executives and investors. They expect that the entrepreneur can quickly and completely describe the key elements of the business. Seasoned entrepreneurs can convey their business description (even for very technical or scientific enterprises) in just a few minutes. This ability indicates that the entrepreneur understands her business enough to convey it to a nonexpert audience. If after a 15-minute presentation by an entrepreneur, the investor asks, "What is it you exactly would do again?", the entrepreneur has failed in her company description.

2. Opportunity or problem in the market to addressed
   Successful entrepreneurs are opportunity-oriented. A phrase often heard from professional investors in the Silicon Valley is, "where is the pain point?" In other words, what problem experienced by consumers or businesses does the entrepreneur intend to solve? How significant is this problem? This must be the focus of a business, rather than producing a product with no clear need. Similar to the basic company description, clearly explaining the problem is critical to a successful business proposal or presentation.

3. How does the product/service address the problem or opportunity?
   Once the entrepreneur has identified the market opportunity or problem, she must, of course, offer a solution to that problem in terms of a product or service. She should be able to clearly describe her product and how it specifically solves the problem met by potential customers. The entrepreneur should be able to demonstrate how her product will diminish specific pain points (e.g., cost, time, aggravation) of the customer.

4. Who are the current and potential competitors, and what is the company's sustainable competitive advantage?
   Once the entrepreneur has demonstrated that she has a product that can *relieve the pain* of the customer, she should clearly indicate who the competition is and how her solution compares to those offered by this list of competitors. Does her product relieve the pain of the customer better, more completely, or more inexpensively? Further, she should indicate what the underlying competitive advantage of her company is in terms of providing this solution. A discussion on achieving sustainable competitive advantage is provided elsewhere in this text; however, in brief, competitive advantage may be attained by creating or possessing intellectual property whose functionality is difficult to replicate, or developing a strong brand, or identifying an exclusive distribution or supply network.

5. Description of the target market in terms of its demographic attributes (e.g., gender, income level, age) and its size
   Primary and secondary market research should be completed by the entrepreneur in order to accurately determine who is the most likely customer, how many of them exist, and how best to market and distribute the product to them. Primary research might begin with a focus group, where a prototype product is given to 5–10 potential customers to comment on, or a survey or interview process might be undertaken. Once this primary research has led to a good description of who is the most likely customer (e.g., in terms of age, gender, income), secondary research

should be completed in order to determine how many of these customers exist. Secondary market research[44] will utilize existing market data to find out how many individuals fit the dimensions or characteristics of the most likely customer as determined by primary research.

6. Marketing and sales strategy to reach target market and an estimate of the projected market penetration over the first five years

   Once the market has been defined through the marketing research process, the entrepreneur must develop a comprehensive marketing strategy to reach that target market. First, the customer must be made aware that the company's product exists and may provide a benefit. Next, the company's product must be made to be felt desirable by that target market segment. This education and persuasion process must fit closely with the customer needs and behaviors. Again, what is the customer's "*pain point*" or felt need that the entrepreneur wishes to solve with the product? How can the product's efficacy be best communicated to the customer? To what media does the customer pay attention? How does the entrepreneur best get the message to the customer? How should the product or service be distributed to the customer once desirability for our product is established? A marketing strategy needs to be specific. How does the entrepreneur get her first customer, then her second and third, and so on? An entrepreneur should avoid indicating the following: "It is a $1 billion potential market nationwide—so if we just get 10% of it—that is $100 million in sales." A written statement or discussion item such as this would end the meeting with a savvy investor. Rather, the marketing strategy helps create a logical argument and estimate for market penetration (the percent of the target market that will buy the product). This penetration estimate along with the market size, determined by market research, leads to the estimate of total sales.

   The sales strategy should explain the process to generate the first sale in great detail. For example, in order to sell to a business, what is the first step? Who in the organization will the entrepreneur contact first? What is the expected length of the sales process to close the sale and collect payment? The clearer the sales strategy, the more realistic the plan will appear to potential investors.

7. Business Model and Strategic Milestones

   The entrepreneur must detail a business model for the proposed business. Specifically, how is the product or service created? What are the primary supply sources? What are the distribution channels to the target markets? How are those distribution channels promoted? What revenue streams are anticipated, and what are the margins? A clear understanding and explanation of the firm's business model by the entrepreneur indicates that she knows her business quite well and is, therefore, more likely to execute on the plan well. The entrepreneur should also specify key strategic milestones that the firm plans to meet.[45] These strategic milestones are often tied to funding requirements. In other words, a round of funding may be contingent on meeting projected milestones. So, the entrepreneur must be sure not to overestimate what can be accomplished.[46]

8. Brief Financial Summary

   While the full business plan will need to detail specific expenses and a sales generation logic with monthly or quarterly entries, a proposal should be much more condensed to allow for a quick assessment by interested investors.[47] For example, a brief summary of projected revenue and profit based on the market size, the penetration of the target market, and estimated expenses for the first five years of the enterprise is normally expected.

Year 1	Year 2	Year 3	Year 4	Year 5
Market Size				
Revenue				
Expenses				
Profit				

9. Management team description and their relevant experience
   Most professional investors will indicate that the management team of a new venture is the top or one of the top criteria they use when evaluating a new business for possible financing. The saying goes, "better to have an 'A' team with a 'B' idea, than an 'A' idea with a 'B' team." That is in part because the original idea for a business will usually be modified, and the management team must be strong enough to be able to adapt. The entrepreneur should indicate previous industry experience as well as experience in launching other companies. Being associated with one or two previous start-up companies that failed is not seen as problematic in Silicon Valley because these experiences are often where the greatest learning occurs. Further, identifying holes in the management team would indicate the need for recruiting for those positions. Finally, integrity and ethics are the essential characteristics of each management team member. If trust is lost between the entrepreneur and the investor, the deal is dead. So, the entrepreneur must never exaggerate or obfuscate. Honesty and sincerity are essential.
10. Amount of money needed from investors and for what purpose
    The entrepreneur must not forget to ask what she wants from investors in terms of financing. This initial financing request should be based on the financial forecast of the business plan. How much capital is needed to launch the venture in terms of needed cash for operations and investment? It is typical to have several rounds of financing as the firm grows. The first round of financing should cover at least 12 months of the company's operations.[48]
11. Current State of the Firm
    As a business plan is a living document, being updated throughout the life of the venture, the entrepreneur may present her plan after operating for several years. So, it is important for the entrepreneur to indicate the current state of the firm in terms of product development, sales, profits, etc. An established firm is more likely to get financial backing because much of the risk of the initial launch has been removed, so the entrepreneur must not be shy about discussing her firm's achievements.
    The preceding business proposal provides the standard outline for organizing a business plan for a new venture in the Silicon Valley. Normally, an entrepreneur will need to develop a comprehensive business plan with extensive market research and financial forecasts in order to extract the essence for this proposal. Still, this guide should help the entrepreneur focus on those essential elements that investors are looking for. Strategic milestones and planning are the backbone of a well-written business plan. The entrepreneur should start there and follow her passion to bring the new enterprise to life.

GLOBAL CAR INDUSTRY CASE

The Daimler–Chrysler Merger: A New World Order— That Was Not[49]

In May 1998, Daimler-Benz, the largest industrial firm in Europe, and Chrysler, the third largest car maker in the United States, merged. The carefully planned merger seemed to be a "strategic fit". Chrysler, with its lower-priced cars, light trucks, pickups, and its successful minivans, appeared to complement Daimler's luxury cars, commercial vehicles, and sport utility vehicles (SUVs). There was hardly any product-line overlap.

The merger followed a trend of other consolidations. General Motors (GM) owns 50 percent of Swedish Saab AB and has subsidiaries Opel in Germany and Vauxhall in England. Ford acquired British Jaguar and Aston Martin. The German car maker BMW acquired British Rover (but later got rid of it and kept only the Mini model), and Rolls Royce successfully sold its interests to Volkswagen and BMW. On the other hand, the attempted merger of Volvo and Renault failed, and Ford later acquired Volvo.

The Daimler–Chrysler cross-cultural merger had the advantage that the CEOs of both companies had international experience and knowledge of both German and American cultures. Chrysler's Robert Eaton had experience in restyling Opel cars in GM's European operation. Mr. Lutz, the co-chair at Chrysler, speaks fluent German, English, French, and Italian and had past work experience with BMW, GM, and Ford. Daimler's CEO, Jürgen Schrempp, had worked in the United States and South Africa, giving him a global perspective.

Background

Lee Iacocca, the colorful Chrysler chairman, left Ford for Chrysler because of a clash with Henry Ford II in 1978. He is credited with saving Chrysler from bankruptcy in 1979/1980 when he negotiated a loan guaranty from the U.S. government. Iacocca also led Chrysler's acquisition of American Motors in 1987, which added the Jeep to the Chrysler line. Robert Eaton, Chrysler's CEO who negotiated the 1998 merger with Daimler, replaced Iacocca in 1992.

At the time of the merger, Daimler was selling fewer vehicles than Chrysler but had higher revenues. Daimler's 300,000 employees worldwide produced 715,000 cars and 417,000 trucks and commercial vehicles in 1997. The company was also in the business of airplanes, trains, and helicopters, with two-thirds of its revenue coming from outside Germany.

So, why would Daimler in Stuttgart, Germany, go to Chrysler in Detroit, USA? The companies had complementary product lines and Chrysler saw the merger as an opportunity to overcome some of the European trade barriers. However, the primary reasons for mergers in the auto industry are technology (which has high fixed costs) and overcapacity (which is estimated at 20 percent). Only those companies with economies of scale can survive. Mr. Park, the president of Hyundai Motor Company, stated that production lines in South Korea operated at about 50 percent of capacity in 1998. The auto industry could produce about one-third more cars. It has been predicted that only six or seven major car makers will be able to survive in the twenty-first century. This makes a merger more of a competitive necessity than a competitive or strategic advantage.

Daimler + Chrysler = New Car Company*

In the late 1980s and the early 1990s, the Japanese made great strides in the auto industry through efficient production methods and high-quality products. However, a new trend was set by the German car maker that changed the car industry with the Daimler–Chrysler merger, in which the former had 53 percent ownership and the latter the rest. The new car company was now the fifth largest in the world and could become the volume producer in the whole product range.

---

* This discussion illustrates the application of the TOWS Merger Matrix introduced in Chapter 5.

The respective strengths were that Daimler was known for its luxury cars and its innovation in small cars (A-Class, Smart car[50]). Chrysler, on the other hand, had an average profit per vehicle that was the highest among the Big 3 (GM, Ford, and Chrysler) in Detroit, thanks to high margins derived from the sale of minivans and Jeeps. The company was also known for its highly skilled management and efficient production. Low costs and simplicity (e.g., the Neon model) were other hallmarks of Chrysler.

Figure C2.3 shows the strengths and weaknesses of Chrysler before the merger with Daimler-Benz. It also lists the external opportunities and threats for the company as well as alternative strategies. Essentially, Chrysler continued its strategy of strengthening its SUV and minivan market in the countries under the North American Free Trade Agreement (NAFTA). At the same time, the company faced increasing competition and the need for expanding to non-NAFTA markets. Furthermore, there was the danger of an "unfriendly" takeover by another company. Exploring a friendly merger with a firm with a good reputation that could supplement its product line and enable it to expand into new markets made a lot of sense.

FIGURE C2.3 TOWS Matrix for Chrysler Corporation before the merger

Internal environment / External environment	Internal strengths (S) • A tradition and brand image in NAFTA • Sales and service network in NAFTA • Balanced portfolio in USA • Jeep image and profitable minivans	Internal weaknesses (W) • Narrow focus on home market and NAFTA • Company little known outside NAFTA • Weak network outside NAFTA • Delicate overall financial situation
External opportunities (O) • Demand for high-margin minivans • Growing SUV market • Advances in information technology	**SO: Maxi-Maxi** • Strengthen SUV and minivan products in NAFTA • Seek merger with a high-tech company	**WO: Mini-Maxi** • Enter non-NAFTA markets • Develop sales and service networks outside NAFTA
External threats (T) • Saturation and stagnation of U.S. market • Increasing SUV and minivan competition (e.g., Nissan, Toyota) • Hostile takeover possibility • Competition (e.g., General Motors, Ford)	**ST: Maxi-Mini** • Use know-how to improve SUV and minivan position • Develop innovative cars • Explore a friendly merger	**WT: Mini-Mini** • Find partner to enter worldwide market

Mercedes-Benz (a part of Daimler Corporation) was known for its excellence in engineering and product quality; the company's brand image was luxury cars. On the other hand, Mercedes lacked a product offering in the lower-priced, high-volume segment as shown in Figure C2.4. The high development costs and the need for gaining economies of scale called for finding a partner that would enable it to offer a complete product line from high-priced to low-priced vehicles.

FIGURE C2.4 TOWS Matrix for Daimler-Benz before the merger

Internal environment / External environment	Internal strengths (S) • Brand image for luxury cars • Engineering expertise • Product quality • Financial power	Internal weaknesses (W) • Focus only on worldwide luxury car market • Lack of high-volume segment • High prices • Weak presence in Asian markets
External opportunities (O) • Need for broad product line • Demand for small luxury cars • Need for new sales channels	**SO: Maxi-Maxi** • Use brand image to enter new area and broaden product line • Develop the Smart car • Use platform concepts to reduce costs • Develop minivans	**WO: Mini-Maxi** • Enter lower-priced segment • Develop products to increase volume • Utilize existing partners • Find new partners in lower-priced segment
External threats (T) • Saturation in home market • Economic problems in emerging markets • Competition in luxury car market (e.g., BMW, Lexus, Infiniti, Accord, Jaguar) • Broadened product line of competitors (e.g., Volkswagen, Audi)	**ST: Maxi-Maxi** • Use technological know-how to fight competitors • Search for cooperating partners	**WT: Mini-Maxi** • Establish a new brand for lower-priced segment

The situational analysis after the merger shows that the strengths and weaknesses of the two companies complement each other (see Figure C2.5). They could now offer a full product line in all segments in their respective home markets. There was little product overlap with the exception of the Jeep Cherokee competing directly with the Mercedes M-Class SUV, which was produced in Alabama. Moreover, the partners could now utilize the innovation in both their particular areas of expertise. Their facilities in various countries could be used for the production and assembly of both low- and premium-priced cars. In all, the merged DaimlerChrysler Corporation aimed to achieve synergy and cost savings.

Despite the potential advantages of the merger, challenges remained. The company had little experience in penetrating the worldwide market of lower-priced products. There was also the potential for conflicts in the integration of the operational and management systems of the merged companies. External threats remained and would get worse. Car markets in the European Union and NAFTA were becoming saturated and economic deterioration in developed and emerging economies reduced and stagnated the growth in those countries. In addition, competition (especially in the luxury segments) became fiercer.

The challenge for Daimler's CEO, Jürgen Schrempp, was to integrate the two companies and achieve the efficiencies that were one of the important aims of the merger. In addition, integrating the organizational cultures of the two companies would be a major challenge.

Strategy Implementation: The Achilles' Heel of the Merger?

The merger strategy was carefully planned and formulated. The global perspectives of Schrempp and Eaton as well as the product lines indicated a potential fit as shown in the TOWS Matrix of the combined company (Figure C2.5). Yet, implementing a well-conceived strategy provides its own challenges. Some Chrysler designers and managers saw the merger more as a takeover by Daimler and consequently left

FIGURE C2.5 TOWS Matrix for Daimler-Chrysler after the merger

Internal environment / External environment	Internal strengths (S) • Full product line; presence in all segments in home markets • Favorable image and brand perception of Mercedes and Jeep brands • Improved car sales in WEU and USA • Sales and service network in WEU and USA • Worldwide assembly and production • Innovation potential and technological know-how • Financial power; productivity	Internal weaknesses (W) • Focus only on luxury segment worldwide • Lack of products for Asian volume segment • Little experience in lower-priced segment in certain regions • Lack of products to enter lower-priced segment • High-priced position • Weak performance in Asia, except in luxury • Potential conflicts in operational and management systems
External opportunities (O) • Establishing existing brands in new markets • Addressing needs in new segments • Developing and introducing new models • Entering niche segments • Utilizing new sales channels • Broadening service (mobility, financing) • Utilizing economies of scale (cost-saving potential in distribution, production, and administration) • Development of fuel cells powered by hydrogen	**SO: Maxi–Maxi** • Make use of brands and products • Utilize business systems and further improve sales performance and efficiency • Further improve reputation of entire brand portfolio and customer awareness • Make use of technological know-how in newly served segments • Make use of synergies to reduce development, production, and administrative costs • Research in fuel cell technology for car offerings around 2004	**WO: Mini–Maxi** • Buy or create brand for lower-priced segment • Acquire or cooperate with other firms to penetrate lower-priced segment, achieve economies of scale, and gain access to new markets (especially Asia) • Develop lower-priced products, especially for Asia • Market products outside home markets • Search for appropriate partners especially in insufficiently served markets
External threats (T) • Saturation and stagnation in WEU and NAFTA • Economic deterioration in emerging markets, reducing demand • Fiercer competition in luxury segment • Broadening product line of (new) competitors. Increasing concentration in automotive sector. Falling stock market value	**ST: Maxi–Mini** • Utilize innovation potential and technological know-how to achieve dominance in all segments • Scan all potential customers to find their needs and offer the "perfect" solution • Attract investors to back up and increase stock market value to protect against hostile investors	**WT: Mini–Mini** • Deliberate cooperation with Asian partners to further grow and improve worldwide setup

NAFTA: North American Free Trade Agreement; WEU: Western European Union.

Figure compiled with the assistance of K. U. Seidenfuss.

the firm to join GM and Ford. Mr. Eaton, the American morale booster, retired soon after the merger. While there was mutual understanding of the country and corporate cultures at the highest organizational level (both CEOs having a global perspective), incorporating the different cultures and managerial styles at lower levels was much more difficult.

German top managers may rely on a 50-page report for discussion and decision making, while Americans prefer one-to-one communication. Below the board level, subordinates typically research an issue and present it to their German boss, who usually accepts the recommendation. American managers, on the other hand, frequently accept the report and file it away, which frustrates German subordinates. Also, Chrysler designers became frustrated with not being involved in the design of Mercedes cars. Although there were two headquarters (Detroit and Stuttgart), a top manager predicted that in the future there would be only one—in Germany. Both the Americans and Germans could learn from each other. Germans needed to write shorter reports, be more flexible, reduce bureaucracy, and speed up managerial decision making. American managers, on the other hand, could learn discipline from the Germans. As one Chrysler employee said: "One of the real benefits to us is instilling some discipline that we know we needed but weren't able to inflict on ourselves."[51]

This employee seemed to have been right because in 2001 Chrysler needed a dramatic shakeup. External threats had increased and the internal environment needed an overall revamp. Externally, demand for the very profitable Chrysler minivans and SUVs dropped, partly because of the slowing economies in the United States and Europe and partly because of increased competition from Toyota, Honda, and Volkswagen. Internally, the past extravagant spending became a drain on Chrysler's resources as well as on the DaimlerChrysler Corporation. To solve the internal problems, Dieter Zetsche from Mercedes took control at Auburn Hills in the United States. In his analysis of the situation, he noted that assumptions underlying the plans were incorrect. Perhaps even more important, the plans lacked proper assessments of Chrysler's strengths and weaknesses.[52] With Zetsche focusing on Chrysler's operation and Schrempp on the overall strategy of DaimlerChrysler, will the merger finally live up to its promise? That was the question!

The Answer to the Question

The Daimler-Chrysler merger was not a new world order model. The company marriage ended in the divorce of the two companies, with Chrysler being sold to Cerberus Capital Management. Many reasons were given for the failure such as:

- It was not a merger of equals—Chrysler was treated as a subsidiary.
- The German leadership was missing for too long. The German management team arrived too late.
- The wage differential between Chrysler and Mercedes created a controversy, with Chrysler employees earning much more than its German counterparts.
- The expected synergies in sales, purchasing, distribution, product design, and research and development did not materialize.
- There was a culture clash below top-level management. The culture-sensitive workshops did not overcome the culture clash.
- Some key Chrysler managers were uncertain about their careers and left for GM and Ford.
- Chrysler share value declined.
- German engineers focused on quality, Chrysler engineers emphasized price.

The analysis of the relative strengths and weaknesses of both companies indicated that in many ways they complemented each other. There was little overlap in the model lineup. Similarly, in the analysis of the opportunities for both companies the outlook was positive. There was an overoptimism about the synergy. This case illustrates the need for the integration of strategy formulation and strategy implementation.

Questions:

1. Evaluate the formulation of the merger between Daimler and Chrysler. Discuss the strategic fit and the different product lines.

2. Assess the international perspectives of Eaton and Schrempp.
3. What are the difficulties in merging the organizational cultures of the two companies?
4. What should have been done to make the strategy implementation successful?

ENDNOTES

1. See James G. March and Herbert A. Simon, *Organizations* (New York: Wiley, 1958).
2. "Suzy Welch's Big Strategic Thought," *Business Week*, May 4, 2009. pp. 56–57.
3. In 1978, Professor Simon received the Nobel Prize for economics. He died in 2001 at the age of 84. See "Herbert Simon," *The Economist*, February 24, 2001, p. 91. His autobiography can be found at www.nobel.se/economics/laureates/1978/simon-autobio.html, accessed January 2, 2016.
4. Melanie Trottman, "Bad Weather, Tough Choices," *The Wall Street Journal*, February 14, 2006.
5. A. Tversky and D. Kahneman, "Judgement Under Uncertainty: Heuristics and Biases," *Science*, 1974, 185: 1124–1131.
6. Richard Daft and Karl E. Weick, "Toward a Model of Organizations as Interpretations Systems", *Academy of Management Review*, 1984, 9 (2): 284–295.
7. P. Shrivastava and G. Lim, Alternative Approaches to Strategic Analysis of Environments. Working Paper: New York University, 1984. C. I. Stubbart and A. Ramaprasad, "Comments on the Empirical Articles and Recommendations for Future Research", in A. S. Huff, ed. *Mapping Strategic Thought* (New York: John Wiley, 1990), pp. 251-288.
8. Mark Cannice and Art Bell, "Metaphors used by Venture Capitalists: Darwinism, Architecture, and Myth," *Venture Capital: An International Journal of Entrepreneurial Finance*, forthcoming 2010.
9. March and Simon, *Organizations*. R. M. Cyert and J. G. March, *A Behavioral Theory of the Firm* (Englewood Cliffs, NJ: Prentice Hall, 1963). I. L. Janis and L. Mann. *Decision Making: A Psychological Analysis of Conflict, Choice, and Commitment* (The Free Press: New York, 1977).
10. Email interview conducted with Mr. Jeb Miller, General Partner, JAFCO Ventures, by Mark Cannice on August 11, 2009.
11. "Taking Off: Boeing," *Fortune*, November 9, 1993, pp. 53–54; George Taninecz, "Blue Sky Meets Blue Sky," *Industry Week*, December 18, 1995, pp. 48–52; Boeing, http://www.boeing.com/commercial/777family/index.html, accessed July 30, 2011.
12. "The Top 25 Managers: Louis V. Gerstner Jr., IBM," *Business Week*, January 14, 2002, p. 54; Andrew Park, Peter Burrows, and Spencer E. Ante, "How Low Can Big Blue Go," *Business Week*, October 22, 2001, pp. 56–57; Fred Vogelstein, "Sun on the Ropes," *Business Week*, January 7, 2002, pp. 82–87; David Kirkpatrick, "The Future of IBM," *Fortune*, February 18, 2002, p. 70.
13. Patrick May, "Uphill Drive," *Contra Costa Times*, July 4, 2010; Tesla's home page http://www.teslamotors.com/ accessed November 16, 2011; Tesla Motors, *The New York Times*, July 6, 2010.
14. See Nissan LEAF, youtube.com/nissanusa accessed January 2, 2016.
15. "2010 Prius Plug-In Hybrid Makes North American Debut at Los Angeles Auto Show," http://pressroom.toyota.com/pr/tms/toyota/2010-prius-plug-in-hybrid-makes-149402.aspx, accessed July 6, 2010.
16. "The Top 25 Managers: Louis V. Gerstner Jr., IBM," *Business Week*, January 14, 2002, p. 54; Park, Burrows, and Ante, "How Low Can Big Blue Go"; Vogelstein, "Sun on the Ropes"; Kirkpatrick, "The Future of IBM."
17. See also the discussion of intuition in decision making by Erik Dane and Michael G. Pratt, "Exploring Intuition and its Role in Managerial Decision Making," *The Academy of Management Review*, January 2007, pp. 33–32.
18. C. K. Prahalad and M. S. Krishnan, *The New Age of Innovation* (New York: McGraw-Hill, 2008), p. 5.
19. See also Robert C. Lichtfield, "Brainstorming: A Goal-Based View," *The Academy of Management Review*, July 2008, pp. 649–668.
20. Alex F. Osborn, *Applied Imagination*, 3rd rev. ed. (New York: Scribner, 1963).
21. Reena Jana, "Inspiration from Emerging Economies", *Business Week*, March 23 and 30, 2009, pp. 38-41.
22. Thomas A. Stewart, "3M Fights Back," *Fortune*, February 5, 1996, pp. 94–99; "3M and Then There Were Two," *The Economist*, November 18, 1995, pp. 74–75; Michael Arndt, "3M: A Lab for Growth?" *Business Week*, January 21, 2002, pp. 50–51; 3M Worldwide, www.3m.com, accessed November 8, 2008.
23. See also Joseph V. Anderson, "Weirder than Fiction: The Reality and Myths of Creativity," *Academy of Management Executive*, November 1992, pp. 40–47.
24. "Mr. Creativity," *The Economist*, August 17, 1996, p. 55.
25. William Buxton, "Innovation vs. Invention," http://www.billbuxton.com/innovationInvention.pdf, accessed January 2, 2016.
26. Ogan Gurel, "Innovation and Invention—Similar Words, Different Concepts," http://www.ipfrontline.com/depts/article.aspx?id=16295&deptid=5, accessed January 2, 2016.
27. "Carrefour at the Crossroads," *The Economist*, October 22, 2005, p. 7, Cecilie Rohwedder, "A New Chief Seeks to Make French Retailing Giant Nimbler," *Wall Street Journal*, November 30, 2006; "Setting Up Shop in India," *The Economist*, November 2, 2006, pp. 73–74. See also "Setting Up Shop in India," http://www.economist.com/business/displaystory.cfm?story_id=8109636, accessed November 15, 2011.
28. Heinz Weihrich, "The TOWS Matrix: A Tool for Situational Analysis," *Long Range Planning*, 1982, 15 (2): 54–66.
29. Heinz Weihrich, "Strategic Career Management—A Missing Link in Management by Objectives," *Human Resource Management* (Summer, Fall, 1982), pp. 58-56.
30. Steve Hammm, "The Trouble with India," op. cit.; "India on Fire," *The Economist*, February 3, 2007, pp. 69–71; Robyn Meredith, *The Elephant and the Dragon* (New York: W.W. Norton & Company, 2008); HDNet World Report, op. cit.
31. Ibid. See also Thomas L. Friedman, *The World is Flat* (New York: Picador and Thomas L. Friedman, 2007).
32. India, http://en.wikipedia.org/wiki/India, accessed December 10, 2009.

33. Jonathan Ablett, Addarsh Baija and others "The 'Bird of Gold': The Rise of India's Consumer Market, *McKinsey*, May 2007.
34. Ganapati Mudur, "Hospitals in India woo foreign patients", *British Medical Journal* June 2004, 328: 1338.
35. Paul Maidment, "India's 40 Biggest Companies," *Forbes*, August 2, 2006.
36. HDNet World Report, op. cit.
37. Steve Hamm, op. cit. p. 50.
38. For a discussion of the Germany apprenticeship system see Heinz Weihrich, Kai-Uwe Seidenfuss, and Volker Goebel, "Managing Vocational Training as a Joint Venture—Can the German Approach of Cooperative Education Serve as a Model for the United States?" *European Business Review*, 1996 at www.usfca.edu/fac-staff/weihrichh, accessed January 2, 2016.
39. Einhorn in Hong Kong, "Hanging Tough in Asia," *Business Week*, September 15, 2008, p.66.
40. See, for example, Heinz Weihrich, "Decision Making for Gaining a Competitive Advantage for the Nation with the TOWS Matrix—An Alternative to Porter's Model—Illustrated by the People's Republic of China," in *Decision Sciences Institute 5th International Conference Proceedings*, Athens, July, 1999.
41. The United States Small Business Administration (www.SBA.gov) provides advice on writing a business plan as well as links to sample business plans.
42. Knowledge of Silicon Valley standards of business planning comes from years of extensive interaction and collaboration with dozens of Silicon Valley venture capitalists and entrepreneurs.
43. Please see the *Silicon Valley Venture Capitalist Confidence Index* Quarterly Reports to gain a sense of what VCs are expecting in terms of the high-growth entrepreneurial environment in the coming quarters (*ProQuest* and www.Cannice.net.)
44. An excellent starting point for gathering national and local customer demographic data is www.census.gov, accessed January 2, 2016.
45. Strategic milestones might include estimated dates of the completion of product development, the beginning of sales, the break-even point in terms of sales level and time, expansion plans, etc.
46. A Silicon Valley rule of thumb for entrepreneurs regarding milestones and projections is to "underpromise and overdeliver."
47. See also Philip J. Adelman and Alan M. Marks, *Entrepreneurial Finance*, 4th edition (Pearson Prentice Hall, 2007).
48. See also Richard C. Dorf and Thomas H. Byers, *Technology Ventures: From Idea to Enterprise* (McGraw Hill, 2005).
49. The case is based on a variety of sources, including Heinz Weihrich and Kai-Uwe Seidenfuss, "Reengineering the Global Car Industry: Will the Daimler–Chrysler Merger Create a New World Order?" in *The Automobile Industry in the 21st Century* (Seoul: Seoul National University, June 2, 1998), pp. 45–46; "Daimler-Chrysler: Crunch Time," *The Economist*, September 25, 1999, pp. 73–74; "Merger Brief: The Daimler-Chrysler Emulsion," *The Economist*, July 29, 2000, pp. 67–68; DaimlerChrysler, www.daimlerchrysler.com (not available 2011); www.daimlerchrysler.com/index_e.htm?/news/top/1999/t90924_e.htm; (not available 2011); Micheline Maynard, "Amid the Turmoil, A Rare Success at DaimlerChrysler," *Fortune*, January 22, 2001, pp. 112C–P; Alex Taylor III, "Can the Germans Rescue Chrysler?" *Fortune*, April 30, 2001; David Stipp, "The Coming Hydrogen Economy," *Fortune*, November 12, 2001, pp. 90–100; http://voices.yahoo.com/change-management-analysis-daimler-chrysler-merger-2351208.html, accessed September 17, 2012; David Waller, *Wheels on Fire: The Amazing Inside Story of the DaimlerChrysler Merger* (London: Hodder & Stoughton, 2001); see also "The DaimlerChrysler Merger, *Tuck School of Business at Dartmouth*, No. 1-0071 http://mba.tuck.dartmouth.edu/pdf/2002-1-0071.pdf, accessed September 17, 2012.
50. Micheline Maynard, "Smart Car: Get Smart," *Fortune*, April 30, 2001.
51. "Daimler-Chrysler: Crunch Time," p. 74.
52. Taylor III, "Can the Germans Rescue Chrysler?"

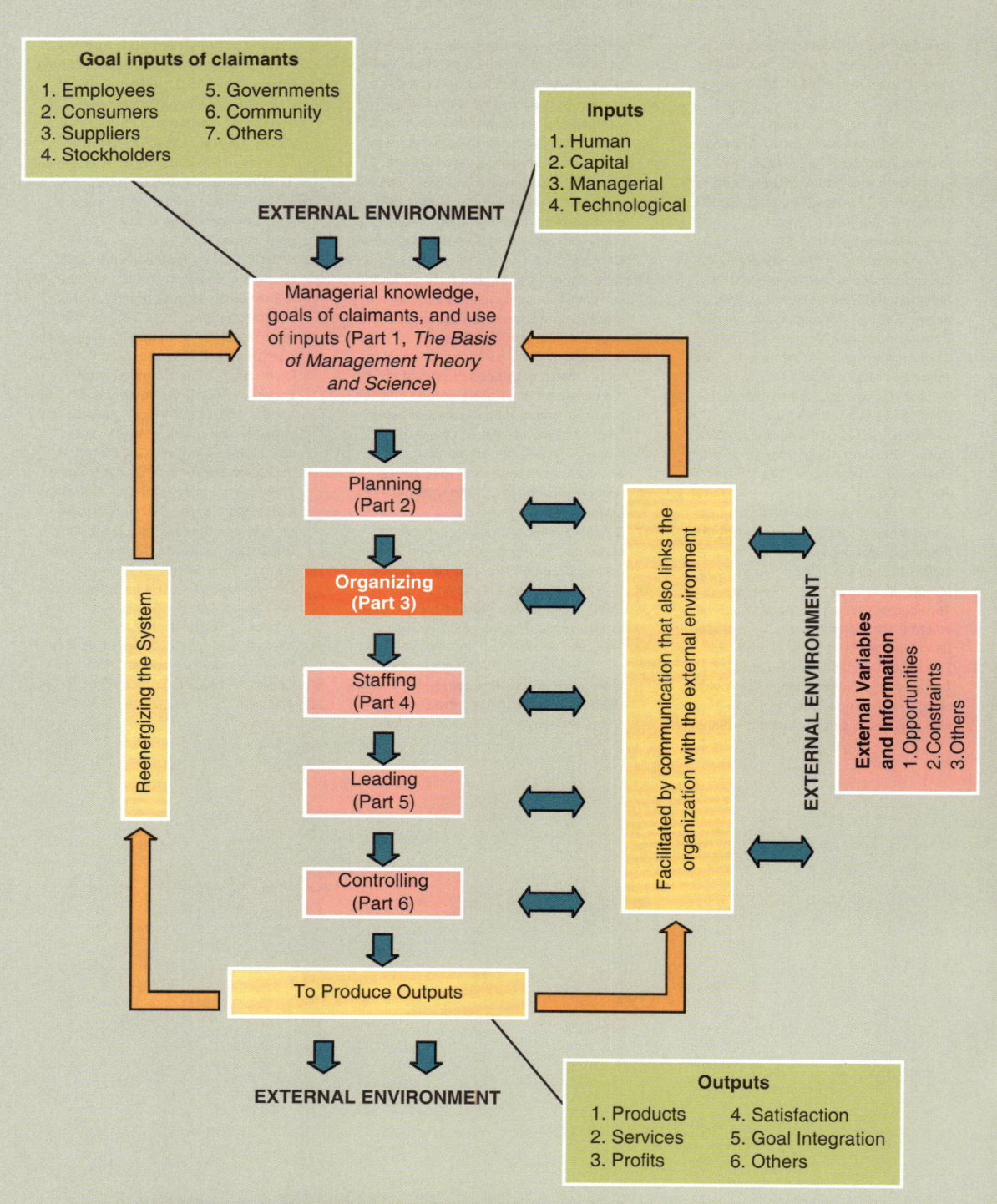

SYSTEMS APPROACH TO MANAGEMENT: ORGANIZING

Goal inputs of claimants
1. Employees
2. Consumers
3. Suppliers
4. Stockholders
5. Governments
6. Community
7. Others

Inputs
1. Human
2. Capital
3. Managerial
4. Technological

EXTERNAL ENVIRONMENT

Managerial knowledge, goals of claimants, and use of inputs (Part 1, *The Basis of Management Theory and Science*)

Planning (Part 2)

Organizing (Part 3)

Staffing (Part 4)

Leading (Part 5)

Controlling (Part 6)

To Produce Outputs

Reenergizing the System

Facilitated by communication that also links the organization with the external environment

EXTERNAL ENVIRONMENT

External Variables and Information
1. Opportunities
2. Constraints
3. Others

EXTERNAL ENVIRONMENT

Outputs
1. Products
2. Services
3. Profits
4. Satisfaction
5. Goal Integration
6. Others

PART 3

Organizing

Chapter 7:   The Nature of Organizing, Entrepreneuring, and Reengineering
Chapter 8:   Organization Structure: Departmentation
Chapter 9:   Line/Staff Authority, Empowerment, and Decentralization
Chapter 10:   Effective Organizing and Organization Culture
Part 3 Closing: Global and Entrepreneurial Organizing

CHAPTER 7

The Nature of Organizing, Entrepreneuring, and Reengineering

Learning Objectives

After studying this chapter, you should be able to:

LO 1   Realize that the purpose of an organization structure is to establish a formal system of roles

LO 2   Understand the meaning of *organizing* and *organization*

LO 3   Draw a distinction between formal and informal organization

LO 4   Show how organization structures and their levels are due to the limitation of the span of management

LO 5   Recognize that the exact number of people a manager can effectively

LO 6   Describe the nature of entrepreneuring and intrapreneuring

LO 7   Understand the key aspects and limitations of reengineering

LO 8   Demonstrate the logic of organizing and its relationship to other managerial functions

LO 9   Appreciate that organizing requires taking situations into account

It is often said that good people can make any organizational structure work. Some people even assert that vagueness in organization is a good thing in that it forces teamwork, since people know that they must cooperate to get anything done. However, there can be no doubt that good people and those who want to cooperate will work together most effectively if they know the parts they are to play in any team operation and the way their roles relate to one another. This is as true in business or government as it is in football or in a symphony orchestra. Designing and maintaining these systems of roles is basically the managerial function of organizing.

For an **organizational role** to exist and be meaningful to people, it must incorporate (1) verifiable objectives, which, as indicated in Part 2, are a major part of planning; (2) a clear idea of the major duties or activities involved; and (3) an understood area of discretion or authority so that the person filling the role knows what he or she can do to accomplish goals. In addition, to make a role work out effectively, provision should be made for supplying needed information and other tools necessary for performance in that role.

It is in this sense that we think of **organizing** as:

- the identification and classification of required activities
- the grouping of activities necessary for attaining objectives
- the assignment of each group to a manager with the authority (delegation) necessary to supervise it
- the provision for coordination horizontally (on the same or a similar organizational level) and vertically (e.g., between corporate headquarters, division, and department) in the organization structure

An organization structure should be designed to clarify who is to do what tasks and who is responsible for what results in order to remove obstacles to performance caused by confusion and uncertainty of assignment and to furnish decision-making and communication networks reflecting and supporting enterprise objectives.

Organization is a word many people use loosely. Some would say it includes all the behaviors of all participants. Others would equate it with the total system of social and cultural relationships. Still others refer to an enterprise, such as the United States Steel Corporation or the Department of Defense, as an organization. But for most practicing managers, the term **organization** implies a formalized intentional structure of roles or positions. In this book, the term is generally used in reference to a formalized structure of roles, although it is sometimes used to denote an enterprise.

> **Organization**
> Formalized intentional structure of roles or positions.

What does *intentional structure of roles* mean? In the first place, as already implied in the definition of the nature and content of organizational roles, people working together must fill certain roles. In the second place, the roles people are asked to fill should be intentionally designed to ensure that required activities are done and that activities fit together so that people can work smoothly, effectively, and efficiently in groups. Certainly, most managers believe they are organizing when they establish such an intentional structure.

FORMAL AND INFORMAL ORGANIZATION

Many writers on management distinguish between formal and informal organization. Both types are found in organizations, as shown in Figure 7.1. Let us look at them in more detail.

Formal Organization

Formal Organization
The intentional structure of roles in a formally organized enterprise.

In this book, generally, **formal organization** means the intentional structure of roles in a formally organized enterprise. Describing an organization as formal, however, does not mean there is anything inherently inflexible or unduly confining about it. If a manager is to organize well, the structure must furnish an environment in which individual performance, both present and future, contributes most effectively to group goals.

A formal organization must be flexible. There should be room for discretion, for beneficial utilization of creative talents, and for recognition of individual likes and capacities in the most formal of organizations. Yet individual effort in a group situation must be channeled toward group and organizational goals.

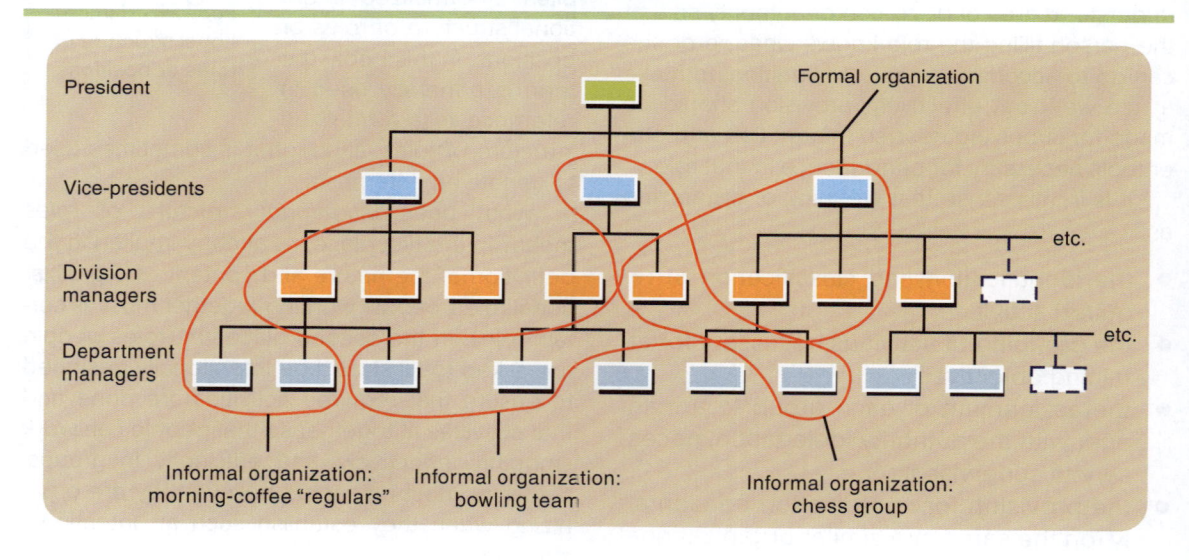

FIGURE 7.1 Formal and informal organizations

President
Vice-presidents
Division managers
Department managers

Formal organization
etc.
etc.

Informal organization: morning-coffee "regulars"
Informal organization: bowling team
Informal organization: chess group

Informal Organization

Chester Barnard, author of the management classic *The Functions of the Executive*, described an informal organization as any joint personal activity without conscious joint purpose, although contributing to joint results.[1] It is much easier to ask for help on an organizational problem from someone you know personally, even if he or she may be in a different department, than from someone you know only as a name on an organization chart. The **informal organization** is a network of interpersonal relationships that arise when people associate with each other. Thus, informal organizations—relationships not appearing on an organization chart—might include the machine shop group, the sixth floor crowd, the Friday evening bowling gang, and the morning coffee "regulars".[2]

> **Informal Organization** Network of interpersonal relationships that arise when people associate with each other.

ORGANIZATIONAL DIVISION: THE DEPARTMENT

One aspect of organizing is the establishment of departments. The word **department** designates a distinct area, division, or branch of an organization over which a manager has authority for the performance of specified activities. A department, as the term is generally used, may be the production division, the sales department, the West Coast branch, the market research section, or the accounts receivable unit. In some enterprises, departmental terminology is loosely applied; in others, especially large ones, a stricter terminology indicates hierarchical relationships. Thus, a vice president may head a division; a director, a department; a manager, a branch; and a chief, a section.

> **Department** Distinct area, division, or branch of an organization over which a manager has authority for the performance of specified activities.

ORGANIZATIONAL LEVELS AND THE SPAN OF MANAGEMENT*

While the purpose of organizing is to make human cooperation effective, the reason for levels of organization is the limitation of the span of management. In other words, organizational levels exist because there is a limit to the number of persons a manager can supervise effectively, though this limit varies depending on situations. The relationships between the span of management and organizational levels are shown in Figure 7.2. A wide span of management is associated with few organizational levels; a narrow span, with many levels.

---

* In much of the literature on management, this is referred to as the *span of control*. Despite the widespread use of this term, in this book *span of management* will be used, since the span is of management and not merely of control, which is only one function of managing.

FIGURE 7.2 Organization structures with narrow and wide spans

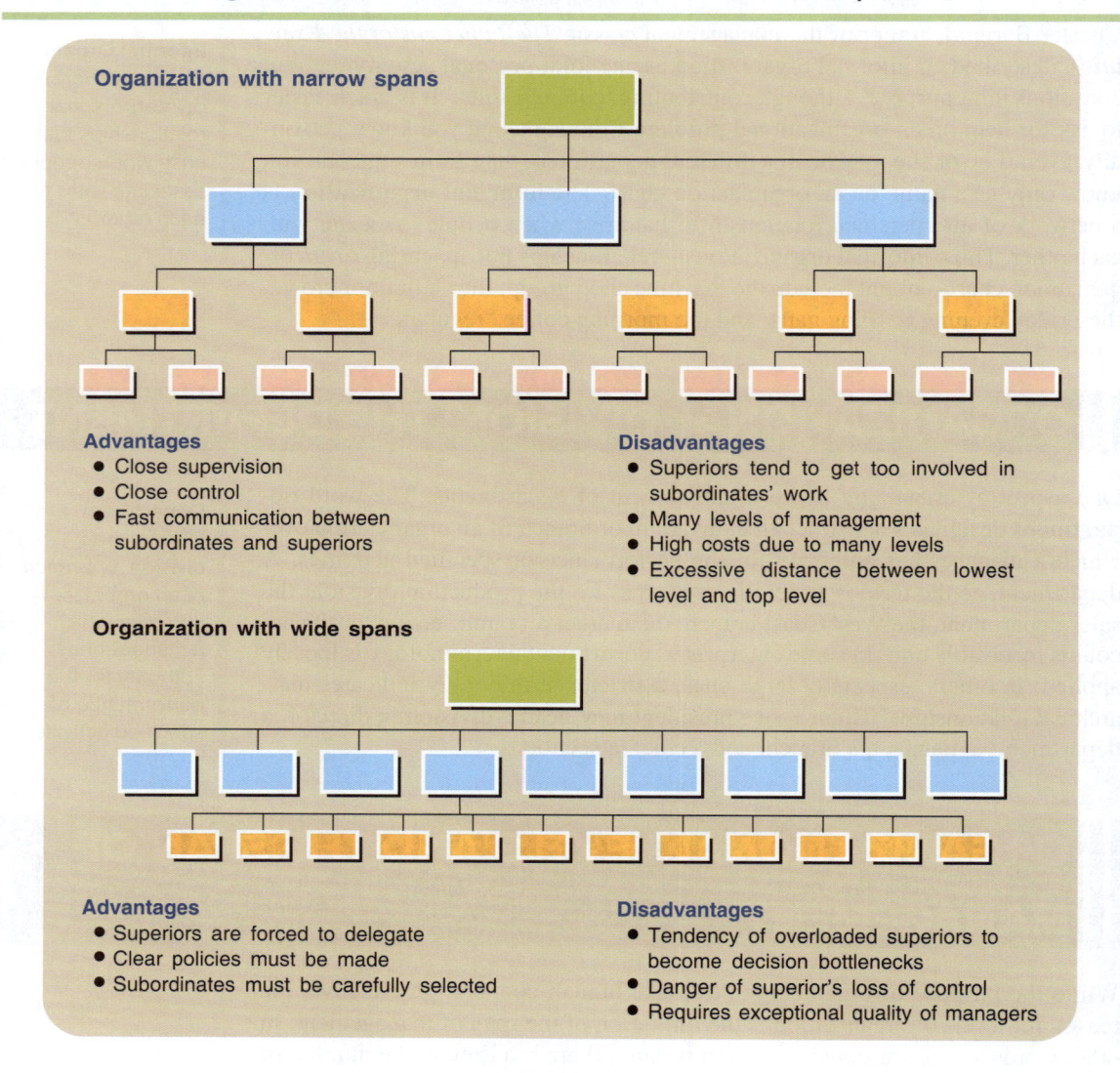

Organization with narrow spans

Advantages
- Close supervision
- Close control
- Fast communication between subordinates and superiors

Disadvantages
- Superiors tend to get too involved in subordinates' work
- Many levels of management
- High costs due to many levels
- Excessive distance between lowest level and top level

Organization with wide spans

Advantages
- Superiors are forced to delegate
- Clear policies must be made
- Subordinates must be carefully selected

Disadvantages
- Tendency of overloaded superiors to become decision bottlenecks
- Danger of superior's loss of control
- Requires exceptional quality of managers

Problems with Organizational Levels

There is a tendency to regard organization and departmentation as ends in themselves and to gauge the effectiveness of organization structures in terms of clarity and completeness of departments and departmental levels. The division of activities into departments and the creation of multiple levels are not completely desirable in themselves.

In the first place, levels are expensive. As they increase, more and more effort and money are devoted to managing because of the additional managers, the staff to assist them, and the necessity of coordinating departmental activities, as well as the cost of facilities for the personnel. Accountants refer to such costs as overhead, burden, or general and administrative, in contrast to so-called direct costs. Real production is accomplished by factory, engineering, or sales employees, who are, or could logically be, accounted for as "direct labor". Levels above the "firing line" are predominantly staffed with managers whose costs it would be desirable to eliminate, if that were possible.

In the second place, departmental levels complicate communication. An enterprise with many levels has greater difficulty communicating objectives, plans, and policies downward through the organization structure than does a firm in which the top manager communicates directly with employees. Omissions and misinterpretations occur as information passes down the line. Levels also complicate communication from the "firing line" to the commanding superiors, which is every bit as important as downward communication. It has been well said that levels are "filters" of information.

Finally, numerous departments and levels complicate planning and control. A plan that may be definite and complete at the top level loses coordination and clarity as it is subdivided at lower levels. Control becomes more difficult as levels and managers are added; at the same time, the complexities of planning and difficulties of communication make this control more important.

The Operational Management Position: A Situational Approach

The classical school approach to the span of management deals with specifying the number of subordinates for an effective span. Operational management theorists have taken the position that there are too many underlying variables in a management situation for us to specify any particular number of subordinates that a manager can effectively supervise. Thus, the **principle of the span of management** states that there is a limit to the number of subordinates a manager can effectively supervise, but the exact number will depend on the impact of underlying factors.

In other words, the dominant current guideline is to look for the causes of limited span in individual situations rather than to assume that there is a widely applicable numerical limit. Examining what consumes the time of managers in their handling of superior—subordinate relationships and ascertaining devices that can be used to reduce these time pressures will be not only a helpful approach for determining the best span in individual cases but also a powerful tool for finding out what can be done to extend the span without destroying effective supervision. There can be no argument that the costs of levels of supervision make it highly desirable for every individual manager to have as many subordinates as can be effectively supervised.

Principle of the span of management There is a limit to the number of subordinates a manager can effectively supervise, but the exact number will depend on the impact of underlying factors.

Factors Determining an Effective Span

The number of subordinates a manager can effectively manage depends on the impact of underlying factors. Apart from such personal capacities as comprehending quickly, getting along with people, and commanding loyalty and respect, the most important determinant is a manager's ability to reduce the time he or she spends with subordinates. This ability naturally varies with managers and their jobs, but several factors materially influence the number and frequency of such contacts and therefore the span of management, as shown in Table 7.1.

TABLE 7.1 Factors influencing the span of management

Narrow spans (a great deal of time spent with subordinates)	Wide spans (very little time spent with subordinates)
Little or no training of subordinates	Thorough training of subordinates
Inadequate or unclear authority delegation	Clear delegation and well-defined tasks
Unclear plans for nonrepetitive operations	Well-defined plans for repetitive operations
Nonverifiable objectives and standards	Verifiable objectives used as standards
Fast changes in external and internal environments	Slow changes in external and internal environments
Use of poor or inappropriate communication techniques, including vague instructions	Use of appropriate techniques, such as proper organization structure and written and oral communication
Ineffective interaction of superior and subordinate	Effective interaction between superior and subordinate
Ineffective meetings	Effective meetings
Greater number of specialties at lower and middle levels	Greater number of specialties at upper levels (top managers concerned with external environment)
Incompetent and untrained manager	Competent and trained manager
Complex task	Simple task
Subordinates' unwillingness to assume responsibility and reasonable risks	Subordinates' willingness to assume responsibility and reasonable risks
Immature subordinates	Mature subordinates

Need for Balance

There can be no doubt that despite the desirability of a flat organization structure, the span of management is limited by real and important restrictions. Managers may have more subordinates than they can manage effectively, even though they delegate authority, conduct training, formulate clear plans and policies, and adopt efficient control and communication techniques. It is equally true that as an enterprise grows, limitations of the span of management force an increase in the number of levels simply because there are more people to supervise.

What is required is more precise balancing, in a given situation, of all pertinent factors. Widening spans and reducing the number of levels may be the answer in some cases; the reverse may be true in others. One must balance all the costs of adopting one course or the other, not only the financial costs, but also costs in morale, personal development, and attainment of enterprise objectives. In a military organization, perhaps, the attainment of objectives quickly and without error would be most important. On the other hand, in a department store operation, the long-run objective of profit may be best served by forcing initiatives and personal development at the lower levels of the organization.

AN ORGANIZATIONAL ENVIRONMENT FOR ENTREPRENEURING AND INTRAPRENEURING[3]

At times, special organizational arrangements need to be made for fostering and utilizing entrepreneurship. Frequently, entrepreneurship is thought to apply to managing small businesses, but many authors now expand the concept to large organizations and to managers carrying out entrepreneurial roles through which they initiate changes to take advantage of opportunities. Although it is common to look for the "entrepreneurial personality" in people, Peter Drucker suggests that this search might not be successful.[4] Instead, one should look for a commitment to systematic innovation, which is a specific activity of entrepreneurs. The essence of entrepreneurship is creation, opportunity orientation, and innovation. Entrepreneurial managers within organizations (e.g. intrapreneurs) identify new market opportunities for their organizations and develop new or improved products to meet those market opportunities.

The Intrapreneur and the Entrepreneur

Gifford Pinchot makes a distinction between the intrapreneur and the entrepreneur.[5] Specifically, an **intrapreneur** is a person who focuses on innovation and creativity and who transforms an idea into a profitable venture by operating *within* the organizational environment. This notion is also sometimes referred to as corporate venturing. In contrast, the **entrepreneur** is a person who creates an organization to take advantage of a market opportunity. Entrepreneurs have the ability to see an opportunity, obtain the necessary capital, labor, and other inputs, and then put together an operation successfully. They are willing to take personal risk of success and failure. In this book, the term *entrepreneur* designates an enterprising person working either within or outside a previously established organization.

Creating an Environment for Entrepreneurship

Because it is a managerial responsibility to create an environment for effective and efficient achievement of group goals, managers must promote opportunities for entrepreneurs to utilize their potential for innovation. Entrepreneurs take personal risks in initiating change, and they expect to be rewarded for it. The taking of reasonable risk will at times result in failure, but this must be tolerated. Finally, entrepreneurs need some degree of freedom to pursue their ideas; this, in turn, requires that sufficient authority be delegated. The personal risks for entrepreneurs who have their own business are of a different kind, and failure may mean bankruptcy.

Innovative persons often have ideas that are contrary to "conventional wisdom." It is quite common that these individuals are not well liked by their colleagues, and their contributions are often not sufficiently appreciated. It is therefore not surprising that many entrepreneurs leave large companies and start their own business. When Steve Wozniak could not get his dream of building a small computer fulfilled at Hewlett-Packard, he left that prestigious firm to form—together with another entrepreneur, Steve Jobs—Apple Computer. Progressive companies, such as 3M, consciously try to develop an organizational environment that promotes entrepreneurship within the company.

Some ways to enhance the environment and, therefore, the likelihood of innovative and entrepreneurial behaviors within an organization include the following:

1. Top management must clearly state that it values innovative and entrepreneurial behavior and create incentives for such activities.
2. Failure in entrepreneurial efforts must be accepted and even celebrated.

---

www.intrapreneur.com

www.entrepreneur.com

Intrapreneur
Person who focuses on innovation and creativity and who transforms an idea into a profitable venture while operating within an established organizational environment.

Entrepreneur
Person who creates an organization to take advantage of market opportunities.

3. A clearly defined and sustainable process of soliciting ideas for new products and services must be promulgated.
4. Time and capital resources must be devoted to allow for creative and innovative activities by employees.
5. Senior management must be evaluated in part by the innovations that come from their departments.
6. Corporate goals should include expectations of new revenues and profits from innovations that are developed.

www.hp.com
www.apple.com
www.3m.com

Only when clear processes and incentives for corporate innovation are in place will the corporate innovators and entrepreneurs provide their optimal contributions to the organization.

Becoming an entrepreneur is an increasing popular career alternative for many individuals for any number of reasons. To account for this increasing interest in entrepreneurship, more and more universities have begun to teach entrepreneurship. In fact, entrepreneurship is a field of learning that is increasingly being offered across university campuses and not just within business schools. Entrepreneurship Programs on university campuses are popular among students as they provide a means by which students can engage with the local entrepreneurial community. Students can test their entrepreneurial acumen in a number of university business plan competitions, where students pitch their business plans to a judging panel of successful entrepreneurs and investors.

Graduate students from around the world can apply to compete at entrepreneurial competitions. These events create international entrepreneurial opportunities for hundreds of students each year. The business community, likewise, values the interaction with universities as campuses provide access to young and energetic minds and emerging technologies. Important requirements for becoming an entrepreneur are self-confidence, willingness to work hard, experience with the product, a good general education, and some financial resources.

ENTREPRENEURIAL PERSPECTIVE

What Is in Your Future?[6]

Harvard professor John P. Kotter in his book *The New Rules: How to Succeed in Today's Post-Corporate World* surveyed the careers of 115 Harvard business graduates of 1974. Some of the findings are surprising. Many of the graduates left big businesses and joined smaller companies. Some who started in large firms switched to smaller firms. They felt that large companies were not open to their creative ideas for change, nor were they receptive to radical changes. In short, traditional big business firms may be stultifying people with new ideas. Kotter suggests that those with unconventional ideas often succeed. In the rapidly changing environment, managers must search for new opportunities, but they must also avoid the hazards.

Small entrepreneurial firms often present more opportunity for advancement, are more open to ambiguous situations, and provide the environment for exerting influence. Although many of the Harvard graduates surveyed preferred smaller firms, they may be connected to large firms as consultants, distributors, suppliers, financiers, or other roles.

What then are some of the implications for managers in carrying out managerial functions? Planning needs to be done in a less bureaucratic manner. A frequent scanning of the environment and a rapid response to changes are essential. Small companies, with a smaller hierarchical structure than large firms, may be more willing to change. With respect to staffing, graduates may want to explore the opportunities in smaller companies. The Harvard graduates who worked for small companies were not only better rewarded financially than those in large firms, but they were also rewarded through job satisfaction.

Innovation and Entrepreneurship[7]

When hearing about innovation and entrepreneurship, one thinks immediately of the success stories of people such as Steve Jobs of Apple Computer and Bill Gates of Microsoft. Entrepreneurs have creative ideas; they use their management skills and resources to meet identifiable needs in the marketplace. If successful, an entrepreneur can become wealthy. Peter Drucker suggests that innovation applies not only to high-tech companies but equally to low-tech, established businesses. Worthwhile innovation is not a matter of sheer luck; it requires systematic and rational work and well organized and managed for results.

What does entrepreneurship imply? It suggests dissatisfaction with how things are and an awareness of a need to do things differently. Innovation comes about because of some of the following situations:

- An unexpected event, failure, or success
- An incongruity between what is assumed and what really is
- A process or task that needs improvement
- Changes in the market or industry structure
- Changes in demographics
- Changes in meaning or in the way things are perceived
- Newly acquired knowledge

INNOVATIVE PERSPECTIVE

Reed Hastings, CEO of NETFLIX—From Peace Corps to Netflix[8]

Reed Hastings, CEO of Netflix, founded the largest online DVD rental company in 1998 with Marc Randolph. After his Marine Corps office training, Hastings joined the Peace Corps teaching mathematics in a high school in Swaziland where he developed his entrepreneurial skills. In 1993, he earned his master's degree in computer science at Stanford University.

Netflix offered DVD rental by mail at a flat rate. The idea for this service derived from his unpleasant experience of paying a big late fee to a movie rental company. Netflix subscription, in contrast, had no due dates and no late fees for the DVDs.

In 2007, Netflix introduced streaming television and movies into computers because Hastings saw a great future for Internet television. Especially, young people under the age of 25 use their laptops, rather than the TV screen. However, in July 2011, a controversy arose when the subscription prices were increased substantially resulting in a customer backlash with many subscription cancellations and reduction in stock price. Hastings reversed his decision and apologized to his customers.

Competitors noting the success of Netflix accelerate their entry into the "streaming" market. For example, when Comcast introduced streaming service at a lower price, Netflix's stock dropped 10%. Other companies, such as Blockbuster, Amazon.com, Verizon, and Hulu are becoming increasingly serious competitors. To counteract the competition, Netflix expanded its library with new titles such as House of Cards and other exclusive titles. Moreover, Netflix attempts to offer Spanish language titles for subscribers in the United States by arranging a deal with Univision Communications.

The innovative management practices at Netflix differed from that of competitors. Salaries were set higher than that of competitors in order to attract the best talents. Moreover, employees could choose annually from receiving their pay in cash or stocks. Those who did not meet expectations received a generous severance package. This way, managers do not feel guilty of firing the employees who do not measure up to the expectation.

www.netflix.com

Innovations based solely on bright ideas may be very risky and at times are not successful. General Electric's ambitious plans for the "factory of the future" may have been a costly mistake. These plans may have been based on unrealistic forecasts and unrealistic expectations for automating industry. The

www.ge.com

concept of the new factory expressed the wish of the chairperson, who wanted to promote entrepreneurship in an organization that was known to be highly structured.

The most successful innovations are often the mundane ones. Take certain Japanese automobile and electronic companies, who make minor innovations (e.g., providing little conveniences that customers like) in their cars or in their electronic equipment. Research has shown that successful large companies listen carefully to the needs of their customers. They establish teams that search for creative alternatives to serve their customers—but within a limiting framework and with clear goals in mind.

GLOBAL PERSPECTIVE

Post-it Note Pads[9]

Even in companies with a policy of promoting entrepreneurship and innovation, the development of new products requires perseverance in transforming an idea into reality.

Art Fry was singing in a church choir. The bookmarks placed in his hymnal fell out after the first church service, making it difficult to find the relevant pages for the second service. The need was clear: an adhesive paper slip that could be easily removed without damaging the page. However, developing an adhesive with the right degree of stickiness was not an easy task. The 3M, where Art Fry worked, was known for products with great adhesion. For Art's purpose, however, a material was needed that not only provides sufficient adhesion, but also allows easy removal. The 3M laboratory did not provide much help in the research and development of such a product, nor did the marketing department think a great deal of this idea. But being an inventor as well as an innovator, Art Fry pursued his goal with great perseverance. The result was the Post-it note pad, which turned out to be a very profitable product for 3M.

www.3M.com

REENGINEERING THE ORGANIZATION[10]

Some time ago, a managerial concept called reengineering entered management literature. It is sometimes called "starting over" because Michael Hammer and James Champy, who popularized the concept, suggested that one asks this question: "If I were recreating this company today (from scratch), knowing what I know now and given current technology, what would it look like?"[11]

More specifically, Hammer and Champy define reengineering as "the *fundamental* rethinking and *radical* redesign of business *processes* to achieve *dramatic* improvements in critical contemporary measures of performance, such as cost, quality, service, and speed."[12] The words in italics are considered key aspects by the authors.

Key Aspects of Reengineering

Let us briefly consider these key aspects. First, hardly anyone would disagree on the need for a *fundamental rethinking* of what the organization is doing and why. One of the authors, while working as a systems analyst, found that systems and procedures were often outdated, inefficient, and completely unnecessary. Seldom did systems users question why the procedures were necessary and the purpose they served. So a fresh look, especially by a "systems outsider", can indeed reveal many inefficiencies. New thinking about management may provide a new perspective at what is being done and why.

The second key aspect in the definition is *radical redesign* of the business processes. In the original publication, the authors suggested that "radical" meant precisely—not a modification, but a reinvention. They also suggested that this is the most important aspect of their approach. Hammer and Champy, in a later paperback edition of the book, admit that they may have been wrong in suggesting that the most important key aspect is radical redesign.[13] Radical redesign often results in radical downsizing with detrimental effects on organizations.

Downsizing or "rightsizing" is not the primary purpose of reengineering, although in many cases it does result in fewer people being needed. Unfortunately, reengineering has primarily been used in a reactive way by managers' intent on reducing costs, without necessarily addressing customer needs and expectations. Another result of radical redesigning is a business system based primarily on the engineering model without due considerations given to the human system. While radical redesign, accompanied by downsizing, may indeed result in short-term cost savings, it may also negatively affect the remaining work force. Teamwork has become increasingly important in the modern organization. But team efforts are built on trust, and trust has to be built over a long period of time. With radical redesign, trust can be destroyed.

The third key term calls for *dramatic results*. Examples are often given to support this key aspect in the definition of reengineering that calls for dramatic improvements. Union Carbide cut $400 million from its fixed costs in 3 years. GTE, the Baby Bell telephone company, developed one-stop shopping; customers, who once had to deal with various departments, can now deal with one person, or they can connect directly with the department providing the specific service sought. But dramatic improvements are moderated by failures.

The fourth key word in the reengineering definition is *processes*. The need for carefully analyzing and questioning business processes is indeed important. However, the process analysis must go beyond operations and must include the analysis and integration of technical systems, human systems, and the total management process including the linkage of the enterprise to the external environment. Engineers may focus on the business process; but to be truly effective, the various subsystems need to be integrated into a total system, as shown in Figure 7.3. The model indicates that the process of transforming the inputs into outputs must go beyond the business process system (the focus of reengineering) to include technological and human aspects, and indeed the total managerial system.

Despite the limitations, reengineering can be a powerful tool; but, it is still only a tool. We suggest integrating reengineering with other systems through a new systems model called management by processes[14] to overcome some of the weaknesses of the narrowly focused reengineering approach.

GLOBAL PERSPECTIVE

Reengineering and Lean Production at Starbucks[15]

Starbucks coffee houses were known of providing a relaxed atmosphere where customers could sip a cup of coffee in a relaxed manner. But, employees costing the company 24% in annual revenue may feel a little less relaxed. The emerging competition and the 2008/2009 recession led to a need for exploring approaches for improving Starbucks's efficiency. The company is, therefore, applying lean product concepts developed by the Japanese in the analysis of Starbucks's operation.

A 10-member lean team is searching for ways to reduce costs and finding ways to improve the drink preparation and exploring other cost savings. The reengineering approach was initially used by analyzing the more complex operations of companies. Similarly, the lean production concepts, first applied by the production of Toyota cars, are now applied in service operations such as Starbucks.

http://www.starbucks.com/

FIGURE 7.3 Management by processes

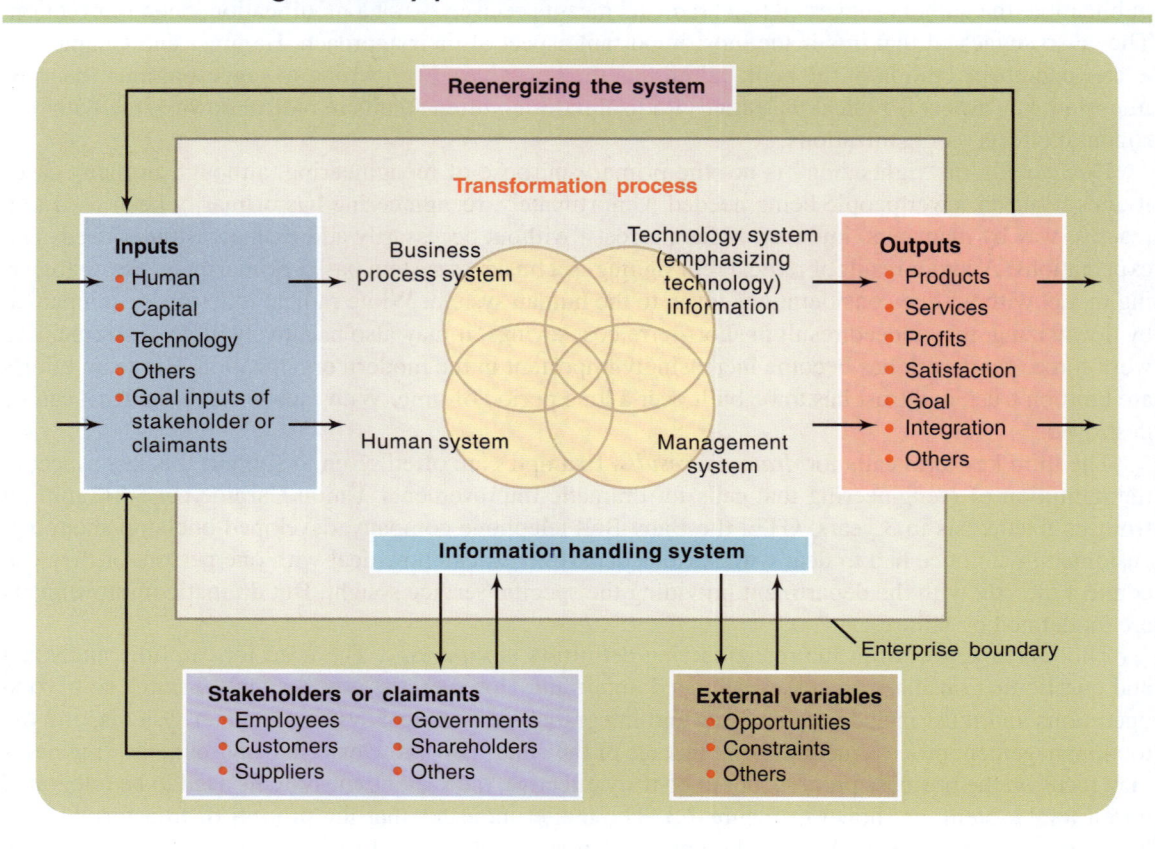

Reenergizing the system

Transformation process

Inputs
- Human
- Capital
- Technology
- Others
- Goal inputs of stakeholder or claimants

- Business process system
- Technology system (emphasizing technology) information
- Human system
- Management system

Outputs
- Products
- Services
- Profits
- Satisfaction
- Goal Integration
- Others

Information handling system

Stakeholders or claimants
- Employees
- Customers
- Suppliers
- Governments
- Shareholders
- Others

External variables
- Opportunities
- Constraints
- Others

Enterprise boundary

THE STRUCTURE AND PROCESS OF ORGANIZING

Looking at organizing as a process requires that several fundamentals be considered. In the first place, the structure must reflect objectives and plans because activities derive from them. In the second place, it must reflect the authority available to an enterprise's management. Authority in a given organization is a socially determined right to exercise discretion; as such, it is subject to change.

In the third place, an organization structure, like any plan, must reflect its environment. Just as the premises of a plan may be economic, technological, political, social, or ethical, so may be those of an organization structure. It must be designed to work, to permit contributions by members of a group, and to help people achieve objectives efficiently in a changing future. In this sense, a workable organization structure can never be static. There is no single organization structure that works best in all kinds of situations: an effective organization structure depends on the situation.

In the fourth place, since the organization is staffed with people, the grouping of activities and the authority relationships of an organization structure must take into account people's limitations and customs. This is not to say that the structure must be designed around individuals instead of around goals and accompanying activities. But an important consideration is the kinds of people who are to staff it.

The Logic of Organizing

There is a fundamental logic to organizing, as shown in Figure 7.4. The organizing process consists of the following six steps, although steps 1 and 2 are actually part of planning:

1. Establishing enterprise objectives
2. Formulating supporting objectives, policies, and plans
3. Identifying, analyzing, and classifying the activities necessary to accomplish these objectives
4. Grouping these activities in light of the human and material resources available and the best way, under the circumstances, of using them
5. Delegating to the head of each group the authority necessary to perform the activities
6. Tying the groups together horizontally and vertically, through authority relationships and information flows

FIGURE 7.4 The organizing process

Feasibility Studies and Feedback

1. Enterprise objectives
2. Supporting objectives, policies, and plans
3. Identification and classification of required activities
4. Grouping of activities in light of resources and situations
5. Delegation of authority
6. Horizontal and vertical coordination of authority and information relationships
7. Staffing
8. Leading
9. Controlling

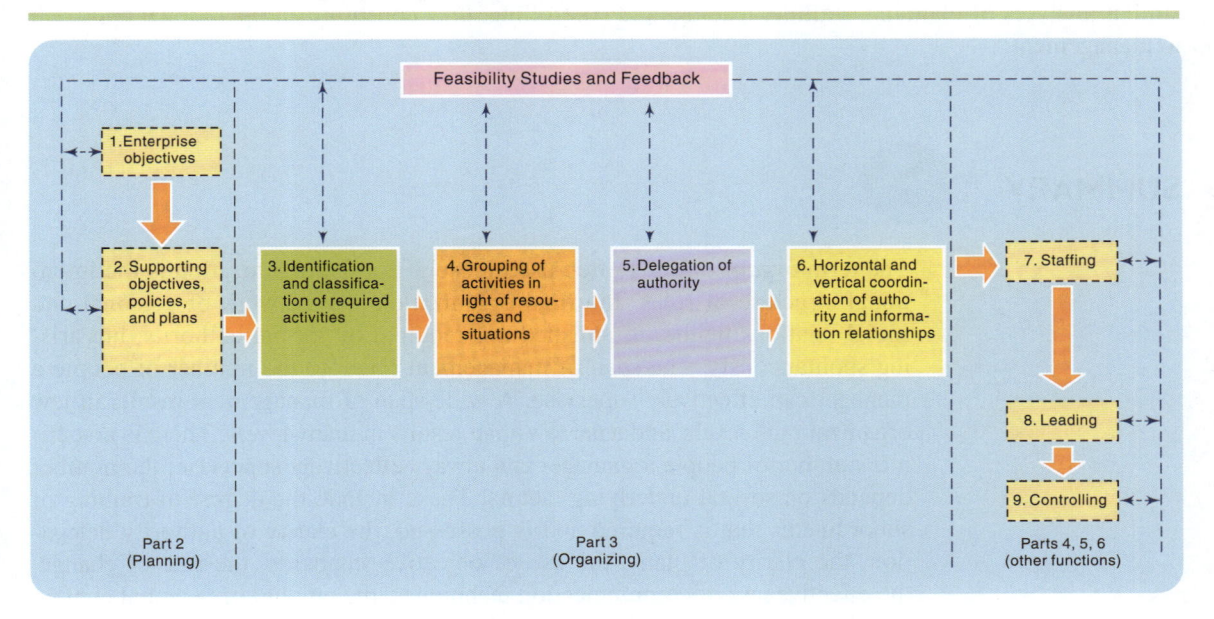

Part 2 (Planning) | Part 3 (Organizing) | Parts 4, 5, 6 (other functions)

Some Misconceptions

Organizing does not imply any extreme occupational specialization, which in many instances makes work uninteresting, tedious, and unduly restrictive. There is nothing in the organization itself that dictates this. To say that tasks should be specific is not to say that they must be limited and mechanical. In any organization, jobs can be defined to allow little or no personal leeway or, conversely, the widest possible discretion. One must not forget that there is no best way to organize and that the application of structural organization theory must take into account the situation.

BASIC QUESTIONS FOR EFFECTIVE ORGANIZING

It is useful to analyze the managerial function of organizing by raising and answering the following questions:

- What determines the span of management and hence the levels of organization? (answered in this chapter)
- What determines the basic framework of departmentation, and what are the strengths and weaknesses of the basic forms? (answered in Chapter 8)
- What kinds of authority relationships exist in organizations? (answered in Chapter 9)
- How should authority be dispersed throughout the organization structure, and what determines the extent of this dispersion? (answered in Chapter 9)
- How should the manager make organization theory work in practice? (answered in Chapter 10)

The answers to these questions form a basis for a theory of organizing. When considered along with similar analyses of planning, staffing, leading, and controlling, they constitute an operational approach to management.

SUMMARY

The term *organization* is often used loosely. Formal organization is the intentional structure of roles. Informal organization is a network of personal and social relations neither established nor required by formal authority, but arising spontaneously. The span of management refers to the number of people a manager can effectively supervise. A wide span of management results in few organizational levels, and a narrow span results in many levels. There is no definite number of people a manager can always effectively supervise; the number depends on several underlying factors. These include the degree of training of subordinates that is required and is possessed, the clarity of authority delegation, the clarity of plans, the use of objective standards, the rate of change, the effectiveness of communication techniques, the amount of personal contact needed, and the level in the organization.

Intrapreneurs and entrepreneurs focus on innovation and creativity. It is the manager's responsibility to create an environment that promotes entrepreneurship.

Reengineering that may require a redesign of business processes has become popular in some companies. The results of these efforts have shown not only positive but also some negative results.

The steps in organizing include formulating objectives and supporting objectives, policies, and plans to achieve the ends (strictly speaking, this is carried out in planning); identifying and classifying activities; grouping these activities; delegating authority; and coordinating authority as well as information relationships.

KEY IDEAS AND CONCEPTS FOR REVIEW

Organizational role
Organizing
Formal organization
Informal organization
Department
Principle of the span of management
Factors determining the span of management
Entrepreneuring and intrapreneuring
Innovation and entrepreneurship
Reengineering, key aspects
Logical steps of organizing
Basic questions for effective organizing

FOR DISCUSSION

1. Since the positions in an organization must be occupied by people, and since an effective organization depends on people, it is often said that the best organization arises when a manager hires good people and lets them do their jobs in their own way. Comment.
2. A formal organization is often conceived of as a communication system. Is it? How?
3. Construct a diagram depicting the formal organization of an enterprise or activity with which you are familiar. How does this organization chart help or hinder the establishment of an environment for performance?
4. Using the same enterprise or activity as in question 3, chart its informal organization. Does it help or hinder the formal organization? Why?
5. When you become a manager, what criteria will you favor to determine your span of management?

EXERCISES/ACTION STEPS

1. Organize a family picnic using the steps suggested in this chapter.
2. Interview a manager in your community and ask him or her how many subordinates he or she has. Are different numbers of subordinates supervised

at the top, the middle, and the bottom of the organizational hierarchy? What really determines the span of management in this organization? Do you think the span is appropriate for the enterprise?
3. Offer to provide a reference to a classmate on LinkedIn.

INNOVATION CASE

Apple's iPad 2: The Tablet to Beat? —Yes, iIt Got Beaten by the New iPad (iPad 3), iPad 4th Generation, iPad Air as well as the iPad Mini and iPad mini with Retina Display[16]

The forerunner to the iPad tablet computer was first introduced by Apple Inc. in 1993 as the Newton Message Pad. Other companies also introduced tablets, often based on the IBM-PC or other architectures. For example, Microsoft introduced the tablet PC in the year 2000. But the tablet computer did not surge in popularity until the introduction of the Apple's iPad in April 2010 and the second generation, the iPad 2, in March 2011. Some industry analysts criticized the functionality of the iPad, contending that as it was neither a computer nor a smart phone; it would not be needed. However, these critics were silenced by the sales success. For example, the first iPad sold 3 million devices during the first 80 days. Furthermore, the initial demand for the iPad 2 resulted in very long lines at the Apple stores amid shortages of the popular device.

Initially, the iPad was developed as a platform especially for audio and visual media such as music, movies, games, and reading books, periodicals, newspapers, and other web content. The iPad shares the operating system with Apple's iPod Touch and the iPhone and can easily integrate with those devices.

The iPad is different from the laptop as it is operated by touch, which means that it has no physical keyboard, but has an on-screen keyboard. Neither does the iPad use a mouse. The various models are connected through Wi-Fi and some even through 3G wireless connection. All the models can be synced with iTunes through a USB cable connected to a personal computer. Therefore, iTunes is used as an interface, connecting not only the iPad, but also the iPod Touch, and the iPhone. Apple's iTunes store allows downloading different kinds of contents, but especially music and videos. iTunes, then, is an important part of Apple's successful strategy for mobile devices.

The original iPad and other Apple products have been a great success. By March 2011:

- Millions of iBooks were downloaded.
- About 15 million iPads were sold in 2010.[17]
- In early 2011, iTunes has more than 350,000 Apps with about 65,000

Apps specifically designed for the iPad. The applications are not only for listening to music and watching videos, but they are used in various ways in schools, hospitals, and businesses —they impact people's lives in many ways.
- Apple retail stores contributed to Apple's success as they provide a place for potential customers eager to learn about Apple's new products with knowledgeable and friendly store associates.
- Apple products are game changers; they are used in everyday's activities.
- Steve Jobs called 2010 the year of the iPad and 2011 the year of iPad 2.
- However, it is with great sorrow that Steve Jobs passed away in 2011.

The second iPad generation, the iPad 2, appears to continue or exceed its success of the first model.

So what are some of the new features of iPad 2? In a nutshell, they are[18]:

- The device is very thin; in fact it is 33% thinner (8.8 mm) than the original iPad and weighs only 1.3 pounds.
- It has rear- and front-facing cameras.
- It is driven by a fast dual-core A5 processor.
- It has a battery life of 10 hours (as the original iPad), but at the same time, the new one is lighter and slimmer.
- The screen is protected by a very slim, elegant, magnetically attached cover in 10 different colors.
- It also has a gyroscope as the one found in Apple's iPhone and iPod Touch.
- The iPad is available in two colors (black and white) and can be connected through AT&T and Verizon to 3G.
- The price is very competitive in America ranging from $499 for the 16GB to $829 for 64GB with 3G connection.
- The iPad 2 was introduced on March 11, 2011, in the United States and shortly afterwards in 26 countries.

Despite its many strong points, the iPad has what many consider weaknesses. For example, the iPad 2 does NOT have a

- Fast 4G connection (but it has 4G in the iPad 3, called the New iPad),
- SD card slot,
- USB connection,
- Flash port,
- Nor does it have the best camera possible (but was greatly improved in the next generation).

There are many applications available for the iPad, and many more are to come. Thousands of application can be used for various business tasks. Colleagues can collaborate on creating, sharing, and analyzing information, or work on a shared business presentation. The iPad is, for example, used in the Ottawa Hospital, replacing the paper medical charts.[19] The doctors can carry the patients' medical records on the iPad in the pocket.

In education, there are Apps for learning about many subjects.[20] In iTunes U, students can listen to lectures, watch videos by distinguished professors from universities such as UC Berkeley, Yale, Stanford, or even presentations from universities abroad such as from the United Kingdom at Oxford and Cambridge, the Beijing Open University, or the University of Tokyo. Books can be downloaded from Apple's iBooks, Amazon's Kindle, or the Gutenberg project. One company, Inkling, has arrangements with McGraw-Hill, the publisher of this book, to link the iPad to textbooks.[21] These are just a few examples of the many applications. In short, iPad can change the way we work.

The Year 2011 may be the "Year of the Tablet Computers."[22] Despite iPad's success, Apple has also many competitors such as

- Motorola's Xoom,
- Samsung's Galaxy Tab 10,
- RIM's BlackBerry PlayBook,
- Dell's Streak 7 Wi-Fi Table,
- LG's OptimusPad,
- HTC's upcoming tables,
- Acer's Iconia Tab A500,
- HP's Touch Pad, or
- Amazon's Kindle that is dedicated for book reading.[23]

The question remains: Is Apple's iPad 2: The Tablet to Beat?

iPad 3 t–The New iPad

Yes, iPad 2 got beaten, not by a competitor, but by Apple's iPad 3 called "New iPad."[24]

In March 2012, the third generation of the iPad was introduced. By many people, this iPad is called iPad 3, but Apple decided the name New iPad. This can be confusing to many people.

The New iPad builds on the features of iPad 2, but also has improvements. The new one has virtually the same dimensions as the previous iPad, except that is it a little thicker than iPad 2 (8.8 mm versus 9.4 mm). The New iPad has the faster A5X chip and has the Retina display with more pixels. The camera now has 5 megapixels and allows for better video recording. Besides Wi-Fi, the new model can be bought with a 4G connection with AT&T or Verizon. But the choice of the provider has to be made at the time of purchase because the systems are different (this was also the case with iPad 2). The battery life of some 10 hours is the same for iPad 2 and the New iPad. The lowest prices 16GB for $499 (in the United States) sells for the same as the introductory price of the iPad 2. However, the iPad 2 is now available at $399, a $100 price drop.

Both generation iPads have now a competitor, the Kindle Fire by Amazon. The Fire is less expensive that the iPads (it costs $200 in the United States in 2012), but it is less powerful. It has a touch screen interface and is connected to a huge library with streaming videos, TV shows, Kindle eBooks, and Amazon music. But the Fire has limitations such as a missing 3G connection and has a smaller Apps selection. Although it has a shiny face with some glare, it is quite good for reading outside. The biggest advantage is probably its lower price than both the iPad 2 as well as the New iPad.

iPad 4th Generation, iPad Air, iPad Mini, and iPad mini with Retina Display

The iPad, the product many predicted would not succeed because it would fall in between the iPhone and the laptop, exceeded the expectations of many.

The iPad 3rd generation was superseded by the 4th generation (introduced in 2012) and the iPad Air introduced in late 2013. The latest one has an A7 chip which performs faster than the previous model and still has a battery capacity for up to 10 hours, has an advanced wireless connection, has an iOS 7 operating system which allows for smarter multitasking, and has a dictionary for many languages. The lowest-priced model is still $499 in America.

In addition, Apple introduced the iPad mini in 2012 followed by the iPad mini with Retina display in 2013. This 2nd-generation iPad mini has a 7.9-inch Retina display, a fast A 7 chip, and the iOS 7 operating system. It also comes free with Pages, the word processing program, Keynote for presentations, iPhoto, iMovie, and Garage Band for playing, recording, mixing, and learning music.

In 2014, the long awaited touch-friendly Microsoft Office for iPad application became available for the 9.7-inch iPad and the 7.9-inch iPad mini. It includes Word, Excel, and PowerPoint applications for both-sized iPads. It is free for viewing the documents, but requires a subscription for editing and creating documents.

Despite the iPad's success, there are some threatening trends coming from Android tablets such as Google Nexus, Samsung Galaxy Note, LG G Pad, Asus Transformer Pad, and others.

Questions:

1. Why has Apple been so successful? What are Apple's strengths?
2. What are the features of the Apple iPad (and especially iPad 2) that makes the tablet so successful?
3. What are the weaknesses of the iPad and what features should be added?
4. If you have an iPad 2, would you buy an iPad 3, called the New iPad, or the 4th-generation iPad, or the iPad Air? Are the improvements worth the price? Why or why not?
5. Why would Apple introduce the 7.9-inch iPad? Would this model take away sales from the 9.7 model?
6. Will the Apple iPad be able to successfully compete with the various (usually less expensive) Android tablets?

INTERNET RESEARCH

Use a search engine and type "post-it-notes" to find out more about the yellow stickers that have been very profitable for 3M.

ENDNOTES

1. Chester I. Barnard, *The Functions of the Executive* (Cambridge, MA: Harvard University Press, 1938, 1964). See also http://www.hup.harvard.edu/catalog/BARFUX.html, accessed September 30, 2006.
2. See also Catherine Truss, "Complexities and Controversies in Linking HRM with Organizational Outcomes," *Journal of Management Studies*, December 2001.
3. See also John Schwartz, "Finding Some Middle Ground in a World Obsessed with the New and Impatient with the Old," *New York Times*, October 9, 2000; Thomas Steward, "Finding the Fault Line Where a New Business Can Grow," *Fortune*, October 30, 2000.
4. Peter F. Drucker, "The Discipline of Innovation," *Harvard Business Review*, May–June 1985, pp. 67–72, rev. November–December 1998, pp. 3–8. See also Drucker, "A Prescription for Entrepreneurial Management," *Industry Week*, April 29, 1985, pp. 33–40; Bruce Rosenstein, "All about Drucker: Drucker Wrote the Book on Innovation," *Information Outlook*, March 2002, p. 34ff; Peter F. Drucker, *Management – Revised Edition* (New York: Harper Collins, 2008).
5. Gifford Pinchot III, *Intrapreneuring* (New York: Harper & Row, 1985); www.pinchot.com, accessed August 1, 2011.
6. John P. Kotter, *The New Rules: How to Succeed in Today's Post-Corporate World* (New York: Free Press, 1995); Keith Hammonds, "Thumbing Their Nose at Corporate America," *Business Week*, March 20, 1995, p. 14; John P. Kotter, *What Leaders Really Do* (Boston: Harvard Business School Press, 1999).
7. Gene Bylinsky, "Heroes of U.S. Manufacturing: Through Innovation and Entrepreneurship, They Have Slashed Costs, Speeded Automation, and Developed Products of Exceptional Quality and Reliability," *Fortune*, March 18, 2002, p. 130; Raphael Amit and Christoph Zott, "Value Creation in E-Business," *Strategic Management Journal*, June–July 2001, p. 493ff.
8. Netflix, http://www.fastcompany.com/most-innovative-companies/2011/profile/netflix.php, accessed March 3, 2012; "Netflix Trying to Counter Competitors, Stock Streaming to $133" http://www.forbes.com/sites/greatspeculations/2012/03/01/netflix-trying-to-counter-competitors-stock-streaming-to-133/, accessed March 3, 2012; Annika Olson and Eddie Yoon, "Netflix Will Rebound Faster than You Think," accessed January 4, 2016.
9. The Post-it story has been reported in various sources, including the videotape. "In Search of Excellence"; Pinchot, *Intrapreneuring*; see also http://www.intrapreneur.com, accessed January 4, 2016; Lester C. Krogh, "Can the Entrepreneurial Spirit Exist within a Large Company?" executive message from 3M delivered at the Conference Board, Conference on Research and Development, New York, April 25, 1984; Brian Dumaine, "Ability to Innovate," *Fortune*, January 29, 1990, pp. 43–46; www.3m.com, accessed August 1, 2011.
10. Michael Hammer and James Champy, *Reengineering the Corporation* (New York: HarperBusiness, 1993). See also Michael C. Gray at www.profitadvisors.com/reengin.shtml, accessed November 10, 2008.
11. Hammer and Champy, *Reengineering the Corporation*, p. 31.
12. Ibid., p. 32.
13. Ibid., p. 219.
14. Heinz Weihrich and Salvatore Belardo, "Beyond Reengineering: Toward a Systems Approach to Management by Processes (MBP)," in Ralph Berndt, ed. *Business Reengineering* (Berlin: Springer, 1997), pp. 19–32; Weihrich and Belardo, "Reengineering Revisited: Toward a Systems Approach to Management by Processes," in *World Management Forum*, Proceedings of the IFSAM Management Conference 1997, Shanghai, organized by the International Federation of Scholarly Association of Management (IFSAM) and the China National Economic Management Association (CNEMA), Special Issue '97, p. 352.
15. Julie Jargon, "Latest Starbucks Buzzword: 'Lean' Japanese Techniques," *The Wall Street Journal*, August 4, 2009; Susan Berfield, "Howard Schultz Versus Howard Schultz," *Business Week*, August 17, 2009.
16. Apple, www.apple.com accessed March 30, 2014. Microsoft http://office.microsoft.com/en-us/mobile?tab=1&ac-q=365&CR_CC=200061904&WT.srch=1&WT.mc_id=PS_Google_Wilbur_office_for_ipad_Text, retrieved April 23, 2014, Tablets, http://www.cnet.com/topics/tablets/best-tablets/android-tablets/ accessed April 24, 2014.
17. "Apple's iPad 2: Competition Ahead," http://www.thestreet.com/story/11034058/1/apples-ipad-2-competition-ahead.html, accessed March 30, 2014.
18. For iPad 2 features, see http://www.huffingtonpost.com/2011/03/02/ipad-2-features-photos_n_830258.html#s247995&title=New_Design,

http://www.apple.com/ipad/?cid=w-wa-us-seg-ipad10, http://events.apple.com.edgesuite.net/1103pijanbdvaaj/event/index.html, accessed March 30, 2012.

19. "1,800 iPads Ordered by Ottawa Hospital," http://www.cbc.ca/news/canada/ottawa/story/2011/04/20/ottawa-ipads-hospital374.html, accessed March 30, 2014 and "See Your Business Like Never Before, http://www.apple.com/ipad/business/ accessed March 30, 2012.

20. "iPad in Education", http://www.apple.com/education/ipad, accessed March 30, 2014.

21. Liz Gannes, "Textbook Makers Fund Inkling for Interactive iPad Editions," http://networkeffect.allthingsd.com/20110323/textbook-makers-fund-inkling-for-interactive-ipad-editions/?mod=ATD_iphone, accessed March 30. 2014.

22. Melissa J. Perenson, "Which Apple is Best for You?" *PC World*, June 2011, pp. 68–74 and "Latest iPad Best Competitors for 2011" at http://techietonic.com/latest-ipad-best-competitors-for-2011-new-list-and-comparison/, accessed June 22, 2011.

23. Various tablets are available at Amazon, http://www.amazon.com/b?ie=UTF8&node=1232597011&ref_=amb_link_37889822_5, accessed March 30, 2014.

24. The New iPad, http://www.apple.com/, accessed March 30, 2012; The New iPad 3: Everything You Should Know, http://www.digitaltrends.com/mobile/the-new-ipad-3-everything-you-should-know/, accessed March 30, 2012; "Kindle Fire vs. iPad: How to Decide," http://www.tuaw.com/2011/11/23/kindle-fire-vs-ipad-how-to-decide/, accessed March 30, 2012.

CHAPTER 8

Organization Structure: Departmentation

Learning Objectives

After studying this chapter, you should be able to:

LO 1 Identify the basic patterns of traditional departmentation and their advantages and disadvantages

LO 2 Analyze matrix organizations

LO 3 Explain strategic business units

LO 4 Examine organization structures for global enterprises

LO 5 Understand the virtual and boundaryless organizations

LO 6 Recognize that there is no single best pattern of departmentation

---

The limitation on the number of subordinates that can be directly managed would restrict the size of enterprises, if it were not for the device of departmentation. Grouping activities and people into departments makes it possible to expand organizations—at least in theory—to an indefinite degree. Departments, however, differ with respect to the basic patterns used to group activities. The nature of these patterns, developed out of logic and practice, and their relative merits will be dealt with in the following sections.

At the outset, it must be emphasized that there is no single best form of departmentation that is applicable to all organizations or to all situations. The pattern used will depend on the given situations and on what managers believe will yield the best results for them in the situation they face. The pattern may also be based on the concepts of reengineering, discussed in the previous chapter.

DEPARTMENTATION BY ENTERPRISE FUNCTION

Grouping activities in accordance with the functions of an enterprise—functional departmentation—embodies what enterprises typically do. Because all enterprises undertake the creation of something useful and desired by others, the basic enterprise functions are production (creating utility or adding utility to a product or service), selling (finding customers, patients, clients, students, or members who will agree to accept the product or service at a price or for a cost), and financing (raising and collecting, safeguarding, and expending the funds of the enterprise). It has been logical to group these activities into such departments as engineering, production, selling or marketing, and finance. Figure 8.1 shows a typical functional grouping for a manufacturing company.

Departmentation by enterprise function Grouping of activities according to the functions of an enterprise, such as production, sales, and financing.

Often, these particular functional designations do not appear in the organization chart. First, there is no generally accepted terminology: a manufacturing enterprise employs the terms production, sales, and finance; a wholesaler is concerned with such activities as buying, selling, and finance; and a railroad is involved with operations, traffic, and finance.

A second reason for the variance of terms is that basic activities often differ in importance: hospitals have no sales departments; churches have no production departments. This does not mean that these activities are not undertaken; rather, these are so unspecialized or narrower in scope that these are combined with other activities.

A third reason for the absence of sales, production, or finance departments in many organization charts is that other methods of departmentation may have been deliberately selected. Those responsible for the enterprise may decide to organize on the basis of product, customer, territory, or marketing channel (the way goods or services reach the user).

Functional departmentation is the most widely used basis for organizing activities and is present in almost every enterprise at some level in the organization structure. The characteristics of the selling, production, and finance functions of enterprises are so widely recognized and thoroughly

FIGURE 8.1 A functional organization grouping (in a manufacturing company)

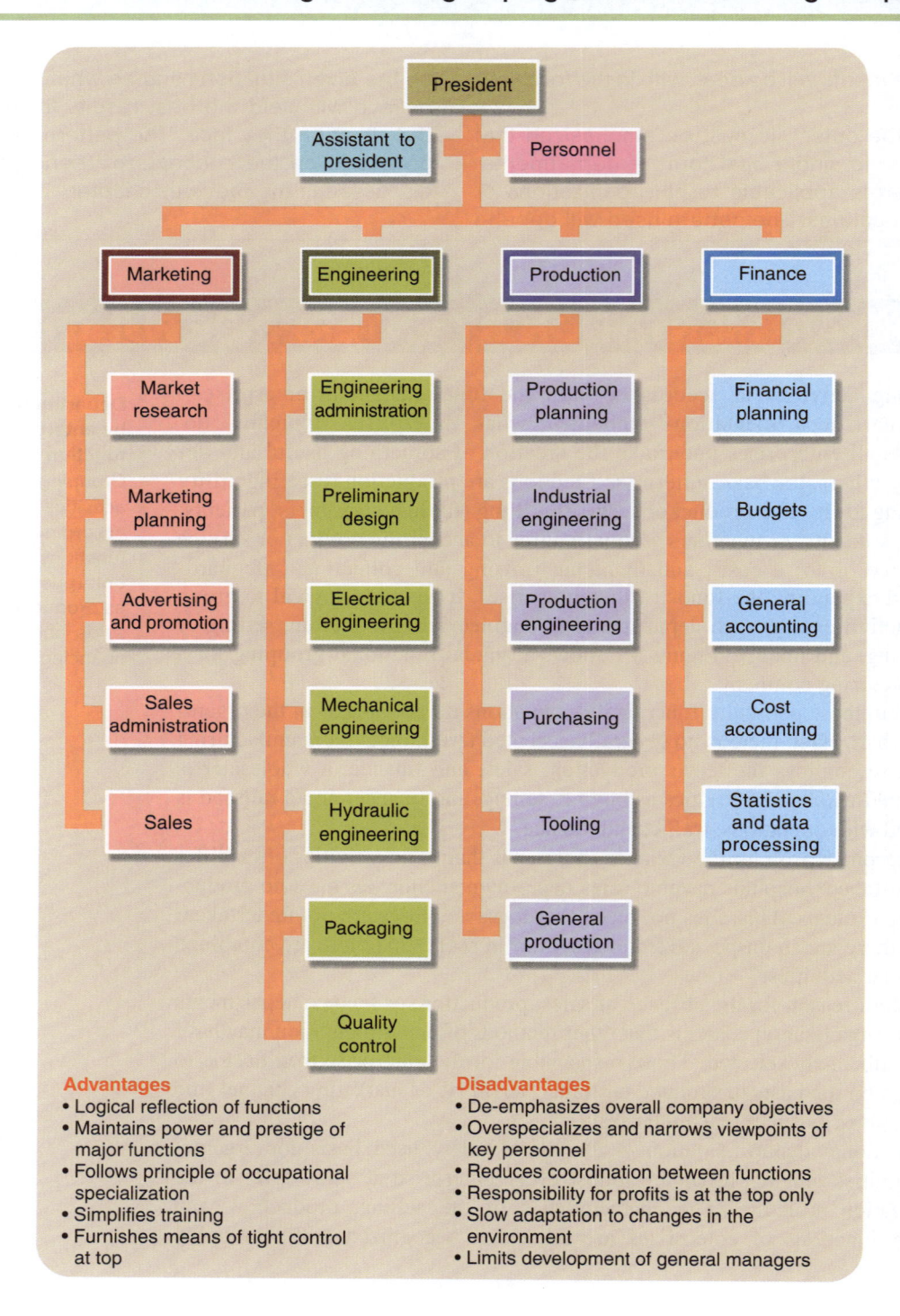

```
                                President
                      Assistant to        Personnel
                      president
        ┌─────────────────┬─────────────────┬─────────────────┐
     Marketing        Engineering        Production         Finance
        │                 │                 │                 │
      Market          Engineering       Production         Financial
      research        administration    planning           planning
        │                 │                 │                 │
     Marketing        Preliminary       Industrial          Budgets
     planning         design            engineering
        │                 │                 │                 │
     Advertising      Electrical        Production         General
     and promotion    engineering       engineering        accounting
        │                 │                 │                 │
      Sales           Mechanical        Purchasing         Cost
     administration   engineering                          accounting
        │                 │                 │                 │
      Sales           Hydraulic         Tooling            Statistics
                      engineering                          and data
                                                           processing
                          │                 │
                       Packaging         General
                                         production
                          │
                       Quality
                       control
```

Advantages
- Logical reflection of functions
- Maintains power and prestige of major functions
- Follows principle of occupational specialization
- Simplifies training
- Furnishes means of tight control at top

Disadvantages
- De-emphasizes overall company objectives
- Overspecializes and narrows viewpoints of key personnel
- Reduces coordination between functions
- Responsibility for profits is at the top only
- Slow adaptation to changes in the environment
- Limits development of general managers

understood that these are the basis not only of departmental organization but also, most often, of departmentation at the top level.

Some firms that are faced with shortening product life cycles and the need for rapid innovation create internal venture capital divisions. These divisions seek out smaller technology firms in which to make an investment. These investments may give new insight or access to newly emerging technologies. These investments may also have the objectives of helping support the development of an ecosystem of other companies that either use or support the primary products of the parent organization.

INNOVATIVE PERSPZECTIVE

Intel Capital

Intel Capital was established in 1991 and has invested over $10 billion in more than a thousand companies around the world. Many of the firms in which it has invested have become public companies in their own right.1 Other firms in which it invests are more of a strategic nature; in that they provide technologies that Intel may eventually use itself or provide elements crucial to an ecosystem in which Intel products may reach more users. Some notable firms that Intel Capital has invested in include: Broadcom Corporation, Inktomi Corporation, Red Hat and Research in Motion and WebMD. Corporate venture capital like independent venture capital firms play a key role in supporting independent entrepreneurship and corporate innovation.

Coordination of activities among departments may be achieved through rules and procedures, various aspects of planning (e.g., goals and budgets), the organizational hierarchy, personal contacts, and sometimes liaison departments. Such a department may be used to handle design or change problems between engineering and manufacturing. The advantages and disadvantages of departmentation by enterprise function are listed in Figure 8.1.

DEPARTMENTATION BY TERRITORY OR GEOGRAPHY

Departmentation based on territory is common in enterprises that operate over wide geographic areas. In this case, it may be important that activities in a given area or territory be grouped and assigned to a manager, for example, as shown in Figure 8.2.

Although territorial departmentation is especially attractive to large-scale firms or other enterprises whose activities are physically or geographically dispersed, a plant that is local in its activities may assign the personnel in its security department on a territorial basis, placing two guards at each of the south and west gates, for example. Department stores assign floorwalkers on this basis, and it is a common way to assign janitors, window washers, and

Departmentation by territory or geography Grouping of activities by area or territory is common in enterprises operating over wide geographic areas.

FIGURE 8.2 A territorial, or geographic, organization grouping (in a manufacturing company)

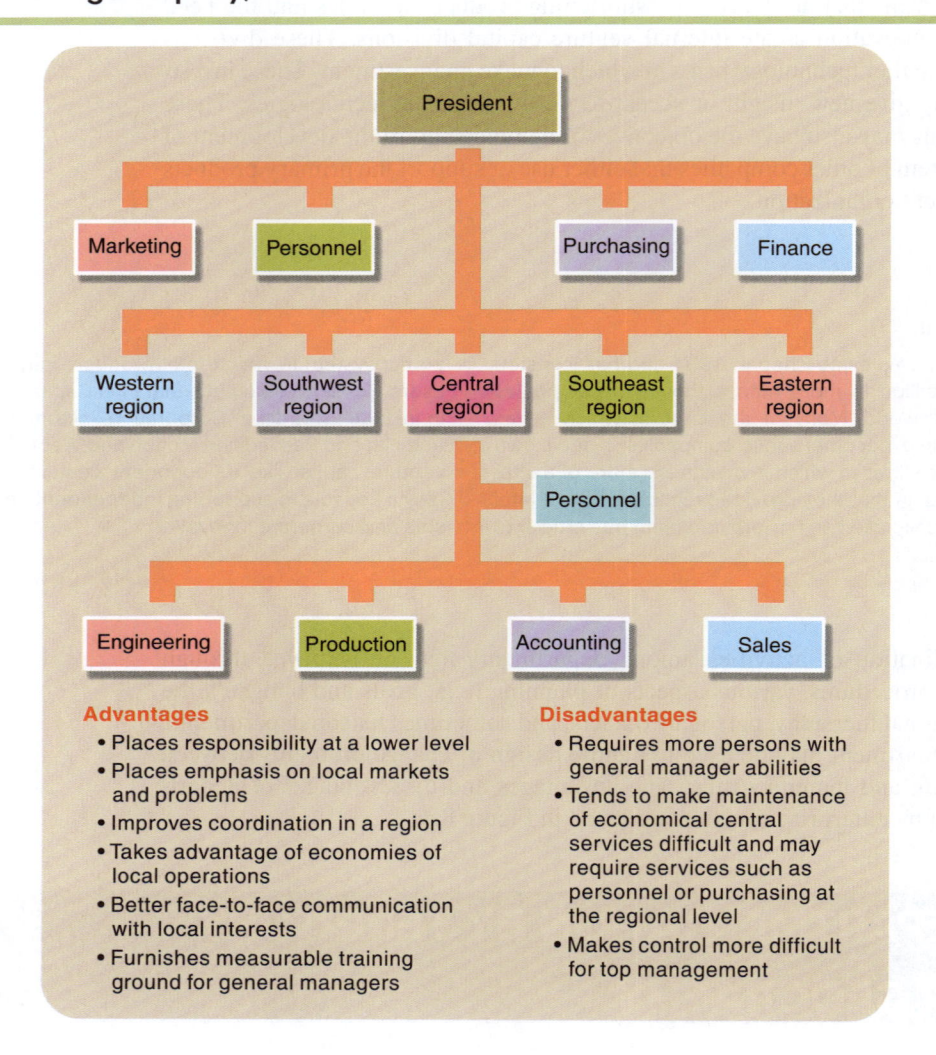

```
                            President
        ┌──────────┬────────────┬──────────┬──────────┐
     Marketing  Personnel    Purchasing  Finance
        ┌──────────┬────────────┬──────────┬──────────┐
     Western    Southwest    Central    Southeast   Eastern
     region     region       region     region      region
                                │
                            Personnel
        ┌──────────┬────────────┬──────────┐
    Engineering  Production  Accounting   Sales
```

Advantages
- Places responsibility at a lower level
- Places emphasis on local markets and problems
- Improves coordination in a region
- Takes advantage of economies of local operations
- Better face-to-face communication with local interests
- Furnishes measurable training ground for general managers

Disadvantages
- Requires more persons with general manager abilities
- Tends to make maintenance of economical central services difficult and may require services such as personnel or purchasing at the regional level
- Makes control more difficult for top management

the like. Business firms resort to this method when similar operations are undertaken in different geographic areas, as in automobile assembling, chain retailing and wholesaling, and oil refining. Many government agencies—the tax department, the central bank, the courts, and the postal service, among others—adopt this basis of organization in their efforts to provide like services simultaneously across the nation. Territorial departmentation is most often used in sales and in production; it is not used in finance, which is usually concentrated at the headquarters.

The advantages and disadvantages of departmentation by territory or geography are shown in Figure 8.2.

DEPARTMENTATION BY CUSTOMER GROUP

Grouping activities so that they reflect a primary interest in customers is common in a variety of enterprises. Customers are the key to the way activities are grouped when each customer group is managed by one department head. The industrial sales department of a wholesaler that also sells to retailers is a case in point. Business owners and managers frequently arrange activities on this basis to cater to the requirements of clearly defined customer groups.

Departmentation by customer group Grouping of activities that reflects a primary interest in customers.

For the structure and the advantages and disadvantages of customer departmentation, see Figure 8.3.

DEPARTMENTATION BY PRODUCT

Grouping activities on the basis of products or product lines have been growing in importance in multiline, large-scale enterprises. It can be seen as an evolutionary process. Typically, companies and other enterprises adopting this form of departmentation were organized by enterprise functions. With the growth of the firm, production managers, sales and service managers, and engineering executives encountered problems of size. The managerial job became complex, and the span of management limited the managers' ability to increase the

FIGURE 8.3 Customer departmentation (in a large bank)

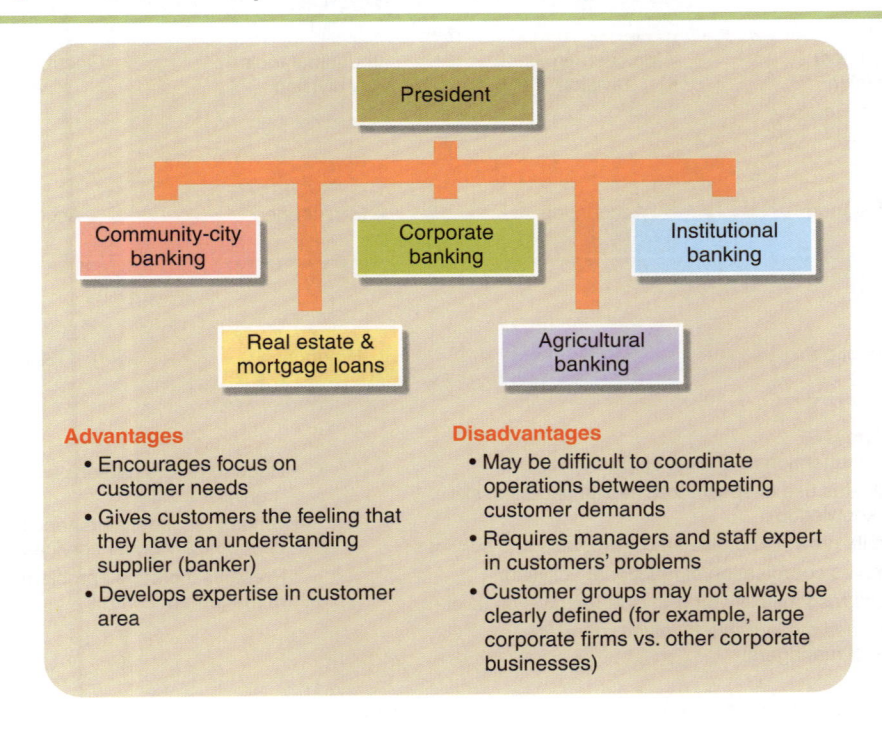

Organization chart:
- President
  - Community-city banking
    - Real estate & mortgage loans
  - Corporate banking
    - Agricultural banking
  - Institutional banking

Advantages
- Encourages focus on customer needs
- Gives customers the feeling that they have an understanding supplier (banker)
- Develops expertise in customer area

Disadvantages
- May be difficult to coordinate operations between competing customer demands
- Requires managers and staff expert in customers' problems
- Customer groups may not always be clearly defined (for example, large corporate firms vs. other corporate businesses)

> **Departmentation by product**
> Grouping of activities according to products or product lines, especially in multiline, large-scale enterprises.

number of immediate subordinate managers. At this point, reorganization on the basis of product division became necessary. This structure permits top management to delegate to a division executive extensive authority over the manufacturing, sales, service, and engineering functions that relate to a given product or product line and to exact a considerable degree of profit responsibility from each of these managers. Figure 8.4 shows an example of a typical product organization grouping for a manufacturing company*, together with the advantages and disadvantages of such departmentation.

FIGURE 8.4 A product organization grouping (in a manufacturing company)

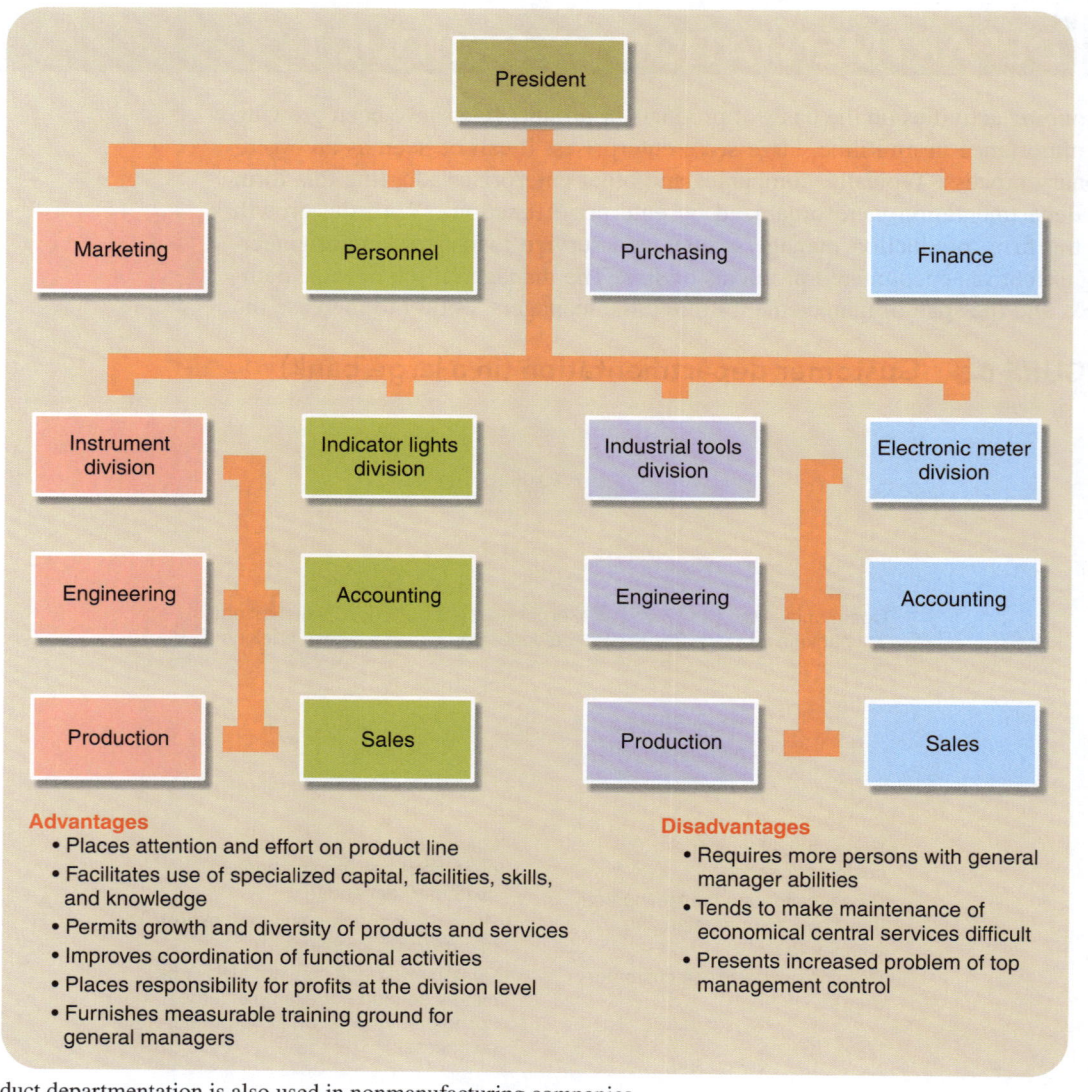

```
                           President
        ┌──────────┬──────────────┬──────────────┐
     Marketing  Personnel      Purchasing      Finance

   Instrument   Indicator lights   Industrial tools   Electronic meter
   division     division           division           division

   Engineering  Accounting         Engineering        Accounting

   Production   Sales              Production         Sales
```

Advantages
- Places attention and effort on product line
- Facilitates use of specialized capital, facilities, skills, and knowledge
- Permits growth and diversity of products and services
- Improves coordination of functional activities
- Places responsibility for profits at the division level
- Furnishes measurable training ground for general managers

Disadvantages
- Requires more persons with general manager abilities
- Tends to make maintenance of economical central services difficult
- Presents increased problem of top management control

*Product departmentation is also used in nonmanufacturing companies.

In considering advantages, it is essential to avoid oversimplification. Product-line managers may be saddled with heavy overhead costs, allocated from the expense of operating the headquarters office, perhaps a central research division, and, frequently, many central service divisions. Product managers understandably resent being charged with costs over which they have no control.

Organizing the Chrysler Fiat Strategy[2]

Within a span of 3 years, Chrysler has had three new owners. First, it was Daimler Chrysler, then it was Cerberus Capital Management, and now it is the Italian Fiat** company headed by CEO Sergio Marchionne. His communication to the Chrysler employees is straightforward, telling them the mediocrity will not be tolerated. In addition, he has little tolerance for organizational hierarchy and tends to emphasize delegation. He sets goals and expects his managers to report about the process of achieving the aims.

Chrysler has been organized into three separate companies: the Dodge, Jeep, and Chrysler lines, each with its own CEOs. Marchionne wants to use Fiat's advantage in small car technologies and Chryslers' strength in SUVs, pickups, and minivans. Fiat gained a good reputation in small, fuel-efficient cars, which is a weakness of Chrysler. The small car innovation included the development of a diesel engine, a technology Fiat had to sell to the German Bosch company because of Fiat's need for cash. Sergio Marchionne's aim is to use the respective strengths of Fiat and Chrysler and his organization skills to succeed in the very competitive global car market.

Three years into the Chrysler Fiat Merger, significant progress has been made. Fiat owns 58.5% of Chrysler and intends to have a complete merger by 2014.[3] The merged company has become an unexpected success—offering new models and demonstrating increasing financial stability since the financial crisis of 2008. Clearly, strong management by Marchionne and his team has made this success possible.

MATRIX ORGANIZATION

Another kind of departmentation is matrix or grid organization or project or product management. However, pure project management need not imply a grid or matrix. The essence of matrix organization normally is the combining of functional and project or product patterns of departmentation in the same organization structure. As shown in Figure 8.5, which depicts matrix organization in an engineering department, there are functional managers in charge of engineering functions and an overlay of project managers responsible for the end product. While this form is common in engineering and in research and development, it has also been widely used, although seldom drawn as a matrix, in product marketing organization.

This kind of organization occurs frequently in construction (e.g., building a bridge), in aerospace (e.g., designing and launching a weather satellite), in marketing (e.g., an advertising campaign for a major new product), in the installation of an electronic data processing system, or in management consulting firms where management experts work together on a project.

Matrix organization
The combining of functional and project or product patterns of departmentation in the same organization structure.

**U.S. taxpayers and unions are technically part-owners.

FIGURE 8.5 Matrix organization (in engineering)

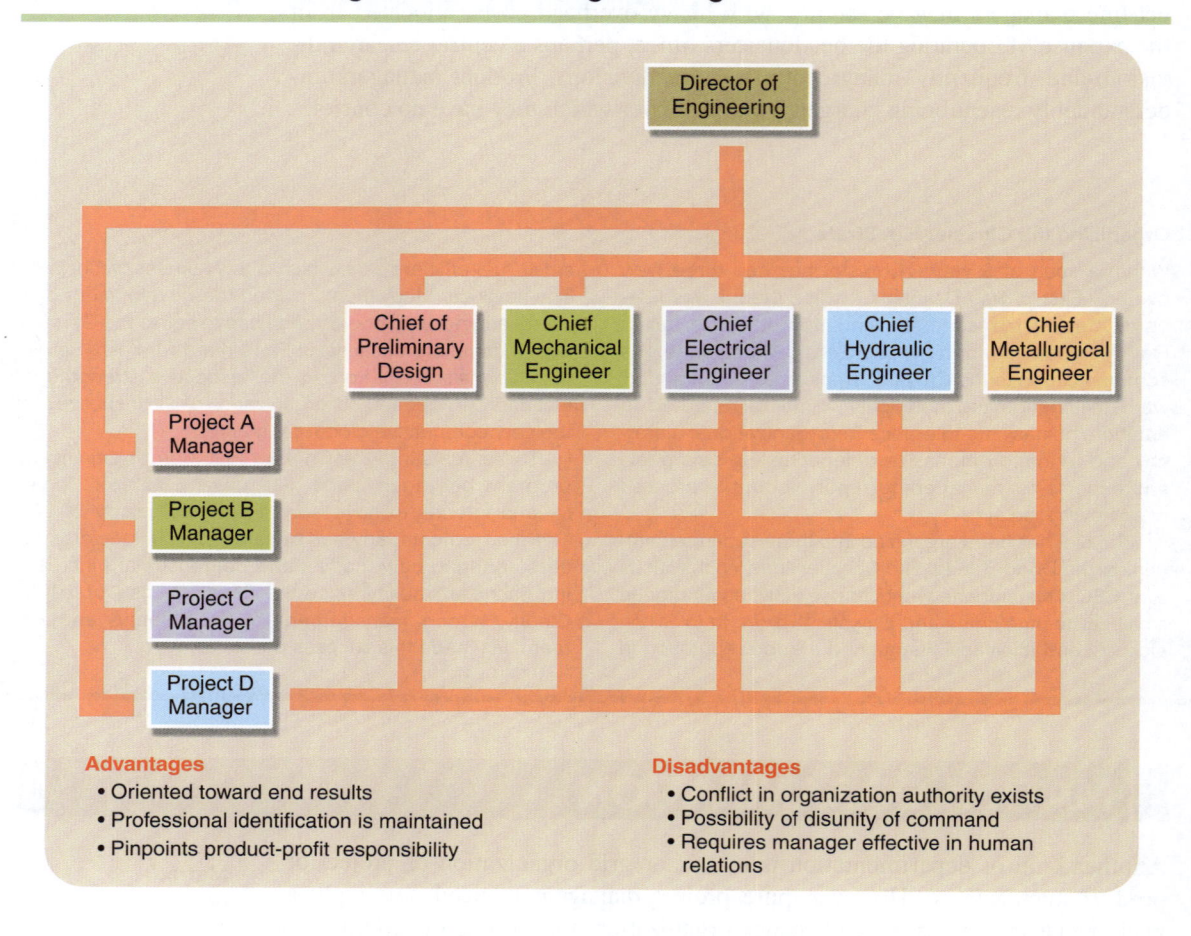

```
                           Director of
                           Engineering
                               │
      ┌────────────┬──────────┼──────────┬────────────┐
   Chief of      Chief      Chief      Chief        Chief
  Preliminary  Mechanical  Electrical  Hydraulic  Metallurgical
    Design     Engineer    Engineer    Engineer     Engineer

Project A
 Manager ───────┼──────────┼──────────┼──────────┼──────────┤

Project B
 Manager ───────┼──────────┼──────────┼──────────┼──────────┤

Project C
 Manager ───────┼──────────┼──────────┼──────────┼──────────┤

Project D
 Manager ───────┼──────────┼──────────┼──────────┼──────────┤
```

Advantages
- Oriented toward end results
- Professional identification is maintained
- Pinpoints product-profit responsibility

Disadvantages
- Conflict in organization authority exists
- Possibility of disunity of command
- Requires manager effective in human relations

Guidelines for Making Matrix Management Effective

Matrix management can be made more effective by following these guidelines:

- Define the objectives of the project or task.
- Clarify the roles, authority, and responsibilities of managers and team members.
- Ensure that influence is based on knowledge and information, rather than on rank.
- Balance the power of functional and project managers.
- Select an experienced manager for the project who can provide leadership.
- Undertake organization and team development.
- Install appropriate cost, time, and quality controls that report deviations from standards in a timely manner.
- Reward project managers and team members fairly.

STRATEGIC BUSINESS UNITS

Companies have been using an organizational device generally referred to as a **strategic business unit** (SBU). SBUs are distinct businesses set up as units in a larger company to ensure that certain products or product lines are promoted and handled as though each were an independent business. One of the earlier users of this organizational device was General Electric, which wanted to ensure that each product or product line of the hundreds offered by the company would receive the same attention as it would if it were developed, produced, and marketed by an independent company. In some cases, companies have also used the device for a major product line. Occidental Chemical Company, for example, used it for such products as phosphates, alkalies, and resins.

To be called an SBU, generally, a business unit must meet specific criteria. For example, it must have its own mission, distinct from the missions of other SBUs; have definable groups of competitors; prepare its own integrative plans, fairly distinct from those of other SBUs; manage its own resources in key areas; and be of an appropriate size, neither too large nor too small. Obviously, in practice, it might be difficult to establish SBUs that meet all these criteria.

For each SBU, a manager (usually a business manager) is appointed with the responsibility of guiding and promoting the product from the research laboratory through product engineering, market research, production, packaging, marketing, and with bottom-line responsibility for its profitability. Thus, an SBU is given its own mission and goals as well as a manager who, with the assistance of full-time or part-time staff (people from other departments assigned to the SBU on a part-time basis), will develop and implement strategic and operating plans for the product. The organization of a typical SBU, such as that for phosphates in Occidental Chemical, is shown in Figure 8.6. Note that reporting to the business manager for phosphates are all the functions that would be found necessary in a separate company.

Obviously, the major benefit of utilizing an SBU organization is to provide assurance that a product will not get "lost" among other products (usually those with larger sales and profits) in a large company. It preserves the attention and energies of a manager and staff whose job is to guide and promote a product or product line. It is thus an organizational technique for preserving the entrepreneurial attention and drive so characteristic of the small company. In fact, it is an excellent means of promoting entrepreneurship, which is likely to be lacking in a large company.

> **Strategic business units** Distinct businesses set up as units in a larger company to ensure that certain products or product lines are promoted and handled as though each were an independent business.
>
> www.ge.com, www.oxychem.com

Potential Problems with SBUs[4]

C. K. Prahalad and Gary Hamel, two professors in strategic management, suggest that companies should invest in their core competencies and watch out for the tyranny of SBUs. The **core competency** is the organization's collective learning, especially the capability to coordinate the different production skills and the integration of these skills into what they call "streams of technology". For example, for car maker Honda, engines are the core products to which

> **Core competency** Collective learning, coordination, and integration of skills to obtain "streams of technology".

FIGURE 8.6 Typical SBU organization (in a large industrial chemical company)

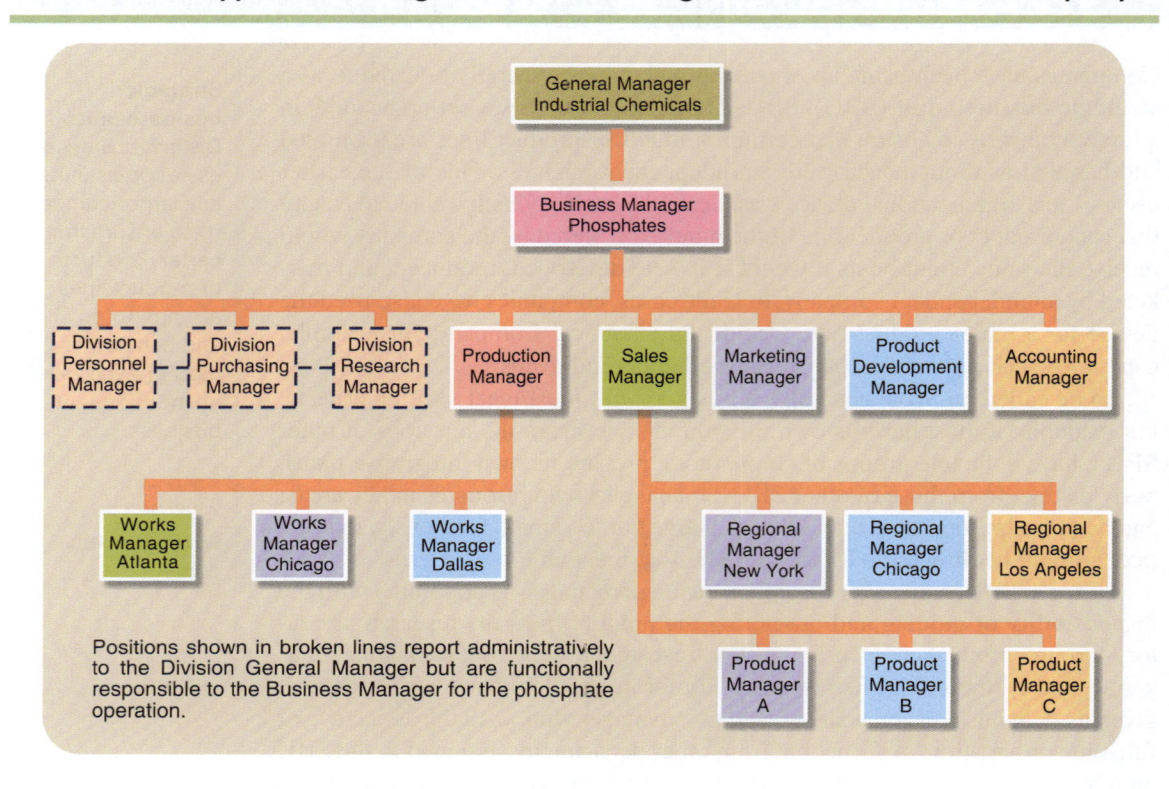

Chart showing: General Manager Industrial Chemicals → Business Manager Phosphates. Reporting to Business Manager Phosphates: Division Personnel Manager (dashed), Division Purchasing Manager (dashed), Division Research Manager (dashed), Production Manager, Sales Manager, Marketing Manager, Product Development Manager, Accounting Manager. Under Production Manager: Works Manager Atlanta, Works Manager Chicago, Works Manager Dallas. Under Sales Manager: Regional Manager New York, Regional Manager Chicago, Regional Manager Los Angeles. Under Marketing Manager/Product Development/Accounting area: Product Manager A, Product Manager B, Product Manager C.

Positions shown in broken lines report administratively to the Division General Manager but are functionally responsible to the Business Manager for the phosphate operation.

design and development skills are directed that result in end products such as cars and motorcycles. If the motorcycle division had received resources for development, it may not share this technology with a car division. The allocation of resources to individual SBUs can result in the underinvestment in core competencies (such as in engines) that benefit the total organization. Also, SBU managers may not be willing to share talented people and may hide them rather than lending them to another SBU.

ORGANIZATION STRUCTURES FOR THE GLOBAL ENVIRONMENT

Organization structures differ greatly for enterprises operating in the global environment. The kind of structure depends on a variety of factors, such as the degree of international orientation and commitment. A company may begin internationalizing its operation by simply creating at its headquarters an international department, headed by an export manager. As the company expands its international operation, foreign subsidiaries and later international divisions may be established in various countries, reporting to a manager in charge of global operation at headquarters or possibly the chief executive officer (CEO). With further growth of the international operations, several countries may be grouped into regions, such as Africa, Asia, Europe, and South America. Furthermore, the European division (and other divisions as well) may then be divided into groups of countries, such as the European Union (EU) countries, non-EU countries, and Eastern European countries.

> **GLOBAL PERSPECTIVE**
>
> **Organizational Challenges at the TATA Conglomerate[5]**
>
> The Tata Group is India's biggest conglomerate with about 100 companies operating in some 40 businesses. How does such a company organize? For one, there is no central strategy at TATA. The company has only a small staff comprised mostly of Tata's sons. Critical for the organization is the Bombay House with a board of senior executives. One of the task is mentoring managers and to promote the philosophy of the importance to social responsibility. Another important aspect of filling the positions in the organization structure is the Management Center in Pune. Success requires not only a good strategy, but also an effective organization structure as well as human resource planning and development.

Companies may also choose other forms of departmentation in addition to the geographic pattern. For example, an oil company may subdivide the functional group for exploration according to regions, such as exploration in Alaska or in the Persian Gulf. Similarly, the functional groups of refining and marketing may be subdivided into various regions. Clearly, petroleum products may be marketed in areas other than those where exploration or production takes place.

THE VIRTUAL ORGANIZATION[6]

The virtual organization is a rather loose concept of a group of independent firms or people that are connected through, usually, information technology. These firms may be suppliers, customers, and even competing companies. The aim of the virtual organization is to gain access to another firm's competence, to gain flexibility, to reduce risks, or to respond rapidly to market needs. Virtual organizations coordinate their activities through the market where each party sells its goods and services.

The virtual organization has advantages and disadvantages. When IBM developed the personal computer in 1981, all major components were acquired from other companies. This enabled IBM to market the product in 15 months. The microprocessor was bought from Intel and the software was developed by Microsoft. The "open" architecture was based on well-known standards, and components could be purchased from many vendors. By using outside parties, IBM had to invest little for its decentralized strategy. Later, however, the open architecture strategy revealed its downside. Other firms could purchase

Virtual Organization
A rather loose concept of a group of independent firms or people that are connected through, usually, information technology.

> www.ibm.com,
> www.microsoft.com

microprocessors directly from Intel and the software operating system from Microsoft.

Virtual organizations may have neither an organization chart nor a centralized office building. The modern library may not be a building with lots of bookshelves. One may never have to visit a library—a database, a computer, a modem, and a password may be all that is necessary to access the library. The Open University in the United Kingdom may be one example of a university without a place. It has a home base with an administrative body but no students. The students are spread all over the world, and so are the professors. They may never meet each other. The technological possibilities are exciting, but how do we manage people we never see? Clearly, many unanswered questions surround the virtual organization.

> www.open.ac.uk

THE BOUNDARYLESS ORGANIZATION

> www.ge.com, accessed February 16, 2006

Jack Welch, former CEO of General Electric, stated his vision for the company as a "boundaryless company". By this he meant an "open, anti-parochial environment, friendly toward the seeking and sharing of new ideas, regardless of their origin"[7]. The purpose of this initiative was to remove barriers between the various departments as well as between domestic and international operations. To reward people for adopting the "integration model," bonuses were awarded to those who not only generated new ideas but also shared them with others.

INNOVATION PERSPECTIVE

Post-it Note Pads[8]

Even in companies with a policy of promoting entrepreneurship and innovation, the development of new products requires perseverance in transforming an idea into reality.

Art Fry was singing in a church choir. The bookmarks placed in his hymnal fell out after the first church service, making it difficult to find the relevant pages for the second service. The need was clear: an adhesive paper slip that could be easily removed without damaging the page. However, developing an adhesive with the right degree of stickiness was not an easy task. The 3M, where Art Fry worked, was known for products with great adhesion. For Art's purpose, however, a material was needed that not only provides sufficient adhesion but also allows easy removal. The 3M laboratory did not provide much help in the research and development of such a product, nor did the marketing department think a great deal of this idea. But being an inventor as well as an innovator, Art Fry pursued his goal with great perseverance. The result was the Post-it note pad, which turned out to be a very profitable product for 3M.

> www.3M.com

CHOOSING THE PATTERN OF DEPARTMENTATION[9]

There is no one best pattern of departmentation that is applicable to all organizations and all situations. Managers must determine what is best by looking at the situation they face: the jobs to be done and the way they should be done, the people involved and their personalities, the technology employed in the department, the users being served, and other internal and external environmental factors in the situation. However, if they know the various departmentation patterns, and the advantages, disadvantages, and dangers of each, practicing managers should be able to design the organization structure most suitable for their particular operations.

The Aim: Achieving Objectives

Departmentation is not an end in itself, but is simply a method of arranging activities to facilitate the accomplishment of objectives. Each method has its advantages and disadvantages. Consequently, the process of selection involves a consideration of the relative advantages of each pattern at each level in the organization structure. In all cases, the central question concerns the type of organizational environment that the manager wishes to design and the situation being faced. The preceding discussion of the alternative methods of departmentation shows that each method yields certain gains and involves certain costs.

LEADERSHIP PERSPECTIVE

Marisa Bellisario Leading Italian ITALTEL[10]

When Marisa Bellisario became director and CEO of ITALTEL, a state-owned telecommunication equipment manufacturer in Italy, the company was in trouble: high losses, large debts, insufficient research and development, and an overstaffed, unionized organization. Ms. Bellisario took some major steps to turn the company around and to improve productivity. Here are examples of the new direction:

- Restructuring the organization into business units, which was accomplished through open communication and cooperation with the union
- Leading the company into electronics, which required retraining of employees
- Developing a program to upgrade low-skilled women in the workforce
- Pushing for intra-European cooperation with companies in France, England, and Germany
- Improving efficiency through innovation in products and manufacturing processes

Leadership such as this has to be analyzed in terms of the characteristics of the leader (technical, human, conceptual, and design skills); relations with the followers, especially the unionized workforce; and the situation, which demanded a strong leader to deal with the crisis. Changing an organization structure to achieve enterprise objectives is difficult, but Marisa Bellisario achieved this in a difficult environment.

www.italtel.it

Mixing Types of Departmentation

Another point to be highlighted concerns the mixing of types of departmentation within a functional area. For example, a wholesale drug firm has grouped the buying and selling activities relating to beverages in one product department, but it has grouped, on the same level, all other selling activities on a territorial basis. A manufacturer of plastic goods has territorialized both the production and the sale of all its products except dinnerware, which is itself a product department. A functional department manager may, in other words, employ two or more bases for grouping activities on the same organizational level. Such practices may be justified on logical grounds. The objective of departmentation is not to build a rigid structure, balanced in terms of levels and characterized by consistency and identical bases, but to group activities in the manner that will best contribute to achieving enterprise objectives. If a variety of bases does this, there is no reason why managers should not take advantage of the alternatives before them.

SUMMARY

The grouping of activities and people into departments makes organizational expansion possible. Departmentation can be done by enterprise function, by territory or geography, and by the kinds of customers served. Other kinds of departmentation are the product organization grouping, matrix or grid organization, project organization, and the SBU. The organization structure for the global environment may vary greatly, ranging from having an export department at the headquarters to regional groupings, with many variations in between. In addition, companies may have also one or more functionally organized groupings within a region. The virtual organization is a loose concept of a group of independent companies or people that are connected often through computer technology.

There is no single best way to organize; the most appropriate pattern depends on various factors in a given situation. These factors include the kind of job to be done, the way the task must be done, the kinds of people involved, the technology, the people served, and other internal and external considerations. At any rate, the selection of a specific departmentation pattern should be done so that organizational and individual objectives can be achieved effectively and efficiently. Accomplishing this goal often requires mixing forms of departmentation.

KEY IDEAS AND CONCEPTS FOR REVIEW

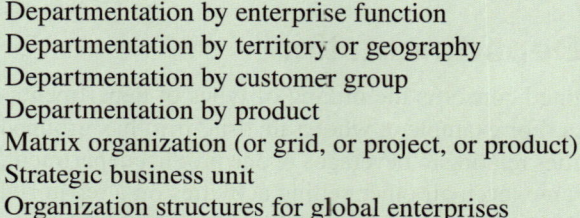

Departmentation by enterprise function
Departmentation by territory or geography
Departmentation by customer group
Departmentation by product
Matrix organization (or grid, or project, or product)
Strategic business unit
Organization structures for global enterprises
Virtual organization
Boundaryless organization

FOR DISCUSSION

1. Some sociologists tell us that organization structuring is a social invention. What do you think they mean? Do they imply that there is a "right" or "wrong" way to organize? What would you suggest as a test of whether an organization structure is "right"?
2. If you were the president of a company that was organized along functional lines and a consultant suggested that you organize along territorial or product lines, what might concern you in following this recommendation?
3. Why do most large department store and supermarket chains organize their stores on a territorial basis and the internal store units by products? Give examples from your own experience.
4. Why do most small companies use functionally organized departments?
5. Why are so many national government agencies organized primarily on a territorial basis?
6. Do you see any reasons why managing by objectives may result in increased use of matrix organization structures?
7. How does this chapter illustrate a situational approach to management?

EXERCISES/ACTION STEPS

1. Divide the class into groups of four or five students (depending on class size). Assign one pattern of departmentation to each group (assign two to each if the class is small). The groups should discuss (a) the nature of the assigned departmentation, (b) companies that use this departmental arrangement, and (c) the advantages and disadvantages of this form of departmentation.
2. Select a company and identify the departmentation pattern (or patterns) it uses. Draw an organization chart for the firm. Why do you think the company selected the type of departmentation it did? Would you recommend it?
3. Select several interest groups to follow on your LinkedIn account.

INTERNET RESEARCH

1. Search the Internet for the term "matrix organization" to find examples of the grid. Also, note the difficulties those companies may have encountered.
2. Search the Internet for the term "SBUs". Look for the ways that various organizations are utilizing such units to enhance their management.

GLOBAL CASE

GM: General Motors, Generous Motors, Government Motors[11]

On June 1, 2009, the once-powerful General Motors (GM) with a distinguished history, applied for protection from its creditors by declaring bankruptcy. Up to 2008, GM was the largest car company in the world.

Under the leadership of Alfred Sloan, the long-time president (1923) and chairman (1937) of GM, established the concept of the modern organization, with brand names such as Chevrolet, Pontiac, Oldsmobile, Buick, and Cadillac with a price structure ranging from the lowest to the highest. While Ford Motor Company focused on low-priced, mass-produced cars (Model T), GM produced cars for "every purse and purpose" according to the needs of its diverse customers.

Problems began during the oil crisis in the early 1970s. GM did not well respond to the customers' demand for fuel-efficient cars which Japanese and German carmakers offered. Rather than responding to the environmental changes, GM focuses on producing profitable pickups and fuel-inefficient SUVs.

GM, called by some "Generous Motors", agreed to generous pay and benefit packages demanded by the United Auto Workers (UAW), the powerful union. The high health and pension costs eventually added about $1,400 to the cost of their cars. In contrast, Japanese carmakers in America were not burdened by similar costs which, in turn, allowed them to price their cars competitively. In addition, foreign auto firms had a reputation for producing reliable cars. Especially, young people were attracted by the offerings of Toyota, Honda, Mercedes, and BMW cars. Many of those cars were produced at lower cost in the United States, but outside the Detroit car capital.

This downward slide resulted in the 2009 bankruptcy with the U.S. government owning 60.8% in stock of the company, the Canadian government receiving 11.7%, the UAW trust 17.5%, and bondholders 10%. With the high percentage of government ownership, some called GM "Government Motors." After the government bailout of billions of dollars, the influence of the government has been clearly felt with the former CEO, Rick Wagoner, being ousted and by being replaced by Fritz Henderson.

With the fall of GM, what will be its future role in the global car industry? Certainly, most car companies suffered greatly which resulted in a loss of hourly and white-collar jobs. However, GM's Chapter 11 proceedings eventually saved many jobs, although it resulted in the sale of the Hummer, Saturn, and Saab brands. Moreover, by 2012, GM largely repaid its loan and posted a record profit for 2011.[12] Still, with a favorable car market situation in 2012, GM's market share of 17.5%, it is a lowest in 90 years. Nevertheless, GM is optimistic because of the new or improved car lineup with cars such as the Chevrolet Cruze, Sonic, and the electric Volt.

Questions:

1. What should GM do now after the bankruptcy?
2. If GM can produce a competitively priced car (less pricey than comparable cars), would you buy one? Why or why not?
3. In your country, which automobile company is the market leader? Is it GM? If not, which company is it? Why?

ENDNOTES

1. http://www.intelcapital.com/, accessed March 20, 2013.
2. David Welch, David Kiley, and Carol Matlack, "Tough Live at Chrysler – The carmaker's new chief is embracing unconventional methods – such as a fostering internal competition—as he races to rev up the company," *Business Week*, August 24 and 31, 2009, pp. 25–28 and Carol Matlack, "The Hidden Edge at Fiat – the automaker has advance fuel-efficiency techniques that may give Chrysler a strategic boost," *Business Week*, August 24 and 31, 2009, p. 28.
3. http://www.intel.com/about/companyinfo/capital/info/earnings.htm (accessed September 30, 2012).
4. C. K. Prahalad and Gary Hamel, "The Core Competence of the Corporation," *Harvard Business Review*, May–June 1990, pp. 79–91; Gary Hamel and C. K. Prahalad, *Competing for the Future* (Boston, MA: Harvard Business School Press, 1994). For a review of the preceding book, see Judith K. Broida, "Competing for the Future: Breakthrough Strategies for Seizing Control of Your Industry and Creating the Markets for Tomorrow," *Academy of Management Executive*, November 1994, pp. 90–91. See also C. K. Prahalad and Venkatram Ramaswamy, "Co-opting Customer Competence," *Harvard Business Review*, January–February 2000, pp. 79–87.
5. Pete Engardio, "The Last Rajah," *Business Week*, August 13, 2007; see also Management Changes, http://uk.biz.yahoo.com/28112007/323/india-s-tata-steel-revamps-organisational-structure-names-group-heads.html, accessed September 20, 2008; see also Tata Consultancy Services Unveils New, Agile Organization Structure to Fuel Next..., http://www.reuters.com/article/pressRelease/idUS162043+12-Feb-2008+PRN20080212, accessed August 1, 2011.
6. Henry W. Chesbrough and David J. Teece, "When Is Virtual Virtuous? Organizing for Innovation," *Harvard Business Review*, January–February 1996, pp. 65–73; Charles Handy, "Trust and the Virtual Organization," *Harvard Business Review*, May–June 1995, pp. 40–50; Larue Tone Hosmer, "Trust: The Connecting Link between Organizational Theory and Philosophical Ethics," *Academy of Management Review*, April 1995, pp. 379–403; Charles Wardell, "The Art of Managing Virtual Teams: Eight Key Lessons," *Harvard Management Update*, November 1998, pp. 3–4, http://www.reuters.com/article/2012/09/27/us-autoshow-paris-fiat-veba-idUSBRE-88Q1H420120927, accessed September 30, 2012.
7. "GE's Two-Decade Transformation: Jack Welch's Leadership," Harvard Business School Case 9-399-150, rev. May 3, 2005.
8. The Post-it story has been reported in various sources, including the videotape. "In Search of Excellence"; Pinchot, *Intrapreneuring*; see also, accessed November 16, 2011; Lester C. Krogh, "Can the Entrepreneurial Spirit Exist within a Large Company?" executive message from 3M delivered at the Conference Board, Conference on Research and Development, New York, April 25, 1984; Brian Dumaine, "Ability to Innovate," *Fortune*, January 29, 1990, pp. 43–46; www.3m.com, accessed November 16, 2011.
9. See also Gregory G. Dess, Abdul M. A. Rasheed, Kevin J. McLaughlin, and Richard L. Priem, "The New Corporate Architecture," *Academy of Management Executive*, August 1995, pp. 7–18; Henry Lucas, *The T-Form Organization* (San Francisco, CA: Jossey-Bass, 1996). See also Lucas's book reviewed in *The Executive*, May 1996.
10. Based on a variety of sources, including personal correspondence.
11. "Detroitosaurus Wreck", *The Economist*, June 6–12, 2009, p. 9; "A Giant Falls" *The Economist*, June 6–12, 2009, pp. 60–62; see various sources at https://www.google.com/#hl=en&cp=10&gs_id=14&xhr=t&q=General+Motors&tok=XkctEveQIzPKbaqV1LfNSw&pf=p&sclient=psy-ab&source=hp&pbx=1&oq=General+Mo&aq=0&aqi=g4&aql=&gs_sm=&gs_upl=&bav=on.2,or.r_gc.r_pw.,cf.osb&fp=e79311b35f21cafc&biw=754&bih=600, accessed August 15, 2012; "President Barack Obama Campaign Video Says Auto Companies 'repaid their loans'," *PolitiFact.com* March 15, 2012; "About GM: GM Sustainability," http://www.gm.com/company/aboutGM/gm_sustainability.html, accessed August 15, 2012; "As Market Takes Off, GM's Share Hits A 90-Year Low," http://www.forbes.com/sites/michelinemaynard/2012/04/10/as-market-takes-off-gms-share-hits-a-90-year-low/, accessed August 15, 2012; "GM, Ford Poised to Move Into Higher Gear," http://online.wsj.com/article/SB10001424052702303933404577502881118602586.html, accessed January 4, 2016; "The First Electric Car That Runs On More Than Electricity", http://www.chevrolet.com/volt-electric-car.html, accessed August 15, 2012 and January 4, 2016.
12. Jerry Hirsch, "Resurgent General Motors Posts Record Profit for 2011," http://articles.latimes.com/2012/feb/16/business/la-fi-mo-general-motors-profits-20120215, accessed December 4, 2016.

CHAPTER 9

Line/Staff Authority, Empowerment, and Decentralization

Learning Objectives

After studying this chapter, you should be able to:

LO 1   Understand the nature of authority, power, and empowerment

LO 2   Distinguish between line, staff, and functional authority

LO 3   Discuss the nature of decentralization, centralization, and delegation of authority

LO 4   Recognize the importance of obtaining balance in the centralization and decentralization of authority

Now that the patterns of departmentation have been discussed, it is time to consider another essential question: What kind of authority is found in an organization structure? The question has to do with the nature of authority relationships—the problem of line and staff. This chapter will also deal with the question of how much authority should be delegated. The answer concerns the decentralization of authority. Without authority—the power to exercise discretion in making decisions—properly placed in managers, departments cannot become smoothly working units harmonized for the accomplishment of enterprise objectives.

Authority relationships, whether vertical or horizontal, are the factors that make organization possible, facilitate departmental activities, and bring coordination to an enterprise.

AUTHORITY AND POWER

Before concentrating on the authority in organization, it will be useful to distinguish between authority and power. **Power**, a much broader concept than authority, is the ability of individuals or groups to induce or influence the beliefs or actions of other persons or groups.[1] **Authority** in organization is the right in a position (and, through it, the right of the person occupying the position) to exercise discretion in making decisions affecting others. It is of course one type of power, but power in an organizational setting.

Although there are many different **bases of power**, the power of primary concern in this book is *legitimate power*.[2] It normally arises from position and derives from our cultural system of rights, obligations, and duties whereby a "position" is accepted by people as being "legitimate". In a privately owned business, authority of position arises primarily from the social institution (a "bundle of rights") of private property. In government, this authority arises basically from the institution of representative government. A traffic officer who gives you a traffic ticket has the power to do so because we have a system of representative government in which we have elected legislators to make laws and provide for their enforcement.

Power may also come from the *expertness* of a person or a group. This is the power of knowledge. Physicians, lawyers, and university professors may have considerable influence on others because they are respected for their specialized knowledge. Power may further exist as *referent power*, that is, influence those people or groups may exercise because people believe in them and their ideas. Thus, Martin Luther King had very little legitimate power but by the force of his personality, his ideas, and his ability to preach, he was able to strongly influence the behavior of many people. Likewise, a movie star or a military hero might possess considerable referent power.

In addition, power arises from the ability of some people to grant rewards. Purchasing agents, with little position power, might be able to exercise considerable influence through their ability to expedite or delay a much-needed spare part. Likewise, university professors have considerable *reward power*: they can grant or withhold high grades. *Coercive power* is still another type. Closely related to reward power and normally arising from legitimate power, it is the power to punish, whether by firing a subordinate or by withholding a merit pay increase.

While organizational authority is the power to exercise discretion in decision making, it almost invariably arises from the power of position, or legitimate power. When people speak of authority in managerial settings, they are usually

Power Ability of individuals or groups to induce or influence the beliefs or actions of other persons or groups.

Authority Right in a position to exercise discretion in making decisions affecting others.

EMPOWERMENT

Empowerment Employees at all levels in the organization are given the power to make decisions without asking their superiors for permission.

In recent years, it has become fashionable to advocate a variety of empowerment approaches. **Empowerment** means that employees, managers, or teams at all levels in the organization are given the power to make decisions without asking their superiors for permission. The notion underlying empowerment is that those closest to the task are best able to make the decision—provided that they have the required competencies. Actually, the notion of empowerment is historically based on suggestion schemes, job enrichment, and worker participation.[3] Moreover, concepts of delegation discussed later in this chapter are also closely related to empowerment.

INNOVATIVE PERSPECTIVE

Empowerment at Zappos[4]

Zappos is an online retailer of shoes and other apparel, and it is renowned for its great customer service. Zappos achieved this reputation in great customer service, at least in part, through its culture that encourages the empowerment of its employees to "deliver happiness" to the customer by whatever means each employee sees fit. That may mean spending an hour on a phone call to make sure the customer is fully satisfied or expediting a return even if the return does not exactly conform to policy. Zappos core values encourage employee empowerment. For example, core value 3 is to "create fun and a little weirdness", and core value 4 is "be adventurous, creative, and open-minded". In this way, empowerment helps lead to innovation in an enterprise and also creates a key competitive advantage at Zappos as it delivers profits along with customer happiness.

Both delegation and empowerment are a matter of degree.[5] They also require that employees and teams accept responsibility for their actions and tasks. Conceptually, this can be illustrated as follows:

- Power should be equal to responsibility (P = R).
- If power is greater than responsibility (P > R), then this could result in autocratic behavior of the superior who is not held accountable for his or her actions.
- If responsibility is greater than power (R > P), then this could result in frustration because the person has not the necessary power to carry out the task for which he or she is responsible.

The increasing interest in empowerment is due in part to the rise in global competitiveness, the need to respond quickly to the demands and expectations of customers, and a better-educated workforce that demands greater autonomy. Empowerment of subordinates means that superiors have to share their authority and power with their subordinates. Thus, an autocratic leadership style, when used as the only way to manage, is often inappropriate for the 21st-century organizations. Most employees want to be involved and want to participate in decisions; this participation creates a sense of belonging and achievement and raises self-esteem.

Effective management requires that empowerment be sincere, based on mutual trust, accompanied by relevant information for the employees to carry out their tasks, and given to competent people.[6] Moreover, employees should be rewarded for exercising their decision authority.

LINE/STAFF CONCEPTS AND FUNCTIONAL AUTHORITY

Line authority gives a superior a line of authority over a subordinate. It exists in all organizations as an uninterrupted scale or series of steps. Hence, the **scalar principle** in organization: the clearer the line of authority from the ultimate management position in an enterprise to every subordinate position, the clearer will be the responsibility for decision making and the more effective will be organizational communication. In many large enterprises, the steps are long and complicated; but even in the smallest, the very fact of organization introduces the scalar principle.

It therefore becomes apparent from the scalar principle that **line authority** is that relationship in which a superior exercises direct supervision over a subordinate—an authority relationship in a direct line or steps.

The nature of **staff relationship** is advisory. The function of people in a pure staff capacity is to investigate, research, and give advice to line managers.

Functional authority is the right delegated to an individual or a department to control specified processes, practices, policies, or other matters relating to activities undertaken by persons in other departments. One can better understand functional authority by thinking of it as a small slice of the authority of a line superior. If the principle of unity of command were followed without exception, authority over these activities would be exercised only by the relevant line superiors. But numerous reasons—including a lack of specialized knowledge, a lack of ability to supervise specified processes, and the danger of diverse interpretations of policies—explain why these managers are occasionally not allowed to exercise this authority. In such cases, line managers are deprived of some authority, which is delegated by their common superior to a staff specialist or to a manager in another department. For example, a company controller is ordinarily given functional authority to prescribe the system of accounting throughout the company, but this specialized authority is really a delegation from the chief executive.

> **Scalar principle** The clearer the line of authority, the clearer will be the responsibility for decision making and the more effective will be organizational communication.
>
> **Line authority** Relationship in which a superior exercises direct supervision over a subordinate.
>
> **Staff relationship** is advisory.
>
> **Functional authority** Right delegated to an individual or a department to control specified processes, practices, policies, or other matters relating to activities undertaken by persons in other departments.

DECENTRALIZATION OF AUTHORITY

The previous section focused on the kinds of authority relationships, such as line, staff, and functional authority. This section emphasizes the dispersion of authority in the organization.

The Nature of Decentralization

Decentralization
Tendency to disperse decision-making authority in an organized structure.

Organizational authority is merely the discretion conferred on people to use their judgment to make decisions and issue instructions. **Decentralization** is the tendency to disperse decision-making authority in an organized structure. It is a fundamental aspect of delegation, to the extent that authority that is delegated is decentralized. How much should authority be concentrated in or dispersed throughout the organization? There could be absolute centralization of authority in one person, but that implies no subordinate managers and, therefore, no structured organization. Some decentralization exists in all organizations. On the other hand, there cannot be absolute decentralization; for if managers delegated all their authority, their status as managers would cease, their position would be eliminated, and there would, again, be no organization. Centralization and decentralization are tendencies, as indicated in Figure 9.1.

FIGURE 9.1 Centralization and decentralization as tendencies

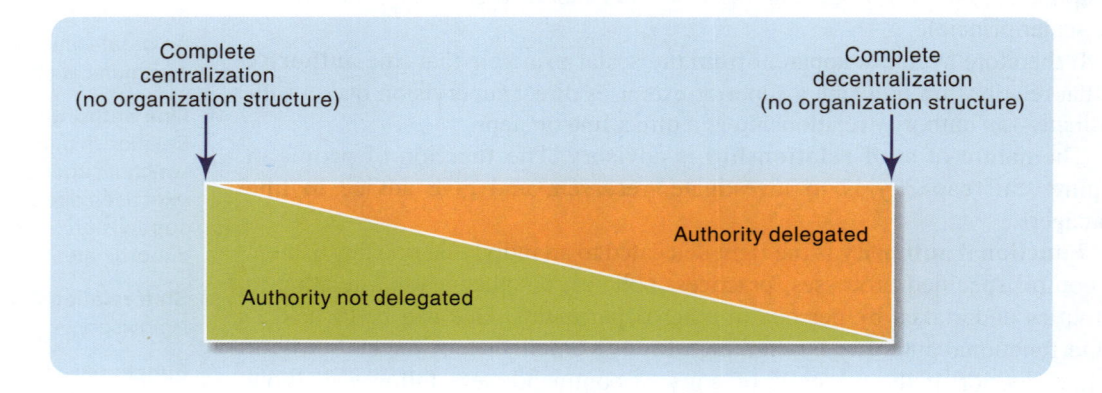

Complete centralization (no organization structure)

Complete decentralization (no organization structure)

Authority delegated

Authority not delegated

Different Kinds of Centralization

The term *centralization* has several meanings:

- *Centralization of performance* pertains to geographic concentration; it characterizes, for example, a company operating in a single location.
- *Departmental centralization* refers to concentration of specialized activities, generally in one department. For example, maintenance for a whole plant may be carried out by a single department.
- *Centralization of management* is the tendency to restrict delegation of decision making. A high degree of authority is held by managers at or near the top of the organizational hierarchy.

Decentralization as a Philosophy and Policy

A Philosophy is a set of principles that guide practical actions. Decentralization implies more than delegation: It reflects a philosophy of organization and management. It requires careful selection of which decisions to push down the organization structure and which to hold near the top, specific policy making to guide the decision making, proper selection and training of people, and adequate controls. A policy of decentralization affects all areas of management and can be looked upon as an essential element of a managerial system. In fact, without it, managers could not use their discretion to handle the ever-changing situations they face.

> **GLOBAL PERSPECTIVE**
>
> **GE's Decentralization Under the Leadership of Jeff Immelt[7]**
>
> General Electric under the leadership of Jack Welch was a different company when compared to Jeff Immelt's GE today. Immelt became GE's CEO in 2001. Fourteen years later, GE has disposed of major businesses and invested heavily in data and analytics. The businesses are not only broad but also very deep. Not only GE has changed, but so has the leadership style of Immelt. Jack Welch's style of command-and-control and centralization would not be appropriate today.
>
> What has changed at GE? When Immelt became CEO, 70 percent of the business was in the United States. Today, GE has some 40 percent market share in the Chinese health care business. In today's volatile environment with relatively slow growth, depth is important. GE has to focus on things based on the core competencies, its strengths, to take advantage of changes in the global and technological environment. This also means that the company has a narrower, but deeper strategy when compared to the past.
>
> In his 14 years as GE's CEO, Immelt has become, as he described it, a better learner and better questioner and more reflective and humble. The controlling approach of Jack Welch would not work today. It has to be more decentralized, more nimble, and more able to adapt to changes in the environment. The evolvement of the GE giant illustrates that the leadership of one person at a particular time may be inappropriate at a different time.
>
> As GE performance has declined in recent years as evidenced by its declining stock price, yet a new leader has been named—John Flannery. Mr. Flannery's charge has been to stabilize GE and rationalize its businesses.

DELEGATION OF AUTHORITY

Authority is delegated when a superior gives a subordinate discretion to make decisions. Clearly, superiors cannot delegate authority they do not have, whether they are board members, presidents, vice presidents, or supervisors.

The **process of delegation** involves (1) determining the results expected from a position, (2) assigning tasks to the position, (3) delegating authority for accomplishing these tasks, and (4) holding the person in that position responsible for the accomplishment of the tasks. In practice, it is impossible to split this process, since expecting a person to accomplish goals without giving him or her the authority to achieve them is impractical, as is delegating authority without knowing the end results to which it will be applied. Moreover, since the superior's responsibility cannot be delegated, a boss must hold subordinates responsible for completing their assignments.

THE ART OF DELEGATION

Most failures in effective delegation occur not because managers do not understand the nature and principles of delegation, but because they are unable or unwilling to apply them. Delegation is, in a way, an elementary act of managing. Yet, studies almost invariably find that poor or inept delegation is one of the causes of managerial failures. Much of the reason lies in personal attitudes toward delegation.

Personal Attitudes toward Delegation

Although charting an organization and outlining managerial goals and duties will help in making delegation decisions, and knowledge of the principles of delegation will furnish a basis for it, certain personal attitudes underlie real delegation.

Receptiveness

An underlying attribute of managers who will delegate authority is a willingness to give other people's ideas a chance. Decision making always involves some discretion, and a subordinate's decision is not likely to be exactly the one a superior would have made. The manager who knows how to delegate must have a minimum of the "NIH (not invented here) factor" and must be able not only to welcome the ideas of others but also to help others come up with ideas and to complement them on their ingenuity.

Willingness to Let Go[8]

A manager who will effectively delegate authority must be willing to release the right to make decisions to subordinates. A major fault of some managers who move up the executive ladder—or of the pioneer who has built a large business from a small beginning of, say, a garage machine shop—is that they want to continue making decisions for the positions they have left. Corporate presidents and vice presidents who insist on confirming every purchase or approving the appointment of every laborer or secretary do not realize that doing so takes their time and attention away from far more important decisions.

If the size or complexity of the organization forces delegation of authority, managers should realize that there is a "law of comparative managerial advantage", somewhat like the law of comparative economic advantage that applies to nations. Well known to economists and logically sound, the law of comparative economic advantage states that a country's wealth will be enhanced, if it exports what it produces most efficiently and imports what it produces least efficiently, even though it could produce the imported goods more cheaply than any other nation. Likewise, managers will enhance their contributions to the firm if they concentrate on tasks that contribute most to the firm's goals and assign to subordinates other tasks, even though they could accomplish them better themselves.

INNOVATIVE PERSPECTIVE

Suitable Technologies produces smart presence systems that allow for a more functional presence of remote individuals for their organizations. Its Beam Smart Presence Device is a remotely moveable device with a screen that simulates the presence of the remote individual. This capability allows employees to provide their insights to organizational locales more effectively that simply calling in or being confined to a static screen. In fact, the Beam Store in Palo Alto is remotely managed by employees using these devices with no other physical presence. Welcome to the art of delegation in the age of robotics! (www.suitabletech.com).

Willingness to Allow Mistakes by Subordinates

Although no responsible manager would sit idly by and let a subordinate make a mistake that might endanger the company or the subordinate's position in the company, continual checking on the subordinate to ensure that no mistakes are ever made will make true delegation impossible. Since everyone makes mistakes, a subordinate must be allowed to make some, and their cost must be considered an investment in personal development.

Serious or repeated mistakes can be largely avoided without nullifying delegation or hindering the development of a subordinate. Patient counseling, asking leading or discerning questions, and carefully explaining the objectives and policies are some of the methods available to the manager who would delegate well. None of these techniques involve discouraging subordinates with intimidating criticism or harping on their shortcomings.

Willingness to Trust Subordinates

Superiors have no alternative to trusting their subordinates, for delegation implies a trustful attitude between them. This trust is sometimes hard to come by. A superior may put off delegation with the thought that subordinates are not yet experienced enough, that they cannot handle people, that they have not yet developed judgment, or that they do not appreciate all the facts bearing on a situation. Sometimes these considerations are true, but then a superior should either train subordinates or else select others who are prepared to assume the responsibility. Too often, however, bosses distrust their subordinates because they do not wish to let go, are threatened by subordinates' successes, do not delegate wisely, or do not know how to set up controls to ensure proper use of the authority.

Willingness to Establish and Use Broad Controls

Since superiors cannot delegate responsibility for performance, they should not delegate authority unless they are willing to find means of getting feedback, that is, of assuring themselves that the authority is being used to support enterprise or departmental goals and plans. Obviously, controls cannot be established and exercised unless goals, policies, and plans are used as basic standards for judging the activities of subordinates. More often than not, reluctance to delegate and to trust subordinates comes from the superior's inadequate planning and understandable fear of loss of control.

Overcoming Weak Delegation

The following practical guide will facilitate successful delegation:

- *Define assignments and delegate authority in light of results expected.* Or, to put it another way, grant sufficient authority to make possible the accomplishment of goal assignments.
- *Select the person in light of the job to be done.* Although the good organizer will approach delegation primarily from the standpoint of the task to be accomplished, in the final analysis staffing as a part of the total system of delegation cannot be ignored.
- *Maintain open lines of communication.* Since the superior does not delegate all authority or abdicate responsibility and therefore managerial independence does not exist, decentralization should not lead to insulation. There should be free flow of information between superior and subordinate, furnishing the subordinate with the information needed to make decisions and to interpret properly the authority delegated. Delegation, then, does depend on situations.
- *Establish proper controls.* Because no manager can relinquish responsibility, delegation should be accompanied by techniques for ensuring that the authority is properly used. But if controls are to enhance delegation, they must be relatively broad and be designed to show deviations from plans, rather than interfering with routine actions of subordinates.
- *Reward effective delegation and successful assumption of authority.* Managers should be ever watchful for means of rewarding both effective delegation and effective assumption of authority. Although many of these rewards will be monetary, the granting of greater discretion and prestige—both in a given position and by promotion to a higher position—is often even more of an incentive.

RECENTRALIZATION OF AUTHORITY[9] AND BALANCE AS THE KEY TO DECENTRALIZATION

Recentralization
Centralization of authority that was once decentralized; normally not a complete reversal of decentralization, as the authority delegated is not wholly withdrawn.

At times, an enterprise can be said to recentralize authority—to centralize authority that was once decentralized. **Recentralization** is normally not a complete reversal of decentralization, as the authority delegation is not wholly withdrawn by the managers who made it. The process is a centralization of authority over a certain type of activity or function, wherever in the organization it may be found. To avoid pitfalls, any program for decentralization of authority must take into consideration the advantages and limitations shown in Table 9.1.

TABLE 9.1 Advantages and limitations of decentralization

Advantages
1. Relieves top management of some burden of decision making and forces upper-level managers to let go.
2. Encourages decision making and assumption of authority and responsibility.
3. Gives managers more freedom and independence in decision making.
4. Promotes establishment and use of broad controls that may increase motivation.
5. Makes comparison of performance of different organizational units possible.
6. Facilitates setting up of profit centers.
7. Helps product diversification.
8. Promotes development of general managers.
9. Aids in adaptation to fast-changing environment.

Limitations
1. Makes it more difficult to have a uniform policy.
2. Increases complexity of coordination of decentralized organizational units.
3. May result in loss of some control by upper-level managers.
4. May be limited by inadequate control techniques.
5. May be constrained by inadequate planning and control systems.
6. Can be limited by the lack of qualified managers.
7. Involves considerable expenses for training managers.
8. May be limited by external forces (national labor unions, governmental controls, tax policies).
9. May not be favored by economies of scale of some operations.

SUMMARY

There are a number of different bases of power. Power can be legitimate, expert, referent, reward, or coercive. Empowerment enables people to make decisions without asking their superiors for permission. Line authority is that relationship in which a superior exercises direct supervision over subordinates. The staff relationship, on the other hand, consists of giving advice and counsel. Functional authority is the right to control selected processes, practices, policies, or other matters in departments other than a person's own. It is a small slice of a line manager's authority and should be used sparingly.

Another important concept is decentralization, which is the tendency to disperse decision-making authority. Centralization, on the other hand, is the concentration of authority. It may refer to geographic concentration, departmental centralization, or the tendency to restrict delegation of decision making. The process of delegation of authority includes determining the results to be achieved, assigning tasks, delegating authority for accomplishing the tasks, and holding people responsible for results.

Failures in effective delegation are often due to personal attitudes. Weak delegation can be overcome by considering the tasks and the goals, maintaining open communication, establishing proper controls, and motivating through appropriate rewards. Previously decentralized authority may be recentralized. Balance is the key to proper decentralization.

KEY IDEAS AND CONCEPTS FOR REVIEW

Power
Authority
Bases of power
Empowerment
Scalar principle
Line
Staff
Functional authority
Decentralization
Three kinds of centralization
Process of delegation
Attitudes toward delegation
Recentralization
Advantages and limitations of decentralization

FOR DISCUSSION

1. What are the kinds of power exercised in your organization or school?
2. Take as examples a number of positions in any kind of enterprise (business, church, government, etc.). Classify each as line or staff.
3. How many cases of functional authority in your organization have you seen? Analyzing a few, do you agree that they could have been avoided? If avoidance had been possible, would you have eliminated them? If they could not have been avoided or if you had not wanted to eliminate them, how would you remove most of the difficulties that might arise?
4. If you were asked to advise a young college graduate who has accepted a staff position as assistant to a factory manager, what suggestions would you make?
5. Why is poor delegation of authority often found to be the most important cause of managerial failure?
6. In many countries, companies often have grown from within and are family owned. In these companies, very little authority is decentralized. What do you think would explain this tendency? What effect does it have?
7. If you were a manager, would you decentralize authority? State several reasons for your answer. How would you make sure that you did not decentralize too much?
8. Should authority be pushed down in an organization as far as it will go? Why or why not?

EXERCISES/ACTION STEPS

1. Interview a line manager and a staff person at a local company. Ask them what they like and dislike about their jobs. Reflect on the interviews and ask yourself whether a line or a staff position is the major aim of your career plan.
2. Interview two line managers about their views on delegation. Do they think that their superiors delegate sufficient authority to them? Also inquire how they feel about delegating authority to their subordinates.
3. Identify a company that you would like to work for and analyze its organizational structure of positions and authority.
4. Be sure to include a professional photograph in your LinkedIn profile.

INTERNET RESEARCH

1. Search the Internet for the term "employee empowerment" and read what others think about the empowerment theory. Also find out what "disempowerment" and "disempowerment" are.
2. Search the Internet using the key words "scalar principle". Find out the details of the principle.

INNOVATION CASE

Amazon.Com—America's Biggest Retailer[10]

Amazon, the largest online retail company in the United States, was founded by Jeff Bezos, the powerful CEO, in 1995. The name Amazon was chosen in reference to the Amazon River, one of the largest rivers in the world. The company started as an online bookstore, but later added CDs, DVDs, software, electronics, apparels, toys, food, and a variety of other products. Besides operating in the United States, the company also has websites in Austria, Canada, China, France, Germany, Italy, Japan, and the United Kingdom. Over the years, Amazon made many acquisitions such as Bookpages.co.uk an online book company, BookSurge a print-on-demand firm, Shophop a retailer of designer clothing and women's accessories, Zappos an online retailer for shoes and apparel. Amazon also has rather interesting partnerships with other companies such as Target, Timex, Lacoste, and many others.

One well-known product is the Kindle which is a wireless e-book reader. But it does much more than for reading books. It allows for downloading newspapers and magazines, blogs, and other media. There are several Kindle products available, ranging from the mainline to the large-screen DX line. The DX is especially suitable for reading textbooks or magazines. Kindle books can be downloaded on a computer. In 2011 Amazon sold more Kindle books than printed books.[11] Using the "Kindle for PC" program allows for purchases using a personal computer or even an iPhone or iPod Touch.

Many of Amazon's sales are derived from third-party sellers, called "Amazon Associates" and third-party sellers. The offices, called fulfillment centers, are located throughout North America, Europe, and Asia. They are often near airports, which enhances speedy delivery.

Amazon has its critics and complaints ranging from patent infringement, price discrimination, antiunion efforts, and libel, to the publication of questionable books. One current issue pertains to the collection of U.S. sales taxes on the sales of its products. The tax is collected in only a few states in the

United States. Brick-and-mortar stores, on the other hand, have to collect sales taxes and they consider the Amazon.com advantage as being anticompetitive.

Late in 2011, Amazon unveiled the Kindle Fire tablet computer which some consider a competition to the iPad. The Kindle price of $199 is substantially lower that the iPad 2 which starts at $499. Therefore the Kindle Fire tablet may be appealing to those consumers looking for a less expensive alternative to the iPad 2. Magazine publishers welcome the Kindle Fire as an alternative to the iPad. Amazon has the advantage of Apple that it not only sells music, videos, books, and other items, but it also sells toys, clothes, appliances, and many other items—an advantage for Amazon.

Amazon is a successes story. The company that had a humble beginning in 1995 has grown to become the biggest online retailer in the United States.

Questions:

1. Why was Amazon successful?
2. Would you buy an item on Amazon.com? Why or why not?
3. Do you prefer reading a book, including a textbook, on the Kindle or do you prefer the printed text? Give your reasons.
4. Do you think that the Kindle Fire tablet computer is a challenge to Apple's iPad? Why or why not?
5. What is the future of Amazon.com?

> European cars such as the Mercedes and the BMW.

ENDNOTES

1. The concept of power has been widely discussed in the literature. See, for example, Loren Gary, "Power: How Its Meaning in Corporate Life Is Changing," *Harvard Management Update*, October 1, 1996, pp. 3–5; Thomas A. Teal, "The Human Side of Management," *Harvard Business Review*, November–December 1996, pp. 4–10; John P. Kotter, "What Effective General Managers Really Do," *Harvard Business Review*, March–April 1999, pp. 3–12.
2. John R. P. French, Jr., and Bertram Raven, "The Bases of Social Power," in Walter E. Natemeyer, ed. *Classics of Organizational Behavior* (Oak Park, IL: Moore Publishing, 1978), pp. 198–210.
3. Tony Eccles, "The Deceptive Allure of Empowerment," in Arthur A. Thompson, Jr., A. J. Strickland III, and Tracy Robertson Kramer, eds. *Readings in Strategic Management*, 5th ed. (Chicago: Irwin, 1995), pp. 496–509. See also Kathleen Kane, "A Framework for Understanding Dysempowerment in Organizations," *Human Resource Management*, November 1999.
4. www.Zappos.com, accessed August 6, 2011.
5. Robert C. Ford and Myron D. Fottler, "Empowerment: A Matter of Degree," *Academy of Management Executive*, August 1995, pp. 21–29; Chris Argyris, "Empowerment: The Emperor's New Clothes," *Harvard Business Review*, May–June 1998, p. 76ff.
6. James W. Dean, Jr., and James R. Evans, *Total Quality: Management, Organization, and Strategy* (Minneapolis/St. Paul, MN: West Publishing, 1994), chap. 8; Alan Randolph, "Real Empowerment? Manage the Boundaries," *Harvard Management Update*, 2000, 5 (7): 10; Michael Schrage, "More Power to Whom?" *Fortune*, July 23, 2001, p. 270; Vera Titunik, "Plenty of Power, Not a Man in Sight," *Fortune*, April 1, 2002, p. 40.
7. GE's Jeff Immelt on Evolving a Corporate Giant, Interview, McKinsey, http://www.mckinsey.com/Insights/Organization/GEs_Jeff_Immelt_on_evolving_a_corporate_giant?cid=ceointerview-eml-alt-mip-mck-oth-1510, accessed October 30, 2015.
8. Robert Waterman, the former senior director at McKinsey and coauthor of the bestseller *In Search of Excellence*, pointed out in an interview that managers hate to give up power. See William C. Bogner, "Robert H. Waterman, Jr., on Being Smart and Lucky,"

Academy of Management Executive, February 2002, pp. 45–50.

9. For a discussion of recentralizing the information systems organization, see Ernest M. von Simson, "The 'Centrally Decentralized' IS Organization," *Harvard Business Review*, July–August 1990, pp. 158–162.

10. "2010 Form 10-K, Amazon.com, Inc." United States Securities and Exchange Commission and http://www.sec.gov/Archives/edgar/data/1018724/000119312511016253/d10k.htm accessed April 24, 2014; "The Institutional Yes," http://hbr.org/2007/10/the-institutional-yes/ar/pr accessed January 4, 2016; "Amazon Now Sells More Kindle Books Than Print Books," http://news.searchofficespace.com/sos-news/amazon-now-sells-more-kindle-books-than-print-books.html, accessed January 4, 2016; William Donckels, *"Amazon's New 'Kindle Fire'" Tablets is the Portal to an Amazon Universe,"* http://technorati.com/technology/gadgets/article/amazons-new-kindle-fire-tablet-is/, accessed April 24, 2014; Dylan Tweney, "Can the Kindle Fire Disrupt the Tablet Market? Not So Fast*," Mobile Beat*, http://venturebeat.com/2011/10/02/kindle-fire-disruption/ accessed January 4, 2016.

11. "Introducing Amazon Kindle," http://phx.corporate-ir.net/phoenix.zhtml?c=176060&p=irol-newsArticle&ID=1079388, accessed January 4, 2016.

CHAPTER 10

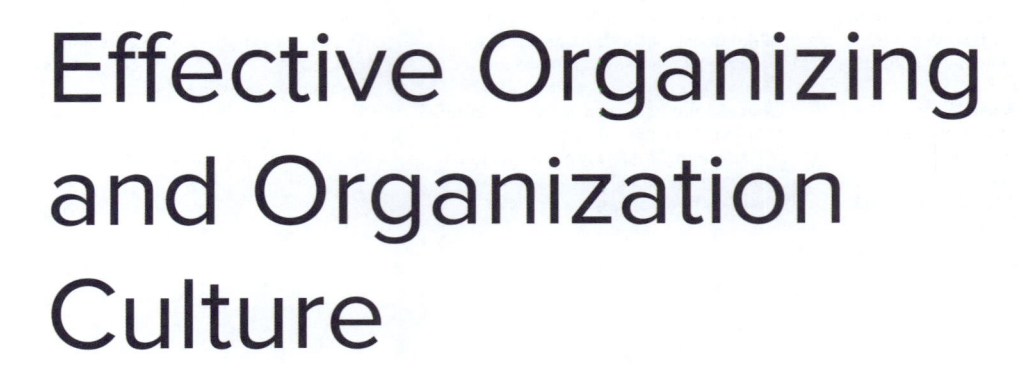

Effective Organizing and Organization Culture

Learning Objectives

After studying this chapter, you should be able to:

LO 1 Avoid mistakes in organizing by planning

LO 2 Show how organizing can be improved by maintaining flexibility and by making staff more effective

LO 3 Avoid conflict by clarifying the organization structure and ensuring an understanding of organizing

LO 4 Promote and develop an appropriate organization culture

Organizing involves developing an intentional structure of roles for effective performance. It requires a network of decision and communication centers for coordinating efforts toward group and enterprise goals. To work, an organization structure must be understood, and principles must be put into practice. As emphasized earlier, in organizing, as elsewhere in managing, there is no one best way. What works will always depend on the specific situation.

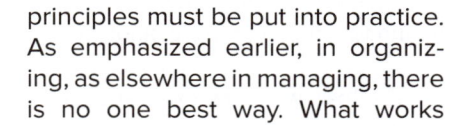

> In organizing, there is no one best way; it depends on the specific situation.

AVOIDING MISTAKES IN ORGANIZING BY PLANNING

As with the other functions of managing, establishment of objectives and orderly planning are necessary for good organization. As Lyndall Urwick said in his classic book *The Elements of Administration*, "Lack of design [in organization] is illogical, cruel, wasteful, and inefficient."[1]

Planning for the Ideal

The search for an ideal organization to reflect enterprise goals under given circumstances is the impetus to planning. The search entails charting the main lines of organization, considering the organizational philosophy of the enterprise managers (e.g., whether authority should be centralized as much as possible or whether enterprise operations should be divided into semi-independent product or territorial divisions), and sketching out consequent authority relationships. The ultimate form established, like all other plans, seldom remains unchanged, and continual remolding of the ideal plan is normally necessary. Nevertheless, an ideal organization plan constitutes a standard; and by comparing the present structure with it, enterprise leaders know what changes should be made when possible.

> Establishment of objectives and orderly planning are necessary for good organization.

An organizer must always be careful not to be blinded by popular notions in organizing because what may work in one enterprise may not work in another. Principles of organizing have general application, but the background of each enterprise's operation and needs must be considered in applying these principles. Organization structure needs to be tailor-made.

Modification for the Human Factor

If the available personnel do not fit into the ideal structure and cannot or should not be pushed aside, the only choice is to modify the structure to fit individual capabilities, attitudes, or limitations. Although this modification may seem like organizing around people, in this case, one is first organizing around the goals to be met and activities to be undertaken and only then making modifications for the human factor. Thus, planning will reduce compromising the necessity for principal whenever changes occur in personnel.

Advantages of Organization Planning

Planning the organization structure helps determine future personnel needs and required training programs. Unless it knows what managerial personnel will be needed and what experience should be demanded, an enterprise cannot intelligently recruit people and train them.

Furthermore, organization planning can disclose weaknesses. Duplication of effort, unclear lines of authority, overlong lines of communication, excessive red tape, and obsolete practices show up best when desirable and actual organization structures are compared.

> **Planning** the organization structure helps determine future personnel needs and required training programs.

AVOIDING ORGANIZATIONAL INFLEXIBILITY

One basic advantage of organization planning is the avoidance of organizational inflexibility. Many enterprises, especially those that have been in operation for many years, become too rigid to meet the first test of effective organization structure: the ability to adapt to a changing environment and meet new contingencies. This resistance to change can cause considerable loss of efficiency in organizations.

Some older companies provide ample evidence of inflexibility: an organization pattern that is no longer suited to the times, a district or regional organization that could be either abolished or enlarged because of improved communication, or a structure that is too highly centralized for an enlarged enterprise requiring decentralization.

Avoiding Inflexibility through Reorganization

Although reorganization is intended to respond to changes in the enterprise environment, there may be other compelling reasons for reorganization. Those related to the business environment include changes in operation caused by the acquisition or sale of major properties, changes in product line or marketing methods, business cycles, competitive influences, new production techniques, labor union policy, government regulatory and fiscal policies, and the current state of knowledge about organizing. New techniques and principles may become applicable, such as developing managers by allowing them to manage decentralized semi-independent units of a company. Or new methods may come into use, such as gaining adequate financial control with a high degree of decentralization.

Moreover, a new chief executive officer (CEO) and new vice presidents and department heads are likely to have some definite organizational ideas of their own. Shifts may be due merely to the desire of new managers to make changes based on ideas formulated through their previous experience or to the fact that their methods of managing and their personalities require a changed organization structure.

Furthermore, reorganization may be caused by demonstrated deficiencies in an existing structure. Some of these arise from organizational weaknesses: excessive spans of management, an excessive number of committees, lack of uniform policy, slow decision-making, failure to accomplish objectives, inability to meet schedules, excessive costs, or a breakdown of financial control. Other deficiencies may stem from inadequacies of managers. Failure due to lack of knowledge or skill of a manager who for some reason cannot be replaced may be avoided by organizing in a way that moves much of the authority for decision-making to another position.

Personality clashes between managers also may be solved by reorganization. Staff–line conflict may develop to such an extent that it can be resolved only by reorganization.

The Need for Readjustment and Change

In addition to pressing reasons for reorganization, there is a certain need for moderate and continuing readjustment merely to keep the structure from becoming stagnant. "Empire building" (i.e., building up a large organization so that the manager appears to be more important) is not so attractive when those involved know that their positions are subject to change. As a company president told his subordinates, "Don't bother to build any empires because I can assure you that you won't be in the same position three years from now." Some managers, realizing that an organization structure must be a living thing, make structural changes merely to accustom subordinates to change.

INNOVATION PERSPECTIVE

Trouble at Apple!—The Early Days[2]

Apple is one of the most innovative companies. But this was not always the case. Steve Jobs and Steve Wozniak invented the personal computer in the garage in 1976. Jobs at age 21 had to sell his Volkswagen to finance his idea. The assembly of the first personal computer was followed by financing help from friends. In 1978, the first computer was launched. At that time, IBM was the dominant company in the big computer market. But it was Steve Jobs, the entrepreneur, not IBM, who conceived the first personal computer. IBM in 1981 began to realize the potential of the personal computer and entered the market. Jobs countered with the Macintosh which was noted for the creative style and design. Jobs dropped out of college, but the course he took in calligraphy, which introduced him to serif and sans serif typography, influenced the innovative typefaces and proportionally spaced fonts in the Mac computer.

As the company grew, Jobs hired John Sculley who was successful in creating the "Pepsi Challenge" and other advertising campaigns at Pepsi. Soon the company's vision was led by Sculley rather than Jobs. Sculley's strategy aimed at competing directly with IBM through an ordinary computer while Jobs envisioned a differentiation strategy for Apple. Eventually, Jobs, the creator of Apple, was fired by Sculley, but Sculley's strategy did not work. In 1993, Sculley was replaced as CEO by Michael Spindler who continued focusing on cost cutting rather than innovative differentiation. But the losses continued. Then, in 1996, Spindler was replaced by Gilbert Amelio. Apple continued being in financial trouble and the board of directors rehired Steve Jobs as an interim CEO.

Jobs' return to Apple resulted in dramatic restructuring and changes in the strategy direction. Several products were discontinued, manufacturing was outsourced to Taiwan region, products were sold directly to customers online, the open-source operating system was introduced, Intel processors were used in the products, and Apple retail stores were opened. Although this was a risky strategy, it made the company profitable again. Indeed, the company change was illustrated by the 1997 advertising slogan "Think Different." Undeniably, the restructured company under the leadership of Steve Jobs moved in a different direction resulting in innovations such as the introduction of the iPod, the iPhone, and the iPad, all discussed in different parts of the book.

www.apple.com

MAKING STAFF WORK EFFECTIVE

The line–staff problem is not only one of the most difficult that organizations face but also the source of an extraordinarily large amount of inefficiency. Solving this problem requires great managerial skill, careful attention to principles, and patient teaching of personnel.

Understanding Authority Relationships

Managers must understand the nature of authority relationships if they want to solve the problems between line and staff. As long as managers regard line and staff as groups of people or groupings of activities, confusion will result. Line and staff are authority relationships, and many jobs have elements of both. The line relationship involves making decisions and acting on them. The staff relationship, on the other hand, implies the right to assist and counsel. In short, the line may "tell", but the staff must "sell" (its recommendations).

www.gm.com

Ensuring Line Listen to Staff

Line managers should be encouraged or required to consult with staff. Enterprises would do well to adopt the practice of compulsory staff assistance where line must listen to staff. At General Motors (GM), for example, product division managers would consult with the headquarters staff divisions before proposing a major program or policy to the top executive or the finance committee. They may not be required to do so, but they are likely to find that this practice results in smoother sailing for their proposals; and if they can present a united front with the staff division concerned, there will unquestionably be a better chance for the adoption of their proposals.

Keeping Staff Informed

Common criticisms of staff are that specialists operate in a vacuum, fail to appreciate the complexity of the line manager's job, and overlook important facts in making recommendations. To some extent, these criticisms are warranted because specialists cannot be expected to know all the fine points of a manager's job. Specialists should take care that their recommendations deal only with matters within their competence, and operating managers should not lean too heavily on a recommendation if it deals only with part of a problem.

Many criticisms arise because staff are not kept informed on matters within their field. Even the best staff cannot advise properly in such situations. If line managers fail to inform their staff of decisions affecting their work or if they do not pave the way—through announcements and requests for cooperation—for staff to obtain the requisite information on specific problems, the staff cannot function as intended. In relieving their superiors of the necessity for gathering and analyzing such information, staff largely justify their existence.

Requiring Complete Staff Work

Staff often overlook the fact that, in order to be most helpful, their recommendations should be complete enough to enable a line manager to make a simple positive or negative answer. Staff should be problem solvers and not problem creators. They create problems for managers when their advice is indecisive or vague, when their conclusions are wrong, when they have not taken into account all the facts or have not consulted the persons seriously affected by a proposed solution, or when they do not point out to superiors the pitfalls as well as the advantages of a recommended course of action.

Complete staff work implies presentation of a clear recommendation based on full consideration of a problem, clearance with persons who will be greatly affected, suggestions about avoiding any difficulties involved, and, often, preparation of the paperwork—letters, directives, job descriptions, and specifications—so that a manager can accept or reject the proposal without further study, long conferences, or unnecessary work. Should a recommendation be accepted, thorough staff work provides line managers with the machinery to put it into effect. People in staff positions who have acquired these capabilities can find themselves highly valued and appreciated.

Making Staff Work as a Way of Organizational Life

An understanding of staff authority lays the foundation for an organizational way of life. Wherever staff are involved, their responsibility is to develop and maintain a climate of favorable personal relations. Essentially, the task of staff is to make the responsible line managers "look good" and to help them do a better job. A staff person should not attempt to assume credit for an idea. Not only is this a sure way of alienating line teammates who do not like being shown up by a staff person, but operating managers who accept ideas and actually bear responsibility for the implementation of the proposals.

Companies also employ the assistance of professional firms, such as consultants to provide advice to line managers. The relationships between line and outside staff are similar to those discussed above. However, outside assistance is often only for a limited time, and it is even more difficult to hold outside staff accountable, especially when they are not involved in the implementation of their recommendations.

AVOIDING CONFLICT BY CLARIFICATION

A major reason for conflict in organizations is that people do not understand their assignments and those of their coworkers. No matter how well conceived an organization structure may be, people must understand it to make it work. Understanding is aided materially by the proper use of organization charts, accurate job descriptions, spelling out of authority and informational relationships, and introduction of specific goals for specific positions.

Organization Charts

Every organization structure, even a poor one, can be charted, for a chart merely indicates how departments are tied together along the principal lines of authority. It is therefore somewhat surprising to find top managers occasionally taking pride in the fact that they do not have an organization chart or, if they do have one, feeling that the chart should be kept a secret.

Organization chart Indicates how departments are tied together along the principal lines of authority.

ENTREPRENEURIAL PERSPECTIVE

Linkedin's Organizational Chart for its IPO S-1 Filing[3]

Linkedin is the world's largest professional network on the Internet today. Linkedin is now a public company and in the process to become a public company (like all other companies that wish to list on a U.S. public exchange) filed an S-1. The S-1 is a legal document that details many financial, organizational, product, and legal aspects of a company. The S-1 provides a glimpse of the proposed organizational structure of Linkedin. In its case, it denotes the CEO, Jeffrey Weiner, and four senior vice presidents (CFO, SVP of Global Sales, SVP of Operations and Planning, and SVP of Products and User Experience). The designation of the top managerial jobs, in this case focusing on global sales, operations, and products, gives a sense of the priorities and direction of the firm. Students of entrepreneurship can develop insight into new high-growth firms as they file to go public through an examination of the S-1 and other required legal documents. Since its public offering Linkedin has performed well as a public firm, especially when compared to some other social media firms, boasting a market capitalization of nearly $30 billion before being acquired by Microsoft in 2017.

Advantages of Organization Charts

A prominent manufacturer once said that, although he could see some use for an organization chart for his factory, he had refused to chart the organization above the level of factory superintendent. His argument was that charts tend to make people overly conscious of being superiors or inferiors, destroy team feeling, and give persons occupying boxes on the chart too great a feeling of "ownership." Another top executive once said that an organization can be changed more easily if it is left uncharted and that the absence of a chart also encourages a competitive drive for higher executive positions by the uncharted middle management group.

These reasons for not charting organization structures are clearly unsound. Subordinate–superior relationships exist not because of charting but, rather, because of essential reporting relationships. As for a chart's creating a too-comfortable feeling and causing a lack of drive in those who have "arrived", these are matters of top leadership—of reorganizing whenever the enterprise environment demands, of developing a tradition of change, and of making subordinate managers continue to meet adequate and well-understood standards of performance. Managers who believe that team spirit can be produced without clearly spelling out relationships are fooling themselves and preparing the way for politics, intrigue, frustration, buck passing, lack of coordination, duplicated effort, vague policy, uncertain decision-making, and other evidence of organizational inefficiency.

Since a chart maps lines of decision-making authority, sometimes merely charting an organization can show inconsistencies and complexities and thus lead to their correction. A chart also reveals to managers and new personnel how they tie into the entire structure.

Organization chart Shows formal authority relationships and omits the many significant informal and informational relationships.

Limitations of Organization Charts

Organization charts are subject to important limitations. A chart shows only formal authority relationships and omits the many significant informal and informational relationships. Figure 10.1 shows many, but not nearly all, of the informal and informational relationships found in a typical organized enterprise. It shows also the major line, or formal, relationships. It does not show how much authority exists at any point in the structure. While it would be interesting to chart an organization with lines of different widths to denote formal authority of varying degrees, authority is not subject to such measurement. And if the multiple lines of informal relationships and of communication were drawn, they would so complicate a chart that it could not be understood.

FIGURE 10.1 Formal and informal or informational organizations

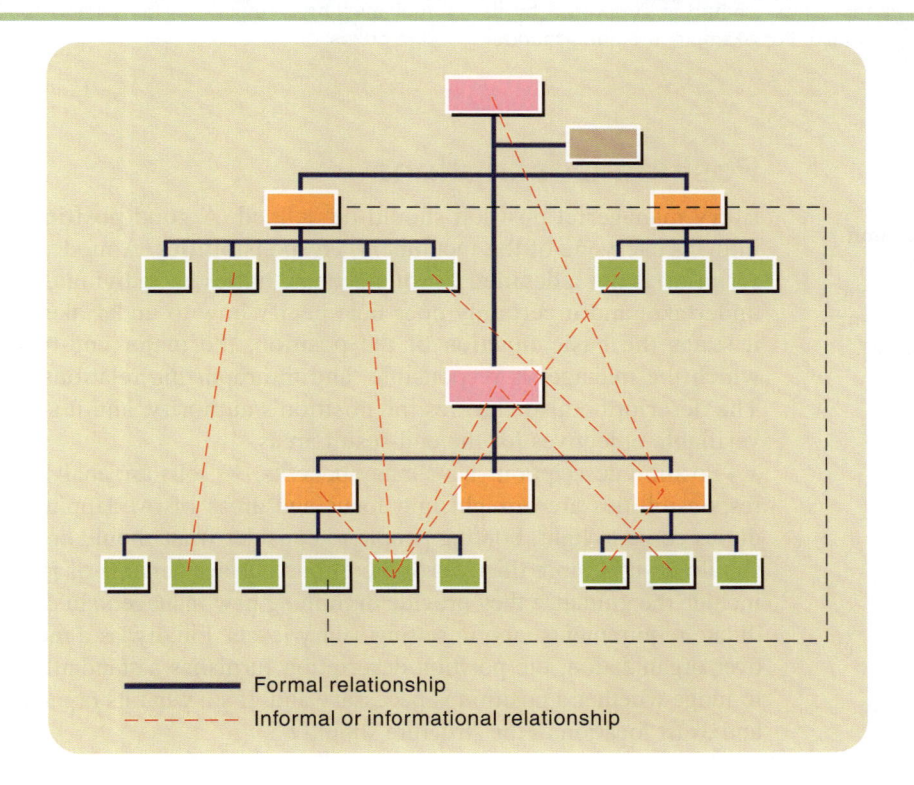

―――― Formal relationship
------ Informal or informational relationship

Many charts show structures as they are supposed to be or used to be, rather than as they really are. Managers hesitate or neglect to redraft charts, forgetting that organization structures are dynamic and that charts should not be allowed to become obsolete.

Another difficulty with organization charts is that individuals may confuse authority relationships with status. The staff officer reporting to the corporation's president may be shown at the top of the organization chart, while a regional line officer may be shown one or two levels lower. Although good charting attempts to make levels on the chart conform to levels of enterprise importance, it cannot always do so. This problem can be handled by clearly spelling out authority relationships and by using that best indicator of status—salary and bonus levels. No one is likely, for example, to hear that the general manager of Chevrolet in GM feels a sense of inferiority because his position on the chart is below that of the company secretary.

www.chevrolet.com

INNOVATIVE PERSPECTIVE

Pandora

Pandora is an Internet radio firm whose mission is "to play only music you'll love."[4] This mission has helped create a certain organizational culture that focuses on developing an extensive knowledge of music and delivering music tailored to each of its listeners. Listeners of Pandora can create multiple unique radio stations that are refined with listener feedback to every song. The culture that Pandora has created is supported by its corporate governance. For example, the firm's founder, Tim Westergren, is Pandora's chief strategy officer, and, thus, can continue to provide guidance and inspiration to top management and the firm employees. Additionally, the company's code of conduct and other corporate documents are available on the firm's website for all to review.[5] A company's culture and organizational structure can be a powerful influence on performance and so they must be carefully considered and nourished as the firm grows.

Position Descriptions

> A good **position description** informs everyone of the incumbent's responsibilities.

Every managerial position should be defined. A good **position description** informs everyone of the incumbent's responsibilities. A modern position description is not a detailed list of all the activities an individual is expected to undertake, and it certainly does not specify how to undertake them. Rather, it states the basic function of the position, the major end-result areas for which the manager is responsible, and the reporting relationships involved. The description also clarifies the position's authority, and it states the set of verifiable objectives for the end-result areas.

Position descriptions have many benefits. As jobs are analyzed, duties and responsibilities are brought into focus and areas of overlapping or neglected duties come to light. Forcing people to consider what should be done and who should do it is more than worth the effort. Further benefits of job descriptions include the guidance they provide in training new managers, in drawing up candidate requirements, and in setting salary levels. Finally, as a means of control over organization, the position description furnishes a standard against which to judge whether a position is necessary and, if so, what its organizational level and exact location in the structure should be.

ENSURING UNDERSTANDING OF ORGANIZING

All the members of an enterprise must understand the structure of their organization in order for that structure to work. This requires teaching. Also, since formal organization is supplemented by informal organization, members of an enterprise must understand the general workings of informal as well as formal organization.

INNOVATIVE PERSPECTIVE

The Third Wave: The Knowledge Age

The first-wave economy was based on land and farm labor. The second wave centered on machines and large industries. The third-wave economy is the knowledge age, which encompasses data, images, symbols, culture, ideology, values, and information. Being at the frontiers of the new technologies, society must rethink the way it structures itself and how it strikes a balance between freedom and restrictions (e.g., how to manage or control the massive amount of information available on the Internet). Cyberspace is a bioelectronic environment that exists wherever one can find telephone and coaxial cables, fiber-optic lines, or electromagnetic waves. It requires a rethinking of centralization versus decentralization, organizational hierarchy versus empowerment, and vertical versus horizontal organization structures, just to mention a few.

Teaching the Nature of Organizing

Many soundly conceived organization plans fail because organization members do not understand them. A well-written organization manual—containing a statement of organizational philosophy, programs, charts, and an outline of job descriptions—goes far toward making organizing understandable. If an organization structure is put into written words and charts, it has a better chance of being clear than if it is not. However, even the best-written words and charts do not always clearly convey the same meaning to every reader; so effective managers cannot stop with written clarification. They must teach those in their operation the meaning of the organization structure, their position in it, and the relationships involved. Managers may do this by individual coaching, through staff or special meetings, or by simply watching how the structure works.

Recognizing the Importance of Informal Organization and the Grapevine

Another way of making the formal organization work effectively is to recognize and take full advantage of informal organization. The nature of informal organization and its distinction from formal organization were discussed in Chapter 7. Many informal organizations arise from the formal organization in which they operate. They include interrelationships that are not usually charted, such as the unwritten rules of organizational conduct, the way to "learn the ropes," the people in an enterprise who have power not implied by or coming from an organizational position, and gossip. One of the best-known examples of informal organization, one which seems to exist in every department and organization, is the "grapevine".

The Grapevine

Informal organization tends to exist when members of a formal organization (perhaps a company department) know one another well enough to pass on information—sometimes only gossip—that is in some way connected with the enterprise. In the typical enterprise—whose members spend many hours a day deriving material security and status, as well as social satisfaction, from the grapevine—the desire for information concerning the organization and its people is strong enough for such information to be rapidly transmitted between persons who know and trust one another.

The grapevine, of course, thrives on information not openly available to the entire group, whether because that information is regarded as confidential or because formal lines of communication are inadequate to spread it or because it is of the kind, like much gossip, that would never be formally disclosed.

Even managers who conscientiously inform employees through company bulletins or newspapers never so completely or quickly disclose all information of interest as to make the grapevine purposeless.

Since all forms of informal organization serve essential human communication needs, the grapevine is inevitable and valuable. Indeed, an intelligent top manager would probably be wise to feed it accurate information, since it is very effective for quick communication. There is much to be said for a manager's getting a place—personally or through a trusted staff member or secretary—on the company grapevine.

Benefits of the Informal Organization

Informal organization brings a kind of cohesiveness to formal organization. It imparts to members of a formal organization a sense of belonging, status, self-respect, and satisfaction. Many managers, understanding this fact, consciously use informal organizations as channels of communication and molders of employee morale.

PROMOTING AN APPROPRIATE ORGANIZATION CULTURE[6]

> The **effectiveness** of an organization is influenced by the organization culture.

The **effectiveness** of an organization is also influenced by the organization culture, which affects the way the managerial functions of planning, organizing, staffing, leading, and controlling are carried out. Illustrations of organization culture are given in Table 10.1. Given the choice, most people would probably prefer to work in an organization with an environment such as B, in which one can participate in the decision-making process, one is evaluated on the basis of performance criteria rather than on the basis of friendship, one has open communication channels in all directions, and one has the opportunity to exercise a great deal of self-control. In their search for excellent companies, Thomas Peters and Robert Waterman, the authors of a best-selling book on management, found that the dominance of a coherent culture characterized these organizations.[7]

But the recognition of the importance of corporate culture is not new at all (although some management gurus want you to believe it is). Over 2,000 years ago, in 431 B.C., Pericles in ancient Greece eloquently urged the Athenians, who were at war with the Spartans, to adhere to values such as those inherent in democracy: informality in communication, the importance of individual dignity, and promotion based on performance. Pericles realized that the underlying values might mean victory or defeat. These values are not so different from those espoused by many U.S. companies.

TABLE 10.1 Illustrations of organization culture and management practice

Environment A	Environment B
Planning	
Goals are set in an autocratic manner.	Goals are set with a great deal of participation.
Decision-making is centralized.	Decision-making is decentralized.
Organizing	
Authority is centralized.	Authority is decentralized.
Authority is narrowly defined.	Authority is broadly defined.
Staffing	
People are selected on the basis of friendship.	People are selected on the basis of performance criteria.
Training is in a narrowly defined specialty.	Training is in many functional areas.
Leading	
Managers exercise directive leadership.	Managers practice participative leadership.
Communication flow is primarily top-down.	Communication flow is top-down, bottom-up, horizontal, and diagonal.
Controlling	
Superiors exercise strict control.	Individuals exercise a great deal of self-control.
Focus is on financial criteria.	Focus is on multiple criteria.

Defining Organization Culture

As it relates to organizations, culture is the general pattern of behavior, shared beliefs, and values that members have in common.[8] Culture can be inferred from what people say, do, and think within an organizational setting. It involves the learning and transmitting of knowledge, beliefs, and patterns of behavior over a period of time, which means that an organization culture is fairly stable and does not change fast. It often sets the tone for the company and establishes implied rules for the way people should behave. Many company slogans give a general idea of what a particular company stands for. Here are some examples: For General Electric, it is "Progress is our most important product." AT&T is proud of its "universal service". Du Pont makes "better things for better living through chemistry". Delta Airlines describes its internal climate as "the Delta family feeling". KLM Royal Dutch Airlines wants to be known as "the reliable airline". Its president, Jan F. A. de Soet, stated that KLM is not a flamboyant airline; instead, the organization culture reflects the Dutch dislike of ostentation.

Similarly, IBM wants to be known for its service, Sears for quality and price, Caterpillar for its 24-hour parts service, and so on. Indeed, the orientation of these companies, often expressed in slogans, contributed to the successful conduct of their businesses.

Asea Brown & Boveri (a giant electrical company), which comprises a Swedish and a Swiss firm, is guided by a culture illustrated by the phrase "think globally, act locally".[9] The organization culture of the highly decentralized

Organization culture General pattern of behavior, shared beliefs, and values that organization members have in common.

www.ge.com
www.att.com
www.dupont.com
www.delta.com
www.klm.com

www.ibm.com
www.sears.com
www.caterpillar.com

company with more than 200,000 employees around the world is integrated with the culture of the country in which the division operates. On the other hand, its managers act globally with respect to sourcing. For example, depending on the prevailing financial market conditions, goods and services are acquired in the country where it is most favorable to do so.

www.abb.com

Value fairly permanent belief about what is appropriate and what is not that guides the actions and behavior of employees in fulfilling the organization's aims.

The Influence of the Leader on Organization Culture

Managers, especially top managers, create the climate for the enterprise. Their values influence the direction of the enterprise. Although the term *value* is used differently, a value can be defined as a fairly permanent belief about what is appropriate and what is not that guides the actions and behavior of employees in fulfilling the organization's aims. Values can be thought of as forming an ideology that permeates everyday decisions.

GLOBAL PERSPECTIVE

Transformational Leadership of Mother Teresa[10]

When one thinks of powerful, transformational leaders, most people envision a political or business leader but not an Albania-born Catholic nun ministering to the poor in India. Yet, Mother Teresa, the Nobel Peace Prize winner, was introduced to the United Nations as the most powerful woman. She founded the Missionaries of Charity in Calcutta and received India's highest civilian honor, the Bharat Ratna in 1980, the prize that was initiated by President Rajendra Prasad in 1954 for services that recognize scientific, literary, artistic, and public service.[11] She opened the first home for the dying in Calcutta in 1952. Later, her order opened leper houses, hospices, orphanages, and foundations in India, Venezuela, Rome, Austria and other countries in Europe, Africa, Asia, and the United States. Mother Teresa did not learn her organizational skills in any business school; she probably never read a management book, but her vision and implementing it through example resulted in an organization that spread around the world with 610 missions in 123 countries at the time of her death in 1997. She even was a model for leadership and compassion for Jerry Brown, the current governor of California (2011), who worked with her in the home for the dying in India.

In many successful companies, value-driven corporate leaders serve as role models, set the standards for performance, motivate employees, make the company special, and are a symbol to the external environment. It was Edwin Land, the founder of Polaroid, who created a favorable organizational environment for research and innovation. It was Jim Treybig of Tandem, in the Silicon Valley near San Francisco, who emphasized that every person is a human being and deserves to be treated accordingly. It was William Cooper Procter of Procter & Gamble who ran the company with the slogan "Do what is right". It was Theodore Vail of AT&T who addressed the needs of customers by emphasizing service. It was Du Pont's CEO Woolard who initiated the "Adopt a Customer" program, through which workers are encouraged to visit their customers monthly to find out their needs and concerns. The organization culture created by corporate leaders can result in managerial functions being carried out in quite different ways.

www.polaroid.com

www.pg.com

While the CEO must indicate the direction, some contend that change must come from the bottom of the organization. At Du Pont's Towanda plant in Pennsylvania, people are organized in self-directing teams. Employees have a great deal of freedom to set their own schedules, solve their own problems, and even participate in selecting coworkers. Indicative of this culture is that managers are called facilitators rather than superiors.

Changing a culture may take a long time, even 5–10 years. It demands changing values, symbols, myths, and behavior. It may require, first, understanding the old culture, then identifying a subculture in the organization, and rewarding those living this new culture. Rewards do not have to be in financial terms. In Sharp's factory in Japan, top performers are rewarded by becoming members of the "gold badge" team that reports directly to the president. At any rate, CEOs must symbolize the culture they want to promote.

www.sharp-world.com

A clear vision of a common purpose elicits commitment. Moreover, when people participate in the decision-making process and exercise self-direction and self-control, they feel committed to their own plans. But espoused values need to be reinforced through rewards and incentives, ceremonies, stories, and symbolic actions.

SUMMARY

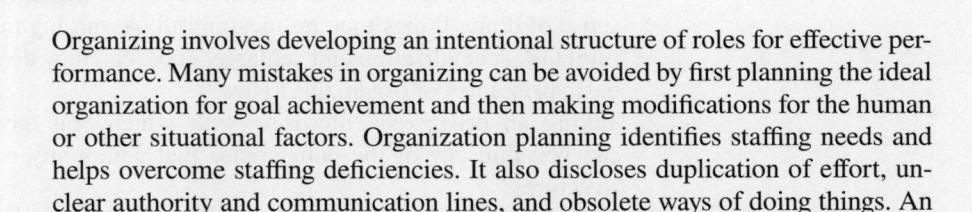

Organizing involves developing an intentional structure of roles for effective performance. Many mistakes in organizing can be avoided by first planning the ideal organization for goal achievement and then making modifications for the human or other situational factors. Organization planning identifies staffing needs and helps overcome staffing deficiencies. It also discloses duplication of effort, unclear authority and communication lines, and obsolete ways of doing things. An effective organization remains flexible and adjusts to changes in the environment.

To make staff work effective, it is important to clarify authority relationships, to make line listen to staff, and to keep staff informed. Furthermore, effectiveness demands that staff prepare complete recommendations and that the utilization of staff becomes a way of organizational life.

Organizational conflict can be reduced by the use of organization charts and position descriptions. Organizing is improved by teaching its nature and by recognizing the informal organization and the grapevine. Moreover, effective enterprises develop and nurture an appropriate organization culture.

KEY IDEAS AND CONCEPTS FOR REVIEW

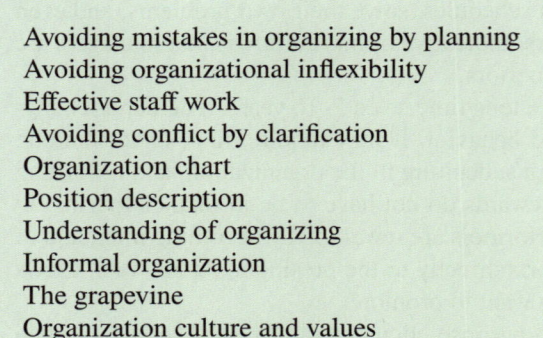

Avoiding mistakes in organizing by planning
Avoiding organizational inflexibility
Effective staff work
Avoiding conflict by clarification
Organization chart
Position description
Understanding of organizing
Informal organization
The grapevine
Organization culture and values

FOR DISCUSSION

1. Many psychologists have pointed to the advantage of job enlargement, which refers to assigning tasks that are not so specialized that an individual loses a sense of doing things that are meaningful. Assuming that managers wish to limit task specialization and "enlarge" jobs, can they do so and still apply the basic principles of organizing? How?
2. Taking an organized enterprise with which you have some familiarity, can you find any of the deficiencies that commonly occur in organization structures?
3. It is sometimes stated that the typical organization chart is undemocratic, in that it emphasizes the superiority and inferiority of people and positions. Comment.
4. What would you need to know to plan an organization structure? How far ahead should you plan it? How would you go about making such a plan?
5. Take an organization that you know and discuss its culture. Is the culture helping or hindering the organization with respect to the achievement of its goals? In what ways?

EXERCISE/ACTION STEPS

Visit a company in your area that is considered a model of effective management. Get any information on this company that gives you some insight into its operation. What makes this organization excellent? Would you like to work for this enterprise? Why or why not?

INTERNET RESEARCH

1. Search the Internet for the term "organization planning" and locate the resources of organization planning on the Web.
2. Search the Internet for reviews of the book *In Search of Excellence* by Peters and Waterman.

GLOBAL CAR COMPANY CASE

Restructuring at South Korea's Daewoo[12]

Daewoo was founded in 1967 by its hardworking, relentlessly driven chairman Kim Woo-Choong. After its initial success in exporting textiles, the company expanded into trade, autos, machinery, consumer electronics, construction, heavy shipping, computers, telephones, and financial services, becoming South Korea's fourth largest business group. It became a textile supplier for Sears, Christian Dior, Calvin Klein, and London Fog. It also engaged in a joint venture with GM to build the Le Mans car. However, labor and other problems limited car shipments.

Chairman Kim's philosophy of hard work and the value placed in people were important factors in the firm's success. However, in the late 1980s and early 1990s, the company faced several problems. For one, Kim was concerned that, with the increasing prosperity of Koreans, the workforce might lose the spirit of hard work. Moreover, there was growing discontent among younger workers and decreasing motivation.

Through Kim's hands-off approach to managing, some of the companies in the Daewoo group went out of control. For example, in the unprofitable heavy shipping unit, he noticed many unnecessary expenses. The elimination of company-sponsored barbershops saved the company $8 million a year. In general, Daewoo's workforce was young and well educated. In contrast to similar positions in many other Korean companies, top positions at Daewoo were occupied by managers with no family ties.

Although Daewoo was a major company with its 91,000 employees, it was not dominant in any one industry. The strategy of being a supplier for major foreign companies, such as Caterpillar, GM, and Boeing, may have led to opportunities being bypassed for becoming a major marketer of its own brands. Now in the 1990s, Kim was also looking at opportunities in Europe; for example, he formed a joint venture with a distribution company in France.

The massive restructuring had already shown some positive effects. Kim sold some steel, financial, and real estate units. The hands-off managerial style had been replaced by a hands-on style, resulting in recentralization. Managers were "retired" or otherwise let go. Thousands of positions were also eliminated.

Things were looking better in 1991. The company lost money in 1988 and 1989 but made some profit in 1990 partly because of the sale of some major assets. The joint venture with GM registered a healthy growth. The company was also optimistic about the future of the new compact car Espero. Still, Daewoo had to cope with its labor costs and Japanese competition.

What looked good in the early 1990s dramatically changed in the latter part of that decade and especially in the years 2000–2002. In 2000, Ford planned to buy Daewoo Motor for some $7 billion. However, the deal fell apart later that year. Moreover, the company went bankrupt in November 2000. Chairman Kim mysteriously disappeared. He liked to think big, and he also left behind a company with big debts. Several billion dollars were also unaccounted for. With Ford out of the picture, GM entered seriously into negotiations with Daewoo, which was once Korea's second biggest car maker. On April 30, 2002, GM agreed to buy the bankrupt company, which was renamed GM-Daewoo. What is in it for GM? The acquisition was a key component of its global strategy.

In 2011, the Daewoo brand was discontinued and replaced with the GM Chevrolet brand. Korea has become an important GM engineering center for small-car platforms such as Opel in Germany, Vauxhall in England, Holden in Australia, Chevrolet in the U.S., and GM cars in China.

Questions:
1. What are the advantages and disadvantages of a hands-off, decentralized management approach?
2. What were some of the controllable and uncontrollable factors in this case? How should Mr. Kim have responded to those factors?
3. What do you think of Daewoo's expansion into Europe? What are the advantages and risks for the company?
4. Why do you think GM acquired the company, while Ford did not?
5. Why was the Daewoo brand discontinued?
6. How important is GM's presence in Korea now?

PART 3 CLOSING

Global and Entrepreneurial Organizing

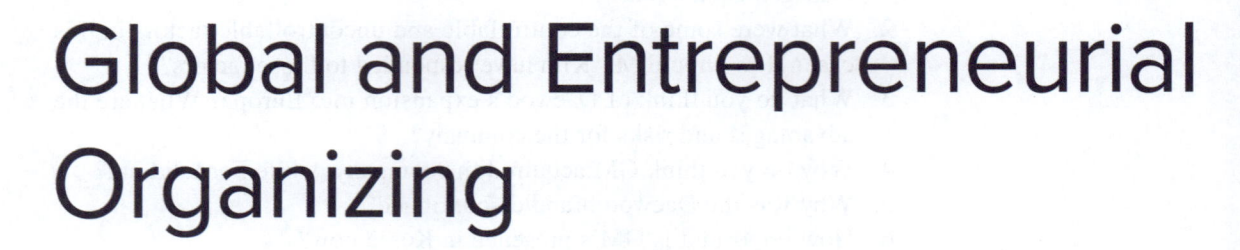

This part closing is about Global and Entrepreneurial Organizing. First, the international focus is on companies known for excellent service. Second, the entrepreneurial focus is on the legal forms and the organizational and intellectual property (IP) of new ventures. Finally, the global car industry case is illustrated by the Lexus car company.

INTERNATIONAL FOCUS: PERSPECTIVE: WHO ARE THE CUSTOMER SERVICE CHAMPS?[13]

At the time of financial crisis, some companies try to reduce costs through layoffs and other measures. Yet, a greater focus on better quality and giving customers better service may be called for. Easier said than done? Yet companies that have done so may profit. In fact, the ranking of Customer Service Champs showed that treating the better customers well might pay out. While trying to reduce back-office expenses, they may want to maintain frontline personnel, sometimes by using inexpensive technology. For example, BMW dealerships provided their customers Wi-Fi services to use their time on the Internet while waiting for their vehicles to be serviced. This resulted in lower costs because fewer customers were taking advantage of free loaner cars, a costly benefit provided by the company.

The Business Week survey identified and ranked 25 companies as service champs. Here are some examples and their rankings in different industries:

1. Amazon.com, online/catalog retail
3. Jaguar, auto
4. Lexus, auto
5. Ritz-Carlton, hotels
8. Hewlett-Packard, consumer electronics
10. ACE Hardware, home improvement and electronics retail
13. Nordstrom, department store
17. American Express, credit card
18. Trader Joe's, super market
20. Apple, consumer electronics
22. BMW, autos
25. JW Marriott, hotel

While these may not always be the most profitable companies, the service reputation may improve profitability in the long run.

ENTREPRENEURIAL FOCUS: LEGAL FORMS OF ORGANIZATION AND IP OF NEW VENTURES

Organizing in an entrepreneurial context often refers to the initial steps that the founders of a new venture take to legally establish the organization. This organizational step is essential as the new venture does not officially exist until it has some governmental recognition of its status. This means that the founders and managers of the organization must take certain legal steps to establish the venture. New businesses may take one of several legal forms. These legal forms normally fall into one of three categories: a sole proprietorship, a partnership, or a corporation.[14]

A sole proprietorship is a recognized legal form of an organization; however, the organization is not distinguished from the owner of the business. For example, John Smith may establish "ABC" company as a sole proprietorship for the purpose of doing business, but the law recognizes that ABC company is an extension of John Smith and he is, therefore, personally responsible for all of its affairs (expenses and liabilities). The sole proprietorship is a common legal form of business in the United States because it is easy and inexpensive to form. However, it does not provide a mechanism for raising significant amounts of capital, nor does it provide for limits of business liability for the entrepreneur/founder.

A partnership is another commonly formed business entity where two or more founders own the business enterprise and share the profits and liability of the organization. Organizing a business as a partnership has benefits in that the partners share the costs and bring unique talents and resources to the business. However, all partners are equally responsible for the liabilities of the enterprise. A partnership agreement should be written to clearly delineate the responsibilities of all partners.

A corporation is ideal for organizations that need to raise significant amounts of equity capital. As a corporation is a separate legal entity from the owners, portions (stock) of the corporation can be sold for cash to finance the operations and investment of the company. Furthermore, as the corporation is a separate legal entity, the owners are not liable for the debts of the corporation beyond their own equity ownership.[15]

Table C3.1 below provides a summary of specific control, management, and liability issues of various types of organizational forms. These are provided by Hason Bridgett Marcus Vlahos and Rudy, LLP, a top corporate law firm in San Francisco. It may serve as a useful guide for entrepreneurial managers considering launching a new venture in the Silicon Valley or elsewhere.

The choice of legal entity is a crucial management action as it both facilitates and limits the type of organizational choices available. These initial organizational decisions by the firm's managers determine in large measure the future course of a new company. As noted in Table C3.1, control and management of the organization are determined, in part, by the legal form of the firm. Is the firm best organized as an equal partnership or corporation owned by shareholders and directed by board members? How shall profits be divided? Who is liable for the firm's expenses and liabilities? These issues are determined in

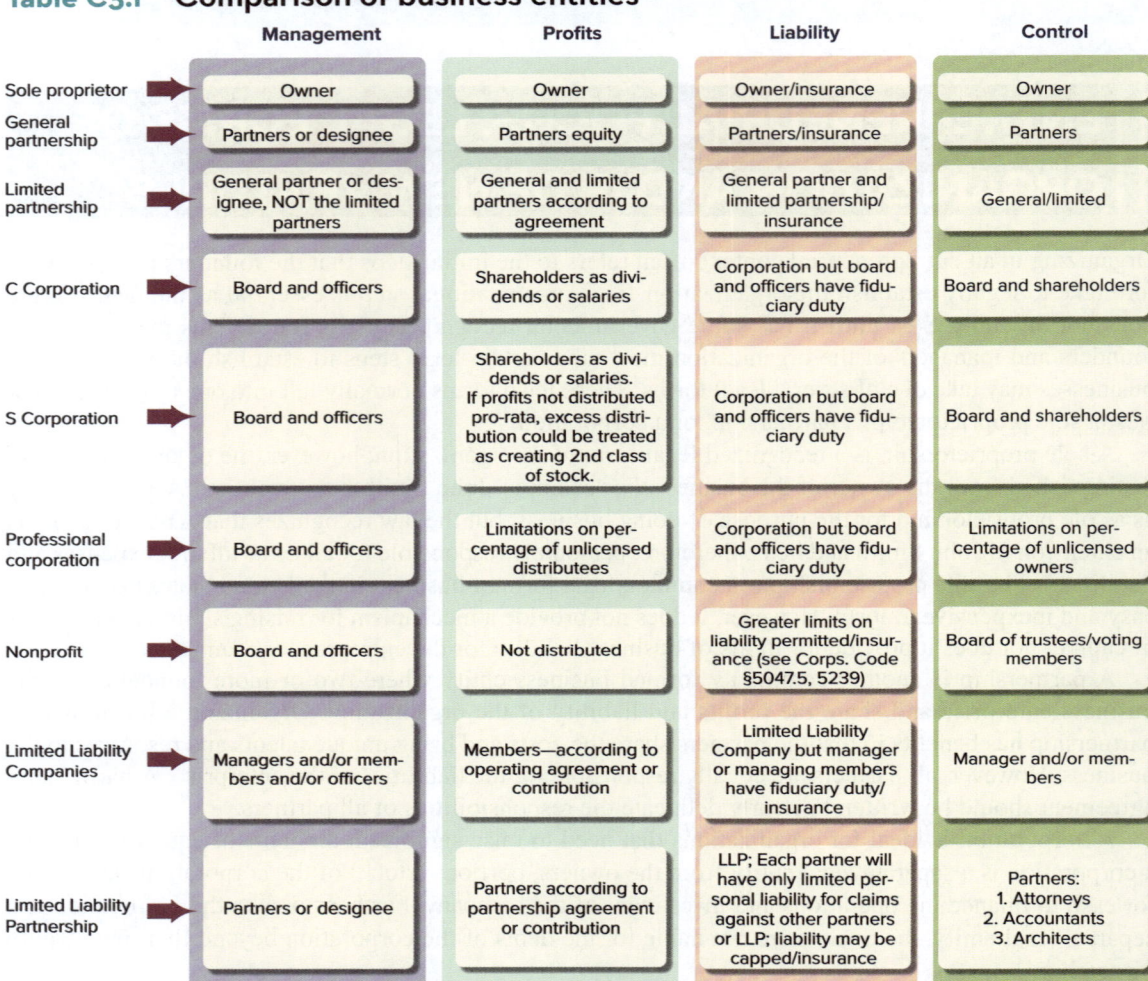

Table C3.1 Comparison of business entities[16]

	Management	Profits	Liability	Control
Sole proprietor	Owner	Owner	Owner/insurance	Owner
General partnership	Partners or designee	Partners equity	Partners/insurance	Partners
Limited partnership	General partner or designee, NOT the limited partners	General and limited partners according to agreement	General partner and limited partnership/insurance	General/limited
C Corporation	Board and officers	Shareholders as dividends or salaries	Corporation but board and officers have fiduciary duty	Board and shareholders
S Corporation	Board and officers	Shareholders as dividends or salaries. If profits not distributed pro-rata, excess distribution could be treated as creating 2nd class of stock.	Corporation but board and officers have fiduciary duty	Board and shareholders
Professional corporation	Board and officers	Limitations on percentage of unlicensed distributees	Corporation but board and officers have fiduciary duty	Limitations on percentage of unlicensed owners
Nonprofit	Board and officers	Not distributed	Greater limits on liability permitted/insurance (see Corps. Code §5047.5, 5239)	Board of trustees/voting members
Limited Liability Companies	Managers and/or members and/or officers	Members—according to operating agreement or contribution	Limited Liability Company but manager or managing members have fiduciary duty/insurance	Manager and/or members
Limited Liability Partnership	Partners or designee	Partners according to partnership agreement or contribution	LLP; Each partner will have only limited personal liability for claims against other partners or LLP; liability may be capped/insurance	Partners: 1. Attorneys 2. Accountants 3. Architects

Source: Jonathan Storper, "Comparison of Business Entities", Corporate Entity Table.

large part by the choice or legal entity. Therefore, managers must be thorough in their understanding of the needs of the firms they lead and the best legal entity to help them organize this venture.

Intellectual Property

When organizing a company, managers must be able to develop and leverage the intellectual assets of the firm. Ideas and knowledge created by the company's employees can be transformed into assets of the firm through the development of IP rights. IP can be a vital resource for firms—often serving as a core competency of the company that can be developed into many different products and services. IP can take a number of forms. Common types of IP include copyright, trademark, patent and trade secrets.

A brief overview of these types of IP is offered in Table C3.2. It is provided by Cecily Anne O'Regan, JD, LLM, a patent attorney with Greenberg Traurig, LLP, a highly respected law firm with offices in Silicon Valley and around the world.

Table C3.2 Intellectual property overview

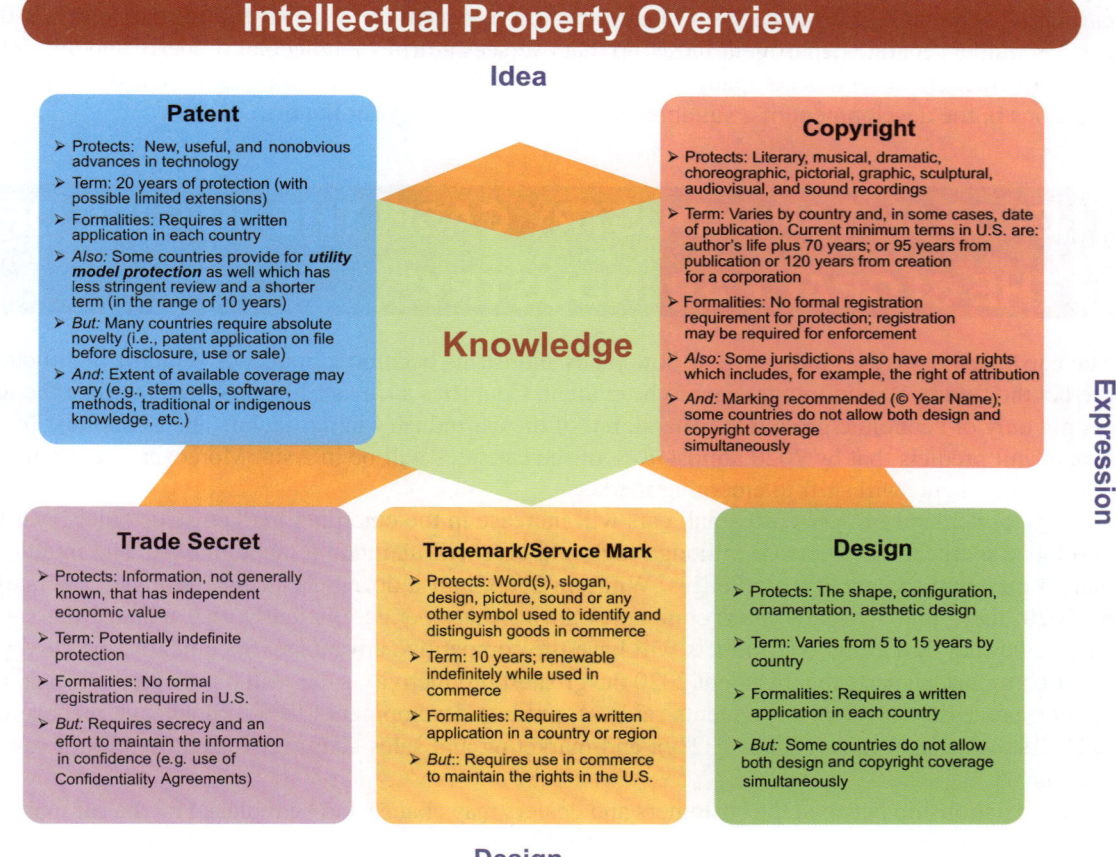

Intellectual Property Overview

Axes: Advantage (left) — Expression (right); Idea (top) — Design (bottom); **Knowledge** (center).

Patent
- Protects: New, useful, and nonobvious advances in technology
- Term: 20 years of protection (with possible limited extensions)
- Formalities: Requires a written application in each country
- Also: Some countries provide for **utility model protection** as well which has less stringent review and a shorter term (in the range of 10 years)
- But: Many countries require absolute novelty (i.e., patent application on file before disclosure, use or sale)
- And: Extent of available coverage may vary (e.g., stem cells, software, methods, traditional or indigenous knowledge, etc.)

Copyright
- Protects: Literary, musical, dramatic, choreographic, pictorial, graphic, sculptural, audiovisual, and sound recordings
- Term: Varies by country and, in some cases, date of publication. Current minimum terms in U.S. are: author's life plus 70 years; or 95 years from publication or 120 years from creation for a corporation
- Formalities: No formal registration requirement for protection; registration may be required for enforcement
- Also: Some jurisdictions also have moral rights which includes, for example, the right of attribution
- And: Marking recommended (© Year Name); some countries do not allow both design and copyright coverage simultaneously

Trade Secret
- Protects: Information, not generally known, that has independent economic value
- Term: Potentially indefinite protection
- Formalities: No formal registration required in U.S.
- But: Requires secrecy and an effort to maintain the information in confidence (e.g. use of Confidentiality Agreements)

Trademark/Service Mark
- Protects: Word(s), slogan, design, picture, sound or any other symbol used to identify and distinguish goods in commerce
- Term: 10 years; renewable indefinitely while used in commerce
- Formalities: Requires a written application in a country or region
- But:: Requires use in commerce to maintain the rights in the U.S.

Design
- Protects: The shape, configuration, ornamentation, aesthetic design
- Term: Varies from 5 to 15 years by country
- Formalities: Requires a written application in each country
- But: Some countries do not allow both design and copyright coverage simultaneously

Source: Cecily Anne O'Regan © 2013.

Properly organizing a firm's IP can lead to significant returns for the firm's stakeholders.[17] Among technology firms, significant attention has been paid to organizing an effective patent portfolio and to the strategic use of patent filing. In essence, a company can stake out ground related to its core products by filing patents on technologies or processes that are related to its line of business. This type of patent organizational strategy adds value to the firm in two ways. It increases the value of the options of future product development related to the firm's patent portfolio (e.g., possible future products that build on of a particular technology now owned by the firm). Holding a broad portfolio of patents also increases potential licensing opportunities as other firms that wish to develop products related to a technology owned by the firm holding the patents are legally obliged to pay the firm for the rights to produce and sell a product that utilizes that technology.

While much attention is often paid to patents, effective use of trade secrets, copyrights, and trademarks can also enhance firm value. Organizational structure can play a part in managing IP. For example, who should have access to which elements of a firm's patent portfolio? How can a firm's patents best be utilized among various organizational units? Can the innovative capacity of a firm be enhanced by the organization of its intellectual property? Which departmentation structure is most suitable for a firm's particular IP portfolio? What degree of centralization or decentralization of control over a firm's IP is best? Should a separate department be set up that oversees a firm's intellectual property and authorizes its use to other elements of a company? An entrepreneurial manager must seek the best answers for these questions in the development of a suitable organizational strategy for the firm.

GLOBAL CAR INDUSTRY CASE: THE FUTURE OF THE GLOBAL CAR INDUSTRY[18]

The car industry may be indicative of how many industries become globalized. While it is difficult to predict the future, certain trends seem to be evident. Countries such as China and India will be the drivers not only of economic growth in general, but of the car industry in particular. The Economist Intelligence Unit predicts that by 2020 almost 40% of the car sales will be in Asia. Moreover, the production of car components will shift to emerging markets.

A great demand for low-cost, small cars will increase in the emerging markets. Customer loyalty in developed markets will decrease although high-end cars will maintain a niche market. The middle-car market may find the greatest challenges. While in 2005, half a dozen car firms dominated the market, by 2020, there may be many more companies. Firms that operate efficiently, that manage the supply chain, and that develop good products will have the competitive advantage. Specifically, the survey by The Economist suggests that by about 2020 the greatest productivity gains will be in operations and production processes (60% of respondents said so), product development (40%), knowledge management (32%), supply-chain management (32%), and marketing and sales activities (listed by 32% of respondents).

The relationship between the customers and dealers may change and be replaced by the car manufacturer's direct relations with the car buyers. Dr. Carl Hahn, the former chairman of Volkswagen AG said "Retailing will be revolutionized towards Wal-Mart type structures,"[19] and Dr. Kai-Uwe Seidenfuss, vice presidents at Daimler in Japan, suggested: "It could well be that we will see an 'Apple-follower' type of car buyer, favoring simplicity."[20]

The car industry's future certainly will have many challenges ranging from less loyal customers to the need to improve productivity to the demand for producing low-cost mass market vehicles and the maintenance of small top-end vehicle market.

Questions:

1. Do you agree with Dr. Hahn that retailing will move toward Wal-Mart type structures? Why or why not?
2. Do you agree with the statement by Dr. Seidenfuss? Why or why not?
3. Describe the car industry structure in your country?

ENDNOTES

1. Lyndall Urwick, *The Elements of Administration* (New York: Harper & Row, 1944), p. 38.
2. David B. Yoffie and Michael Slind, Apple Inc. 2008, Harvard Business School 2008.
3. Linkedin.com, accessed August 6, 2011.
4. Pandora, http://www.pandora.com/about, accessed January 4, 2016.
5. Pandora, http://investor.pandora.com/phoenix.zhtml?c=227956&p=irol-gov-Highlights, accesses January 4, 2016.
6. See also William C. Bogner, "Robert H. Waterman, Jr., on Being Smart and Lucky," *Academy of Management Executive*, February 2002, pp. 45–50; Taylor Cox, Jr., "The Multicultural Organization," *Academy of Management Executive*, May 1991, pp. 34–47.
7. Thomas J. Peters and Robert H. Waterman, Jr., *In Search of Excellence* (New York: Harper & Row, 1982). For more on this and the authors' other books, see note in Chapter 1.
8. Edgar Schein, *Organizational Culture and Leadership*, 2nd ed. (San Francisco, CA: Jossey-Bass, 1992). Organizational Culture & Leadership http://www.tnellen.com/ted/tc/schein.html, accessed January 4, 2016.
9. Charlene Marmer Solomon, "Translating Corporate Culture Globally," in Arthur A. Thompson, Jr., A. J. Strickland III, and Tracy Robertson Kramer (eds.), *Readings in Strategic Management*, 5th ed. (Chicago: Irwin, 1995), pp. 623–634.
10. "Blessed Mother Teresa," http://www.britannica.com/EBchecked/topic/587877/Blessed-Mother-Teresa, accessed January 4, 2016; See also YouTube "India – Calcutta: The Legacy of Mother Teresa, YouTube, http://www.youtube.com/watch?v=8Q_sepFXPCU, accessed January 4, 2016.
11. Govt Changes Criteria for Bharat Ratna; Now Open for All, http://www.thehindu.com/news/national/article2720348.ece, accessed July 31, 2012.
12. The case is based on a variety of sources, including Eryn Brown and Melanie Warner, "Daewoo's Daring Drive into Europe," *Fortune*, May 13, 1996, pp. 145–152; "After Japan," *The Economist*, October 5, 1996, pp. 17–18; Laxmi Nakarmi, "Ford to Daewoo: Forget It!" *AsianWeek.com*, September 29, 2000; Peter Cordingley and Laxmi Nakarmi, "In Search of Daewoo's Kim," *AsianWeek.com*, February 16, 2001; Moon Ihlwan, "Daewoo: Stuck in Neutral," *Business Week*, February 18, 2002, p. 54; "One Step Forward, One Step Back," *Business Week*, May 4, 2002, p. 61; Daewoo Motor, www.daewoomotor.com, accessed August 18, 2012; GM Daewoo, http://www.autozine.org/Manufacturer/Korea/Daewoo.html, accessed January 4, 2016.
13. Jena McGregor, "When Service Means Survival," *Business Week*, March 2, 2009, p. 32. Although these are mostly American companies, many operate in a global environment.
14. Please see California Corporation Law by Harold Marsh, R. Roy Finkle, and Larry W. Sonsini, *Aspen Law and Business Publishers*, 4th Ring Edition, January 2000, for an exhaustive discussion on all aspects of California Corporate Law.
15. Please see Entrepreneurship: Starting and Operating a Small Business, by Steve Mariotti, Pearson Prentice Hall, 2007, for a brief discussion on the advantages and disadvantages of each type of legal entity.
16. Extracted from Corporate Entity Table created by Jonathan Storper, Law Partner with Hanson Bridgett Marcus Vlahos & Rudy, LLP.
17. Please also see Technology Ventures: From Idea to Enterprise, by Richard C. Dorf and Thomas H. Byers, McGraw Hill, 2007, 2nd Edition, for a discussion of intellectual property in high tech growth ventures.
18. "Foresight 2020 Economic, Industry, and Corporate Trends," *The Economist Intelligence Unit 2006*, (April 23, 2006); "Chinese Cars – One to Watch," *The Economist*, February 24, 2007; p. 79; "Briefing Germany's Car Industry – The Big Car Problem," *The Economist*, February 24, 2007, pp. 81–83.
19. Foresight 2020, op. cit., p. 27.
20. Foresight 2020, op. cit., p. 26.

Goal inputs of claimants
1. Employees
2. Consumers
3. Suppliers
4. Stockholders
5. Governments
6. Community
7. Others

Inputs
1. Human
2. Capital
3. Managerial
4. Technological

EXTERNAL ENVIRONMENT

Managerial knowledge, goals of claimants, and use of inputs (Part 1, *The Basis of Management Theory and Science*)

- Planning (Part 2)
- Organizing (Part 3)
- **Staffing (Part 4)**
- Leading (Part 5)
- Controlling (Part 6)

To Produce Outputs

Reenergizing the System

Facilitated by communication that also links the organization with the external environment

EXTERNAL ENVIRONMENT

External Variables and Information
1. Opportunities
2. Constraints
3. Others

EXTERNAL ENVIRONMENT

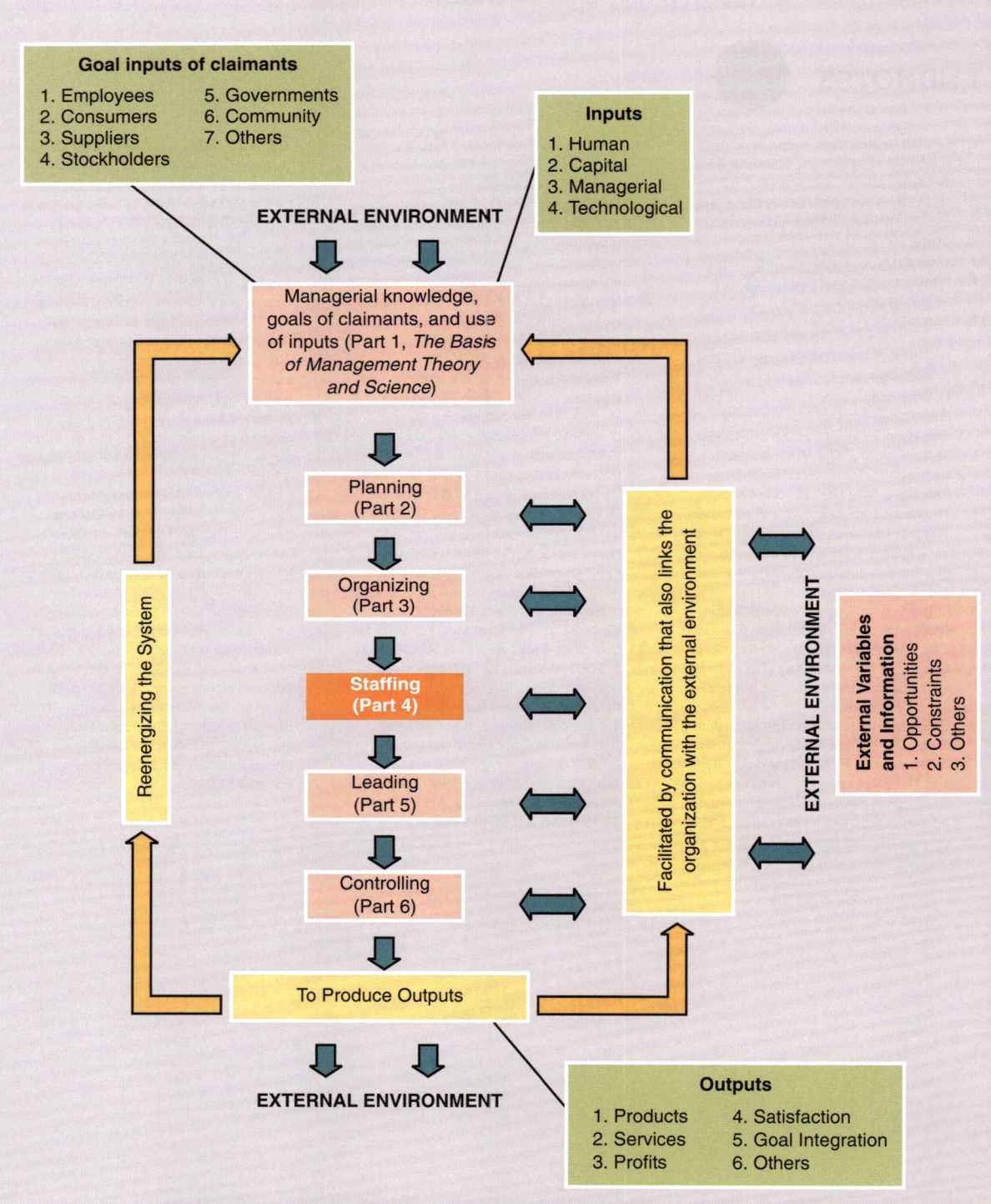

Outputs
1. Products
2. Services
3. Profits
4. Satisfaction
5. Goal Integration
6. Others

SYSTEMS APPROACH TO MANAGEMENT: STAFFING

PART 4

Staffing

Chapter 11: Human Resource Management and Selection
Chapter 12: Performance Appraisal and Career Strategy
Chapter 13: Managing Change through Manager and Organization Development
Part 4 Closing: Global and Entrepreneurial Staffing

CHAPTER 11

Human Resource Management and Selection

Learning Objectives

After studying this chapter, you should be able to:

LO 1   Define the managerial function of staffing

LO 2   Describe the systems approach to human resource management

LO 3   Explain the management inventory and the factors in the external and internal environments affecting staffing

LO 4   Explain the policy of open competition and ways to make staffing more effective

LO 5   Summarize important aspects of the systems approach to manager selection

LO 6   Analyze position requirements, important characteristics of job design, and personal characteristics needed in managers

LO 7   Describe the process of matching manager qualifications with position requirements

LO 8   Discuss the orientation and socialization process for new employees

Few executives would argue with the fact that talented people are vital for the effective operation of a company. Managers often say that people are their most important asset. Yet, the "human assets" are virtually never shown on the balance sheet as a distinct category, although a great deal of money is invested in the recruitment, selection, and training of people. It is for this reason that the late Rensis Likert and his colleagues suggested maintaining accounts of the valuable human assets. They refer to this process as "human resource accounting". This approach is not without its problems, and there is even conflict among management experts, between the proponents of human resource accounting and the financial people who have to develop the system for measuring human assets.[1] What is important here is the recognition that staffing is a crucial function of managers, one that may well determine the success or failure of an enterprise.

This chapter begins with a definition of the managerial function of staffing and an explanation of the role of the manager in this function. It then provides an overview of the systems approach to human resource management before concluding with a discussion of the various aspects of selecting the right person.

DEFINITION OF STAFFING

The managerial function of **staffing** is defined as filling, and keeping filled, positions in the organization structure. This is done by identifying workforce requirements, inventorying the people available, and recruiting, selecting, placing, promoting, appraising, planning the careers of, compensating, and training or otherwise developing both candidates and current jobholders so that they can accomplish their tasks effectively and efficiently. It is clear that staffing must be closely linked to organizing, that is, the setting up of intentional structures of roles and positions.

Staffing filling, and keeping filled, positions in the organization structure.

Many writers on management theory discuss staffing as a phase of organizing. In this book, however, staffing is identified as a separate managerial function for several reasons. First, the staffing of organizational positions includes knowledge and approaches not usually recognized by practicing managers, who often think of organizing as just setting up a structure of roles and give little attention to filling these roles. Second, making staffing a separate function facilitates placing an even greater emphasis on the human element in personnel selection, appraisal, career planning, and manager development. Third, an important body of knowledge and experience has been developed in the area of staffing. The fourth reason for separating staffing is that managers often overlook the fact that staffing is their responsibility—not that of the personnel department. To be sure, this department provides valuable assistance, but it is the job of managers to fill the positions in their organization and to keep them filled with qualified people.

THE SYSTEMS APPROACH TO HUMAN RESOURCE MANAGEMENT: AN OVERVIEW OF THE STAFFING FUNCTION[2]

Figure 11.1 shows how the managerial function of staffing relates to the total management system. Specifically, enterprise plans become the basis for organization plans, which are necessary in order to achieve enterprise objectives. The present and projected organization structures determine the number and kinds of managers required. These demands are compared with available talent through the management inventory. On the basis of this analysis, external and internal sources are utilized in the processes of recruitment, selection, placement, promotion, and separation. Other essential aspects of staffing are appraisal, career strategy, and training and development of managers.

Staffing, as seen in the model, affects leading and controlling. For instance, well-trained managers create an environment in which people, working together in groups, can achieve enterprise objectives and at the same time accomplish personal goals. In other words, proper staffing facilitates leading. Similarly, selecting quality managers affects controlling, for example, by preventing many undesirable deviations from becoming major problems.

Staffing requires an open-system approach. It is carried out within the enterprise, which in turn is linked to the external environment. Therefore, internal factors of the firm—such as personnel policies, the organizational climate, and the reward system—must be taken into account. Clearly, without adequate rewards,

FIGURE 11.1 Systems approach to staffing

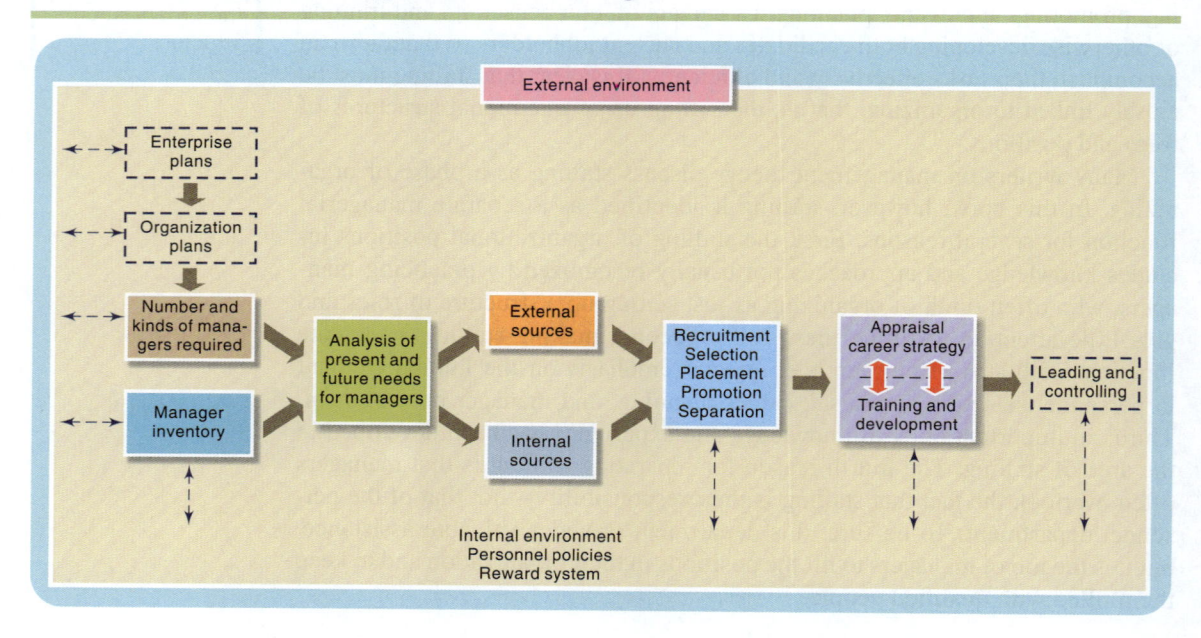

The figure is an overview of the staffing function. The variables not discussed in Part 4, but which also affect staffing, are enclosed with broken lines. Enterprise plans are discussed in Part 2, organization plans in Part 3, and leading and controlling in Parts 5 and 6.

it is impossible to attract and keep quality managers. The external environment cannot be ignored either: high technology demands well-trained, well-educated, and highly skilled managers. Inability to meet the demand for such managers may well prevent an enterprise from growing at a desired rate.

Factors Affecting the Number and Kinds of Managers Required

The number of managers needed in an enterprise depends not only on its size but also on the complexity of the organization structure, the plans for expansion, and the turnover rate of managerial personnel. The ratio between the number of managers and the number of employees does not follow any law. It is possible, by expanding or contracting the delegation of authority, to modify a structure so that the number of managers in a given instance will increase or decrease regardless of the size of an operation.

Although the need for determining the number of managers required has been stressed here, it is clear that numbers are only part of the picture. Specifically, the qualifications for individual positions must be identified so that the best-suited managers can be chosen. This kind of detailed analysis of position requirements will be discussed later in this chapter.

Determination of Available Managerial Resources: The Management Inventory

It is common for any business, as well as for most nonbusiness enterprises, to keep an inventory of raw materials and goods on hand to enable it to carry on its operation. It is far less common for enterprises to keep an inventory of available human resources, particularly managers, despite the fact that the required number of competent managers is a vital requirement for success. Keeping abreast of the management potential within a firm can be done by the use of an inventory chart (also called management replacement chart), which is simply an organization chart of a unit with managerial positions indicated and keyed as to the promotability of each incumbent.

Figure 11.2 depicts a typical manager inventory chart. At a glance, the controller can see where he or she stands with respect to the staffing function. The controller's successor is probably the manager of general accounting, and this person in turn has a successor ready for promotion. Supporting that person, in turn, is a subordinate who will be ready for promotion in a year, but below that position are one person who does not have potential and two newly hired employees.

LEADERSHIP PERSPECTIVE

Brain Drain at BMW[3]

BMW, the maker of luxury cars that wants to be known for producing the "ultimate driving machine," encountered the exodus of key managers after the failed association with British Rover. Bernd Pischetsrieder, the chief executive officer (CEO), left for Volkswagen; the production manager, Carl-Peter Forster, left for Opel; Wolfgang Reitzle of the development and purchasing group moved to Ford, while his successor, Wolfgang Ziebart, is now at Continental Tire. One may wonder if a company with so much managerial talent drain can survive in the very competitive car industry.

Mr. Milberg, BMW's CEO, ex-professor, and machine fitter apprentice in his formative years, is confident that BMW will do well as a niche player with 20 new models in the planning stage. The conventional wisdom is that organization size is essential to survival in the very competitive car industry; yet Mr. Milberg states that "There's no reason for BMW to merge with anyone."[4] Still, the strength or weakness of his managerial talent inventory must be on his mind.

FIGURE 11.2 Manager inventory chart

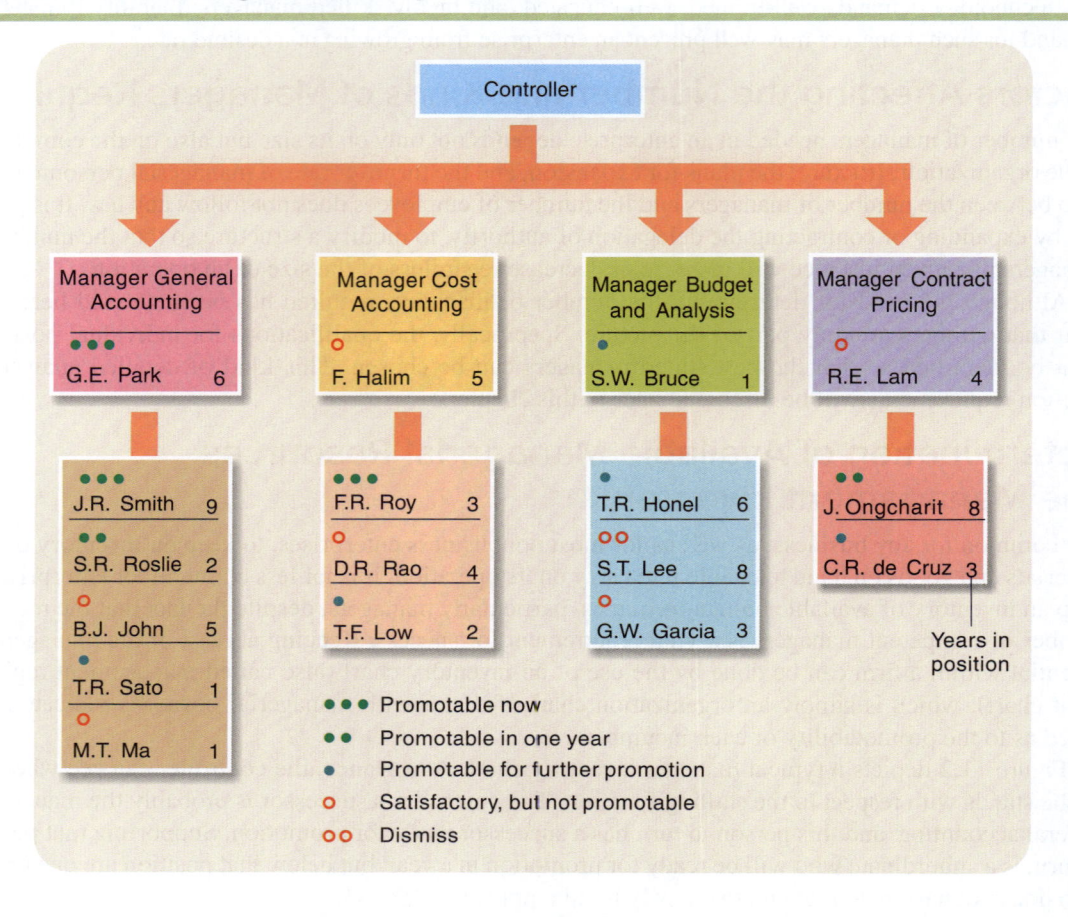

```
                        Controller
           ┌───────────────┬──────────────┬───────────────┐
    Manager General   Manager Cost   Manager Budget   Manager Contract
      Accounting       Accounting    and Analysis        Pricing
      •••              ○              •                  ○
      G.E. Park  6     F. Halim  5    S.W. Bruce  1      R.E. Lam  4

      •••              •••            •                  ••
      J.R. Smith  9    F.R. Roy  3    T.R. Honel  6      J. Ongcharit  8
      ••               ○              ○○                 •
      S.R. Roslie  2   D.R. Rao  4    S.T. Lee  8        C.R. de Cruz  3
      ○                •              ○                              ↑
      B.J. John  5     T.F. Low  2    G.W. Garcia  3          Years in position
      •
      T.R. Sato  1
      ○
      M.T. Ma  1
```

••• Promotable now
••   Promotable in one year
•   Promotable for further promotion
○   Satisfactory, but not promotable
○○   Dismiss

Analysis of the Need for Managers: External and Internal Information Sources

As shown in Figure 11.1, the need for managers is determined by enterprise and organization plans and, more specifically, by an analysis of the number of managers required and the number available as identified through the management inventory. But there are other factors, internal and external, that influence the demand for and supply of managers. The external forces include economic, technological, social, political, and legal factors (which were discussed in Chapters 2 and 3). For example, economic growth may result in increased demand for a product, which in turn requires an expansion of the workforce, thus increasing the demand for managers. At the same time, competing companies may also expand and recruit from a common labor pool, thus reducing the supply of managers. One must also consider the trends in the labor market, the demographics, and the composition of the community with respect to knowledge and skills of the labor pool and the attitude toward the company. Information about the long-term trends in the labor market may be obtained from several sources. The U.S. government, for example, publishes the *Monthly Labor Review* and the annual *Manpower Report of the President*, which makes long-term projections. Some trade associations and unions also project the demand for labor.

FIGURE 11.3 Personnel actions based on manager supply and demand within the enterprise

	Supply of managers	
Demand for managers	**High**	**Low**
High	Selection Placement Promotion	Internal: Training and Development Compensation External: Recruitment
Low	Change in company plans Outplacement Layoffs Demotions Early retirement	Training and development if change in demand is expected in the future

The need for and the availability of personnel give rise to four demand and supply situations, each requiring a different emphasis in personnel actions. This is illustrated in the matrix shown in Figure 11.3.

The demand for and supply of labor must not be viewed from a national, or even local, perspective only. On a global scale, we find the imbalance of demand and supply increasing. In the past, labor was very much a fixed factor of production. But in several developing countries, such as South Korea, Poland, and Hungary, the demand for qualified labor and managers has increased with their rapid economic development, resulting in labor shortages. The educational level of the global workforce is also changing, with the proportion of college graduates rising in developing countries such as China and Brazil.

Other Important Aspects in the Systems Approach to Staffing

After the need for managerial personnel has been determined, a number of candidates may have to be *recruited* (see Figure 11.1). This involves attracting qualified candidates to fill organizational roles. From these, managers or potential managers are *selected*; this is the process of choosing from among the candidates the most suitable ones. The aim is to *place* people in positions that allow them to utilize their personal strengths and, perhaps, overcome their weaknesses by getting experience or training in those skills in which they need improvement. Finally, placing a manager within the enterprise in a new position often means a *promotion*, which normally involves more responsibility. Since recruitment, selection, placement, and promotion are complex processes, these will be discussed in greater detail later in this chapter. Similarly, appraisal, career strategy, training, and development

The **staffing model** shows that managers have to be recruited, selected, placed, and promoted.
www.infosys.com

will be discussed in the following staffing chapters. The reference to leading and controlling in Figure 11.1 indicates that effective staffing influences these functions.

> **INTERNATIONAL PERSPECTIVE**
>
> **Looking for a Company to Work For? Try Infosys**
>
> Located in Bangalore, India, Infosys is one of the largest information technology companies in India. It is a multinational company with several development centers in India and more than 80 offices around the world including offices in the United States, the UK, Canada, France, the United Arab Emirates, Argentina, Europe, and other countries. The company started in Pune in 1981 with very little money. *Business Today* rated Infosys as being the best employer in 2001. Other awards followed, such as being "India's Most Respected Company in 2002."[5] It was also the first Indian firm to be listed in the NASDAQ 100 (National Association of Securities Dealers Automated).[6]

SITUATIONAL FACTORS AFFECTING STAFFING

The actual process of staffing shown in Figure 11.1 is affected by many environmental factors. Specifically, external factors include the level of education, the prevailing attitudes in society (such as the attitude toward work), the many laws and regulations that directly affect staffing, the economic conditions, and the supply of and demand for managers outside the enterprise.

There are also many internal factors that affect staffing. They include organizational goals, tasks, technology, organization structure, the kinds of people employed by the enterprise, the demand for and the supply of managers within the enterprise, the reward system, and various kinds of policies. Some organizations are highly structured; others are not. For some positions, such as that of a sales manager, skill in human relations may be of vital importance, while the same skill may be less critical for a research scientist working fairly independently in the laboratory. Effective staffing, then, requires recognition of many external and internal situational factors, but the focus here is on those that have a particular relevance to staffing.

The External Environment

Factors in the external environment do affect staffing to various degrees. These influences can be grouped into educational, sociocultural, legal–political, and economic constraints or opportunities. For example, the high technology used in many industries requires extensive and intensive education. Similarly, managers in the sociocultural environment in the United States generally do not accept orders blindly, but would want to become active participants in the decision-making process. Furthermore, now and in the future, managers will have to be more oriented toward the public than they have been in the past, responding to the public's legitimate needs and adhering to high ethical standards.

The economic environment, including the competitive situation, determines the external supply of and the demand for managers. Legal and political constraints require that organizations follow laws and guidelines issued by various levels of government. As examples, Table 11.1 summarizes major U.S. federal laws relating to fair employment that influence the staffing function. The following discussion focuses on equal employment opportunity and the role of women in management, as well as on the staffing of international businesses.

TABLE 11.1 Major U.S. federal laws governing equal employment opportunity

Law	Provision
Equal Pay Act (1963)	Equal pay for equal work regardless of sex
Title VII of the Civil Rights Act (1964) (as amended in 1972)	Equal employment opportunity regardless of race, color, religion, sex, and national origin
Age Discrimination in Employment Act (1967) (as amended from ages 65 to 70 in 1978)	Equal employment opportunity for ages 40 to 70
Vocational Rehabilitation Act (1973)	Equal employment opportunity and reasonable affirmative action for handicapped people
Pregnancy Discrimination Act (1978)	Equal employment opportunity during pregnancy
Immigration Reform and Control Act (1986)	Making illegal the hiring, recruitment, or referral of a person known to be an unauthorized alien
Americans with Disabilities Act (1990)	Better access for disabled persons to services and jobs
Older Workers Benefit Protection Act (1990)	Protection for employees above 40 years with respect to fringe benefits; requirement that employees be given time to consider early-retirement offer
Civil Rights Act (1991)	Allowing women, persons with disabilities, and persons who are religious minorities to a jury trial as well as to suing for punitive damages in certain situations
Family and Medical Leave Act (1993)	Allowing qualified persons to have prolonged unpaid leave for family- and health-related reasons without fear of job loss
Sarbanes-Oxley Act (2002)	Passed partly in response to major corporate and accounting scandals including Enron and Tyco. It requires businesses to provide more disclosure and to adopt higher standards

Sources: Keith Davis and John W. Newstrom, *Human Behavior at Work: Organizational Behavior*, 8th ed. (New York: McGraw-Hill, 1990); Lloyd L. Byars and Leslie W. Rue, *Human Resource Management*, 5th ed. (Chicago: Irwin, 1997); Family and Medical Leave Act of 1993, *www.dol.gov/esa/regs/statutes/whd/fmla.htm*, accessed June 5, 2002.

Equal Employment Opportunity

Several laws have been passed in the United States that provide for equal employment opportunity. They prohibit employment practices that discriminate on the basis of race, color, religion, national origin, sex, or age (in specified age ranges). These laws impact on staffing, as recruitment and selection for promotion must be in compliance with them. This means that managers making decisions in these areas must be knowledgeable about these laws and the way they apply to the staffing function.

Diversity in the Workplace[7]

Organizations today have a very diverse workforce. This is not only true in the United States, but also in other countries. In addition to higher ethnic and gender diversity, the average American worker and manager is also older. However, increasing diversity is also seen in education and the economic backgrounds.

The diverse workforce has implications for staffing such as recruitment, selection, training and development, work schedule flexibility, affirmative actions, provisions for preventing sexual harassment, and the establishment of an appropriate organization culture.

Working in a diverse workplace has many advantages, but also poses challenges for managers. The advantages may include bringing different perspectives to management and nonmanagerial issues, learning tolerating different views, developing behavioral flexibility, and accepting that everyone is different.

The managerial challenges deal with communication problems, difficulty of reaching agreement, shifting from a monoculture to pluralism, and overcoming the ethnocentric outlook that assumes that his or her position is the only correct one. Many companies, especially large corporations, have established diversity management programs.[8] McDonald's, Ford Motor Company, Allstate Insurance, IBM, Dole Food, and Xerox are just a few of those firms. Yet, conflicts will remain and need to be managed effectively as we have discussed in Chapter 10 and will again address in Chapter 13 where we discuss managing conflict.

Staffing in the International Environment[9]

One must look beyond the immediate external environment and recognize the worldwide changes brought about primarily by advanced communication technology and by the existence of multinational corporations. It is not unusual for large international firms to have top management teams composed of managers of many different nationalities. The geocentric attitude is the basis for viewing the organization as a worldwide entity engaged in global decision-making, including staffing decisions.

Companies have three sources for staffing the positions in international operations: (1) managers from the home country of the firm, (2) managers from the host country, and (3) managers from third countries. In the early stages of the development of an international business, managers are often selected from the home country. Some of the reasons include the managers' experience at the head office and their familiarity with products, personnel, enterprise goals and policies, and so on. This facilitates not only planning but also control. On the other hand, the home-country national may be unfamiliar with the language or the environment of the foreign country. Moreover, it is usually more expensive to send managers and their families abroad, and the family often finds it difficult to adjust to the new environment of a foreign country. Also, host countries may pressure the parent firm to employ host-country managers.

Managers who are host-country nationals speak the local language and are familiar with their country's environment. Employing them is generally less costly, and it may not require relocating them and their families. The problem is that those managers may not be familiar with the firm's products and operations, and thus control may be more difficult.

The other alternative is to employ third-country nationals, who often are international career managers. Still, the host country may prefer to have its own nationals in the positions of power. One has to be also cautious in selecting managers from countries that had political conflicts in the past. There are of course many other factors that have to be taken into account when operating abroad.

GLOBAL PERSPECTIVE

Wipro's Development Center in Atlanta[10]

India's global information technology services company, Wipro, chose Atlanta for its software development center. The plan is to start small, but expand later. The idea is to use local people who know local business needs. Around Atlanta are 12 universities from which the center will draw local talent. But this global expansion of Wipro is not new because it has already more than 12 offices in the United States.

The Internal Environment

The internal factors selected for this discussion concern staffing managerial positions—with personnel from within the firm as well as from the outside—and determining the responsibility for staffing.

Promotion from within

Originally, promotion from within implied that workers proceeded into first-line supervisory positions and then upward through the organization structure. Thus, a firm was pictured as receiving a flow of nonmanagerial employees from which future managers emerged. As used to be said in the railroad industry, "When a president retires or dies, we hire a new office worker."

As long as the matter is considered in general terms, there is little doubt that employees overwhelmingly favor a policy of promotion from within. The banning of outsiders reduces competition for positions and gives employees an established monopoly on managerial openings. Employees come to doubt the wisdom of the policy, however, when they are confronted with a specific case of selection of one of their own for promotion. This feeling is present at all levels of the organization, largely because of jealousy or because of rivalry for promotion. The difficulty becomes most evident when a general manager is being selected from among the sales, production, finance, or engineering managers. Top managers are often inclined to choose the easy way and avoid problems by selecting an outsider.

Promoting from within the enterprise not only has positive values relating to morale, employees' long-run commitment to the company, and the firm's reputation, but also allows the enterprise to take advantage of the presence of potentially fine managers among its employees. However, although these positive but unmeasurable values are important, executives should not be blind to the dangers of either overemphasizing this source or relying on it exclusively.

A danger presented by a policy of exclusively promoting from within is that it may lead to the selection of persons who have, perhaps, only imitated their superiors. This is not necessarily a fault, especially if only the best methods, routines, and viewpoints are cultivated, but this is likely to be an unapproachable ideal. The fact is that enterprises often need people from the outside to introduce new ideas and practices. Consequently, there is good reason to avoid a policy of exclusive promotion from within.

Promotion from within in Large Companies

On the other hand, a policy of promotion from within may be quite suitable for very large companies such as Sears, Du Pont, or General Motors. Large business and nonbusiness organizations usually have so many qualified people that promotion from within actually approaches a condition similar to an open-competition policy. Even in these large companies, however, it may be necessary to go outside, as General Motors did when it hired a university professor as vice president to head its environmental control staff.

www.sears.com

www.dupont.com

www.gm.com

GLOBAL PERSPECTIVE

Managing Human Resources at Wal-Mart[11]

Wal-Mart is the largest U.S. private employer with over a million people. Sam Walton, the founder of the company, had a special rapport with his employees, called associates. Although he died in 1992, he is lovingly remembered for his caring, his concern, his listening to them, and his open-door policy. His legacy continues. He was lovingly called Mr. Sam, who showed his concern for people by initiating a policy of paying a time and a half for working on Sundays. Wal-Mart paid low wages, yet employees were generally happy, which was one of the reasons the company grew rapidly. The importance of people is also shown in the associates' handbook: "The undeniable cornerstone of Wal-Mart's success can be traced back to our strong belief in the dignity of each individual."

Sam's successors tried to maintain the organizational climate—and succeeded to a great extent. But things are changing, ranging from the elimination of the 50% extra pay for Sunday work to demands created by the long store hours, such as unsuitable working hours in stores that are open 24 hours. The change in orientation may also be shown by the slogan on the blue aprons associates wear. It changed from "Our people make the difference" to "How may I help you?", which could be interpreted as a change in focus from the associate to the customer. Taking advantage of the concern of some associates, labor unions try to recruit members in some locations.

Although Wal-Mart is still very successful, its growth has slowed. The challenge is to maintain a concerned human organization despite its size.

The Policy of Open Competition

> **Principle of open competition**
> Vacant positions should be opened to the best-qualified persons available, whether inside or outside the enterprise.

Managers must decide whether the benefits of a policy of promotion from within outweigh its shortcomings. There are clear-cut reasons for implementing the **principle of open competition** by opening vacant positions to the best-qualified persons available, whether inside or outside the enterprise. It gives the firm, in the final analysis, the opportunity to secure the services of the best-suited candidates. It counters the shortcomings of a policy of exclusive promotion from within, permits a firm to adopt the best techniques in recruiting managers, and motivates the complacent "heir apparent". To exchange these advantages for the morale advantages attributed to internal promotion would appear questionable.

A policy of open competition is a better and more honest means of ensuring managerial competence than is obligatory promotion from within. However, it does put the managers who use it under a special obligation. If morale is to be protected in applying an open-competition policy, the enterprise must have fair and objective methods of appraising and selecting its people. It should also do everything possible to help them develop so that they can qualify for promotion.

When these requirements are met, it would be expected that every manager making an appointment to a vacancy or a new position would have available a roster of qualified candidates within the entire enterprise. If people know that their qualifications are being considered, if they have been fairly appraised and have been given opportunities for development, they are far less likely to feel a sense of injustice if an opening goes to an outsider. Other things being equal, present employees should be able to compete with outsiders. If a person has the ability for a position, he or she has the considerable advantage of knowing the enterprise and its personnel, history, problems, policies, and objectives. For the superior candidate, the policy of open competition should be a challenge and not a hindrance to advancement.

Responsibility for Staffing

While responsibility for staffing should rest with every manager at every level, the ultimate responsibility is with the CEO and the policy-making group of top executives. They have the duty of developing policy, assigning its execution to subordinates, and ensuring its proper application. Policy considerations include decisions about the development of a staffing program, the desirability of promoting from within or securing managers from the outside, the sources of candidates, the selection procedure to follow, the kind of appraisal program to use, the nature of manager and organization development, and the promotion and retirement policies to follow.

Line managers should certainly make use of the services of staff members, usually from the personnel department, in recruiting, selecting, placing, promoting, appraising, and training people. In the final analysis, however, it is the manager's responsibility to fill positions with the best-qualified persons.

SELECTION: MATCHING THE PERSON WITH THE JOB

Plant, equipment, materials, and people do not make a business any more than airplanes, tanks, ships, and people make an effective military force. One other element is indispensable: effective managers. The quality of managers is one of the most important factors determining the continuing success of any organization. It necessarily follows, therefore, that the selection of managers is one of the most critical steps in the entire process of managing. **Selection** is the process of choosing from among candidates, from within the organization or from outside, the most suitable person for the current position or for future positions.

Selection Choosing from among candidates, from within or outside the organization, the most suitable person for a position.

THE SYSTEMS APPROACH TO SELECTION: AN OVERVIEW

Since qualified managers are critical to the success of an enterprise, a systematic approach is essential to manager selection and to the assessment of present and future needs for managerial personnel. An overview of the systems approach to selection is illustrated in Figure 11.4. The managerial requirements plan is based on the firm's objectives, forecasts, plans, and strategies. This plan is translated into position requirements and job design, which are matched with such individual characteristics as intelligence, knowledge, skills, attitudes, and experience. To meet organizational requirements, managers recruit, select, place, and promote people. This, of course, must be done with due consideration for the internal environment (e.g., company policies, manager supply and demand, and the organizational climate) and the external environment (e.g., laws,

FIGURE 11.4 Systems approach to selection. Variables marked with broken lines are staffing and other activities that are discussed in other chapters

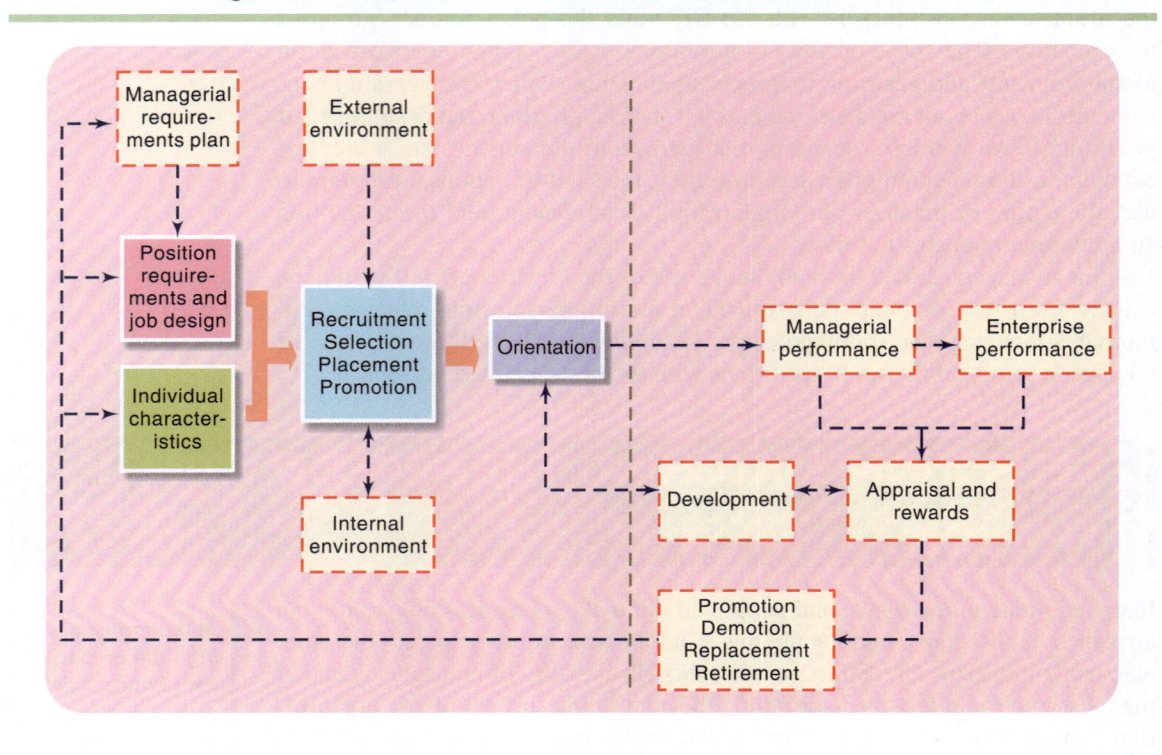

regulations, and availability of managers). After people have been selected and placed in positions, they must be introduced to the new job. This orientation involves learning about the company, its operation, and its social aspects.

The newly placed managers then carry out their managerial and nonmanagerial functions (such as marketing), and the resulting managerial performance will eventually determines enterprise performance. Subsequently, managerial performance is appraised, and managers who meet their performance goals are rewarded (see Chapter 12). On the basis of this evaluation, manager and organization development is initiated (Chapter 13). Finally, appraisal may also become the basis for promotion, demotion, replacement, and retirement decisions.

That is the selection model in brief; now, each major variable in the model will receive closer attention.

ENTREPRENEURIAL PERSPECTIVE

What Do You Do After you Retire or Get Fired?[12]

Companies such as Dow Chemical encourage former employees to stay in contact with the firm, similar to universities that keep in touch with their *alma mater*. The idea is to develop an alumni social network by using networks such as Twitter, LinkedIn, or Facebook. This may benefit the company as well as the employee. One such benefit is the sharing of knowledge that may also result in reemployment after separation. There is, however, a potential downside. A fired or laid-off employee may use the social network for venting grievances against the company. Social networking, like most technologies, has the potential not only for benefits but also for nondesired consequences.

POSITION REQUIREMENTS AND JOB DESIGN

Selecting a manager effectively requires a clear understanding of the nature and purpose of the position that is to be filled. An objective analysis of position requirements must be made and, as far as possible, the job must be designed to meet organizational and individual needs. In addition, positions must be evaluated and compared so that the incumbents can be treated equitably. Among other factors to consider are the skills required, since they vary with the level in the organizational hierarchy, and the personal characteristics desired in managers.

Identifying Job Requirements

In identifying job requirements, firms must answer questions such as these: What has to be done in this job? How is it done? What background knowledge, attitudes, and skills are required? Since positions are not static, additional questions may have to be considered: Can the job be done differently? If so, what are the new requirements? Finding answers to these and similar questions requires that the job be analyzed. This can be done through observation, interviews, questionnaires, or even a systems analysis. Thus, a job description, based on job analysis, usually lists important duties, authority–responsibility, and the relationship to other positions. Many firms also include objectives and expected results in job descriptions.

There is of course no foolproof rule for designing managerial jobs. Nevertheless, firms can avoid mistakes by following some guidelines.

Appropriate Scope of the Job

A job too narrowly defined provides no challenge, no opportunity for growth, and no sense of accomplishment. Consequently, good managers will be bored and dissatisfied. On the other hand, a job must not be so broad that it cannot be effectively handled. The result will be stress, frustration, and loss of control.

Meeting Managerial Skills Required by Job Design

Generally, the design of the job should start with the tasks to be accomplished. The design is usually broad enough to accommodate people's needs and desires. But, some writers on management suggest that it may be necessary to design the job to fit the leadership style of a particular person. It may be especially appropriate to design jobs for exceptional persons in order to utilize their potential. The problem, of course, is that such a position would probably have to be restructured every time a new manager occupies it. The job description, then, must provide a clear idea of the performance requirements for a person in a particular position but must also allow some flexibility so that the employer can take advantage of individual characteristics and abilities.

Any position description is contingent on the particular job and the organization. For example, in a bureaucratic and fairly stable organizational environment, a position may be described in relatively specific terms. In contrast, in a dynamic organization with an unstable, fast-changing environment, a job description may have to be more general and most likely will have to be reviewed more frequently. A situational approach to job description and job design is called for.

Job Design

People spend a great deal of time on the job, and it is therefore important to design jobs so that individuals feel good about their work. This requires an appropriate job structure in terms of content, function, and relationships.

Design of Jobs for Individuals and Work Teams

The focus of job design can be on the individual position or on work groups. First, individual jobs can be enriched by grouping tasks into natural work units. This means putting tasks that are related into one category and assigning an individual to carry out the tasks. A second related approach is to combine several tasks into one job. For example, rather than having the tasks of assembling a water pump carried out by several persons on the assembly line, workstations can be established with individuals doing the whole task of putting the unit together and even testing it. A third way of enriching the job is to establish direct relationships with the customer or client. Rather than reporting to his or her superior, who would then make the recommendations to top management, a systems analyst may present findings and recommendations directly to the managers involved in the systems change. Fourth, prompt and specific feedback should be built into the system whenever appropriate. In one retail store, for example, salespersons received sales figures for each day and summary figures for each month. Fifth, individual jobs can be enriched through vertical job loading, which means increasing individuals' responsibility for planning, doing, and controlling their job.

Similar arguments can be made for improving the design of jobs for work teams. Jobs should be designed so that groups have a complete task to perform. Moreover, teams may be given a great deal of autonomy in the form of authority and freedom to decide how well the jobs shall be performed. Within the team, individuals can often be trained so that they can rotate to different jobs within the group. Finally, rewards may be administered on the basis of group performance, which tends to induce cooperation rather than competition among team members.

Considerable research has been done on what makes for strong entrepreneurial teams. Founding teams face considerable amounts of uncertainty and so must be able to adapt to this uncertainty while achieving important milestones for the business. Research has shown that larger founding teams tend to outperform smaller founding teams and team cohesion (the closeness and trust exhibited by team members) tends to be associated with higher performance. Clarity in roles also tends to enhance firm performance. Finally, conflict is inevitable; however, research has shown that cognitive conflict (disagreement over ideas) tends to be productive whereas affective conflict (personal conflict) tends to be detrimental to firm performance.[13]

Factors Influencing Job Design

In designing jobs, the requirements of the enterprise have to be taken into account. But other factors must also be considered in order to realize maximum benefits; they include individual differences, the technology involved, the costs associated with restructuring the jobs, the organization structure, and the internal climate.

People have different needs. Those with unused capabilities and a need for growth and development usually want to have their job enriched and to assume greater responsibility. While some people prefer to work by themselves, others with social needs usually work well in groups. The nature of the task and the technology related to the job must also be considered. While it may be possible for work teams to assemble automobiles, as it was done at a Volvo plant in Sweden, it may not be efficient to use the same work design for the high production runs at General Motors in the United States. The costs of changing to new job designs must also be considered. It makes a great deal of difference whether a plant is newly designed or an old plant has to be redesigned and changed to accommodate new job design concepts.

www.volvo.com
www.gm.com

The organization structure must also be taken into account. Individual jobs must fit the overall structure. Autonomous work groups, for example, may work well in a decentralized organization, but they may be inappropriate in a centralized structure. Similarly, the organizational climate influences job design. Groups may function well in an atmosphere that encourages participation, job enrichment, and autonomous work, while they may not fit into an enterprise with an autocratic, top-down approach to managerial leadership.

The Impact of Technologies on Human Resource Management[14]

We live in a time when many activities formerly performed by people are now being done by technology. For example, many of the flights are now guided by the autopilot instead by a person, and passengers themselves do the check-in at many airports now instead by an airline person behind the desk. On the telephone, it is often very difficult to talk to a real person, but instead one talks to voice-recognizing machines. What are the effects of these developments on human resources? An extensive study by McKinsey suggests that many of the jobs will be redefined rather than eliminated. The McKinsey study identified 2,000 work activities. Some 45% of them could be automated with already existing technology. Advances in artificial intelligence cloud probably increase this percentage.

It has been estimated that fewer than 5% of the occupations can be completely automated. But many more occupations can be partially automated. It is clear that many job definitions will need to be changed. Not only the labor-saving costs will be reduced but also the persons in the highest-paid jobs will be aided by technology. For example, lawyers already use text-mining technology to scan thousands of documents, tasks that were performed previously by a clerk. It is estimated that more than 20% of the CEO's time could be automated by technologies that already exist today. Clearly, technology greatly impacts on human resource management.

INNOVATION PERSPECTIVE

SKILLS AND PERSONAL CHARACTERISTICS NEEDED IN MANAGERS

To be effective, managers need various skills: technical, human, conceptual, and design. The relative importance of these skills varies according to the level in the organization, as discussed in Chapter 1. In addition, analytical and problem-solving abilities and certain personal characteristics are sought in managers.

Analytical and Problem-Solving Abilities

One of the frequently mentioned skills desired of managers is analytical and problem-solving ability. As Alan Stoneman, former president of Purex Corporation, used to say, "We have no problems here; all are opportunities; all a problem should be is an opportunity." In other words, managers must be able to identify problems, analyze complex situations, and, by solving the problems encountered, exploit the opportunities presented. They must scan the environment and identify, through a rational process, those factors that stand in the way of opportunities. Thus, analytical skills should be used to find the needs of present customers—or potential ones—and then to satisfy those needs with a product or service. It has been amply demonstrated that this opportunity-seeking approach can mean corporate success. For example, Edwin H. Land of Polaroid filled the needs of people who wanted instant photographs. But problem identification and analysis are not enough. Managers also need the will to implement the solutions; they must recognize the emotions, needs, and motivations of the people involved in initiating the required change as well as of those who resist change.

www.purex.com

Personal Characteristics Needed in Managers

In addition to the various skills that effective managers need, several personal characteristics are also important. They are a desire to manage; the ability to communicate with empathy; integrity and honesty; and experience as manager, which is a very significant characteristic.

Desire to Manage

The successful manager has a strong desire to manage, to influence others, and to get results through the team efforts of subordinates. To be sure, many people want the privileges of managerial positions, which include high status and salary, but they lack the basic motivation to achieve results by creating an environment in which people work together toward common aims. The desire to manage requires effort, time, energy, and, usually, long hours of work.

Communication Skills and Empathy

Another important characteristic of managers is the ability to communicate through written reports, letters, speeches, and discussions. Communication demands clarity, but, even more, it demands empathy. This is the ability to understand the feelings of another person and to deal with the emotional aspects of communication. Communication skills are important for effective **intragroup communication**, that is, communication with people in the same organizational unit. As one moves up in the organization, however, **intergroup communication** becomes increasingly important. This is communication not only with other departments but also with groups outside the enterprise: customers, suppliers, governments, the community, and the stockholders in business enterprises.

> **Intragroup communication:** Communication with people in the same organizational unit.
>
> **Intergroup communication:** Communication with other departments as well as with groups outside the enterprise.
>
> www.ford.com

Integrity and Honesty

Managers must be morally sound and worthy of trust. Integrity in managers includes honesty in money matters and in dealing with others, adherence to the full truth, strength of character, and behavior in accordance with ethical standards.

Many of these qualities, and others, have been cited by top executives of major companies. For example, Henry Ford II, former chairman of Ford Motor Company, considers honesty, candor, and openness as appealing qualities.

Past Performance as Manager

Another very important characteristic for selection is past performance as a manager. It is probably the most reliable forecast of a manager's future performance. Of course, an assessment of managerial experience is not possible in selecting first-line supervisors from the ranks since they have not had such experience. But, past accomplishments are important considerations in the selection of middle- and upper-level managers.

MATCHING QUALIFICATIONS WITH POSITION REQUIREMENTS

After the positions are identified, managers are obtained through recruitment, selection, placement, and promotion (see Figure 11.4). There are basically two sources of managerial personnel: (1) promotion or transfer of people from within the enterprise and (2) hiring from outside. For internal promotions, a computerized information system may help identify qualified candidates. It can be used in conjunction with a comprehensive human resource plan. Specifically, it can be utilized to anticipate staff requirements, new openings, attritions, development needs, and career planning.

There are several external sources available, and the enterprise may use different channels to find qualified managers. Many employment agencies—public and private—and executive recruiters (sometimes called headhunters) locate suitable candidates for positions. Other sources of managers are professional associations, educational institutions, referrals from people within the enterprise, and unsolicited applications from persons interested in the firm.

Recruitment of Managers

Recruiting
Attracting candidates to fill positions in the organization structure.

Recruiting involves attracting candidates to fill the positions in the organization structure. Before recruiting begins, the position's requirements, which should relate directly to the task, must be clearly identified to facilitate recruitment from the outside. Enterprises with a favorable public image find it easier to attract qualified candidates. A company such as Sony has a well-recognized image, while small firms—which frequently offer excellent growth and development opportunities—may have to make great efforts to communicate to applicants the kind of business they do and the opportunities they offer.

GLOBAL PERSPECTIVE

Where Do Chinese Companies Recruit?[15]

As Chinese companies become more globally oriented, many now hire Western managers. Lenovo, the biggest computer maker in China, hired Bill Amelio as CEO. Mr. Amelio was the head of Dell Computer's Asia–Pacific region. Similarly, Phil Murtaugh migrated from General Motors to Shanghai Automotive Industry Corp (SAIC), which is China's largest car company that may produce cars for export. As can be expected, some local Chinese firms have reservations about such practices, but increasingly top jobs in China became attractive for Western executives. Still, for those executives, such a switch is risky because they are not familiar with the detailed knowledge of Chinese culture. A number of Chinese companies now hire Chinese executives with Western experience who have the advantage of being familiar with the Chinese environment.

There is also a great need for middle managers in China. As Chinese companies become globally oriented, the need for top as well as middle managers is increasing which opens attractive opportunities for some westerners.

Selection, Placement, and Promotion

Two approaches to filling positions: selection and placement.

Selecting a manager is choosing from among the candidates the one who best meets the position requirements. Since the selection may be for a specific job opening or for future managerial requirements, there are two approaches to filling organizational positions. In the *selection approach*, applicants are sought to fill a position with rather specific requirements; while in the *placement approach*, the strengths and weaknesses of the individual are evaluated, and a suitable position is found or even designed.

Promotion is a move within the organization to a higher position that has greater responsibilities and requires more advanced skills. It usually involves a raise in status and in pay. The various facets of selection generally apply also to promotion, which may be a reward for outstanding performance or a result of the firm's desire to better utilize an individual's skills and abilities. Promotions may be a reward for past performance, but only if there is evidence of potential competency; otherwise, the persons may be promoted to a level at which they are incompetent.

The Peter Principle

Errors in selection are possible, perhaps even common. According to Laurence J. Peter and Raymond Hall, authors of *The Peter Principle*, managers tend to be promoted to the level of their incompetence.[16] Specifically, if a manager succeeds in a position, this very success may lead to promotion to a higher position, often one requiring skills that the person does not possess. Such a promotion may involve work that is over the manager's head. While the possibility of individual growth must not be overlooked, the Peter Principle can serve as a warning not to take the selection and promotion process lightly.

SELECTION PROCESS, TECHNIQUES, AND INSTRUMENTS

This section presents an overview of the selection process, followed by a discussion of a number of selection instruments and techniques, including interviews, tests, and the assessment center approach. For good selection, the information about the applicant should be both valid and reliable. When people ask if data are valid, they are asking if the data are measuring what they are supposed to be measuring. In selection, **validity** is the degree to which the data predict the candidate's success as a manager. The information should also have a high degree of **reliability**, a term that refers to the accuracy and consistency of the measurement. For example, a reliable test, if repeated under the same conditions, would give essentially the same results.

Validity Degree to which the data predict the candidate's success as a manager.

Reliability Accuracy and consistency of the measurement.

ENTREPRENEURIAL PERSPECTIVE

How to Staff an Entrepreneurial Firm?[17]

How do entrepreneurial managers staff their firms? Do they look for a certain kind of person to work in a high-growth venture?

These questions were posed to Venky Ganesan, a partner and managing director of Globespan Capital Partners, a San Francisco Bay Area venture capital firm that assists portfolio firms in developing a global presence. Venky Ganesan previously served as Vice President of JAFCO Ventures and cofounded Trigo Technologies, which was acquired by IBM. When asked what entrepreneurial managers look for in potential staff, he replied, "They look for flexible good general athletes rather than very domain focused experts. Early on (in a venture) it is about learning and flexibility and you want people open and eager for market feedback rather than 'experts' who have a predetermined view of the market. They (entrepreneurial managers) look for high energy, smart people who are relentless in their execution, people who look at every problem as an opportunity to solve rather than a barrier..." When asked what attracts individuals to work in high-intensity environments with long work hours and uncertain futures, Ganesan responded, "Individuals are attracted by the fast-paced, high-intensity culture that gives them great room to grow and learn. The high degree of learning and camaraderie of start-ups make up for the long work hours and uncertain future. Also, most young companies have little bureaucracy and very little middle management so people can actually do things as opposed to moving paper and filling out reports."

Clearly, the risks and rewards of staffing and joining a new venture make for an exciting and fast-paced work environment. It is essential that entrepreneurial managers recognize the unique needs of high-growth ventures and properly select those candidates whose expectations and talents fit this unique environment.

Process Fairness and Transparency

Selections for hire or advancement impact the person hired or selected, but also others in the organization. To help ensure that new hires and promoted individuals have the necessary legitimacy to be effective, the hiring/promotion process must be considered fair and transparent by organization employees as well as management. If a national search for a particular position is the norm, then deviations from this norm must be thoroughly explained or else there is a great risk of creating distrust in management. This distrust will likely make it more difficult for the new hire or promoted person to do the job assigned.

The Selection Process

There are some variations of the specific steps in the selection process. For example, the interview of a candidate for a first-line supervisory position may be relatively simple when compared with the rigorous interviews for a top-level executive. Nevertheless, the following broad outline is indicative of the typical process.

First, the selection criteria are established, usually on the basis of current, and sometimes future, job requirements. These criteria include such items as education, knowledge, skills, and experience. The candidate is then requested to complete an application form (this step may be omitted if the candidate is from within the organization). A screening interview follows to identify the more promising candidates. Additional information may be obtained by testing the candidate's qualifications for the position. Formal interviews are then conducted by the manager, his or her superior, and other persons within the organization. The information provided by the candidate is checked and verified. A physical examination may be required. Finally, on the basis of the information gathered, the candidate is either offered the job or informed that he or she has not been selected for the position. Let us examine some parts of the selection process in greater detail.

Interviews

Virtually, every manager hired or promoted by a company is interviewed by one or more people. Despite its general use, the interview is considerably distrusted as a reliable and valid means for selecting managers. Different interviewers may weigh or interpret the gathered information differently. Interviewers often do not ask the right questions. They may be influenced by the interviewee's general appearance, which may have little bearing on job performance. They also frequently make up their minds early in the interview, before they have all the information necessary to make a fair judgment.

Several techniques can be used to improve the interviewing process and overcome some of these weaknesses. First, interviewers should be trained so that they know what to look for. For example, in interviewing people from within the enterprise, they should analyze and discuss past records. They should study the results achieved as well as the way key managerial activities were performed. Chapter 12, on performance appraisal, shows in greater detail how this can be done. When selecting managers from outside the firm, these data are more difficult to obtain, and interviewers usually get them by checking with the listed references.

Second, interviewers should be prepared to ask the right questions. There are structured, semistructured, and unstructured interviews. In an *unstructured* interview, an interviewer may say something like "Tell me about your last job." In the *semistructured* interview, the interviewer follows an interview guide but may also ask other questions. In a *structured* interview, the interviewer asks a set of prepared questions.

A third way to improve selection is to conduct multiple interviews utilizing different interviewers. Thus, several people can compare their evaluations and perceptions. However, not all interviewers should vote in selecting a candidate; rather, their role is to provide additional information for the manager who will be responsible for the final decision.

Fourth, the interview is just one aspect of the selection process. It should be supplemented by data from the application form, the results of tests, and the information obtained from persons listed as references.

Reference checks and letters of recommendation may be necessary to verify the information given by the applicant. For a reference to be useful, the person must know the applicant well and give a truthful and complete assessment of the applicant. Many people are reluctant to provide information that may jeopardize an applicant's chances, and so the applicant's strong points are often overemphasized while shortcomings may be omitted or glossed over. In the United States, the Privacy Act of 1974 and related legislation and judicial rulings have made it even more difficult to obtain objective references. Under the Privacy Act, the applicant has a legal right to inspect letters of reference, unless this right is waived. This is one of the reasons that teachers are sometimes reluctant to make objective and accurate job referrals for their students.

Tests

The primary aim of testing is to obtain data about applicants that help predict their probable success as managers. Some of the benefits from testing include finding the best person for the job, obtaining a high degree of job satisfaction for the applicant, and reducing turnover. Some of the commonly used tests can be classified as follows:

- *Intelligence tests* are designed to measure mental capacity and to test memory, speed of thought, and ability to see relationships in complex problem situations.
- *Proficiency and aptitude tests* are constructed to discover interests, existing skills, and potential for acquiring skills.
- *Vocational tests* are designed to indicate a candidate's most suitable occupation or the areas in which the candidate's interests match the interests of people working in those areas.
- *Personality tests* are designed to reveal a candidate's personal characteristics and the way the candidate may interact with others, thereby giving a measure of leadership potential.

Tests have a number of limitations, however. First, competent industrial psychologists agree that tests are not accurate enough to be used as the sole measure of candidates' characteristics, but must be interpreted in light of each individual's entire history. Second, the test user must know what tests do and what their limitations are. One of the major limitations is uncertainty about whether tests are really applicable; even psychologists are not highly confident that present-day tests are effective in measuring managerial abilities and potentials. Third, before any test is widely used, it should be tried out, if possible on existing personnel, to see whether it is valid for employees whose managerial abilities are already known. Fourth, it is also important that tests be administered and interpreted by experts in the field. Finally, tests should not discriminate unfairly and should be consistent with laws and government guidelines.

Assessment Centers

The **assessment center** is not a location but a technique for selecting and promoting managers. This approach may be used in combination with training.

Assessment center Technique for selecting and promoting managers.

www.att.com

Assessment centers were first used for selecting and promoting lower-level supervisors, but now they are applied to middle-level managers as well. They seem, however, to be inappropriate for top executives. The assessment center technique is not new. It was used by the German and British military in World War II and the American Office of Strategic Services. But its first corporate use in the United States is generally attributed to the American Telephone and Telegraph Company in the 1950s.

Intended to measure how a potential manager will act in typical managerial situations, the usual center approach is to have candidates take part in a series of exercises. During this period, they are observed and assessed by psychologists or experienced managers. A typical assessment center will have the candidates do the following: take various psychological tests; engage in management games in small groups; engage in "in-basket" exercises in which they are asked to handle a variety of matters that they might face in a managerial job; participate in a leaderless group discussion of some problem; give a brief oral presentation on a particular topic or theme, usually recommending a course of desirable action to a mythical superior; and engage in various other exercises, such as preparing a written report.

During these exercises, the candidates are observed by their evaluators, who also interview them from time to time. At the end of the assessment center period, the assessors summarize their own appraisal of each candidate's performance; then they compare their evaluations, come to conclusions concerning each candidate's managerial potential, and write a summary report on each candidate. These reports are made available to appointing managers for their guidance. They are also often used as guides for management development. In many cases, candidates are given feedback on their evaluation; in other cases, feedback is given only when candidates request it. Sometimes, the overall evaluation as to promotability remains confidential, even though candidates may be informed by assessors about their performance in the various exercises.

Evidence of the usefulness of the assessment center approach, although not conclusive, is encouraging. On the other hand, there is controversy over to whom, by whom, and under what circumstances this and other tests should be administered and as to who should receive the test results.

Assessment centers do present some problems. First, they are costly in terms of time, especially since many effective programs extend over a 5-day period. Second, training assessors is a problem, particularly in companies that believe, with some justification, that the best assessors are likely to be experienced line managers rather than trained psychologists. Third, although a number of different exercises are used to cover the kinds of things a manager does, questions have been raised as to whether these exercises are the best criteria for evaluation. An even greater problem exists in determining which evaluation measures should be applied to each exercise. Most assessment centers, being highly oriented to individual and interpersonal behavior under various circumstances, may be overlooking the most important element in selecting managers, especially those about to enter the managerial ranks for the first time. That element is motivation—whether or not a person truly wants to be a manager. To be so motivated, candidates must know what managing is, what it involves, and what is required to be a successful manager. Obviously, motivation is a difficult quality to evaluate. However, by making clear to a candidate what managing involves and requires and then asking the candidate to think this over, the interviewer can give the candidate a good basis on which to determine whether he or she really wants to be a manager.

Limitations of the Selection Process

The diversity of selection approaches and tests indicates that there is no one perfect way to select managers. Experience has shown that even carefully chosen selection criteria are still imperfect in predicting performance. Furthermore, there is a distinction between what persons can do—that is, their ability to perform—and what they will do, which relates to motivation. The latter is a function of the individual and the environment. For example, a person's needs may be different at various times. The organizational environment also changes. The climate of an enterprise may change from one that encourages initiative to one that restricts it because a new top management introduces a different managerial philosophy. Therefore, selection techniques and instruments are not a sure way to predict what people will do, even though they may have the ability to do it.

Testing itself, especially psychological testing, has limitations. Specifically, seeking of certain information may be considered an invasion of privacy. In addition, it has been charged that some tests unfairly discriminate against women or members of minority groups. These complex issues are not easily resolved, yet they cannot be ignored when an enterprise is selecting managers.

Still other concerns in selection and hiring are the time and costs involved, including advertising, agency fees, tests, interviews, reference checks, medical examinations, relocation, orientation, and start-up time required for the new manager to get acquainted with the job. When recruiting costs are recognized, it becomes evident that turnover can be very expensive to an enterprise.

GLOBAL PERSPECTIVE[18]

HRM in India and Other Countries

Outsourcing has become very popular with globalization. India is often the favorite place for outsourcing. The benefits for outsourcing are obtaining a lower cost service which may increase the competitive advantage of the firm doing the outsourcing. But, outsourcing is not without risk because cultural differences may result in some difficulty in communication even though English is widely spoken. Other considerations are the differences in time zones that may hinder, for example, providing assistance to Dell customers in the United States. On the other hand, communication through the internet is rather inexpensive. But India has no monopoly on the information technology and outsourcing. In Asia, the workforce in the Philippines also offers IT services and China is in the process of going into the IT business.

These developments have important implications on staffing and leading. Human resource managers have now a greater and more diverse tool for selecting suitable persons for the tasks. Traditional tools for selecting the right candidate may not be appropriate for candidates in other countries. Moreover, training and performance evaluation may have to be adapted to the local environment. Compensation, motivation, local needs, and requirements, as well as expectations differ among countries. Companies need to adapt to the local situation. This is true for India as well as for other countries.

ORIENTING AND SOCIALIZING NEW EMPLOYEES

The selection of the best person for the job is only the first step in building an effective management team. Even companies that make great efforts in the recruitment and selection process often ignore the needs of new managers after they have been hired. Yet, the first few days and weeks can be crucial for integrating the new person into the organization.

Orientation involves the introduction of new employees to the enterprise—its functions, tasks, and people. Large firms usually have a formal orientation program that explains these features of the company: history, products and services, general policies and practices, organization (divisions, departments, and geographic locations), benefits (insurance, retirement, and vacations), requirements for confidentiality and secrecy (especially with regard to defense contracts), as well as safety and other regulations. These may be further described in detail in a company booklet, but the orientation meeting provides new employees with

Orientation
Introduction of new employees to the enterprise—its functions, tasks, and people.

an opportunity to ask questions. Although staff from the personnel department usually conduct these formal programs, the primary responsibility for orienting the new manager still rests with the superior.

GLOBAL PERSPECTIVE

Creating an Environment that People Enjoy[19]

In the new millennium, companies are fiercely competing for talent in a very competitive job market. Losing a valuable employee may cost a company $50,000 to $100,000. How, then, can a company retain its intellectual capital?

Leaders such as Herb Kelleher at Southwest Airlines and Jack Welch at General Electric have done much to inspire their employees by providing an environment with challenging work and opportunities for personal and professional growth. Companies have pursued various strategies to retain employees. Firms with a good reputation, such as Southwest Airlines and General Electric, can highlight to their employees the competitive advantage of their firm and the opportunities in a growing organization. Companies in a market leadership position also have an advantage in retaining employees, as they can point out that leaving the company may be a step down. Other firms have created a feeling of community and family in their organization. Employees also like the flexibility of gaining different kinds of experience in various parts of the company. Empowerment through broad delegation gives employees decision-making authority and a sense of responsibility. Cisco Systems constantly makes its employees aware that they are welcomed. General Electric makes heavy investments in the best people through training and mentoring. Southwest Airlines pays much attention to finding the right people during the selection process by hiring people who fit the organization culture.

While companies face serious challenges in recruiting and retaining employees, people preparing for a career in management or as a staff person find in this situation a great opportunity.

www.southwest.com
www.ge.com
www.cisco.com

Organizational socialization
Acquisition of work skills and abilities, adoption of appropriate role behaviors, and adjustment to the norms and values of the work group.

There is another and perhaps even more important aspect of orientation: the socialization of new managers. **Organizational socialization** is defined in several different ways. A global view includes three aspects: acquisition of work skills and abilities, adoption of appropriate role behaviors, and adjustment to the norms and values of the work group. So, in addition to meeting the specific requirements of the job, new managers will usually encounter new values, new personal relationships, and new modes of behavior. They do not know whom they can ask for advice, they do not know how the organization works, and they have a fear of failing in the new job. All this uncertainty can cause a great deal of anxiety for a new employee, especially a management trainee. Because the initial experience in an enterprise can be very important for future management behavior, the first contact of trainees should be with the best superiors in the enterprise, people who can serve as models for future behavior.

MANAGING HUMAN RESOURCES WHILE MOVING TOWARD 2020[20]

The future is difficult to predict; yet managers do have to make decisions now to prepare for the future. The Economist Intelligence Unit surveyed some 1,650 executives from around the world asking how they see changes while moving toward the year 2020. The areas that have the greatest potential for improving productivity are managing knowledge, providing services and support to customers, improving operations and production processes, developing businesses and strategies, managing marketing and sales activities, managing human resources and training, as well as other areas. These views of executives do have important implications for human resource management.

The contributions of knowledge workers may be most critical for gaining a competitive advantage. Moreover, collaboration within the organization as well as with the outside will be very important. This, of course, requires people with good interpersonal relationships. They need to be able to operate in different cultural environments and communicate well. The staffing functions of recruitment, selection, training, and development will play important roles in preparing for the future. Similarly, effective leading, motivation, and communication, functions discussed in Part 5 in this book, will be essential to compete in the global environment.

The Future of Work[21]

Globalization and technology are changing our jobs. It is, of course, difficult to predict the future; but, some of the trends can already be seen in companies. The new CEO may be a global networker. Although organization structure will still be needed, the cubical culture will be reduced or eliminated. This means the office boundaries will be removed and offices and office desks will become less important or even disappear. The workforce will be even more multicultural that is it now. Wellness programs will aim to keep the workers healthy and employees may choose from a variety of benefits ("cafeteria" approach). Projects will be multidisciplinary with a scalable workforce to adjust to the work demands. In some ways, the future is already here.

SUMMARY

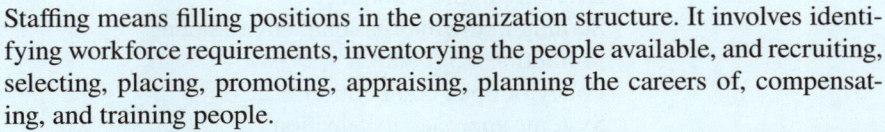

Staffing means filling positions in the organization structure. It involves identifying workforce requirements, inventorying the people available, and recruiting, selecting, placing, promoting, appraising, planning the careers of, compensating, and training people.

In the systems approach to staffing, enterprise and organization plans become important inputs for staffing tasks. The number and quality of managers required to carry out crucial tasks depend on many different factors. One major step in staffing is to determine the people available by making a management inventory, which can be done in the form of an inventory chart.

Staffing does not take place in a vacuum; one must consider many situational factors, both internal and external. Staffing requires adherence to equal employment opportunity laws so that practices do not discriminate, for example, against minorities or women. Also, one must evaluate the pros and cons of promoting people from within the organization or selecting people from outside.

In the systems model for selection, the comprehensive managerial requirements plan is the basis for position requirements. In designing jobs, the enterprise must see that the job has an appropriate scope, is challenging, and reflects required skills. The job structure must be appropriate in terms of content, function, and relationships. Jobs can be designed for individuals or work teams. The importance of technical, human, conceptual, and design skills varies with the level in the organizational hierarchy. The position requirements have to be matched with the various skills and personal characteristics of individuals. The matching is important in recruitment, selection, placement, and promotion.

Errors in selection can lead to actualization of the Peter Principle, which states that managers tend to be promoted to the level of their incompetence. Although the advice of several people should be sought, the selection decision should generally rest with the immediate superior of the candidate for the position.

The selection process may include interviews, various tests, and the use of assessment centers. To avoid dissatisfaction and employee turnover, companies must ensure that new employees are introduced to and integrated with other persons in the organization.

KEY IDEAS AND CONCEPTS FOR REVIEW

Staffing
Systems approach to human resource management
Management inventory
Situational factors affecting staffing
Equal employment opportunity
Women in management
Diversity in the workplace
Staffing in the international environment
Promotion from within
Policy of open competition
Systems approach to selection
Position and job requirements
Job design
Recruitment
Selection
Placement
Promotion
Peter Principle
Validity and reliability
Selection process
Interview
Kinds of tests
Assessment center
Orientation and socialization
The future of managing human resources

FOR DISCUSSION

1. Why is the function of staffing seldom approached logically? Briefly describe the systems approach to staffing. How is staffing related to other managerial functions and activities?
2. List and evaluate external factors affecting staffing. Which ones are most critical today? Explain.
3. What are the dangers and difficulties in applying a policy of promotion from within? What is meant by a policy of open competition? Do you favor such a policy? Why or why not?
4. What is the systems approach to selection of managers? Why is it called a systems approach? How does it differ from other approaches?
5. What are some of the factors that are important in designing individual jobs and jobs for work teams? Which ones seem most important to you? Why?
6. The Peter Principle has been widely quoted in management circles. What do you think of it? Do you think that it could ever apply to you? Does it mean that all chief executives are incompetent? Explain.
7. What is an assessment center? How does it work? Would you like to participate in such a center? Why or why not?

EXERCISES/ACTION STEPS

1. Select an organization that you have an interest in and evaluate the effectiveness of its recruitment and selection of people. How systematically are these and other staffing activities carried out? Make an inquiry to this firm and determine how to arrange for an informational interview.
2. Go to the library and research the background of successful CEOs. You may begin by looking at *Fortune* magazine or reading the biography of a CEO. What makes the CEOs successful?

INTERNET RESEARCH

1. Use one of the popular search engines to search for "workforce.com". What are some of the current topics human resource managers concerned about?
2. What does equal employment opportunity mean? Search the Web, then select a topic and present it to the class.

GLOBAL CASE

Recruiting Talent at Infosys[22]

Infosys, founded in 1981 in Pune by N. R. Narayana Murthy and his colleagues, is one of the biggest IT (Information Technology) companies in India. Two years later, the firm moved its headquarters to Bangalore. In 1987, Infosys began its international expansion by opening its first sales office in Boston. By 2008, the company with more than 90,000 employees (mostly professionals) expanded its operation to more than 30 worldwide offices. How does one recruit competent people for this global organization?

Operating in the software industry, Infosys provides services to many businesses in a variety of industry segments including banking, communication media, entertainment, manufacturing, energy and utilities, retail businesses, consumer products and services, and many others.

In 1996, the company created a foundation, headed by Mrs. Sudha Murthy, that works in a variety of areas such as healthcare, arts, culture, social activities, and education. Some of the initiatives include a program called Academic Entente that involves activities such as arranging academic conferences, research collaboration, a global internship program, and study tours to the company's development center. This initiative provides the link to academic institutions. The global internship program also provides opportunities for recruiting undergraduates, graduates, as well as Ph.D. students. The disciplines are not restricted to business students, but also include liberal arts majors. Such programs aim at getting young people interested in information technology and computer science.

The $120 million Global Education Center in Mysore, about 90 miles from Bangalore, is one of the largest company training centers. It has been said that it is more difficult to be admitted to the Infosys training program than to get into Harvard. Only 1% of applicants get invited to the campus, which is like a modern university; it also includes a large gym, a swimming pool, a bowling alley, and even a hair salon. But the campus is run by strict rules, such as alcohol prohibition. Yet, the "freshers", as the new recruits are called, do not complain—indeed, it is considered a dream come true to be invited to the program, which not only focuses on technical skills but also includes communication and team-building classes. The participants come from many countries and the aim is to train some 10,000 employees at a time.

Questions:

1. People are the key to success of enterprises. Assess the recruitment efforts for finding and recruiting such talents at Infosys.
2. Would you be interested in working for Infosys operating in many diverse businesses or would you prefer to become an entrepreneur working for a relative or establishing your own business?
3. List the advantages and disadvantages working for a company like Infosys or being an entrepreneur.

ENDNOTES

1. See also human asset accounting for the economy at www.knowledgeu.com/human_capital.html, accessed June 5, 2002.
2. For a discussion of human resource management in German and U.S. firms, see Helmut Wagner and Marion Linke, "Internationales Management der Humanressourcen in deutschen und amerikanischen Unternehmen," in Ralph Berndt (ed.), *Global Management* (Berlin: Springer, 1996), pp. 457–475. See also the Society for Human Resource Management, www.shrm.org, accessed August 18, 2011.
3. Christine Tierney and Joann Muller, "BMW: Speeding into a Tight Turn," *Business Week*, November 5, 2001, pp. 54–55. See also BMW, *www.bmw.com*, accessed November 16, 2011.
4. Tierney and Muller, "BMW: Speeding into a Tight Turn," p. 55.
5. Business World (2004) "BW Most Respected Company Awards 2004," accessed April 28, 2014.
6. Infosys Makes it to NASDAQ 100, Infosys Press release and "Infosys Looks Beyond Nasdaq 100 -Global Ambitions for Pioneering Indian Firm," http://www.infoworld.com/t/architecture/infosys-looks-beyond-nasdaq-100-642, accessed April 28, 2014.
7. Parshotam Dass and Barbara Parker, "Strategies for Managing Human Resource Diversity: From Resistance to Learning," *The Academy of Management Executive*, May 1999, pp. 68–80. See also http://money.cnn.com/magazines/fortune/bestcompanies/minorities, accessed August 31, 2006; Richard W. July and Carol D. A'Amico, *Workforce 2020* (Indianapolis: Hudson Institute, August 1999); see also Kathryn A. Canas and Harris Sondak, *Opportunities and Challenges of Workplace Diversity* (Upper Saddle River, NJ, 2008); Scott E. Page, "Making the Difference: Applying a Logic of Diversity," *The Academy of Management Perspectives,* November 2007, pp. 6–29; Myrtle P. Bell and Daphne P. Berry, "Viewing Diversity Through Different Lenses," *The Academy of Management Perspectives*, November 2007, pp. 21–25.
8. www.mcdonalds.com/corp/values/diversity.html, accessed August 31, 2006; www.rmhc.org/usa/good/people.html, accessed August 31, 2006; media. ford.com/newsroom/feature_display.cfm?release=17674, accessed November 13, 2008.
9. Arvind V. Phatak, *International Dimensions of Management*, 4th ed. (Cincinnati, OH: South-Western, 1995), Chap. 6; Arvind V. Phatak, *International Management* (Cincinnati, OH: South-Western, 1997), Chap. 13.
10. "Wipro Chooses Atlanta for Development Center," *The Wall Street Journal*, August 29, 2007.
11. Mark Gimein, "Sam Walton Made Us a Promise," *Fortune*, March 18, 2002, pp. 120–130; *Wal-Mart*, www.walmart.com, accessed August 18, 2011.
12. Stephen Baker, "You're Fired – But Stay in Touch," *Business Week*, May 4, 2009, pp. 54–55.
13. R. Blatt (2009). "Tough Love: How Communal Schemas and Contracting Practices Build Relational Capital in Entrepreneurial Teams", *Academy of Management Review*, 2009, 34 (3): 533–551. M. Ensley, A. Pearson, and A. Amason, "Understanding the Dynamics of New Venture Top Management Teams: Cohesion, Conflict, and New Venture Performance," *Journal of Business Venturing*, 2002, 17: 365–386.
14. Hui, James Manyika, and Mehdi Miremadi, "Four Fundamentals of Workplace Automation," *McKinsey Quarterly*, November 2015.
15. "Management in China – Go East, My Son," *The Economist*, August 12, 2006, p. 53.
16. Laurence J. Peter and Raymond Hall, *The Peter Principle* (New York: Bantam, 1969). See also Laurence J. Peter, *The Peter Pyramid: Or Will We Ever Get the Point?* (New York: Morrow, 1986) and its review by Peter Shaw, "A Management Guru Peters Out," *Wall Street Journal*, January 24, 1986. For the application of the Peter Principle to software development, see Craig Kirkwood, "Adobe and the Peter Principle," www.planetpublish.com, April 17, 2002, accessed June 5, 2002.
17. Interview conducted with Venky Ganesan, Managing Director with Globespan Capital Partners, on January 2, 2007 by Mark Cannice.
18. Singha Chiamsiri, Sri Devi Bulusu & Mithlesh Agarwal, "Information Technology Offshore Outsourcing in India: A Human Resource Management Perspective", http://rphrm.curtin.edu.au/2005/issue2/india.html, accessed January 5, 2016; Pawan S. Budhwar, "HRM in Context," http://ccm.sagepub.com/cgi/content/abstract/1/3/333, accessed January 5, 2016.
19. Nicholas Stein, "Winning the War to Keep Top Talent," *Fortune*, May 29, 2000, pp. 132–138.
20. "Foresight 2020, Economic, Industry, and Corporate Trends," Economist Intelligence Unit 2006 (London: *The Economist*, 2006); see also 2020 Management Insight: Management Development, http://www.2020.eu.com/content/view/15/30, accessed August 18, 2011; Stephan Manning, Silvia Massine, and Arie Y. Lewin, "A Dynamic Perspective on Next Generation Offshoring: The Global Sourcing of Science and Engineering Talent," *The Academy of Management Perspective,* August 2008, pp. 35–54; see also Work Rules, Laszlo Bock, https://www.workrules.net/, accessed October 2015.
21. Various Authors, "The Future of Work," *Business Week,* August 20 and 27, 2007, pp. 41–95.
22. Infosys Tops India's Most-Admired Companies, *The Wall Street Journal Asian Edition,* November 2, 2010, http://online.wsj.com/article/SB10001424052702304173704575577683613256368.html, accessed January 5, 2015.

CHAPTER 12

Performance Appraisal and Career Strategy

Learning Objectives

After studying this chapter, you should be able to:

LO 1   recognize the importance of effectively appraising managers

LO 2   identify the qualities that should be measured in appraising managers

LO 3   present a system of managerial appraisal based on evaluating performance against verifiable objectives and performance as a manager

LO 4   describe the team approach to evaluation

LO 5   recognize the rewards and stress of managing

LO 6   identify important aspects of career planning

LO 7   write your own professional biography

LO 8   write your own 10-year professional development plan

Managerial appraisal has sometimes been referred to as the Achilles' heel of managerial staffing, but it is a major key to managing itself. It is the basis for determining who is promotable to a higher position. It is also important to management development because it is difficult to determine whether development efforts are aimed in the right direction if a manager's strengths and weaknesses are not known. Appraisal is, or should be, an integral part of a system of managing. Knowing how well a manager plans, organizes, staffs, leads, and controls is really the only way to ensure that those occupying managerial positions are actually managing effectively. If a business, a government agency, a charitable organization, or even a university is to reach its goals effectively and efficiently, ways of accurately measuring management performance must be found and implemented.

There are other reasons why effective managerial appraisal is important. One of the most compelling reasons in the United States arises from the provisions of Title VII of the Civil Rights Act of 1964 (as amended in 1972) and the regulations of the Equal Employment Opportunity Commission and the Office of Federal Contract Compliance. These agencies have been highly critical of many appraisal programs, finding that they often result in discrimination, particularly in areas of race, age, and sex. Courts have supported the federal agencies in their insistence that, to be acceptable, an appraisal program must be reliable and valid and that these agencies set rigorous standards is apparent.

Effective performance appraisal should also recognize the legitimate desire of employees for progress in their professions. One way to integrate organizational demands and individual needs is through career management, which can be a part of performance appraisal, as this chapter will explain.

| www.eeoc.gov |

CHOOSING APPRAISAL CRITERIA

The appraisal should measure performance in accomplishing goals and plans as well as performance as a manager. No one wants a person in a managerial role who appears to do everything right as a manager but who cannot turn in a good record of profit making, marketing, controllership, or whatever the area of responsibility may be. Nor should one be satisfied to have a "performer" in a managerial position who cannot operate effectively as a manager. Some star performers may have succeeded by chance and not through effective managing.

Performance in Accomplishing Goals

In assessing performance, systems of appraising against verifiable preselected goals have extraordinary value. Given consistent, integrated, and understood planning designed to reach specific objectives, probably, the best criteria of managerial performance relate to the ability to set goals intelligently, to plan programs that will accomplish those goals, and to succeed in achieving them. Those who have operated under some variation of this system often claim that these criteria are inadequate and that elements of luck or other factors beyond the manager's control are not excluded when arriving at any appraisal. In too many cases, managers who achieve results owing to sheer luck are promoted, and those who do not achieve the expected results because of factors beyond their control are blamed for failures. Thus, appraisal against verifiable objectives is, by itself, insufficient.

Performance as Managers

The system of measuring performance against preestablished objectives should be supplemented by an appraisal of the manager as a manager. Managers at any level also undertake nonmanagerial duties, and these cannot be overlooked. However, the primary purpose for which managers are hired and against which they should be measured is their performance as managers, which means they should be appraised on the basis of how well they understand and undertake the managerial functions of planning, organizing, staffing, leading, and controlling. The standards to use in this area are the fundamentals of management; but, first, appraising against performance objectives should be examined.

> The system of measuring performance against preestablished objectives should be supplemented by an appraisal of the manager as a manager.

APPRAISING MANAGERS AGAINST VERIFIABLE OBJECTIVES

One widely used approach to managerial appraisal is the system of evaluating managerial performance against the setting and accomplishing of verifiable objectives. As was noted in Chapter 4, a **network** of meaningful and attainable objectives is basic to effective managing. This is simple logic, since people cannot be expected to accomplish a task with effectiveness or efficiency unless they know what the end points of their efforts should be. Nor can any organized enterprise be expected to do so.

> A **network** of meaningful and attainable objectives is basic to effective managing.

The Appraisal Process

Once a program of managing by verifiable objectives is operating, appraisal is a fairly easy step. Superiors determine how well managers set objectives and how well they have performed against them. In cases where appraisal by results has failed or has been disillusioning, the principal reason is that managing by objectives was seen only as an appraisal technique. The system is not likely to work if used only for this purpose. Management by objectives must be a way of managing, a way of planning, as well as the key to organizing, staffing, leading, and controlling. When this is the case, appraisal boils down to whether managers have established adequate and reasonably attainable objectives and how they have performed against them in a certain period. Look at the systems approach to management by objectives in Figure 4.4 in Chapter 4. As shown in the figure, appraising is merely a last step in the entire process.

There are other questions to consider too. Were the goals adequate? Did they call for "stretched" (high but reasonable) performance? These questions can be answered only through the judgment and experience of a person's superior, although this judgment can become sharper with time and experience, and it may be even more objective if the superior can use the goals of other managers in similar positions for comparison.

In assessing the accomplishment of goals, the evaluator must take into account such considerations as whether the goals were reasonably attainable in the first place, whether factors beyond a person's control unduly helped or hindered the person in accomplishing goals, and what the reasons for the results were. The reviewer should also note whether an individual continued to operate against obsolete goals when situations changed and revised goals were called for.

Different Views on Appraisal Issues

People hold different views on performance appraisal issues. We will focus on three of them.

Subjective versus Objective Evaluation

There are those who still maintain that subjective rating of subordinates is sufficient. After all, it is argued that managerial performance is difficult to evaluate. On the other side of the argument are those who maintain that an appraisal must be completely objective and only numbers count; either a person achieves the previously set objective or not.

Appraisal should focus on results, but one must be careful to avoid the "numbers game". Figures can be manipulated to suit the individual, thus defeating the purpose of appraisal. Also, pursuing a limited number of verifiable criteria may ignore other, not formally stated objectives, as one cannot set objectives for all tasks. It is, therefore, not only important to look at performance figures but also at the causes of positive or negative deviations from standards, although this may involve some subjective judgment.

> **Appraisal** should focus on results, but one must be careful to avoid the "numbers game."

Judging versus Self-Appraisal

There is the view that managers have the authority vested in their position, and therefore, they should be the sole judge in assessing the performance of their subordinates. But many managers dislike being placed in the role of a judge, especially when they are asked to evaluate subordinates on personality characteristics. Similarly, employees feel uncomfortable being judged on factors that have questionable relationships to the tasks they are doing. The other view holds that people should be asked to appraise themselves. It is realized that some subordinates may be harsher on themselves than their superior would be; but other individuals may rate themselves unreasonably high, especially if the rating influences their salary.

The management-by-objectives philosophy places emphasis on self-control and self-direction. But this presupposes that verifiable objectives have been previously set (primarily by the subordinate in conjunction with the superior), against which performance can be measured. Indeed, if this is done well, appraising is relatively easy. There should be no surprises during the appraisal

> The management-by-objectives philosophy places emphasis on self-control and self-direction.

meeting: subordinates know what they want to achieve and superiors know what contributions they can expect from their subordinates. Besides the comprehensive appraisal, periodic and constant monitoring of performance can uncover deviations from standards. Generally, then, subordinates should have an opportunity to exercise self-control, but the superior still has the veto power in case of controversy about the objective that is the basis for performance appraisal.

Assessing Past Performance versus Future Development

Some managers see the purpose of appraisal primarily as assessing past performance, but others focus on the developmental aspects of appraisal. The improvement orientation in the latter is toward the future.[1]

With the emphasis on self-appraisal and responsible self-direction, the judgmental aspect in appraisal is considerably reduced. To be sure, one should learn from past mistakes, but one should use these insights for translating them into development plans for the future. Clearly, appraisal can be an excellent opportunity to emphasize a person's strengths and to prepare action plans for overcoming weaknesses, as discussed in the career planning section later in this chapter.

> One should learn from past mistakes and translate these insights into development plans for the future.

Three Kinds of Reviews

The simplified model of performance appraisal shown in Figure 12.1 indicates three kinds of appraisals: (1) a comprehensive review, (2) progress or periodic reviews, and (3) continuous monitoring.

There is a general agreement that a *formal comprehensive appraisal* should be conducted at least once a year, but some people suggest that such discussions should take place more frequently. Some enterprises do all the reviews within a short period of time each year, while others schedule the appraisals throughout the year, often at the employment anniversary. A case could be made against any rigid schedule of annual performance reviews. Instead, it may be argued with good reason that performance should be reviewed, for example, after the completion of a major project. Obviously, no universally applicable suggestion can be made about the time frame for the formal comprehensive review. It depends on the nature of the task, past company practices, and other situational factors. Once, twice, or even three times may be appropriate for a particular organization or a person who is new in a job.

> The formal comprehensive appraisal should be conducted at least once a year, with discussions taking place more frequently. It should be supplemented by frequent progress or periodic reviews as well as continuous monitoring.

What is important is that the formal comprehensive review should be supplemented by frequent *progress or periodic reviews*. These reviews can be short and relatively informal, but they help identify problems or barriers that hinder effective performance. They also keep communication open between the superior and the subordinates. Furthermore, priorities can be rearranged and objectives can be renegotiated if warranted by changed situations. It certainly is inappropriate to pursue obsolete or even unsuitable objectives that were agreed on in an environment of uncertainties.

FIGURE 12.1 The appraisal process

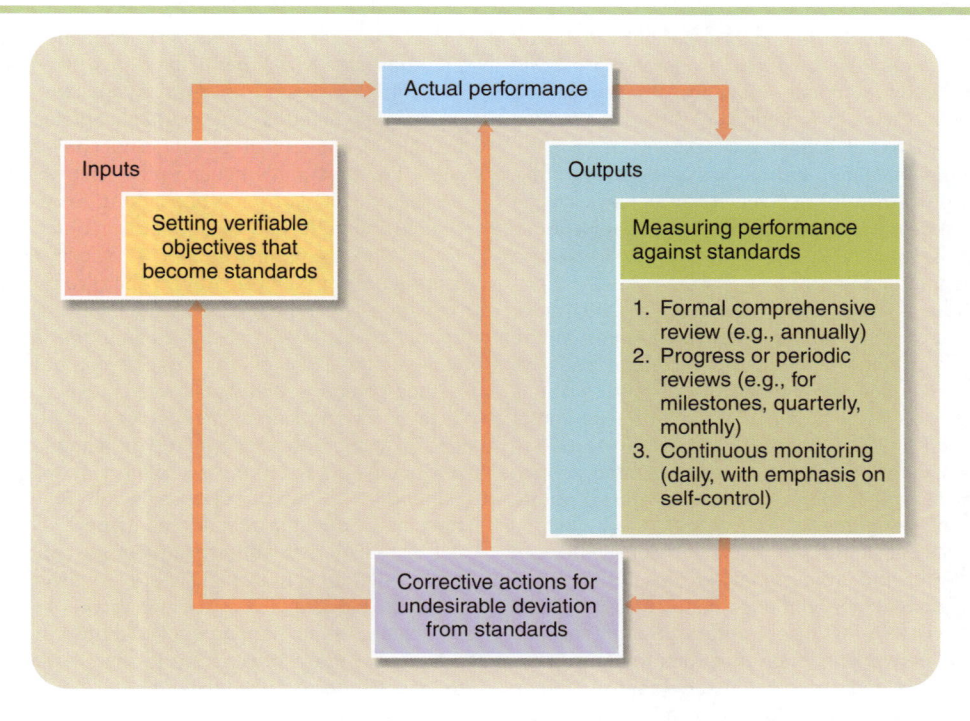

Redrawn from Heinz Weihrich, *Management Excellence: Productivity through MBO* (New York: McGraw-Hill, 1985), p. 125.

Finally, there is *continuous monitoring* of performance. With this system, when performance deviates from plans, one does not have to wait for the next periodic review to correct it. The superior and the subordinate discuss the situation immediately so that corrective actions can be taken at once in order to prevent a small deviation from developing into a major problem.

Strengths of Appraisal against Verifiable Objectives

The strengths of appraising against accomplishment of objectives are almost the same as those of managing by objectives. Both are part of the same process, both are basic to effective managing, and both are means of improving the quality of managing.

In the area of appraising, there are other special and important strengths. Appraising on the basis of performance against verifiable objectives has the great advantage of being operational. Appraisals are not apart from the job that managers do, but are a review of what they actually did as managers.

There are always questions of how well a person did; of whether goals were missed or accomplished, and for what reasons; and of how much in the way of goal attainment should be expected. But information about what a person has done, measured against what that individual agreed was a reasonable target, is available. This information furnishes strong presumptions of objectivity and reduces the element of pure judgment in appraisal. Besides, the appraisal can be carried on in an atmosphere in which superiors work cooperatively with subordinates rather than sitting in judgment of them.

ENTREPRENEURIAL PERSPECTIVE

Interview with Shomit Ghose, Venture Capitalist Partner with Onset Ventures, on Evaluating Managers of Venture-Backed Portfolio Firms[2]

Shomit Ghose is a venture capitalist partner with Onset Ventures in Menlo Park, California. Onset Ventures, with over $1 billion under management and eight successful funds launched since its founding in 1984, has a proven record of successful investment in early-stage information, communication, and medical technology firms. Onset is well known for actively collaborating with the firms it finances, helping entrepreneurs develop business models, identifying new markets, and recruiting ideal management teams.

Mr. Ghose joined Onset Ventures in 2001 after 19 years of working at high-tech companies in the Silicon Valley. During his career, he participated in several successful IPOs, including those of Sun Microsystems and Broadvision. Prior to joining Onset, he was Senior Vice President (VP) of Operations at Tumbleweed Communications, where he managed the marketing, professional services, applications engineering, and corporate development departments. He helped the company through a successful IPO in 1999. Previously, he was VP of the Worldwide Professional Services Organization at Broadvision and helped that company through a successful IPO in 1996. At Onset Ventures, Shomit focuses on software, networking, and infrastructure companies. He also mentors and provides management resources to portfolio companies to help maximize their success.

Given Shomit's deep experience on guiding successful ventures, we asked him about his approach to appraising managers. Mr. Ghose told us, "At the coarsest level of granularity, as a start-up investor, I evaluate chief executive officers (CEOs) based on two principal metrics: the ability to raise money, and the ability to hire well. Implicit in the former is the ability to espouse a strategic vision, the ability to validate that vision via customer wins, and the ability to deliver a compelling business model. If you've been able to do these three, then you'll always be able to raise money at positive valuations. So the ability to get the interest of new investors and raise money is truly a capstone metric, a proxy, that allows you to objectively evaluate a business' – and hence the CEO's – progress." He continued, "Of course, start-ups can only grow if they have the right staff to scale the business. This certainly applies to companies in growing markets, and perhaps applies even more acutely in markets that are facing challenges. So my other key metric in evaluating the success or failure of a start-up CEO is by the quality and experience of the direct-reports they've succeeded in hiring."

Mr. Ghose emphasized that "The ability to hire well is a great proxy for an executive's ability to provide people management and effective leadership within the organization. It's a perfect capstone metric that allows you to evaluate the CEO's skill as a people manager and leader of their company. With quality staff in place the business always has a fighting chance to overcome any obstacles and grow. No one ever got fired for hiring too well, while not hiring well is the most surefire way to find yourself out of a job." From our discussion with Shomit Ghose, it became evident that management appraisal is an essential capability of a successful venture capital firm, and central elements of this ability are identifying and evaluating appropriate proxies for management performance. In the case of top management of venture-backed enterprise case, these proxies are top management's ability to raise financing and to hire well.

Mr. Ghose also detailed his evaluation criteria for functional managers, stating, "As for C-level executives below the CEO, I evaluate them primarily on their ability to contribute to the bottom line. For VPs of sales, it's based on their being able to build a scalable selling model with customers that matter. For VPs of marketing, it's the ability to generate reliable lead-flow for the sales team; they need to be able to make Sales' job *bonehead easy*. For VPs of engineering, it's the ability to deliver a product that meets the needs of the customer within the very finite time frames that are typical in start-up ventures." Clearly, evaluation criteria will vary with the level and mandate of the managers involved. What are best proxies for effective management in the enterprise you are associated with?

Weaknesses of Appraisal Against Verifiable Objectives

As noted in Chapter 4, there are certain weaknesses in the implementation of managing by objectives. These apply with equal force to appraisal. One of them is that it is entirely possible for persons to meet or miss goals through no effort or fault of their own. Luck often plays a part in performance. A new product's acceptance may be far beyond expectations, and its success will make a marketing manager look exceptionally good, even though the quality of the marketing program and its implementation might actually be poor. Or an unpredictable cancellation of a major military contract might make the record of a division manager look unsatisfactory. There may also be an overemphasis on output quantity and not enough attention given to the quality of the product or service.[3]

Most evaluators will say that they always take uncontrollable or unexpected factors into account in assessing goal performance, and to a very great extent they do. But it is extremely difficult to do so. In an outstanding sales record, for example, how can anyone be sure how much was due to luck and how much to competence? Outstanding performers are rated highly, at least as long as they perform. Nonperformers can hardly escape having a cloud cast over them.

With its emphasis on accomplishing operating objectives, the system of appraising against these may overlook needs for individual development. Goal attainment tends to be short run in practice. Even if longer-range goals are put into the system, seldom are they so long range as to allow for adequate long-term development of managers. Managers concerned primarily with results might be driven by the system to take too little time to plan, implement, and follow through with programs required for their development and that of their subordinates.

On the other hand, since managing by objectives gives better visibility to managerial needs, development programs can be better pinpointed. If individual development is to be ensured, goals in this area should be specifically set.

From an appraisal as well as an operating management point of view, perhaps the greatest deficiency of management by objectives is that it appraises operating performance only. Not only is there the question of luck, but also there are other factors to appraise, notably an individual's managerial abilities. This is why an adequate appraisal system must appraise performance as a manager as well as performance in setting and meeting goals.

GLOBAL PERSPECTIVE

How About a Twitter Performance Evaluation?[4]

Twitter is a social networking program that is limited by 140 words communication. In the Twitter and Facebook age, people want immediate feedback. However, traditional performance reviews are done mostly once or twice a year. Accenture has developed a Facebook-type program "Performance Multiplier". People post two- or three-weekly goals, project status updates, and even include photos. Another program, called "Ripple" lets people post up to 140 words questions requesting anonymous feedback. This allows people to post questions, for example, about the assessment of a presentation or how to conduct a more effective meeting. Posting goals and updating them from time to time keeps others informed. Supervisors can note the progress of their employees and also identify those who do not post their objectives. This approach seems to be congruent with the MBO approach which requires stating objective clearly, updating not only the superior but also the colleagues about the progress toward the goals. At this time, this 140 Twitter keystrokes approach may not be widely used, but it is an alternative, or rather a supplement, to the dreaded yearly performance evaluation.

APPRAISING MANAGERS AS MANAGERS: A SUGGESTED PROGRAM

The most appropriate standards to use for appraising managers as managers are the fundamentals of management. It is not enough to appraise a manager broadly, evaluating only performance of the basic functions of the manager; appraisal should go further.

The best approach is to utilize the basic techniques and principles of management as standards. If they are basic, as they have been found to be in a wide variety of managerial positions and environments, they should

> The most appropriate standards to use for appraising managers as managers are the fundamentals of management.

serve as reasonably good standards. As crude as they may be, and even though some judgment may be necessary in applying them to practice, they give the evaluator some benchmarks for measuring how well subordinates understand and are following the functions of managing. They are definitely more specific and more applicable for evaluation than such broad standards as work and dress habits, cooperation, intelligence, judgment, and loyalty. They at least focus attention on what may be expected of a manager as a manager. And when used in conjunction with appraisal of the performance of plans and goals, they can help remove much of the weakness in many management appraisal systems.

In brief, the appraisal program that we suggest involves classifying the functions of the manager as done in this book and then dealing with each function by a series of questions. The questions are designed to reflect the most important fundamentals of managing in each area. Although the whole list of 73 key questions, the form used, the system of ratings, and the instructions for operating the program are too extensive to be treated in this book, sample "checkpoints" in the areas of planning and organizing are presented in Table 12.1.

TABLE 12.1   Sample questions for appraising managers as managers

Planning
• Does the manager set for the department both short- and long-term goals in verifiable terms that are related in a positive way to those of the superiors and of the company?
• In choosing from among alternatives, does the manager recognize and give primary attention to those factors that are limiting or critical to the solution of a problem?
• Does the manager check plans periodically to see if they are still consistent with current expectations?

Organizing
• Does the manager delegate authority to subordinates on the basis of results expected of them?
• Does the manager refrain from making decisions in that area once authority has been delegated to subordinates?
• Does the manager regularly teach subordinates, or otherwise make sure that they understand, the nature of line and staff relationships?

Source: Harold Koontz and Heinz Weihrich, *Measuring Managers: A Double-barreled Approach* (New York: AMACOM, 1981).

Semantics has always been a problem in management. Therefore, it is wise to use a standard book on management (such as this one) and refer to the pages that correspond to the questions. This approach leads to a fair degree of managerial development.

Managers are rated on how well they perform the activities. The scale used is from 0 for "inadequate" to 5 for "superior". To give the numerical ratings more rigor, each rating is defined. For example, "superior" means "a standard of performance that could not be improved under any circumstances or conditions known to the rater".

To further reduce subjectivity and to increase the discrimination between performance levels, the program requires that (1) in the comprehensive annual appraisal, incident examples be given to support certain ratings; (2) the ratings be reviewed by the superior's superior; and (3) the raters be informed that their own appraisal will depend in part on how well they discriminate on the ratings of performance levels when evaluating their subordinates. Obviously, objectivity is enhanced by the number and the specificity of the checkpoint questions.

Advantages of the Program

Experience with this program in a multinational company showed certain advantages. By focusing on the essentials of management, this method of evaluation gives operational meaning to what management really is. Also, the use of a standard reference text for interpretation of concepts and terms removes many of the semantic and communication difficulties so commonly encountered. Such things as variable budgets, verifiable objectives, staff, functional authority, and delegation take on consistent meaning. Likewise, many management techniques become uniformly understood.

The system, furthermore, has proved to be a tool for management development. In many cases, it has brought to managers' attention certain basics that they may have long disregarded or not understood. In addition, it has been found useful in pinpointing areas in which weaknesses exist and to which development should be directed. Finally, as intended, the program acts as a supplement to, and a check on, appraisal of managers' effectiveness in setting and achieving goals. If a manager has a record of outstanding performance in goal accomplishment but is found to be a less-than-average manager, those in charge will look for the reason. Normally, one would expect a truly effective manager to be effective also in meeting goals.

Weaknesses of the Program

There are, however, a number of weaknesses or shortcomings in the approach. It applies only to managerial aspects of a given position and not to such technical qualifications as marketing or engineering abilities that might also be important. These, however, can be weighed on the basis of goals selected and achieved. There is also the apparent complexity of the 73 checkpoints; rating on all of them does take time, but the time is well spent.

Perhaps the major shortcoming in appraising managers as managers is the subjectivity involved. Some subjectivity in rating each checkpoint is unavoidable. However, the program still has a high degree of objectivity and is far more objective than appraisal of managers only on the broader areas of the managerial functions. At least, the checkpoints are specific and pertain to the essentials of managing.

A TEAM EVALUATION APPROACH[5]

Another approach to performance appraisal has been introduced. The criteria selected for evaluation are in part similar to the ones mentioned above and include planning, decision-making, organizing, coordinating, staffing, motivating, and controlling. But other factors, such as selling skills, may also be included.

The appraisal process involves the person being evaluated and consists of the following steps:

- Selection of job-related criteria
- Development of examples of observable behavior

- Selection of four to eight raters (peers, associates, other supervisors, and, naturally, the immediate superior)
- Preparation of the rating forms applicable to the job
- Completion of the forms by the raters
- Integration of the various ratings
- Analysis of the results and preparation of the report

This approach has been used not only for appraisal but also for the selection of people for promotion and for personnel development, and even for dealing with alcoholism.

The advantages suggested by the originators of this approach include a rather high degree of accuracy in appraising people by obtaining several inputs rather than input from the superior only. The program can be used to identify raters' bias (e.g., rating consistently high or low, or giving such ratings to certain groups of people, such as women or people of minority groups). The persons being rated apparently would consider this approach quite fair, since they are involved in selecting the evaluation criteria as well as the raters. It also allows comparison of individuals with each other. Although this approach has been used by a variety of enterprises, further assessment seems necessary.

APPLICATION OF PERFORMANCE REVIEW SOFTWARE[6]

The annual review of performance is often disliked by both the superior and the subordinate. Moreover, it is time consuming. One study at Cornell University found that in large firms, managers spend about 6 hours per year for each employee.[7] More recently, several companies developed software that may make the evaluations among superiors more consistent by providing a structure to the appraisal. The paper-based evaluation may be replaced or complemented with web-based appraisal. Of course, the computer-based program is no substitute for the human interaction between the superior and the subordinate. However, the software may include a number of valuable features.

A manager may complete electronically the evaluation form that can be reviewed by other managers who can provide additional inputs and by the employee himself or herself before it is submitted to the human resource department. The database can then be used for identifying training needs and management development and for identifying those individuals who are ready for promotions to a position within the total organization.

Managers who do not submit the evaluations of their employees in time can be reminded automatically through the software program. This increases the on-time completion of appraisals. While it is not a cure-all to the often much dreaded annual appraisal, it can save time and make this important task easier.

Enterprise applications have become more available in recent years to make the process of managing human capital more effective and efficient. For example, Workday is a cloud-based human capital management application that can help managers maximize their organization's human resources. Management students would do well to familiarize themselves with modern enterprise software so that they are prepared to enter the workforce with the appropriate technical competencies.

REWARDS AND STRESS OF MANAGING

Managers are different: they have different needs, desires, and motives. The essentials of motivation will be discussed in Chapter 14; the concern here is with some of the general and financial rewards, as well as the stressful aspects, of managing.

Rewards of Managing: General Aspects

Since managerial candidates differ widely in age, economic position, and level of maturity, their needs and wants vary, but they usually include opportunity, power, and income. Most managerial candidates desire the opportunity for a progressive career that provides depth and breadth of managerial experience. Related to this is the challenge found in meaningful work. Most people, but perhaps managers in particular, want to feel that they have the power to make a significant contribution to the aims of an enterprise and even to society.

In addition, managers want to be, and should be, rewarded for their contributions, although the size of financial rewards has been criticized.

Pay for Performance

There is probably no other item as controversial as the relationship between appraisal of performance and pay. At General Electric (GE), workers get paid for performance: they are paid bonuses when they achieve challenging goals instead of according to a person's title or the length of service. Such an approach requires that the goals be clear and people know what is expected of them. Also, it must be explained to employees what the total compensation is, including fringe benefits. At one university, for example, faculty members get a benefit statement that shows not only the annual salary but also the university's contribution to the health plan, the faculty assistance program, life insurance, dental insurance, long-term disability insurance, worker's compensation, travel accident insurance, social security tax, and the university's retirement contribution.

| www.ge.com |

The reward should be timely. This means that it should be given shortly after the work was done well. The GE Medical Systems group, for example, has a Quick Thanks program that lets employees nominate a colleague for an exceptional performance. The $25 gift certificate can be used in selected stores and restaurants. The positive psychological effect may be even more important than the monetary reward.

| www.gemedical-systems.com |

An increase in salary can hardly ever be reversed. A bonus, on the other hand, can be made contingent on outstanding performance. Steven Kerr at GE recommends variable compensation based on performance, but he also recognizes that this may not be suitable in some countries. A cash bonus could be considered a bribe in Japan because it may be seen as paying for work that is a part of the job anyway. Also, some employees may prefer an extra vacation instead of a cash payment. Therefore, cultural differences should be taken into account when using variable compensation.

INNOVATIVE PERSPECTIVE

Pay for Performance at Lincoln Electric[8]

Lincoln Electric's incentive plan has been the model for other companies for years. Yet even its successful pay-for-performance system is beginning to change.

The family-controlled company, making welding equipment and supplies, has been known for its unique compensation system. Its 3,400 employees are paid for work, with no pay for holidays or sick leave; they are considered self-managing entrepreneurs. Twice a year, they are held accountable for their output, quality, cooperation, dependability, and ideas. Their average hourly pay is only slightly above the average manufacturing wage in the area around Cleveland, but their bonuses averaged 56% of annual wages in 1995. Substantial? Yes, but lower than in some previous years. Because of the bonuses, the pay differential among workers is substantial, ranging from about $32,000 to more than $100,000.

The pressure to perform is great. Yet the turnover rate is less than 4% among those who survived at least the first 180 days in the company. When Lincoln Electric lost money in 1992 and 1993 because of an unwise foreign acquisition, it borrowed money to pay bonuses to its workers.

But things began to change somewhat when the company made public offerings in 1996 so that outsiders gained a 40% stake in the firm. While the unique bonus system is to remain, the bonuses may be reduced. With global competition, the company expects to modernize its facilities, expand abroad, and recruit more outsiders.

www.lincolnelectric.com

Should doctors be paid for performance? This is the big question for 80 physicians with specialties in psychiatry, neurology, general pediatrics, as well as adolescent and emergency medicine at the Children's Hospital in Oakland, California.[9] The proposed plan would provide bonuses for the doctors instead of being paid for the time they worked. Although the performance criteria are not quite clear, they might include the number of visits and other factors. Most of the physicians are opposed to the plan arguing that the incentive plan would result that doctors would spend less time with each patient, give greater attention to private-pay patients and less to those covered by Medi-Cal. While pay-for-performance system is generally accepted in companies, the concept may be more difficult to apply in certain fields such as medical care.

Stress in Managing[10]

Stress Adaptive response, mediated by individual differences and/or psychological processes, that is, a consequence of any external action, situation, or event that places excessive psychological and/or physical demands on a person.

Stress is a very complex phenomenon. It is therefore no surprise that there is no commonly accepted definition. A widely used working definition is an adaptive response, mediated by individual differences and/or psychological processes, that is, a consequence of any external (environmental) action, situation, or event that places excessive psychological and/or physical demands on a person.

Hans Selye, probably the leading authority on the concept of stress, describes stress as "the rate of all wear and tear caused by life"[11]. There are many physical sources of stress, such as work overload, irregular work hours, loss of sleep, loud noises, bright light, and insufficient light. Psychological sources of stress may be due to a particular situation, such as a boring job, inability to socialize, lack of autonomy, responsibility for results without sufficient authority, unrealistic objectives, role ambiguity or role conflict, or a dual-career marriage. But what might be stressful to one person may be less so to another; people react differently to situations.

Stress can have various effects on the individual as well as on the organization.[12] There are the physiological effects that may be linked to a variety of illnesses. Then, there are psychological effects such as burnout or boredom. Various kinds of behavior, such as drug and alcohol abuse, inordinate food consumption, accidents, or withdrawal from the stressful situation (absenteeism, excessive labor turnover), may be a reaction to stress. Clearly, not only does the individual suffer, but the organization may also be affected by the turnover or impaired decision-making of its managers and nonmanagers alike.

Individuals and organizations have attempted to deal with stress in various ways. Individuals may try to reduce stress through better time management, healthful nutrition, exercise, career planning, a change in jobs, promotion of psychological health, relaxation, meditation, and prayer. Organizations may provide counseling or recreation facilities or may improve the job design by matching the person with the job.

Fitting the Needs of the Individual to the Demands of the Job

Managing, then, offers rewards but also involves stress. An individual aspiring to a managerial position should evaluate both the advantages and the disadvantages of managing before pursuing this career. A proper fit between individual needs and the demands of the task will benefit both the individual and the enterprise. Career management will help to achieve this fit.

INNOVATIVE PERSPECTIVE

How to Lead the Generation Xers?[13]

Baby boomers often lead Generation Xers. What are the implications for staffing and leading? The term "baby boomers" refers to people born after World War II, generally in the middle of the 20th century; let's say about from 1945 to 1964. The term *Generation X* was introduced in the early 1950s by Robert Capa and generally refers to the people born in the 1960s ending in the late 1970s to early 1980s. The time frames are, of course, approximate. The Generation Xers grew up in an environment of computers and cell phones and other technological application. It was also a rather uncertain environment characterized by corporate downsizing and job changers. Generation Xers are often led by baby boomers. Managing the Generation Xers has implications for staffing and leading. This is what some experts suggest for leading the Xers:

- Give them challenging assignment so that they can use their entrepreneurial talents
- Let them work in teams
- Involve them in planning
- Give reasons for instructions
- Give them feedback on their performance promptly
- Provide counseling for their career path

These suggestions, of course, should be also considered for leading older employees, but they may be especially important for the Generation Xers.

FORMULATING THE CAREER STRATEGY[14]

The appraisal of performance should identify the strengths and weaknesses of an individual; this identification can be the starting point for a career plan. The personal strategy should be designed to utilize strengths and overcome weaknesses in order to take advantage of career opportunities. Although there are different approaches to career development,[15] it is considered here as a process of developing a personal strategy that is conceptually similar to an organizational strategy. This process is summarized in Figure 12.2 and is elaborated below.

FIGURE 12.2 Formulation of a career strategy

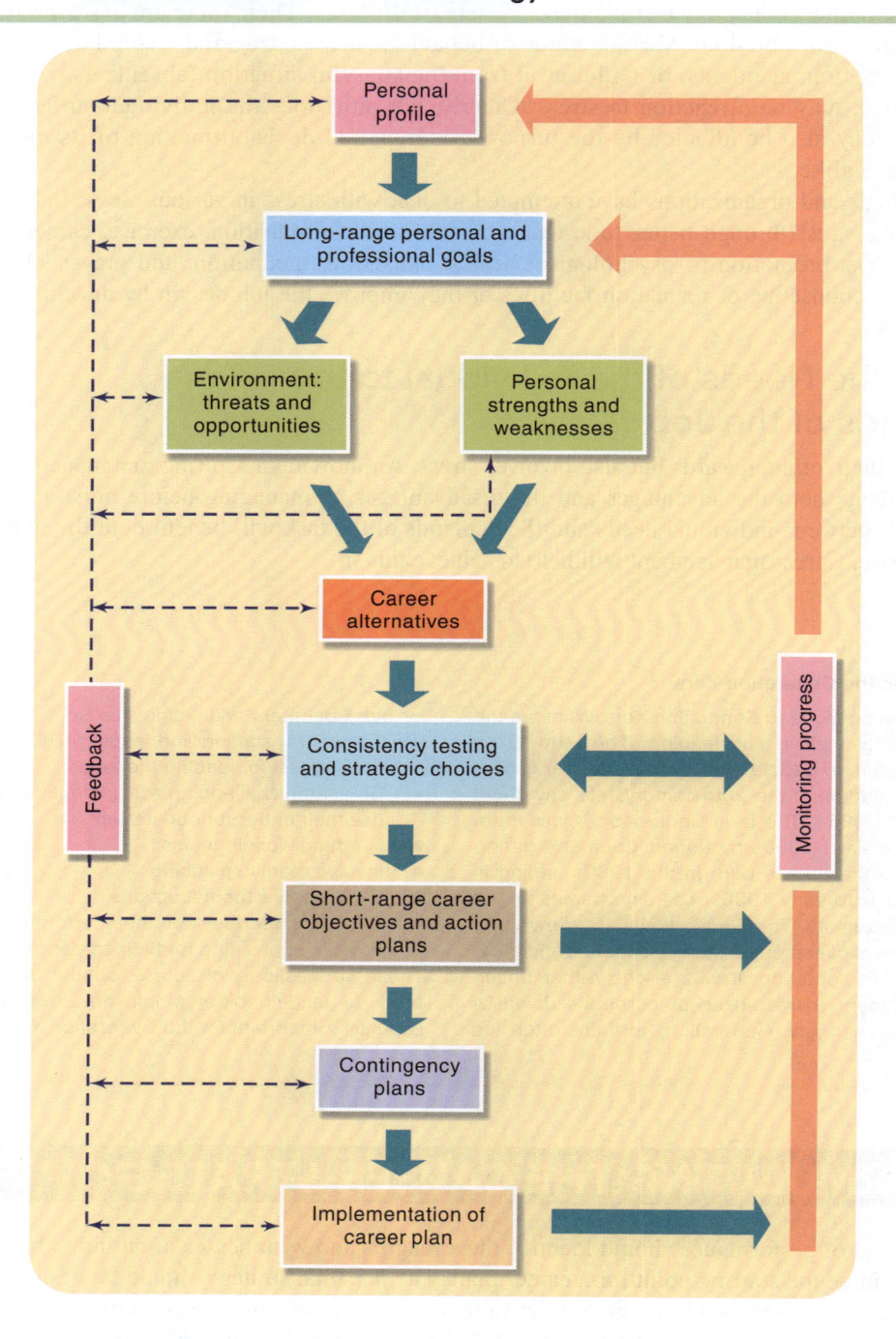

1. Preparation of a Personal Profile

One of the most difficult tasks is gaining insight into oneself; yet this is an essential first step in developing a career strategy. Managers should ask themselves: Am I an introvert or an extrovert? What are my attitudes toward time, achievement, work, material things, and change? The answers to these and similar questions and a clarification of values will help in determining the direction of the professional career.

2. Development of Long-Range Personal and Professional Goals

No airplane would take off without a flight plan including a destination. Yet how clear are managers about the direction of their lives? People often resist career planning because it involves making decisions. By choosing one goal, a person gives up opportunities to pursue others; if an individual studies to become a lawyer, he or she cannot become a doctor at the same time. Managers also resist goal setting because uncertainties in the environment cause concern about making commitments. Furthermore, there is the fear of failing to achieve goals because failure is a blow to one's ego.

But by understanding the factors that inhibit goal setting, one can take steps to increase commitment. First, when the setting of performance goals becomes a part of the appraisal process, identifying career goals is easier. Besides, one does not set career goals all at once. Rather, goal setting is a continuing process that allows flexibility; professional goals can be revised in light of changing circumstances. Another factor that reduces resistance to goal setting is the integration of long-term aims with the more immediate requirement for action. For example, the aim of becoming a doctor makes one accept the study of boring subjects that are necessary for the medical degree.

How far in advance should one plan? The answer may be found in the commitment principle. It states that planning should cover a period of time necessary for the fulfillment of commitments involved in the decision made today. Therefore, the time frame for career planning will differ with the circumstances. For example, if a person wants to become a professor, it is necessary to plan for university studies of 7–9 years. On the other hand, if the career goal is to become a taxi driver, the time span is much shorter. At any rate, the long-term aim has to be translated into short-term objectives. Before this is done, it is necessary to make a careful assessment of the environment, including its threats and opportunities.

3. Analysis of the Environment: Threats and Opportunities

In the analysis of the environment, internal and external, many diverse factors need to be taken into account. They include economic, social, political, technological, and demographic factors; they also include the labor market, competition, and other factors relevant to a particular situation. For example, joining an expanding company usually provides more career opportunities than working for a mature company that is not expected to grow. Similarly, working for a mobile manager means a higher probability that the position of the superior will become vacant, or one might "ride on the coattails" of a competent mobile superior by following him or her through a series of promotions up the organizational hierarchy. At any rate, successful career planning requires a systematic scanning of the environment for opportunities and threats.

One has to be concerned not only about the present but also about the future environment. This requires forecasting. Since there are a great many factors that need to be analyzed, planning one's career necessitates being selective and concentrating on those factors critical to personal success.

4. Analysis of Personal Strengths and Weaknesses[16]

For successful career planning, the environmental opportunities and threats must be matched with the strengths and weaknesses of individuals. Capabilities may be categorized as technical, human, conceptual, or design. As Figure 1.2 in Chapter 1 illustrates, the relative importance of these skills differs for the various positions in the organizational hierarchy, with technical skills being very important on the supervisory level, conceptual and design skills being crucial for top managers, and human skills being important at all levels.

GLOBAL PERSPECTIVE

What is Your Career Path?[17]

Effective human resource management should involve charting your career path. Your career strategy should be goal oriented, but flexible enough to take advantage of opportunities. Probably, many students can identify with the early career of Lee Scott, Wal-Mart's CEO. While studying at Pittsburg State University in Kansas, he worked at night making steel molds at a local factory. After earning his business degree, he worked for the trucking company Yellow Freight System as a dispatcher.

The first contact with Wal-Mart was in 1977 when he tried to collect a $7,000 bill. But Wal-Mart rejected the request. Nevertheless, during the dispute, Mr. Scott impressed Mr. Glass at Wal-Mart who offered him a job as assistant director of transportation, a job that involved setting up Wal-Mart's truck fleet. Fourteen years later, in 1993, Mr. Scott was promoted to executive VP of logistics, an area in which Wal-Mart later gained a competitive advantage. This was followed by the advancement to executive VP for merchandising in 1995, executive VP of Mal-Mart's stores division in 1998, vice chairman and chief operating officer in 1999, and CEO in 2000. In 2002, Wal-Mart under the leadership of Lee Scott became the largest public corporation in the world, based on revenue.

Mr. Scott did not get an MBA from Harvard or Stanford or any other Ivy League school, but he offered Wal-Mart some special knowledge he gained while working for Yellow Freight. What are your strengths and what do you have to offer your potential employer that sets you on a path to success?

---

5. Development of Strategic Career Alternatives

In developing a career strategy, one usually has several alternatives. The most successful strategy would be to build on one's strengths to take advantage of opportunities. For example, if a person has an excellent knowledge of computers and many companies are looking for computer programmers, he or she should find many opportunities for a satisfying career. On the other hand, if there is a demand for programmers and if an individual is interested in programming but lacks the necessary skills, the proper approach would be a development strategy to overcome the weakness and develop the skills in order to take advantage of the opportunities.

It may also be important to recognize the threats in the environment and develop a strategy to cope with them. If a person with excellent managerial and technical skills is working in a declining company or industry, the appropriate strategy might be to find employment in an expanding firm or in a growing industry.

6. Consistency Testing and Strategic Choices

In developing a personal strategy, one must realize that the rational choice based on strengths and opportunities is not always the most fulfilling alternative. Although one may have certain skills demanded in the job market, a career in that field may not be congruent with personal values or interests. For example, a person may prefer dealing with people to programming computers. Some may find great satisfaction in specialization, while others prefer to broaden their knowledge and skills.

Strategic choices require trade-offs. Some alternatives involve high risks and others low risks. Some choices demand action now; other choices can wait. Careers that were glamorous in the past may have an uncertain future. Rational and systematic analysis is just one step in the career-planning process, for a choice also involves personal preferences, personal ambitions, and personal values.

7. Development of Short-Range Career Objectives and Action Plans

So far, concern has centered on career direction. But the strategy has to be supported by short-term objectives and action plans, which can be a part of the performance appraisal process. Thus, if the aim is to reach a certain management position that requires a Master of Business degree, the short-term objective may be to complete a number of relevant courses. Here is an example of a short-term verifiable objective: to complete the course Fundamentals of Management by May 30 with a grade of A. This objective is measurable, as it states the task to be done, the deadline, and the quality of performance (the grade).

Objectives often must be supported by action plans. Continuing with the example, the completion of the management course may require preparing a schedule for attending classes, doing the homework, and obtaining the understanding and support of the spouse for sacrificing family time to attend the course. It is obvious that the long-term strategic career plan needs to be supported by short-term objectives and action plans.

8. Development of Contingency Plans

Career plans are developed in an environment of uncertainty, and the future cannot be predicted with great accuracy. Therefore, contingency plans based on alternative assumptions should be prepared. While one may enjoy working for a small, fast-growing venture company, it may be wise to prepare an alternative career plan based on the assumption that the venture may not succeed.

Managers in today's economy may be advised to consider developing a *personal entrepreneurial strategy*. That is to say, a manager, even one who has worked in large corporations her entire career, may want to consider entrepreneurial alternatives. These alternatives may range from, of course, launching her own business to joining a venture-backed firm and to inventing a new career track within her current firm. Having a personal entrepreneurial strategy may allow for greater freedom of expression of one's own unique talents and may also provide career security in uncertain environmental conditions.

9. Implementation of the Career Plan

Career planning may start during the performance appraisal. At that time, the person's growth and development should be discussed. Career goals and personal ambitions can be considered in selecting and promoting and in designing training and development programs.

10. Build a Professional Development Plan

Create a 10-year individual professional development plan—with annual career milestones. Provide a detailed strategy to enter industry of your choice. Provide an overview of industry—description, size, trends, outlook (e.g., cyber security industry, marketing analytics industry, biotech industry) footnote all sources. List an overview of key players in the industry—three companies and three executives. Note your preferred functional area in your target industry(s) (e.g., marketing) and description of likely job and job title for you (e.g., marketing director in your target industry or company). Include brief biographies of three key executives in your target function (e.g., marketing, sales) in your industry/company. Use this as a guide for your career path.

11. Monitoring Progress

Monitoring is the process of evaluating progress toward career goals and making necessary corrections in the aims or plans. An opportune time for assessing career programs is during the performance appraisal. This is the time not only to review performance against objectives in the operating areas but also to review the achievement of milestones in the career plan. In addition, progress should be monitored at other times, such as at the completion of an important task or project.

12. Write Your Own Biography

As individuals progress in their careers they will often be invited to participate in various events and conferences. A brief biography of the invited speaker will often be requested. Prepare now and complete your professional biography now and update it every few months. This is also a good exercise to review what you have accomplished and what the cost in time and effort was for these accomplishments. This biography is also a great way to help establish your own reputation in professional circles. Your biography should include your current assignments and recent accomplishments and education as well as a short reference to a personal interest (e.g., avid sailor or marathon runner).

Build Your Own Mentor Panel

Build your own professional mentor panel of three to four executives in your function or industry. One mentor should be from your home region who knows you well and at least one mentor from the region where you would like to build a career, and at least one mentor in your target functional area (e.g., marketing) and/or your target industry (biotech). Mentors can provide regular guidance, feedback (e.g., biweekly e-mail correspondence and monthly conversations), and referrals on your professional development through your career.

GLOBAL PERSPECTIVE

Career Planning in the New Economy

The traditional career model in which people prepared plans for working themselves up in a single organization needs to be modified. Today, people change jobs more frequently or even may work from their homes. There are more job opportunities. This is especially true for California's high-tech firms in the Silicon Valley with its rapidly changing business environment. While there are many opportunities in such an environment, job insecurity also increases. It is not unusual for a 32-year-old to have worked for nine different firms. California workers stay a medium of about 3 years with a company. Job seekers there are better informed as the Internet provides data on job openings as well as pay scales. It has been estimated that the turnover rate in the Silicon Valley is almost 20% a year.

But the Silicon Valley is not representative of America in general. Generally, Americans work longer hours than people in most European countries, such as France, Germany, and Sweden. On the other hand, Japanese workers put in similar hours as the Americans. The Japanese practice of lifelong employment is beginning to change, replaced by job insecurity. Furthermore, the use of temporary workers has also increased in Japan.

Perhaps more than ever before, developing a career strategy, or a personal entrepreneurial strategy, is important. Have a clear goal in mind, but be flexible and find alternative ways to reach it. Many people switch from big manufacturing firms to small service companies during the course of their career. In addition, it is essential to develop new skills needed for the new economy, join professional organizations, and invest in education and reeducation because the rapid changes in the work environment demand new skills.

Strategy for Dual-Career Couples[18]

An effective career strategy requires that consideration be given to the career of the spouse. Dual-career couples, with both partners working, sometimes have to make very stressful choices. For example, if both partners have successful careers, the opportunity for a promotion that requires relocation poses a particularly painful situation. Some companies are accommodating the special needs of dual-career couples by having a flexible approach to transfers that involve relocation, considering the needs of both partners in career planning, helping to find employment for the spouse either within the company or outside, and providing maternity leave and day-care services for children. With the large number of married women in the workforce, an increasing number of companies have recognized the stressful situation of dual-career couples and incorporated more flexibility in their policies, in career planning, and in personnel selection, placement, and promotion.

SUMMARY

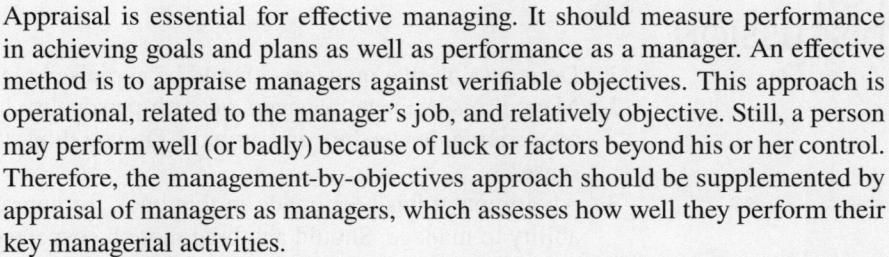

Appraisal is essential for effective managing. It should measure performance in achieving goals and plans as well as performance as a manager. An effective method is to appraise managers against verifiable objectives. This approach is operational, related to the manager's job, and relatively objective. Still, a person may perform well (or badly) because of luck or factors beyond his or her control. Therefore, the management-by-objectives approach should be supplemented by appraisal of managers as managers, which assesses how well they perform their key managerial activities.

There are three kinds of reviews: (1) the formal comprehensive appraisal, (2) progress or periodic reviews, and (3) continuous monitoring. In a suggested appraisal program, key managerial activities are presented as checklist questions and grouped under the categories of planning, organizing, staffing, leading, and controlling.

Since managers differ greatly, they look for different rewards, such as opportunity and income. The job of a manager is also stressful, and this can affect the individual as well as the organization. Therefore, various ways of coping with stress have evolved.

Career planning can be effectively integrated with performance appraisal. Although the specific steps in developing a career strategy may vary, the process is similar to developing an organizational strategy. Since dual-career couples are quite common today, an effective career strategy must include consideration of the spouse's career.

KEY IDEAS AND CONCEPTS FOR REVIEW

Three kinds of reviews
Appraisal against verifiable objectives
Appraising managers as managers
Team evaluation approach
Rewards of managing
Stress in managing
Ten steps in formulating a career strategy
Career strategy for dual-career couples

FOR DISCUSSION

1. Do you think that managers should be appraised regularly? If so, how?
2. Many firms evaluate managers on such personality factors as aggressiveness, cooperation, leadership, and attitude. Do you think this kind of rating makes sense?
3. An argument has been made in this book for appraising managers on their ability to manage. Should anything more be expected of them?
4. How do you feel about an appraisal system based on results expected and realized? Would you prefer to be appraised on this basis? If not, why not?
5. On what basis should your performance in college be appraised?
6. What would you say to a student who tells you that he studied at least 4 hours every day in preparation for the midterm examination and still got only a C?
7. Describe the most rewarding and most stressful aspects of your job or your college experience.
8. What is your career goal? Have you developed a plan to achieve your goal? If not, why not?

EXERCISES/ACTION STEPS

1. Interview two managers. Ask them what criteria are used for their performance appraisal. Are the criteria verifiable? Do these managers think that the performance evaluation measures their performance in a fair manner?
2. Develop a career plan for yourself. Identify a personal profile for yourself and state your long-range personal and professional goals. What are your strengths and weaknesses? Follow the steps explained in this chapter to develop a comprehensive strategic career plan for yourself.
3. Write your own professional biography of 100–250 words. Get feedback from your professor or classmates.
4. Find a calendar of professional events in your location. Attend two or three events and make it a point to meet at least two people at each event. Keep a logbook of who you met and what you learned at each event. (See www.Techvenue.com for a list of potential events.)

INTERNET RESEARCH

1. Access *Fortune* magazine's website and read on three topics in the "Careers" section. How can these sources help you in developing a career strategy?
2. Search the Internet for "performance appraisal". What criteria are used for evaluating performance? On what criteria would you like to be evaluated as a student, a subordinate, or a manager?

GLOBAL CASE

Female CEO Manages by the Textbook[19]

The demand for managers with an international background is great. Consider Marisa Bellisario, who was one of the most sought-after executives in Europe. She was the first woman to head a major industrial firm in Italy, the state-controlled ITALTEL Societa Italiana. This company is the largest telecommunication equipment manufacturer in Italy. Bellisario's background, however, was international. After receiving her degree in economics and business administration from Turin University, she worked at Olivetti in the electronics division. When Olivetti sold its data processing unit to GE, she spent time in Miami working on GE's worldwide marketing strategy for computers. She left GE to head corporate planning at Olivetti. As the CEO at ITALTEL, she turned the company around to show a small profit. (The firm had experienced huge losses in the past.) Her managerial approach had been characterized as "straight out of the textbook", and companies such as GTE Corporation, IBM, AT&T, and other European and Japanese firms were interested in recruiting her.

Questions:

1. Why was Ms. Bellisario a much sought-after CEO? What was her career path?
2. What special problems may she have encountered as a woman heading a major company in Italy?
3. If she was successful managing by the textbook, why do some managers still think that management cannot be taught?

ENDNOTES

1. Susan Scherreik, "Your Performance Review: Make It Perform," *Business Week*, December 12, 2001, pp. 139–140.
2. E-mail interview conducted on August 16, 2009, with Mr. Shomit Ghose, Partner, Onset Ventures, by Mark Cannice.
3. Jai Ghorpade and Milton M. Chen, "Creating Quality-driven Performance Appraisal Systems," *Academy of Management Executive*, February 1995, pp. 32–39.
4. Jena McGregor, "Job Review in 140 Keystrokes," *Business Week*, March 23 and 30, 2009, p. 58.
5. Mark R. Edwards, Walter C. Borman, and J. Ruth Sproull, "Solving the Double Bind in Performance Appraisal: A Saga of Wolves, Sloths, and Eagles," *Business Horizons*, May–June 1985, pp. 59–68; Mark R. Edwards and J. Ruth Sproull, "Team Talent Assessment: Optimizing Assessee Visibility and Assessment Accuracy," *Human Resource Planning*, Autumn 1985, pp. 157–171; Mark R. Edwards, *360 Degree Feedback: A New Model for Employee Development and Performance Improvement* (New York: AMACOM, 1996); Ginka Toegel and Jay A. Conger, "360-Degree Assessment: Time for Reinvention," *Academy of Management Learning & Education*, September 2003, pp. 297–311, the authors argue for the development of two separate tools: one for performance feedback and the other for management development.
6. Michael Totty, "The Dreaded Performance Review," *The Wall Street Journal*, November 27, 2006, http://www.halogensoftware.com, accessed November 13, 2008.
7. Robert D. Bretz Jr. et al., "Comparing the Performance Appraisal Practices in Large Firms with the Directions in Research Literature: Learning More and More about Less and Less," http://digitalcommons.ilr.cornell.edu/cahrswp/414, accessed August 18, 2011.
8. Zachary Schiller, "A Model Incentive Plan Gets Caught in a Vise," *Business Week*, January 22, 1996, pp. 89–90; Carolyn Wiley, "Incentive Plan Pushes Production," in Arthur A. Thompson, Jr., A. J. Strickland III, and Tracy Robertson Kramer (eds.), *Readings in Strategic Management*, 5th ed. (Chicago: Irwin, 1995), pp. 590–599; "Incentive Performance: A Cornerstone of Our Culture," www.lincolnelectric.com/corporate/career, accessed November 22, 2012.
9. Rebecca Vesely, "Doctors Protest Move from Hospital Payroll," *Contra Costa Times*, December 9, 2006.
10. Harry Levinson, "Burn Out," *Harvard Business Review*, July–August 1996, pp. 152–163; Stuart D. Diddle, "Workplace Stress Management Interventions: What Works Best", *The Academy of Management Perspectives,* August 2008, pp. 110–112.
11. Hans Selye, *The Stress of Life*, rev. ed. (New York: McGraw-Hill, 1976), p. viii.
12. See, for example, "Undue Diligence," *The Economist*, August 24, 1996, pp. 47–49.
13. *Doug Owram, Born at the Right Time* (Toronto: Univeristy of Toronto Press, 1997; Fred Luthans*, Organizational Behavior: An Evidence-Based Approach*, 12th Ed. (New York: McGraw-Hill, Irwin, 2011), p. 447.
14. For a variety of perspectives on careers by various authors, see the special issue on "Careers in the 21st Century" of the *Academy of Management Executive*, November 1996.
15. Stanley B. Malos and Michael A. Campion, "An Options-based Model of

Career Mobility in Professional Service Firms," *Academy of Management Review*, July 1995, pp. 611–644.
16. Richard Nelson Bolles, *What Color Is Your Parachute 2011* (Berkeley, CA: Ten Speed Press, 2011). See also www.jobhuntersbible.com, accessed January 5, 2016.
17. Ann Zimmerman, "Wal-Mart Boss's Unlikely Role: Corporate Defender-in-Chief", *The Wall Street Journal*, July 26, 2005. See also Wal-Mart CEO Vows "Unfiltered Truth", http://www.usatoday.com/money/industries/retail/2005-01-12-walmart-usat_x.htm, accessed January 5, 2016.
18. See also the Dual Career Network at Ohio University, http://www.ohio.edu/hr/employment/dual_career.cfm, accessed August 18, 2011.
19. "ITALTEL's New Chief Gets What She Wants," *Business Week*, April 30, 1984, p. 51; Robert Ball, "Italy's Most Talked-about Executive," *Fortune*, April 2, 1984, pp. 99–102; Marisa Bellisario, "The Turnaround at ITALTEL," *Long Range Planning*, 1985, 18 (6): 21–24.

CHAPTER 13

Managing Change through Manager and Organization Development

Learning Objectives

After studying this chapter, you should be able to:

LO 1   Distinguish between manager development, managerial training, and organization development

LO 2   Discuss the manager development process and training

LO 3   Describe the various approaches to manager development

LO 4   Identify changes and sources of conflict and show how to manage them

LO 5   Describe the characteristics and process of organization development

LO 6   Understand the learning organization

This chapter deals with change. First, the focus is on the change of individuals, specifically manager development and training. However, people do not operate in isolation. Consequently, in the second part of this chapter, the emphasis shifts to groups of individuals and organizations.

Excellent executives look to the future and prepare for it. One important way to do this is to develop and train managers so that they are able to cope with new demands, new problems, and new challenges. Indeed, executives have a responsibility to provide training and development opportunities for their employees so that they can reach their full potential.

The term "**manager development**" refers to long-term, future-oriented programs and the progress a person makes in learning how to manage. **Managerial training**, on the other hand, pertains to the programs that facilitate the learning process and is mostly a short-term activity to help managers do their jobs better. In this book, **organization development** is a systematic, integrated, and planned approach to improving the effectiveness of groups of people and of the whole organization or a major organizational unit. Organization development uses various techniques for identifying and solving problems.

Essentially, then, organization development focuses on the total organization (or a major segment of it), while manager development concentrates on individuals. These approaches support each other and should be integrated to improve the effectiveness of both the managers and the enterprise.

> **Manager development** Use of long-term, future-oriented programs to develop a person's ability in managing.
>
> **Managerial training** Use of mostly short-term programs that facilitate the learning process to help managers do their jobs better.
>
> **Organization development** Systematic, integrated, and planned approach to improving the effectiveness of groups of people and of the whole organization or a major organizational unit.

MANAGER DEVELOPMENT PROCESS AND TRAINING

Before specific training and development programs are chosen, three kinds of needs must be considered. First, the needs of the organization include such items as the objectives of the enterprise, the availability of managers, and turnover rates. Second, needs related to operations and the job itself can be determined from job descriptions and performance standards. Third, data about individual training needs can be gathered from performance appraisals, interviews with the jobholder, tests, surveys, and career plans for individuals. Let us look more closely at the steps in the manager development process, focusing first on the present job, then on the next job in the career ladder, and finally on the long-term future needs of the organization. The steps in manager development are depicted in Figure 13.1.

FIGURE 13.1 Manager development process and training

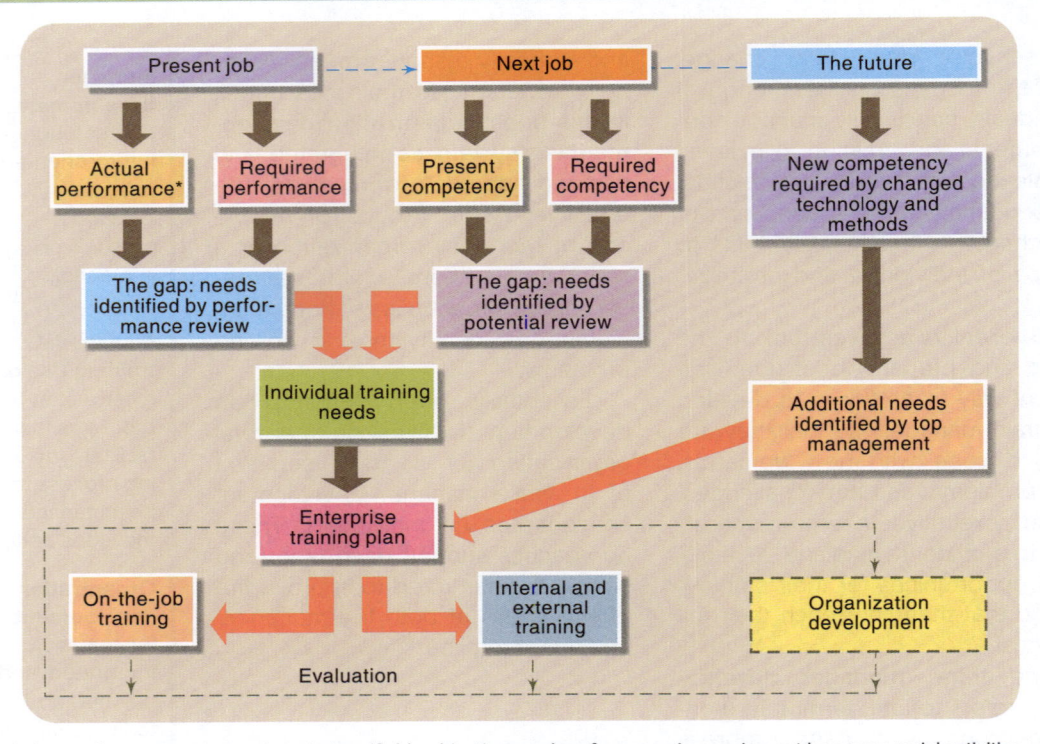

*This includes performance measured against verifiable objectives and performance in carrying out key managerial activities.
Source: John W. Humble, "Manager Development Process and Training", Improving Business Results.*

India's Leadership Needs[1]

With India's growth, companies need leadership. Salaries of expatriate managers are increasing the costs of goods and services. Moreover, they often do not have the experience dealing with the diverse labor force, which is shaped by many cultures. On the other hand, there is a lack of local people with managerial and leadership skills. Indian companies, in order to sustain their success, need to pay more attention to develop managerial talent. Since people are the most important assets, the focus should be on the critical variables in the systems approach to staffing as previously shown in Figure 11.1. Moreover, the manager development process and training model shown in Figure 13.1 indicates the need not only to focus on the present job but also on the next job and on the future. The systematic analysis of the individual and organizational training needs become the basis for the enterprise training plan, which may be the key factor for success.

Present Job

Manager development and training must be based on a needs analysis derived from a comparison of actual performance and behavior with required performance and behavior. Such an analysis is shown in Figure 13.2. A district sales manager has decided that 1,000 units is a reasonable sales expectation, but

FIGURE 13.2 Analysis of training needs

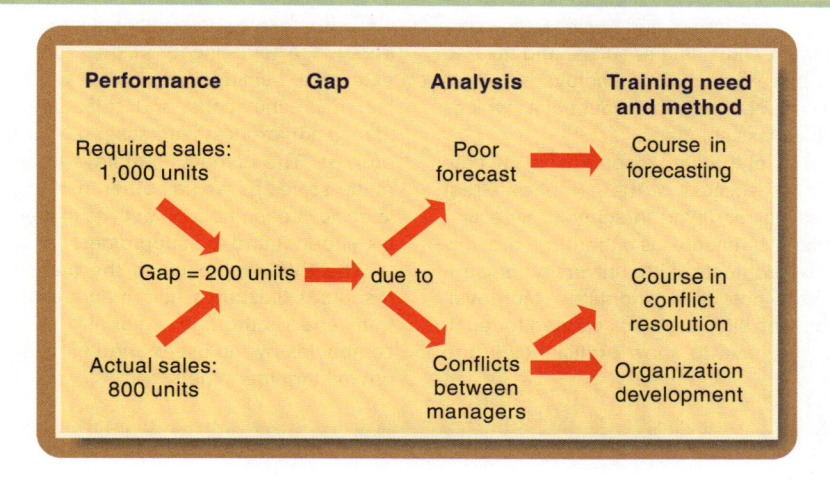

Performance	Gap	Analysis	Training need and method
Required sales: 1,000 units		Poor forecast	Course in forecasting
	Gap = 200 units due to		Course in conflict resolution
Actual sales: 800 units		Conflicts between managers	Organization development

the actual sales are only 800, which is 200 units short of the target. Analysis of the deviation from the target might indicate that the manager lacks the knowledge and skills for making a forecast and that conflict between subordinate managers hinders effective teamwork. On the basis of this analysis, training needs and methods for overcoming the deficiencies are identified. Consequently, the district sales manager enrolls in courses in forecasting and conflict resolution. Furthermore, organization development efforts are undertaken to facilitate cooperation among organizational units.

Next Job

As shown in Figure 13.1, a similar process is applied in the identification of the training needs for the next job. Specifically, present competency is compared with the competency demanded by the next job. A person who has worked mainly in production may be under consideration for a job as a project manager. This position requires training in functional areas such as engineering, marketing, and even finance. This systematic preparation for a new assignment certainly is a more professional approach than simply thrusting a person into a new work situation without training.

Future Needs

Progressive organizations go one step further in their training and development approach: they prepare for the more distant future. This requires that they forecast what new competencies will be demanded by changing technology and methods. For example, energy shortages may again occur, and this requires that managers be trained not only in the technical aspects of energy conservation but also in energy-related long-range planning and creative problem solving. In the new millennium, training in e-business is essential. In Europe especially, the impact of m-business (mobile and wireless business) has been taught in training programs. These changes, created by the external environment, have to be integrated into enterprise training plans, with a focus on the present as well as the future. These plans are contingent not only on the training needs but also on the various approaches to manager development that are available.

INNOVATIVE PERSPECTIVE

Managing Human Resources at PriceWaterhouseCoopers in China[2]

PriceWaterhouseCoopers (PWC) is the largest company in China that provides assurance and business advisory services, management consulting services, and tax and legal services. Its more than 3,000 employees, with a wealth of local experience, help international as well as local clients with business solutions.

The management of human resources is of critical importance for the success of the company. Great emphasis is placed on recruiting in schools. Selecting from among the many candidates is a thorough process that includes close contacts with university personnel who can identify potential candidates. Moreover, résumés posted on web sites are also scanned for qualified candidates, who have to show proficiency in the English language.

The selection process includes initial interviews, workshop exercises, additional interviews, and the hiring decision. After being hired, the recruits have to undergo extensive training that includes lectures, audiovisual material, simulations, and self-study programs. Performance and progress are assessed through the appraisal process. The company employs behaviorally anchored rating scales as well as other instruments that focus on specific, measurable objectives that are agreed upon by the superior and the subordinate.

The PWC approach to the management of human resources illustrates how managerial practices can be transferred through global companies by the use of modern management tools.

www.pwcglobal.com

APPROACHES TO MANAGER DEVELOPMENT: ON-THE-JOB TRAINING

Many opportunities for development can be found on the job. Trainees can learn as they contribute to the aims of the enterprise. However, because this approach requires competent higher-level managers who can teach and coach trainees, there are limitations to on-the-job training.

Planned Progression

Planned progression gives managers a clear idea of their path of development.

Planned progression is a technique that gives managers a clear idea of their path of development. Managers know where they stand and where they are going. For example, a lower-level manager may have available with him an outline of the path from superintendent to works manager and eventually to production manager. The manager then knows the requirements for advancement and the means of achieving it. Unfortunately, there may be an overemphasis on the next job instead of on good performance of present tasks. Planned progression may be perceived by trainees as a smooth path to the top, but it really is a step-by-step approach, which requires that tasks be done well at each level.

Job Rotation

Job rotation is intended to broaden the knowledge of managers or potential managers in different enterprise functions.

The purpose of job rotation is to broaden the knowledge of managers or potential managers. Trainees learn about the different enterprise functions by rotating into different positions. They may rotate through (1) nonsupervisory work, (2) observation assignments (observing what managers do, rather than actually managing), (3) various managerial training positions, (4) middle-level "assistant" positions, and even (5) various managerial positions in different departments such as production, sales, and finance.

The idea of job rotation is good, but there are difficulties. In some job rotation programs, participants do not actually have managerial authority. Instead, they observe or assist line managers, and they do not have the responsibility they would have if they were actually managing. Even in rotations to managerial positions, the participants in the training program may not remain long enough in each position to prove their future effectiveness as managers. Furthermore, when the rotation program is completed, there may be no suitable positions available for the newly trained managers. Despite these drawbacks, if both managers and trainees understand the inherent difficulties, job rotation has positive aspects and should benefit trainees.

Creation of "Assistant-to" Positions

"Assistant-to" positions are frequently created to broaden the viewpoints of trainees by allowing them to work closely with experienced managers who can give special attention to the development needs of trainees. Managers can, among other things, give selected assignments to test the judgment of trainees. As in job rotation, this approach can be very effective when superiors are also qualified teachers who can guide and develop trainees until they are ready to assume full responsibilities as managers.

> **"Assistant-to" positions** are often created to broaden the viewpoints of trainees through working closely with experienced managers.

Temporary Promotions

Individuals are frequently appointed as "acting" managers when, for example, the permanent manager is on vacation, is ill, or is making an extended business trip, or even when a position is vacant. Thus, temporary promotions are a developmental device as well as a convenience to the enterprise.

When the acting manager is given the authority to make decisions and to assume full responsibility, the experience can be valuable. On the other hand, if such a manager is merely a figurehead, makes no decisions, and really does not manage, the developmental benefit may be minimal.

> **Temporary appointment** to acting manager is used to cover the responsibilities of the absent manager.

Committees and Junior Boards

Committees and junior boards, also known as multiple management, are sometimes used as developmental techniques. These give trainees the opportunity to interact with experienced managers. Furthermore, trainees, usually from the middle but sometimes from the lower level, become acquainted with a variety of issues that concern the whole organization. They learn about the relationships between different departments and the problems created by the interaction of these organizational units. Trainees may be given the opportunity to submit reports and proposals to the committee or the board and to demonstrate their analytical and conceptual abilities. On the other hand, trainees may be treated in a paternalistic way by senior executives and may not be given opportunities to participate, an omission that might frustrate and discourage them. The program would then be detrimental to their development.

> **Committees and junior boards**, also known as multiple management, give trainees the opportunity to interact with experienced managers.

Coaching

On-the-job training is a never-ending process. A good example of on-the-job training is athletic coaching. To be effective, coaching, which is the responsibility

> **Coaching** must be done in a climate of confidence and trust, with the aim of developing subordinates' strengths and overcoming their weaknesses.

of every line manager, must be done in a climate of confidence and trust between the superior and the trainees. Patience and wisdom are required of superiors, who must be able to delegate authority and give recognition and praise for jobs well done. Effective coaches will develop the strengths and potentials of subordinates and help them overcome their weaknesses. Coaching requires time; but if done well, it will save time and money and will prevent costly mistakes by subordinates. Thus, in the long run, it will benefit all—the superior, the subordinates, and the enterprise.

APPROACHES TO MANAGER DEVELOPMENT: INTERNAL AND EXTERNAL TRAINING[3]

As indicated in Figure 13.1, besides on-the-job training, there are many other approaches to manager development. These programs may be conducted within the company or they may be offered externally by educational institutions and management associations.

Conference Programs

Conference programs expose managers or potential managers to the ideas of speakers who are experts in their fields.

Conference programs may be used in internal or external training. They expose managers or potential managers to the ideas of speakers who are experts in their fields. Within the company, employees may be instructed in the history of the firm and its purposes, policies, and relationships with customers, consumers, and other groups. External conferences may vary greatly, ranging from programs on specific managerial techniques to programs on broad topics, such as the relationship between business and society.

These programs can be valuable if they satisfy a training need and are thoughtfully planned. A careful selection of topics and speakers will increase the effectiveness of this training device. Furthermore, conferences can be made more useful by including discussions, as two-way communication allows participants to ask for clarification of topics that are particularly relevant to them.

INNOVATIVE PERSPECTIVE

Innovation Education in the United States and Europe[4]

The importance of innovation is widely recognized. The Academy of Management formed the Technology and Innovation Management (TIM) division in 1987 that promotes interdisciplinary dialogue on management innovation and technology change. The division has over 2,000 members. The topics range from strategic, managerial, and operational aspects of innovation. The TIM division also uses cases such as Hewlett-Packard: the Flight of the Kitty Hawk (Harvard Business School (HBS) case), Tivo (HBS), iMotors (INSEAD), Intel Corp. (HBS), WebMD (HBS), and other cases for teaching innovation.

In Europe, the European Management Academy is a new academic institution that explores applied innovation management. The mission of the IMPROVE Academy is to conduct research and share the results for improving the economic competitiveness of Europe. The aim is also to work with the academic community, which could lead to integrating innovation management into curriculum of bachelor, master, or executive programs. The benefits are the integration of academic research and practical application of the research findings.

University Management Programs

Besides offering undergraduate and graduate degrees in business administration, many universities now conduct courses, workshops, conferences, and formal programs for training managers. These offerings may include evening courses, short seminars, live-in programs, a full graduate curriculum, or even programs tailored to the needs of individual companies. Some executive development centers even provide career development assistance with programs designed to fit typical training and development needs of first-line supervisors, middle managers, and top executives.

> **University management programs** expose managers to theories, principles, and new developments in management.

These university programs expose managers to theories, principles, and new developments in management. In addition, there is usually a valuable interchange of experience among managers who, in similar positions, face similar challenges.

INNOVATIVE PERSPECTIVE

How to Get into the Business School of Your Choice[5]

Even experienced managers may decide to go back to school. Disappointment may occur when applicants are told that they are denied admission or that they are "wait-listed". But such a notice should not discourage, rather stimulate the search for the reason for their unsuccessful application. Here are some ideas about what admissions officers may look for: Is there a gap in the employment record? What does a candidate offer in special skills or knowledge? Are the strengths of the candidate effectively articulated?

What does the person want to do with the degree? Does the candidate show that he or she is different (e.g., speaking different languages, having international experience)? Does the career path show a rapid promotion?

A generic application letter is usually not sufficient. The applicant should learn about the school and, if possible, visit the university and meet faculty members and students. An advanced degree or special courses may be the pathway to a successful career.

In-House "Universities"

One of the earliest in-house educational facilities was established by General Electric's CEO Ralph Cordiner in the mid- to late 1950s in Crotonville, New York. Jack Welch, the recently retired GE CEO, liked to teach at Crotonville on his favorite strategy theme of making GE's units No. 1 and No. 2 in the market.[6] Crotonville became GE's center for learning.

Another well-known center for in-company learning is McDonald's University near Chicago. It has its own library and modern electronic classrooms in which managers study how to operate McDonald's restaurants. Similar universities are located strategically in several parts of the world. Many companies have established their own universities.

Other companies engaged in their own training and development of managers are Intel, FedEx, Capital One, and many others. German companies known for their comprehensive apprenticeship training have expanded their programs to include managerial education. For example, SAP (known for its software offerings) and BASF (a multinational chemical firm) have supplemented their programs with a program at the University of Applied Sciences in Ludwigshafen.

Still another example of in-house development is the IBM's Peace Corps-Type Training.[7] IBM is well known for its classroom training of its personnel. But the real world is different from the classroom. Therefore, the HR department initiated a program that is modeled after the U.S. Peace Corps program. The objective of the program is to teach managers how the real world works. In this innovative program, IBMers spend a month in countries such as India, Brazil, Malaysia, South Africa, and others to learn about the culture and to become a kind of global citizen. This means living in circumstances different from their home country—not luxury hotels with CNN connections, but guest houses eating local food. Program participants work in teams with local governments, universities, businesses to help them upgrade their technologies and improving the water quality. This one-month program will not make the participants instant global experts, but they learn that the earth is flatter in which people from different cultures work together to achieve common goals.

> **INNOVATIVE PERSPECTIVE**
>
> **Thinking about the Future at Singularity University**[8]
>
> Located at the NASA Ames Research Center in California, Singularity University is not a traditional university. Instead, the aim is to attract executives who deal with disruptive technologies in the rapidly changing environment dealing with such topics as robotics. The participants work in small groups to explore new ideas. Applicants from some 60 countries explore, for example, the future of the application of artificial intelligence to assume certain functions of the brain.

Readings, Television, Video Instruction, and Online Education[9]

www.education.com
www.ucla.edu
www.phoenix.edu
www.uchicago.edu
www.columbia.edu
www.stanford.edu
www.lse.ac.uk
www.cmu.edu
www.cardean.edu
www.blackboard.com
www.webct.com

www.towson.edu/~absel

Another approach to development is planned reading of relevant and current management literature. This is essentially self-development. A manager may be aided by the training department, which often develops a reading list of valuable literature. This learning experience can be enhanced through discussion of articles and books with other managers and the superior.

Increasingly, management and other topics are featured in television instruction programs. For certain programs, college credits can be obtained. Moreover, videotapes on a variety of subjects are available for instruction and learning in the university or company classroom.

Investment in online education is growing. The providers of online education can be categorized into three groups: (1) schools, (2) universities, and (3) business and commercial training organizations.[10] Universities use the new technologies for graduate programs and extension courses. At the University of California, Los Angeles, most of the 3,000 undergraduate courses are accompanied by websites containing lecture notes and supplementary material; even tests can be taken online. The University of Phoenix mixes distance learning with evening classes. Business schools such as the University of Chicago, Columbia University, Stanford University, the London School of Economics, and Carnegie Mellon University work with Cardean University to offer complete online courses. Firms such as Blackboard and WebCT have developed platforms for placing course material on the web. Although online education can be helpful, skeptics question the profitability and effectiveness of the application of the new technologies.

Business Simulation and Experiential Exercises

Business games and experiential exercises have been used for some time, but the introduction of computers has made these approaches to training and development even more popular. The computer, however, is only one of several tools; many of the exercises do not require any hardware at all.

The great variety of business simulations is best illustrated by the topics discussed at the meetings of the Association for Business Simulation and Experiential Learning (ABSEL). The approaches range from behavioral exercises dealing, for example, with attitudes and values to simulations in courses such as marketing, accounting, decision support systems, and business policy and strategic management.

E-Training[11]

With operations in many places, companies such as McDonald's, Thrifty Car Rental, and Circuit City offer web-based training classes, which may be more cost-effective than traditional classroom training. McDonald's, for example, started its pilot web training in 2001 with 3,000 employees in four languages in six countries. Various approaches are possible. One is the off-the-shelf content. Another approach is to create a virtual classroom with the teacher interacting with students. Synchronous e-learning with live instructions appears to be more effective than self-paced learning that requires self-discipline. Live instructions can be adapted to the needs of students at the particular time by integrating overhead transparencies, slides, and lecture notes. One approach is to blend off-the-shelf programs with live e-training.

www.mcdonalds.com
www.thrifty.com
www.circuitcity.com

E-learning has been successfully used in knowledge-intensive companies, such as IBM's Basic Blue e-learning approach. More recently, e-training is employed for teaching skills. The U.S. Internal Revenue Service uses web-based training, and so does Neptune Orient Lines, the large transporter of containers. The container company has to train its global workforce in various countries in Europe, Asia, South America, and other regions. Instead of sending trainers around the world, it uses live e-learning as a cost-effective alternative.

www.ibm.com
www.irs.gov
www.nol.com.sg

The trend of e-learning is just in its early stages. More research will have to be done to make it more effective and to find the proper balance between self-paced learning and instructor-led training.

Innovation in Higher Education: edX and Coursera Online Programs[12]

"Half of the business schools in this country could be out of business in 10 years."[13]

Most threatened are those schools that rely on executive education programs and part-time students. One way to mitigate the situation would be through distant learning programs. Even elite schools such as Wharton and Stanford University offer online programs. The University of California Los Angeles offers a hybrid program with in-class and online courses. Two approaches to online learning and researching are edX and Coursera. Let us look at them for more details, shown in the mindmap figure below.

edX

This program is an online course platform using open-source software. It was founded by MIT and Harvard in 2012 and is offered without charge worldwide. In 2014, it had more than 2 million users who could take advantage of more than 170 courses.

The programs are in partnership with institutions in the United States, China and India. Member institutions are in Australia, Canada, China, Japan, Switzerland, Belgium, Germany, India, the Netherlands, South Korea, and Sweden.

Online Programs Mind Map

- **Online Programs**
  - **Coursera** (What)
    - for-profit educational firm
      - Founded by Stanford University professors
      - Mobile app
        - iPhone
        - Android
      - More than 7 million users in 2014
      - More than 108 institutions
        - University of California, Irvine
        - Duke University
        - Uni. of Pennsylvania
        - Princeton U
        - Others
      - Working with State Department teaching in foreign countries
      - Offering many online courses
        - Physics
        - Mathematics
        - Engineering
        - Biology
        - Medicine
        - Business
        - Computer Science
        - Humanities
        - More than 600 courses
        - Many free online courses
    - Courses
      - Video lectures
        - One to two hours per week
      - Six to ten weeks long
      - Quizzes
      - Exercises
      - Sometimes final exam
      - Use of web forums-students meet face to face
  - **edX**
    - online course platform
    - Open-source software
    - Founded by MIT and Harvard 2012
    - Worldwide no charge
    - More than 2 million users in early 2014
    - At this time more than 170 courses
    - Organization
      - Use: learning, distance education, research
      - Partnerships with institutions in
        - US
        - China
        - India
      - Blended classrooms
        - Traditional classes with online interactive component
      - Learning examples
        - Short videos
        - Learning exercises
        - Use of slides or tablets
        - Use of online textbooks
        - Online discussion forums
      - EdX certificates but no course credit
        - Colleges may give credit
    - Members sample
      - US
        - MIT
        - Harvard
        - Boston University
        - Cornell U.
        - UC Berkeley
        - Others
      - Other countries
        - Australia
        - Canada
        - China
        - Japan
        - Switzerland
        - Belgium
        - Germany
        - India
        - Netherlands
        - South Korea
        - Sweden
    - Sample courses
      - Solar Energy
      - Introduction to Computer Science
      - Challenges of Global Poverty
      - Descriptive Statistics
      - Energy
      - China
  - **Other**
    - Expensive
    - For-Profit
    - Udacity

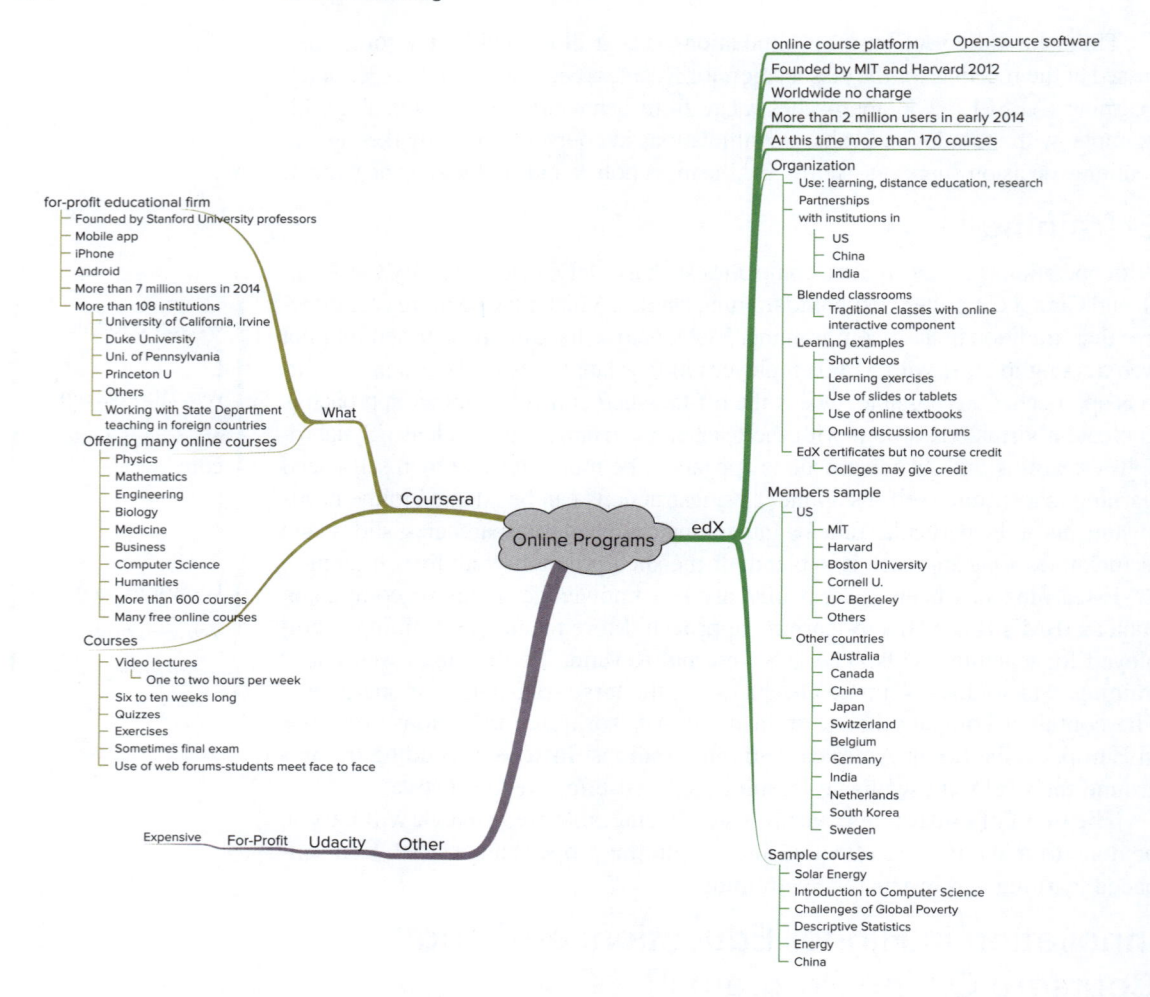

Some programs offer blended classrooms that include traditional classes with online interactive components. The learning experiences may include short videos, learning exercises, the use of tablets and slides. Also online textbooks may be used. The online discussion forums allow interactions among students. The edX program does not offer course credit, but the participating colleges may do so. Here are some sample courses offered through edX: Introduction to Computer Science, Solar Energy, Statistics, Challenges to Global Poverty, and many other courses.

Coursera

Another online program is the for-profit educational firm Coursera. It was founded by Stanford University professors. It had over 7 million users in 2014. More than 108 institutions participate, including the University of California at Irvine, Duke University, the University of Pennsylvania, Princeton University, and others. Coursera also works with the U.S. State Department offering courses for the military stationed in several countries.

The more than 600 courses are offered in various disciplines such as physics, mathematics, engineering, biology, medicine, business, computer science, and humanities. The courses typically include video lectures, quizzes, exercises, and sometimes a final exam. Web forums allow students to meet face to face. The courses are generally six to ten weeks long.

Education may be the key to prosperity in countries around the world. There are several experimental approaches today. Distance learning, using online programs such as edX and Coursera, may be one way to teach and to conduct research worldwide.

Coding Bootcamps

The increasing demand for individuals skilled in programming and software design has led to a proliferation of coding boot camps (e.g., Codecademy). In these intensive training programs, students receive training in highly demanded software skills (e.g., Full Stack, Python) that may help students attain employment in higher paying careers. Whether the trend in these training programs continues or whether traditional universities respond with similar offerings remains to be seen.

Special Training Programs

Management development must take an open-system approach that responds to the needs and demands of the external environment. There is an increasing awareness of the need for training programs specifically designed for members of minority groups and for the physically handicapped. Many firms have made special efforts to train these people so that they may utilize their full potential while contributing to the aims of the enterprise.

Companies may also offer special programs on selected subjects. The topic of ethics may be discussed to give the workforce guidelines on ethical behavior. The subject of corporate culture may be addressed in a formal or informal manner. Japanese companies, in particular, are known for making special efforts to instill the company philosophy in employees to promote a desirable corporate culture.

GLOBAL PERSPECTIVE

Cisco's Talent Development in India and Elsewhere[14]

For several years, Cisco has focused on emerging markets. For example, the company used a hyperactive approach for recruiting and developing people in India. The second headquarters in Bangalore allows Cisco to recruit from the local talent. In addition, Cisco started the Global Talent Acceleration Program operating in Saudi Arabia, Jordan, and South Africa, looking for people who worked in two continents and speak two languages. The recruits get six months training in selling and finance. Mentoring is done by assigning those recruits to experienced managers. This program encourages employees to contribute $100 to help micro-startups in the rural areas in India. The idea is that another "Bill Gates" may be discovered.

EVALUATION AND RELEVANCE OF TRAINING PROGRAMS

Determining the effectiveness of training programs is difficult. It requires measurements against standards and a systematic identification of training needs and objectives.

In general, development objectives include (1) an increase in knowledge, (2) development of attitudes conducive to good managing, (3) acquisition of skills, (4) improvement of management performance, and (5) achievement of enterprise objectives.

Determining the effectiveness of training programs requires measurements against standards and a systematic identification of training needs and objectives.

If training is to be effective, it is extremely important that the criteria used in the classroom situation resemble as closely as possible criteria relevant to the working environment. Manager development requires a situational approach in which training objectives, techniques, and methods are sufficiently congruent with the values, norms, and characteristics of the environment.

> **INNOVATIVE PERSPECTIVE**
>
> **Making Management Education Relevant**
>
> In order to make business courses more meaningful, many schools invite guest speakers from industry to share their experiences. This creates close ties between business schools and enterprises. Executives become aware of the quality of each school's curriculum, and students may find it advantageous to know about the companies when they are looking for a job. Moreover, executives often serve on school advisory boards, and this makes the schools aware of the needs of the business community. This does not mean, however, that market-driven schools should adopt any management fad. Instead, management education must be broad enough to encompass the teaching of all key managerial activities in planning, organizing, staffing, leading, and controlling.

MANAGING CHANGE[15]

The forces for change may come from the external environment, from within the organization, or from the individuals themselves.

The forces for change may come from the environment external to the firm, from within the organization, or from the individuals themselves.

Changes That Affect Manager and Organization Development

Several trends, some of them already occurring, will have implications for developing human resources. Here are illustrations:

- The proportion of knowledge workers will increase and the need for skill workers will decrease, which may require more training in knowledge, conceptual, and design skills.
- The shift from manufacturing to service industries requires retraining in preparation for new positions.
- The choice of educational opportunities will expand. For example, many companies already are conducting their own training programs.
- There may be greater cooperation and interdependence between the private and the public sector, at least in some countries, such as Canada.
- Internationalization will continue, so managers must learn to communicate with and to adapt to managers in other countries. Companies need to train with a global perspective.

There are various ways to respond to these forces. One approach is simply to react to a crisis. Unfortunately, this is usually not the most effective response. Another approach is to deliberately plan the change. This may require new objectives or policies, organizational rearrangements, or a change in leadership style and organization culture.

FIGURE 13.3 Moving an organizational equilibrium

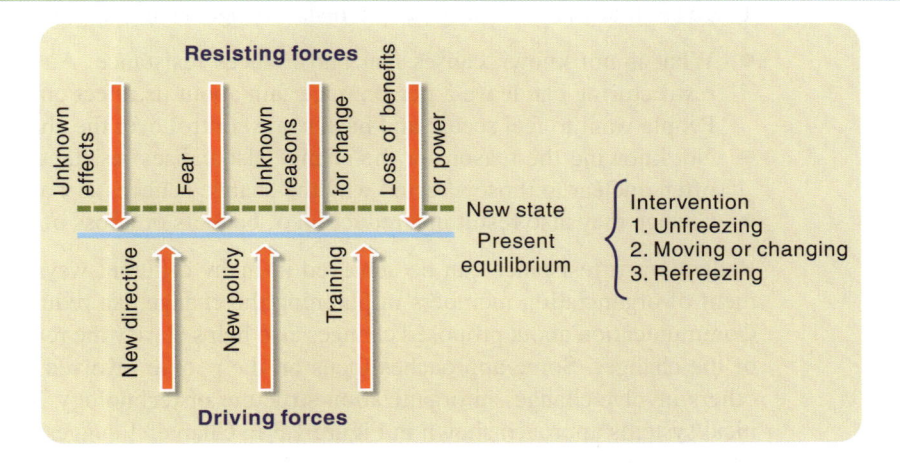

Figure shows Lewin's force field model with resisting forces (Unknown effects, Fear, Unknown reasons, Loss of benefits or power) pushing down against driving forces (New directive, New policy, Training) pushing up, between a Present equilibrium line and New state line. Intervention: 1. Unfreezing, 2. Moving or changing, 3. Refreezing.

Techniques for Initiating Change

Organizations may be in a state of equilibrium, with forces pushing for change on the one hand and forces resisting change by attempting to maintain the status quo on the other. Kurt Lewin expressed this phenomenon in his **field force theory**, which suggests that an equilibrium is maintained by *driving* forces and *restraining* forces, as shown in Figure 13.3.[16] In initiating change, the tendency is to increase the driving forces. This may indeed produce some movement, but it usually also increases resistance by strengthening the restraining forces. Another approach, one that is usually more effective, is to reduce or eliminate the restraining forces and then move to a new level of equilibrium. In organizations, a change in policy is less resisted when those affected by it participate in the change.

The change process involves three steps: (1) unfreezing, (2) moving or changing, and (3) refreezing.[17] The first stage, unfreezing, creates the motivation for change. If people feel uncomfortable with the present situation, they may see the need for change. However, in some cases, an ethical question may arise regarding the legitimacy of deliberately creating discomfort that may initiate change.

The second stage is the change itself. This change may occur through assimilation of new information, exposure to new concepts, or development of a different perspective. The third stage, refreezing, stabilizes the change. Change, to be effective, has to be congruent with a person's self-concept and values. If the change is incongruent with the attitudes and behaviors of others in the organization, chances are that the person will revert to the old behavior. Thus, reinforcement of the new behavior is essential.

In a recent McKinsey Quarterly Article, lessons on how leaders may best effect change were provided based on three recent corporate change programs that McKinsey Consultants were engaged in. The lessons for more effective change included: connecting training to business goals, working with managers who were already influential in their respective departments, providing executive sponsorship to the managers leading the change, and creating networks of change leaders to prevent positive change being limited to silos.[18]

> **Field force theory**
> Equilibrium is maintained by driving forces and restraining forces.

Resistance to Change

There are many reasons why people resist change. Here are examples:

- What is not known causes fear and induces resistance. An organizational restructuring can leave a person uncertain about its effect on his or her job. People want to feel secure and have some control over the change.
- Not knowing the reason for the change also causes resistance. In fact, it is often unclear to those affected why the change is necessary at all.
- Change may also result in a reduction of benefits or a loss of power.

Reduction of resistance can be achieved in many different ways. The involvement of organization members in planning the change can reduce uncertainty. Communication about proposed changes also helps clarify the reasons or effects of the changes. Some approaches focus on the people involved in the change; others involve changes in organization structure or technology. The sociotechnical systems approach shown in Figure 1.3 in Chapter 1 suggests that effective organization requires consideration of both the social and the technical dimensions in an enterprise.

ORGANIZATIONAL CONFLICT

Conflict Part of organizational life and may occur within the individual, between individuals, between the individual and the group, and between groups.

Conflict is a part of organizational life and may occur within the individual, between individuals, between the individual and the group, and between groups. While conflict is generally perceived as dysfunctional, it can also be beneficial because it may cause an issue to be presented in different perspectives. Cognitive conflict, the debating of ideas, is often seen as productive, while affective conflict, personal disagreements, is typically seen as unproductive. As one top executive of a major company maintained, if there was no conflict on an issue, it could not have been sufficiently analyzed, and the final decision on the issue was usually postponed until all aspects were critically evaluated.

Sources of Conflict

There are many potential sources of conflict. Today's organizations are characterized by complex relationships and a high degree of task interdependence, so friction can easily occur. Moreover, the goals of the parties are often incompatible, especially when the parties compete for limited resources. People also have different values and different perceptions of issues. A production manager may take the position that streamlining the product line and concentrating on a few products can make the organization more productive, while a sales manager may desire a broad product line that will satisfy diverse customer demands. An engineer may want to design the best product regardless of cost or market demand considerations.

Conflict can arise from other sources as well. There may be conflict between people in line and staff positions. A superior's autocratic leadership style may cause conflict. Differing educational backgrounds are potential sources of conflict. Perhaps most often mentioned is lack of communication. Many of these topics are discussed in various chapters of this book.

Managing Conflict

Conflict can be managed in different ways, some focusing on interpersonal relationships and others on structural changes. Avoidance of the situation that causes the conflict is an example of an interpersonal approach. Another way of coping with conflict is through smoothing, emphasizing the areas of agreement and common goals and deemphasizing disagreements. A third way is forcing, pushing one's own view on others; this will of course cause overt or covert resistance. A traditional way of coping with conflict is to compromise, agreeing in part with the other person's view or demand.

Conflict can be managed in different ways, some focusing on interpersonal relationships and others on structural changes.

Attempts can also be made to change the behavior of individuals, a very difficult task indeed. At times, it may also be possible to reassign an individual to another organizational unit. In many situations, conflict is resolved by a person higher up in the organization who has sufficient authority to decide an issue. However, if the solution is perceived as being unfair, the loser may attempt to get even with the winner at a later time, thus perpetuating the conflict. In the problem-solving approach to organizational conflict, differences are openly confronted and the issues are analyzed as objectively as possible.

Another way of coping with conflict is to make structural changes. This means modifying and integrating the objectives of groups with different viewpoints. Moreover, the organization structure may have to be changed and authority–responsibility relationships clarified. New ways of coordinating activities may have to be found. Tasks and work locations can also be rearranged. In one workroom in a firm, for example, machines were placed in a way that prevented conflicting parties from interacting with one another. Often one must not only decide on the necessary changes but also select the appropriate process. For this reason, the next section focuses on organization development.

ORGANIZATION DEVELOPMENT

As explained earlier, organization development, typically shortened to OD, is a systematic, integrated, and planned approach to improving enterprise effectiveness. It is designed to solve problems that decrease operating efficiency at all levels. Such problems may include lack of cooperation, excessive decentralization, and poor communication.

The techniques of OD may involve laboratory training (e.g., people communicating in a group situation), managerial-grid training, and survey feedback. Some OD practitioners also use team building, process consultation, job enrichment, organizational behavior modification, job design, stress management, career and life planning, and management by objectives as part of their approach.

The Organization Development Process

OD is a situational or contingency approach to improving enterprise effectiveness. Although various techniques are utilized, the process often involves the steps shown in Figure 13.4. An example can illustrate the application of the model.

FIGURE 13.4 A model of the organization development process

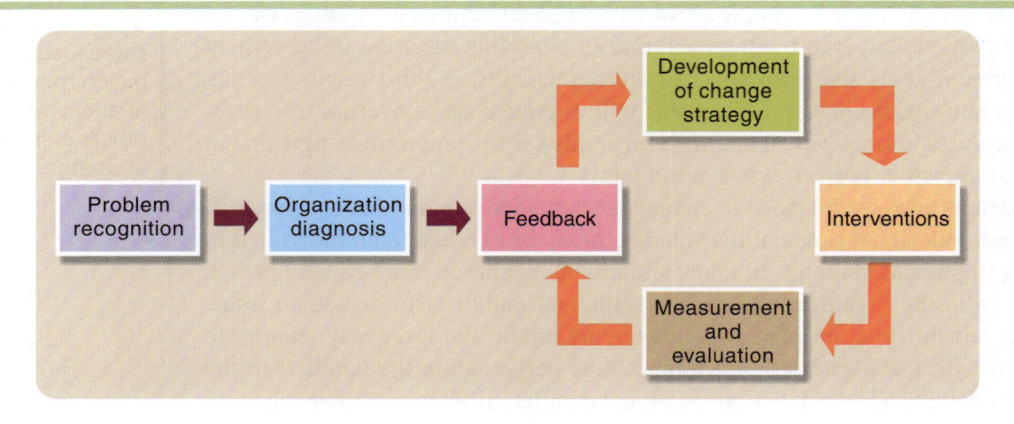

Source: H. M. F. Rush, "A Model of the Organization Development Process", *Organizational Development: A Reconnaissance.*

Consider a firm that experiences certain problems: conflict between organizational units, low morale, customer complaints, and rising costs (*problem recognition* in the model). The chief executive contacts an OD expert to discuss the situation. The two agree on the necessity of an *organizational diagnosis*. The consultant then collects information from several organizational units, using questionnaires, interviews, and observation. The data are analyzed and prepared for feedback.

The executive confers with other managers to set up a meeting with them. At the meeting, after some introductory comments, the consultant presents the findings under the headings "relations between departments", "enterprise goals", and "customer relations" (*feedback*). The group then ranks the problems in order of their importance. With the guidance of the consultant, the group discusses the difficulties, identifies the underlying causes, and explores possible solutions.

The role of the consultant is that of a coach facilitating the process. Short lectures and exercises on decision making, team building, and problem solving are integrated into the process. At times, subgroups are established to deal with specific issues. The emphasis is on openness and objectivity. The meeting ends with an agreement on a *change strategy*.

The specific *interventions* may include a change in the organization structure, a more effective procedure for handling customer complaints, and the establishment of a team charged with the responsibility of implementing a cost reduction program. Furthermore, the group agrees to meet again in three months to *measure and evaluate* the effectiveness of the OD efforts.

Although three phases complete the OD cycle, the effort does not end. Instead, OD becomes a continuous process—planned, systematic, and focused on change—that aims at making the enterprise more effective.

INNOVATIVE PERSPECTIVE

Successful Teamwork[19]

The position of the chief operating officer (COO) is often considered a stepping stone for the top position of the chief executive officer (CEO). But this may be changing in favor of teams that implement corporate strategy. Instead of having the COO implementing the strategy, teams may carry out this task. This would eliminate a level in the organizational hierarchy.

The chief characteristic of teams is a shared commitment to a common purpose. Team members share accountability not only to each other but also to the common aim. However, team skills have to be learned. Not all teams succeed; in fact, many fail.

What makes successful teams? Team members need to be trained in skills such as communication, including listening. They must learn about setting team objectives, staying focused, and making decisions that contribute not only to the team's goals but also to the aims of the total organization. Moreover, the reward system must be based more on team performance and less on individual accomplishments. Teams also need to have access to important information (which some top managers may not want to share), thus a culture of openness is essential. Perhaps most important, team training is not an individual event or a one-time program, but a continuing process.

THE LEARNING ORGANIZATION

A learning organization is one that can adapt to changes in the external environment through continuous renewal of its structure and practices. Peter Senge, who popularized the concepts of the learning organization with his book *The Fifth Discipline*,[20] suggests five techniques that help the organization to learn: (1) systems thinking, (2) personal mastery, (3) mental models, (4) a shared vision, and (5) team learning. The learning organization is generally associated with concepts such as sharing the vision of the enterprise, self-examining the prevailing assumptions and practices, considering radically new organization structures, creating learning teams, and establishing linkages with parties outside the enterprise for generating new ideas and perspectives.

David Garvin offers the following definition: "A learning organization is an organization skilled at creating, acquiring, and transferring knowledge, and at modifying its behavior to reflect new knowledge and insights."[21] This means that organizations engage in systematic problem solving, experimenting, and continuously searching for new knowledge. There must also be tolerance for failure because experimentation may not succeed; the aim is of course to learn from past failures. The learning should not be restricted to one's own experience. One can learn a great deal from others, inside and outside the organization. Learning from other organizations is often achieved through benchmarking, which requires the search for the best practices not only within the same industry but also in other industries. What is learned needs to be shared through, for example, reports, plant tours, and education and training programs. Individuals or groups should be encouraged to share their specialized knowledge and disseminate it throughout the organization. Acquiring knowledge is not enough; knowledge has to be applied. Unless behavior is changed, little is gained from the efforts of creating a learning organization. Therefore, progress and improvement need to be measured through questionnaires, surveys, interviews, and observation of behavior. Department stores may, for example, use shoppers to assess the service of their sales assistants. Assessors at the department store L.L. Bean shop by telephone to evaluate the service of its operators. A comprehensive learning audit may include a variety of measurements.

Learning organization An organization that can adapt to changes in the external environment through continuous renewal of its structure and practices.

www.llbean.com

GLOBAL PERSPECTIVE

Wal-Mart's Global Learning[22]

When Wal-Mart's U.S. market became saturated, it needed international markets for its expansion. By 2006, its international sales accounted for some 20 percent of total sales. But the expansion abroad into some 15 counties was not without its problems—even in countries where the company was relatively successful.

- In Germany, Wal-Mart had problems with employees, customers, and the low-price competitor Aldi Einkauf GmbH. Employees objected to the policy that does not allow employees to engage in romantic relationships between supervisors and employees. Customers considered the friendly smiles by cashiers as flirting. Perhaps most important, Aldi was already well established in Germany by offering a limited number of products but at low prices. Also, certain consumers did not consider Wal-Mart's image as a low-priced leader. Wal-Mart was not profitable and left Germany.
- In the United Kingdom, Wal-Mart's subsidiary Asda fared better because the company was recognized for its low prices. Moreover, Asda responded to local zoning laws by opening smaller stores.
- Since 2002, Wal-Mart operated in Japan where it invested in Seiyu Ltd., a chain selling groceries and apparels. Its competitor, Aeon Co., apparently was impressed by the Wal-Mart business model that it sent its employees to China and South Korea to study the operation. On the other hand, other Japanese competitors also reduced prices and opened single-story supercenters.
- But the supercenter model did not work well in Brazil where consumers prefer the local market. Also, pushing golf clubs in the land of soccer was not appropriate. But Wal-Mart's Brazilian managers helped to adjust the company's approach by offering, for example, more food items in their stores.
- In China, where many consumers have limited transportation choices, Wal-Mart offered free shuttle service and home delivery for heavy items such as refrigerators. Although the market share in 2005 was only 2 percent, it is estimated that an increase to 3 percent could gain it $20 billion in annual sales. But the company faces tough competition from the French retailer Carrefour SA.
- Mexico is a very important market for Wal-Mart. It learned that ice skates are not important to the consumers. On the other hand, certain Mexicans are familiar with Wal-Mart from their experiences in the United States.
- Wal-Mart is planning for the future. Although India does not allow foreign retailers into the country, Wal-Mart is studying this market carefully to be ready if and when the restrictions will be lifted.

With international sales accounting for 20 percent of Wal-Mart's sales, the global market is crucial for Wal-Mart's future. Yes, mistakes have been made by not understanding the cultural environment abroad. However, Wal-Mart is learning from its mistakes because international customers are vital for its growth.

www.aldi.com
www.asda.co.uk
www.seiyu.co.jp/english/index.shtml
www.aeon.info/en/
www.carrefour.com/english/

SUMMARY

Manager development refers to the progress a manager makes in learning how to manage effectively. Frequently, it also pertains to development programs. OD, on the other hand, is a systematic, integrated, and planned approach to making the whole organization or an organizational unit effective.

Good results can be achieved through a systematic approach to manager development and training. On-the-job training includes planned progression, job rotation, creation of "assistant-to" positions, temporary promotions, use of committees and junior boards, and coaching. Manager development may include a variety of internal and external training programs.

There are many sources of conflict. Ways of managing conflict include avoiding the situation, smoothing, forcing, compromising, changing behavior, reassigning individuals, resolving the conflict at higher levels, and problem solving. Another approach is to make structural changes: modifying objectives, developing new methods of coordination, as well as rearranging authority–responsibility relationships, tasks, and work locations.

The typical OD process includes the recognition of problems, diagnosis of an organization, feedback of information on the organization, development of a change strategy, interventions, and measurement and evaluation of the change efforts. The learning organization adapts quickly to changes in the environment through continuous learning.

KEY IDEAS AND CONCEPTS FOR REVIEW

Manager development
Managerial training
Organization development
Manager development process
On-the-job training
Internal and external training and development
Business simulation and experiential exercises
E-training
Field force theory
Sources of organizational conflict
Ways of managing organizational conflict
Organization development process
Learning organization

FOR DISCUSSION

1. It has been argued that firms have an obligation to train and develop all employees with managerial potential. Do you agree? Why or why not?
2. What are some typical failures in manager development and training? Can you explain these failures? What would you recommend to overcome the shortcomings?
3. Evaluate the advantages and limitations of different approaches to on-the-job training.

4. In the job that you now have or that you expect to have in the future, what kind of coaching and management development would be most beneficial to you?
5. What are the main characteristics of organization development? How does organization development differ from manager development? Do you think organization development might work in your organization? Explain why or why not.

EXERCISES/ACTION STEPS

1. Select an organization that you know and analyze its management development efforts.
2. What kinds of conflicts have you experienced in an organization with which you are familiar? What were the causes of the conflicts? What was done, if anything, about resolving these conflicts?

INTERNET RESEARCH

1. Search the Internet for "open university". What are the advantages and disadvantages of the Open University? Compare the Open University with the traditional university.
2. Search for "organization development" on the Internet. Discuss your findings with the class.

GLOBAL CASE

Jack Welch Leading Organizational Change at GE[23]

When Jack Welch, the chairman and CEO at General Electric (GE) retired in 2001, he could look back at a very successful career. He became CEO in 1981 at the age of 45. At that time, GE had a very complex organization structure with considerable bureaucratic rules.

One of his first changes was to initiate a strategy formulation process with the guideline that each of the businesses should be number 1 or 2 in their respective areas. If this was not the case, managers had the options of fixing the problem, selling their particular business, or closing it. In an effort to streamline the organization, Welch removed the sector level and eliminated thousands of salaried and hourly employee positions. Because of these drastic measures, he earned the nickname "Neutron Jack". The reorganization increased the span of management (also called span of control) for many managers so that they would have 10 or even 15 subordinates.

The restructuring was followed by changing the organization culture and the managerial styles of GE's managers. One such program was the Work-Out. Groups of managers were assembled to share their views openly in three-day sessions. At the beginning of the meetings, the superior presented the challenges for his or her organizational unit. Then the superior had to leave, requesting the groups to find solutions to the problems. Facilitators helped these discussions. On the last day, the superior was presented with problem solutions. He or she then had three choices: to accept the proposal, not to accept it, or to collect more information. This process put great pressure on the superior to make decisions.

Another program to improve effectiveness and efficiency was Best Practices. The aim was to learn from other companies how they obtained customer satisfaction, how they related to their suppliers, and in what ways they developed new products. This helped the GE people to focus on the processes in their operations that would improve the company's performance.

Jack Welch was personally involved in developing managers at GE's training center in Crotonville. Leaders, Welch suggested, are not only those who achieve results but also those who share the values of the company. Managers who shared the company values but did not achieve results got another opportunity to improve performance, while managers who achieved results but did not share the values received coaching aimed at changing their value orientation. There was little hope for managers who did not achieve results nor shared the company's values.

The stretch initiative at GE emphasized "dream targets" with little consideration of how to achieve them. This approach is similar to the setting of creative objectives used in some management-by-objectives programs by other companies. These dream targets did not replace the traditional objective-setting approach but supplemented it.

To improve quality, the Six Sigma approach, which was used by Motorola, was introduced at GE. The Six Sigma program suggests a quality level of not more than 3.4 defects for a million operations. Managers were required to participate in the program, and their bonuses were related to the achievement of the quality level. With the strong conviction of relating performance to rewards, an appraisal system was also introduced that ranked employees in five categories ranging from the top 10 percent to the bottom 10 percent. The top 25 percent received stock options as their reward.

While some managers were in favor of the organizational transformation because they felt greater freedom and were rewarded for good performance and value sharing, others saw flaws in the system.

Questions:

1. Do you think it is ethical to engage in restructuring and delayering that result in massive reduction of positions?
2. How would you feel if you were the boss in the Work-Out session being asked to leave the meeting while your subordinates discuss problems and suggest solutions to which you have to say "yes", "no", or "require further study"?
3. Why would other companies agree to their best practices being studied?
4. What do you think of evaluating the performance of managers not only on the achievement of results but also on the degree to which they share the organizational values?
5. How would you feel about setting unrealistic (stretch) objectives?
6. Should managers be ranked within their organizational unit? What would you suggest if one such unit is far superior to another unit with most of its managers being generally good managers and yet you still have to identify the bottom 10 percent?
7. Overall, how would you evaluate GE's approach to organizational change? What are the advantages and possible problems?

PART 4 CLOSING

Global and Entrepreneurial Staffing

This part closing is about Global and Entrepreneurial Staffing. First, the international focus is on the German/European model for training and development. The second issue is about attracting talent for a high-intensity new venture. Finally, the global car industry case focuses on the chief executives of carmakers.

GLOBAL FOCUS: TRAINING AND DEVELOPMENT FOR THE GLOBAL MARKET: THE GERMAN/EUROPEAN MODEL

Germany has been slow in accepting the idea that management is learnable and teachable. Because managerial education provided by universities is insufficient, companies have developed their own programs or made cooperative arrangements with schools. One such cooperative arrangement is the apprenticeship system.

Internal and External Training Combined: The Apprenticeship System

An apprentice obtains practical experience by working in the company and learns theoretical concepts that can be applied on the job by attending a vocational school.[24] University of Chicago professor Gary Becker said that the German approach to vocational training may be useful for reducing the number of high school dropouts in the United States.[25] He suggested that some young people would prefer to be in a training–employment program rather than continue their studies in high school. Owing to their lack of interest in academic subjects, some students simply drop out of school.

Although they are not managerial training programs as such, the in-company apprenticeship programs play a vital role in preparing future managers for their job. These programs, supplemented by additional education, provide the foundation for the development of first-line supervisors in Germany.

Young people who choose the three-year apprenticeship training work three to four days a week and spend one or two days a week in the vocational school. The government sets the standards for over 400 occupations. For example, an apprentice auto mechanic may be required to learn some basic skills, such as how to use a file, lathe, and drill, while working in the company. These activities may be supervised by a trainer (each supervising 10 to 15 young people), a manager, and a director. The apprentices' work usually does not contribute to the short-term profit of the firm. Typically, these apprentices engage in projects that are then carefully evaluated for accuracy, surface preparation, proper and precise angles, and so on. Advanced auto mechanic training requires working on more complex car components, such as automatic transmissions or engines.

In addition to having apprentices attend vocational training courses, many large firms offer in-house classroom training. Thus, apprentices not only learn about the products or services of the firm but also may be taught foreign languages, which are important for technicians or managers sent to other countries. Social activities are not neglected either during the apprenticeship training. For example, apprentices have opportunities to participate in company-sponsored hiking tours, competitive sports such as soccer or track-and-field events, and other recreational activities. In a sense, apprenticeship training is really a continuation of basic schooling with an emphasis on job skills. This is reflected in the fact that, at the end of the training, apprentices take an examination administered by the public vocational school. In addition, they must meet company requirements. It is interesting to note that Daimler-Benz's chief executive officer (CEO), Jürgen Schrempp, started his career as an auto mechanic apprentice.[26]

Although the wages for the apprentices are relatively low, the training is quite costly to the company, especially since a trainee may leave the company after completing the program. Hewlett-Packard in Germany hired about 80 apprentices each year at a cost of about $5,000 per apprentice. Most apprentices stay with their company and so the long-term investment pays off for the firm. Without apprenticeship programs, German firms would not have been so successful in producing the quality products and services that they sell around the world.

The German airline Lufthansa has an advertisement showing apprentices inspecting an airplane engine. The message is that investment in the training of technicians results in higher product and service quality. About half a million German firms train 1.8 million teenagers, or 6 percent of the workforce, and about 70 percent of Germany's high school students choose vocational education.[27]

One benefit of the apprenticeship system is that by teaching skilled workers and trained technicians, the theoretical foundation of their work creates professionals who will continually make efforts to improve productivity.

The Vocational Academy

While apprenticeship training emphasizes technical knowledge and skills, it usually does not teach managerial skills. When the need for teaching managerial skills and integrating theory with practice became recognized, a new program, the Vocational Academy (Berufsakademie), was devised to address this need. Because of its success, a more detailed discussion is in order.

In 1974, the German state of Baden-Wuerttemberg, together with firms such as Daimler-Benz and Bosch, started the Vocational Academy (also called the Stuttgarter Educational Model, named after the city of Stuttgart). This managerial training model, which focuses on technology, social sciences, and business, rather than on academic subjects, has been considered an important alternative to university studies. The academy has the following characteristics[28]:

- Theoretical and vocational studies are closely integrated. The educational process consists of two sets of learning modules, one for theory and the other for practice.
- Students must have a vocational contract with an enterprise or a social institution to be admitted to the academy.
- The academy and the enterprises have equal authority in determining the educational goals.
- The first step in the program is achieved after two years, when students must take a state-recognized vocation-qualifying examination.
- The complete educational process spans three years, or six semesters. The students must take a second examination, and upon passing it they receive a degree that is similar to a university degree in engineering.

Ten years after the inception of the academy, surveys indicated that professional opportunities were considerably higher for its graduates than for those who did not receive this training. Applications for admission to the academy far exceed available places, with as many as 20 young people competing for one educational slot. While the Vocational Academy programs originated in the cities of Stuttgart and Mannheim, they are now established in eight cities, with approximately 3,000 enterprises participating, offering 22 curriculums.[29]

One can conclude that the Stuttgarter Educational Model, integrating theory and practical experience, fills an important business education gap not filled by traditional universities and apprenticeship programs. This relatively new cooperative model, involving the academy, industry, and government, has shown encouraging results. It may stimulate companies in other countries to search for alternative training methods for developing managers and increasing productivity.

The New European Manager

So far, the discussion has centered on training and development for lower- and middle-level managers; now the focus shifts to training for upper-level management. Managers in many European firms have been criticized for insufficient knowledge and skills necessary for managing globally. Specifically, demands on today's global managers include the ability to think globally, an understanding of the mentalities of managers in other countries, managerial experience abroad, and proficiency in speaking at least two foreign languages.

The European Community 1992 program (now the European Union) underscores the need for developing globally minded managers. A research study of 11 European firms by the international consulting group Korn/Ferry found that many managers did not meet the European demands of the future, although respondents in the study recognized the need for international managerial experience. Not only do European managers need to gain experience abroad, but multinational corporations also should realize that they need to recruit and train non-European managers for their foreign operations. The following examples illustrate the exception rather than the rule under which companies operate. The Deutsche Bank has a development program for foreign managers, who spend at least one year at its Frankfurt headquarters. Bosch, a manufacturer of a variety of products ranging from refrigerators to auto accessories, invites foreigners, Spaniards in particular, to Germany for training. It also requires its German trainees to spend at least six months abroad. While these international opportunities are attractive for young managers, there is concern, especially among older managers, that being away from headquarters may inhibit their career advancement.

According to Korn/Ferry, the following characteristics are very important for the ideal European manager[30]:

- Having a university or college education
- Having work experience abroad
- Understanding economics
- Being a generalist
- Being proficient in English and French as foreign languages

The research study found that German, French, and Italian managers had little work experience abroad. German and Italian managers lacked general managerial experience, while German and British managers were not proficient in the French language. In team orientation and global thinking, the Germans and Italians ranked low. The Germans also ranked low in communication and motivation abilities. With respect to the question pertaining to "the willingness to contribute above average", English and French managers ranked low; while in decision making, Italian managers got a low rating. Although these are generalizations, they indicate that many European managers are not sufficiently prepared for the competitive environment that will be created by the European Union.

Business Schools in Europe

While German universities have not been adequately preparing managers for the global environment, there are many MBA schools throughout the rest of Europe, including the following[31]:

- Rotterdam School of Management (RSM) in the Netherlands
- International Institute for Management Development (IMD) in Lausanne, Switzerland
- Graduate School of Business Administration (GSBA) in Zurich, Switzerland
- Institute Superieur des Affaires (ISA) in Jouy-en-Josas, France
- Manchester Business School in England
- Scuola Di Direzione Aziendale Dell' Universita Luigi Bocconi (SDA Bocconi) in Milan, Italy
- Institut Europeen d'Administration des Affaires (INSEAD) in Fontainebleau, France
- Nijenrode School of Business in Breukelen, the Netherlands
- Escola Superior d'Administració i Direcció d'Empreses (ESADE) in Barcelona, Spain
- London Business School in England

The 21st century is marked by fierce global competition in which only the most productive organizations will survive. This competitive environment necessitates a second look at human resource training and development. Managers should evaluate the suitability of cooperative training by industry and educational institutions as practiced in Germany. The model of the new European manager may inspire more effective and relevant approaches for training future executives.

ENTREPRENEURIAL FOCUS: ATTRACTING TALENT FOR THE HIGH-INTENSITY VENTURE

How do entrepreneurial managers staff their firms? Do they look for a certain kind of person to work in a high-growth venture? How do they manage the cost of staff when cash is a prime concern for new ventures on a budget? To what extent do entrepreneurial managers employ outsourcing to maximize the efficiency of their staffing decisions? Finally, what attracts individuals to work in high-intensity environments with long work hours and an uncertain future?

We know that the success or failure of firms frequently rests on the ability of the firms' managers to execute an appropriate strategy for the company. People make the firm, and good people are necessary for the firm to succeed. But does this equation differ somehow in an entrepreneurial context?

High-growth entrepreneurial firms in the Silicon Valley are noted for the high demands they place on their employees. These high demands are a function of the necessity for a small number of start-up firms' managers to accomplish a multitude of tasks. Entrepreneurial managers must not only make and sell superior products. They must also raise significant financing to fund the operations and investment in the company, develop a network of industry relationships, build an attractive company brand, negotiate legal issues on corporate structure and intellectual property protection, and, of course, hire more staff. In the early months and years of a high-growth venture, all or most of these tasks frequently fall upon just the firm's early leadership. Given the high demands of a new high-growth venture and the necessity of each person to fill numerous tasks, the early hiring decisions are crucial to the survival and success of the enterprise.[32]

Due to the heavy workload and overlapping responsibilities of high-growth start-up ventures, early employees of these types of enterprises need to possess a tolerance for increased levels of stress and ambiguity. The stress and ambiguity come not only from the workload of these positions but also from the uncertainty of the firm's future.[33] Further, compensation for employees often comes in the form of stock options in addition to salaries that are sometimes less than what might be received at larger organizations. This compensation package (lower salary coupled with stock options) is consistent with the low-cash position of a new venture where cash must be conserved wherever possible. Further, stock options tend to align the priorities of the new employee better with the firm than pure cash compensation. Still, new employees must truly *buy into* the firm they are joining as their compensation package is more closely aligned to the firm's success than at larger more established companies. Hiring managers of start-up ventures need to clarify these risks and rewards to potential employees and extend offers only to those whose tolerance for risk and ability to perform under stress match the needs of the company.

Other ways that entrepreneurial managers may staff effectively but also conserve cash is the prudent use of outsourcing and offshoring. Outsourcing, as discussed in Chapter 20 of this text, is essentially the movement of some elements of a firm's activities to outside vendors who are more effective or efficient in the production of aspects of a firm's value chain of activities. Offshoring is the movement of certain business processes from one country to another country.[34] This movement of activities may be either through international subsidiaries owned by the firm or foreign contractors. India, with its large supply of well-educated English-speaking workers at low real wages, is the number one destination for U.S. firms seeking to reduce costs of development and implementation of their business model. In fact, according to a study completed by Santa Clara University, more than half of Silicon Valley firms outsource some of their activities internationally and more than half of those outsourced activities are occurring in India.[35] For example, Cisco Systems, a Silicon Valley technology powerhouse, recently announced it is investing $1.2 billion in Bangalore, India, to establish a new R&D campus that will employ 3000 people.[36] China is also an increasingly popular destination of offshoring of a firm's activities. For example, Hewlett Packard has nearly 5000 employees in China as of late 2006.[37]

The offshoring of activities is not confined to large multinational firms. New growth enterprises that expect funding by venture capitalists must consider potential outsourcing and offshoring strategies for their firms. Funding decisions for new ventures are based on financing those activities that bring distinctive advantage to a new company. Savvy venture firms are most interested in financing those activities that lead directly to competitive advantage in a growing market and expect the management team to complete other noncore activities as efficiently as possible. These efficiencies can often be found in coherent outsourcing and offshoring tactics. In fact, start-ups are increasingly being prodded to hire overseas as a cost strategy.[38] However, this process needs to be intertwined in a long-term strategy of rationalizing a firm's production and distribution process rather than be a knee-jerk reaction to an impulse to cut costs, as managing an overseas workforce requires time in oversight and entails some risks such as loss of technology, quality control, and others.

In sum, what attracts employees to a start-up firm and how are these employees best managed? Similar to entrepreneurs themselves, employees for new high-growth firms knowingly accept some additional risk for potentially higher rewards—both financial and aspirational. It is up to the entrepreneurial leaders of a firm to first find the right types of persons who are motivated and excel in this business environment, and then to continue to motivate new staff to excel through the articulation of a vision of the firm's purpose that goes beyond pure profits. Guy Kawasaki, in his most recent book, *The Art of the Start*, discusses the importance of firms to "make meaning" with their enterprises.[39] With this, he refers to the impact that firms have on society beyond revenues and expenses. Rather, what part does the firm play in enhancing the world we live in? Kawasaki emphasizes that entrepreneurial managers need to recruit their employees every day to make sure they want to come back the next day. It is this continuous motivational energy and the articulation of an inspirational vision that attracts and retains staff in a start-up firm and what is essential to effective entrepreneurial management.

GLOBAL CAR INDUSTRY CASE

Career Paths of CEOs at Toyota, Volkswagen (VW), Ford, and General Motors (GM).

Organizational strategies are to a great extent determined by CEOs. It is, therefore, important to learn about the career paths of the top executives. The focus is on the CEOs of the major car manufacturers of Toyota, Volkswagen, Ford, and General Motors.

AKIO TOYODA, PRESIDENT AND CEO OF TOYOTA[40]

Mr. Toyoda, the grandson of the founder of Toyota, was born in 1956. He earned a law degree from Keio University in Japan and a Master of Business Administration from Babson College in the United States. He joined Toyota in 1984, became executive vice president in 2005, and president in 2009 at the time the company had an extensive car recall campaign for quality defects. Shortly after assuming the position, he apologized to the US Congress for the vehicle recalls. At age 53, he is a young president by Japanese standards. He took the office when Toyota reported the biggest annual loss.

He spent seven years in the United States and speaks fluent English. When asked about comparing life in America and Japan, he liked the feeling of freedom in the United States while life is more restricted in Japan because it is a small country and people live close together, which requires consideration for others.

He enjoyed working on the factory floor more than sitting in the office and is interested in racing cars. He views the challenge for the car industry as using the available energy resources effectively and efficiently. This is one of the reasons Toyota focuses on the development of the fuel-efficient hybrid cars, illustrated by the best-selling Prius model.

In his early tenure as president, Akio Toyoda had to face many challenges such as the financial condition of the company, the car recall, and the damage caused by the 2011 earthquake disaster.

Martin Winterkorn, Volkswagen (VW) CEO and Chairman of the Board[41]

Mr. Winterkorn was born in 1947 and became Chairman of the Volkswagen Board in 2007. He studied metallurgy and metal physics at the University of Stuttgart from 1966 to 1973. In 1977 he earned his doctorate from the prestigious Max-Planck Institute for metal research and metal physics. He then joined Robert Bosch GmbH working in the refrigerant compressor group. In 1993 he became the director of the Group Quality Assurance at Volkswagen and worked in various technical fields. In 2002, he became head of the Audi group, which includes brands such as SEAT and Lamborghini.

The Volkswagen Group includes passenger cars and large vehicles. The International Group consists of Volkswagen of America, Brazil, China, India, and Ireland. The company also has major interests in Porsche AG, MAN SE, Suzuki Motor Corporation, Italdesign Giugiaro and others.

The goal of Martin Winterkorn is to make Volkswagen the largest car company by 2018. Winterkorn's strategy is to overtake, by sales volume, the current leader Toyota. Some of the first moves are the expansion of the operations in China and in Chattanooga, Tennessee, United States where the midsize Passat will be built. Some specific goals are to be an attractive employer, achieve the greatest customer satisfaction and have a pretax return on sales of over 8 percent. Winterkorn also plans to improve the brands like Audi, SEAT, and Skoda.

Alan Mulally, President and CEO of Ford Motor Company[42]

Mr. Mulally, who considers himself as being an engineer and businessman, was born in 1945. He graduated with the bachelor of science degree and the master of science degree in astronautical engineering from the University of Kansas. He also earned a master's degree in management as a Sloan Fellow at MIT. Before joining Ford, he served as executive vice president of Boeing Company and CEO of Boeing's commercial airplanes group. Mulally started at Boeing as an engineer in 1969 and has been credited with making Boeing competitive with Airbus, the European consortium.

In 2006, Mulally became CEO and president of Ford. He was named one of "The Best Leaders of 2005" by *Business Week* magazine and *AUTOWEEK* called him Top CEO. During the financial crisis in the late 2000s, Ford was the only American automobile manufacturer that avoided government-sponsored bankruptcy.

Daniel F. Akerson, Chairman and Executive Officer at General Motors (GM)[43]

Mr. Akerson was born in 1948. He earned his bachelor of science degree from the U.S. Naval Academy in 1970 and his master of science degree from the London School of Economics. Since 2010, he is the CEO of GM and became chairman in 2011. He joined the GM board as a representative of the government.

Before joining GM, he was the managing director of the Carlyle Group, a private equity company (2003 to 2010). In addition he also had extensive experience with several other companies, including XO Communication (1999 to 2003), Nextel Communication (1996–1999), General Instrument (1993–1995), and MCI Communication (1983–1993).

While with the Carlyle Group, he gained experience in company buyouts in Asia and Europe as well as providing other services in Japan and America. For example, he formulated and implemented MCI's global strategy. At Nextel, he helped the company to become a national digital wireless provider. Clearly, he has a strong background in telecommunication.

Before becoming GM's CEO, he served on GM's Board as well as on the Board of the American Express firm. With his background in the financial industry, he is attractive to GM investors, but he is not a person with hands-on car experience. Akerson is relatively unknown in the car industry. However, his goal is to make GM cars better than those from competitors such as BMW.

Questions:

1. Which CEO do you think has the best experience for succeeding in the automobile industry? Why?
2. Do you think that management skills are transferable between industries? If you say "no", how successful do you think Daniel Akerson will be at General Motors?
3. What is your career path? Is it in a technical field, finance, marketing, operations or is it another path?
4. Do you want to work in a line or staff position? Why? What makes a line or staff position attractive to you?

ENDNOTES

1. "Leadership: India Inc's Biggest Challenge," http://www.rediff.com/money/2008/jun/05lead.htm, accessed January 5, 2016.
2. See PWC in China, www.pwcglobal.com/cn, accessed August 18, 2011; Information was also obtained from persons familiar with the operation.
3. For a discussion of European and North American management education, see Daniel J. McCarthy, Sheila M. Puffer, and Heinz Weihrich, "Contributions to Management Practice by European and North American Management Education Programs," in Ralph Berndt (ed.), *Global Management* (Berlin: Springer, 1996), pp. 3–18; Paul W. Beamish et al., *International Management* (Burr Ridge, IL: Irwin/McGraw-Hill, 2000), pp. 191–192.
4. IMPROVE Academy, https://www.improve-innovation.eu/academy/about-the-academy/, accessed March 5, 2012; IMP^{3}rove—"Pushing the Frontier: New Ideas to Promote Service Innovation Through Structural Funds", http://www.europe-innova.eu/c/document_library/get_file?folderId=366487&name=DLFE-11061.pdf, accessed March 5, 2012; TIM Cases, http://aomtim.org/index.php?option=com_content&task=view&id=27&Itemid=48, accessed March 5, 2012.
5. Ann Harrington, "Or Not to B," *Fortune*, March 4, 2002, pp. 223–224.
6. Jack Welch with John A. Byrne, *Jack—Straight from the Gut* (New York: Warner Brooks, 2001), Chapter 12.
7. Steve Hamm, "The Globe is IBM's Classroom," *Business Week,* March 23 and 30, 2009, p. 56.
8. Ellen Gibson, "The School of Future Knocks," *Business Week*, March 23 and 30, 2009, pp. 44–45.
9. One can also listen to podcast on *Business Today*. Go to: http://businesstoday.digitaltoday.in/podcast, accessed January 5, 2016.
10. "Online Education: Lessons of a Virtual Timetable," *The Economist*, February 17, 2001, pp. 69–71.
11. Lisa Vaas, "The E-Training of America," *PC Magazine*, December 26, 2001, Internet Business Insert pp. 1–4; Elisabeth Goodridge, "Slowing Economy Sparks Boom in E-Learning: Online Training Lets Companies Provide More Employee Instruction for Less Money," *Information Week*, November 12, 2001, p. 100; "Harvard Adds Online Courses," *Information Week*, October 15, 2001, p. 67; William C. Symonds, "Giving It the Old Online Try", *Business Week*, December 3, 2001, pp. 76–80.
12. Online B-Schools Threaten the Traditional Classroom, Bloomberg Businessweek, May 5–11, 2014, pp. 51–54; edX at https://www.edx.org, accessed May 20, 2014; Coursera at https://www.coursera.org, accessed May 20, 2014; "Harvard EdCast: edX Marks the Spot," http://www.gse.harvard.edu/news-impact/2013/11/harvard-edcast-edx-marks-the-spot, accessed January 5, 2016; "edX" at https://www.edx.org/edx-terms-service, accessed May 21, 2014; edX, "Schools and Partners," https://www.edx.org/schools-partners, accessed 2014; "Harvard and MIT Put $60-Million Into New Platform for Free Online Courses", at http://chronicle.com/blogs/wiredcampus/harvard-and-mit-put-60-million-into-new-platform-for-free-online-courses/36284, accessed January 5, 2016; Coursera, Our Mission, How It Works, Our Approach, https://www.coursera.org/about, accessed May 21, 2014; "How Coursera, a Free Online Education Service, Will School Us All," in FastCompany, at http://www.fastcompany.com/3000042/how-coursera-free-online-education-service-will-school-us-all, accessed January 5, 2016.
13. Online B-Schools Threaten the Traditional Classroom, *Bloomberg Businessweek*, May 5–11, 2014, pp. 51.
14. Peter Burrows, "Cisco: Tuning a Workforce to Local Markets," *Business Week*, March 23 and 30, 2009, p. 55.
15. See, for example, Timothy J. Galpin, *The Human Side of Change: A Practical Guide to Organization Redesign* (San Francisco, CA: Jossey-Bass, 1996). For reviews of various career trends, see the special issue of the *Academy of Management Executive*, November 1996, pp. 8–103.
16. Kurt Lewin, *Field Theory in Social Science: Selected Theoretical Papers* (New York: Harper, 1951).
17. Edgar H. Schein, *Organizational Psychology*, 3rd ed. (Englewood Cliffs, NJ: Prentice Hall, 1980), chap. 13; D. D. Warrick, *Managing Organization Change and Development* (Chicago: Science Research Associates, 1984).
18. Aaron De Smet, Johanne Lavoie, and Elizabeth Hioe, "Developing Better Change Leaders", *McKinsey Quarterly*, 2012, 2: 98–104.
19. Diane Brady, "An Executive Whose Time Has Gone," *Business Week*, August 28, 2000; "Why Some Teams Succeed (and So Many Don't)," *Harvard Management Update*, January 2000. See also Jack D. Orsburn and Linda Moran, *The New Self-directed Work Teams: Mastering the Challenge*, 2nd ed. (New York: McGraw-Hill, 2000).
20. Peter M. Senge, *The Fifth Discipline* (New York: Doubleday, 1990); Peter M. Senge, Art Kleiner, Charlotte Roberts, Richard B. Ross, and Bryan J. Smith, *The Fifth Discipline Fieldbook* (New York: Doubleday, 1994).
21. David A. Garvin, "Building a Learning Organization", *Harvard Business Review*, July–August 1993; http://doi.contentdirections.com/mr/hbsp.jsp?doi=10.1225/93402, accessed November 22, 2012.
22. Geraldo Samor, Cecilie Rohwedder, and Ann Zimmerman, "Innocents Abroad?" *The Wall Street Journal*, May 5, May 16, 2006; http://www.sbaer.uca.edu/research/allied/2004/international-Business/pdf, accessed September 5, 2006. See also Vijay Govindarajan and Anil K. Gupta, "Taking Wal-Mart Global: Lessons from Retailing's Giant", http://www.strategy-business.com/press/16635507/13866, accessed August 18, 2011.
23. Several sources were consulted, including the following: John A. Byrne, "Jack: A Close-up Look at How America's #1 Manager Runs GE", *Business Week*, June 8, 1998, p. 92ff.; Julie Schlosser, "Jack? Jack Who? Six CEOs Who Have Outperformed GE's Welch", *Fortune*, September 17, 2001; several Harvard Business School cases that discuss GE and Jack Welch; Jack Welch with John A. Byrne, *Jack: Straight from the Gut* (New York: Warner Books, 2001); GE at www.ge.com, accessed August 18, 2011; Motorola at www.motorola.com, accessed August 18, 2011 and "What Is Six Sigma?" at www.ge.com/sixsigma, accessed January 5, 2016.

24. Peter F. Drucker, "What We Can Learn from the Germans", *Wall Street Journal*, March 6, 1986.
25. Gary S. Becker, "Tuning in to the Needs of High School Dropouts", *Business Week*, July 3, 1989.
26. "Juergen Schrempp", www.manager-magazin.de/koepfe/mdj/0,2828,167372,00.html, accessed January 5, 2016.
27. Nancy J. Perry, "The New, Improved Vocational School", *Fortune*, June 19, 1989, pp. 127–138. German schools have also been criticized: see "Vocational Schools under Scrutiny", *BBC News*, January 28, 2002.
28. Informationen zu den Berufsakademien des Landes Baden-Wuerttemberg (undated); Michael Leitl, "Berufsakademien: Doppelt Genaeht", *Manager Magazine*, September 6, 2001, www.manager-magazin.de/koepfe/uniguide, accessed October 1, 2006.
29. "Interesenten Stehen Schlange", *IWD* (Institut der Deutschen Wirtschaft), 1986. See also the home page of the Berufsakademie in Stuttgart, www.ba-stuttgart.de, accessed October 2006.
30. Brigitta Lentz, "Der polyglotte Supermann", *Manager Magazine*, May 1989, pp. 257–270.
31. *MBA-Schulen auf dem Pruefstand: Die Top Ten 1988* (Frankfurt: Cox Communication, 1988); Albert Staehli, "Helvetische Spitzenausbildung fuer Europas Topmanagers", in *The Best of Switzerland* (Zurich: Jean Frey AG, 1989); Andrew Fisher, "Putting Europe's Business Schools under the Microscope", *Financial Times*, September 22, 1989; William H. Cox and Ingrid Cox, *Der MBA in Europa* (Frankfurt: Allgemeine Zeitung, 1987); brochures by the institutions; "The MBA Tour: Graduate Programs in Management", www.thembatour.com/fairs/sme.htm, accessed June 10, 2002.
32. A rule of thumb regarding hiring in the Silicon Valley states that "A" players (highly talented managers) tend to hire other "A" players. Highly talented managers tend to hire other highly talented managers because they are confident in their own abilities and seek other strong managers to help the firm succeed. However, "B" players (modestly talented managers) tend to hire "C" players (barely competent managers) because the B managers are less confident in their own abilities and, therefore, hire those who are less capable than they are so that their own jobs are more secure. Once this scenario is played out, we can see that the early hiring decisions to recruit "A" players are so crucial in order to ensure a well-staffed enterprise and the success of the venture.
33. Start-up firms, by their nature, are in a race to achieve profitability before their financing runs out. When considering joining a start-up venture, potential employees should verify the level of financing the firm currently has and how quickly the firm is "burning" that financing (how long can the firm survive given its negative monthly cash flow and level of financing). Knowing this information can relieve some of the risk and stress in joining a start-up company.
34. "Offshoring—Definition of Offshoring", http://operationstech.about.com/od/glossary/g/Offshoring.htm, accessed August 2, 2012.
35. Dawn Kawamoto, "More than Half of the Silicon Valley Firms are Outsourcing", http://services.silicon.com/itoutsourcing/0,3800004871,39152881,00.htm, accessed August 18, 2011.
36. Keith Naughton, *Newsweek*, March 6, 2006 issue, http://www.msnbc.msn.com/id/11571580/site/newsweek/, accessed January 28, 2007.
37. "Outsourcing in China", http://www.computerworld.com/action/article.do?command=viewArticleBasic&articleId=268501&pageNumber=2, accessed November 22, 2012.
38. "Siliconvalley.com", http://www.siliconvalley.com/mld/siliconvalley/business/special_packages/venture_capital_survey/8679984.htm, accessed August 18, 2011.
39. Guy Kawasaki, "The Art of the Start", Portfolio, 2004.
40. Alex Taylor III, "Toyota's New Man At The Wheel", http://money.cnn.com/2009/06/23/autos/akio_toyoda_toyota_new_president.fortune/index, accessed January 6, 2016 "Toyota's New Man At the Wheel," http://money.cnn.com/2009/06/23/autos/akio_toyoda_toyota_new_president.fortune/index.htm?postversion=2009062605, accessed January 5, 2016; "Akio Toyoda", http://people.forbes.com/profile/akio-toyoda/80520, accessed July 9, 2011; "Toyota Global Vision, Mission Statement Announced on March 9, 2011" see video at http://www.toyota-global.com/company/message_from_president/, accessed January 5, 2016.
41. "Volkswagen Extends C.E.O. Martin Winterkorn's Contract", http://wheels.blogs.nytimes.com/2011/01/04/volkswagen-extends-c-e-o-martin-winterkorns-contract/, accessed January 5, 2016; "The Next Step is the Electric Car", http://www.spiegel.de/international/business/0,1518,719730,00.html, accessed January 5, 2016; "Martin Winterkorn", http://topics.wsj.com/person/W/martin-winterkorn/414, accessed January 5, 2016.
42. "Ford Motor Co", http://investing.businessweek.com/businessweek/research/stocks/people/person.asp?personId=370889&ticker=F:US, accessed July 5, 2011; "Magazine Names Ford's Alan Mulally Top CEO: according to Autoweek", https://www.google.com/#hl=en&cp=66&gs_id=4&xhr=t&q=Magazine+Names+Ford%E2%80%99s+Alan+Mulally+Top+CEO%3A+according+to+Autoweek%2C&tok=ZevSHam5tSVefndki6LF3Q&pf=p&sclient=psy-ab&site=&source=hp&p-bx=1&oq=Magazine+Names+Ford%E2%80%99s+Alan+Mulally+Top+CEO:+according+to+Autoweek,&aq=f&aqi=&aql=&gs_sm=&gs_upl=&bav=on.2,or.r_gc.r_pw.,cf.osb&fp=7ddfadd03e25da7c&biw=754&bih=609, accessed July 5, 2011; "What Other Automakers Can Learn from Alan Mulally", http://www.fastcompany.com/1573670/what-other-automakers-can-learn-from-alan-mulally, accessed July 9, 2011; "Alan Mulally, CEO Ford Motor Company", http://fpolom.wordpress.com/2011/02/27/alan-mulally-ceo-ford-motor-company, accessed July 9, 2011.
43. "Who is Dan Akerson? Seven Facts You Should Know about General Motors' Incoming CEO", accessed July 4, 2011; http://people.forbes.com/profile/daniel-f-akerson/4686, accessed July 4, 2011; "About GM", http://www.gm.com/company/aboutGM/GM_Corporate_Officers/daniel_f_akerson.html, accessed July 9, 2011; "Why Attacking Your Company Can Make it Stronger", http://management.fortune.cnn.com/2011/07/06/why-attacking-your-company-can-make-it-stronger/, accessed July 9, 2011; "Daniel Akerson, GM CEO: We Want to Beat BMW Go Into 'Attack Mode'", http://www.huffingtonpost.com/2010/09/08/gm-ceo-wants-to-beat-bmw_n_709541.html, accessed July 4, 2011; http://www.nndb.com/people/365/000124990/, accessed July 4 2011; "New GM Chief Daniel Akerson Not Usual 'Car Guy'", http://www.usatoday.com/money/autos/2010-08-13-gmearns13_ST2_N.htm, accessed January 6, 2016.

Goal inputs of claimants
1. Employees
2. Consumers
3. Suppliers
4. Stockholders
5. Governments
6. Community
7. Others

Inputs
1. Human
2. Capital
3. Managerial
4. Technological

EXTERNAL ENVIRONMENT

Managerial knowledge, goals of claimants, and use of inputs (Part 1, *The Basis of Management Theory and Science*)

Planning (Part 2)

Organizing (Part 3)

Staffing (Part 4)

Leading (Part 5)

Controlling (Part 6)

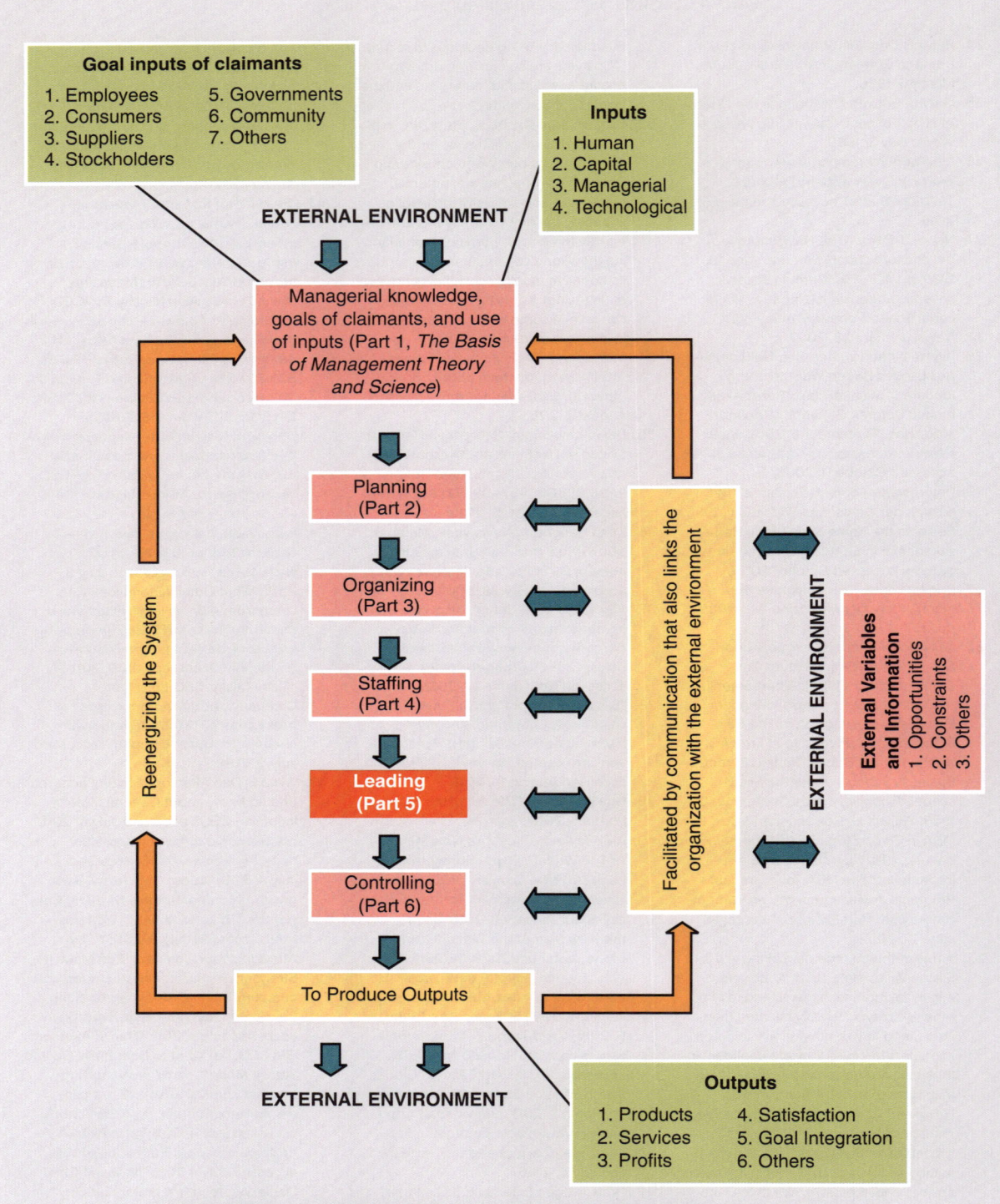

To Produce Outputs

Reenergizing the System

Facilitated by communication that also links the organization with the external environment

EXTERNAL ENVIRONMENT

External Variables and Information
1. Opportunities
2. Constraints
3. Others

EXTERNAL ENVIRONMENT

Outputs
1. Products
2. Services
3. Profits
4. Satisfaction
5. Goal Integration
6. Others

SYSTEMS APPROACH TO MANAGEMENT: LEADING

PART 5

Leading

Chapter 14:   Human Factors and Motivation
Chapter 15:   Leadership
Chapter 16:   Committees, Teams, and Group Decision Making
Chapter 17:   Communication
Part 5 Closing: Global and Entrepreneurial Leading

CHAPTER 14

Human Factors and Motivation

Learning Objectives

After studying this chapter, you should be able to:

LO 1   Define the nature of leading and leadership

LO 2   Describe the basic human factors that affect managing

LO 3   Explain the meaning of motivation

LO 4   Describe the various theories of motivation and their strengths and weaknesses

LO 5   Analyze motivational techniques, with emphasis on the role of money, participation, the quality of working life, and job enrichment

LO 6   Present a systems and situational approach to motivation

Management and leadership are often thought of as the same thing. Although it is true that the most effective manager will almost certainly be an effective leader and that leading is an essential function of managers, there is more to managing than just leading. As indicated in previous chapters, managing involves doing careful planning, setting up an organization structure that will aid people in achieving goals, and staffing the organization structure with people who are as competent as possible. The measurement and correction of people's activities through controlling is also an important function of management, as Part 6 will show. However, all these managerial functions accomplish little if managers do not know how to lead people or understand the human factors in their operations in such a way as to produce desired results.

The managerial function of **leading** is defined as the process of influencing people so that they will contribute to organizational and group goals. As the discussion of this function will show, it is in this area that the behavioral sciences make their major contribution to managing. In its analysis of the pertinent knowledge in leading, Part 5 of this book will focus on the human factors, motivation, leadership, and communication.

In this chapter, discussion centers on a variety of human factors. **Managing** requires the creation and maintenance of an environment in which individuals work together in groups toward the accomplishment of common objectives. This chapter emphasizes the importance of knowing and taking advantage of human and motivating factors, but that does not mean managers should become amateur psychiatrists. The manager's job is not to manipulate people but, rather, to recognize what motivates people.

> **Leading** Process of influencing people so that they will contribute to organizational and group goals.

> **Managing** requires the creation and maintenance of an environment in which individuals work together toward the accomplishment of common objectives.

HUMAN FACTORS IN MANAGING

It is obvious that, while enterprise objectives may differ somewhat between organizations, employees also have needs and objectives that are especially important to them. Through the function of leading, managers help people see that they can satisfy their own needs and utilize their potential while contributing to the aims of an enterprise. Managers should thus have an understanding of the roles assumed by people and the individuality and personalities of people.

Multiplicity of Roles

Individuals are much more than a productive factor in management's plans. They are members of social systems of many organizations; they are consumers of goods and services, and thus they vitally influence demand; and they are members of families, schools, churches, trade associations, and political parties. In these different roles, they establish laws that govern managers, ethics that guide behavior, and a tradition of human dignity that is a major characteristic of our society. In short, managers and the people they lead are interacting members of a broad social system.

No Average Person

People act in different roles, but they are also different themselves. There is no average person. Yet, in organized enterprises, the assumption is often made that there is. Firms develop rules, procedures, work schedules, safety standards, and position descriptions—all with the implicit assumption that people are essentially alike. Of course, this assumption is necessary to a great extent in organized efforts, but it is equally important to acknowledge that individuals are unique—they have different needs, different ambitions, different attitudes, different desires for responsibility, different levels of knowledge and skills, and different potentials.

Unless managers understand the complexity and individuality of people, they may misapply the generalizations about motivation, leadership, and communication. Principles and concepts, although generally true, have to be adjusted to fit specific situations. In an enterprise, not all the needs of individuals can be completely satisfied, but managers do have considerable latitude in making individual arrangements. Although position requirements are usually derived from enterprise and organization plans, this fact does not necessarily exclude the possibility of arranging the job to fit the person in a specific situation.

INNOVATIVE PERSPECTIVE

Interview with Dr. Kern Peng, Project Manager with Intel Corporation

Dr. Kern Peng has more than 26 years of people and project management experience in engineering and manufacturing, with the last 20 years at Intel Corporation. He has extensive skills in engineering and manufacturing management and has proven results in finding innovative solutions to business and engineering problems. He has been accorded more than 50 career awards in the areas of engineering design; software development; technical paper publication; problem resolution; project management and execution; teamwork; and leadership.

Given Dr. Peng's extensive experience in innovation with one of the world's technology leaders, we asked him how Intel encourages innovation among its employees. He responded that "Intel believes that setting up the right corporate culture has significant impact on innovation. Under the Intel Values, you will find phrases such as 'Foster innovation and creative thinking', 'Embrace change and challenge the status quo', and 'Encourage and reward informed risk taking'. The Intel Values are posted in all conference rooms and printed on a card with the calendar given to every employee to be attached with the ID badge." Dr. Peng continued, saying, "In addition to process innovation and product innovation, strategic innovation (i.e. new market) and continuous improvement are also under the innovation umbrella at Intel, which essentially means innovation is in every employee's job scope, from executives, to engineers, to technicians. To encourage innovation, courses such as 'Innovation 101 for Employees' and 'Innovation 101 for Managers' are offered. An internal web site called 'Innovation center' is in place to recommend an approach to bring innovation into a daily work environment and offer systemic innovation tools and resources to assist teams and individuals to increase the use of innovation in their daily work. Employees can submit ideas on line and rewards are given to selected ideas. Annual Innovation Day is arranged with series of activities targeted at building and promoting Intel's technical and innovation leadership."

Concept of individual dignity People must be treated with respect, no matter what their position in the organization is.

The Importance of Personal Dignity

Managing involves achieving enterprise objectives. Achieving results is important, but the means must never violate the dignity of people. The **concept of individual dignity** means that people must be treated with respect, no matter what their position in the organization is. The president, vice president, manager, first-line supervisor, and worker all contribute to the aims of the enterprise.

Each is unique, with different abilities and aspirations, but all are human beings and all deserve to be treated as such.[1]

Consideration of the Whole Person

We cannot talk about the nature of people unless we consider the whole person, not just separate and distinct characteristics such as knowledge, attitude, skills, or personality traits. A person has them all to different degrees. Moreover, these characteristics interact with one another, and their predominance in specific situations changes quickly and unpredictably. The human being is a total person influenced by external factors. People cannot divest themselves of the impact of these forces when they come to work. Managers must recognize these facts and be prepared to deal with them.

GLOBAL PERSPECTIVE

Disillusioned Middle Managers[2]

The recent trend of downsizing organizations and the merger of enterprises has had a traumatic effect on middle managers in many organizations. In the drive to improve efficiency, many middle-level manager jobs have been eliminated. The drastic reduction in personnel in many U.S. enterprises has had unexpected consequences. For example, it was assumed that the working life of the remaining managers would be enriched by more meaningful jobs. The reality is that many managers now feel that they are overworked and that their contributions go unappreciated.

The restructuring of organizations has resulted in great job insecurity and low morale. Managers are often reluctant to share information because they want to protect their jobs. Moreover, they hesitate to speak freely in meetings because they do not want to risk crossing their boss. Middle managers feel that they do not get sufficient information from top managers, who often do not provide vision and leadership for the enterprise.

Whatever the situation, the bitterness and alienation of many lower-level managers affect morale and productivity. If companies want to be competitive, employees must be committed to enterprise goals. To elicit this dedication requires corporate concern for the individual, recognition of his or her dignity as a human being, and reasonable job security with an opportunity for personal growth and development.

MOTIVATION

Human motives are based on needs, whether consciously or subconsciously felt. Some are primary needs, such as the physiological needs for water, air, food, sleep, and shelter. Other needs may be regarded as secondary, such as self-esteem, status, affiliation with others, affection, giving, accomplishment, and self-assertion. Naturally, these needs vary in intensity and over time between individuals.

Motivation is a general term applying to the entire class of drives, desires, needs, wishes, and similar forces. To say that managers motivate their subordinates is to say that they do things which they hope will satisfy these drives and desires and induce the subordinates to act in a desired manner.

Motivation General term applying to the entire class of drives, desires, needs, wishes, and similar forces.

INNOVATION PERSPECTIVE

Self-motivation

Managers are responsible for providing an environment conducive to performance. But individuals themselves are responsible for self-motivation. One approach is through strategic career management (which was discussed in Chapter 12). George Odiorne, a management professor, scholar, and experienced consultant, made specific recommendations for motivating yourself. Here are some:

- Set a goal for yourself and do not lose sight of it. Lee Iacocca (former president of Chrysler) set the goal of becoming vice president at Ford Motor Company by age 35, and for 15 years this aim motivated him and guided his behavior.
- Supplement your long-term objectives with short-term goals and specific actions. It has been said that to get something done is to begin.
- Learn a challenging new task each year. Learning to become a manager does not stop with a bachelor's or master's degree in business. A degree is the real beginning, not the end, of learning. Learning and applying microcomputer technology might be considered a challenging task.
- Make your job a different one. Set improvement objectives for your position. With some imagination, you probably can considerably increase your productivity.
- Develop an area of expertise. Build on your strengths or develop one of your weaknesses into strength. You might want to be known as the best accountant or the best engineer in your specific area of competence.
- Give yourself feedback and reward yourself. Setting verifiable goals provides you with a standard against which you can measure your performance. Why not have a special dinner to celebrate your accomplishments?

www.chrysler.com

www.ford.com

AN EARLY BEHAVIORAL MODEL: McGREGOR'S THEORY X AND THEORY Y

McGregor's Theory X and Theory Y Two sets of assumptions about the nature of people.

One view about the nature of people has been expressed by Douglas McGregor in his Theory X and Theory Y.[3] Managing, McGregor suggests, must start with the basic question of how managers see themselves in relation to others. This viewpoint requires some thought on the perception of human nature. Theories X and Y are two sets of assumptions about the nature of people. McGregor chose these terms because he wanted neutral terminology without any connotation of being "good" or "bad".

Theory X Assumptions

The "traditional" assumptions about the nature of people, according to McGregor, are included in Theory X as follows:

- Average human beings have an inherent dislike of work and will avoid it if they can.
- Because of this human characteristic of disliking work, most people must be coerced, controlled, directed, and threatened with punishment to get them to put forth adequate effort toward the achievement of organizational objectives.
- Average human beings prefer to be directed, wish to avoid responsibility, have relatively little ambition, and want security above all.

Theory Y Assumptions

McGregor sees the assumptions under Theory Y as follows:

- The expenditure of physical and mental effort in work is as natural as play or rest.
- External control and the threat of punishment are not the only means for producing effort toward organizational objectives. People will exercise self-direction and self-control in the service of objectives to which they are committed.
- The degree of commitment to objectives is in proportion to the size of the rewards associated with their achievement.
- Average human beings learn, under proper conditions, not only to accept responsibility but also to seek it.
- The capacity to exercise a relatively high degree of imagination, ingenuity, and creativity in the solution of organizational problems is widely, not narrowly, distributed in the population.
- Under the conditions of modern industrial life, the intellectual potentialities of the average human being are only partially utilized.

These two sets of assumptions obviously are fundamentally different. Theory X is pessimistic, static, and rigid. Control is primarily external, imposed on the subordinate by the superior. In contrast, Theory Y is optimistic, dynamic, and flexible, with an emphasis on self-direction and the integration of individual needs with organizational demands. There is little doubt that each set of assumptions will affect the way managers carry out their managerial functions and activities.

Clarification of the Theories

McGregor was apparently concerned that Theory X and Theory Y might be misinterpreted. The following points will clarify some of the areas of misunderstanding and keep the assumptions in proper perspective. First, theories X and Y assumptions are just that: they are assumptions only. They are not prescriptions or suggestions for managerial strategies. Rather, these assumptions must be tested against reality. Furthermore, they are intuitive deductions and are not based on research. Second, theories X and Y do not imply "hard" or "soft" management. The "hard" approach may produce resistance and antagonism. The "soft" approach may result in laissez-faire management and is not congruent with Theory Y. The effective manager recognizes the dignity and capabilities, as well as the limitations, of people and adjusts behavior as demanded by the situation. Third, theories X and Y are not to be viewed as being on a continuous scale, with X and Y on opposite extremes. They are not a matter of degree; rather, they are completely different views of people.

Fourth, the discussion of Theory Y is not a case for consensus management, nor is it an argument against the use of authority. Under Theory Y, authority is seen as only one of the many ways a manager exerts leadership. Fifth, the variety of tasks and situations requires different approaches to management. At times, authority and structure may be effective for certain tasks, as found in the research by John J. Morse and Jay W. Lorsch.[4] They suggest that different approaches are effective in different situations. Thus, the productive enterprise is one that fits the task requirements to the people and the particular situation. We shall describe in the following section various theories of motivation.

INNOVATIVE PERSPECTIVE

Can the Khan Academy Change Education and Motivate Students?[5]

Too many students are dropping out of lower level education. Educators as well as noneducators are trying to find new ways to motivate students to study and stay in school. One such motivational approach is the Khan Academy which is "the world's first free, world-class virtual school where anyone can learn anything". The Academy provides tutorials and exercises on YouTube. The teaching approach also provides for measuring the students' progress so that the teacher can help those students who are struggling with a topic. On the other hand, gifted students can progress to more advanced subjects. The program offers free of charge more than 3,000 micro lectures on topics such as Banking and Money, Chemistry, Computer Science, Economics, Finance, Healthcare, History, Mathematics, Physics, Venture Capital and Capital Market, and many more subjects. These topics are available to anyone anywhere in the world. Offline teaching is also made available for students in Asia, Latin America, and Africa. Bill Gates at Microsoft was so impressed by the Khan Academy that he made a sizable contribution to the Academy, as did Google. Mr. Gates felt that mathematics is often a stumbling block for a person's career and Khan's YouTube videos help to overcome this hurdle.

Actually the Khan Academy started when Salman Khan was asked to tutor his 13-year-old cousin in mathematics. Soon he was asked to do the same for other students, eventually resulting in the Academy. Khan has an impressive background with two bachelor degrees from MIT in mathematics and electrical engineering and computer science. In addition, he also earned a master's degree at MIT in the same subject and an MBA at the Harvard Business School. While tutoring his cousin, he worked as a hedge fund analyst at Connective Capital Management. He quit his job as an analyst and started the Khan Academy.

The Khan video approach to teaching has received praise from educators, noneducators, and students, with some 2 million users watching the videos every month. But there are also critics who argue that the videos are repetitive drilling exercises rather than promoting the student–teacher interaction. Khan, however rejects this criticism. On the contrary, he argues, students can watch the video at home which, in turn, leaves more time for creative activities in the classroom. So far, many students have benefited greatly from the video YouTube learning experience, motivating them to tackle the tough subjects such as mathematics and other topics by learning that takes into account the levels of competency of individuals—because there is no average person.

http://www.khanacademy.org/

MASLOW'S HIERARCHY OF NEEDS THEORY

Maslow's needs theory when one set of needs is satisfied, this kind of need ceases to be a motivator.

One of the most widely mentioned theories of motivation is the hierarchy of needs theory put forth by psychologist Abraham Maslow.[6] Maslow saw human needs in the form of a hierarchy, ascending from the lowest to the highest; and he concluded that, when one set of needs is satisfied, this kind of need ceases to be a motivator.

The Needs Hierarchy

The basic human needs placed by Maslow in an ascending order of importance and shown in Figure 14.1 are these:

1. *Physiological needs*. These are the basic needs for sustaining human life itself, such as food, water, warmth, shelter, and sleep. Maslow took the position that, until these needs are satisfied to the degree necessary to maintain life, other needs will not motivate people.
2. *Security, or safety, needs*. People want to be free of physical danger and of the fear of losing a job, property, food, or shelter.

3. *Affiliation, or acceptance, needs*. Since people are social beings, they need to belong, to be accepted by others.
4. *Esteem needs*. According to Maslow, once people begin to satisfy their need to belong, they tend to want to be held in esteem both by themselves and by others. This kind of need produces such satisfactions as power, prestige, status, and self-confidence.
5. *Need for self-actualization*. Maslow regards this as the highest need in his hierarchy. It is the desire to become what one is capable of becoming—to maximize one's potential and to accomplish something.

FIGURE 14.1 Maslow's hierarchy of needs

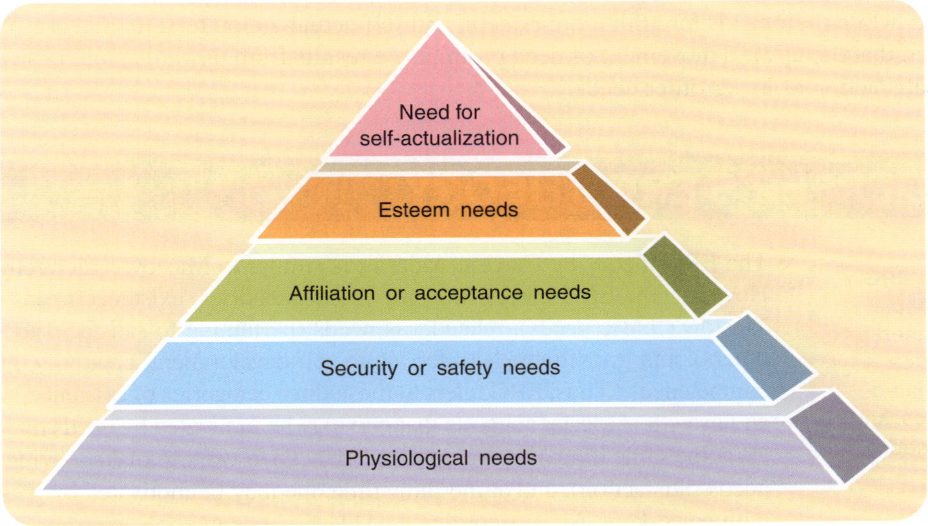
Need for
self-actualization
Esteem needs
Affiliation or acceptance needs
Security or safety needs
Physiological needs

ENTREPRENEURIAL PERSPECTIVE

How to Manage Entrepreneurial Managers

Entrepreneurs reside not only in new ventures they create but also in larger organizations. How can these entrepreneurial managers be motivated and managed? Entrepreneurs tend to value freedom and the chance to pursue opportunities they perceive exist. Rather than trying to oversee them closely, organizational leaders are encouraged to unleash their entrepreneurial managers to pursue new innovations and opportunities for the company. They will find that these entrepreneurial managers will appreciate the freedom and achieve amazing things for their supportive organizations. Often, though, middle-level managers exert too much control and squash the creative capacity and motivation of these corporate entrepreneurs. Organizational leaders are advised to protect their entrepreneurial managers as their vision may in time become the future of the organization.

Questioning the Needs Hierarchy

Maslow's concept of a hierarchy of needs has been subjected to considerable research. Edward Lawler and J. Lloyd Suttle collected data on 187 managers in two different organizations over a period of 6 to 12 months.[7] They found little evidence to support Maslow's theory that human needs form a hierarchy. They did note, however, that there are two levels of needs—biological and other needs—and that the other needs would emerge only when biological needs are reasonably satisfied. They found further that at the higher level the strength of needs varies with the individual: in some individuals social needs predominate, while in others self-actualization needs are strongest.

In another study of Maslow's needs hierarchy involving a group of managers over a period of five years, Douglas T. Hall and Khalil Nougaim did not find strong evidence of a hierarchy.[8] They found that, as managers advance in an organization, their physiological and safety needs tend to decrease in importance, while their needs for affiliation, esteem, and self-actualization tend to increase. They insisted, however, that the upward movement of need prominence results from upward career changes and not from the satisfaction of lower-order needs.

ALDERFER'S ERG THEORY

Alderfer's ERG theory People are motivated by existence needs, relatedness needs, and growth needs.

The ERG theory by Clayton Alderfer is similar to Maslow's hierarchy of needs. However, the ERG theory has only three categories: existence needs (similar to Maslow's basic needs), relatedness needs (pertaining to satisfactorily relating to others), and growth needs (referring to self-development, creativity, growth, and competence).[9] Thus, ERG refers to those three categories of existence, relatedness, and growth. Alderfer suggests that one may be motivated by needs on several levels at the same time. For example, one may go to work to make a living (existence needs satisfaction), and at the same time one may be motivated by good relations with coworkers. Also, according to Alderfer, when people experience frustration on one level, they may focus on the needs at a lower-level needs category.

HERZBERG'S MOTIVATION–HYGIENE THEORY

Herzberg's two-factor theory Dissatisfiers, also called maintenance, hygiene, or job-context factors, are not motivators, while satisfiers are motivators and are related to job content.

Maslow's needs approach has been considerably modified by Frederick Herzberg and his associates.[10] Their research purports to find a **two-factor theory** of motivation. In one group of needs are such things as company policy and administration, supervision, working conditions, interpersonal relations, salary, status, job security, and personal life. These were found by Herzberg to be only *dissatisfiers* and not motivators. In other words, if they exist in a work environment in high quantity and quality, they yield no dissatisfaction. Their existence does not motivate in the sense of yielding satisfaction; their lack of existence would, however, result in dissatisfaction. Herzberg calls them *maintenance, hygiene, or job-context factors*.

In the second group, Herzberg lists certain *satisfiers*—and therefore motivators—all related to *job content*. They include achievement, recognition, challenging work, advancement, and growth in the job. Their existence will yield feelings of satisfaction or no satisfaction (not dissatisfaction). As Figure 14.2 indicates, the satisfiers and dissatisfiers identified by Herzberg are similar to the factors suggested by Maslow.

FIGURE 14.2 Comparison of Maslow's and Herzberg's theories of motivation

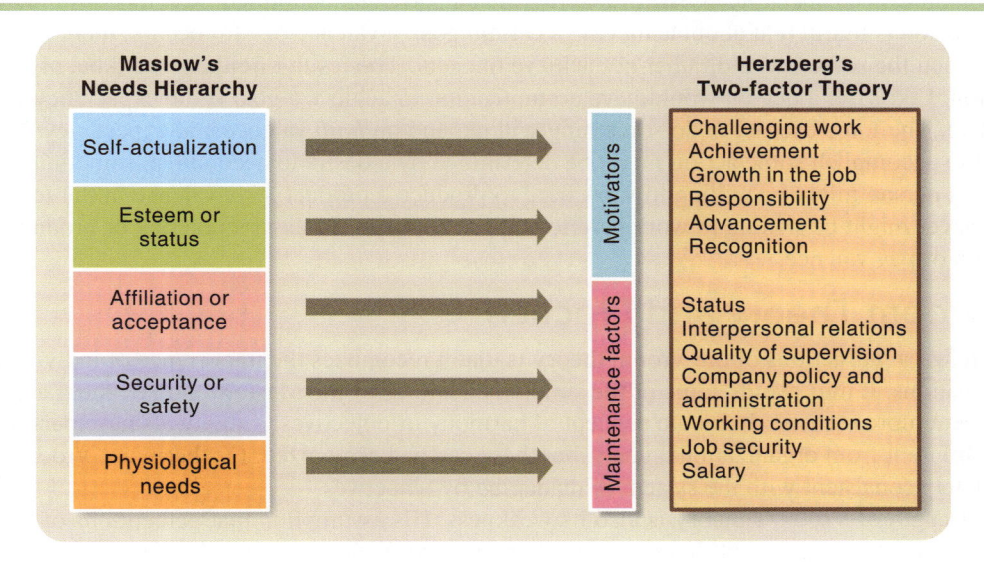

Maslow's Needs Hierarchy		Herzberg's Two-factor Theory
Self-actualization	Motivators	Challenging work Achievement Growth in the job Responsibility Advancement Recognition
Esteem or status		
Affiliation or acceptance	Maintenance factors	Status Interpersonal relations Quality of supervision Company policy and administration Working conditions Job security Salary
Security or safety		
Physiological needs		

The first group of factors (the dissatisfiers) will not motivate people in an organization; yet they must be present, or dissatisfaction will arise. The second group, or the job-content factors, were found to be the real motivators because they have the potential of yielding a sense of satisfaction. Clearly, if this theory of motivation is sound, managers must give considerable attention to upgrading job content.

The Herzberg research has not gone unchallenged. Some researchers have questioned Herzberg's investigation methods, which they said tended to prejudice the results. For example, the well-known tendency of people to attribute good results to their own efforts and to blame others for poor results is thought to have prejudiced Herzberg's findings. Other researchers, not following his methods, have arrived at conclusions that do not support the theory.

THE EXPECTANCY THEORY OF MOTIVATION

Another approach, one that many believe goes far in explaining how people are motivated, is the expectancy theory. One of the leaders in advancing and explaining this theory is the psychologist Victor H. Vroom. He holds that people will be motivated to do things to reach a goal if they believe in the worth of that goal and if they can see that what they do will help them in achieving it.[11] In a sense, this is a modern expression of what the German priest Martin Luther observed centuries ago when he said, "Everything that is done in the world is done by hope."

In greater detail, Vroom's theory is that people's motivation toward doing anything will be determined by the value they place on the outcome of their effort (whether positive or negative) multiplied by the confidence they have that

Vroom's expectancy theory People will be motivated to do things to reach a goal if they believe in the worth of that goal and if they can see that what they do will help them in achieving it.

their effort will materially aid in achieving a goal. In his own terms, Vroom's theory may be stated as

$$\text{Force} = \text{Valence} \times \text{Expectancy}$$

where *force* is the strength of a person's motivation, *valence* is the strength of an individual's preference for an outcome, and *expectancy* is the probability that a particular action will lead to a desired outcome. When a person is indifferent about achieving a certain goal, a valence of zero occurs; there is a negative valence when the person would rather not achieve the goal. The result of either would be, of course, no motivation. Likewise, a person would have no motivation to achieve a goal if the expectancy were zero or negative. The force exerted to do something will depend on *both* valence and expectancy. Moreover, a motive to accomplish some action might be determined by a desire to accomplish something else. For example, a person might be willing to work hard to produce a product for a valence in the form of pay. Or a manager might be willing to work hard to achieve company goals in marketing or production for a promotion or pay valence.

The Vroom Theory and Practice

One of the great attractions of the Vroom theory is that it recognizes the importance of individual needs and motivations. It thus avoids some of the simplistic features of the Maslow and Herzberg approaches. It does seem more realistic. It fits the concept of harmony of objectives: individuals have personal goals that are different from organizational goals, but these can be harmonized. Furthermore, Vroom's theory is completely consistent with the system of managing by objectives.

The strength of Vroom's theory is also its weakness. His assumption that perceptions of value vary between individuals at different times and in different places appears to fit real life more accurately. It is consistent also with the idea that a manager's job is to *design* an environment for performance, necessarily taking into account the differences in various situations. On the other hand, the theory is difficult to apply in practice. Despite its difficulty in application, the logical accuracy of Vroom's theory indicates that motivation is much more complex than the approaches of Maslow and Herzberg seem to imply.

The Porter and Lawler Motivation Model

Lyman W. Porter and Edward E. Lawler derived a substantially more complete model of motivation, built in large part on expectancy theory. In their study, they applied this model primarily to managers.[12] It is summarized in Figure 14.3.

As this model indicates, the amount of effort (the strength of motivation and energy exerted) depends on the value of a reward plus the amount of energy a person believes is required and the probability of receiving the reward. The perceived effort and probability of actually getting a reward are, in turn, influenced by the experience of actual performance. Clearly, if people know they can do a job or if they have done it, they have a better appreciation of the effort required and know better the probability of getting a reward.

Actual performance in a job (the doing of tasks or the meeting of goals) is determined principally by effort expended. But it is also greatly influenced by an individual's ability (knowledge and skills) to do the job and by his or her perception of what the required task is (the extent to which the person understands the goals, required activities, and other elements of a task). Performance, in turn, is seen as leading to intrinsic rewards (such as a sense of accomplishment or self-actualization) and extrinsic rewards (such as working conditions and status). These rewards, tempered by what the individual sees as equitable, lead to satisfaction. But performance also influences sensed equitable rewards. Understandably, what the individual sees as a fair reward for effort will necessarily affect the satisfaction derived. Likewise, the actual value of rewards will be influenced by satisfaction.

FIGURE 14.3 Porter and Lawler's motivation model

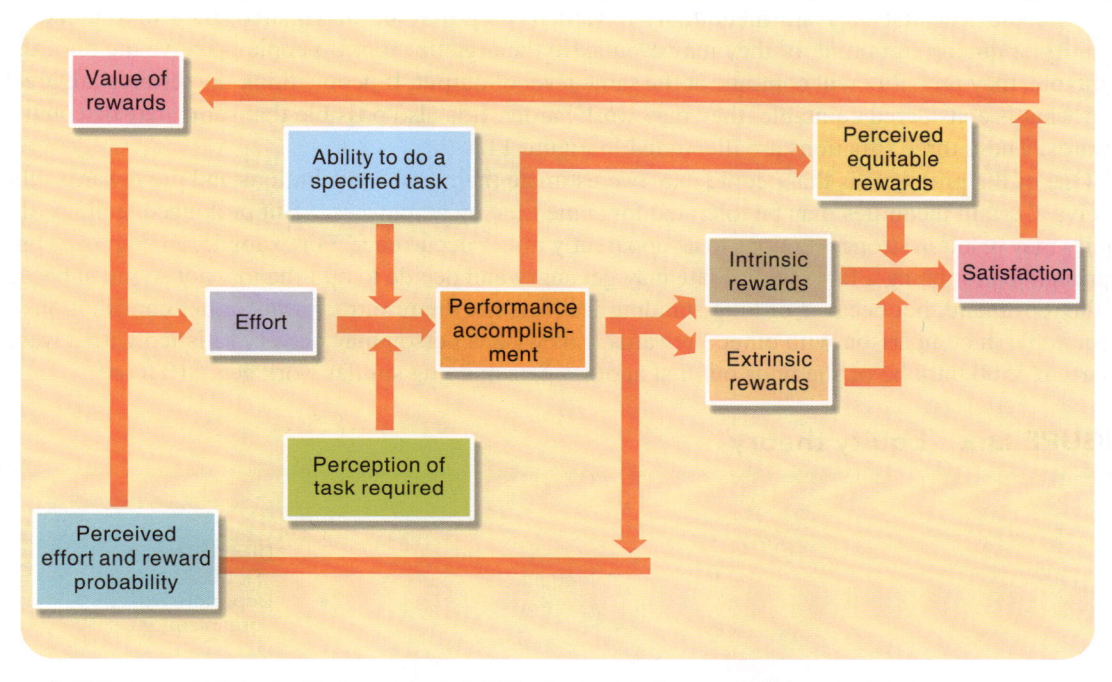

Source: L. W. Porter and E. E. Lawler, "Porter and Lawler's Motivation Model", *Managerial Attitudes and Performance*.

Implications for Practice

The Porter and Lawler model of motivation, while more complex than other theories of motivation, is almost certainly a more adequate portrayal of the system of motivation. To the practicing manager, this model means that motivation is not a simple cause-and-effect matter. It means, too, that managers should carefully assess their reward structures. Through careful planning, managing by objectives, and clearly defining duties and responsibilities through a good organization structure, the effort–performance–reward–satisfaction system can be integrated into an entire system of managing.

EQUITY THEORY

An important factor in motivation is whether individuals perceive the reward structure as being fair. One way of addressing this issue is through the use of equity theory, which refers to an individual's subjective judgment about the fairness of the reward he or she gets, relative to the inputs (which include many factors, such as effort, experience, and education), in comparison with the rewards of others. J. Stacy Adams has received a great deal of credit for the formulation of the equity (or inequity) theory.[13] The essential aspect of the theory may be expressed as follows:

$$\frac{\text{Outcomes by a person}}{\text{Inputs by a person}} = \frac{\text{Outcomes by another person}}{\text{Inputs by another person}}$$

Equity theory
Motivation is influenced by an individual's subjective judgment about the fairness of the reward he or she gets, relative to the inputs, compared with the rewards of others.

There should be a balance of the outcomes/inputs relationship for one person in comparison with that for another person.

If people feel that they are inequitably rewarded, they may be dissatisfied, they may reduce the quantity or quality of output, or they may even leave the organization. If people perceive the rewards as equitable, they probably will continue at the same level of output. If people think the rewards are greater than what is considered equitable, they may work harder. It is also possible that some may discount the rewards. These three situations are illustrated in Figure 14.4.

One of the problems is that people may overestimate their own contributions and the rewards others receive. Certain inequities may be tolerated for some time by employees.[14] But prolonged feelings of inequity may result in strong reactions to an apparently minor occurrence. For example, an employee being reprimanded for being a few minutes late may get angry and decide to quit the job, not so much because of the reprimand, but because of long-standing feelings that the rewards for his or her contributions are inequitable in comparison with others' rewards. Likewise, a person may be very satisfied with a weekly salary of $500 until he or she finds out that another person doing similar work gets $10 more.

FIGURE 14.4   Equity theory

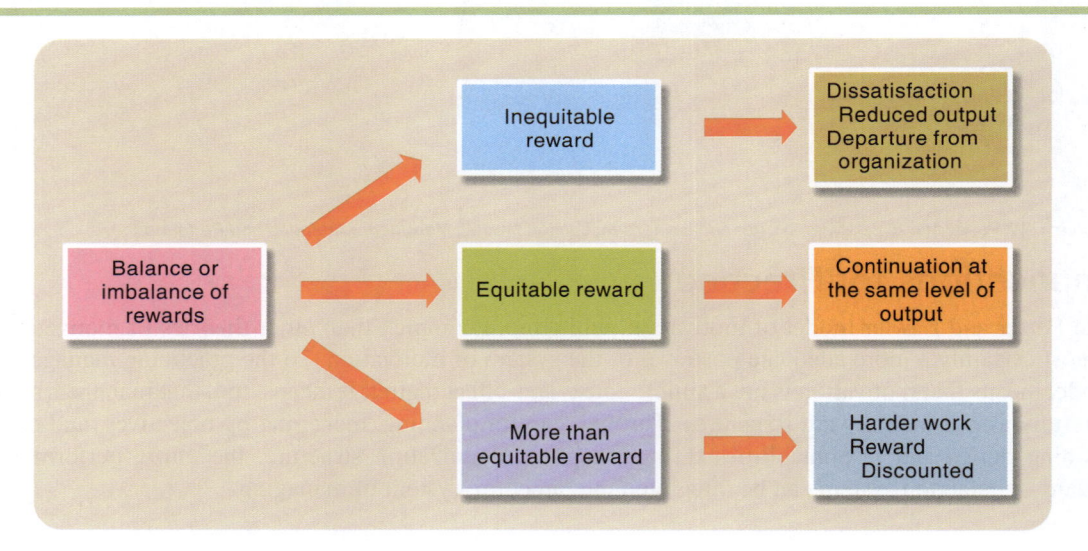

GOAL SETTING THEORY OF MOTIVATION[15]

In Chapter 4, the systems approach to management by objectives (MBO) was introduced. The model shown in Figure 4.4 in that chapter shows a comprehensive view of MBO. Research has shown that, to be effective, many key managerial activities have to be integrated into a comprehensive system. Still, an important part of this system pertains to the steps required, of setting objectives, planning actions, implementation, and control and appraisal, as shown in Figure 14.5. You will recall that the terms *objectives* and *goals* are often used interchangeably in the management literature.

For objectives to be meaningful, they must be clear, attainable, and verifiable.

The proposition is that, for objectives to be meaningful, they must be clear, attainable, and verifiable. Indeed, clear goals, if accepted, are motivating. People

FIGURE 14.5 Objective or goal setting for motivation

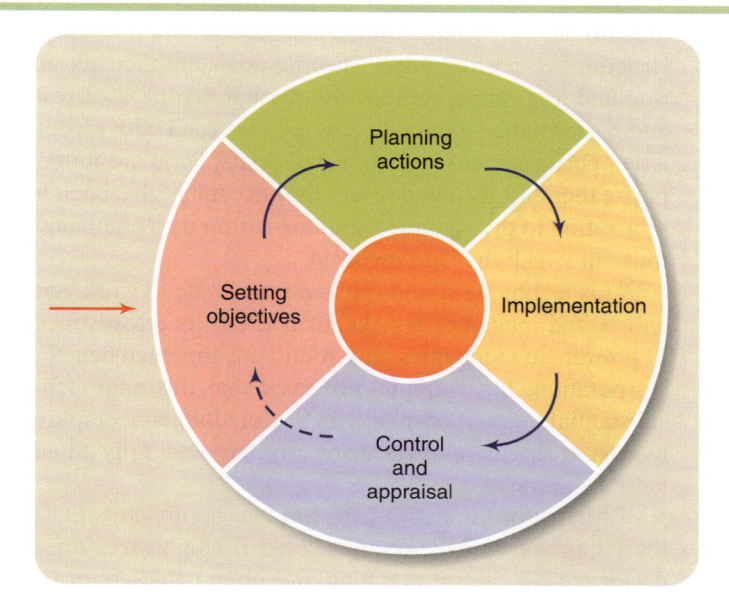

want to know what is expected of them. However, several conditions must be met, including that the objectives must be verifiable, which means that at the end of the period one must be able to measure whether the objectives have been achieved and to what extent. Objectives such as "getting the best grades possible in school" are not verifiable, but graduating with a 3.8 grade point average is. The objectives must be challenging, yet they must also be reasonable. Completely unrealistic objectives that cannot be achieved are demotivating rather than motivating, which is an important aim of MBO.

To gain commitment to achieving the goals, true participation in setting them is essential. In the proper environment, individuals should be encouraged to set them by themselves. The superior, of course, should review and approve them. Chances are that, in the proper environment, people tend to set goals higher than their superior would set them.

For additional conditions for effective goal setting that improve motivation, see the checklist in Table 4.2 in Chapter 4.

> **Positive reinforcement** or **behavior modification** Individuals can be motivated by proper design of their work environment and by praise for their performance, while punishment for poor performance produces negative results.

SKINNER'S REINFORCEMENT THEORY

The psychologist B. F. Skinner of Harvard developed an interesting, but controversial, technique for motivation. This approach, called **positive reinforcement** or **behavior modification**,[16] holds that individuals can be motivated by proper design of their work environment and by praise for their performance and that punishment for poor performance produces negative results.

Skinner and his followers do far more than praise good performance. They analyze the work situation to determine what causes workers to act the way they do, and then they initiate changes to eliminate troublesome areas and obstructions to performance. Specific goals are then set with workers' participation and assistance, prompt and regular feedback of results is made available, and performance improvements are rewarded with recognition and praise. Even when performance does not equal goals, ways are found to help people and to praise them for the good things they do. It has also been found highly useful and motivating to give people full information on a company's problems, especially those in which they are involved.

This technique sounds almost too simple to work, and many behavioral scientists and managers are skeptical about its effectiveness. However, a number of prominent companies have found the approach beneficial. Emery Air Freight Corporation, for example, observed that this approach saved the company a substantial amount of money by merely inducing employees to take great pains to ensure that containers were properly and fully filled with small packages before shipment.

www.emeryworld.com

Perhaps the strength of the Skinner approach is that it is so closely akin to the requirements of good managing. It emphasizes removal of obstructions to performance, careful planning and organizing, control through feedback, and the expansion of communication.

McCLELLAND'S NEEDS THEORY OF MOTIVATION

McClelland's needs theory Basic motivating needs are the need for power, the need for affiliation, and the need for achievement.

David C. McClelland has contributed to the understanding of motivation by identifying three types of basic motivating needs.[17] He classifies them as the need for power, need for affiliation, and need for achievement. Considerable research has been done on methods of testing people with respect to these three types of needs, and McClelland and his associates have done substantial research, especially on the need for achievement.

All three drives—power, affiliation, and achievement—are of particular relevance to management, since all must be recognized to make an organized enterprise work well.

Need for Power

McClelland and other researchers have found that people with a high need for power have a great concern with exercising influence and control. Such individuals generally are seeking positions of leadership; they are frequently good conversationalists, though often argumentative; they are forceful, outspoken, hardheaded, and demanding; and they enjoy teaching and public speaking.

Need for Affiliation

People with a high need for affiliation usually derive pleasure from being loved and tend to avoid the pain of being rejected by a social group. As individuals, they are likely to be concerned with maintaining pleasant social relationships, to enjoy a sense of intimacy and understanding, to be ready to console and help others in trouble, and to enjoy friendly interaction with others.

Need for Achievement[18]

People with a high need for achievement have an intense desire for success and an equally intense fear of failure. They want to be challenged, and they set moderately difficult (but not impossible) goals for themselves. They take a realistic approach to risk; they are not likely to be gamblers but, rather, prefer to analyze and assess problems, assume personal responsibility for getting a job done, and like specific and prompt feedback on how they are doing. They tend to be restless, like to work long hours, do not worry unduly about failure if it does occur, and tend to like to run their own shows.

How McClelland's Approach Applies to Managers

In research studies by McClelland and others, entrepreneurs—people who start and develop a business or some other enterprise—showed very high need-for-achievement and fairly high need-for-power drives but were quite low in their need for affiliation. Managers generally showed high on achievement and power and low on affiliation, but not as high or as low as entrepreneurs.

McClelland found the pattern of achievement motivation clearest in people in small companies, with the president normally having very high achievement motivation. In large companies, what is quite interesting is that he found chief executives to be only average in achievement motivation and often stronger in power and affiliation drives. Managers in the upper-middle level of management in such companies rated higher than their presidents in achievement motivation. Perhaps, as McClelland indicated, these scores are understandable. The chief executive has "arrived", while those below are striving to advance.

The question is often raised as to whether all managers should rate high on achievement motivation. People who do rate high tend to advance faster than those who do not. But because so much of managing requires other characteristics besides achievement drive, every company should probably have many managers who, while possessing fairly strong achievement motivation, also have a high need for affiliation. This latter need is important for working with people and for coordinating the efforts of individuals working in groups.

SPECIAL MOTIVATIONAL TECHNIQUES

After looking at the theories of motivation, one may well ask what they mean to managers. What motivational techniques can managers use? While motivation is so complex and individualized that there can be no single best answer, some of the major motivational techniques can be identified.

Money[19]

Money can never be overlooked as a motivator. Whether in the form of wages, piecework (getting paid for units produced at a certain quality level) or any other incentive pay, bonuses, stock options, company-paid insurance, or any of the other things that may be given to people for performance, money is important. And as some writers have pointed out, money is often more than monetary value; it can also mean status or power, or other things.

Money is often more than monetary value; it can also mean status or power, or other things.

Economists and most managers have tended to place money high on the scale of motivators, while behavioral scientists tend to place it low. Probably neither view is right. But, if money is to be the kind of motivator that it can and should be, managers must remember several things.

First, money, as money, is likely to be more important to people who are raising a family, for example, than to people who have "arrived" in the sense that their financial needs are not so urgent. Money is an urgent means of achieving a minimum standard of living, although this minimum has a way of getting higher as people become more affluent. An individual who was once satisfied with a small house and a low-priced car may now be able to derive the same satisfaction only from a large and comfortable house and a fairly luxurious automobile. And yet it is impossible to generalize even in these terms. For some people money will always be of the utmost importance, while for others it may never be.

GLOBAL PERSPECTIVE

The Other Side of the Coin

The lure of money and power can lead to inappropriate and illegal actions. Ivan F. Boesky was accused of insider trading that resulted in huge personal profits—and a $100 million fine. The scandal, one of the worst on Wall Street since the 1920s, shook public confidence with the fear that stock trading may be rigged.[20]

A more recent investment scandal by was committed by Bernard Madoff and others through his wealth management business. Madoff admitted that his investment fund was "basically a giant Ponzi scheme"[21]. The size of the loss to investors is difficult to determine, but it is estimated that if all the funds were recovered, the investors' net loss would be below $10 billion.

While money is often used for motivating, it also addresses itself to human greed, which dulls the conscience and may result in unethical and illegal behavior.

Second, it is probably quite true that in most kinds of businesses and other enterprises, money is used as a means of keeping an organization adequately staffed and not primarily as a motivator. Enterprises usually make wages and salaries competitive within their industry and their geographic area to attract and hold people.

Third, money as a motivator tends to be dulled somewhat by the practice of making the salaries of the various managers in a company reasonably similar. In other words, organizations often take great care to ensure that people on comparable levels are given the same, or nearly the same, compensation. This is understandable, since people usually evaluate their compensation in light of what their equals are receiving.

Fourth, if money is to be an effective motivator, people in various positions, even though at a similar level, must be given salaries and bonuses that reflect their individual performance. Even if a company is committed to the practice of comparable wages and salaries, a well-managed firm need never be bound to the same practice with respect to bonuses. In fact, it appears that, unless bonuses for managers are based to a major extent on individual performance, an enterprise is not buying much motivation with them. The way to ensure that money has meaning, as a reward for accomplishment and as a means of giving people pleasure from accomplishment, is to base compensation as much as possible on performance.

It is almost certainly true that money can motivate only when the prospective payment is large relative to a person's income. The trouble with many wage and salary increases, and even bonus payments, is that they are not large enough to motivate the receiver. They may keep the individual from being dissatisfied and from looking for another job, but they are not likely to be a strong motivator, unless they are large enough to be felt.

Traditionally, pay and promotion in Japan are based on seniority. However, in some Japanese companies, merit pay has been introduced. The reason is that some young Japanese professionals are leaving secure positions for exciting work in Internet companies. In order to keep employees, companies use merit pay based on performance.

Executive Pay for Performance[22]

During the global financial meltdown in 2008–2009, many executives of companies with very poor performance received big pay packages. This created a public outcry. Spring is the time when compensation committees have to decide on the paychecks of business leaders.

Richard R. Floersch, the executive vice president of McDonald's Corporation and chairman of the Center on Executive Compensation, argues that compensation should be an integral part of the company's strategy. While compensation has been used as a tool for recruitment and retention, other things should be considered. Compensation, for example, communicates the company's values and culture and its relationship with its workforce. Pay should go up with good performance and down with poor company results.

In determining executive pay, questions should be raised such as:

Is both performance and sustainability considered? Short-term results could result in negative long-term performance. It has also been argued that the executives should own considerable amount of stocks to be held over a long period. This may discourage making decisions that may result in short-term performance (and increased pay) at the expense of long-term company sustainability. Many of the Fortune 100 companies have a "clawback—or recoup—policy" which goes into effect on the company that does not perform as expected. Thus, a pay-for-performance policy should also take into account the long-term effect on the company of executives' decisions.

GLOBAL PERSPECTIVE

Other Rewards Considerations

Implicit in most motivation theories are intrinsic and extrinsic rewards. *Intrinsic rewards* may include a feeling of accomplishment, or even self-actualization. *Extrinsic rewards* include benefits, recognition, status symbols, and of course money. Some compensation plans may not provide a strong incentive, such as the hourly, weekly, or even annual salary. On the other hand, *incentive plans* may be based on piecework, sales commission, merit pay, bonus plans, profit or gain (e.g., productivity gain) sharing, and stock options. In Chapter 12 on performance appraisal, we illustrated the incentive plan at the Lincoln Electric Company. Some companies offer "cafeteria" compensation plans tailored to the needs and preferences of the individual employee.

The pay may be based on individual, group, and organizational performance. When the pay is based solely on *individual performance*, people may compete against each other, which may make teamwork and cooperation difficult. On the other hand, if *group performance* is the sole criterion for merit pay, some individuals may not contribute their fair share of effort. Considering *organizational performance* as a criterion of bonuses, reward system is based on the notion that employees contributed to the outstanding performance and therefore should be rewarded. To realize the benefits of individual, group, and organizational reward systems, some companies use a combination of plans.

Intrinsic rewards Include a feeling of accomplishment and self-actualization.

Extrinsic rewards Include benefits, recognition, status symbols, and money.

Pay may be based on individual, group, and organizational performance.

Participation

There is increased awareness and use of a technique that has been given strong support by motivation theory and research, and that is participation. Only rarely are people not motivated by being consulted on action affecting them—by being "in on the act". In addition, most people at the center of an operation have knowledge both of problems and of solutions to them. As a consequence, the right kind of participation yields both motivation and knowledge valuable for enterprise success.

Participation is also a means of recognition. It appeals to the need for affiliation and acceptance. Above all, it gives people a sense of accomplishment. But encouraging participation should not mean that managers weaken their position. Although they encourage participation of subordinates on matters with which the latter can help, and although they listen carefully, they must themselves decide on matters requiring *their* decision.

Quality of Working Life

One of the most interesting approaches to motivation is the quality of working life (QWL) program, which is a systems approach to job design and a promising development in the broad area of job enrichment, combined with a grounding in the sociotechnical systems approach to management (see Chapter 1). QWL is not only a very broad approach to job enrichment but also an interdisciplinary field of inquiry and action combining industrial and organizational psychology and sociology, industrial engineering, organization theory and development, motivational and leadership theory, and industrial relations. Although QWL rose to prominence only in the 1970s, there are now hundreds of case studies and practical programs and a number of QWL centers, primarily in the United States, Great Britain, and Scandinavia.

www.qwl.com

QWL has received enthusiastic support from a number of sources. Managers have regarded it as a promising means of dealing with stagnating productivity, especially in the United States and Europe. Workers and union representatives have also seen it as a means of improving working conditions and productivity and as a means of justifying higher pay. Government agencies have been attracted to QWL as a means of increasing productivity and reducing inflation and as a way of obtaining industrial democracy and minimizing labor disputes.

> **INNOVATIVE PERSPECTIVE**
>
> **QWL in Action**
>
> In the development of a QWL program, certain steps are normally undertaken. Usually, a labor–management steering committee is set up, ordinarily with a QWL specialist or staff, which is charged with finding ways of enhancing the dignity, attractiveness, and productivity of jobs through job enrichment and redesign. The participation of workers and their unions (if an operation is unionized) in the effort is thought to be very important, not only because of the exercise of industrial democracy but also because of the great practical advantage it offers: people on a job are the ones who are best able to identify what would enrich the job for them and make it possible for them to be more productive. This typical QWL technique tends to solve the problem encountered in many job enrichment programs in which workers are not asked what would make the job more interesting for them.
>
> Out of the deliberations of this committee, a number of changes may be suggested in the design of jobs and in the entire working environment. The recommendations of the committee may extend to such matters as reorganization of the enterprise, means of improving communication, problems that may never have surfaced before and their solutions, changes in work arrangements through technical modifications such as the redesign of an assembly line, better quality control, and other things that might improve organizational health and productivity.

www.gm.com
www.pg.com
www.alcoa.com
www.att.com

It is no wonder that QWL, with such possible important yields, has been spreading fast, especially in larger companies. Nor is it a surprise that leaders in adopting QWL programs should be such well-managed companies as General Motors, Procter & Gamble, American Aluminum (ALCOA), and AT&T.

JOB ENRICHMENT

Research on and analysis of motivation point to the importance of making jobs challenging and meaningful. This applies to the jobs of managers as well as to those of nonmanagers. Job enrichment is related to Herzberg's theory of motivation, in which factors such as challenge, achievement, recognition, and responsibility are seen as the real motivators. Even though his theory has not gone unchallenged, it has led to widespread interest worldwide in developing ways to enrich job content, particularly for nonmanagerial employees.

Job enrichment should be distinguished from job enlargement (but some authors do not make this distinction). **Job enlargement** attempts to make a job more varied by removing the dullness associated with performing repetitive operations. It means enlarging the scope of the job by adding similar tasks without enhancing responsibility. For example, a production line worker may install not only the bumper on a car but also the front hood. Critics would say that this is simply adding one dull job to another, since it does not increase the worker's responsibility. In **job enrichment**, the attempt is to build into jobs a higher sense of challenge and achievement. Jobs may be enriched by variety. But they also may be enriched by (1) giving workers more freedom in deciding about such things as work methods, sequence, and pace or the acceptance or rejection of materials; (2) encouraging participation of subordinates and interaction between workers; (3) giving workers a feeling of personal responsibility for their tasks; (4) taking steps to make sure that workers can see how their tasks contribute to a finished product and to the welfare of the enterprise; (5) giving people feedback on their job performance, preferably before their supervisors get it; and (6) involving workers in the analysis and change of physical aspects of the work environment, such as the layout of the office or plant, temperature, lighting, and cleanliness.

Job enlargement
Enlarging the scope of the job by adding similar tasks without enhancing responsibility.

Job enrichment
Building into jobs a higher sense of challenge and achievement.

Limitations of Job Enrichment

Even the strongest supporters of job enrichment readily admit that there are limitations in its application. One of these is technology. With specialized machinery and assembly-line techniques, it may not be possible to make all jobs very meaningful. Another limitation is costs. General Motors tried six-person and three-person teams in the assembly of motor homes but found that this approach was too difficult, slow, and costly. On the other hand, two Swedish auto manufacturers, Saab and Volvo, have used the team approach and have found costs to be only slightly higher, and they believe that this increase is more than offset by reduction in absenteeism and turnover.

www.gm.com
www.saab.com
www.volvo.com

There is also some question as to whether workers really want job enrichment, especially of the kind that changes the basic content of their jobs. Various surveys of worker attitudes, even the attitudes of assembly-line workers, have shown that a high percentage of workers are not dissatisfied with their jobs and that few want "more interesting" jobs. What these workers seem to want above all is job security and pay. Moreover, workers are concerned that changing the nature of tasks to increase productivity may mean a loss of jobs.

The limitations of job enrichment apply mainly to low-skill jobs. The jobs of highly skilled workers, professionals, and managers already contain varying degrees of challenge and accomplishment. Perhaps they could still be enriched considerably more than they are. But this can probably be done best by management techniques such as managing by objectives, utilizing more policy guidance with delegation of authority, introducing more status symbols in the form of titles and office facilities, and tying bonus and other rewards more closely to performance.

Making Job Enrichment Effective

Several approaches can be used to make job enrichment appeal to higher-level motivations. First, organizations need a better understanding of what people want. As a number of motivation researchers have pointed out, wants vary with people and situations. Research has shown that workers with few skills want such factors as job security, pay, benefits, less restrictive rules, and more sympathetic and understanding supervisors. As people move up the ladder in an enterprise, they find that other factors become increasingly important. But little job enrichment research has been done on high-level professionals and managers.

Second, if productivity improvement is the main goal of enrichment, the program must show how workers will benefit. In one company with fleets of unsupervised two-person service trucks, a program of giving these employees 25 percent of the cost savings from increased productivity, while still making it clear that the company would profit from their efforts, resulted in a startling rise in output and a much greater interest in these jobs.

Third, people like to be involved, to be consulted, and to be given an opportunity to offer suggestions. They like to be considered as people. In one aerospace missile plant, increased morale and productivity, as well as greatly reduced turnover and absenteeism, resulted from the simple technique of having all employees' names on placards at their workstations and having each program group—from parts production and assembly to inspection—work in an area in which machines and equipment were painted a different color for each group.

Fourth, people like to feel that their managers are truly concerned with their welfare. Workers like to know what they are doing and why. They like feedback on their performance. They like to be appreciated and recognized for their work.

A SYSTEMS AND CONTINGENCY APPROACH TO MOTIVATION

Motivation must be considered from a systems and contingency point of view.

The foregoing analysis of theory, research, and application demonstrates that **motivation** must be considered from a systems and contingency point of view. Given the complexity of motivating people with individual personalities and in different situations, the risk of failure exists when any single motivator, or group of motivators, is applied without taking into account these variables. Human behavior is not a simple matter but must be looked upon as a complex system of variables and interactions of which certain motivating factors are an important element.

SUMMARY

Leading is the process of influencing people so that they will contribute to organizational and group goals. People assume different roles, and there is no average person. While working toward goals, a manager must take into account the dignity of the whole person.

Motivation is not a simple concept; rather, it pertains to various drives, desires, needs, wishes, and other forces. Managers motivate by providing an environment that induces organization members to contribute.

There are different views and assumptions about human nature. McGregor called his sets of assumptions about people Theory X and Theory Y. Maslow's theory holds that human needs form a hierarchy ranging from the lowest-order needs (physiological needs) to the highest-order need (the need for self-actualization). Alderfer's ERG theory, which has only three categories (Maslow has five), suggests that a person may be motivated in more than one category at the same time. According to Herzberg's two-factor theory, there are two sets of motivating factors. In one set are the dissatisfiers, which are related to the job context (circumstances, conditions). The absence of these factors results in dissatisfaction. In the other set are the satisfiers, or motivators, which are related to the content of the job.

Vroom's expectancy theory of motivation suggests that people are motivated to reach a goal if they think that the goal is worthwhile and they can see that their activities will help them achieve the goal. The Porter and Lawler model has many variables. Essentially, performance is a function of ability, the perception of the task required, and effort. Effort is influenced by the value of rewards and the perceived effort–reward probability. Performance accomplishment, in turn, is related to rewards and satisfaction.

Equity theory refers to an individual's subjective judgment about the fairness of the reward received for inputs in comparison with the rewards of others. Skinner's reinforcement theory suggests that people are motivated by praise for desirable behavior; people should participate in setting their goals and should receive regular feedback with recognition and praise. Goals can motivate if they are attainable, verifiable, and understood and accepted by the people who have to achieve them. McClelland's theory is based on the need for power, the need for affiliation, and the need for achievement.

Special motivational techniques include using money and other rewards considerations, encouraging participation, and improving the QWL. Job enrichment aims at making jobs challenging and meaningful. Although there have been some successes at job enrichment, certain limitations must not be overlooked.

The complexity of motivation requires a contingency approach that takes into account environmental factors.

KEY IDEAS AND CONCEPTS FOR REVIEW

Leading
Human factors in managing
Individual dignity
Motivation
McGregor's Theory X and Theory Y
Maslow's needs hierarchy
Alderfer's ERG theory
Herzberg's motivation–hygiene theory
Vroom's expectancy theory
Porter and Lawler's motivation model
Equity theory
Goal setting theory of motivation
Positive reinforcement or behavior modification
McClelland's needs theory
Money and other rewards considerations
Quality of working life
Job enrichment
Systems and contingency approach to motivation

FOR DISCUSSION

1. What is motivation? How does effective managing take advantage of, and contribute to, motivation?
2. What are Theory X and Theory Y assumptions? State your reasons for agreeing or disagreeing with these assumptions. What are some misunderstandings of these theories?
3. Why has the Maslow theory of needs been criticized? To what extent is it valid?
4. Compare and contrast the Maslow and Herzberg theories of motivation. On what grounds has the Herzberg theory been criticized? Why would you suspect that Herzberg's approach has been very popular with practicing managers?
5. Explain Vroom's expectancy theory of motivation. How is it different from the Porter and Lawler approach? Which appeals to you as being more accurate? Which is more useful in practice?
6. Explain McClelland's theory of motivation. How does it fit into a systems approach?

7. "You cannot motivate managers. They are self-propelled. You just get out of their way if you really want performance." Comment.
8. To what extent, and how, is money an effective motivator?
9. What motivates you in striving toward excellence in your work at school? Are these motivating forces shown in any of the models discussed in this chapter?

EXERCISES/ACTION STEPS

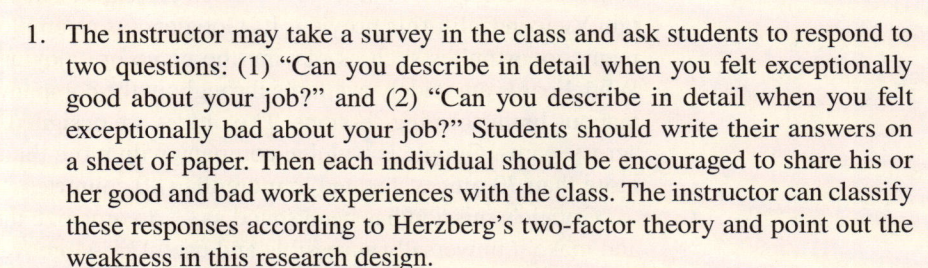

1. The instructor may take a survey in the class and ask students to respond to two questions: (1) "Can you describe in detail when you felt exceptionally good about your job?" and (2) "Can you describe in detail when you felt exceptionally bad about your job?" Students should write their answers on a sheet of paper. Then each individual should be encouraged to share his or her good and bad work experiences with the class. The instructor can classify these responses according to Herzberg's two-factor theory and point out the weakness in this research design.
2. Collect information on an organization that you know and identify the reasons why people contribute to the goals of the enterprise.

INTERNET RESEARCH

1. Surf the Internet for the term "motivation". You will get many "hits". Select one for class discussion.
2. Use a popular search engine and type the first and last name of any authors discussed in this chapter. Do you find information that goes beyond what has been discussed in this chapter? If so, what is it?

INNOVATIVE PERSPECTIVE

How Does Google Motivate Its Employees?[23]

Google is often cited for its unique organizational culture and for motivating its employees. Forbes magazine in its 2011 search of "the best company to work for" ranked Google fourth. Fortune even ranked Google first in 2012.

What does Google do to motivate its employees? The corporate culture and the perks are often mentioned. These perks include free gourmet meals, the availability of a spa and swimming pool, a gym for workout, or getting a massage, and free shuttle service. The reasons for the perks are to attract the best people and keep them—they also help employees to work long hours and get relieved from the every-day chores. Google employees like the organizational culture, the company's vision, values, and open communication all designed for finding and hiring smart and determined people who share the common vision and goals of the company. The workforce speaks several languages that reflect the global environment of the users. The culture also makes people feel comfortable and encourage them sharing ideas freely. Communication is fostered by the weekly meetings as well as the gathering in the many cafes or playing video games and engaging in other recreational activities. The headquarters in Mountain View in California provides its Googlers (as its employees are known) with many opportunites such as playing the piano or enjoying the swimming pool. Whiteboards are widely available throughout the company for conducting spontaneous brainstorming sessions. The offices are designed to foster conversation across teams. Google is a global company with more than 30,000 employees in more than 70 offices, located in more than 40 countries.

Google's mission has been stated as "...to organize the world's information and make it universally accessible and useful"[24]. Moreover, Google has a list of 10 things that are believed to be true.[25] Here are some examples:

- "Focus on the user and all else will follow"
- "Fast is better than slow"
- "You can make money without doing evil"

Although people liked the perks and opportunities at Google, some left the company. Some even joined the club of ex-Googlers. There may be several reasons why people left the firm: Some felt that the company is too large and not a start-up company anymore; they felt that they do not make a big impact with their ideas. Others left to start their own company or joined competitors such as Foursquare or Facebook.

Google certainly is an exciting company that offers many attractive and unique perks and opportunities. The challenge is whether the company can grow and retain is organizational culture for motivating its Googlers.

Questions:

1. Several things are listed that are believed to be true. What are the others in the list of 10 things? Use the Internet to find out.
2. Would you like to work for Google requiring long hours? You may discuss your view on the balance of life.
3. Find on the Internet the 10 things that are believed to be true. Discuss them. Are they applicable for your organization or one you know?
4. What should Google do to maintain the organization culture?

ENDNOTES

1. This is also one of the important messages in the *Second Draft—Pastoral Letter on Catholic Social Teaching and the U.S. Economy*, October 7, 1985, and *Economic Justice for All: Catholic Social Teaching and the U.S. Economy* (Washington, DC: National Conference of Catholic Bishops, 1996).
2. See also http://www.management-issues.com/2006/8/24/research/organisations-get thumbs-down-from-disillusioned-managers.asp, accessed February 3, 2007 and http://www.blackwell-synergy.com/doi/pdf/10.1111/j.1365-2934.2005.00612.x?cookieSet=1, accessed February 3, 2007.
3. Douglas McGregor, *The Human Side of Enterprise* (New York: McGraw-Hill, 1960).
4. John J. Morse and Jay W. Lorsch, "Beyond Theory Y," *Harvard Business Review*, May–June 1970, pp. 61–68. For other publications by Lorsch at Harvard Business School, see http://dor.hbs.edu, accessed August 19, 2011.
5. How Khan Academy Is Changing the Rules of Education? http://www.wired.com/magazine/2011/07/ff_khan/all/1, accessed March 13, 2012; Khan Academy, http://www.alexa.com/siteinfo/khanacademy.org#, accessed July 28, 2012; James Temple (2009-12-14). "Salman Khan, math master of the Internet", sfgate.com, December 14, 2009, http://www.sfgate.com/cgi-bin/article.cgi?f=/c/a/2009/12/13/BUKV1B11Q1.DTL&tsp=1, accessed September 12, 2009.
6. Abraham Maslow, *Motivation and Personality* (New York: Harper & Row, 1954). For Maslow's publications, see www.maslow.com, accessed August 19, 2011.
7. Edward Lawler III and J. Lloyd Suttle, "A Causal Correlation Test of the Need-Hierarchy Concept," *Organizational Behavior and Human Performance*, April 1972, 265–287.
8. Douglas T. Hall and Khalil Nougaim, "An Examination of Maslow's Hierarchy in an Organization Setting," *Organizational Behavior and Human Performance*, February 1968, 12–35. For an additional evaluation of the needs hierarchy theory, see John B. Miner, *Theories of Organizational Behavior* (Hinsdale, IL: Dryden Press, 1980), chap. 2.
9. C. P. Alderfer, *Existence, Relatedness, and Growth: Human Needs in Organizational Settings* (New York: Free Press, 1972).
10. Frederick Herzberg, Bernard Mausner, Robert A. Peterson, and D. Capwell, *Job Attitudes: Review of Research and Opinion* (Pittsburgh: Psychological Services of Pittsburgh, 1957); Frederick Herzberg, Bernard Mausner, and Barbara B. Snyderman, *The Motivation to Work* (New York: Wiley, 1959).
11. Victor H. Vroom, *Work and Motivation* (New York: Wiley, 1964). See also David A. Nadler and Edward E. Lawler III, "Motivation: A Diagnostic Approach," in J. Richard Hackman, Edward E. Lawler III, and Lyman W. Porter, eds. *Perspectives on Behavior in Organizations*, 2nd ed. (New York: McGraw-Hill, 1983), pp. 67–87.
12. Lyman W. Porter and Edward E. Lawler III, *Managerial Attitudes and Performance* (Homewood, IL: Irwin, 1968); Cynthia M. Pavett, "Evaluation of the Impact of Feedback on Performance and Motivation," *Human Relations*, July 1983, pp. 641–654.
13. J. Stacy Adams, "Toward an Understanding of Inequity," *Journal of Abnormal and Social Psychology*, 1963, 67: 422–436; J. Stacy Adams, "Inequity in Social Exchange," in L. Berkowitz, ed. *Advances in Experimental Social Psychology* (New York: Academic Press, 1965), pp. 267–299.
14. Richard A. Cosier and Dan R. Dalton, "Equity Theory and Time: A Reformulation," *Academy of Management Review*, April 1983, pp. 311–319. See also Richard C. Huseman, John D. Hatfield, and Edward W. Miles, "A New Perspective on Equity Theory: The Equity Sensitivity Construct," *Academy of Management Review*, April 1987, pp. 222–234.
15. Considerable research has been done on the motivational aspects of goal setting. See Edwin A. Locke and Judith F. Bryan, "Performance Goals as Determinants of Level of Performance and Boredom," *Journal of Applied Psychology*, April 1967, pp. 120–130; Edwin A. Locke, "The Relationship of Intentions to Level of Performance," *Journal of Applied Psychology*, February 1966, pp. 60–66; Edwin A. Locke, "The Ubiquity of the Technique of Goal Setting in Theories of and Approaches to Employee Motivation," *Academy of Management Review*, July 1978, pp. 594–601; Heinz Weihrich, "A Study of the Integration of Management by Objectives with Key Managerial Activities and the Relationship to Selected Effectiveness Measures," doctoral dissertation, University of California, Los Angeles, 1973. For computerized goal setting at Cypress Semiconductor, see T. J. Rogers, "No Excuses Management," *Harvard Business Review*, July–August 1990, pp. 84–98. See also Heinz Weihrich, *Management Excellence: Productivity through MBO* (New York: McGraw-Hill, 1985), chap. 5.
16. Fred Luthans and Robert Kreitner, *Organizational Behavior Modification and Beyond: An Operant and Social Learning Approach* (Glenview, IL: Scott, Foresman and Company, 1984).
17. David C. McClelland, *The Achievement Motive* (New York: Appleton-Century-Crofts, 1953); *Studies in Motivation* (New York: Appleton-Century-Crofts, 1955); and *The Achieving Society* (Princeton, NJ: Van Nostrand, 1961). See also his "Achievement Motivation Can Be Developed," *Harvard Business Review*, January–February 1965, pp. 6–24, 178; and (with David G. Winter) *Motivating Economic Achievement* (New York: Free Press, 1969).
18. David C. McClelland, "That Urge to Achieve," in Max D. Richards. ed. *Readings in Management*, 7th ed. (Cincinnati, OH: South-Western, 1986), pp. 367–375.
19. For a variety of human resource issues and studies, including benefits, see http://was.hewitt.com/hewitt, accessed June 12, 2002.
20. William B. Glaberson, Jeffrey M. Laderman, Christopher Power, and Vicky Cahan, "Who'll Be the Next to Fall?" *Business Week*, December 1, 1986, pp. 28–30; Chris Welles and Gary Weiss, "A Man Who Made a Career of Tempting Fate," ibid., pp. 34–35.
21. David Margolick, "The Madoff Chronicles, Part III: Did the Sons Know", *Vanity Fair*, July 2009.
22. Richard R. Floersch, "The Right Way to Determine Executive Play," *The Wall Street Journal*, March 5, 2009.
23. "Headhunter Dishes on Why People Leave Google", http://news.cnet.com/8301-10784_3-9934527-7.html, accessed October 10, 2012. "What It's Like Leaving Google to Go Work at Facebook", http://www.businessinsider.com/what-its-like-leaving-google-to-go-work-at-facebook-2012-3?op=1, accessed January 5, 2016. "The Best Companies to Work For", http://www.forbes.com/sites/jacquelynsmith/2011/12/15/the-best-companies-to-work-for/2/, accessed January 5, 2016.
24. "Google's Mission is to Organize the World's Information and Make it Universally Accessible and Useful", http://www.google.com/about/company/, accessed January 5, 2016.
25. Ten Things We Know to Be True, http://www.google.com/about/company/philosophy/, accessed January 5, 2016.

CHAPTER 15

Leadership

Learning Objectives

After studying this chapter, you should be able to:

LO 1   Define leadership and its ingredients

LO 2   Describe the trait approaches and charismatic leadership approach and their limitations

LO 3   Discuss various leadership styles based on the use of authority

LO 4   Identify the two dimensions of the managerial grid and the resulting extreme leadership styles

LO 5   Recognize that leadership can be seen as a continuum

LO 6   Explain the contingency approach to leadership

LO 7   Describe the path–goal approach to leadership effectiveness

LO 8   Distinguish between transactional and transformational leaders

Although some people treat the terms *managership* and *leadership* as synonyms, the two should be distinguished. As a matter of fact, there can be leaders of completely unorganized groups, but there can be managers, as conceived here, only where organized structures create roles. Separating leadership from managership has important analytical advantages. It permits leadership to be singled out for study without the encumbrance of qualifications relating to the more general issue of managership.

Leadership is an important aspect of managing. As this chapter will show, the ability to lead effectively is one of the keys to being an effective manager; also, undertaking the other essentials of managing—doing the entire managerial job—has an important bearing on ensuring that a manager will be an effective leader. Managers must exercise all the functions of their role in order to combine human and material resources to achieve objectives. The key to doing this is the existence of a clear role and a degree of discretion or authority to support managers' actions.

Leadership and motivation are closely interconnected. By understanding motivation, one can appreciate better what people want and why they act as they do. Leaders may not only respond to subordinates' motivations but also arouse or dampen them by means of the organizational climate they develop. Both these factors are as important to leadership as they are to managership.

INNOVATIVE PERSPECTIVE

Jim Sinegal, Costco's CEO—A Leader with Heart or Smart?[1]

Costco's warehouse club is one of the most successful U.S. retailers of its kind. It is led by its CEO Jim Sinegal. While many CEOs insist on fancy offices and other perks, not so Sinegal (who likes to be called "Jim"), who has a simple office with two folding tables. His wardrobe is from his own warehouse rather than from fashion designers and he wears a name tag when visiting his stores. In his interview with the *Wall Street Journal*, he discussed his plan of opening about 30 new stores in the United States in 2007. He also considers opportunities in China and India. Costco already operates in Mexico and Japan.

Competing with Wal-Mart, which wants to be known for its low prices, Costco pays better salaries than Wal-Mart and most of Costco's rivals. Sinegal said in the interview: "If you hire good people, pay them good wages and provide good jobs and careers, good things will happen in your business. We think that's proven true in our case. We are the low-cost provider of merchandise, and yet we pay the highest wages." It may be smart to lead with the heart.

> **Leadership** and **motivation** are closely interconnected.

DEFINING LEADERSHIP[2]

Leadership has different meanings to different authors.[3] Harry Truman, former American president, said that leadership is the ability to get men (women) to do what they don't like to do and like it. In this book, leadership is defined as influence, that is, the art or process of influencing people so that they will strive willingly and enthusiastically toward the achievement of group goals.[4] Ideally, people should be encouraged to develop not only willingness to work but also willingness to work with zeal and confidence. Zeal is ardor, earnestness, and intensity in the execution of work; confidence reflects

Leadership Art or process of influencing people so that they will strive willingly and enthusiastically toward the achievement of group goals.

experience and technical ability. Leaders act to help a group attain objectives through the maximum application of its capabilities. They do not stand behind a group to push and prod; they place themselves before the group as they facilitate progress and inspire the group to accomplish organizational goals. A good example is an orchestra leader, whose function is to produce coordinated sound and correct tempo through the integrated effort of the musicians. The performance of the orchestra will depend on the quality of the director's leadership.

LEADERSHIP PERSPECTIVE

Leadership on the New York Hudson River[5]

The "Miracle on the Hudson" is an example of how a company not known for good service gained an excellent reputation by treating the 149 passengers on Flight 1549 in a fair and exemplary way. Through the airmanship of the pilot, the plane landed on the Hudson River in New York. Seen as a miracle, no passenger was killed due to the skills of the pilot and the flight attendants guiding the passengers to safety. The quickly dispatched "Care Team" provided the passengers with sweat suits, emergency cash for buying personal items, medicines, toiletries, and prepaid cell phones. Passengers had a choice of staying in a New York hotel, arranging for a new flight, obtaining a train ticket, or a rental car. Since passengers may have lost their drivers licenses during the plane evacuation, U.S. Airways contacted Hertz rental to accommodate their customers who also received three letters with a ticket refund and $5,000 advance check. Claim adjusters visited those customers with higher value loss.

INGREDIENTS OF LEADERSHIP[6]

www.chrysler.com

www.ge.com

www.microsoft.com

Ingredients of leadership Power; a fundamental understanding of people; the ability to inspire followers to apply their full capabilities; the leader's style; and the development of a conducive organizational climate.

Leaders envision the future; they inspire organization members and chart the course of the organization. Former CEOs Lee Iacocca at Chrysler and Jack Welch at General Electric as well as Bill Gates at Microsoft have provided a vision for their companies. Leaders must instill values—whether they are concern for quality, honesty, and calculated risk-taking or concern for employees and customers.

Every group of people that performs near its total capacity has some person as its head who is skilled in the art of leadership. This skill seems to be a compound of at least four major ingredients: (1) the ability to use power effectively and in a responsible manner, (2) the ability to comprehend that human beings have different motivating forces at different times and in different situations, (3) the ability to inspire, and (4) the ability to act in a manner that will develop a climate conducive to responding to and arousing motivations.

The first ingredient of leadership is power. The nature of power and the difference between power and authority were discussed in Chapter 9. The second ingredient of leadership is a fundamental understanding of people. As in all other practices, it is one thing to know motivation theory, kinds of motivating forces, and the nature of a system of motivation but another thing to be able to apply this knowledge to people and situations. A manager or any other leader who at least knows the present state of motivation theory and who understands the elements of motivation is more aware of the nature and strength of human needs and is better able to define and design ways of satisfying them and to administer so as to get the desired responses.

The third ingredient of leadership is the rare ability to inspire followers to apply their full capabilities to a project. While the use of motivators seems to center on subordinates and their needs, inspiration comes from group heads who may have qualities of charm and appeal that give rise to loyalty, devotion, and a strong desire on the part of followers to promote what leaders want. This is not a matter of needs satisfaction; it is, rather, a matter of people giving unselfish support to a chosen champion. The best examples of inspirational leadership come from hopeless and frightening situations: an unprepared nation on the eve of battle, a prison camp with exceptional morale, or a defeated leader undeserted by faithful followers. Some may argue that such devotion is not entirely unselfish, that it is in the interests of those who face catastrophe to follow a person they trust. But few would deny the value of personal appeal in either case.

Steve Job's Entrepreneurial Leadership[7]

Steve Jobs, after combating serious health issues for several years, resigned as the CEO of Apple on August 24, 2011. Steve Jobs, the founder of Apple and Pixar, is widely acknowledged as a creative genius as well as one of the top CEOs of his generation. Jobs' passion for excellence in detail and design led Apple from near bankruptcy, after his earlier firing from the Apple board, to one of the most valuable companies in the world. His passion, high standards, and techno-chic ability to wow customers helped him lead Apple to a series of unparalleled products (e.g., iPod, iPhone, iPad). The inspiring entrepreneurial leadership embodied by Steve Jobs is a touchstone for future leaders and will stand as a profile in creativity and courage for generations to come. Several years after Jobs' passing, Apple continues to lead the world in innovative products that delight customers.

ENTREPRENEURIAL PERSPECTIVE

The fourth ingredient of leadership has to do with the style of the leader and the organizational climate he or she develops. As the previous chapter has shown, the strength of motivation greatly depends on expectancies, perceived rewards, the amount of effort believed to be required, the task to be done, and other factors that are part of an environment, as well as on organizational climate. Awareness of these factors has led to considerable research on leadership behavior and to the development of various pertinent theories. The views of those who have long approached leadership as a psychological study of interpersonal relationships have tended to converge with the personal viewpoint expressed in this book—that the primary tasks of managers are the design and maintenance of an environment for performance.

John Gabarro and John Kotter added another ingredient: effective managers must develop a healthy relationship with their boss.[8] It means that this relationship is based on mutual dependence. Thus, the manager must understand the boss's goals and pressures and give attention to his or her concerns.

Almost every role in an organized enterprise is made more satisfying for participants and more productive for the enterprise by those who can help others fulfill their desire for such things as money, status, power, and pride of accomplishment. The fundamental **Principle of Leadership** is this: since people

Principle of Leadership Since people tend to follow those who offer them a means of satisfying their personal goals, the more managers understand what motivates their subordinates and the more they reflect this understanding in their actions, the more effective they are likely to be as leaders.

tend to follow those who, in their view, offer them a means of satisfying their personal goals, the more managers understand what motivates their subordinates and how these motivators operate, and the more they reflect this understanding in carrying out their managerial actions, the more effective they are likely to be as leaders.

Because of the importance of leadership in all kinds of group action, there is a considerable volume of theory and research concerning it. It is difficult to summarize such a large body of research in a form relevant to day-to-day management. However, examined below are several major types of leadership theory and research, together with outlines of some basic kinds of leadership styles.

LEADERSHIP PERSPECTIVE

Ratan N. Tata: Leadership at the TATA Group[9]

Ratan Tata is the chairman of the TATA Group, India's biggest conglomerate with the responsibility of guiding the group of some 100 companies. He is a modest person who likes weekend solitude in his self-designed beachfront home. With an architectural degree from Cornell University (1962), he is now the architect of big strategies and big deals for the TATA group.

During his travel to China, he was impressed by the rapid economic development which encouraged him to undertake major projects for the TATA Group. For example, he arranged for the investment binge of acquiring the truck unit of South Korea's Daewoo Motors, hotels, Indonesian coal mines, steel mills in Singapore, Thailand, and Vietnam. He also acquired Tyco International Undersea telecom cables, the Corus Group, the Dutch-British steel giant.

He is considered a tough manager (e.g., in dealing with unions) at the same time, he is promoter of social responsibility. His passion for cars is discussed in conjunction with the now famous $2,500 car discussed elsewhere in this book. The question is: Who will be his successor to continue the leadership role upon Mr. Ratan's retirement?

TRAIT APPROACHES TO LEADERSHIP[10]

Prior to 1949, studies of leadership were based largely on an attempt to identify the traits that leaders possess. Starting with the "great man" theory that leaders are born and not made, a belief dating back to the ancient Greeks and Romans, researchers have tried to identify the physical, mental, and personality traits of various leaders. That theory lost much of its acceptability with the rise of the behaviorist school of psychology.

Many studies of traits have been made. Ralph M. Stogdill found that various researchers had identified specific traits related to leadership ability: 5 physical traits (such as energy, appearance, and height), 4 intelligence and ability traits, 16 personality traits (such as adaptability, aggressiveness, enthusiasm, and self-confidence), 6 task-related characteristics (such as achievement drive, persistence, and initiative), and 9 social characteristics (such as cooperativeness, interpersonal skills, and administrative ability).[11]

The discussion of the importance of traits to leadership goes on. More recently, the following key leadership traits have been identified: drive (including achievement, motivation, energy, ambition, initiative, and tenacity), leadership motivation (the aspiration to lead but not to seek power as such), honesty and integrity, self-confidence (including emotional stability), cognitive ability, and an understanding of the business. Less clear is the impact of creativity, flexibility, and charisma on leadership effectiveness.

In general, the study of leaders' traits has not been a very fruitful approach to explaining leadership. Not all leaders possess all the traits, and many nonleaders may possess most or all of them. Also, the trait approach gives no guidance as to *how much* of any trait a person should have. Furthermore, the dozens of studies that have been made do not agree as to which traits are leadership traits or what their relationships are to actual instances of leadership. Most of these so-called traits are really patterns of behavior.

CHARISMATIC LEADERSHIP APPROACH

Charismatic leadership is closely related to the above discussion. One of the early studies of charismatic characteristics was done by Robert J. House.[12] He and other authors indicate that charismatic leaders may have certain characteristics, such as being self-confident, having strong convictions, articulating a vision, being able to initiate change, communicating high expectations, having a need to influence followers and supporting them, demonstrating enthusiasm and excitement, and being in touch with reality.[13] While these may be admirable characteristics, as we will note later in this chapter, other factors such as the characteristics of the followers and the situation may impact on effective leadership.

LEADERSHIP BEHAVIOR AND STYLES

There are several theories on leadership behavior and styles. This section focuses on (1) leadership based on the use of authority, (2) the managerial grid, and (3) leadership involving a variety of styles, ranging from a maximum to a minimum use of power and influence.

Styles Based on Use of Authority

Some earlier explanations of leadership styles classified the styles on the basis of how leaders use their authority. Leaders are seen as applying three basic styles. The **autocratic leader** commands and expects compliance, is dogmatic and positive, and leads by the ability to withhold or give rewards and punishment. The **democratic**, or **participative**, **leader** consults with subordinates on proposed actions and decisions and encourages participation from them. This type of leader ranges from the person who does not take action without subordinates' concurrence to the one who makes decisions but consults with subordinates before doing so.

The **free-rein leader** uses his or her power very little, if at all, giving subordinates a high degree of independence in their operations. Such leaders depend largely on subordinates to set their own goals and the means of achieving them, and they see their role as one of aiding the operations of followers by furnishing them with information and acting primarily as a contact with the group's external environment. Figure 15.1 illustrates the flow of influence in the three leadership situations.

There are variations within this simple classification of leadership styles. Some autocratic leaders are seen as "benevolent autocrats". Although they listen considerately to their followers' opinions before making a decision, the deci-

> **Autocratic leader** commands and expects compliance, is dogmatic and positive, and leads by the ability to withhold or give rewards and punishment.
>
> **Democratic**, or **participative**, **leader** consults with subordinates and encourages their participation.
>
> **Free-rein leader** uses power very little, if at all, giving subordinates a high degree of independence.

FIGURE 15.1 The flow of influence with three leadership styles

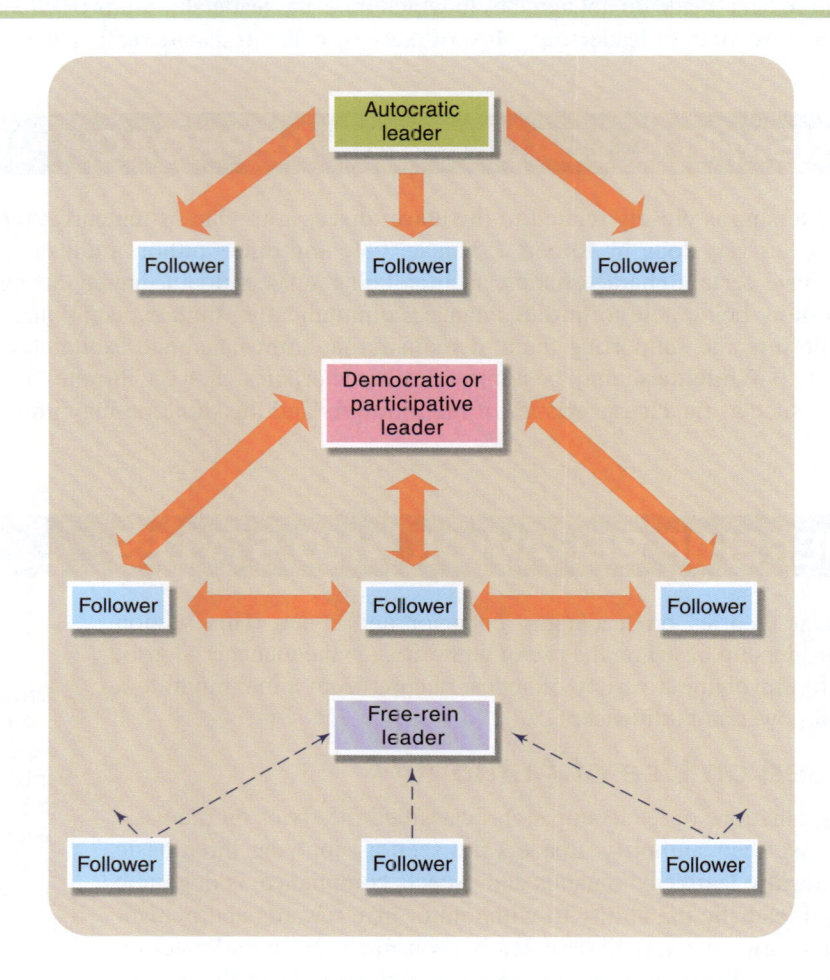

sion is their own. They may be willing to hear and consider subordinates' ideas and concerns, but when a decision is to be made, they may be more autocratic than benevolent.

A variation of the participative leader is the person who is supportive. Leaders in this category may look upon their task as not only consulting with followers and carefully considering their opinions but also doing all they can to support subordinates in accomplishing their duties.

The use of any style will depend on the situation. A manager may be highly autocratic in an emergency; one can hardly imagine a fire chief holding a long meeting with the crew to consider the best way of fighting a fire. Managers may also be autocratic when they alone have the answers to certain questions.

A leader may gain considerable knowledge and a better commitment from the people involved by consulting with them. As already noted, this is true in developing verifiable objectives under systems of managing by objectives. Furthermore, a manager dealing with a group of research scientists may give them free rein in developing their inquiries and experiments. But the same manager might be quite autocratic in enforcing a rule stipulating that employees wear a protective covering when they are handling potentially dangerous chemicals.

INNOVATIVE PERSPECTIVE

Leading in Innovation: Interview with Kern Peng at Intel Corporation[14]

Dr. Peng holds two doctorate degrees, one in mechanical engineering specializing in nanocomposite materials, and the other in business administration specializing in operations management. Given his technical and business expertise and experience at Intel, we asked him how Intel plans and organizes for innovation. Dr. Peng stated, "Intel is a unique case where innovation is emphasized in two main paths: process innovation and product innovation. Process innovation is on how chips are manufactured, which has a very clear direction—keeping up with Moore's Law. Proposed by Intel founder Gordon Moore in 1965, Moore's Law states that the number of transistors on a chip will double approximately every two years. It has been the guiding principle since day 1 when Intel started in 1968. Such clear objective sets the stage for the process innovation as the development activities are planned around it. The recent 3D Tri-Gate transistor technology is an example of Intel's latest innovation to extend Moore's Law."

Dr. Peng, continued, sharing "In the product innovation space, where a specific and clear direction is typically lacking, Intel's approach is relying on 1) investing on path finding researches through the organization called 'Intel Labs' which have research partnerships with universities, governments, and industries and 2) promoting an 'can-do' culture and pushing innovation at every level of the organization down to the technicians and operators level." He concluded, saying, "Intel defines innovation as 'ideation x execution' so Intel plans the execution by using the Tick Tock model, which unites the process innovations and product innovations to bring real values to the market."

The Managerial Grid

A well-known approach to defining leadership styles is the managerial grid, developed decades ago by Robert Blake and Jane Mouton.[15] Building on previous research that showed the importance of a manager having concern both for production and for people, Blake and Mouton developed a clever device to dramatize this concern. This grid, shown in Figure 15.2, has been used throughout the world as a means of training managers and of identifying various combinations of leadership styles.

The Grid Dimensions

The grid has two dimensions: concern for people and concern for production. As Blake and Mouton emphasize, their use of the phrase *concern for* is meant to convey *how* managers are concerned about production or *how* they are concerned about people, and not such things as *how much* production they are concerned about getting out of a group.

Concern for production includes the attitude of a supervisor toward a wide variety of things, such as the quality of policy decisions, procedures and processes, creativeness of research, quality of service, work efficiency, and volume of output. Concern for people is likewise interpreted in a broad way. It includes such elements as the degree of personal commitment toward goal achievement, maintenance of the self-esteem of workers, placement of responsibility on the basis of trust rather than obedience, provision of good working conditions, and maintenance of satisfying interpersonal relations.

> The **managerial grid** has two dimensions: concern for people and concern for production.

The Four Extreme Styles

Blake and Mouton recognize four extremes of style. Under the 1.1 style (referred to as impoverished management), managers concern themselves very little with

FIGURE 15.2 Managerial grid

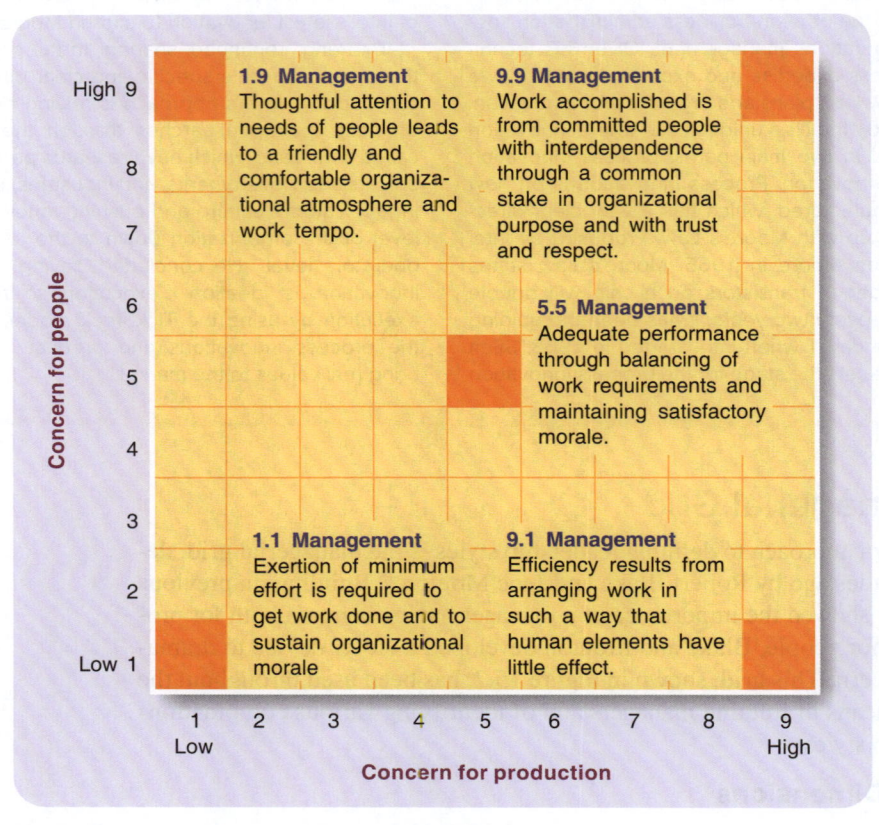

1.9 Management
Thoughtful attention to needs of people leads to a friendly and comfortable organizational atmosphere and work tempo.

9.9 Management
Work accomplished is from committed people with interdependence through a common stake in organizational purpose and with trust and respect.

5.5 Management
Adequate performance through balancing of work requirements and maintaining satisfactory morale.

1.1 Management
Exertion of minimum effort is required to get work done and to sustain organizational morale

9.1 Management
Efficiency results from arranging work in such a way that human elements have little effect.

Y-axis: Concern for people (Low 1 to High 9)
X-axis: Concern for production (Low 1 to High 9)

Source: R. R. Blake and J. S. Mouton, "Managerial Grid", *The Managerial Grid*.

either people or production and have minimum involvement in their jobs; to all intents and purposes, they have abandoned their jobs and only mark time or act as messengers communicating information from superiors to subordinates. At the other extreme are the 9.9 managers, who display in their actions the highest possible dedication both to people and to production. They are the real "team managers", who are able to mesh the production needs of the enterprise with the needs of individuals.

Another style is 1.9 management (called country club management by some), in which managers have little or no concern for production but are concerned only for people. They promote an environment in which everyone is relaxed, friendly, and happy and no one is concerned about putting forth coordinated effort to accomplish enterprise goals. At another extreme are the 9.1 managers (sometimes referred to as autocratic task managers), who are concerned only with developing an efficient operation, who have little or no concern for people, and who are quite autocratic in their style of leadership.

By using these four extremes as points of reference, every managerial technique, approach, or style can be placed somewhere on the grid. Clearly, 5.5 managers have medium concern for production and for people. They obtain adequate, but not outstanding, morale and production. They do not set goals too high and are likely to have a rather benevolently autocratic attitude toward people.

The managerial grid is a useful device for identifying and classifying managerial styles, but it does not tell us *why* a manager falls into one part or another of the grid. To determine the reason, one has to look at underlying causes, such as the personality characteristics of the leader or the followers, the ability and training of managers, the enterprise environment, and other situational factors that influence how leaders and followers act.

Leadership as a Continuum

The adaptation of leadership styles to different contingencies has been well characterized by Robert Tannenbaum and Warren H. Schmidt, developers of the leadership continuum concept. As Figure 15.3 shows, they see leadership as involving a variety of styles, ranging from one that is highly boss-centered to one that is highly subordinate-centered. The styles vary with the degree of freedom a leader or manager grants to subordinates. Thus, instead of suggesting a choice between the two styles of leadership—authoritarian or democratic—this approach offers a range of styles, with no suggestion that one is always right and another is always wrong.

Leadership continuum concept Leadership involves a variety of styles, ranging from one that is highly boss-centered to one that is highly subordinate-centered.

The continuum theory recognizes that the appropriate style of leadership depends on the *leader*, the *followers*, and the *situation*. To Tannenbaum and Schmidt, the most important elements that may influence a manager's style can be seen along a continuum as (1) the forces operating in the manager's personality, including his or her value system, confidence in subordinates, inclination toward leadership styles, and feelings of security in uncertain situations; (2) the forces in subordinates (such as their willingness to assume responsibility, their knowledge and experience, and their tolerance for ambiguity) that will affect the manager's behavior; and (3) the forces in the situation, such as organizational values and traditions, the effectiveness of subordinates working as a unit, the nature of a problem and the feasibility of safely delegating the authority to handle it, and the pressure of time.

The appropriate leadership style depends on the leader, the followers, and the situation.

In reviewing their continuum model in 1973 (it was first formulated in 1958), Tannenbaum and Schmidt placed circles around the model, as shown in Figure 15.3, to represent the influences on style imposed by both the organizational environment and the societal environment.[16] This was done to emphasize the open-system nature of leadership styles and the various impacts of the organizational environment and the social environment outside an enterprise. In their 1973 commentary, they put increased stress on the interdependency of leadership style and environmental forces—such as labor unions, greater pressures for social responsibility, the civil rights movement, and the ecology and consumer movements—that challenge the rights of managers to make decisions or handle their subordinates without considering interests outside the organization.

FIGURE 15.3 Continuum of manager–nonmanager behavior

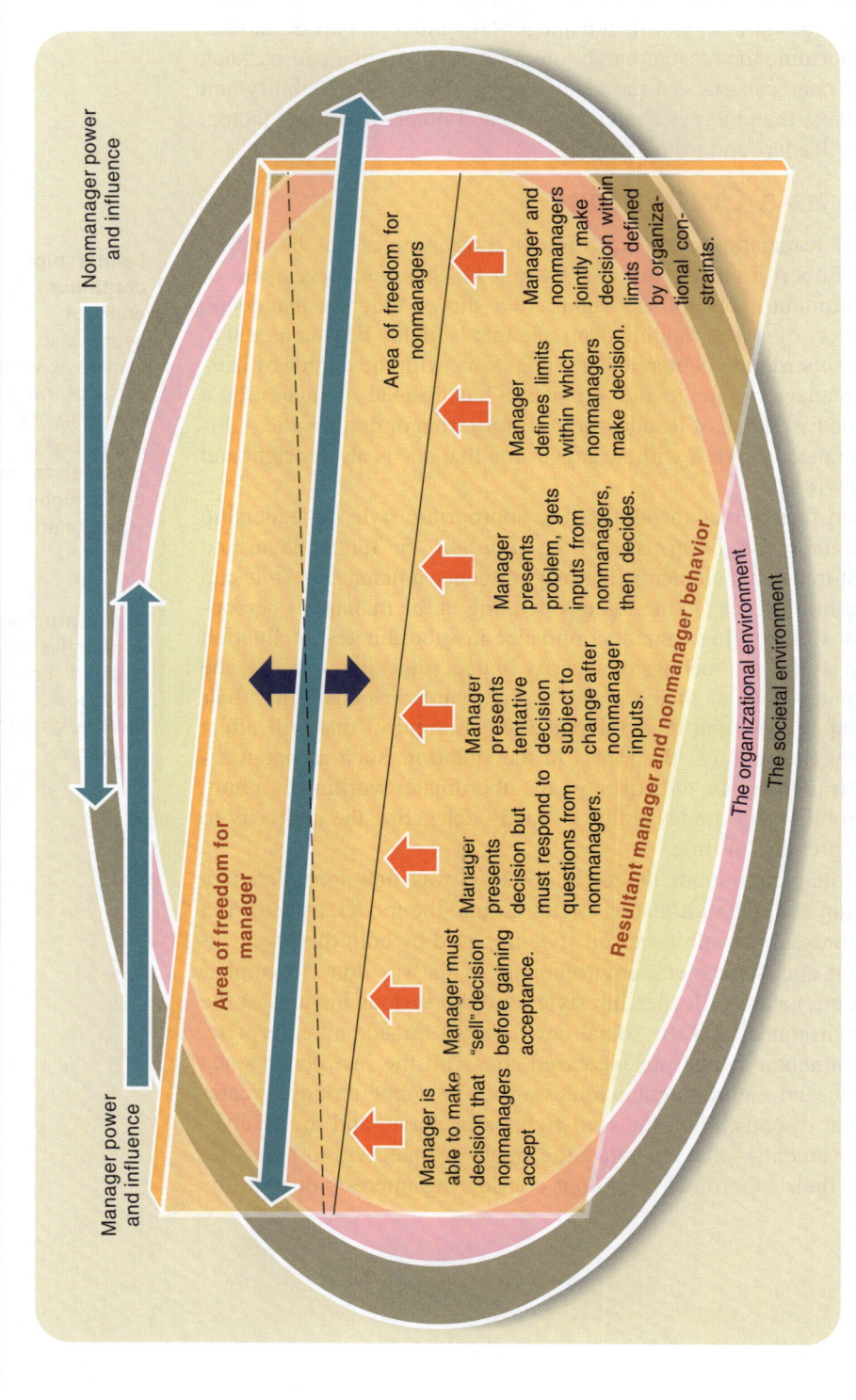

Manager power and influence							Nonmanager power and influence

Area of freedom for manager ⟷ **Area of freedom for nonmanagers**

Resultant manager and nonmanager behavior

- Manager is able to make decision that nonmanagers accept
- Manager must "sell" decision before gaining acceptance.
- Manager presents decision but must respond to questions from nonmanagers.
- Manager presents tentative decision subject to change after nonmanager inputs.
- Manager presents problem, gets inputs from nonmanagers, then decides.
- Manager defines limits within which nonmanagers make decision.
- Manager and nonmanagers jointly make decision within limits defined by organizational constraints.

The organizational environment
The societal environment

Source: R. Tannenbaum and W.H. Schmidt, "Continuum of manager-nonmanager behaviour", *Harvard Business Review.*

LEADERSHIP PERSPECTIVE

Leading by Example—Pope Francis[17]

Since 1927, the respected *Time* magazine selected the "Man of the Year", now appropriately called the "Person of the Year". In 2013, Pope Francis was selected and shown on the magazine cover. Similarly, other magazines also wrote favorably about Pope Francis' ability to communicate, primarily his leadership style. *Rolling Stones* magazine had a feature article on the pope and so did the New Yorker. *Fortune* magazine considered him the fourth most powerful person in the world and *Forbes* described him among the world's top thinkers. *The Economist* suggested that the Harvard Business School should study him and the *British Guardian* considered him the clearest voice against the status quo. *The Financial Times* described him as a global symbol of compassion and humility.

Several books discussed his approach to managing, especially as it relates to leadership. John J. Allen Jr. wrote *Against the Tide, The Radical Leadership of Pope Francis*, Jeffry A. Krames discussed the pope's managerial ability in his book *Lead with Humility—12 Leadership Lessons from Pope Francis*, published by the American Management Association, AMACOM. The question clearly is what makes Pope Francis so special? Let's focus on how he is carrying out managerial activities.

In this chapter we discuss several theories of leadership. Tannenbaum and Schmidt suggest that leadership can be analyzed by considering three sets of variables (see leadership as a continuum): 1) The characteristics of the leader, 2) the followers, and 3) the situation. We will focus on the first, the characteristics of the leader.

Pope Francis believes in the dignity of all people, as we discussed in Chapter 1 in this book. He shows respect for others even those who disagree. In fact, in his 2016 set of New Year Resolutions he states: "Befriend those who disagree." He is considered as being authentic, not selfish. He is often cited for being close to the people, or as Tom Peters, the author of the best-selling management book *In Search for Excellence* suggested, being close to the customers. Similarly, Wal-Mart's late Sam Walton advocated "managing by walking around" or in Pope Francis' words, avoiding insularity.

During his early life in Argentina, where he was born, he learned that authoritarian, top-down management does not work. Instead, now he tries to obtain inputs from many sources, especially from those who may disagree with him. He realizes that he does not have all the answers. In organizing, he prefers a structure that moves from centralization to decentralization. He takes time to select the right people and then gives them a great deal of freedom.

In his decision making, he encourages participation and consultation. He also encourages others to work toward the greater good in their decision making, rather than being driven by self-interest. His focus is on the poor and powerless as illustrated by many of his decisions.

The pope also demonstrated skills in controlling. Shortly after being selected pope, he assembled prominent financiers from around the world with the goal of restructuring and controlling the Vatican Bank. *Fortune* magazine wrote: "He's an elite manager who's reforming the Vatican's troubled finances."[18]

Perhaps most important, he leads by example, leading with humility. He walks the talk. He lives in the guesthouse, not the official residence; he drives an old car whenever he can, rather than being driven in the limousine and he pays his own hotel bills. He communicates his ideas through authentic communication with an open door policy.

We see how Pope Francis, without having had a managerial background, carries out effectively and efficiently many aspects of planning, organizing, staffing, leading, and controlling. One can be an effective manager without an MBA—but most of us need to learn about management principles and practices as discussed in this book.

SITUATIONAL, OR CONTINGENCY, APPROACHES TO LEADERSHIP

As disillusionment with the "great man" and trait approaches to understanding leadership increased, attention turned to the study of situations and the belief that leaders are the product of given situations. A large number of studies have been made on the premise that leadership is strongly affected by the situation from which the leader emerges and in which he or she operates. That this is a persuasive approach is indicated by the emergence of Franklin Delano Roosevelt in the Great Depression of the 1930s in the

United States and the rise of Mao Zedong in China in the period after World War II. This approach to leadership recognizes that there exists an interaction between the group and the leader. It supports the follower theory that people tend to follow those whom they perceive (accurately or inaccurately) as offering them a means of accomplishing their personal desires. The leader, then, is the person who recognizes these desires and does things, or undertakes programs, designed to meet them.

Situational, or contingency, approaches obviously have much meaning for managerial theory and practice. They also tie into the system of motivation discussed in Chapter 14, and they are important for practicing managers, who must consider the situation when they design an environment for performance.

Fiedler's Contingency Approach to Leadership

Although their approach to leadership theory is primarily one of analyzing leadership style, Fred E. Fiedler and his associates at the University of Illinois came up with a **contingency theory of leadership**.[19] The theory holds that people become leaders not only because of the attributes of their personalities but also because of various situational factors and the interactions between leaders and group members.

Contingency theory of leadership People become leaders not only because of their personality attributes but also because of various situational factors and the interactions between leaders and group members.

Critical Dimensions of the Leadership Situation

On the basis of his studies, Fiedler describes three critical dimensions of the leadership situation that help determine what style of leadership will be most effective:

1. *Position power.* This is the degree to which the power of a position, as distinguished from other sources of power, such as personality or expertise, enables a leader to get group members to comply with directions. In the case of managers, this is the power arising from organizational authority. As Fiedler points out, a leader with clear and considerable position power can obtain good followership more easily than one without such power.
2. *Task structure.* With this dimension, Fiedler has in mind the extent to which tasks can be clearly spelled out and people held responsible for them. If tasks are clear (rather than vague and unstructured), the quality of performance can be more easily controlled and group members can be held more definitely responsible for performance.
3. *Leader–member relations.* Fiedler regards this dimension as the most important from a leader's point of view, since position power and task structure may be largely under the control of an enterprise. It has to do with the extent to which group members like and trust a leader and are willing to follow that leader.

Leadership Styles

To approach his study, Fiedler set forth two major styles of leadership. One of these is primarily task-oriented, with the leader gaining satisfaction from seeing tasks performed. The other is oriented primarily toward achieving good interpersonal relations and attaining a position of personal prominence.

To measure leadership styles and determine whether a leader is chiefly task-oriented, Fiedler used an unusual testing technique. He based his findings on two types of sources: (1) scores on the *least preferred coworker* (LPC) scale, which are ratings made by people in a group of members with whom they would least like to work; and (2) scores on the *assumed similarity between opposites* (ASO) scale, which are ratings based on the degree to which leaders see group members as being like themselves, on the assumption that people will like best, and work best with, those who are seen as most like themselves. Today, the LPC scale is most commonly used in research. In developing this scale, Fiedler asked respondents to identify the traits of a person with whom they could work well. Respondents described the person by rating 16 items on a scale of attributes, such as the following:[20]

Pleasant |___|___|___|___|___|___|___|___| Unpleasant

Rejecting |___|___|___|___|___|___|___|___| Accepting

On the basis of his studies with this method, as well as studies done by others, Fiedler found that people who rated their coworkers high (i.e., in favorable terms) were those who derived major satisfaction from successful interpersonal relationships. People who rated their "least preferred coworker" low (i.e., in unfavorable terms) were seen as deriving their major satisfaction from task performance.

From his research, Fiedler came to some interesting conclusions. Recognizing that personal perceptions may be unclear and even quite inaccurate, he nonetheless found the following to be true:

Leadership performance depends as much on the organization as it depends on the leader's own attributes. Except perhaps for the unusual case, it is simply not meaningful to speak of an effective leader or an ineffective leader; we can only speak of a leader who tends to be effective in one situation and ineffective in another. If we wish to increase organizational and group effectiveness, we must learn not only how to train leaders more effectively but also how to build an organizational environment in which the leader can perform well.[21]

Fiedler's contingency model of leadership is presented as a graph in Figure 15.4. This figure is really a summary of Fiedler's research, in which he found that in "unfavorable" or "favorable" situations the task-oriented leader would be the most effective. **Favorableness of situation** is defined by Fiedler as the degree to which a given situation enables a leader to exert influence over a group. In other words, when leader position power is weak, the task structure is unclear, and leader–member relations are moderately poor, the situation is unfavorable for the leader and the most effective leader will be one who is task-oriented (see the lower right corner of the graph). At the other extreme, where position power is strong, the task structure is clear, and leader–member relations are good—a favorable situation for the leader—the task-oriented leader will also be most effective. However, if the situation is only moderately unfavorable or favorable (the middle of the horizontal scale in the figure), the relationship-oriented leader will be most effective.

In a highly structured situation, such as in the military during a war, where the leader has strong position power and good relations with members, there is a favorable situation in which task orientation is the most appropriate. The other extreme, an unfavorable situation with moderately poor relations, an unstructured task, and weak position power, also suggests task orientation by the leader, which may reduce the anxiety or ambiguity that could be created by the loosely structured situation. Between the two extremes, the suggested approach emphasizes cooperation and good relations with people.

Fiedler's Research and Management

In reviewing Fiedler's research, one finds that there is nothing automatic or "good" in either the task-oriented or the people-oriented style. Leadership effectiveness depends on the various elements in the group environment. This might be expected. Cast in the desired role of leaders, managers who apply knowledge to the realities of the group reporting to them will do well to recognize that they are practicing

FIGURE 15.4 Fiedler's model of leadership

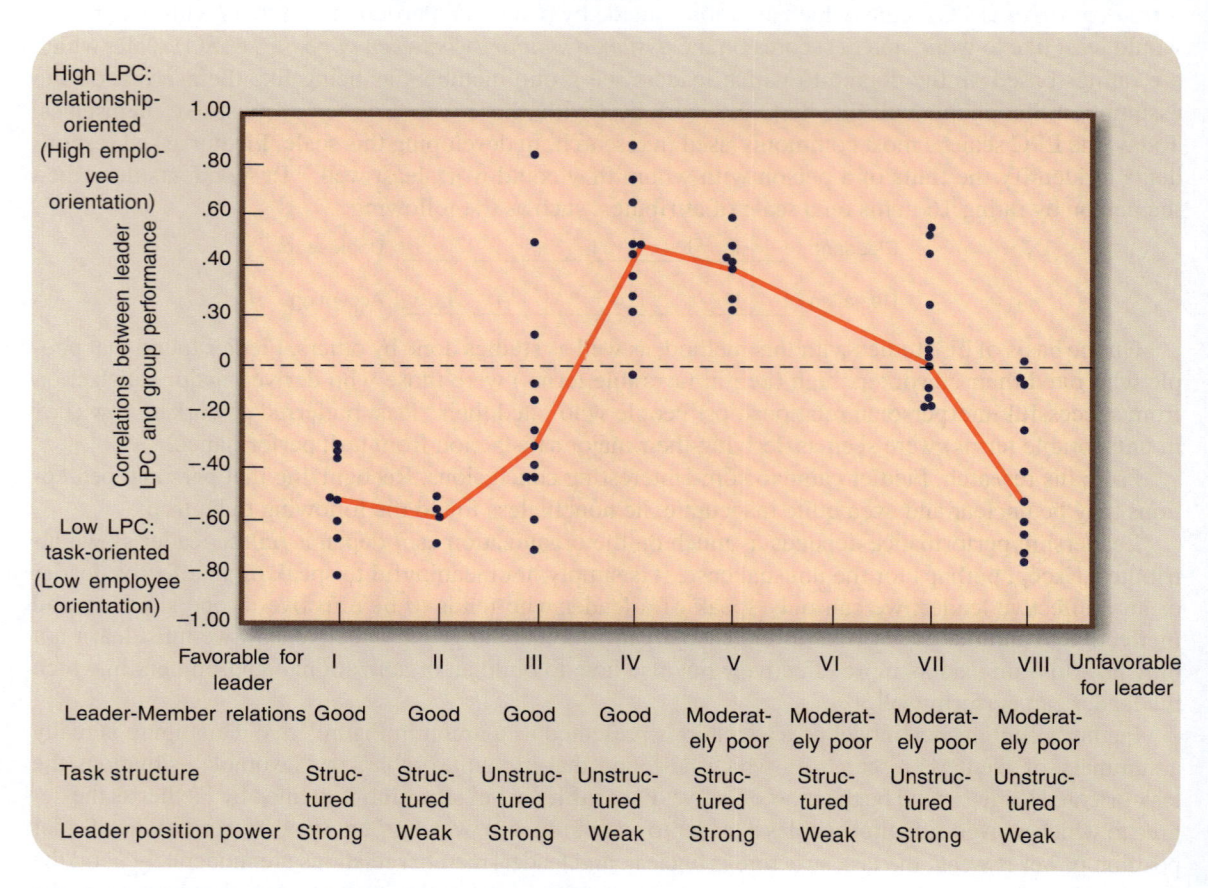

	I	II	III	IV	V	VI	VII	VIII
	Favorable for leader							Unfavorable for leader
Leader-Member relations	Good	Good	Good	Good	Moderately poor	Moderately poor	Moderately poor	Moderately poor
Task structure	Structured	Structured	Unstructured	Unstructured	Structured	Structured	Unstructured	Unstructured
Leader position power	Strong	Weak	Strong	Weak	Strong	Weak	Strong	Weak

Y-axis: Correlations between leader LPC and group performance, ranging from −1.00 (Low LPC: task-oriented / Low employee orientation) to 1.00 (High LPC: relationship-oriented / High employee orientation).

Each dot in the graph represents findings from a research study.
Source: F. E. Fiedler, "Fiedler's Model of Leadership", *A Theory of Leadership Effectiveness*.

an art. But in doing so, they will necessarily take into account the motivations to which group members will respond and their ability to satisfy the members in the interest of attaining enterprise goals.

Several scholars have put Fiedler's theory to the test in various situations. Some have questioned the meaning of the LPC score, and others have suggested that the model does not explain the causal effect of the LPC score on performance. Some of the findings are not statistically significant, and situational measures may not be completely independent of the LPC score.

Despite such criticisms, it is important to recognize that effective leadership style depends on the situation. Although this idea may not be new, Fiedler and his colleagues drew attention to this fact and stimulated a great deal of research.

The Path–Goal Approach to Leadership Effectiveness

The **path–goal theory** suggests that the main function of the leader is to clarify and set goals with subordinates, help them find the best path for achieving the goals, and remove obstacles. Proponents of this approach have studied leadership in a variety of situations; and as stated by Robert House, the theory builds on various motivational and leadership theories of others.[22]

The theory proposes that situational factors contributing to effective leadership should be considered. These factors include (1) the characteristics of subordinates, such as their needs, self-confidence, and abilities; and (2) the work environment, including such components as the task, the reward system, and the relationship with coworkers (see Figure 15.5).

The theory categorizes leader behavior into four groups:

1. *Supportive leadership* behavior gives consideration to the needs of subordinates, shows concern for their well-being, and creates a pleasant organizational climate. It has the greatest impact on subordinates' performance when they are frustrated and dissatisfied.
2. *Participative leadership* allows subordinates to influence the decisions of their superiors, which may increase motivation.
3. *Instrumental leadership* gives subordinates rather specific guidance and clarifies what is expected of them. It involves aspects of planning, organizing, coordinating, and controlling by the leader.
4. *Achievement-oriented leadership* involves setting challenging goals, seeking improvement of performance, and having confidence that subordinates will achieve high goals.

Path–goal theory The main function of the leader is to clarify and set goals with subordinates, help them find the best path for achieving the goals, and remove obstacles.

FIGURE 15.5 Path-goal approach to leadership effectiveness

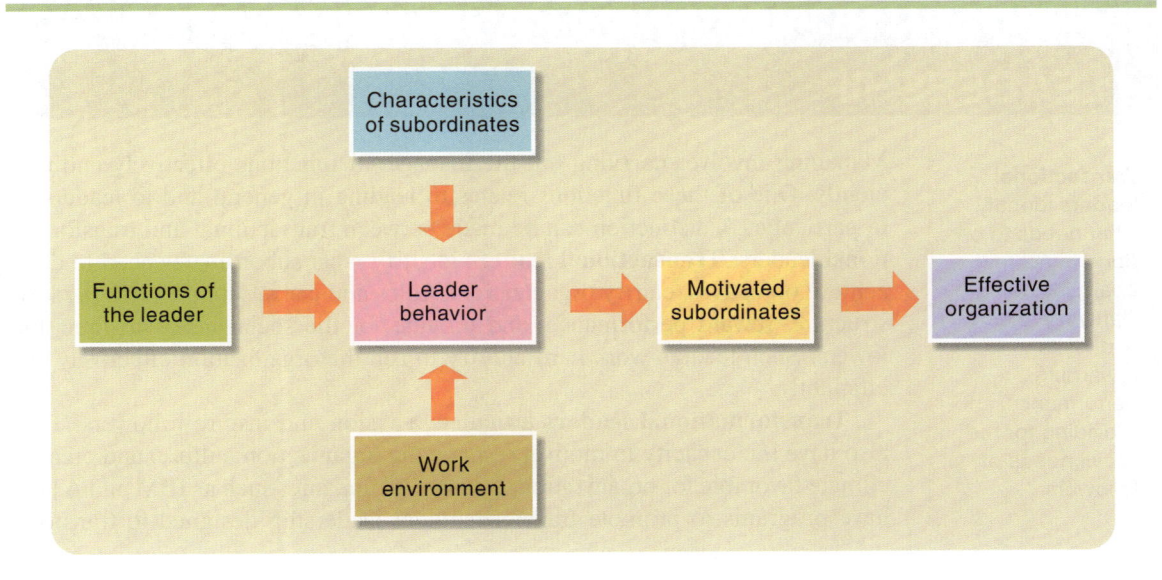

Rather than suggesting that there is one best way to lead, this theory suggests that the appropriate style depends on the situation. Ambiguous and uncertain situations can be frustrating for subordinates, and a more task-oriented style may be called for. In other words, when subordinates are confused, then the leader may tell them what to do and show them a clear path to goals. On the other hand, for routine tasks, such as those found on the assembly line, additional structure (usually provided by a task-oriented leader) may be considered redundant; subordinates may see such efforts as overcontrolling, which in turn may be dissatisfying. To put it differently, employees want the leader to stay out of their way because the path is already clear enough.

The theory proposes that the behavior of the leader is acceptable and satisfies subordinates to the extent that they see it as a source of their satisfaction. Another proposition of the theory is that the behavior of the leader increases the effort of subordinates—that is, it is motivating—insofar as (1) this behavior makes satisfaction of the needs of subordinates dependent on effective performance and (2) the behavior enhances the subordinates' environment through coaching, directing, supporting, and rewarding.

The key to the theory is that the leader influences the path between behavior and goals. The leader can do this by defining positions and task roles, by removing obstacles to performance, by enlisting the assistance of group members in setting goals, by promoting group cohesiveness and team effort, by increasing opportunities for personal satisfaction in work performance, by reducing stresses and external controls, by making expectations clear, and by meeting members' expectations.

The path–goal theory makes a great deal of sense to the practicing manager. At the same time, one must realize that the model needs further testing before the approach can be used as a definite guide for managerial action.

TRANSACTIONAL AND TRANSFORMATIONAL LEADERSHIP

Transactional leaders identify what needs to be done to achieve goals, including clarifying roles and tasks, rewarding performance, and providing for the social needs of followers.

Managing involves carrying out the managerial functions effectively and efficiently. One of these functions relates to leading in general and to leadership in particular. A distinction can be made between transactional and transformational leaders. **Transactional leaders** identify what subordinates need to do to achieve objectives, clarify organizational roles and tasks, set up an organization structure, reward performance, and provide for the social needs of their followers. Such leaders work hard and try to run the organization effectively and efficiently.

Transformational leaders articulate a vision and inspire followers. They also have the capacity to motivate, shape the organization culture, and create a climate favorable for organizational change. Companies such as IBM and AT&T have programs to promote transformational leadership designed to transform their organizations quickly to respond to the rapid changes in the environment. There are many similarities between transformational leaders and charismatic leaders, with the former being noted for initiating innovation and change. When one thinks of charismatic leaders, one thinks of people such as Winston Churchill, Martin Luther King, and Mother Teresa, who inspired people through their selfless service to the poor.

Transformational leaders articulate a vision, inspire and motivate followers, and create a climate favorable for organizational change.

www.ibm.com

www.att.com

ENTREPRENEURIAL PERSPECTIVE

Leadership at the Chinese Haier Group and Volkswagen[23]

Mr. Zhang Ruimin is the founder and CEO of the Haier Group, the most widely recognized home appliances manufacturer in China. Its many products include refrigerators, air conditioners, freezers, and microwave ovens. During China's Cultural Revolution, Mr. Zhang was sent to work in a metal processing plant, which may have helped him later in leading the appliance firm.

With the opening of China, Zhang became familiar with Harvard professor Michael Porter's book on competitive strategy, which emphasizes the importance of recognizing customer needs. Moreover, General Electric's approach to quality management and the emphasis on corporate culture illustrated by its CEO, Jack Welch, also influenced Zhang's view of managing.

Quality was Mr. Zhang's major concern. When visiting his refrigerator company, he noted that many of the products were defective. To demonstrate his passion for quality, he had the brand new refrigerators destroyed in a dramatic fashion. Needless to say, the workers were impressed, not only by Zhang's commitment to quality but also by his 14-hour daily work schedule. Uncommon in China at that time, he tied good performance of employees to monetary rewards and promotions. He also adopted other managerial practices learned from his German partner company, Liebherr.

His leadership by example transformed the bureaucratic enterprise into the Haier Group, which is now the best-known Chinese refrigerator company and operates in many countries, including the United States. But a leader cannot rest on accomplishments; a leader must articulate a vision for the future. Guided by Mr. Zhang's foresight, Haier ventured into computers and pharmaceuticals. The entrance of China into the World Trade Organization in 2001 not only has opened opportunities but also presents new challenges for the Haier Group. Mr. Zhang's leadership illustrates that Western management practices can be transferred to countries such as China.

While Mr. Zhang Ruimin may have benefited from the German managerial practices, Volkswagen's top manager Wolfgang Bernhard adopted some managerial approaches from the Americans. Bernhard received his M.B.A. from the Columbia Business School. He worked for the McKinsey consulting firm and later DaimlerChrysler. He then was hired by Mercedes being put on the fast-track promotion path. When this path was cut short, he got a top management position at Volkswagen being responsible for the VW brand. His task was to reduce the cost and develop new models, a task he did previously at Chrysler. Using his Chrysler experience, he ordered a study that found that VW needed twice the time to assemble a car when compared with its most efficient competitor.

Rather than following the traditional German way of delegating tasks to the appropriate departments, Bernhard assembled 200 VW people in an auditorium with the objective to reduce the costs of the newly planned Sport Utility Vehicle by $2,500. They were not to go back to their workplace until the objective was reached. Each evening, Bernard watched the progress of the teams who worked until late at night to complete their task. After four weeks of hard work, the goal was achieved through team effort. This illustrates that German managers as they gain international experience can transfer their skills and approaches to their home country.

www.haier.com

www.ge.com

www.liebherr.com

http://www.vw.com

OTHER LEADERSHIP THEORIES AND APPROACHES[24]

With the great interest in leadership, many approaches developed as discussed in this book. In addition, there are others such as the *emotional intelligence* approach that focuses on personal competence (self-awareness and self-regulation) and social competence (social awareness and relationship management).

Still another popular situational model was developed by *Hersey and Blanchard* that discusses delegating, participating, selling, and telling. In addition, Fred Luthans lists some new, emerging theories such as e-leadership, contextual, political, positive, primal, relational, responsible, servant, and shared leadership. Luthans and Avolio then introduce their own approach which they called *authentic leadership*.

SUMMARY

Leadership is the art or process of influencing people so that they contribute willingly and enthusiastically toward group goals. Leadership requires followership. There are various approaches to the study of leadership, ranging from the trait to the contingency approach. One such approach focuses on three styles: autocratic, democratic or participative, and free-rein.

The managerial grid identifies two dimensions: concern for production and concern for people. On the basis of these dimensions, four extreme styles and a "middle-of-the-road" style are identified. Leadership can also be viewed as a continuum. At one extreme of the continuum, the manager has a great deal of freedom, while subordinates have very little. At the other extreme, the manager has very little freedom, whereas subordinates have a great deal.

Still another approach to leadership, built on the assumption that leaders are the product of given situations, focuses on the study of situations. Fiedler's contingency approach takes into account the position power of the leader, the structure of the task, and the relations between the leader and group members. The conclusion is that there is no one best leadership style and that managers can be successful if placed in appropriate situations. The path–goal approach to leadership suggests that the most effective leaders help subordinates achieve enterprise as well as personal goals. Transactional leaders clarify roles and tasks, set up a structure, and help followers achieve objectives. Transformational leaders articulate a vision, inspire others, and transform the organization. Transformational and charismatic leadership concepts are similar.

KEY IDEAS AND CONCEPTS FOR REVIEW

Leadership
Ingredients of leadership
Principle of leadership
Leadership traits
Charismatic leadership
Leadership styles based on the use of authority
Managerial grid
Leadership as a continuum
Situational approach to leadership
Fiedler's contingency theory
Path–goal approach to leadership
Transactional leader
Transformational leader

FOR DISCUSSION

1. What do you see as the essence of leadership?
2. How are leadership theory and styles related to motivation?
3. Why has the trait approach as a means of explaining leadership been so open to question?
4. Can you see why the managerial grid has been so popular as a training device?
5. Select a business or political leader whom you admire, and identify his or her style of leading by applying the managerial grid or the continuum-of-behavior model of Tannenbaum and Schmidt.
6. What is Fiedler's theory of leadership? Applying it to cases of leaders whom you have known, do you perceive it as being accurate?
7. What are the advantages and limitations of the path–goal approach to leadership?
8. If you were selected to be the group leader for a class project (e.g., to make a case study of a particular company), which leadership style or what behavior would you use? Why?

EXERCISES/ACTION STEPS

1. Analyze a situation in which you were the leader. Which leadership approach discussed in this chapter helps explain why you were a leader?
2. Analyze a case in this book using the group approach. Specifically, the class should be divided into groups of about five students. Each group should select a spokesperson, who will present the case analysis to the class. For each group, one observer (this person should not be a participant in the case discussion) should describe the interactions in the group. Was there a leader in the group? If the answer is yes, why was he or she considered a leader? Was it owing to his or her personality, the other group members (followers), or the nature of the task (situation)? Explain the group processes in light of any leadership theory or concepts discussed in this chapter.

INTERNET RESEARCH

1. Use any search engine to find sources for the term "business leadership". Do you find different views on leadership?
2. Jack Welch of General Electric is considered by many an effective leader and manager. Scan the Internet for "Jack Welch" and identify his leadership behavior.

INNOVATION CASE

Profiles of Two Visionaries: Bill Gates and Steve Jobs[25]

Two men who gave their hearts and souls to developing their visions have driven the personal computer (PC) revolution. However, the way in which either of these men went about this quest has been different. Steve Jobs and Bill Gates have changed the way the world does business, but the story of their leadership styles is even more compelling than the success and innovation spawned by Apple and Microsoft.

Bill Gates versus Steve Jobs: The Early Years
Bill Gates started developing his computer skills with his childhood friend Paul Allen at the Lakeside School in Seattle. At the age of 14, the two had formed their first computer company. After high school, Allen and Gates left Seattle for Boston. Gates went off to Harvard and Allen began working for Honeywell. After only

two years at Harvard, Gates left and Allen left Boston for Albuquerque to develop a computer language for the new Altair 8080 PC. This computer language would become BASIC and the foundation for Microsoft, which was created as a partnership in 1975.

After five years in New Mexico, Microsoft relocated to Bellevue, Washington, in 1980 with BASIC and two other computer languages (COBOL and FORTRAN) in its arsenal. Later that year, IBM began developing its first PC and was in need of an operating system. Microsoft developed the Microsoft disk operating system (MS-DOS) for IBM while two other companies created competing systems. Eventually, Gates's determination and persuasion made MS-DOS IBM's default platform.

As Microsoft became more successful, Gates realized that he needed help for running the company. His enthusiasm, vision, and hard work were the driving force behind the company's growth, but he recognized the need for professional management. Gates hired one of his friends from Harvard, Steve Ballmer who had worked for Procter & Gamble after graduating from Harvard and was pursuing his MBA at Stanford. Gates persuaded Ballmer to leave school and join Microsoft. Over the years, Ballmer became an indispensable asset to both Gates and Microsoft. In 1983, Gates continued to show his brilliance by hiring Jon Shriley, who brought order to Microsoft and streamlined the organization structure, while Ballmer served as an advisor and sounding board for Gates. Microsoft continued to grow and prosper in the 1990s, dominating both the operating system market with its Windows and the office suite software market with Microsoft Office.

Gates recognized that his role was to be the visionary of the company, but he needed professional managers to run Microsoft. He combined his unyielding determination and passion with a well-structured management team to make Microsoft the giant it is today.

The other visionary, Steve Jobs and his friend Steve Wozniak started Apple Computer in Jobs's garage in Los Altos, California, in 1976. In contrast to Bill Gates, Jobs and Wozniak were hardware experts and started with a vision for a personal computer that was affordable and easy to use. When Microsoft offered the BASIC program to Apple, Jobs immediately dismissed the idea on the basis that he and Wozniak could create their own version of BASIC in a weekend. This was typical Jobs: decisive and almost maniacal at times. Jobs eventually agreed to license Microsoft's BASIC while pursuing his own vision of developing a more usable and friendly interface for the computer.

Many see Jobs as the anti-Gates. He is a trailblazer and a creator as opposed to Gates, who is more of a consolidator of industry standards. Jobs's goal was to change the world with his computers. He was also very demanding of his employees. Clearly Jobs was different from Gates, Allen, and Wozniak. He was not a hardcore computer programmer but the person selling the idea of the PC to the public. Jobs made the decision to change the direction of Apple by developing the Macintosh (Mac) using a new graphical user interface that introduced the world to the mouse and on-screen icons. Jobs's strategy forced people to choose between the Microsoft–IBM operating system and his Mac operating system. In the beginning, Jobs was the visionary who changed the computer world. With its early success, a major problem began brewing at Apple: Steve Jobs was overconfident and did not see Gates and Microsoft as a serious threat to Apple.

Soon after the release of the Macintosh computer, Jobs asked Microsoft to develop software for the Mac operating system. Gates obliged and proceeded to launch a project copying and improving Apple's user interface. The outcome of that venture was Microsoft Windows.

A cocky attitude and lack of management skills made Jobs a threat to Apple's success. He never bothered to develop budgets, and his relationship with his employees was criticized. Wozniak left Apple after the release of the Mac because of differences with Jobs. In 1985, John Scully, CEO of PepsiCo, replaced Steve Jobs as president and CEO of Apple Computer.

Microsoft and Apple at the Turn of the Century: An Industry Giant and a Revitalized Leader

With the success of Windows, the Office application suite, and Internet Explorer, Microsoft became a household name and Bill Gates was hailed as a business genius. The fact that Microsoft's competitors, the press, and the U.S. Justice Department have called Microsoft a monopoly reinforced Gates's determination to succeed. Many people questioned whether Microsoft could survive the Justice Department's decision. Bill Gates, however, did show that he was the master of adapting to changing market conditions and technologies.

Apple did go in the opposite direction in the 1990s. The outdated operating system and falling market share eventually led to a decrease in software development for the Mac. Something needed to be done. In 1998, Steve Jobs returned to Apple as the "interim" CEO. His vision, once again, resulted in the innovative iMac. The design is classic Jobs. In the 1980s, he created the simple-to-operate Mac to attract people who were using IBM PCs and their clones. He developed a simple, stylish, and Internet-friendly computer that added much-needed excitement in the computer market. After his return to Apple, Jobs had also changed as a manager and as a leader. He had matured and looked to his professional staff for advice and ideas. Although he was the interim CEO, Jobs did sell all but one share of his Apple stocks. Larry Ellison, Oracle's CEO and Apple board member, attributes Jobs's ability to lead Apple to this statement: "He owns only one share of Apple stock, yet he clearly owns the product and the idea behind the company. The Mac is an expression of his creativity, and Apple as a whole is an expression of Steve. That's why, despite the 'interim' in his title, he'll stay at Apple for a long time."[26] Many people agreed that Jobs's return would lead to continued success for Apple and a renewed battle between Gates and Jobs.

Gates and Jobs in 2011[27]

While the battle between Apple and Microsoft continued, Steve Jobs passed away in October 2011 and Bill Gates stepped down as CEO in the year 2000 and is now occupied with his philanthropic work at the Bill & Melinda Gates Foundation. Steve Jobs will be remembered for his innovations like other pioneers such as Henry Ford and Thomas Edison that also had a major impact on our lives.

Questions:

1. How did Bill Gates and Steve Jobs differ in their leadership style?
2. Compare and contrast the managerial practices of Gates and Jobs.
3. What do you think about the future of Microsoft and Apple Computer?

ENDNOTES

1. Kris Hudson, "Turning Shopping Trips into Treasure Hunts", *The Wall Street Journal,* August 27, 2007. Alan B. Goldberg and Bill Ritter, "Costco CEO Finds Pro-Worker Means Profitability", *20/20 ABC News,* August 2, 2006.
2. See also James O'Toole, "The True Measure of a CEO—Aristotle Has Something to Say About Than", in Fred H. Maidment, ed. *Annual Editions—Management* (New York: McGraw-Hill 2009), pp. 92–95 and Noel M. Tichy and Warren G. Bennis, "Making Judgment Calls—The Ultimate Act of Leadership", in Fred H. Maidment, ed. *Annual Editions-Management* (New York: McGraw-Hill 2009), pp. 96–102.
3. John Kotter distinguishes between management and leadership. He views management as dealing with complexities, practices, and procedures, primarily responding to emergencies in large organizations. In contrast, leadership is considered as coping with change. Leadership and management are considered complementary. See John P. Kotter, "What Leaders Really Do", *Harvard Business Review*, December 2001 (first published 1990).
4. For other definitions of leadership, see Warren Bennis and James O'Toole, "Don't Hire the Wrong CEO," *Harvard Business Review*, May–June 2000.
5. Dean Foust, "US Airways: After the 'Miracle on the Hudson'", *Business Week,* March 2, 2009, p. 31.
6. See also Howard Gardner, *Leading Minds: An Anatomy of Leadership* (New York: Basic Books, 1995); Warren Bennis, "The Leader as Storyteller," *Harvard Business Review*, January–February 1996, pp. 154–160.
7. "Letter from Steve Jobs", http://www.apple.com/pr/library/2011/08/24Letter-from-Steve-Jobs.html, accessed January 5, 2016.
8. John J. Gabarro and John P. Kotter, "Managing Your Boss," *Harvard Business Review*, January–February 2000.
9. C. Pete Engardio, "The Last Rajah," *Business Week,* August 13, 2007; http://www.rediff.com/cms/print.jsp?docpath=//money/2007/aug/08tata.htm, accessed November 17, 2011; "Complementing for Complexity: Leading Through Managing," http://www.etgmr.com/jan_mar05/style.html, accessed January 5, 2016; "Tata, Leadership with Trust," http://www.tata.com/, accessed May 9, 2014.
10. One popular approach in classifying personality traits is the Meyers-Briggs Type Indicator (MBTI). Carl Jung, *Psychological Types* (London Routledge and Kegan Paul, 1923); N. L. Quenk, *Essentials of Myers-Briggs Type Indicator Assessment* (New York: Wiley, 2000).
11. Ralph M. Stogdill, *Handbook of Leadership: A Survey of Theory and Research* (New York: Free Press, 1974). See also his earlier study, "Personal Factors Associated with Leadership: A Survey of the Literature," *Journal of Psychology*, 1948, 25: 35–71. For a discussion of Russian leadership traits, see Sheila M. Puffer, "Understanding the Bear: A Portrait of Russian Business Leaders," *Academy of Management Executive*, February 1994, pp. 41–54.
12. Robert J. House, "A 1976 Theory of Charismatic Leadership," in J. G. Hunt and L. L. Larson, eds. *Leadership: The Cutting Edge* (Carbondale, IL: Southern Illinois University Press, 1977).
13. See, for example, Jay A. Conger and Rabrinda N. Kanung, *Charismatic Leadership in Organizations* (Thousand Oaks, CA: Sage, 1996); R. W. Rowden, "The Relationship between Charismatic Leadership Behaviors and Organizational Commitment," *Leadership and Organization Development Journal*, January 2000, pp. 30–35; D. Goleman, *Emotional Intelligence* (New York: Bantam, 1995).
14. Interview conducted by Mark Cannice with Kern Peng of Intel by email in October 2012.
15. *The Managerial Grid* (Houston, TX: Gulf Publishing Company, 1954) and *Building a Dynamic Corporation Through Grid Organization Development* (Reading, MA: Addison-Wesley Publishing Company, Inc., 1969). The grid concept has been further refined in Robert R. Blake and Jane S. Mouton, *The Versatile Manager: A Grid Profile* (Homewood, IL: Richard D. Irwin, 1981); and by the same authors, *The Managerial Grid III* (Houston, TX: Gulf Publishing Company, 1985).
16. Robert Tannenbaum and Warren H. Schmidt, "How to Choose a Leadership Pattern," reprinted with a commentary by the authors, *Harvard Business Review*, May–June 1973, pp. 162–180.
17. Chris Lowney, *Pope Francis: Why He Leads the Way He Leads* (Chicago: Loyola Press. Kindle Edition retrieved, 2016); Austen Ivereigh, *The Great Reformer—Francis and the Making of a Radical Pope* (New York: Henry Holt and Company, 2014); John L. Allen, Jr. *Against the Tide—The Racial Leadership of Pope Francis* (Liguori Missouri: Liguori Publications, 2014); Jeffrey A. Krames, *Lead with Humility—12 Leadership Lessons from Pope Francis* (New York: AMACOM, Jeffrey A. Krames 2015).
18. Shawn Tully, "This Pope Means Business," *Fortune*, August 14, 2014.
19. Fred E. Fiedler, *A Theory of Leadership Effectiveness* (New York: McGraw-Hill, 1967). See also Fred E. Fiedler and Martin M. Chemers, *Leadership and Effective Management* (Glenview, IL: Scott, Foresman and Company, 1974); Fred E. Fiedler and Martin M. Chemers, with Linda Mahar, *Improving Leadership Effectiveness* (New York: Wiley, 1977).
20. Fiedler, *A Theory of Leadership Effectiveness*, p. 41.
21. Ibid., p. 261.
22. Robert J. House, "A Path–Goal Theory of Leadership Effectiveness," *Administrative Science Quarterly*, September 1971, pp. 321–338; Robert J. House and Terence R. Mitchell, "Path–Goal Theory of Leadership," in Harold Koontz, Cyril O'Donnell, and Heinz Weihrich, eds. *Management: A Book of Readings*, 5th ed. (New York: McGraw-Hill, 1980), pp. 533–40; Alan C. Filley, Robert J. House, and Steven Kerr, *Managerial Process and Organizational Behavior* (Glenview, IL: Scott, Foresman and Company, 1976), chap. 12.
23. "Zhang Ruimin, CEO, Haier Group China," *Business Week Online*, www.businessweek.com, June 14, 1999; "Haier Rises through Reform and Opening Up," *People's Daily*, August 8, 2001; "The Haier Group (A)," Harvard Business School Case 9-398-101, rev. July 13, 1999; Michael Arndt, "Can Haier Freeze out Whirlpool and GE?" *Business Week*, April 11, 2002; Stephen Power, "Top Volkswagen Executive Tries U.S.-Style Turnaround Tactics," *The Wall Street Journal*, July 18, 2006.
24. Daniel Goleman, "Leadership That Gets Results," *Harvard Business Review*, (March-April 2000); Paul Hersey and Kenneth H. Blanchard, *Management and Organizational Behavior* (Englewood Cliffs, N.J. Prentice Hall, 1988); Fred Luthans, *Organizational Behavior, An Evidence-Based Approach* (New York: McGraw-Hill, 2011), Chapter 13.
25. A variety of sources have been used, including Philip Rosenzweig, "Bill Gates and the Management of Microsoft," Harvard Business School Case, July 8, 1993; Philip Elmer-DeWitt, "Steve Jobs: Apple's Anti-Gates," *Time*, December 7, 1998, p. 205ff.; Susan King, "Pirates of a Modern Age," *Los Angeles Times*, June 20, 1999, p. 3ff.; Walter Isaacson, "In Search of the Real Bill Gates," *Time*, January 13, 1997, p. 44ff.; Bill Gates, *The Road Ahead* (New York: Penguin, 1996); Jay Green and others, "On to the Living Room: Can Microsoft Control the Digital Home?" *Business Week*, January 21, 2002, pp. 68–71; Cliff Edwards, "Come on, Steve, Think beyond the Mac," ibid., p. 72; "Microsoft: Extending Its Tentacles," *The Economist*, October 20, 2001, pp. 59–61; Steve Jobs, CEO, www.apple.com/pr/bios/jobs.html, accessed August 19, 2011; See also Apple Computer, www.apple.com, accessed August 19, 2011. Microsoft, "Microsoft," www.microsoft.com, accessed August 19, 2011; IBM, "IBM," www.ibm.com, accessed August 19, 2011.
26. Brent Schlender, "The Three Faces of Steve," *Fortune*, November 9, 1998, p. 96ff.
27. "Walt Mossberg: Jobs Will be Remembered Like Ford, Edison", http://marketplace.publicradio.org/display/web/2011/10/06/am-walt-mossberg-jobs-will-be-remembered-like-ford-edison, accessed January 5, 2016.

CHAPTER 16

Committees, Teams, and Group Decision Making

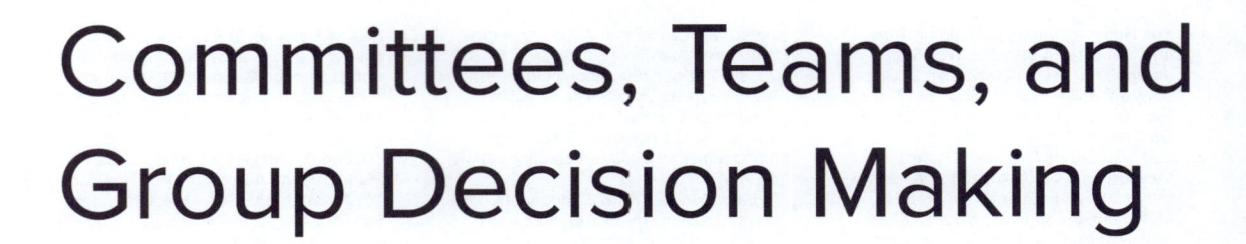

Learning Objectives

After studying this chapter, you should be able to:

LO 1	Explain the nature of various types of committees and groups
LO 2	Outline the reasons why committees and groups are used, with special attention to their use in decision making
LO 3	Present the disadvantages of committees, especially in decision making
LO 4	Discuss the requirements for using committees effectively
LO 5	Explain various group concepts
LO 6	Understand the nature of teams, team building, self-managing teams, and virtual teams
LO 7	Recognize conflict in committees, groups, and organizations

One of the most ubiquitous devices of organization is the committee. Whether it is referred to as a board, commission, task force, team, self-managing team, self-managed work group, or autonomous work group, its essential nature is similar. A **committee** is a group of persons to whom, as a group, some matter is committed. It is this characteristic of group action that sets the committee and team apart from other organizational devices, although, as will be seen, not all committees involve group decision making. As shown later in this chapter, the definition of *team* is similar. Therefore, much of the discussion of committees also pertains to teams, although this term may not be repeatedly used.

> **Committee** Group of persons to whom, as a group, some matter is committed.

THE NATURE OF COMMITTEES AND GROUPS

Because of variation in the authority assigned to committees, much confusion has resulted as to their nature.

Group Processes in Committees

Some say that groups go through four stages: (1) *forming*, when the members of the group get to know each other; (2) *storming*, when the members of the group determine the objective of the meeting and conflict arises; (3) *norming*, when the group agrees on norms and some rules of behavior; and (4) *performing*, when the group gets down to the task. While these characteristics may be found in most groups, they may not necessarily follow these sequential steps.

People play certain roles in committees. Some seek information; others give information. Some try to encourage others to contribute; others are followers. Finally, some try to coordinate the group's effort or to achieve a compromise when disagreements occur, while others take a more aggressive role.

To be effective in a group, one must not only listen to what is said but also observe the nonverbal behavior. Furthermore, noting the seating of members may give clues as to the social bonds among the group participants. Those who know each other often sit next to each other. The seating arrangement may have an impact on the group interaction. Often the chairperson sits at the head of a rectangular table. However, at Daimler-Benz, the maker of Mercedes-Benz cars, the board of directors sits at a round table to deemphasize the position of the chairperson.

> Four stages of group development: forming, storming, norming, and performing.

> www.mercedes.com

Functions and Formality of Committees and Groups

Some committees and teams undertake the managerial functions of planning, organizing, staffing, leading, and controlling, while others do not. Some make decisions, while others merely deliberate on problems without authority to decide. Some have authority to make recommendations to a manager, who may or

Plural executive Line committee that also carries out managerial functions, such as the board of directors.

may not accept them, while others are formed to receive information, without making recommendations or decisions.

A committee may have either line or staff functions, depending on its authority. If its authority involves decision making affecting subordinates it is responsible for, it is a **plural executive**—a *line committee* that also carries out managerial functions, such as the board of directors. If its authority relationship to a superior is advisory, then it is a *staff committee*.

GLOBAL PERSPECTIVE

Corporate Governance[1]

Recently, the boards of directors in U.S. companies have come under intense scrutiny by the Securities and Exchange Commission and other groups because of accounting impropriety at organizations such as Tyco (a conglomerate), WorldCom (a telecommunication company), and Enron (an energy trader) that led to two of the largest bankruptcy cases in U.S. history. There is a call for strengthening the board of directors, a plural executive committee. Among the recommendations by various groups are the following:

- Change the accounting standards and audit regulations.
- Publish ethical and corporate governance guidelines on the company's web site.
- Strengthen the role of independent directors.
- Make the board accountable to shareholders and involve shareholders in selecting board members.
- Obtain greater involvement of institutional investors (such as pension fund managers).
- Separate the job of the chairperson from that of the chief executive officer (CEO).
- Get the board more actively involved in selecting the CEO.

Other countries are also reviewing corporate governance. For example, German companies have two boards. The supervisory board provides oversight, while the management board is responsible for managing the firm. Recently, there is a drive to publish the pay of top managers, which in the past was considered a private matter. There is also the push to increase the supervisory board's supervision of the activities of the management board. In France and Italy, the governance issue has not yet become a major issue. For example, in the Italian Fiat Company, families hold a large portion of shares. Still, the publicity on corporate scandals may raise awareness of the role of corporate governance.

www.tyco.com

www.enron.com

Committees may also be formal or informal. If established as part of the organization structure, with specifically delegated duties and authority, they are *formal*. Most committees with any permanence fall into this class. Committees that are *informal* are organized without specific delegation of authority, usually by some person desiring group thinking or a group decision on a particular problem. For example, a manager may have a problem on which he or she needs advice or agreement from other managers or specialists outside his or her department. The manager may therefore call a special meeting for the purpose of solving the problem.

Committees may be relatively *permanent*, or they may be *temporary*. One would expect formal committees to be more permanent than the informal ones, although this is not necessarily so. A formal committee might be established by order of a company president, with appropriate provision in the organization structure, for the sole purpose of studying the advisability of building a new factory and be disbanded immediately upon the completion of its task.

And an informal committee set up by the factory manager to advise on the improvement of product quality or to help coordinate delivery dates with sales commitments might continue indefinitely.

REASONS FOR USING COMMITTEES AND GROUPS

One need not look far for reasons for the widespread use of committees and teams. Although the committee is sometimes regarded as having democratic origins and as being characteristic of democratic society, the reasons for its existence go beyond mere desire for group participation. Committees are widely used even in authoritarian organizations.

Group Deliberation and Judgment

Perhaps the most important reason for the use of committees is the advantage of gaining group deliberation and judgment—a variation of the adage that "two heads are better than one". Very few important business problems fall entirely into one single enterprise function such as production, engineering, finance, or sales. Most problems require more knowledge, experience, and judgment than any individual possesses.

It should not be inferred that group judgment can be obtained only through the use of committees. The staff specialist who confers individually with many persons in a given phase of a problem can obtain group judgment without the formation of a committee. Similarly, an executive may ask key subordinates or other specialists for their analyses and recommendations. At times, group judgment can be obtained more efficiently this way, in terms of time, than by using the deliberations of a committee.

Dominant Logic

The dominant logic of the firm may be defined as a mindset or a worldview or a conceptualization of the business.[2] An organization's dominant logic can be thought of as the aggregation or subtlety negotiated compromise of the individual heuristics or biases of the firm's top decision makers. Individual biases may interact with each other in organizational decisions involving multiple contributors, whose cooperation and commitment are necessary for the organization to act.

CEOs may evolve unified, internally reinforcing configurations or "gestalts" among elements of strategy, structure and process. Organizations first coalesce and then rigidify around a leader's gestalt.[3] It is the combined or hierarchically determined impact of the top management team which forms the dominant logic of the firm, and from which strategic decisions are based. Their dominant logic is further ingrained, as the leaders of the firm look to past successes and formulate current strategies based on them. Dominant logic may then limit the choices that the committees or groups may consider.

Entrepreneurial teams may also be influenced by the dominant logic of the firm which develops from the founding team. Consider the dominant logic of Apple under Steve Jobs or Amazon under Jeff Bezos or Twitter under Jack Dorsey. How might the vision of the founder influence the dominant logic and performance of the to management team or the outcome of committees?

Fear of Too Much Authority in a Single Person

Another reason for the widespread use of committees is the fear of delegating too much authority to a single person. This fear, especially pronounced in government, dictated to the framers of the American Constitution not only the establishment of a two-house legislature and a multimember Supreme Court

www.supreme-courtus.gov

www.house.gov

www.whitehouse.gov

but also the division of the powers of government among the Congress, the Supreme Court, and the President. Despite this fear of centralized authority, the founders of the American republic placed the administration of laws in the hands of a single top executive. Yet, as President Nixon discovered, the legislature has the power to remove, or force the resignation, of the chief executive.

Representation of Interested Groups

Representation plays a part in the establishment and staffing of committees. Boards of directors are often selected on the basis of groups interested in the company and, perhaps more often, on the basis of groups in which the company has an interest. When executives have a particularly difficult internal problem involving managers and specialists in various departments and activities, they may choose members in such a way as to give these interested parties representation.

Coordination of Departments, Plans, and Policies

There is general agreement that committees are very useful for coordinating activities among various organizational units. They are also useful for coordinating plans and policies as well as their implementation. The dynamics of modern enterprises place a heavy burden on the managers to integrate plans and activities. A committee permits individuals not only to obtain first-hand knowledge of the plans and of their own role in the execution of them, but also to make suggestions for the improvement of plans.

Transmission and Sharing of Information

Committees are useful for transmitting and sharing information. All group members affected by a mutual problem or project can learn about it simultaneously, and decisions and instructions can be received uniformly with opportunities for clarification. This may save time. The spoken word may clarify a point better than even carefully written memorandums.

Consolidation of Authority

A manager in a department, branch, or section often has only a portion of the authority necessary to accomplish a program. This is known as *splintered authority*. One way to handle a problem in this situation is to refer it upward in the organizational hierarchy until it reaches a point at which the requisite authority exists. But this place is often in the office of the president, and the problem may not be of sufficient importance to be decided at that level.

For example, a customer of a machine tool manufacturer may wish a slight but unusual change in the design of a piece of equipment. The customer approaches the sales department, which (if there is no established procedure for handling this change) cannot act without the authority of the engineering, production, and cost estimating departments. In such a case, the sales manager might establish a special purpose team to study the problem, to agree on the nature and cost of the change, and to use the combined authority of its members to approve the request.

The informal use of committees gives much flexibility to an organization. However, consolidating splintered authority through a committee should be considered carefully. It should be determined whether the organization structure itself should be changed in order to concentrate in one position the appropriate authority to make recurring decisions.

Motivation Through Participation

Committees permit wide participation in decision making. People who take part in planning a program or making a decision usually feel more enthusiastic about accepting and executing it. Even limited participation can be helpful.

DISADVANTAGES AND MISUSE OF COMMITTEES

Although there are good reasons for using committees, there are also disadvantages of doing so. They are costly. They may result in compromises at the least common denominator rather than in an optimal decision. They may lead to indecision. They also can split responsibility. Finally, they can lead to a situation in which a few persons impose their will on the majority, not allowing participation of other members.

The committee form has often fallen into disrepute through misuse. In general, committees should not be used as a replacement for a manager, for research study, for unimportant decisions, and for decisions beyond the participants' authority.

GLOBAL PERSPECTIVE

What People Say about Committees

Disparaging attitudes toward committees are reflected in such sayings as the following:

- "A camel is a horse invented by a committee."
- "A committee is made up of the unfit selected by the unwilling to do the unnecessary."
- "A committee is a place where the loneliness of thought is replaced by the togetherness of nothingness."

SUCCESSFUL OPERATION OF COMMITTEES AND GROUPS

Managers spend a great deal of time in committees. The use of committees is due not only to the democratic tradition but also to a growing emphasis on group management and group participation in organizations. In attempting to overcome some of the disadvantages of committees, managers may find the following guidelines useful.

Authority

A committee's authority should be spelled out so that its members know whether their responsibility is to make decisions, make recommendations, or merely deliberate and give the chairperson some insights into the issue under discussion.

FIGURE 16.1 Increased complexity of relationships through increase in group size

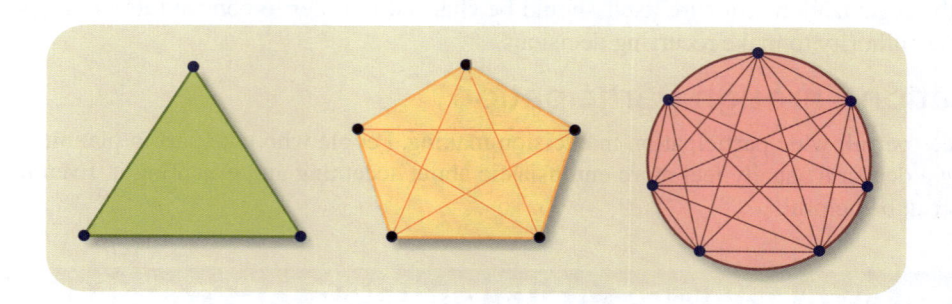

Size

> The **complexity of interrelationships** greatly increases with the size of the group.

The size of a committee is very important. As shown in Figure 16.1, the **complexity of interrelationships** greatly increases with the size of the group. If the group is too large, there may not be enough opportunities for adequate communication among its members. On the other hand, if the group consists of only three persons, there is the possibility that two may form a coalition against the third member. No precise conclusions can be drawn here about the appropriate size. As a general rule, a committee should be large enough to promote deliberation and include the breadth of expertise required for the job, but not so large as to waste time or foster indecision. It is obvious that the larger the group, the greater the difficulty in obtaining a "meeting of the minds" and the more time needed to allow everyone to contribute.

Membership

The members of a committee must be selected carefully. If a committee is to be successful, the members must be representatives of the interests they are expected to serve. They must also possess the required authority and be able to perform well in a group. Finally, the members should have the capacity for communicating well and reaching group decisions by integrated group thinking rather than by inappropriate compromise.

Subject Matter

The subject must be carefully selected. Committee work should be limited to subject matter that can be handled in group discussion. Certain kinds of subjects lend themselves to committee action, while others do not. Jurisdictional disputes and strategy formulation, for example, may be suitable for group deliberation, while an expert in the relevant specialized field may better solve certain isolated, technical problems. Committees will be more effective if an agenda and relevant information are circulated well in advance so that members can study the subject matter before the meeting.

Chairperson

The selection of the chairperson is crucial for an effective committee meeting. Such a person can avoid the wastes and drawbacks of committees by planning the meeting, preparing the agenda, seeing that the results of research are available to members ahead of time, formulating definite proposals for discussion or action, and conducting the meeting effectively. The chairperson sets the tone of the meeting, integrates the ideas, and keeps the discussion from wandering.

Minutes

Effective communication in committees usually requires circulating minutes and checking conclusions. At times, individuals leave a meeting with varying interpretations as to what agreements were reached. This can be avoided by taking careful minutes of the meeting and circulating them in draft form for correction or modification before the committee approves the final copy.

Cost-Effectiveness

A committee must be worth its costs. It may be difficult to count the benefits, especially such intangible factors as morale, enhanced status of committee members, and the committee's value as a training device to enhance teamwork. But the committee can be justified only if the costs are offset by tangible and intangible benefits.

ADDITIONAL GROUP CONCEPTS[4]

Although the committee is of special importance as an organizational device, it is really only one of many types of groups that are found in organizations. In addition to committees, there are teams, conferences, task forces, and negotiation sessions, all involving group activities.

A **group** may be defined as two or more people acting interdependently in a unified manner toward the achievement of common goals. A group is more than a collection of individuals; rather, through their interactions, new forces and new properties are created that need to be identified and studied in themselves. The goals may pertain to specific tasks, but they may also mean that the people share some common concerns or values or an ideology. Thus, group members are attracted to each other by some social bonds.

> **Group** Two or more people acting interdependently in a unified manner toward the achievement of common goals.

Characteristics of Groups

Groups—and the focus is on groups in an organization—have a number of characteristics. First, group members share one or more common goals, such as the goals of a product group to develop, manufacture, and market a new product. A second characteristic of groups is that they normally require interaction and communication among members. It is impossible to coordinate the efforts of group members without communication. Third, members within a group assume roles. In a product group, various individuals are responsible for designing, producing, selling, or distributing a product. Naturally, the roles are in some kind of relationship to each other in order to achieve the group task. Fourth, groups usually are a part of a larger group. The product group may belong to a product division that produces many products of a similar nature. Large groups may also consist of subgroups. Thus, within the product group may be a subgroup specializing exclusively in the selling of the product. Also, groups interface with other groups. Thus, product group A may cooperate with product group B in the distribution of their products. It is evident, then, that the systems point of view, which focuses on the interrelatedness of parts, is essential in understanding the functioning of groups.

There are a number of other sociological characteristics of groups that must be recognized. Groups develop **norms**, which refer to the expected behavior of the group members. If individuals deviate from the norms, pressure is exerted to make them comply. This can be functional when, for example, a person who frequently shows up late for work is admonished by other group members. But there are also situations in which groups may be dysfunctional. For example, ambitious, highly motivated employees may be pressed to produce in congruence with generally accepted norms rather than according to their abilities.

Norms Expected behavior of group members.

GLOBAL PERSPECTIVE

Pressure Toward Conformity: How Would You Respond?

In a widely publicized experiment, S. E. Asch showed the impact of group pressure toward conformity.[5] Members of a small group were asked to match a standard line (8 inches long) with three comparison lines (6¼, 8 and 6¾ inches long) (see Figure 16.2). One member of the group (the naive subject) was not aware that all the other students in the group (confederates of the experimenter) were instructed to occasionally give wrong answers, such as saying that the 6¾-inch line was as long as the 8-inch standard line. The setting was arranged so that the naive subject was one of the last ones to make a judgment. It was found that an "innocent" member made wrong choices when the confederates did so unanimously. In later interviews, subjects reported that they wanted to agree with the majority. This illustrates that, even in a rather uncomplicated task, people may decide against their better judgment owing to group pressure. These findings explain to some extent the influence of group pressure toward conformity and how it may result in managerial decisions that are less than optimal.

FIGURE 16.2 Which comparison line is the same length as the standard line?

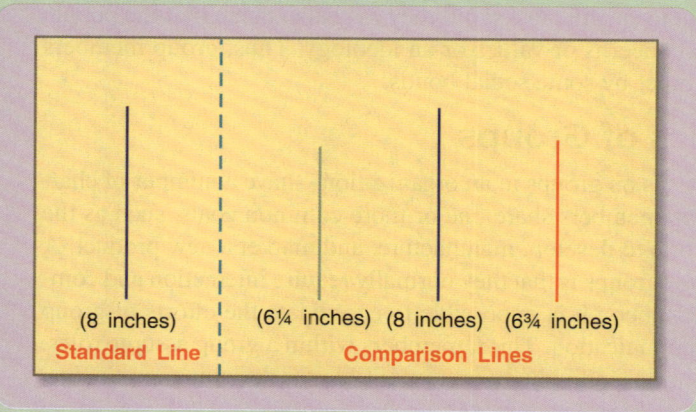

(8 inches)
Standard Line

(6¼ inches) (8 inches) (6¾ inches)
Comparison Lines

A Special Kind of Group: The Focus Group

Focus groups have been used for some time in market research. For example, actual or potential customers are asked in a group setting to comment on a product or service before large-scale research is undertaken. The comments may be taped or notes may be taken. The responses are then analyzed to determine the customers' attitudes, perceptions, or satisfaction with regard to the product or service.

Elements of focus groups have also been used in Europe. Germany's public participated in value forums to determine long-term energy policies. The experience indicated that the public can contribute to value forums, the participants were satisfied with this kind of procedure, and they were eager to help resolve inconsistencies.

Focus groups may also be used for evaluating managerial aspects within an organization. The Public Service Company of New Mexico established six focus groups to elicit responses about its performance appraisal, compensation, and benefits systems. On the basis of the findings, the company implemented a more flexible benefits program, a job redesign program, and a new decision-making process. Rather than imposing organizational changes, the company allowed the employees to become actively involved in the change process.

www.pnm.com

Functions and Advantages of Groups[6]

Groups have many functions. They are powerful in changing behavior, attitudes, and values and in disciplining members. As noted, deviant members may be pressured to adhere to group norms. In addition, groups are used for decision making, negotiating, and bargaining. Thus, group members with diverse backgrounds may bring different perspectives to the decision-making process. This does not mean, however, that group decisions are always better than individual decisions.

Group concepts are very important for the topics covered in other chapters in this book. Specifically, different group structures influence *communication* patterns. Thus, communication will differ when it is channeled through one key member or when it flows freely among all the group members. One can hardly consider a number of people as a team when each member communicates only with the boss; teamwork requires open communication among all members. Effective group interaction may also affect *motivation*. For example, group members participating in setting objectives may become committed to the achievement of group goals. Finally, *leadership* must be seen in the context of group processes. A grasp of group concepts helps in understanding the interactions between leaders and followers as well as among all the group members. In short, an understanding of groups is important for carrying out all managerial functions, particularly the function of leading. Groups are a fact of organized and unorganized life. It is important to know how they work and to use them in an effective and efficient manner in situations that favor group actions.

Groups also have advantages for individuals. Groups do provide social satisfaction for their members, a feeling of belonging, and support for the needs of individuals. Another benefit of groups is that they promote communication.

It may be the give-and-take in a formal meeting, or it can take the form of the grapevine, which is the informal communication through which group members become aware of "what is really going on in the organization". Groups also provide security. Labor unions are sometimes formed precisely for this reason—to give job security to their members. Finally, groups provide opportunities for promoting self-esteem through recognition from and acceptance by peers.

TEAMS[7]

Team Small number of people with complementary skills who are committed to a common purpose, set of performance goals, and approach for which they hold themselves mutually accountable.

www.boeing.com

A team consists of a number of people who are empowered to achieve team goals. As mentioned at the beginning of the chapter, committees, groups, and teams have similar characteristics. A **team** can be defined as "a small number of people with complementary skills who are committed to a common purpose, set of performance goals, and approach for which they hold themselves mutually accountable"[8]. As with committees, there are different types of teams. Some make recommendations, others have the power to make decisions, and still others actually run operations. Some teams are created to solve problems, such as quality circles; others engage in activities that cross functional areas, such as design, marketing, finance, manufacturing, personnel, and so on. Such cross-functional teams may be used for developing a new product or to improve the quality of a product or service. For example, in the design and development of the Boeing 777 airliner, some 200 cross-functional teams were involved. It is clear that what has been said about committees also applies to teams.

Team Building[9]

There are no definite rules for building effective teams. The following approaches, however, were found to be useful. Team members must be convinced that the team's purpose is worthwhile, meaningful, and urgent. Team members should also be selected according to the skills needed to achieve the purpose. Teams should have the right mix of skills, such as functional or technical skills, problem-solving and decision-making skills, and of course human relations skills. The team needs to be guided by rules for group behavior, such as regular attendance, confidentiality, discussions based on facts, and everyone contributing. Goals and required tasks should be identified early in team formation. Members should encourage each other through recognition, positive feedback, and rewards.

Self-Managing Teams[10]

Self-managing team Group with members who have a variety of skills needed to carry out a relatively complete task.

Recently, organizations have used self-managing teams, which usually consist of members who have a variety of skills needed to carry out a relatively complete task. Thus, such a team may have the power to determine what needs to be done, how it will be done, when it needs to be completed, and who is going to do it. Team members may also be evaluated and rewarded as a group. Especially when the team has a great deal of power, it may be called a *high-performance team* or even a *super team*.

Virtual Teams

In the rapidly changing environment, a company has to respond fast to take advantage of opportunities. This, in turn, may require **virtual management**, which has been described as "the ability to run a team whose members aren't in the same location, don't report to you, and may not even work for your organization"[11]. Not being in the same location and not even reporting to the same superior make managing those teams even more difficult. Therefore, it is important to have a clear purpose, to define clearly the tasks and assumptions, and to communicate effectively by such means as e-mail, fax, telephone, and perhaps even a project web site. It is also essential to carefully watch for possible conflict so that it can be resolved quickly.

> **Virtual management** Running a team whose members are not in the same location, do not report to the person managing it, and may not even work for the same organization.

INNOVATIVE PERSPECTIVE

Interview with Mr. Reginald Chatman, Senior Manager of Corporate Quality Solutions, Cisco Systems, on Managing Work Teams[12]

While managing work teams in globally connected enterprises requires managerial and technical expertise, we expect that maximizing the joint contribution of a sophisticated and culturally diverse work group also requires a certain social adroitness. To ascertain how the global manager maximizes the potential of an international work team, we spoke to Mr. Reginald Chatman of Cisco Systems. Mr. Chatman is a Senior Manager of Corporate Quality Solutions with Cisco and has extensive experience in managing work teams that are geographically diverse.

We asked Reginald Chatman to share his thoughts on successfully managing work groups in the Cisco context. Mr. Chatman stated, "To successfully manage work groups and teams in today's fast-paced business environment, one must exhibit leadership skills to overcome three challenges: influencing without authority, communicating through new platforms, and working with remote team members around the globe." He continued, "Team leadership now involves motivating members to execute to a vision without the ability to formally direct. That requires development of the kind of soft skills that are not commonly taught. Chief among them is the need to develop a rapport with team members and engender mutual trust and respect. Communicating in the age of wikis, instant messaging, social networks, blogs, and Twitter means adapting the message to ensure information is readily available, clear and consistent, and appropriate for local cultures. Finally, to lead in a world where team members are working and contributing in every time zone means being sensitive to the different work schedules, smart about assessing talent and assigning work to ensure team members can be successful, and helping remote workers feel connected to the rest of the team."

While advances in communication and information technology have made global collaboration possible, these technologies are still wielded by human beings who require respect, inspiration, and consideration. It will be those business leaders, who can provide these essential elements to those they manage, who will achieve the potential that today's global workforce can provide.

CONFLICT IN COMMITTEES, GROUPS, AND TEAMS[13]

Despite the many advantages of committees, groups, and teams, conflict will arise. In the discussion of committees, we pointed out the disadvantages of committees; they also apply to groups and teams. In addition, there is a great deal of literature dealing with work-group and team conflict.[14] **Conflict** may arise between individuals (interpersonal conflict), between groups (intergroup conflict), and between the organization and its environment, such as with other organizations. There can also be resentment toward "free riders", individuals who do not contribute their fair share yet share in group rewards.

> **Conflict** may arise between individuals, between groups, and between the organization and its environment.

SUMMARY

A committee is a group of persons to whom, as a group, some matter is committed. Committees may be line or staff, formal or informal, permanent or temporary. Committees are used for obtaining group deliberation and judgment, for preventing one person from accumulating too much authority, and for presenting the views of different groups. Committees are also used for coordinating departments, plans, and policies as well as for sharing information. At times, a manager may not have all the authority needed for making a decision; authority is therefore consolidated through committees. Moreover, committees often increase motivation by letting people participate in the decision-making process.

Committees also have disadvantages: they can be costly, their actions may result in compromises at the least common denominator, their discussions may lead to indecisions, and they have the tendency to be self-destructive when one person dominates the meetings. Another drawback is that responsibility is split, with no one person feeling responsible for a decision. Moreover, a small group of committee members may insist on the acceptance of their unwarranted view against the will of the majority.

Effective operation of a committee requires determining its authority, choosing an appropriate size, selecting members carefully, using it only for the proper subject matter, appointing an effective chairperson, taking and circulating minutes, and using it only when its benefits exceed its costs.

The experiment by Asch shows the impact of group pressure toward conformity. The focus group is a special kind of group that elicits responses from customers, the public, or employees. Before an organization uses group actions, it must consider the advantages and disadvantages of groups. A committee is one kind of group; another kind is a team. In the self-managing team, members have a variety of skills needed to carry out relatively complete tasks. In virtual management, team members are not in the same place, do not report to the same superior, and may not work for the same organization. With the wide use of committees, groups, and teams, interpersonal and intergroup conflict may arise. In addition, conflict between organizations as well as between organizations and their environments needs to be dealt with.

KEY IDEAS AND CONCEPTS FOR REVIEW

Committee
Four stages in group processes
Plural executive and board of directors
Line and staff committees
Formal and informal committees
Permanent and temporary committees
Reasons for using committees
Disadvantages and misuse of committees
Recommendations for making committees successful
Characteristics of groups
Norms
Asch's experiment on group pressure
Focus group
Functions and advantages of groups
Team and team building
Self-managing team
Virtual team
Conflict in committees, groups, and teams

FOR DISCUSSION

1. A prominent novelist-critic of the management scene has said: "I don't think we can go on very much longer with the luxurious practice of hiring ten men to make one man's decision. With all its advantages, professional management tends to encourage bureaucratic corpulence." Comment.
2. Distinguish between a committee, a team, and a group.
3. What are the reasons for using committees? If there are good reasons, why are committees criticized so much?
4. What is the relative effectiveness of individual and committee action in functional activities? Identify the activities that can be undertaken most effectively by a committee.
5. Describe and discuss the nature of misapplications of committees.
6. What would you recommend for making committees effective?
7. Go to the Internet and find out what has been written about team management.
8. What are the major characteristics of groups in organizations?

EXERCISES/ACTION STEPS

1. Discuss the case in this chapter in groups. Divide the class into groups of various sizes (e.g., groups of 3, 6, 9, and 12 students). Each group is to analyze the case and make recommendations. A spokesperson should be selected in each group to present the group's view on the case. On what basis was the spokesperson selected? What are the similarities and differences between a spokesperson and a chairperson? Discuss the advantages and problems encountered in the groups of various sizes. What do you think is the ideal group size?
2. Interview two managers and ask about their experiences in committees. Do they have a positive or a negative view of committees? What have they found to be most important for making committees effective and efficient? What do they think is the ideal size of a committee?
3. Are you on a team at school? Try to apply some of the team building and committee principles from this chapter to your team. Report on the results.
4. Build a virtual team of students from other universities to work on a project and compare the outcome to projects you develop with students in your own class.
5. Identify two or more commercial software packages that facilitate the operation of teams. What are their advantages and disadvantages?

INTERNET RESEARCH

1. Search the Internet for the term "virtual team" and see how companies develop and apply tools for virtual teams in real situations.
2. Search the Internet using the key words "Asch effect" or "Asch experiment". Find out the details of the experiment.

GLOBAL CASE

To Merge or Not to Merge: That Is the Question for HP, Compaq, and CEO Fiorina[15]

The high-tech business is changing rapidly. Some companies, such as Dell and IBM, have gained strengths and pose a threat to other companies, such as

Hewlett-Packard (HP) and Compaq. It appeared to make sense for the latter two to merge—or did it? At the center of the merger decision was HP's CEO, Carleton (Carly) S. Fiorina, who was instrumental in engineering the proposed merger. On the other side was Walter B. Hewlett, the son of one of the founders of HP Corporation, which was known for its humane organization culture. Hewlett, representing the HP Foundation, opposed the merger. Thus, the final decision on the merger would be a group decision.

Ms. Fiorina, an outsider, was brought in to head HP with the aim of reinvigorating the organization and move the company in a new direction. There were arguments supporting a merger with Compaq, but there were also reasons for not pursuing such a strategy. After the merger was announced, both companies' stocks fell.

Each company has its strengths and weaknesses, but there is also an overlap of their respective products and services. HP's strengths are in imaging and printing systems. Its software and service businesses have growth potential, although they are only a small part of the total business. The company also is strong in UNIX servers, an area that was dominated by Sun Microsystems.[16] Perhaps most important, HP has an excellent reputation for innovation and quality. Compaq's strengths, on the other hand, are in the hardware business and its strong distribution channels. Moreover, it is known for its information technology services providing one-stop solutions.

But both companies also have weaknesses. For HP, one is the declining growth of the personal computer (PC) market, where it is difficult to compete with IBM and Dell. It is also weak in the server market, which has profit potential (but note that Dell is also moving into this market). The company's direction is somewhat vague and it is not aggressive enough in the market, a problem Fiorina was supposed to solve. Instead, she lost the confidence of a portion of the workforce.

One of Compaq's weaknesses at the time of the proposed merger, was its high inventory. In contrast, its competitor Dell took orders and customized its computers, thus reducing inventory costs. Similarly, Dell's strength in online business showed up Compaq's weakness in this area.

It is clear that a merger between HP and Compaq could be beneficial by combining products and services (despite some overlaps), although there were several arguments that could be made against the merger. One would be the difficulty of merging two large firms (150,000 people in some 160 countries). Moreover, the PC market is losing importance, and competitors such as IBM and Dell are better positioned in that field. It would also be difficult to merge two companies with very different organization cultures. Certainly, the opposition to the merger by Walter Hewlett, who was on the HP board, was also hindering such a strategic move.

HP and Compaq maintained that the competitive situation seemed to demand such a merger, which could result in cost savings (estimated at $2.5 billion by the year 2004, but this may be too optimistic). Also, the sharing of technology and consolidation of the customers of both companies would benefit the merged new HP, which would rival IBM in size.

Although Fiorina strongly argued for the proposed merger, she also had to realize the risks in the merger and weigh the pros and cons of this strategic move—risks not only for the company but also for her survival at HP. The decision to merge or not to merge was a group decision. The David and Lucile Packard Foundation, led by the children of the founders of the company, voted against the merger. The legal attempt by Mr. Packard was not successful and the merger proceeded.[17]

Questions:

1. List and discuss the pros and cons for the merger.
2. What are the personal risks for Ms. Fiorina?
3. How did she influence members of the group to approve the merger between HP and Compaq?
4. Why do you think Fiorina lost the confidence of the workforce?
5. What should Fiorina have done to build a cohesive management team of the combined company?

ENDNOTES

1. "Corporate Governance: Under the Board Talk," *The Economist*, June 15, 2002, pp. 13–14; "Designed by Committee," ibid., pp. 69–71; John A. Byrne, "Restoring Trust in Corporate America," *Business Week*, June 24, 2002, pp. 31–35; Emily Thornton and David Henry, "Big Guns Aim for Change," ibid., pp. 36–39. See also Enron, www.enron.com, accessed August 19, 2011; Tyco, "Tyco," www.tyco.com, accessed August 19, 2011.
2. C.K. Prahalad and Richard A. Bettis, "The Dominant Logic: A New Linkage between Diversity and Performance", *Strategic Management Journal*, 1986, 7 (6): 485–501.
3. D. Miller and P. H. Friesen, "Momentum and Revolution in Organization Adaptation", *Academy of Management Journal*, 1980, 23: 591–614.
4. See also Harold J. Leavitt and Jean Lipman-Blumen, "Hot Groups," *Harvard Business Review*, July–August 1995, pp. 109–116.
5. See David Krech, Richard S. Crutchfield, and Egerton L. Ballachey, *Individual in Society* (New York: McGraw-Hill, 1962), pp. 507–508; see also Jerry B. Harvey, "The Abilene Paradox: The Management of Agreement", *Organizational Dynamics* (Summer 1988), pp. 17–43.
6. Erich Brockmann, "Removing the Paradox of Conflict from Group Decisions," *Academy of Management Executive*, May 1996, pp. 61–62.
7. See Darrel Ray and Howard Bronstein, *Teaming Up* (New York: McGraw-Hill, 1995). Teams may work better in the Japanese culture than in the U.S. environment, according to Afsaneh Nahavandi and Eileen Aranda, "Restructuring Teams for the Re-engineered Organization," *Academy of Management Executive*, November 1994, pp. 58–68. For managing international teams, see Nicola Phillips, *Managing International Teams* (Burr Ridge, IL: Irwin, 1994); Don Mankin, Susan G. Cohen, and Tora K. Bikson, *Teams and Technology* (Boston, MA: Harvard Business School Press, 1996); Ann Donnellon, *Team Talk* (Boston, MA: Harvard Business School Press, 1996).
8. Jon R. Katzenbach and Douglas K. Smith, "The Discipline of Teams," in Arthur A. Thompson, Jr., A. J. Strickland III, and Tracy Robertson Kramer, eds. *Readings in Strategic Management*, 5th ed. (Chicago: Irwin, 1995), pp. 483–495.
9. Nancy Katz, "Sport Teams as a Model for Workplace Teams: Lessons and Liabilities," *Academy of Management Executive*, August 2001, pp. 56–67.
10. Katzenbach and Smith, "The Discipline of Teams"; James R. Barker, "Tightening the Iron Cage: Concertive Control in Self-managing Teams," *Administrative Science Quarterly*, September 1993, pp. 408–37; Ron Williams, "Self-directed Work Teams: A Competitive Advantage," *Quality Digest*, November 1995, pp. 50–52; Michael Donovan, "Maximizing the Bottom-line Impact of Self-directed Work Teams," *Quality Digest*, June 1996, pp. 34–39; Chantell E. Nicholls, Henry W. Lane, and Mauricio Brehm Bechu, "Taking Self-Management Teams to Mexico," *Academy of Management Executive*, August 1999, pp. 15–25.
11. Charles Wardell, "The Art of Managing Virtual Teams: Eight Key Lessons," *Harvard Management Update*, November 1998, p. 4. See also Anthony M. Townsend, Samuel M. DeMarie, and Anthony R. Hendrickson, "Virtual Teams: Technology and the Workplace in the Future," *Academy of Management Executive*, August 1998; Wayne F. Cascio, "Managing a Virtual Workplace,"

Academy of Management Executive, August 2000, pp. 81–90.

12. Interview conducted by email with Mr. Reginald Chatman of Cisco Systems, on August 30, 2009 by Mark Cannice.

13. Russ Forrester and Allan B. Drexler, "A Model for Team-based Organization Performance," *Academy of Management Executive*, August 1999, pp. 36–49.

14. See, for example, K. A. Jehn, "A Multimethod Examination of the Benefits and Detriments of Intergroup Conflict," *Administrative Science Quarterly*, June 1995, pp. 256–282.

15. A variety of sources have been consulted, including the following: Peter Burrows, Andrew Park, and Jim Kerstetter, "Carly's Last Stand?" *Business Week*, December 24, 2001, pp. 63–70; Andrew Park, "Can Compaq Survive as a Solo Act?" ibid., p. 71; "In the Family's Way," *The Economist*, December 15, 2001, p. 56.

16. But Sun has to battle with IBM in the server market. See "Sun Microsystems: Stealing Each Other's Clothes," *The Economist*, October 13, 2001, pp. 61–63.

17. Ms. Fiorina was fired in February 2005 and succeeded by Mark Hurd. Observers said that he brought stability to the company. See Pui-Wing Tam, "Hitting the Ground Running," *The Wall Street Journal*, April 4, 2005; Pui-Wing Tam, "Hurd's Big Challenge at H-P: Overhauling Corporate Sales," *The Wall Street Journal*, April 3, 2006; Nicole C. Wong, "HP Has Prospered in CEO Hurd's First Year," *The Wall Street Journal,* April 7, 2006. Ms. Fiorina discussed the details of her ouster in her memoir; see Don Clark, "Fiorina Memoir Details H-P Board Conflicts Preceding Her Ouster," *The Wall Street Journal*, October 6, 2006.

CHAPTER 17

Communication

Learning Objectives

After studying this chapter, you should be able to:

LO 1   Describe the purpose of communication and the basic communication process

LO 2   Explain the flow of communication in an organization

LO 3   Describe the characteristics of written, oral, and nonverbal communication

LO 4   Identify barriers and breakdowns in communication and suggest approaches to improve it

LO 5   Understand the role of the electronic media in communication

---

Although communication applies to all phases of managing, it is particularly important in the function of leading. **Communication** is the transfer of information from a sender to a receiver, with the information being understood by the receiver. This definition forms the basis for the communication process model discussed in this chapter. The model focuses on the sender, the transmission, and the receiver of the message. It also draws attention to "noise", which interferes with good communication, and feedback, that facilitates communication. This chapter also examines the impact of the electronic media on communication.

Communication
Transfer of information from a sender to a receiver, with the information being understood by the receiver.

THE PURPOSE OF COMMUNICATION

In its broadest sense, the purpose of communication in an enterprise is to effect change—to influence action toward the welfare of the enterprise. Communication is essential for the *internal* functioning of enterprises because it integrates the managerial functions. Especially, communication is needed (1) to establish and disseminate the goals of an enterprise; (2) to develop plans for their achievement; (3) to organize human and other resources in the most effective and efficient way; (4) to select, develop, and appraise members of the organization; (5) to lead, direct, motivate, and create a climate in which people want to contribute; and (6) to control performance.

Figure 17.1 graphically shows not only that communication facilitates the managerial functions but also that communication relates an enterprise to its *external* environment. It is through information exchange that managers become aware of the needs of customers, the availability of suppliers, the claims of stockholders, the regulations of governments, and the concerns of the community. It is through communication that any organization becomes an open system interacting with its environment, a fact whose importance is emphasized throughout this book.

FIGURE 17.1 The purpose and function of communication

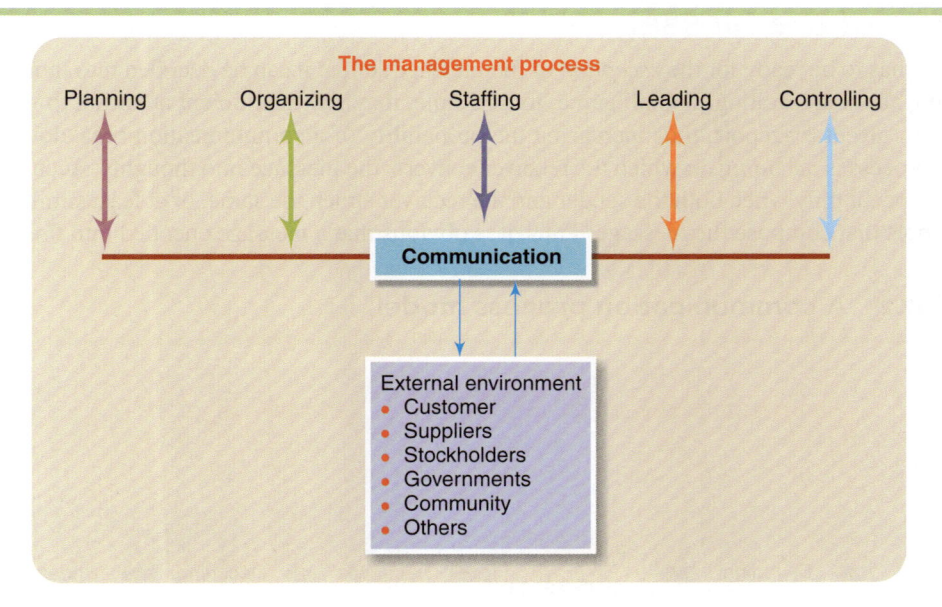

THE COMMUNICATION PROCESS

Simply stated, the communication process, diagrammed in Figure 17.2, involves the sender, the transmission of a message through a selected channel, and the receiver. Let us examine closely the specific steps in the process.

Sender of the Message

Communication begins with the sender, who has a *thought* or an idea, which is then encoded in a way that can be understood by both the sender and the receiver. While it is usual to think of *encoding* a message into a spoken language, there are many other ways of encoding, such as translating the thought into computer language.

Use of a Channel to Transmit the Message

The information is then transmitted over a channel that links the sender with the receiver. The message may be oral or written, and its *transmission* may be through a memorandum, a computer, telephone, a telegram, e-mail, television, or other media. Television, of course, also facilitates the transmission of gestures and other visual clues. At times, two or more channels are used. In a telephone conversation, for instance, two people may reach a basic agreement that they later confirm by a letter. Since many choices are available, each with advantages and disadvantages, the proper selection of the channel is vital for effective communication.

Receiver of the Message

The receiver has to be ready for the *reception* of the message so that it can be decoded into thoughts. A person thinking about an exciting football game, for example, may pay insufficient attention to what is being said about an inventory report, thus increasing the probability of a communication breakdown. The next step in the process is *decoding*, in which the receiver converts the message into thoughts. Accurate communication can occur only when both the sender and the receiver attach the same, or at least similar, meanings to the symbols that compose the message. Thus, it is obvious that a message encoded into French requires

FIGURE 17.2 A communication process model

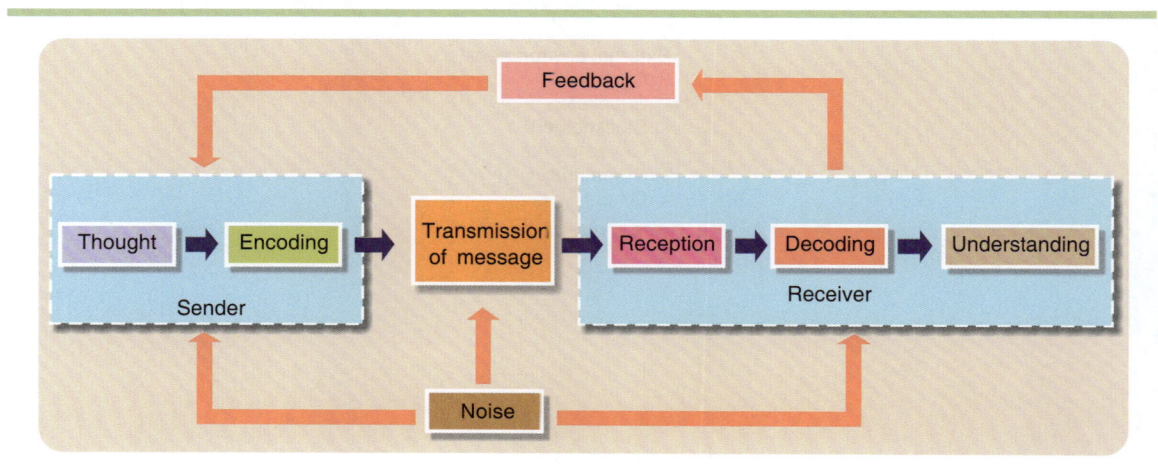

a receiver who understands French. Less obvious, and frequently overlooked, is the fact that a message in technical or professional jargon requires a recipient who understands such language. So communication is not complete unless it is understood. *Understanding* is in the mind of both the sender and the receiver. Persons with closed minds will normally not completely understand messages, especially if the information is contrary to their value system.

GLOBAL PERSPECTIVE

Cross-Cultural Barriers

Misunderstandings increase when communication is made in different languages. The German language, for example, is rather distinct in its formality and the way people are addressed. The formal *Sie* is seldom replaced by *Du*. Only after people know each other for a long time and only after they know each other very well is the informal *Du* used. Similarly, adults usually address each other with *Herr* (Mr.) or *Frau* (Mrs.). The use of the first name is common only among relatives, very close friends, or children and teenagers. A non-German who is addressed with the formal *Sie* or the formal *Frau* or *Herr* may interpret such usage as meaning that the person does not like him or her, or wants to maintain a social distance. This may not be true at all; the usage is simply dictated by cultural norms. On the other hand, if a German casual acquaintance is addressed in German by his or her first name, that person may be offended. While such distinctions in a language may appear unimportant to a non-German, they not only create communication barriers but also may result in damaged relationships and possibly in a loss of business.

Noise Hindering Communication

Unfortunately, communication is affected by "*noise*", which is anything—whether in the sender, the transmission, or the receiver—that hinders communication. Here are examples of "noise":

- A noise or a confined environment may hinder the development of a clear thought.
- Encoding may be faulty because of the use of ambiguous symbols.
- Transmission may be interrupted by static in the channel, such as may be experienced in a poor telephone connection.
- Inaccurate reception may be caused by inattention.
- Decoding may be faulty because the wrong meaning may be attached to words and other symbols.
- Understanding can be obstructed by prejudices.
- A desired change that is communicated may not occur because of the fear of possible consequences of the change.
- In cross-cultural communication, not only verbal expression but also gestures and posture can cause miscommunication.

Noise Anything—whether in the sender, the transmission, or the receiver—that hinders communication.

Feedback in Communication

To check the effectiveness of communication, a person must have *feedback*. One can never be sure whether or not a message has been effectively encoded, transmitted, decoded, and understood until it is confirmed by feedback. Similarly, feedback indicates whether individual or organizational change has taken place as a result of communication.

ENTREPRENEURIAL PERSPECTIVE

Accepting Negative Feedback

Entrepreneurs are by nature optimistic. They believe in themselves and their vision for their companies. Along their path, though, they will and must receive blunt feedback about their new venture vision. How the entrepreneur accepts and uses this feedback is critical to the survival of her venture. Venture capitalists and others will try to find holes or problems in the business plan of an entrepreneur. The entrepreneur must respectfully take this feedback and do her best to respond to it. The entrepreneur should never become defensive or combative about negative feedback, as this is a deal ender with most investors. Rather, the entrepreneur should acknowledge the criticism, provide a rational response if she has one, or agree to explore and correct the deficiency noted.

Situational and Organizational Factors in Communication

> The **communication process** is affected by many situational and organizational factors.

Many situational and organizational factors affect the **communication process**. Such factors in the external environment may be educational, sociological, legal–political, and economic. For example, a repressive political environment will inhibit the free flow of communication. Another situational factor is geographic distance. A direct face-to-face communication is different from a telephone conversation with a person on the other side of the globe and different from an exchange of cables or letters. Time must also be considered in communication. The busy executive may not have sufficient time to receive and send information accurately. Other situational factors that affect communication within an enterprise include the organization structure, managerial and nonmanagerial processes, and technology. An example of the latter is the pervasive impact of computer technology on the handling of huge amounts of data.

> The **communication model** provides an overview of the communication process, identifies the critical variables, and shows their relationships.

In summary, the **communication model** provides an overview of the communication process, identifies the critical variables, and shows their relationships. This, in turn, helps managers pinpoint communication problems so that they can take steps to solve them or, even better, prevent the difficulties from occurring in the first place.

COMMUNICATION IN THE ORGANIZATION

In today's enterprises, information must flow faster than ever before. Even a short stoppage on a fast-moving production line can be very costly in terms of lost output. It is therefore essential that production problems be communicated quickly for corrective action to be taken. Another important element is the amount of information, which has greatly increased over the years, frequently causing an information overload. What is often needed is not more information but relevant information. It is necessary to determine what kind of information a manager needs to have for effective decision making. Obtaining this information frequently requires getting information from managers' superiors and subordinates and also from departments and people elsewhere in the organization.

CHAPTER 17 Communication

INNOVATIVE PERSPECTIVE

Communicating with Portfolio Firms of a Venture Capital Company: An Interview with Elton Sherwin, Senior Managing Director at Ridgewood Capital

Leadership demands information about what is really going on in the organization. Managers who never leave the office, and who rely on formal communication channels, may receive only the information that places subordinates in a favorable light. To overcome their isolation, managers need to supplement the formal communication channels with informal ones.

Venture-financed firms, in particular, need close attention and guidance. We asked a leading Silicon Valley venture capitalist, Elton Sherwin, how he communicates with the start-up companies that his firm finances. Mr. Sherwin is the senior managing director at Ridgewood Capital where he invests across a broad range of technology companies including cleantech and software. He also authored, *The Silicon Valley Way*, which is a widely used entrepreneur's guide book used around the world as well as *Addicted to Energy, A Venture Capitalist's Perspective on How to Save Our Economy and Our Climate*.

Mr. Sherwin indicated he calls, e-mails, texts, mails books and mp3s, and visits the managers of his portfolio firms. He also spends time one-on-one with multiple members of the executive team, not just the CEO and CFO. Having invested in more that 25 companies, he stated, "Now when I see something that is broken I am tenacious about fixing it."

The Manager's Need to Know

To be effective, a manager needs information necessary for carrying out managerial functions and activities. Yet, even a casual glance at communication systems shows that managers often lack vital information for decision making, or they may get too much information, resulting in overload. It is evident that managers must be discriminating in selecting information. A simple way for a manager to start is to ask, "What do I really need to know for my job?" or "What would happen if I did not get this information on a regular basis?" It is not maximum information that a manager needs, but pertinent information. Clearly, there is no universally applicable communication system; rather, a communication system must be tailored to the manager's needs.

Communication Flow in the Organization

In an effective organization, communication flows in various directions: downward, upward, and crosswise. Traditionally, downward communication was emphasized, but there is ample evidence that problems will develop if communication flows only downward. In fact, one could argue that effective communication has to start with the subordinate, and this means primarily upward communication. Communication also flows horizontally and diagonally. The different kinds of information flows are diagrammed in Figure 17.3 and elaborated below.

FIGURE 17.3   Information flow in an organization

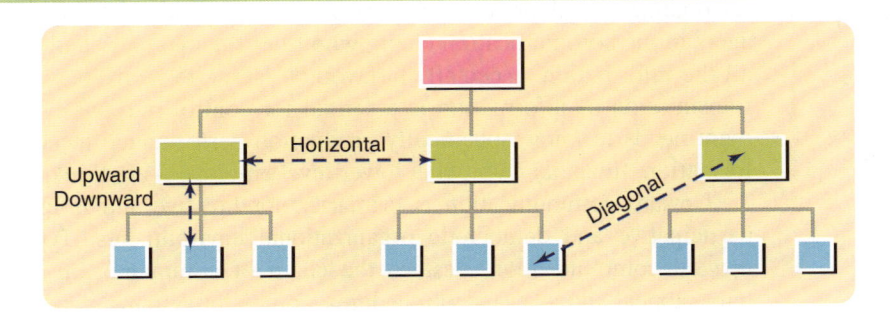

Downward Communication

Downward communication flows from people at higher levels to those at lower levels in the organizational hierarchy.

Downward communication flows from people at higher levels to those at lower levels in the organizational hierarchy. This kind of communication exists especially in organizations with an authoritarian atmosphere. The media used for oral downward communication include instructions, speeches, meetings, the telephone, loudspeakers, and even the grapevine. Examples of written downward communication are memorandums, letters, handbooks, pamphlets, policy statements, procedures, and electronic news displays.

Unfortunately, information is often lost or distorted as it comes down the chain of command. Top management's issuance of policies and procedures does not ensure communication. In fact, many directives are not understood or even read. Consequently, a feedback system is essential for finding out whether information was perceived as intended by the sender.

Downward flow of information through the different levels of the organization is time-consuming. Indeed, delays may be so frustrating that some top managers insist that information be sent directly to the person or group requiring it.

GLOBAL PERSPECTIVE

Transformational Communication by American Presidents[1]

Communication is not only important in organizations, but may have dramatic effects in politics as illustrated by transformational rhetoric by U.S. presidents. Leadership means influencing people. This may be achieved by behavior, but also by rhetoric. Leaders are often remembered by important speeches. The most memorable one is by the U.S. President, John R. Kennedy, in his inaugural address when he said: "And so, my fellow Americans...ask not what your country can do for you—ask what you can do for your country. My fellow citizens of the world: Ask not what America will do for you, but together we can for the freedom of man." This speech may have inspired the founding of the Peace Corps, a volunteer program with the goals of providing technical assistance to other countries, understanding the cultures of other countries and helping other countries to understand U.S. culture.

Another speech by President Ronald Reagan at the Brandenburg Gate in Berlin may have influenced the eventual downfall of the Berlin Wall and the unification of East Germany and West Germany. Reagan said: "General Secretary Gorbachev, if you seek peace, if you seek prosperity for the Soviet Union and Eastern Europe, if you seek liberalization: Come here to this gate! Mr. Gorbachev, open this gate! Mr. Gorbachev, tear down this wall!"

Upward Communication

Upward communication travels from subordinates to superiors and continues up the organizational hierarchy.

Upward communication travels from subordinates to superiors and continues up the organizational hierarchy. Unfortunately, this flow is often hindered by managers in the communication chain, who filter the messages and do not transmit all the information, especially unfavorable news, to their bosses. Yet objective transmission of information is essential for control purposes. Upper management needs to know specifically production performance facts, marketing information, financial data, what lower-level employees are thinking, and so on.

Upward communication is primarily nondirective and is usually found in participative and democratic organizational environments. Typical means of upward communication, besides the chain of command, are suggestion systems, appeal and grievance procedures, complaint systems, counseling sessions, joint setting of objectives, the grapevine, group meetings, the practice of an open-door policy, morale questionnaires, exit interviews, and the ombudsperson.

The concept of the **ombudsperson** was used relatively little in the United States until recently. It originated in Sweden, where a civil servant could be approached by a citizen to investigate complaints about the government bureaucracy. Now some U.S. companies have established a position for a person who investigates employees' concerns. Companies have found that the ombudsperson can provide a valuable upward communication link. Effective upward communication requires an environment in which subordinates feel free to communicate. Since the organizational climate is greatly influenced by upper management, the responsibility for creating a free flow of upward communication rests to a great extent, although not exclusively, with superiors.

> **Ombudsperson**
> Person assigned to investigate employee concerns, thus providing a valuable upward communication link.

LEADERSHIP PERSPECTIVE

Lack of Upward Communication Can Be Disastrous

The lack of upward communication can be disastrous. In the 1986 space shuttle disaster, vital information apparently did not reach the top management at the National Aeronautics and Space Administration (NASA). The Bank of America's top officials were surprised at the poor quality of their mortgage portfolio, which resulted in substantial losses for the bank. The brokerage house E. F. Hutton's executives were apparently unaware of the check-writing fraud of their lower-level managers.

In some organizations, upward communication is hindered by an organization culture and climate that "punishes" managers who communicate bad news or information with which top management does not agree. Indeed, the tendency to report only good news upward is quite common. Yet correct information is absolutely necessary for managing an enterprise.

So what can managers do to facilitate the free flow of information? First, they must create an informal climate that encourages upward communication. An open-door policy is only useful when it is practiced. Second, the formal structure of information flow must be clear. Third, managers can learn a great deal by just wandering through the corridors. Hewlett-Packard is often mentioned as an example of open communication because of the practice of management by wandering around.

www.nasa.gov
www.bofa.com
en.wikipedia.org/wiki/E.F._Hutton_&_Co

Crosswise Communication

Crosswise communication includes the **horizontal flow** of information, among people on the same or similar organizational levels, and the **diagonal flow**, among persons at different levels who have no direct reporting relationships with one another. This kind of communication is used to speed information flow, to improve understanding, and to coordinate efforts for the achievement of organizational objectives. A great deal of communication does not follow the organizational hierarchy but cuts across the chain of command.

The enterprise environment provides many occasions for oral communication. They range from informal meetings of the company bowling team and lunch hours employees spend together to more formal conferences and committee and board meetings. This kind of communication also occurs when members of different departments form task teams or project groups. Finally, communication cuts

> **Horizontal flow**
> of information is among people on the same or similar organizational levels.
>
> **Diagonal flow**
> of information is among persons at different levels who have no direct reporting relationships with one another.

across organizational boundaries when, for example, staff members with functional or advisory authority interact with line managers in different departments.

In addition, written forms of communication keep people informed about the enterprise. These written forms include the company newspaper or magazine and bulletin board notices. Modern enterprises use many kinds of oral and written crosswise communication patterns to supplement the vertical flow of information.

Because information flow may not follow the chain of command, proper safeguards need to be taken to prevent potential problems. Specifically, crosswise communication should rest on the understanding that crosswise relationships will be encouraged wherever they are appropriate, that subordinates will refrain from making commitments beyond their authority, and that subordinates will keep superiors informed of important interdepartmental activities. In short, crosswise communication may create difficulties, but it is a necessity in many enterprises in order to respond to the needs of the complex and dynamic organizational environment.

Written, Oral, and Nonverbal Communication[2]

Written and oral communication media have favorable and unfavorable characteristics; consequently, they are often used together so that the favorable qualities of each can complement the limitations of the other. In addition, visual aids may be used to supplement both oral and written communications. A lecture in a management training session may be made more effective by the use of written handouts, transparencies, videotapes, and films. Evidence has shown that a message that is repeated through several media will be more accurately comprehended and recalled by the receiver.

In selecting the media, one must consider the communicator, the audience, and the situation. An executive who feels uncomfortable in front of a large audience may choose written communication rather than a speech. On the other hand, certain audiences who may not read a memo may be reached and become motivated by direct oral communication.

Written Communication

French managers are almost obsessed with the use of written communication, not only for formal messages but also for informal notes. A French manager stated that something has no reality unless it is written down.

Written communication has the advantage of providing records, references, and legal defenses. A message can be carefully prepared and then directed to a large audience through mass mailings. Written communication can also promote uniformity in policy and procedure and can reduce costs in some cases.

The disadvantages are that written messages may create mountains of paper, may be poorly expressed by ineffective writers, and may provide no immediate feedback. Consequently, it may take a long time to know whether a message has been received and properly understood.

INNOVATIVE PERSPECTIVE

Communicating with White Papers

White papers are a method of written communication among professionals that address important topics that are relevant to a firm, industry or trend of interest. White papers can be technical (e.g., addressing an engineering issue) or conceptual in nature and should focus on a specific challenge and a specific target audience. White papers typically begin with a statement of the challenge faced by a target reader which should be very clear, compelling and relevant, and supported by well-sourced hard data, and timely for the target audience. The argument which addresses this challenge should be airtight and articulate and could be based on archival, first hand or theoretical research (e.g., a scholarly white paper). Well-written white papers are typically appreciated by the target audience and help establish the reputation of the writer as a thoughtful professional. A series of well-written white papers can help establish the writer as a thought leader in her chosen profession.

Oral Communication

A great deal of information is communicated orally. Oral communication can occur in a face-to-face meeting of two people or in a manager's presentation to a large audience, it can be formal or informal, and it can be planned or accidental.

The principal advantage of oral communication is that it makes possible speedy interchange with immediate feedback. People can ask questions and clarify points. In a face-to-face interaction, the effect can be noted. Furthermore, a meeting with the superior may give the subordinate a feeling of importance. Clearly, informal or planned meetings can greatly contribute to the understanding of the issues.

However, oral communication also has disadvantages. It does not always save time, as any manager knows who has attended meetings in which no results or agreements were achieved. These meetings can be costly in terms of time and money.

LEADERSHIP PERSPECTIVE

Can a Person Fearful of Public Speaking Become the Head of the Largest Publicly Owned Corporation?[3]

Consider Lee Scott, the CEO of Wal-Mart. He hated to speak to large groups of people. He recalled that he was afraid speaking in meetings and stated: "I would shake and my voice would crack." Yet, in February 2005, he addressed 500 business leaders in Los Angeles, in just one of many public speeches in which he had to defend criticisms of Wal-Mart. They included providing insufficient health care benefits to its employees, substandard wages, requiring employees to work beyond their shifts, buying overseas thereby hurting U.S. companies, and putting local businesses out of business.

Students sometimes encounter also fear of addressing the class as part of the courser requirement. Could Mr. Scott's example serve as a role model in overcoming the fear of public speaking?

| www.walmart.com |

Nonverbal Communication

People communicate in many different ways. What a person says can be reinforced (or contradicted) by **nonverbal communication**, such as facial expressions and body gestures. Nonverbal communication is expected to support the verbal, but it does not always do so. An autocratic manager may pound a fist on the table while announcing that from now on participative management will be practiced; such contradictory communications will certainly create a credibility gap. Similarly, managers may state that they have an open-door policy, but then they may have a secretary carefully screen people who want to see them; this creates incongruence between what they say and what they do. This is an illustration of "noise" in the communication process model (Figure 17.2). Clearly, nonverbal communication may support or contradict verbal communication, giving rise to the saying that actions often speak louder than words.

Nonverbal communication includes facial expressions and body gestures.

Innovation by Observing Communication

Managers can help initiate and lead innovation efforts in their firms by observing patterns of communications—verbal and non-verbal—of their firms' customers. Observing customer interactions in a sales or service process, with a focus on nonverbal cues may provide truer feedback to a company's service. For example, customers may respond to a survey that they like or dislike a particular feature of a firm's product; however, by observing customers attempts to use the product and taking note of facial expressions and body language, an adept manager may discern deeper truths. IDEO is a global design firm that pioneered a human-centered design approach to helping its clients develop better products and services. Its method for success relies partly on conducting extensive observational research of a client's customers in order to better understand customers' latent needs and desires. Thus, IDEO leverages the power of nonverbal communication to create and innovate and help its clients succeed in the market place.[4]

In addition to leveraging observation for market research, managers may also seek to better understand their organizations through a similar method of observation to best understand and identify problem as well as success factors of the organization. This managerial observation method may provide subtler but perhaps more true insights into the organization than staff interviews or organizational climate surveys.

Communication Methods

There are different methods and channels for communication: some are oral, some are written, and some use information technology. They range from face-to-face communication, group meeting, and the various kinds of written communication discussed above. Technology is used for certain types of communication, such as the wired and wireless telephone, fax, voice mail, e-mail, as well as teleconference and videoconference. We highlighted above some of the advantages and disadvantages of various types of communication, including speed of feedback, ease of use, cost and time, as well as formality and informality. You probably do not want to invite an honored guest by e-mail. On the other hand, for informal communication and if time is of the essence—and the technology is available—you may want to use e-mail rather than "snail mail" (regular mail).

Other communication topics are discussed in other parts of the book. For example, the grapevine, the informal and unofficial communication channel, was discussed in Chapter 10. The impact of technology on communication will be discussed in Chapter 19.

INNOVATION PERSPECTIVE

UPS: From Time Management to Information Technology (IT)[5]

In the delivery business, time is critical for United Parcel Service Inc. (UPS) and FedEx Corporation two fierce competitors. In the 1980s, UPS was known for its low-tech, but labor intensive trucking operations with a focus on intensive time-management studies. But by 2006, the emphasis is on IT, partly driven by FedEx that was known for high-speed, overnight service. To improve speed, UPS customers can prepare their own labels even before the package is picked up by going to the UPS's website or using software provided by the company. By using the satellite global-positioning system the company can quite accurately estimate the delivery time. In the future, UPS may even be able to schedule delivery by appointment.

BARRIERS AND BREAKDOWNS IN COMMUNICATION[6]

It is probably no surprise that managers frequently cite communication breakdowns as one of their most important problems. However, communication problems are often symptoms of more deeply rooted problems. For example, poor planning may be the cause of uncertainty about the direction of the firm. Similarly, a poorly designed organization structure may not clearly communicate organizational relationships. Vague performance standards may leave managers uncertain about what is expected of them. Thus, the perceptive manager will look for the causes of communication problems instead of just dealing with the symptoms. Barriers can exist in the sender, in the transmission of the message, in the receiver, or in the feedback. Specific communication barriers are discussed below.

Lack of Planning

Good communication seldom happens by chance. Too often, people start talking and writing without first thinking, planning, and stating the purpose of the message. Yet giving the reasons for a directive, selecting the most appropriate channel, and choosing proper timing can greatly improve understanding and reduce resistance to change.

Unclarified Assumptions

Often overlooked, yet very important, are the uncommunicated assumptions that underlie messages. A customer may send a note stating that she will visit a vendor's plant. Then she may assume that the vendor will meet her at the airport, reserve a hotel room, arrange for transportation, and set up a full-scale review of the program at the plant. But the vendor may assume that the customer is coming to town mainly to attend a wedding and will make just a routine call at the plant. These unclarified assumptions in both instances may result in confusion and the loss of goodwill.

Semantic Distortion

Another barrier to effective communication is semantic distortion, which can be deliberate or accidental. An advertisement that states "We sell for less" is deliberately ambiguous, begging the question: less than what? Words may evoke different responses. To some people, the word *government* may mean interference or deficit spending; to others, the same word may mean help, equalization, and justice.

Poorly Expressed Messages

No matter how clear the idea is in the mind of the sender of communication, the message may still be marked by poorly chosen words, omissions, lack of coherence, poor organization, awkward sentence structure, platitudes, unnecessary jargon, and a failure to clarify its implications. This lack of clarity and precision, which can be costly, can be avoided through greater care in encoding the message.

Communication Barriers in the International Environment[7]

Communication in the international environment is made more difficult because of different languages, cultures, and etiquette.[8] Translating advertising slogans is very risky. The slogan "Put a Tiger in Your Tank" by Exxon was very effective in the United States, yet it may be an insult to the people in Thailand. Colors have different meanings in different cultures. Black is often associated with death in many Western countries, while in the Far East white is the color of mourning. In business dealings, it is quite common in the United States to communicate on a first-name basis, yet in most other cultures, especially those with a pronounced hierarchical structure, people generally address one another by their surnames.

www.exxon.com

In the Chinese culture, words may not convey what people really mean because they may want to appear humble. For example, when a promotion is offered, the person may say that he or she is not qualified enough to assume great responsibility. But the expectation is that the superior will urge the subordinate to accept the promotion and will mention all the virtues and strengths of the candidate, as well as his or her suitability for the new position.

GLOBAL PERSPECTIVE

Country Differences in Explicit and Implicit Communication

Communication patterns differ between countries with respect to the degree to which they are explicit or implicit. In countries such as Germany and the United States, one expects that people mean what they say. The need for precision is illustrated in the popularity of management by objectives, where goals are stated precisely in quantitative, measurable terms whenever possible. In contrast, Japanese communication is implicit; the meaning has to be inferred. For example, Japanese dislike saying "no" in communication; instead, a negative answer is couched in ambivalent terms. This has been demonstrated many times in trade agreements between Japan and the United States, as well as between Japan and Europe.

While these observations may be, to some extent, an overgeneralization, managers who are aware of the different communication patterns still can benefit from this knowledge.

www.vw.com

To overcome communication barriers in the international environment, large corporations have taken a variety of steps. Volkswagen, for example, provides extensive language training. Furthermore, it maintains a large staff of translators. Frequently, local nationals, who know best the host country's language and culture, are hired for top positions. In the United States, foreign firms find it advantageous to hire students from their own country who are attending U.S. universities.

GLOBAL PERSPECTIVE

The Multilingual CEO[9]

How do executives spend their well-deserved vacations? Some play golf, others learn to sail, and still others learn about Aristotle's ethics. Josef Ackermann, the Deutsche Bank's CEO, used a week's vacation studying Spanish six hours a day with a private tutor. He already knows English, Italian, French, and his native German. With the Deutsche Bank operating in many countries around the globe, Mr. Ackerman thinks that his multilingual skills help him to communicate with employees, customers, and government leaders around the world.

Many U.S. executives rely on their English proficiencies in conducting business around the globe. And indeed, much of the business communication is in English, but the knowledge of other languages promotes business and personal relationships. Time is one of the most critical personal resource and some stressed executives combine leisure with continuing, never-ending education.

www.db.com/index_e.htm

Loss by Transmission and Poor Retention

In a series of transmissions from one person to the next, the message becomes less and less accurate. Poor retention of information is another serious problem. Thus, the necessity of repeating the message and using several channels is rather obvious. Consequently, companies often use more than one channel to communicate the same message.

Poor Listening and Premature Evaluation

There are many talkers but few listeners. Everyone probably has observed people entering a discussion with comments that have no relation to the topic. One reason may be that these persons are pondering their own problems—such as preserving their own egos or making a good impression on other group members—instead of listening to the conversation. Listening demands full attention and self-discipline. It also requires that the listener avoid premature evaluation of what another person has to say. A common tendency is to judge, to approve or disapprove what is being said, rather than trying to understand the speaker's frame of reference. Yet listening without making hasty judgments can make the whole enterprise more effective and more efficient. For example, sympathetic listening can result in better labor–management relations and greater understanding among managers. Specifically, sales personnel may better understand the problems of production people, and the credit manager may realize that an overly restrictive credit policy may lead to a disproportionate loss in sales. In short, listening with empathy can reduce some of the daily frustrations in organized life and result in better communication.

Impersonal Communication[10]

Effective communication is more than simply transmitting information to employees. It requires face-to-face contact in an environment of openness and trust. Improvement of communication often requires not expensive and sophisticated (and impersonal) communication media but the willingness of superiors to engage in face-to-face communication. Such informal gatherings, without status trappings or a formal authority base, may be threatening to a top executive, but the risks involved are outweighed by the benefits that better communication can bring.

Distrust, Threat, and Fear

Distrust, threat, and fear undermine communication. In a climate containing these forces, any message will be viewed with skepticism. Distrust can be the result of inconsistent behavior by the superior, or it can be due to past experiences in which the subordinate was punished for honestly reporting unfavorable, but true, information to the boss. Similarly, in light of threats, whether real or imagined, people tend to tighten up, become defensive, and distort information. What is needed is a climate of trust, which facilitates open and honest communication.

Insufficient Period for Adjustment to Change

The purpose of communication is to effect change that may seriously concern employees: shifts in the time, place, type, and order of work or shifts in group arrangements or skills to be used. Some communications point to the need for further training, career adjustment, or status arrangements. Changes affect people in different ways, and it may take time to think through the full meaning of a message. Consequently, for maximum efficiency, it is important not to force change before people can adjust to its implications.

Information Overload

One might think that more and unrestricted information flow would help people overcome communication problems. But unrestricted flow may result in too much information. People respond to information overload in various ways.[11] First, they may *disregard* certain information. A person getting too much mail may ignore letters that should be answered. Second, overwhelmed with too much information, people may *make errors* in processing it. For example, they may leave out the word "not" in a message, which reverses the intended meaning. Third, people may *delay* processing information, either permanently or with the intention of catching up in the future. Fourth, they may *filter* information. Filtering may be helpful when the most pressing and most important information is processed first and the less important messages receive lower priority. However, chances are that attention will be given first to matters that are easy to handle, while more difficult but perhaps critical messages are ignored. Finally, people respond to information overload by simply *escaping* from the task of communication. In other words, they ignore information or do not communicate it.

Some responses to information overload may be adaptive tactics that can, at times, be functional. For example, delaying the processing of information until the amount is reduced can be effective. On the other hand, withdrawing from the task of communicating is usually not a helpful response. Another way to approach the overload problem is to reduce the demand for information. Within an enterprise, this may be accomplished by insisting that only essential data be processed, such as information showing critical deviations from plans. Reducing external demand for information is usually more difficult because it is less controllable by managers. An example may be the government's demand for detailed documentation on governmental contracts. Companies that do business with the government simply have to comply with these requests.

Other Communication Barriers

There are many other barriers to effective communication. In *selective perception*, people tend to perceive what they expect to perceive. In communication, this means that they hear what they want to hear and ignore other relevant information.

Closely related to perception is the influence of *attitude*, which is the predisposition to act or not to act in a certain way; it is a mental position regarding a fact or state. Clearly, if people have made up their minds, they cannot objectively listen to what is said.

Still other barriers to communication are differences in *status* and *power* between the sender and the receiver of information. Also, when information has to pass through several organizational *levels*, it tends to be distorted.

TOWARD EFFECTIVE COMMUNICATION[12]

The communication process model introduced earlier (Figure 17.2) helps identify the critical elements in the communication process. At each stage, breakdowns can occur: in the encoding of the message by the sender, in the transmission of the message, and in the decoding and understanding of the message by the receiver. Certainly, "noise" can interfere with effective communication at each stage of the process.

ENTREPRENEURIAL PERSPECTIVE

Interview with Lori Teranishi, Co-Principal, IQPR, on Developing an Effective Enterprise Communication Strategy[13]

Lori Teranishi is coprincipal of IQPR, a public relations firm. She has worked extensively with start-ups and multinational corporations to develop their communications strategies and build as well as repair their corporate reputations. We asked Lori Teranishi to comment on the role of internal and external communications in organizational development. Ms. Teranishi indicated,

"One essential component of a successful start-up or growing company that is too often overlooked is communications. An effective communications strategy builds the company's image internally among managers and employees, and externally for investors as well as current and potential customers and suppliers." She emphasized, "Communications establish and maintain a company's reputation within its industry and among the wider public."

With a firm's reputation so closely tied to its communications, we asked Ms. Teranishi to explain the changing role of communications as an organization grows. Lori explained, "From the very beginning, the way a company communicates internally defines its corporate culture. As a start-up grows, communications evolve from hallway meetings and discussions around the founder's desk, to a more formalized process involving a large number of people. What doesn't change is the need to make sure that the staff understands the corporate mission and values; that they understand the products and services that the company sells, and that they, themselves, can communicate this information to each other and to the outside world. Everyone in the company needs to be seen as a potential ambassador." She also noted that as the company grows, communications become more complex and requires knowledge that is more specialized. For example, communicating with investors, regulators or the government may require an investment in additional resources to ensure that effective and accurate messages are transmitted. It becomes clear then that an effective communication strategy is essential to the proper execution of corporate goals and the development and maintenance of a firm's brand and competitive advantage.

Guidelines for Improving Communication

Effective communication is the responsibility of all persons in the organization, managers as well as nonmanagers, in working toward a common aim. Whether communication is effective can be evaluated by the intended results. The following guidelines can help overcome the barriers to communication.

1. Clarify the Purpose of the Message

Senders of messages must clarify in their minds what they want to communicate. This means that one of the first steps in communicating is to clarify the purpose of the message and to make a plan to achieve the intended end.

2. Use Intelligible Encoding

Effective communication requires that encoding and decoding be done with symbols that are familiar to both the sender and the receiver of the message. Thus, the manager (and especially the staff specialist) should avoid unnecessary technical jargon, which is intelligible only to experts in their particular field.

3. Consult Others' Views

The planning of the communication should not be done in a vacuum. Instead, other people should be consulted and encouraged to participate: to collect the facts, analyze the message, and select the appropriate media. For example, a manager may ask a colleague to read an important memo before it is distributed throughout the organization. The content of the message should fit the recipients' level of knowledge and the organizational climate.

4. Consider Receivers' Needs

It is important to consider the needs of the receivers of the information. Whenever appropriate, one should communicate something that is of value to them, in the short run as well as in the more distant future. At times, unpopular actions that affect employees in the short run may be more easily accepted if they are beneficial to them in the long run. For instance, shortening the workweek may be more acceptable if it is made clear that this action will strengthen the competitive position of the company in the long run and avoid layoffs.

5. Use Appropriate Tone and Language and Ensure Credibility

There is a saying that the tone makes the music. Similarly, in communication, the tone of voice, the choice of language, and the congruency between what is said and how it is said influence the reaction of the receiver of the message. An autocratic manager ordering subordinate supervisors to practice participative management will create a credibility gap that will be difficult to overcome.

6. Get Feedback

Too often, information is transmitted without communicating. Communication is complete only when the message is understood by the receiver. And the sender never knows whether the message is understood unless he or she gets feedback. This is accomplished by asking questions, requesting a reply to a letter, and encouraging receivers to give their reactions to the message.

7. Consider Receivers' Emotions and Motivations

The function of communication is more than transmitting information. It also deals with emotions, which are very important in interpersonal relationships between superiors, subordinates, and colleagues in an organization. Furthermore, communication is vital for creating an environment in which people are motivated to work toward the goals of the enterprise while they achieve their personal aims. Another function of communication is control. As explained in the discussion of management by objectives (MBO), control does not necessarily mean top-down control. Instead, the MBO philosophy emphasizes self-control, which demands clear communication with an understanding of the criteria against which performance is measured.

8. Listen

Effective communicating is the responsibility not only of the sender but also of the receiver of the information. Thus, listening is an aspect that needs additional comment.

Listening: A Key to Understanding

The rushed, never-listening manager will seldom get an objective view of the functioning of the organization. Time, empathy, and concentration on the communicator's message are prerequisites for understanding. People want to be heard, want to be taken seriously, want to be understood. Thus, managers must avoid interrupting subordinates and putting them on the defensive. It is also wise both to give and to ask for feedback, for without it one can never be sure whether the message is understood. To elicit honest feedback, managers should develop an atmosphere of trust and confidence and a supportive leadership style, with a deemphasis on status (such as barricading oneself behind an extrawide executive desk).

Listening is a skill that can be developed. John W. Newstrom and Keith Davis propose ten techniques for improving listening: (1) stop talking, (2) put

> **Listening** is a skill that can be developed through appropriate techniques.

the talker at ease, (3) show the talker that you want to listen, (4) remove distractions, (5) empathize with the talker, (6) be patient, (7) hold your temper, (8) go easy on arguments and criticism, (9) ask questions, and (10) stop talking! The first and the last points are the most important: people have to stop talking before they can listen.[14]

Tips for Improving Written Communication

Effective writing may be the exception rather than the rule; nor do education and intelligence guarantee good writing. Many people fall into the habit of using technical jargon that can be understood only by experts in the same field. Common problems in written communication are that writers omit the conclusion or bury it in the report, are too wordy, and use poor grammar, inappropriate words, ineffective sentence structure, and incorrect spelling. Yet a few guidelines may do much to improve written communication[15]:

- Use simple words and phrases.
- Use short and familiar words.
- Use personal pronouns (such as "you") whenever appropriate.
- Give illustrations and examples; use charts.
- Use short sentences and paragraphs.
- Use active verbs, such as "The manager *plans*······."
- Avoid unnecessary words.

John Fielden suggests that the writing style should fit the situation and the effect the writer wants to achieve.[16] Specifically, he recommends a *forceful* style when the writer has power, using a polite but firm tone. The *passive* style is appropriate when the writer is in a position lower than that of the recipient of the message. The *personal* style is recommended for communicating good news and making persuasive requests for action. The *impersonal* style is generally right for conveying negative information. The *lively* or *colorful* style is suitable for good news, advertisements, and sales letters. On the other hand, a less colorful style, combining the impersonal with the passive, may be appropriate for common business writing.

Tips for Improving Oral Communication

For some people, including executives, the thought of having to give a speech may cause nightmares. Yet giving speeches and having fun doing it can be learned. A classic example of how one can learn oral communication is the Greek statesman Demosthenes, who, after being very discouraged following his poorly delivered first public speech, became one of the greatest orators through practice, practice, and practice.

Managers need to inspire, to lead, to communicate a vision. A clear idea of the organizational purpose is essential but insufficient for leading. This vision must be articulated. This means not only to state the facts but also to deliver them in a way that inspires people by catering to their values, their pride, and their personal objectives.

Most of the tips for written communication also apply to oral communication. The following Perspective provides helpful hints for improving oral communication.

INNOVATIVE PERSPECTIVE

Learning from Newscasters[17]

Some of the most effective communicators are American television news anchors, such as NBC's Tom Brokaw, ABC's Peter Jennings, and CBS's Dan Rather. How do they keep the television audience's attention despite the many attractive programs on other channels? Here are some hints you may use:

- Communicate with a large audience as you would do in a one-to-one conversation.
- Tell a story, an anecdote, and give examples.
- Pause—do not rush. In a discussion, a pause shows that you are listening.
- Use visual aids, such as diagrams, charts, overhead slides, and computer graphic presentations.
- Communicate confidence and create trust. This can be done by a strong and clear voice, good posture, and a smile.
- Use a colorful, specific language and show through your body language that you are confident and are in command of the situation.

The next time you watch television, think what you can learn from the highly paid news anchors, who reach sometimes millions of people.

ELECTRONIC MEDIA IN COMMUNICATION[18]

Organizations are increasingly adopting various electronic devices that improve communication. Electronic equipment includes mainframe computers, minicomputers, personal computers, and e-mail systems, as well as cell phones for making calls while on the move and beepers for keeping in contact with the office. The impact of computers on all phases of the management process will be discussed in Chapter 19 in connection with management information systems and will therefore be mentioned only briefly here. Let us first look at telecommunication in general and at the increasing use of teleconferencing in particular.

Telecommunication

Telecommunication is now widely used. Many organizations have already effectively used the new technology in a variety of ways, as shown by the following examples:

- Some banks supply hardware and software to their corporate customers so that they can easily transfer funds to their suppliers.
- Several banks now make phone banking services available, even to individuals.
- Information can be transmitted within seconds or minutes to countries on the opposite side of the globe by fax or e-mail.
- Car makers stay in close contact with their suppliers through telecommunication means to inform them about their needs, thus permitting just-in-time delivery and reducing inventory costs.
- Computerized airline reservation systems facilitate flight booking.
- Many firms now have detailed personnel information, including performance appraisals and career development plans, in a data bank.

As you can see, there are many applications of telecommunication. But to make telecommunication systems effective, technical experts must make every effort to identify the real needs of organizations and their customers and to design systems that are useful and user-friendly. Let us now turn to a specific application of the new technology: teleconferencing.

Teleconferencing

Owing to the wide variety of systems, including audio systems, audio systems with snapshots displayed on a video monitor, and live video systems, the term *teleconferencing* is difficult to define. In general, most people think of a **teleconference** as a group of people interacting with each other by means of audio and video media with moving or still pictures.

Full-motion video is frequently used to hold meetings among managers. Not only do they hear each other but they can also see each other's expressions as well as visual displays. This kind of communication is of course rather expensive, and audio in combination with still video may be used instead. This method of communicating may be useful for showing charts or illustrations during a technical discussion.

Some of the potential advantages of teleconferencing include savings in travel expenses and travel time. Also, conferences can be held whenever necessary, since there is no need to make travel plans long in advance. Because meetings can be held more frequently, communication is improved between, for example, headquarters and geographically scattered divisions.

There are also drawbacks to teleconferencing. Because of the ease in arranging meetings in this manner, they may be held more often than necessary. Moreover, since this approach uses rather new technology, the equipment is more prone to breakdowns. Most important, perhaps, teleconferencing is still a poor substitute for face-to-face meetings. Despite these limitations, increased use of teleconferencing is likely in the future.

> **Teleconference** A group of people interacting with each other by means of audio and video media with moving or still pictures.

The Use of Computers for Information Handling and Networking

Electronic data processing now makes it possible to handle large amounts of data and to make information available to a large number of people. Thus, one can obtain, analyze, and organize timely data quite inexpensively. But it must never be forgotten that data are not necessarily information—information must inform someone. New computer graphics can inform visually, displaying important company information in a matter of seconds. At PepsiCo, Inc., managers used to dig through reams of computer printouts for information; now they can quickly display a colored map showing their competitive picture.

> www.pepsi.com

New technologies for Information Handling and Networking

The new information technology fundamentally changes communication.[19] **Instant messaging** shows whether a friend or colleague is connected to the Internet; if connected, messages can be exchanged instantly. Slack has become a workplace communication tool in recent years. And Zoom and Skype have become central for video conferencing. And WhatsApp and WeChat have become useful for group coordination.

SUMMARY

Communication is important for the internal functioning of the organization and for interaction with the external environment. Communication is the transfer of information from a sender to a receiver, with the information being understood by the receiver. The communication process begins with the sender, who encodes an idea that is sent in oral, written, visual, or some other form to the receiver. The receiver decodes the message and gains an understanding of what the sender wants to communicate. This, in turn, may result in some change or action. But the communication process may be interrupted by "noise", which is anything that hinders communication.

In an organization, managers should have the information necessary for doing a good job. The information may flow not only downward or upward in the organization structure but also horizontally or diagonally. Communication can be in written form, but more information is communicated orally. In addition, people communicate through gestures and facial expressions. A great variety of communication methods are available. For example, technology may be used for wired and wireless telephone, fax, voice, and e-mail as well as teleconferences and video conferences.

Communication is hindered by barriers and breakdowns in the communication process. Recognizing these barriers and listening facilitate not only understanding but also managing. Tips for improving written and oral communication are suggested. Electronic media can improve communication, as illustrated by teleconferencing and the application of computers, two of many approaches to handling the increasing amount of information in organizations and coping with the trend of globalization.

KEY IDEAS AND CONCEPTS FOR REVIEW

Communication
Communication process model
"Noise" in communication
Downward communication
Upward communication
Ombudsperson
Crosswise communication
Written communication: advantages and disadvantages
Oral communication: advantages and disadvantages
Nonverbal communication
Observational Research

Human-Centered Design
Barriers and breakdowns in communication
Responses to information overload
Guidelines for improving communication
Listening as a key to understanding
Teleconferencing
Instant messaging
White Paper

FOR DISCUSSION

1. Briefly describe the communication process model. Select a communication problem and determine the cause (or causes) by applying the model in your analysis.
2. List different channels for transmitting a message. Discuss the advantages and disadvantages of the various channels.
3. What are some kinds of downward communication? Discuss those used most frequently in an enterprise you are familiar with. How effective are the various types?
4. What are some problems in upward communication? What would you suggest for overcoming the difficulties?
5. What are the advantages and disadvantages of written and oral communication? Which do you prefer: written or oral? Under what circumstances?
6. What is information overload? Do you ever experience it? How do you deal with it?
7. How well do you listen? How could you improve your listening skills?
8. Discuss the role of electronic media in communication.

EXERCISES/ ACTION STEPS

1. Recall a situation that occurred at home or at work and identify the communication problems that you observed or experienced. Discuss how the communication model in this chapter can help you locate the problems.
2. Go to the library and do research on a public figure who communicates well. Discuss this person's characteristics as they relate to communication.
3. Spend 30 minutes observing customer and staff interactions at your favorite store. Based on your observations what could be improved in the way the store manages its customer experience?

INTERNET RESEARCH

1. Search the Internet for the term "electronic data processing" or "EDP". Find out the definition of the term and see how it evolved through the history of business communication.
2. Use a search engine to find out about various forms of wireless or mobile communications. How can each type of wireless device enhance your business communication capability?

GLOBAL CASE

Could the Challenger Accident Have Been Avoided?[20]

The Challenger space shuttle accident on January 28, 1986, gripped America more than any other event in the last dozen years or so. It was a tragic accident in which seven people died. There is now evidence that the astronauts may have survived the initial explosion and may have died on impact when the space shuttle hit the water. The purpose of recounting the Challenger accident is to briefly explain what happened, possible reasons for why it happened, how it may have been prevented, and what one can learn from it.

The Challenger mission consisted of two complex systems: the technical system and the managerial system. The technical problem was the troublesome O-rings, which under pressure and low temperatures became ineffective and did not provide the required seal. Engineers and managers were aware of the problem. So why was the go-ahead given for launching the spacecraft? Can it be explained by the way the managerial system worked?

Engineers at Morton Thiokol, the contractor for the rocket booster, argued against the launch, citing previous problems at low temperatures. Management, on the other hand, may have felt pressure from NASA to go ahead with the launch. Roger Boisjoly, one of the engineers who argued strongly against the launch, stated that he received looks from management that seemed to say, "Go away and don't bother us with the facts." He said that he felt helpless. Another engineer was told to take off his engineering hat and put on his management hat.

Eventually, managers gave the go-ahead. Engineers were excluded from the final decision. What, then, were some possible reasons for the disaster? Some argued that there was a lack of communication between engineers and managers. They had different goals: safety versus on-time launching. Others suggested that people with responsibilities did not want to hear the bad news.

CHAPTER 17 Communication

Thus, no listening. Still others suggested that there was insufficient provision for upward communication outside the chain of command. There was also a suggestion that status differences between engineers and managers and between upper- and lower-level managers may have played a role in inhibiting upward communication. Perhaps there was also false confidence in the mission because of past luck. Managers and engineers knew of the problem, but nobody was killed before. Moreover, no one in the organizational unit wanted to be the "bad guy" to halt the launch. Morton Thiokol may also have been concerned about a pending contract.

The result of the series of events was the death of seven Americans: Jarvis, McAuliffe, McNair, Onizuka, Resnik, Scobee, and Smith. The question on our mind is: Could this accident have been prevented?

Questions:

1. What can you learn from this disaster that may be relevant to your organization or an organization you know?
2. What do you think was the cause, or were the causes, of the Challenger disaster?

PART 5 CLOSING

Global and Entrepreneurial Leading

This part closing is on Global and Entrepreneurial Leading. First, the international focus is on selected global aspects of leading, specifically the influence of different cultures. This is followed by the discussion of the possible traits of entrepreneurial leaders and communication with the "elevator pitch". Finally, a global car industry case on Ford's chief executive officers (CEOs) is presented to illustrate managerial leading and leadership styles.

INTERNATIONAL FOCUS: LEADING IN DIFFERENT CULTURES[21]

The managerial function of leading focuses on human interactions among people. Managers operating in the global environment need to understand at least some cultural aspects of the country in which they plan to work. The influence of the nation's culture on the organization culture may not be immediately recognized, yet it is reflected in organizational behavior and managerial practices.

Culture and Managerial Behavior

Culture is not easy to define. One way to describe culture is as a pattern of behavior related to values and beliefs that were developed over a period of time. Symbols, for example, may indicate what members of a society or an organization value. Indeed, one may distinguish between the culture of a nation and that of an organization. The external environment influences the way people interact within an organization. It must also be recognized that within a country the culture may differ widely, not only in countries as large and diverse as the United States but also in geographically small and relatively homogeneous countries such as Germany. Northern Germans behave differently than the people in southern Germany. It is with this precaution that culture and its impact on organizations must be viewed.

Today's managers need to develop a global perspective; a parochial view is inappropriate. In the past, many U.S. corporations (except the multinationals) saw little reason to develop a global view. The immense U.S. market was often sufficient for small- and medium-sized firms. These companies did not see the need to expand beyond the national boundaries and venture to foreign countries, with different cultures, different languages, and increased risks. But now hardly any company can ignore the global environment, even if the firm has no plans to operate abroad. Increasingly, foreign firms are entering the U.S. market. Moreover, many U.S. firms employ people from different nations with different cultures.

Cultural differences affect managerial behavior and practices such as planning (e.g., short- versus long-term orientation), organizing (e.g., the kind of organization structure or the attitude toward delegation), staffing (e.g., selection based on family relationships versus on professional qualifications), leading (e.g., participative versus directive leadership style), and controlling (e.g., tight and close control versus broad control).

Culture also affects interpersonal relations, such as those found in negotiations. In Russia, for example, people in business may not seek long-term relations with their negotiating partners.[22] Also, one should not be surprised to see very few Russians smile in public. In Russian business dealings, toasts are very common, so foreign managers would be well advised not to try to keep up with the way Russians drink alcoholic beverages.

Americans may find doing business with the British relatively easy. Not only do Americans and the British share many cultural aspects, but they also communicate in the same native language, which facilitates interpersonal relations. However, the British do not like to discuss business at the dinner table.

In France, conflict is a common part of daily life. The French attempt to seek the truth in universal laws. They also base their personal trust on the character of the individual, rather than on professional achievement. Moreover, competitive drive is not as pronounced in France as it is in the United States. The social class structure and the status related to this structure are very important for social interactions within and outside the organization.

Since business relationships with Japanese firms are becoming more frequent, and since foreign managers, in particular Westerners are often unaware or uncertain of Japanese cultural aspects in social interactions, some guidelines will be provided.

Understanding the Business Culture in Japan

People from Western countries may feel uncomfortable doing business in Japan. It may be extremely difficult to understand the subtleties of the Japanese culture, so thorough preparation may be vitally important for harmonious business relationships.

Establishing Business Relationships

It is virtually impossible to meet new Japanese business partners without establishing contacts long before the trip to Japan. Appointments need to be preceded by connections and letters planning the meetings. While it may be difficult to learn the Japanese language, one should at least learn greetings and some common phrases. In a male-dominated society such as Japan, Western women may feel uncomfortable at first. However, they are aided by the fact that the Japanese are very polite to foreigners in general. Moreover, even Japanese women have made some career advancement in recent years in Japanese firms.

For the Japanese, face-to-face communication is very important. They want to know their foreign partners very well before doing business with them. Moreover, it must be remembered that Japanese managers try to reach a consensus among themselves before responding to questions or making statements. One of the authors had the opportunity to visit a major Japanese car maker. Questions directed at the Japanese host were first discussed by the managers (in Japanese) before one of the managers provided answers.

Recognizing What the Japanese May Think About Westerners

The Japanese may admire the innovativeness of Westerners as well as their energy in getting things done. On the other hand, foreigners are often viewed as being impatient, making quick acquaintances but shallow friendships. Moreover, the Japanese often feel that deprivation, such as that experienced after World War II, made them hard workers. Some Japanese political and business leaders feel that Japan should now be assuming economic leadership in the world. These same leaders realize that the economic prosperity of their more than 120 million people depends on exports and the operation of Japan's multinational corporations abroad. Furthermore, Japan has only limited natural resources and must import all its oil from abroad.

Understanding the Art of Gift Giving

One can distinguish between two kinds of gifts: personal and corporate. Personal gifts may include picture books or items for which the home country is known. Other items may include golf balls, caps, tie clips, or native jewelry from the home country. If the Japanese partner has children, then T-shirts, children's books, or pens or pencils may be appropriate gifts. Corporate gifts may include pens, T-shirts, bookmarks, or other items with the company logo. These items should be made in the home country, not in Japan.

The way gifts are presented is also important. Presents should be wrapped in colors appropriate for the occasion, such as blue, brown, gray, or green. Showy colors, such as pink or red, and flowered paper are not appropriate. Moreover, black and white, known as funeral colors, should be avoided. Giving and receiving gifts is done with both hands. Gift packages are generally not opened in front of the giver, in case it may embarrass him or her. If a gift consists of several similar items, avoid giving four or nine items of a kind, as this may imply death or choking, respectively.

Meeting with the Japanese

Business meetings in Japan are generally more formal than in the United States. The preliminary aspects take a great deal of time, yet they are essential for a successful meeting. Unless introduced, one introduces oneself first to the senior Japanese businessperson. At this time, business cards are exchanged. If the ranking, or senior, person is not known, it usually becomes evident from the behavior of subordinates, who show great respect toward this person. Moreover, it is usually the senior person who enters the room first. At the meeting, the ranking person usually sits in the middle position at the table or in the middle among his advisors. (Note that there are only few women in top management positions in Japanese companies.)

The presentation of business cards is an essential ritual. Never leave your home without your business card when going to Japan. Ideally, the card should be in English and Japanese. Younger persons, or those of lower ranking, present their card first to the Japanese business partner. However, lower-level foreign managers only give their card when the Japanese CEO has offered his. The card should be presented with both hands, unless the cards are exchanged with a handshake. Also, the printed side (the English side if the other side is in Japanese) should be held face up and in such a way that the recipient can read it without having to turn the card. While the Japanese have a custom of bowing, a friendly nod by the foreign person will suffice.

Meetings serve not only for "making deals" but also for establishing relationships. The Japanese would like to know whether they feel comfortable enough to deal with the counterpart. This means that they want to know whether a person is trustworthy, has a thorough knowledge of the product or service offered, and is listening and being receptive to their needs. Americans are often perceived as being too talkative or too pushy in obtaining a decision.

Modern managers need to develop a perspective with a global geographic and multicultural orientation. Being aware of cultural differences is a prerequisite for personal and organizational success.

ENTREPRENEURIAL FOCUS: CHARACTERISTICS OF ENTREPRENEURIAL LEADERS AND COMMUNICATING WITH THE ELEVATOR PITCH

Are entrepreneurial leaders born or made? This question has been the focus of significant research and debate. Is entrepreneurial ability inherent in all of us? Does it require some external shock to awaken it inside of us? Can we identify the characteristics or traits of great entrepreneurial leaders, and can these traits be taught?[23]

When one thinks of great entrepreneurs, who comes to mind and what characteristics stand out among them? Are they visionary and determined? Are they creative and persuasive? How else can we define what makes people great entrepreneurs? One of the earliest definitions of an entrepreneur can be traced to Richard Cantillon in 1734. Cantillion, an economist, defined entrepreneurship as self-employment with an uncertain return.[24] Joseph A. Schumpeter stated that entrepreneurs are a force for change and make existing products obsolete.[25]

Although studies have shown that personality traits are not very good indicators of future behavior,[26] researchers still examine the impact of the entrepreneur's personal characteristics. For example, Singh and DeNoble (2003) found that the personality characteristic of "openness" is related to entrepreneurship as it "fosters creativity, originality and receptiveness to new experience".[27]

Other traits commonly associated with entrepreneurs include: a drive to excel, risk taking (although—typically calculated risks), self-confidence, and persuasiveness.[28] Art Ciocca, Chairman of the Wine Group, one of the largest wine companies in the United States, shared that, "Almost every entrepreneur I have known has been passionate about his/her endeavor and highly driven to succeed. Most have excellent intra and interpersonal skills and are otherwise largely right brain oriented with excellent feel and intuition. They know how to get in the way of luck!" Brett Bonthron, a former sales manager with Microsoft and serial entrepreneur, reflecting on his experiences stated, "Everyone cites that entrepreneurs are optimists, and I think that is true, but the best entrepreneurs never get so optimistic that they ignore the true core problems their business is facing. Successful entrepreneurs are flexible and can change—this is a bit of a cliché I know—but I have known a lot of entrepreneurs that are so passionate about achieving their vision that they have not been flexible; they have not been able to change in the face of overwhelming evidence." Timmons and Spinelli in their textbook, *New Venture Creation*, state, "Managers of entrepreneurial firms need to recognize and cope with innovation, taking risks, and responding quickly, as well as with absorbing major setbacks. The most effective managers seem to thrive on the hectic, and at times chaotic, pace and find it challenging and stimulating, rather than frustrating or overwhelming."[29]

It is not clear, however, if the aforementioned traits preexist in successful entrepreneurs or if the entrepreneurial experience develops these traits in entrepreneurs. Circumstances do seem to affect entrepreneurial behavior. For example, there is a high coincidence of entrepreneurship among immigrant populations—perhaps because other professional business opportunities are not as available to them as they are for native-born residents of a country. The loss of a job or the decline of an industry may also necessitate entrepreneurial behavior.

So the question remains, what aspects of entrepreneurs are worth emulating? While certain personality traits (e.g., self-confidence) probably do make successful entrepreneurship more likely, we know that the ability to communicate and persuade is vital. The entrepreneur must be able to effectively communicating with investors, customers, partners, potential employees, and various other stakeholders in the potential enterprise. One essential aspect of this communicative ability is sometimes demonstrated by the "elevator pitch".

The notion of the elevator pitch is based on a scenario where a young entrepreneur happens to step into an elevator with a potential investor. The entrepreneur recognizes this fortunate opportunity but also realizes that she likely has only a minute or so to introduce herself and "pitch" her business idea to the potential investor. The goal of the entrepreneur is not to describe in detail every aspect of the business, but, rather, to present enough about the business to spur interest in the investor in order to arrange for another more formal meeting. Therefore, the entrepreneur must be somewhat assertive, very clear and precise in her description of the business and opportunity, and brief. The importance of the ability to communicate clearly and efficiently is magnified in today's increasingly fast-paced business environment. Brevity tends to be even more highly prized by venture investors whose time is limited as they are constantly approached by eager entrepreneurs.

This ability of to effectively pitching a business idea in an efficient and clear way is also increasingly recognized by business schools in their curriculum and in major student entrepreneurial contests that are regularly organized. The "Elevator Pitch Competitions" held annually at the University of San Francisco, Wake Forest University, and other strong entrepreneurial universities have become famous for their intensity, the entrepreneurial opportunity they provide, and their learning value for both the presenters and the spectators.[30]

But what does an elevator pitch actually cover? In essence, it covers much of the same material of a business plan but in a much-abbreviated format. For example, after a brief personal introduction, an elevator pitch should include the following at a minimum.

— Company name and brief description.
  A crisp and clear description of the company is essential. If the company description is not clear, the rest of the pitch is diminished as the audience is still focused on construing the company business while the entrepreneur is describing other items.
— Opportunity or problem that the company is addressing.
  A new venture should be opportunity oriented, as this is the reason for its existence. What problem is the entrepreneur solving? Is this a problem faced by many people or business?
— How does the company's product or service solve this problem or take advantage of this opportunity?
  It should be clear how the entrepreneur's product perfectly or nearly perfectly solves the problem faced by consumers or creates a great new value for them.
— What is the firm's competition and what is the company's competitive advantage?
  In other words, if the entrepreneur has demonstrated that there is a market need and her product can meet that need, a potential investor wants to know who else is also trying to solve this market problem and why is this entrepreneur's firm the best to do it and earn financing dollars.
— An estimate of the market size and the marketing strategy to reach this market.
  It is important to be specific how the entrepreneur will get the first customer.
— Describe the company's business model.
  A business model illustrates how the company works from supply to production to distribution, marketing, and receipts. If time is short, describe the revenue model (how the firm is paid through sales of product, advertising, commissions, etc.)
— If time remains, highlight the management team experience, the amount of financing that is needed, and what the financing will be applied to.

This may seem like a lot to cover in 90 seconds or less (the approximate time of an average elevator ride). It is. But this is an essential communication skill of a successful entrepreneur. It can be done even for technical products and services (e.g., medical devices or software). There is no need to describe exactly how the product works; rather, focus on the problem that the product solves. Try to inspire the listener with the significance of the problem and the promise of the product to solve the problem. For example, the entrepreneur of a medical device company may describe a specific illness affects a large number of people each year. However, the illness is treatable with early detection and the entrepreneur's product will enable that early detection cheaply and accurately and save many lives. If an investor in the life science industries would want to hear more, the elevator pitch was successful.

Onset Ventures, a leading Silicon Valley Venture Capital firm with offices in the United States, India, and Israel, suggests that successful pitches share a common DNA. This DNA includes some of the following elements: 1. Sell rather than explain, 2. Story added to execution leads to valuation, 3. Cite reports to give credibility to your claims, 4. Assemble the right team.

Communication is about clarity, but it can also inspire. Entrepreneurs must be able to inspire with their communication in order to convince friends and strangers to join the quest in the development of a new and potentially risky venture. Practice your own elevator pitch again and again. Be ready to give it at a moments notice, whether you take the elevator or the stairs.

GLOBAL CAR INDUSTRY CASE

Who Will Provide Leadership in the Automobile Industry[31]

Today, most cars depend on gasoline-power for propulsion. The future, however, provides opportunities for many alternative power sources ranging from electricity to hydrogen. Diesel and natural gas engines are still based on old technologies. The developing technologies may be utilized not only for cars, but also for buses, trucks, trains, ships boats, and other vehicles. The focus, however, is on the application of power sources for cars.

New Technologies

At the moment, hybrid cars are very popular and electric cars gaining on importance. Hydrogen-driven cars are still futuristic and the infrastructure is critical for the success of cars using electricity for power

Electric Cars

Companies have been working on electric cars for a long time. But only more recently do we see some viable electric cars on the market. **Tesla** Motors, a Silicon-based company near San Francisco, began producing and selling the high-priced Tesla Roadster. More recently, the company introduced the Model S an electric luxury sedan (with a base price of more than $55.000), It is still expensive, but much less than the Roadster. Tesla cars use lithium-ion batteries with a driving range of more than 200 miles. The Roadster accelerates very quickly and is even more efficient than Toyota's popular Prius. The Tesla car may have inspired General Motors (GM) to develop the Chevrolet Volt electric car.

GM introduced the plug-in Chevrolet Volt with much fanfare. But shortly after its introduction, the company planned a five-week production stop, temporary laying off 1.300 employees.[32] The reason was a shortfall of its sales expectation. The Volt experienced battery problems that may have contributed to the low-volume sales in America and may have affected the sales of Opel's Ampera, a newer "twin" in Europe. Still, GM is hopeful for the future of electric cars.

Carlos Ghosn, **Nissan's** CEO is a strong advocate for electric cars with significant R&D investments. The electric Leaf vehicle was introduced in 2010 in Europe, Japan, and North America. The company arranged agreements with the U.S. State of Oregon with the objective of encouraging clean energy. Alliances were also formed in Denmark, France, Spain, Portugal, and other countries. Nissan attempts to profit from the new developments in battery technology and formed an alliance with the German Bosch company. Nissan is best known for the Leaf model which has a driving range of some 100 miles, or 160 km. Other models such as the Esflow, Townpod, Nuvu, and Land Glider have been introduced in various motor shows. It is clear, Nissan's strategy is betting on the electric car future.

Hybrid Cars

Besides electric cars from Tesla, GM, and Nissan, hybrid cars have become very popular, especially during the time of high gasoline prices. The hybrid vehicle uses a small combustion engine and an electric motor or even two motors. The combustion engines use mostly gasoline or Diesel fuels. The electric motors are powered by batteries. The combustion engine not only charges the battery, but it is also used for propulsion. The result is an improved fuel consumption and reduced emission. Toyota Motors is at the forefront on the hybrid technology as illustrated by its popular Prius models. The basic Prius model (now in its third generation) has been followed by Prius V, which is larger, the smaller Prius C, and the Prius Plug-In Hybrid which also allows stationary battery charging. Other Toyota models are the Camry Hybrid and the Highlander Hybrid. Clearly, Toyota is betting its future on hybrid vehicles.

Hydrogen Cars

Another approach to prepare for the future is the development of hydrogen vehicles that carry hydrogen fuel in the tank. Many car companies have hydrogen vehicles in the developmental stage, but the vehicles are mostly used for demonstration rather than mass production. The American Ford Motor Company dropped the hydrogen developments and so did Renault–Nisan. GM reduced its efforts and focused on the electric Volt vehicle. Other companies still make some efforts in the hydrogen vehicle development, but the hydrogen fuel cell car got a setback when the U.S. Energy Secretary Steven Chu announced cutting its research funding. In the short-term, there are other more promising alternatives such as the plug-in electric cars.

Infrastructure[33]

With the increased interest in electric plug-in cars, the need for providing opportunities for charging the batteries is evident. Various approaches have been used such as Park & Charge in Europe and the standardized PARVE design in Spain. Charging stations can be found at taxi stands, parking lots, shopping centers, garages, on-street parking, and many other places. An easy way to charge the battery is at the home. Another, innovative approach is to swap the batteries on designated battery switching stations.

Better Place is an American-Israeli venture company located in California, near San Francisco. The idea originated at the World Economic Forum in Davos, Switzerland in 2005. The battery-swapping network was introduced in Israel, Denmark, and Hawaii. Other countries and regions are also interested in the idea. The project is supported by Renault-Nissan which will built vehicles suitable for battery swapping. In such an arrangement, the vehicle would be sold by the car manufacturer and the batteries would be supplied separately. Customers would pay for the battery, and the use of the electric power. Batteries could be swapped in three minutes or even in same cases in one minute. The customer would not even have to get out of the car while the battery is replaced.

Below is a diagram that highlights some of the issues in the future development of car propulsion.

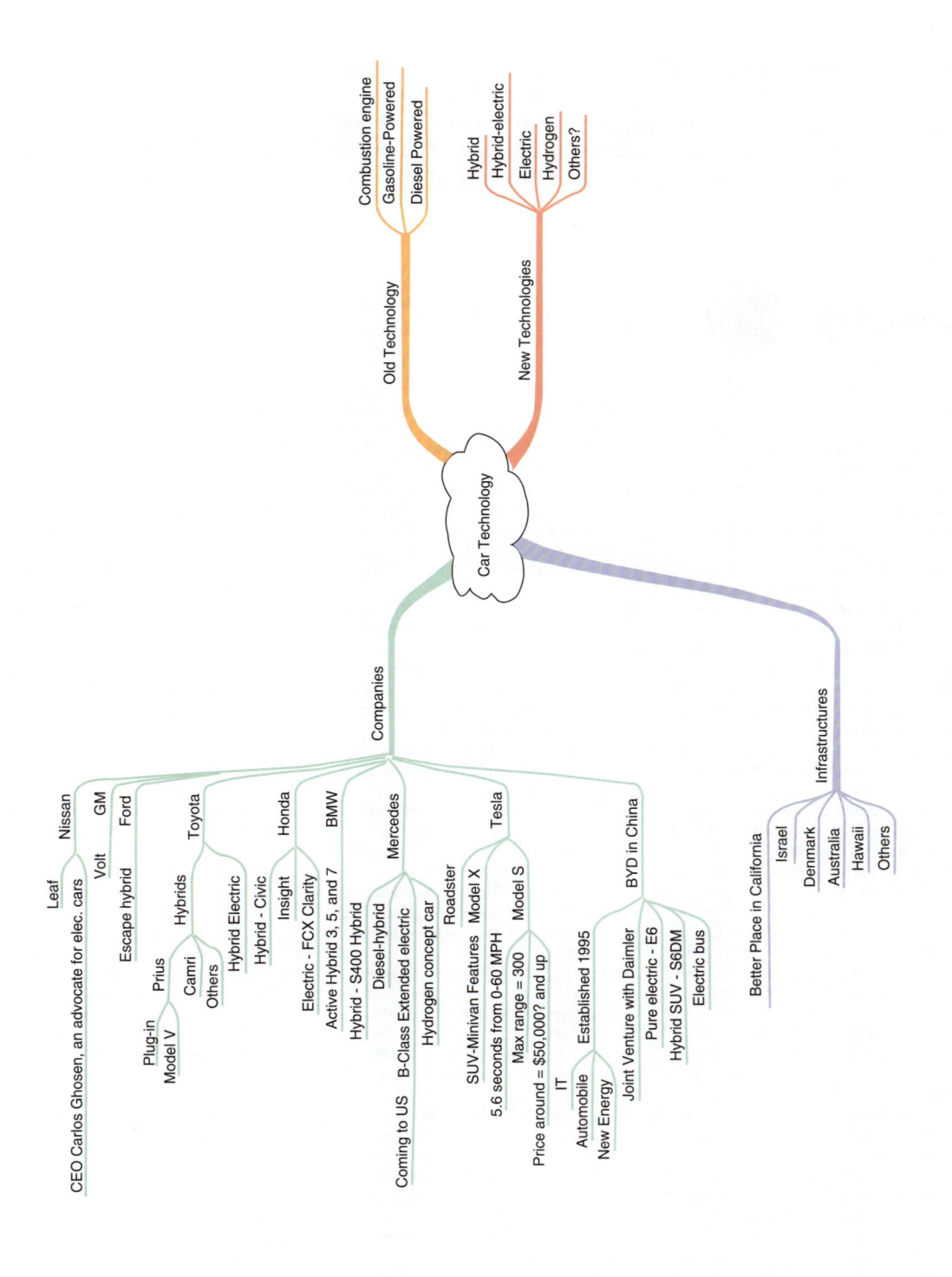

PART 5 CLOSING   Global and Entrepreneurial Leading   457

Car Technology

Old Technology
- Combustion engine
  - Gasoline-Powered
  - Diesel Powered

New Technologies
- Hybrid
- Hybrid-electric
- Electric
- Hydrogen
- Others?

Companies
- Nissan
  - Leaf
  - CEO Carlos Ghosen, an advocate for elec. cars
- GM
  - Volt
- Ford
  - Escape hybrid
- Toyota
  - Prius
    - Plug-in
    - Model V
  - Hybrids
    - Camri
    - Others
  - Hybrid Electric
- Honda
  - Hybrid - Civic
  - Insight
  - Electric - FCX Clarity
- BMW
  - Active Hybrid 3, 5, and 7
  - Hybrid - S400 Hybrid
- Mercedes
  - Diesel-hybrid
  - Coming to US
  - B-Class Extended electric
  - Hydrogen concept car
- Tesla
  - Roadster
  - Model X
    - SUV-Minivan Features
    - 5.6 seconds from 0-60 MPH
    - Max range = 300
  - Model S
    - Price around = $50,000? and up
- BYD in China
  - IT
  - Automobile
  - New Energy
  - Established 1995
  - Joint Venture with Daimler
  - Pure electric - E6
  - Hybrid SUV - S6DM
  - Electric bus

Infrastructures
- Better Place in California
- Israel
- Denmark
- Australia
- Hawaii
- Others

Questions:

1. Which new technology (electric-plug in, hybrid, hybrid electric, hydrogen) will lead and succeed in the car industry, let's say five or ten years from now?
2. Would you buy an electric plug in car with a range of about 100 or 200 miles? Why or why not?
3. Will your next car have a traditional gasoline or diesel combustion engine? If your answer is "Yes", are you concerned about the environmental impact of such a car? Why or why not?

ENDNOTES

1. Jeffery Scott Mio, Ronald E. Riggio, Shana Levin, and Renford Reese, "Presidential Leadership and Charisma: The Effects of Metaphor," *Leadership Quarterly*, 2005, 16: 287; http://www.usa-patriotism.com/quotes/_list.htm, accessed January 5, 2016.
2. See also Deborah Tannen, "The Power of Talk: Who Gets Heard and Why," *Harvard Business Review*, September–October 1995, pp. 138–148. For written communication, see Arthur H. Bell, *NTC's Business Writer's Handbook* (Lincolnwood, IL: NTC, 1996); Joy Clayton, "The Ten Principles of Good Business Writing," *Harvard Management Communication Letter*, September 2000; or the classic book on style by William Strunk, Jr., and E. B. White, *The Elements of Style*, 4th ed. (New York: Longman, 1999).
3. "Wal-Mart Boss's Unlikely Role: Corporate Defender-in-Chief," *The Wall Street Journal*, July 26, 2005.
4. See Ideo.com for an introduction to the IDEO method of human centered design and innovation.
5. Corey Dade, "Moving Ahead – How UPS Went from Low-Tech to IT Power – and Where It's Headed Next," *The Wall Street Journal*, July 24, 2006.
6. See also Stever Robbins, "Communication Breakdown: Nine Mistakes Managers Make," *Harvard Management Communication Letter*, September 2000, pp. 3–5.
7. See also Nancy J. Adler, *International Dimensions of Organizational Behavior*, 3rd ed. (Boston: PWS-Kent, 1997).
8. See, for example, Arvind V. Phatak, *International Management* (Cincinnati, OH: South-Western, 1997), chap. 6.
9. Carol Hymowitz, "Executives Who Make Their Leisure Time Inspiring and Useful," *The Wall Street Journal*, August 14, 2006.
10. Dean Williams, "Ethics: Are You up for the Challenge?" International Association of Business Communication, www.iabc.com/help/ethicsresourcelist.htm, accessed October 2, 2006.
11. For a detailed discussion of this topic, see J. D. Miller's analysis of information overload in Daniel Katz and Robert L. Kahn, *The Social Psychology of Organizations* (New York: Wiley, 1978), pp. 451–455.
12. See also Theodore E. Zorn, "Converging within Divergence: Overcoming the Disciplinary Fragmentation in Business Communication, Organizational Communication, and Public Relations," *Business Communication Quarterly*, March 2002, pp. 44–53.
13. Interview conducted by e-mail with Lori Teranishi of IQFR, on August 26, 2009 by Mark Cannice.
14. John W. Newstrom and Keith Davis, *Organizational Behavior: Human Behavior at Work*, 9th ed. (New York: McGraw-Hill, 1993), p. 109.
15. Keith Davis and John W. Newstrom, *Human Behavior at Work: Organizational Behavior* (New York: McGraw-Hill, 1985), p. 438.
16. John S. Fielden, "What Do You Mean You Don't Like My Style?" *Harvard Business Review*, May–June 1982, pp. 128–138.
17. William Hennefrund, "Learning from Anchors," *The Toastmaster*, June 2002, pp. 17–19.
18. See also Simon Moore, "Disaster's Future – The Prospect for Corporate Crisis Management and Communication", in Fred H. Maidment, ed. *Annual Editions—Management* (New York: McGraw-Hill 2009), pp. 106–113.
19. Don Tapscott and Art Caston, *Paradigm Shift: The New Promise of Information Technology* (New York: McGraw-Hill, 1993); Don Tapscott, *The Digital Economy: Promise and Peril in the Age of Networked Intelligence* (New York: McGraw-Hill, 1996).
20. Information for this case was drawn from a variety of sources, including Congressional hearings and a presentation by Roger Boisjoly. See Robert Elliott Allinson, "A Call for Ethically-centered Management," *Academy of Management Executive*, February 1995, pp. 73–76; Paul W. Mulvey, John F. Veiga, and Priscilla M. Elsass, "When Teammates Raise a White Flag," *Academy of Management Executive*, February 1996, pp. 40–48; NASA, www.nasa.gov, accessed August 19, 2011, 2008.
21. For further reading, see Nancy J. Adler, *International Dimensions of Organizational Behavior*, 4th ed. (Boston: PWS-Kent, 2002); Simcha Ronen, *Comparative and Multinational Management* (New York: Wiley, 1986); Philip R. Harris and Robert T. Moran, *Managing Cultural Differences*, 2nd ed. (Houston, TX: Gulf Publishing, 1987); Christalyn Brannen, *Going to Japan on Business* (Berkeley, CA: Stone Bridge Press and BLC Intercultural, 1991); John C. Condon, *With Respect to the Japanese* (Yarmouth, ME: Intercultural Press, 1984); David J. Lu, *Inside Corporate Japan: The Art of Fumble-Free Management* (Tokyo: Charles E. Tuttle, 1987); Robert Neff, Ted Holden, Karen Lowry Miller, and Joyce Barnathan, "Hidden Japan: The Scandals Start to Reveal How the System Really Works," *Business Week*, August 26, 1991, pp. 34–38; Robert Neff, "Japan's Small Smoke-filled Room," ibid., pp. 42–44; Robert Whiting, *You Gotta Have Wa* (New York: Vintage Books, 1990); Mark Zimmerman, *How to Do Business with the Japanese* (New York: Random House, 1985). For discussions of management in various countries, see the country close-up articles in various issues of the *Academy*

of *Management Executive*: Canada, May 1999; Mexico, August 1999; Japan, November 1999; China, February 2000; India, May 2001; Russia, November 2001; Germany, February 2002.

22. For an excellent discussion of entrepreneurial leadership in Russia, see Sheila M. Puffer and Daniel J. McCarthy, "Navigating the Hostile Maze: A Framework for Russian Entrepreneurship," *Academy of Management Executive*, November 2001, pp. 24–36.

23. Please see "How do you teach entrepreneurship", USF Entrepreneur E-newsletter September 2003, for a roundtable discussion on how several professors teach entrepreneurship. http://www.usfca.edu/sobam/nvc/newsletter/2003/9/3.html.

24. Pramodita Sharma and James J. Chrisman, "Toward a Reconciliation of the Definitional Issue in the Field of Entrepreneurship", *Entrepreneurship Theory and Practice* Spring 1999, pp. 11–27.

25. Michael Morris, Pamela S. Lewis, and Donald L. Sexton, "Reconceptualizing Entrepreneurship: An Input-Output Perspective," *Advanced Management Journal*, Winter 1994, p. 21.

26. Nancy G. Boyd and George S. Vozikis, "The Influence of Self-Efficacy on the Development of the Entrepreneur," *Entrepreneurship Theory and Practice*, Summer 1994.

27. Gangaram Singh and Alex DeNoble, "Views on Self-Employment and Personality: An Exploratory Study," *Journal of Development Entrepreneurship*, December 2003.

28. Please also see "How do Students Learn Entrepreneurship", USF Entrepreneur E-newsletter November 2003, for a roundtable discussion on entrepreneurial characteristics and motivations by student entrepreneurs, http://www.usfca.edu/sobam/nvc/newsletter/2003/11/2.html

29. Jeffry A. Timmons and Stephen Spinelli, *New Venture Creation: Entrepreneurship for the 21st Century*, 7th ed. (McGraw-Hill Irwin, 2007), p. 266.

30. Please see http://www.usfca.edu/sobam/nvc/pub/bpc05mus.html for an audio recording of the 2005 USF Elevator Pitch Competition.

31. Tesla Motors, http://www.teslamotors.com/, accessed March 16, 2012; History of the Automobile, http://inventors.about.com/library/weekly/aacarsgasa.htm, accessed January 5, 2016; "Don't Forget the Combustion Engine", *Washington Post*, http://www.washingtonpost.com/opinions/dont-forget-the-combustion-engine/2011/10/06/gIQAtFNzTL_story.html, accessed January 5, 2016.

32. "G.M. Again Pauses Production of Chevy Volt", http://www.nytimes.com/2012/03/03/business/gm-suspends-production-of-chevrolet-volt.html, accessed January 5, 2016; Toyota, http://www.toyota.com/, accessed March 17, 2012; "Hydrogen Car Goes Like the Hindenburg: DoE Kills the Program, http://blogs.discovermagazine.com/80beats/2009/05/08/hydrogen-car-goes-down-like-the-hindenburg-doe-kills-the-program/, accessed March 18, 2012.

33. Charging Station, http://en.wikipedia.org/wiki/Battery_exchange_station#Battery_swapping, accessed March 18, 2012; Better Place, http://en.wikipedia.org/wiki/Better_Place, accessed March 18, 2012.

Goal Inputs of Claimants
1. Employees
2. Consumers
3. Suppliers
4. Stockholders
5. Governments
6. Community
7. Others

Inputs
1. Human
2. Capital
3. Managerial
4. Technological

EXTERNAL ENVIRONMENT

Managerial knowledge, goals of claimants, and use of inputs (Part 1, *The Basis of Management Theory and Science*)

↓

Planning (Part 2)

↓

Organizing (Part 3)

↓

Staffing (Part 4)

↓

Leading (Part 5)

↓

Controlling (Part 6)

↓

To Produce Outputs

EXTERNAL ENVIRONMENT

Reenergizing the System

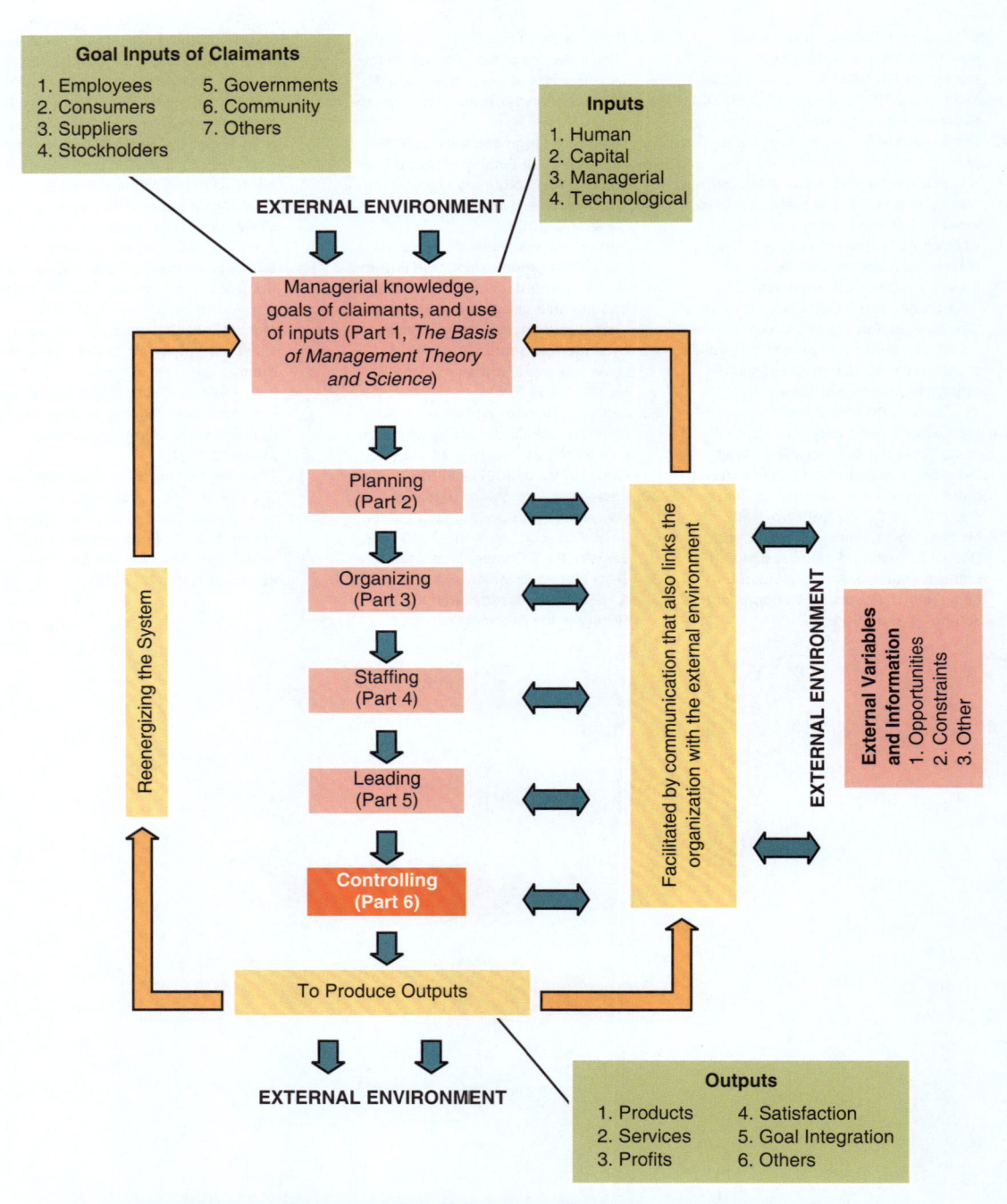

Facilitated by communication that also links the organization with the external environment

EXTERNAL ENVIRONMENT

External Variables and Information
1. Opportunities
2. Constraints
3. Other

Outputs
1. Products
2. Services
3. Profits
4. Satisfaction
5. Goal Integration
6. Others

SYSTEMS APPROACH TO MANAGEMENT: CONTROLLING

PART 6

Controlling

Chapter 18: The System and Process of Controlling
Chapter 19: Control Techniques and Information Technology
Chapter 20: Productivity, Operations Management, and Total Quality Management
Part 6 Closing: Global Controlling and Challenges and Entrepreneurial Controlling

CHAPTER 18

The System and Process of Controlling

Learning Objectives

After studying this chapter, you should be able to:

LO 1 Describe the steps in the basic control process

LO 2 Enumerate and explain the critical control points, standards, and benchmarking

LO 3 Illustrate applications of the feedback system

LO 4 Understand that real-time information will not solve all the problems of management control

LO 5 Show that feedforward control systems can make management control more effective

LO 6 Describe some of the most widely used techniques of overall control of an enterprise

LO 7 Recognize the use and problems of management audits by accounting firms

LO 8 Understand the difference between bureaucratic and clan control

LO 9 List and explain the requirements for effective controls

The managerial function of **controlling** is the measurement and correction of performance in order to make sure that enterprise objectives and the plans devised to attain them are being accomplished. Planning and controlling are closely related. In fact, some writers on management think that these functions cannot be separated. It is wise to separate them conceptually, however, which is why they are discussed individually in Parts 2 and 6 of this book. Still, planning and controlling may be viewed as the blades of a pair of scissors: the scissors cannot work unless there are two blades. Without objectives and plans, control is not possible because performance has to be measured against some established criteria.

> **Controlling** Measurement and correction of performance in order to make sure that enterprise objectives and the plans devised to attain them are being accomplished.

THE BASIC CONTROL PROCESS

Control techniques and systems are essentially the same for controlling cash, office procedures, morale, product quality, and anything else. The basic control process, wherever it is found and whatever is being controlled, involves three steps: (1) establishing standards, (2) measuring performance against these standards, and (3) correcting variations from standards and plans.

Establishment of Standards

Because plans are the yardsticks against which managers devise controls, the first step in the control process logically would be to establish plans. However, since plans vary in detail and complexity, and since managers cannot usually watch everything, special standards are established. **Standards** are simply criteria of performance. They are the selected points in an entire planning program at which measures of performance are made so that managers can receive signals about how things are going and thus do not have to watch every step in the execution of plans.

> **Standards** Criteria of performance.

There are many kinds of standards. Among the best are verifiable goals or objectives, as suggested in the discussion of managing by objectives (see Chapter 4). You will learn more about standards later, especially those that point out deviations at critical points.

Measurement of Performance

Although such measurement is not always practicable, the measurement of performance against standards should ideally be done on a forward-looking basis so that deviations may be detected in advance of their occurrence and avoided by appropriate actions. The alert, forward-looking manager can sometimes predict probable departures from standards. In the absence of such ability, however, deviations should be disclosed as early as possible.

Correction of Deviations

Standards should reflect the various positions in an organization structure. If performance is measured accordingly, it is easier to correct deviations. Managers know exactly where, in the assignment of individual or group duties, the corrective measures must be applied.

Correction of deviations is the point at which control can be seen as a part of the whole system of management and can be related to the other managerial functions. Managers may correct deviations by redrawing their plans or by modifying their goals. (This is an exercise of the principle of navigational change.) Or they may correct deviations by exercising their organizing function through reassignment or clarification of duties. They may correct, also, by additional staffing, by better selection and training of subordinates, or by that ultimate restaffing measure—firing. Another way is to correct through better leading—fuller explanation of the job or more effective leadership techniques.

GLOBAL PERSPECTIVE

Special Considerations in Controlling International Companies

Controlling domestic companies is often difficult, let alone exercising control of operations in different countries. The geographic distances make certain controls, such as observation, very difficult, despite modern jet service. Walmart, for example, has operations around the globe. The same measurement criteria can hardly be applied to all stores.

Control standards have to be adjusted to the local environment. Subsidiaries in low-labor-cost countries may have lower cost budgets than those in countries with a high-cost labor force. And productivity in countries with low labor costs may lag behind that of other countries.

Transfer pricing between the headquarters and the subsidiaries or between subsidiaries may distort the profitability and return-on-investment pictures. A similar distortion can occur through currency fluctuations among the various countries. Moreover, erratic or chronic inflation makes the setting of standards and measurement against those standards difficult.

Other factors should also be considered in controlling. As pointed out in the discussion of organizing, the organization structure should facilitate control. Multinational corporations require a different departmentation from that of domestic firms. Another way to exercise control is to prevent deviations from occurring by selecting competent managers. In the past, multinational corporations sent experienced managers to head their foreign subsidiaries. More recently, however, companies have been selecting and training local managers from the country in which they operate. Furthermore, managers with special skills in cultural adaptation may even come from a third country. At one time, the chief executive officer (CEO) of Volkswagen in America was neither a German nor an American but a Canadian.

The way control is exercised differs between countries. In the United States, attempts are made to pinpoint responsibility for deviations from standards. In many Asian countries, superiors usually try not to let the person responsible lose face. Moreover, standards may not even be set in measurable terms in the first place. How, then, can control be exercised? In countries such as Japan where group work is common, peer pressure may be a very effective means for exercising control.

In short, controlling—setting standards, measuring performance, and taking corrective actions—must be flexible enough to take into account the organizational and country-specific environment.

www.walmart.com
www.vw.com

BUSINESS ANALYTICS

A growing focus of management research and practice has been in the field of business analytics. The focus of business analytics is to make readily available advanced analysis of the treasure trove of data that organizations collect to the manager and decision maker to take better decisions for the course of the organization.[1] Often there can exist a time delay from the collection of data to its analysis and its dissemination to users of this information to make key decisions for the benefit of the enterprise. Business analytics is focused on better systematizing the collection, analysis, and availability of key organizational data sets to allow the firm to act and respond more nimbly to changes in its market and competitive environment.

Some consulting firms such as IBM have built practices on helping their clients leverage the data they have collected. IBM refers to this practice as "Smarter Analytics" with a promise to help its customer act more nimbly than their competitors with regard to identification of customer trends and the development of better business practices to reduce costs and mitigate risks.[2]

A focus on sustainable supply chain management has also come into play with many large enterprises seeking to maximize efficiency but also long-term sustainability of their supply chains. This focus entails not only gathering data to analyze cost but also methods to ensure ethical and environmentally sensitive business decisions.

CRITICAL CONTROL POINTS, STANDARDS, AND BENCHMARKING[3]

Standards are yardsticks against which actual or expected performance is measured. In a simple operation, a manager might control through careful personal observation of the work being done. However, in most operations, this is not possible because of the complexity of the operations and the fact that a manager has far more to do than personally observe performance for a whole day. A manager must choose points for special attention and then watch them to be sure that the whole operation is proceeding as planned.

The points selected for control should be *critical*, in the sense either of being limiting factors in the operation or of being better indicators than other factors of whether plans are working out. With such standards, managers can handle a larger group of subordinates and thereby increase their span of management, with resulting cost savings and improvement of communication. The **principle of critical point control**, one of the more important control principles, states that effective control requires attention to those factors critical to evaluating performance against plans. Another way of controlling is comparing company performance with that of other firms through benchmarking.

Principle of critical point control Effective control requires attention to factors critical to evaluating performance against plans.

Types of Critical Point Standards

Every objective, every goal of the many planning programs, every activity of these programs, every policy, every procedure, and every budget can become a standard against which actual or expected performance might be measured. In practice, however, standards tend to be of the following types: (1) physical standards, (2) cost standards, (3) capital standards, (4) revenue standards, (5) program standards, (6) intangible standards, (7) goals as standards, and (8) strategic plans as control points for strategic control.

Physical Standards

Physical standards are nonmonetary measurements and are common at the operating level, where materials are used, labor is employed, services are rendered, and goods are produced. They may reflect quantities, such as labor-hours per unit of output, pounds of fuel per horsepower per hour, ton-miles of freight traffic carried, units of production per machine-hour, or feet of wire per ton of copper. Physical standards may also reflect quality, such as hardness of bearings, closeness of tolerances, rate of climb of an airplane, durability of a fabric, or fastness of a color.

Cost Standards

Cost standards are monetary measurements and, like physical standards, are common at the operating level. They attach monetary values to specific aspects of operations. Illustrative of cost standards are such widely used measures as direct and indirect costs per unit produced, labor cost per unit or per hour, material cost per unit, machine-hour costs, cost per seat-mile, selling cost per dollar or unit of sales, and cost per foot of oil well drilled.

Capital Standards

There are a variety of capital standards, all arising from the application of monetary measurements to physical items. They have to do with the capital invested in the firm rather than with operating costs and are therefore primarily related to the balance sheet rather than to the income statement. Perhaps the most widely used standard for new investment, as well as for overall control, is return on investment. The typical balance sheet will disclose other capital standards, such as the ratios of current assets to current liabilities, debt to net worth, fixed investment to total investment, cash and receivables to payables, and bonds to stocks, as well as the size and turnover of inventories.

Revenue Standards

Revenue standards arise from attaching monetary values to sales. They may include such standards as revenue per bus passenger-mile, average sales per customer, and sales per capita in a given market area.

Program Standards

A manager may be assigned to install a variable budget program, a program for formally following the development of new products, or a program for improving the quality of a sales force. Although some subjective judgment may have to be applied in appraising program performance, timing and other factors can be used as objective standards.

Intangible Standards

More difficult to set are standards not expressed in either physical or monetary measurements. What standard can a manager use for determining the competence of the divisional purchasing agent or the personnel director? What can one use for determining whether the advertising program meets both short- and long-term objectives? Or whether the public relations program is successful? Are supervisors loyal to the company's objectives? Such questions show the difficulty of establishing standards or goals for clear quantitative or qualitative measurement.

Goals as Standards

With the present tendency for better-managed enterprises to establish an entire network of verifiable qualitative or quantitative goals at every level of management, the use of intangible standards, while still important, is diminishing. In complex program operations, as well as in the performance of managers themselves, modern managers are finding that through research and thinking it is possible to define goals that can be used as performance standards. While the quantitative goals are likely to take the form of the standards outlined above, the definition of qualitative goals represents an important development in the area of standards. For example, if the program of a district sales office is spelled out to include such elements as training sales people in accordance with a plan with specific characteristics, the plan and its characteristics themselves furnish standards that tend to become objective and therefore "tangible".

Strategic Plans as Control Points for Strategic Control

Strategic control requires systematic monitoring at strategic control points and modifying the organization's strategy based on this evaluation. As pointed out earlier, planning and controlling are closely related. Therefore, strategic plans require strategic control. Moreover, since control facilitates comparison of intended goals with actual performance, it also provides opportunities for learning, which in turn is the basis for organizational change. Finally, through the use of strategic control, one gains insights not only about organizational performance but also about the ever-changing environment by monitoring it.

Strategic control Systematic monitoring at strategic control points and modifying the organization's strategy based on this evaluation.

Benchmarking[4]

Benchmarking is a concept that is now widely accepted. It is an approach for setting goals and productivity measures based on best industry practices. Benchmarking developed out of the need to have data against which performance can be measured. What should the criteria be? If a company needs six days to fill a customer's order and the competitor in the same industry needs only five days, then five days does not become the standard if a firm in an unrelated industry can fill orders in four days. The four-day criterion becomes the benchmark even when at first this seems to be an unachievable goal. The process involved in filling the order is then carefully analyzed, and creative ways are encouraged to achieve the benchmark.

Benchmarking Approach for setting goals and productivity measures based on best industry practices.

There are three types of benchmarking. First, *strategic benchmarking* compares various strategies and identifies the key strategic elements of success. Second, *operational benchmarking* compares relative costs or possibilities for product differentiation. Third, *management benchmarking* focuses on support functions such as market planning and information systems, logistics, human resource management, and so on.

Three types of benchmarking: strategic, operational, and management.

The benchmarking procedure begins with the identification of what is to be benchmarked. Then superior performers have to be selected. Data need to be gathered and analyzed, which become the basis for performance goals. During the implementation of the new approach, performance is periodically measured and corrective actions are taken at that time.

CONTROL AS A FEEDBACK SYSTEM

Managerial control is essentially the same basic control process as that found in physical, biological, and social systems. Many systems control themselves through information feedback, which shows deviations from standards and initiates changes. In other words, systems use some of their energy to feed back information that compares performance with a standard and initiates corrective action. A simple feedback system was shown in Figure 4.1 in Chapter 4.

GLOBAL PERSPECTIVE

Examples of Feedback Systems

The house thermostat is a system of feedback and information control. When the house temperature falls below the preset level, an electric message is sent to the heating system, which is then activated. When the temperature rises and reaches the set level, another message shuts off the heater. This continual measurement and turning on and off of the heater keeps the house at the desired temperature. A similar process activates the air-conditioning system. As soon as the temperature exceeds the preset level, the air-conditioning system cools the house to the desired temperature. Likewise, in the human body, a number of feedback systems control temperature, blood pressure, motor reactions, and other conditions. Another example of feedback is the grade a student receives on a midterm test. This is intended, of course, to give the student information about how he or she is doing and, if performance is less than desirable, to send a signal suggesting improvement.

> **Management control is usually perceived as a feedback system similar to the common household thermostat.**

Management control is usually perceived as a feedback system similar to that which operates in the common household thermostat. This can be seen clearly in Figure 18.1, which shows the feedback process in management control. This system places control in a more complex and realistic light than if it is regarded merely as a matter of establishing standards, measuring performance, and correcting for deviations. Managers do measure actual performance, compare this measurement against standards, and identify and analyze deviations. But then, to make the necessary corrections, they must develop a program for corrective action and implement this program in order to arrive at the performance desired.

FIGURE 18.1 Feedback loop of management control

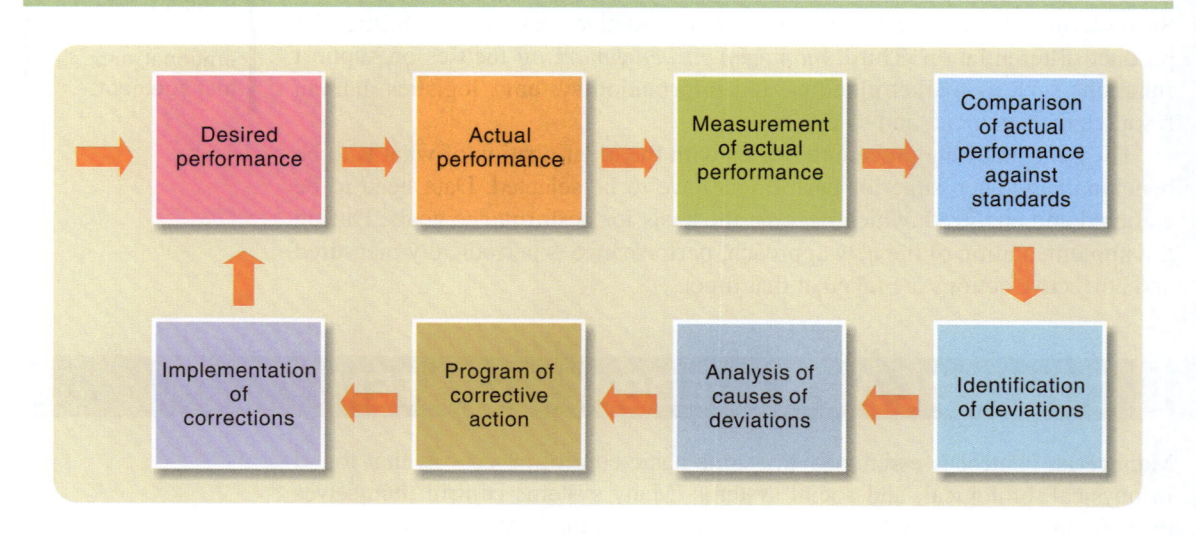

Desired performance → Actual performance → Measurement of actual performance → Comparison of actual performance against standards → Identification of deviations → Analysis of causes of deviations → Program of corrective action → Implementation of corrections → (back to Desired performance)

REAL-TIME INFORMATION AND CONTROL

One of the interesting advances arising from the use of the computer and from electronic gathering, transmission, and storage of data is the development of systems of **real-time information**. This is information about what is happening while it is happening. It is technically possible through various means to obtain real-time data on many operations. For years, airlines have obtained information about seat availability simply by entering a flight number, trip segment (e.g., London to New York), and date into a memory system, which immediately responds with the information. Supermarkets and department stores have electronic cash registers in operation that immediately transmit data on every sale to a central data storage facility, where inventory, sales, gross, profit, and other data can be obtained as sales occur. A factory manager can have a system that reports at any time the status of a production program in terms of such things as the production point reached, labor-hours accumulated, and even whether the project is late or on time in the manufacturing process.

> **Real-time information** about what is happening while it is happening.

Some people see real-time information as a means of getting real-time control in areas of importance to managers—in other words, control effected at the very time information shows a deviation from plans. But reference to the management control feedback loop in Figure 18.1 shows that real-time information does not, except possibly in the simplest and most unusual cases, make possible real-time control. It is possible in many areas to collect real-time data that measure performance. It may also be possible in many of these cases to compare these data with standards and even to identify deviations. But the analysis of causes of deviations, the development of programs of correction, and the implementation of these programs are likely to be time-consuming tasks.

In the case of quality control, for example, it may take considerable time to discover what is causing factory rejects and more time to put corrective measures into effect. In the more complex case of inventory control, particularly in a manufacturing company, which has many items—raw materials, component parts, goods in process, and finished goods—the correction time may be very long. Once it is learned that an inventory is too high, the steps involved in getting it back to the desired level may take a number of months. And so it goes with most other instances of management control problems: time lags are unavoidable.

This does not mean that prompt measurement of performance is unimportant. The sooner managers know that activities for which they are responsible are not proceeding in accordance with plans, the faster they can take action to make corrections. Even so, there is always the question of whether the cost of gathering real-time data is worth the few days saved. Often it is, as in the case of the airline business, in which ready information on seat availability is likely to be crucial to serving customers and filling airplanes. But in a major defense company producing one of the highest-priority defense equipment items, there was little real-time information in an otherwise highly sophisticated information control system. Even for this program, it was thought that the benefit of gathering real-time data was not worth the expense because the correction process took so long.

FEEDFORWARD, OR PREVENTIVE, CONTROL

The time lag in the management control process shows that control must be directed toward the future, if it is to be effective. It illustrates the problem of only using feedback from the output of a system and measuring this output as a means of control. It shows the deficiency of historical data, such as those received from accounting reports. One of the difficulties with such historical data is that they tell business managers in November that they lost money in October (or even September) because of something that was done in July. At this late time, such information is only a distressingly interesting historical fact.

What **managers** need for effective control is a system that will tell them, in time to take corrective action, that certain problems will occur if they do not do something now. Feedback from the output of a system is not good enough for control. It is little more than a postmortem, and no one has found a way to change the past.

Future-directed control is largely disregarded in practice, mainly because managers have been so dependent for purposes of control on accounting and statistical data. To be sure, in the absence of any means of looking forward, reference to history—on the questionable assumption that what is past is prologue—is admittedly better than no reference at all.

> **Managers** need for effective control a system that will tell them potential problems, giving them time to take corrective action before those problems occur.

Feedforward in Human Systems

There are many examples of feedforward control in human systems. A motorist, for example, who wishes to maintain a constant speed in going up a hill would not usually wait for the speedometer to signal a drop in speed before depressing the accelerator. Instead, knowing that the hill represents a disturbing variable in the system, the driver would probably correct for this by pressing the accelerator before speed falls. Likewise, a hunter will always aim ahead of a duck's flight to correct for the time lag between a shot and a hoped-for hit.

Feedforward versus Feedback Systems

Simple feedback systems measure outputs of a process and feed into the system or the inputs of the system corrective actions to obtain desired outputs. For most management problems, because of time lags in the correction process, this is not good enough. **Feedforward systems** monitor *inputs* into a process to ascertain whether the inputs are as planned; if they are not, the inputs, or perhaps the process, are changed in order to obtain the desired results. A comparison of feedforward and feedback systems is depicted in Figure 18.2.

In a sense, a feedforward control system is really a kind of feedback system. However, the information feedback is at the *input* side of the system so that corrections can be made before the system output is affected. Also, even with a feedforward system, a manager would still want to measure the final system output, since nothing can be expected to work perfectly enough to ensure that the final output will always be exactly as desired.

> **Feedforward systems** monitor inputs into a process to ascertain if the inputs are as planned; if they are not, the inputs or the process is changed in order to obtain the desired results.

FIGURE 18.2 Comparison of simple feedback and feedforward systems

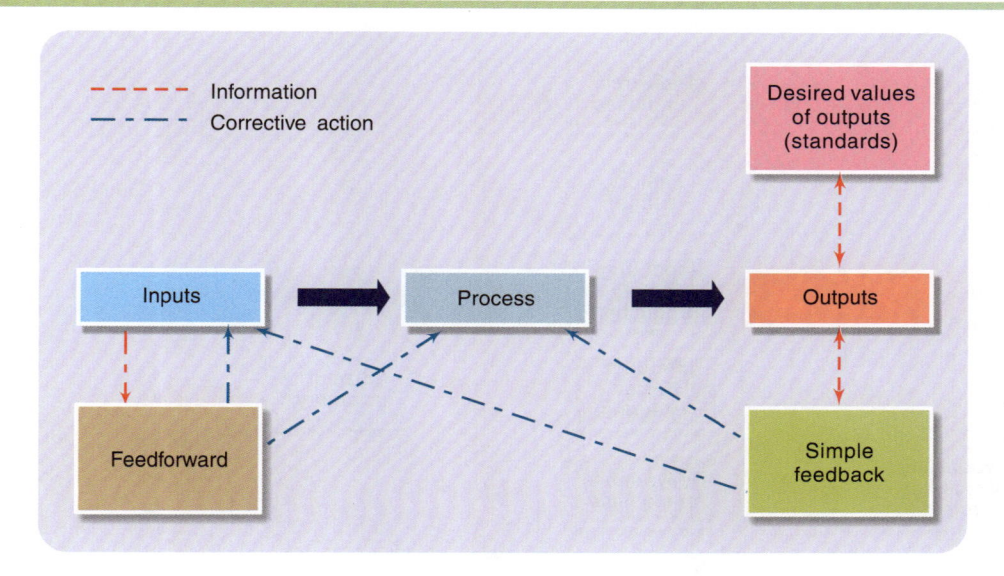

Feedforward in Management

An idea of what feedforward means in management control can be conveyed through the example of inventory planning system. Figure 18.3 illustrates what is involved. The somewhat simplified schematic figure of input variables for inventory planning and control indicates that, if managers are to exercise effective control over inventory, they must identify the variables in the system. Some of the variables have either a negative or a positive effect on inventory.

Also, if the system of variables and their impact on a process are accurately portrayed—and each enterprise should design its own system, appropriate to the realities of its situation—a deviation from any planned input can result in an unplanned output, unless something is done about it in time. For example, in the case of the inventory model, if delivered purchases are greater than planned or if factory usage turns out to be less than planned, the result will be a higher-than-planned inventory, unless corrective action is taken. Of course, to make feedforward work in practice, inputs must be carefully monitored.

One of the problems in all feedforward control systems is the necessity of watching for what engineers call disturbances. These are factors which have not been taken into account in the input model but which may have an impact on the system and the desired end result. Obviously, it would be impracticable to take into account in a model all inputs that might possibly affect the operation of a program. For example, the bankruptcy of a large supplier might be an unanticipated, and unprogrammed, input variable and would delay the shipping of supplies. Since unprogrammed events do sometimes occur and may upset a desired output, monitoring regular inputs must be supplemented by watching for, and taking into account, unusual and unexpected disturbances.

FIGURE 18.3 System of inputs for feedforward inventory control

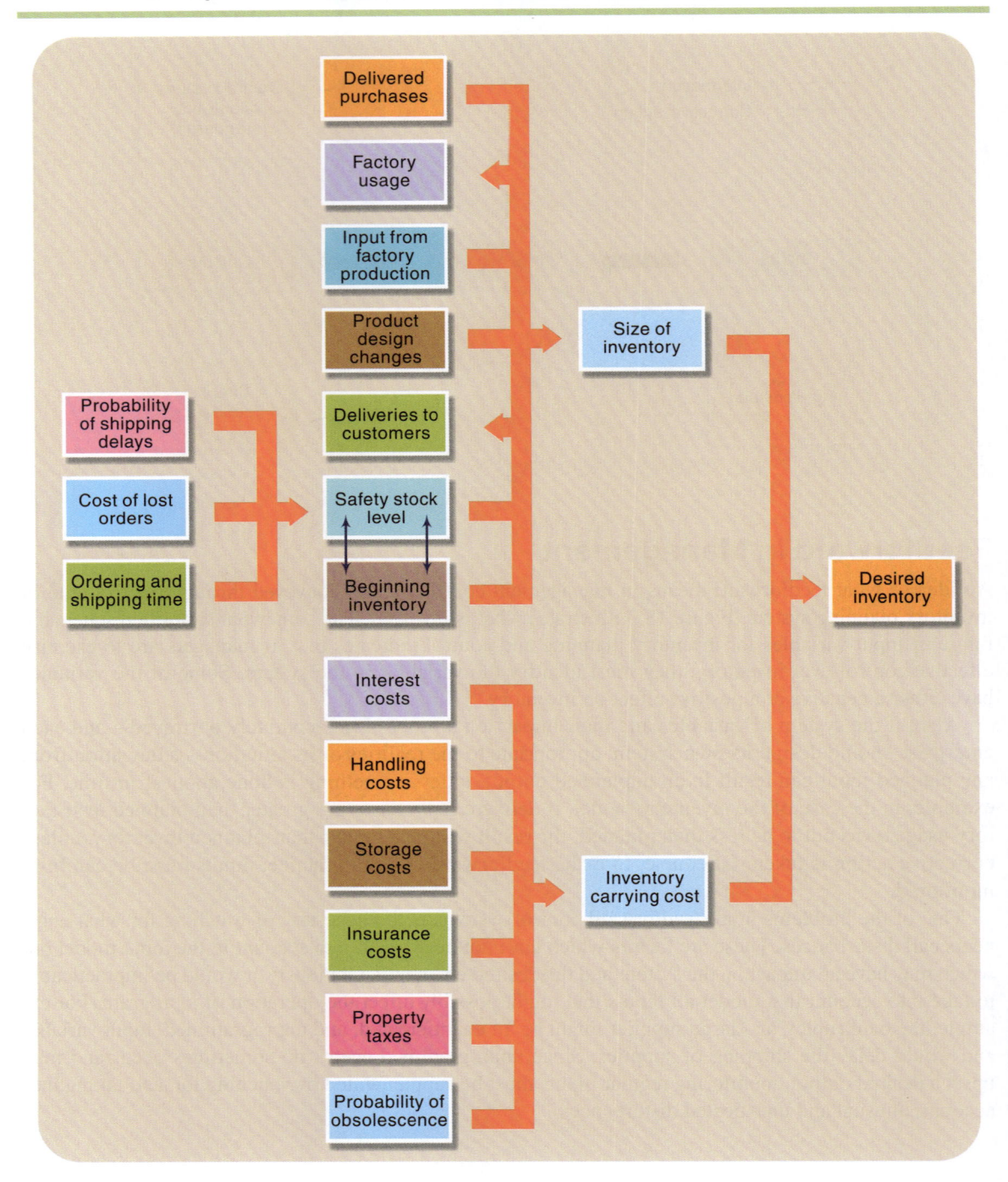

Requirements for Feedforward Control

The requirements for a workable feedforward control system may be summarized as follows:

1. Make a thorough and careful analysis of the planning and control system, and identify the more important input variables.
2. Develop a model of the system.
3. Take care to keep the model up to date; in other words, the model should be reviewed regularly to see whether the input variables identified and their interrelationships continue to represent realities.
4. Collect data on input variables regularly, and put them into the system.
5. Regularly assess variations of actual input data from planned-for inputs, and evaluate the impact on the expected end result.
6. Take action. Like any other technique of planning and control, all that the system can do is indicate problems; people must obviously take action to solve them.

CONTROL OF OVERALL PERFORMANCE[5]

Planning and control are increasingly being treated as an interrelated system. Along with techniques for partial control, control devices have been developed for measuring the overall performance of an enterprise—or an integrated division or project within it—against total goals.

There are many reasons for control of overall performance. In the first place, just as overall planning must apply to enterprise or major division goals, so must overall control be applied. In the second place, decentralization of authority—especially in product or territorial divisions—creates semi-independent units, and these must be subjected to overall control to avoid the chaos of complete independence. In the third place, overall control permits the measurement of an integrated area manager's total effort, rather than parts of it.

Many overall controls in business are, as one might expect, financial. Business owes its continued existence to profit making; its capital resources are a scarce, life-giving element. Since finance is the binding force of business, financial controls are certainly an important objective gauge of the success of plans. Moreover, sophisticated computer programs can use financial records as strategic tools.[6]

> Many overall controls in business are financial.

Financial measurements also summarize, as a common denominator, the operation of a number of plans. Further, they accurately indicate total expenditure of resources in reaching goals. This is true in all forms of enterprises. Although the purpose of an educational or government enterprise is not to make monetary profits, any responsible manager must have some way of knowing what goal achievement has cost in terms of resources. Proper accounting is important not only for business but for government as well.

Financial controls, like any other control, have to be tailored to the specific needs of the enterprise or the position. Doctors, lawyers, and managers at different organizational levels do have different needs for controlling their area of operation. Financial analyses also furnish an excellent "window" through which accomplishment in nonfinancial areas can be seen. A deviation from planned costs, for example, may lead a manager to find the causes in poor planning, inadequate training of employees, or other nonfinancial factors.

PROFIT AND LOSS CONTROL

The income statement for an enterprise as a whole serves important control purposes, mainly because it is useful for determining the immediate revenue or cost factors that have accounted for success or failure. Obviously, if it is first put in the form of a forecast, the income statement is an even better control device in that it gives managers a chance, before things happen, to influence revenues, expenses, and consequently profits.

The Nature and Purpose of Profit and Loss Control

> The **profit and loss statement** shows all revenues and expenses for a given time, so it is a true summary of the results of business operations.

Since the survival of a business usually depends on profits, and since profits are a definite standard against which to measure success, many companies use the income statement for divisional or departmental control. As it is a statement of all revenues and expenses for a given time, it is a true summary of the results of business operations. Profit and loss control, when applied to divisions or departments, is based on the premise that, if it is the purpose of the entire business to make a profit, each part of the enterprise should contribute to this purpose. Thus, the ability of a part to make an expected profit becomes a standard for measuring its performance.

Limitations of Profit and Loss Control

Profit and loss control suffers from the cost of the accounting and paper transactions involving intracompany transfer of costs and revenues. But the use of computers has greatly reduced this cost. Duplication of accounting records, efforts involved in allocating the many overhead costs, and the time and effort required to calculate intracompany sales can make this control costly if it is carried too far.

CONTROL THROUGH RETURN ON INVESTMENT[7]

Another control technique is that of measuring both the absolute and the relative success of a company or company unit by the ratio of earnings to investment of capital. The return-on-investment approach, often referred to simply as ROI, has been the core of the control system of the Du Pont Company. This yardstick is the rate of return that a company or a division can earn on the capital allocated to it. This tool therefore regards profit not as an absolute but as a return on capital employed in the business. The goal of a business is seen, accordingly, not necessarily as optimizing profits but as optimizing return from capital devoted to business purposes. This standard recognizes the fundamental fact that capital is a critical factor in almost any enterprise and, through its scarcity, limits progress. It also emphasizes the fact that the job of managers is to make the best possible use of assets entrusted to them.

MANAGEMENT AUDITS AND ACCOUNTING FIRMS

Although many management consulting firms have undertaken various kinds of appraisals of management systems, usually as part of an organizational study, the greatest interest in pursuing management audits has been demonstrated by accounting audit firms. One of the significant developments has been their entry into the field of management services of a broad consultancy nature. While this has been an attractive field of expansion for these auditing companies, since they are already inside an organization and the financial information to which they have access furnishes a ready window on problems of managing, it does open the question of conflict of interest. In other words, the question is whether the same firm can be in the position of a management consultant furnishing both advice and services and still be completely objective as an accounting auditor. To be sure, accounting firms have attempted to avoid this problem by organizationally separating these two activities.

Accounting firms had enjoyed a great deal of trust, but this changed when U.S. federal prosecutors charged the accounting firm Arthur Andersen with obstruction of justice in connection with the collapse of Enron in 2002.[8]

Return-on-investment control measures both the absolute and the relative success of a company or company unit by the ratio of earnings to investment of capital.

THE BALANCED SCORECARD[9]

The occasional overemphasis on financial data may have led to the popularity of the balanced scorecard. Robert Kaplan and David Norton have written extensively on that topic, but the origin of the concept may be traced to the performance measurement by General Electric in the 1950s and the "dashboard" discussion by French process engineers.

The balanced scorecard is used by business, nonprofit organizations, and government to align the company activities with the organization's vision and strategy as well as the improvement of internal and external communication. Thus, the balanced scorecard is not only for control, but also for strategic planning and managing in general. To accomplish the vision and the strategy, four sets of perspectives need to be considered. First, learning and growth deals with objectives, measures, targets and initiatives. The second perspectives focuses on the internal business processes, that give an indication how well its products and services meet the requirements and expectations of the company's customers in congruence with the mission of the enterprise. The third perspective focuses on the satisfaction of the customer. Even if financial performance is satisfactory, unsatisfied customers may be a leading indicator of future problems. The fourth, the financial perspective, is of course, important, but it should not lead to an unbalanced neglect of the other three perspectives.

The balanced scoreboard approach is congruent with the systems approach used in this book that focuses on the importance of goals and objectives as well as the close relationship between planning and controlling. Moreover, the importance of the total management process has been stressed, as well as the integration of internal strengths and weaknesses with the external opportunities and threats. The importance of meeting or exceeding customers' expectations and their satisfaction with the enterprises' products and services has also been emphasized. Finally, the need for creating a surplus for any organization, profit and not-for-profit, is shown in the integrative management model that provides the framework for this book.

BUREAUCRATIC AND CLAN CONTROL

Bureaucratic control is characterized by the wide use of rules, regulations, policies, procedures, and formal authority.

Clan control is based on norms, shared values, expected behavior, and other cultural variables.

www.nokia.com

Organizations exercise control in different ways. One can distinguish between two kinds of structural control: the bureaucratic and the clan control. **Bureaucratic control** is characterized by a wide use of rules, regulations, policies, procedures, and formal authority. This kind of control requires clear job descriptions, budgets, and often standardized tasks. Employees are expected to comply with the rules and regulations and may have limited opportunities for participation.

Clan control, on the other hand, is based on norms, shared values, expected behavior, and other aspects relating to organization culture, which was discussed in Chapter 10.[10] Clan control can be illustrated by the use of teams and by organizations operating in a very dynamic environment that requires quick adaptation to changes in that environment. Nokia, the largest wireless phone manufacturer in Finland, tries to keep bureaucracy at a minimum and instead creates an environment consistent with Finnish culture.

REQUIREMENTS FOR EFFECTIVE CONTROLS

All alert managers want to have an adequate and effective system of controls to assist them in making sure that events conform to plans. It is sometimes not realized that the controls used by managers must be designed for the specific task and person they are intended to serve. While the basic process and the fundamentals of control are universal, the actual system requires special design.

Indeed, if controls are to work, they must be tailored to plans and positions, to the individual managers and their personalities, and to the needs for efficiency and effectiveness.

Tailoring Controls to Plans and Positions

All control techniques and systems should reflect the plans they are designed to follow. They should also be tailored to positions. What will be appropriate for a vice president in charge of manufacturing will certainly not be suitable for a shop supervisor. Controls should also reflect the organization structure, showing who is responsible for the execution of plans and for any deviation from them.

Tailoring Controls to Individual Managers

Controls must also be tailored to individual managers. Control systems and information are of course intended to help individual managers carry out their function of control. If they are not of a type that a manager can or will understand, they will not be useful. What individuals cannot understand they will not trust. And what they do not trust they will not use.

Designing Controls to Point up Exceptions at Critical Points

One of the most important ways of tailoring controls to the needs for efficiency and effectiveness is to design them to point up exceptions. In other words, controls that concentrate on exceptions from planned performance allow managers to benefit from the time-honored *exception principle* and detect areas that require their attention.

But it is not enough merely to look at exceptions. Some deviations from standards have little meaning, while others have a great deal. Small deviations in certain areas may have greater significance than larger exceptions in other areas. A manager might be concerned if the cost of office labor deviated from the budget by 5 percent but might be unworried if the cost of postage stamps deviated from the budget by 20 percent.

Consequently, the exception principle should be accompanied in practice by the *principle of critical point control*. It is not enough just to look for exceptions; one must look for them at critical points. Certainly, the more that managers concentrate their control efforts on exceptions, the more efficient their control will be. But effective control requires that managers pay primary attention to things that are most important.

> Efficient control requires that managers look for exceptions, while effective control requires that managers pay primary attention to things that are most important.

Seeking Objectivity of Controls

Management necessarily has many subjective elements, but whether a subordinate is doing a good job should ideally not be a matter for subjective determination. If controls are subjective, a manager's or a subordinate's personality may influence judgments of performance and make them less accurate. However, people would have difficulty dismissing control of their performance if the standards and measurements are kept up to date through periodic review. Effective control requires objective, accurate, and suitable standards. McDonald's, for example, is very strict in applying and maintaining the same quality standards in all its restaurants, as you have seen in the McDonald's case discussed in Chapter 1.

> www.mcdonalds.com

Ensuring Flexibility of Controls[11]

Controls should remain workable in the face of changed plans, unforeseen circumstances, or outright failures. If controls are to remain effective despite failure or unexpected changes of plans, they must be flexible.

The need for flexible control can readily be illustrated. A budget system may project a certain level of expenses and grant authority to managers to hire labor and purchase materials and services at this level. If, as is usually the case, this budget is based on a forecast of a certain level of sales, it may become meaningless as a system of control if the actual sales volume is considerably above or below the forecast. Budget systems have been brought into ill repute in some companies because of inflexibility in such circumstances. What is needed, of course, is a system that will reflect sales variations as well as other deviations from plans.

> If controls are to remain effective despite failure or unexpected changes of plans, they must be flexible.

Fitting the Control System to the Organization Culture

To be most effective, any control system or technique must fit the organization culture. If an organization has given its employees considerable freedom and participation, a tight control system may go so strongly against the grain that it will be doomed to failure. On the other hand, if subordinates have been managed by a superior who allows little participation in decision making, a generalized and permissive control system will hardly succeed. People who have little desire to participate or who have not been accustomed to participating are likely to want clear standards and measurements and specific directions. At one time, Mercedes-Benz, the luxury car maker, publicized that each of its cars underwent checks by many inspectors. But later, with a change in organization culture, a great deal of responsibility for quality was given to individual production workers.

> To be most effective, any control system or technique must fit the organization culture.
>
> www.mercedes.com

Achieving Economy of Controls

Controls must be worth their costs. Although this requirement is simple, it is often difficult to accomplish in practice. A manager may have difficulty ascertaining what a particular control system is worth or what it costs. Economy is relative, since the benefits of control vary with the importance of the activity, the size of the operation, the expense that might be incurred in the absence of control, and the contribution the system can make.

> **Controls** must be worth their costs.

Establishing Controls That Lead to Corrective Action

An **adequate system** will disclose where failures are occurring and who is responsible for them, and it will ensure that corrective action is taken. Control is justified only if deviations from plans are corrected through appropriate planning, organizing, staffing, and leading. As mentioned in Chapter 13, General Electric and Motorola aim at Six Sigma quality, or no more than 3.4 defects for a million operations.[12]

> An **adequate control system** will disclose where failures are occurring and who is responsible for them, as well as ensuring that corrective action is taken.

SUMMARY

The managerial function of controlling is the measurement and correction of performance in order to ensure that enterprise objectives and the plans devised to attain them are being accomplished. It is a function of every manager, from president to supervisor.

Control techniques and systems are basically the same regardless of what is being controlled. Wherever it is found and whatever is being controlled, the basic control process involves three steps: (1) establishing standards, (2) measuring performance against these standards, and (3) correcting variations from standards and plans. There are different kinds of standards, and all should point out deviations at critical points. Performance can be measured against best industry practices, an approach known as benchmarking.

Managerial control is usually perceived as a simple feedback system similar to the common household thermostat. However, no matter how quickly information is available on what is occurring (even real-time information, which is information on what is happening as it happens), there are unavoidable delays in analyzing deviations, developing plans for taking corrective action, and implementing these programs. In order to overcome these time lags in control, it is suggested that managers utilize a feedforward control approach and not rely on simple feedback alone. Feedforward control requires designing a model of a process or system and monitoring inputs with a view to detecting future deviations of results from standards and plans, thereby giving managers time to take corrective action before problems occur.

Many overall controls are financial, one of which is profit and loss control. Another is the exercise of control through calculating and comparing return on investment. This approach is based on the idea that profit should be considered not as an absolute measure but as a return on the capital employed in a business or a segment of it. The management audit has also been used as a control device. Bureaucratic control is based on rules, regulations, policies, procedures, and formal authority. On the other hand, clan control is influenced by norms, shared values, and expected behavior.

If controls are to work, they must be specially tailored to plans and positions, to individual managers, and to the needs for efficiency and effectiveness. To be effective, controls also should be designed to point up exceptions at critical points, to be objective, to be flexible, to fit the organization culture, to be economical, and to lead to corrective action.

KEY IDEAS AND CONCEPTS FOR REVIEW

Controlling
Steps in controlling
Critical point control
Types of critical point standards
Benchmarking
Feedback system
Real-time information system
Feedforward control
Profit and loss control
Return-on-investment control
Management audit
Bureaucratic control
Clan control
Requirements for effective controls
Exception principle
Principle of critical point control

FOR DISCUSSION

1. Planning and control are often thought of as a system; control is also often referred to as a system. What do these observations mean? Can both statements be true?
2. Why is real-time information not good enough for effective control?
3. What is feedforward control? Why is it important to managers? Besides the example of inventory control mentioned in this chapter, can you think of any other areas in which feedforward would be used? Select one of these and explain how you would proceed.
4. Why do most controls of overall performance tend to be financial? Should they be? What else would you suggest?
5. "Profit and loss control is defective in that it does not emphasize return on investment; the latter is defective in that it places too great an emphasis on present results, possibly endangering future results." Discuss.
6. If you were asked to institute a system of "tailored" controls in a company, how would you go about it? What would you need to know?
7. In benchmarking, companies compare their performance with best practices. Why do you think firms that have an effective system are willing to share information with other companies?

EXERCISES/ACTION STEPS

1. Design a control system for measuring the progress that you make in your course work. Apply the feedback and feedforward concepts discussed in this chapter.
2. Interview two managers about the controls used in their companies. Can you identify standards against which performance can be accurately measured? How is performance measured against the standards, and how timely is the reporting of deviations? If deviations are detected, how long does it take before corrections are made in specific situations?
3. The widespread use of analytics among organizations requires more people with education in this field. Explore the curriculum of your university to identify classes in analytics or statistics that you may want to take to enhance your capabilities in this emerging field.

INTERNET RESEARCH

1. Search the Internet for the term "feedforward control". How does it differ from feedback control?
2. Search the Internet for the term "profit and loss statement". What is it?

GLOBAL CASE

Walmart in America and Around the Globe[13]

Walmart ranked number 2 in 2011 among the Fortune 500 companies after being number 1 the previous two years. The decline was partly due to declining economy and slow recovery in the United States. While the company had difficulties in the U.S. market, the international market grew.

The company has one of the most sophisticated logistic systems controlled by computers. Yet its headquarters are located in a small town in Bentonville, Arkansas. The small-town orientation in its business approach contributed to its value-based success story.

Success did not come by accident; rather, it is based on careful planning of a unique strategy, a simple organization structure, an effective human resource policy, an inspiring leadership style initiated by founder Sam Walton, and a clever use of information technology to manage its inventory. When the company made mistakes, it learned from them. One concern is whether the strategy of invading rural areas will also work in the urban areas of America and in the global environment.

The Background
It all began in 1962 in a small town in Arkansas when Sam Walton noted the need for serving customers in small towns. Retailers such as Kmart and Sears focused on big towns. This created an opportunity for Walmart to fill people's needs in rural areas. This small-town orientation is reflected in the company's values, which emphasize maintaining good relationships with staff as well as suppliers. Sam Walton's values and his philosophy of simplicity and frugality live on after his death. The focus on cost savings enables the company to offer "everyday low prices", which has become the familiar company slogan.

Planning: From Small Towns to a Global Strategy
Besides the traditional stores, the company has Supercenters with a full line of groceries for one-stop family shopping. They may also include specialties shops with a vision center, tire and lubrication facilities, and photo processing. In addition, Sam's Club is a members-only warehouse club for individual and business members.

Since the early 1990s, Walmart has gone international, starting with a Sam's Club store near Mexico City. Now Walmart operates clubs and stores worldwide in countries such as Argentina, Brazil, Canada, China, South Korea, Mexico, Puerto Rico, and the United Kingdom, employing more than 280,000 people.

The tremendous size of the company gives it a great deal of buying power, which in turn makes it possible to offer goods at low prices, a policy that differentiates Walmart from other retailers. The company is known for its national brand strategy, which allows consumers to compare prices. In addition, Walmart has its own private labels with product offerings in apparel, health and beauty care, dog food, and other items.

In its hub-and-spoke distribution system, merchandise is brought to a distribution center, where it is sorted and prepared for delivery to the stores. These highly automated distribution centers operate 24 hours a day and may serve some 150 stores. Other merchandise is shipped directly from the suppliers to the stores.

Simple Organization Structure: Centralized and Decentralized
While the company's proprietary information system is centralized, the operation is decentralized with a great deal of authority delegated to local managers in, for example, pricing the merchandise according to the local environment. The autonomy given to store managers makes them in a sense a small shopkeeper who can make decisions to adjust inventory according to local needs. Employees, called associates, are informed and celebrated at the Saturday morning meetings, where they are cheered for their accomplishments. The meetings also provide an opportunity to reinforce the notion that the customer is number 1.

Walmart's organization culture is built on three basic values promulgated by Sam Walton. It was established in 1962 and still permeates the organization. The values are (1) respect for the individual, (2) service to the customer, and (3) striving for excellence. Other factors influencing the organization culture include exceeding the expectations of customers, assisting people so that they can make a difference, quickly approaching customers to help, doing today what can be done today rather than postponing it, and pricing for providing value to the customer.

Human Resource Management: People, the Most Important Assets
Clearly, the organization culture has an impact on the staffing function. Associates are treated with respect in this lean organization. Having a great deal of authority motivates people. Training is decentralized with management seminars offered at the distribution centers instead of at the company headquarters. The company atmosphere encourages employees to submit suggestions, many of them being implemented through the "Yes We Can Sam" suggestion system. Associates are rewarded bonuses for cost reduction through the "shrink incentive plan". Supervisors and managers receive a salary as well as incentive compensation based on store performance. Associates can also participate in a profit-sharing plan with Walmart contributing a certain percentage.

Leadership by Example: Simple Frugality Communicated Effectively
Sam Walton, the founder, provided leadership by example. His philosophy influenced his style. Once the richest person in America, he was a very frugal man, flying economy class and driving an old pickup truck. Similarly, Lee Scott, the past CEO and now Chairman, drove a Volkswagen Beetle. Sam Walton was a good communicator during his time as CEO, and his style was described as "management by walking and flying around" because of his frequent visits to his stores. Although he felt that trusting people and giving them responsibility was essential in managing people effectively, he also had the necessary control systems. Although Walton passed away in 1992, his legacy and philosophy still permeate his organization, as shown by the spartanly furnished headquarters in Bentonville.

Controlling a Large Organization: Sharing Information and Technologies with Suppliers
One of the key factors for Walmart's success is the inventory system that uses modern technology. The proprietary computer-controlled logistic system is considered one of the largest in America, ranking just below the Pentagon's system. The store manager can easily find out how his or her department managers are doing and which products are in high demand. Walmart's inventory turns over about twice as fast as the industry average, thus reducing greatly inventory costs. Suppliers, who are considered a part of the Walmart family, also have access to the system and receive real-time data to help them plan for the fast-moving items.

The relationship with suppliers is, however, very businesslike. Contracts are negotiated in no-nonsense rooms with a table and some chairs—no plush offices can be found. What is found, however, is a sign that says Walmart's buyers do not accept bribes, which could influence buying decisions.

Growth and Adaptation
Any company (indeed, any system) has to adapt and respond to the changing environment as illustrated by a few examples:

- In September 2005 after the Hurricane Katrina devastation, Walmart using its sophisticated logistic system responded to the disaster by providing free merchandise, food, and the commitment to provide jobs for displaced workers.[14]
- The company announced initiatives to implement efficiency measures that would increase the fuel efficiency of its trucks and cut solid waste in U.S. stores. It also announced the "Sustainable Produce Index" in a meeting with some 1,500 suppliers. The idea is to evaluate the sustainability of its products.[15]

- In 2011, responding to Mrs. Michelle Obama, Walmart committed the company in improving the nutritional values in its products.
- The company also started a "beta" version of downloading movies through the Internet.
- The "Supermercado de Walmart" stores in America are designed to appeal to the Hispanic communities.[16]
- Walmart Express are smaller discount stores especially located in small towns that are not suitable for the big stores.
- In 2012, increased its stake in Yihaodian, a Chinese Online Supermarket. As it is typical in China, the Chinese government has to approve the deal.[17]

Global Challenges for the Future[18]

Although Walmart has been successful, there are considerable challenges ahead. To continue its growth, Walmart would have to continue aggressively with opening new stores at home and abroad. In addition, product and service offerings need to be expanded. International expansion is another way to grow. The company has been successful in the expansion into Canada and Mexico, but other strategies have been less successful. One such example was the move into Germany, which the company did not plan carefully. Lee Scott, the CEO at that time, attributed the failure to poor management. The company tries to learn from its mistakes and impresses on its associates to provide good service with a smile. In fact, a big problem for the rapidly growing company is developing competent managers and associates.

Domestically, the Walmart image has been hurt by the publicity on the impact of the big retailer on small communities. The "60 Minutes" television program showed how small retailers of small towns could not effectively compete against the giant and were driven out of business. Still, consumers in the small communities were attracted by the everyday low prices. Walmart has also been cited for the low health-care benefits given to its employees. Perhaps partly to divert attention from this issue, the company drew attention to the high health care cost in America with a strategy of reducing drastically prices of several generic drugs in its stores. While critics see this as a publicity move, consumers welcome it.[19]

One of Walmart's attempt to remain the world's largest retailer is to become the neighborhood grocer, which has created fear among other food stores. Food business is big business. People may shop once or more times a week for food. At the same time, they may be enticed to buy other goods Walmart has to offer.[20]

Walmart effectively practiced the managerial functions of planning, organizing, staffing, leading, and controlling, which led to its remarkable success, but challenges remain.

Questions:

1. With a saturation of stores in the rural areas in America, can Walmart employ the same strategies for setting up stores in the cities? Why or why not? What difficulties may the company encounter?
2. Can the organization culture, which was so effective in the United States, be transferred to other countries? What changes, if any, would you suggest?
3. Could competitors copy the inventory system of Walmart?
4. Would you like to be a manager at Walmart? Why or why not?
5. What should Walmart do to be successful in other countries?
6. How can Walmart control the global enterprise?

ENDNOTES

1. Ron Kohavi, Neal Rothleder, and Evangelos Simoudis, "Emerging Trends in Business Analytics", *ACM,* 2002, 45 (8): 45–48.
2. Please see IBM.com/analytics.
3. See also Robert S. Kaplan and David P. Norton, *Balanced Scorecard: Translating Strategy into Action* (Boston, MA: Harvard Business School Press, 1996).
4. Robert C. Camp, "Learning from the Best Leads to Superior Performance," in Arthur A. Thompson, Jr., A. J. Strickland III, and Tracy Robertson Kramer, eds. *Readings in Strategic Management,* 5th ed. (Chicago: Irwin, 1995), pp. 518–524; Y. K. Shetty, "Aiming High: Competitive Benchmarking for Superior Performance," ibid., pp. 525–535; J. M. Juran, "A History of Managing for Quality in the United States, Part 2," *Quality Digest,* December 1995, p. 40; Charles J. Burke, "10 Steps to Best-Practices Benchmarking," *Quality Digest,* February 1996, pp. 23–28. For benchmarking in Europe, see www.benchmarking-in-europe.com, accessed January 11, 2016.
5. Another broad measurement is the balanced scorecard, which focuses on financial, customer, internal process, and learning and growth perspectives in clarifying the enterprise vision and strategy. This is not only a measurement system but also a management system. See "What is a Balanced Scoreboard?" www.balancedscorecard.org/basics/bsc1.html, accessed August 19, 2011.
6. Phillip L. Zweig, John Verity, Stephanie Anderson Forrest, Greg Burns, Rob Hof, and Nicole Harris, "Beyond Bean-Counting," *Business Week,* October 28, 1996, pp. 130–132.
7. See also W. Brian Arthur, "Increasing Returns and the New World of Business," *Harvard Business Review,* July–August 1996, pp. 100–109.
8. Wendy Zellner and Dan Carney, "The Price of Victory over Andersen," *Business Week,* July 1, 2002, p. 38; Joseph Weber, "The Lingering Lessons of Andersen's Fall," ibid., p. 39; Mike France and Dan Carney, "Why Corporate Crooks Are Tough to Nail," ibid., pp. 35–37; Joseph Nocera, "System Failure," *Fortune,* June 24, 2002, pp. 62–74. See also Arthur Andersen, www.arthurandersen.com, accessed August 19, 2011, and Enron, www.enron.com, accessed August 19, 2011.
9. Robert S. Kaplan and David P. Norton, "Using the Balanced Scoreboard as a Strategic Management System," *Harvard Business Review,* January–February 1996; See also Robert S. Kaplan and David P. Norton, *Balanced Scorecard: Translating Strategy into Action* (Boston, MA: Harvard Business School Press, 1996); The balanced scorecard, focuses on financial, customer, internal process, and learning and growth perspectives in clarifying the enterprise vision and strategy. This is not only a measurement system but also a management system; "What is a Balanced Scoreboard?" www.balancedscorecard.org/basics/bsc1.html, accessed November 17, 2011, "Balanced Scorecard Basics," http://www.balancedscorecard.org/BSCResources/AbouttheBalancedScorecard/tabid/55/Default.aspx, accessed January 11, 2016.
10. William Ouchi described clans as a control system. The characteristics of a clan culture can be found in "Managing Corporate Culture through Reward Systems" by Jeffrey Kerr and John W. Slocum, Jr. in *The Academy of Management Executive,* November 2005, pp. 132–133.
11. See also Mary C. Lacity, Leslie P. Willcocks, and David F. Feeny, "IT Outsourcing: Maximize Flexibility and Control," *Harvard Business Review,* May–June 1995, pp. 84–94.
12. See also the articles in the various issues of *Quality Digest.* For example, Steve Fleming and E. Lowry Manson, "Six Sigma and Process Simulation," *Quality Digest,* March 2002, pp. 35–39 and http://www.isixsigma.com/sixsigma/six_sigma.asp, accessed January 11, 2016.
13. "Walmart, Wal around the World," *The Economist,* December 8, 2001, pp. 55–57; "Walmart Stores, Inc.," Harvard Business School Case 9-794-024, rev. August 6, 1996; "Walmart," www.walmartstores.com, accessed November 17, 2011; "H. Lee Scott Jr., Walmart Stores," *Business Week,* January 14, 2002, p. 71; see also Charles Fishman, *The Wall-Mart Effect* (Stratford: Penguin Press, 2006); the book has been reviewed by Daniel T. Gillepspie in *Academy of Management Learning & Education,* September 2006, pp. 378–379; "Walmart," http://www.walmart.com, accessed November 17, 2011; Charles Fishman, "The Walmart Effect and a Decent Society: Who Know Shopping Was So Important," *The Academy of Management Perspective,* August 2006, pp. 6–25. See also other articles in *The Academy of Management Perspective,* August 2006; 2. Walmart stores, http://money.cnn.com/magazines/fortune/fortune500/2012/snapshots/2255.html, accessed September 21, 2011.
14. "Walmart at Forefront of Hurricane Relief", *The Washington Post,* September 6, 2005.
15. "Walmart Announces Sustainable Product Index," http://news.walmart.com/news-archive/2009/07/16/walmart-announces-sustainable-product-index, accessed January 11, 2016.
16. "Walmart woos Hispanics with new Supermercado" http://www.reuters.com/article/2009/07/08/us-walmart-supermercado-idUSTRE5676N820090708, accessed January 11, 2016.
17. "Walmart Raises Stake to 51% in Chinese Website Yihaodian," http://www.bloomberg.com/news/2012-02-20/Walmart-raises-stake-to-51-in-chinese-website-yihaodian.html, accessed September 21, 2012.
18. See also Peter Drucker, "The Next Society," *The Economist,* November 3, 2001, Insert pp. 3–20.
19. "Walmart—High Risk, High Reward," *The Economist,* October 14, 2006, p. 32.
20. Brian O'Keefe, "Meet Your New Neighborhood Grocer," *Fortune,* May 13, 2002, pp. 93–96; Robert Berner and Stephanie Anderson Forest, "Walmart Is Eating Everybody's Lunch," *Business Week,* April 15, 2002, p. 43.

CHAPTER 19

Control Techniques and Information Technology

Learning Objectives

After studying this chapter, you should be able to:

LO 1   Explain the nature of budgeting and the types of budgets

LO 2   Describe zero-base budgeting

LO 3   Discuss nonbudgetary control devices

LO 4   Explain time–event network analysis as a major technique of planning and control

LO 5   Understand the nature and applications of information technology

LO 6   Recognize the importance of computers in handling information

LO 7   Explain the opportunities as well as challenges created by the new information technology

LO 8   Discuss the digital economy as well as developments in e-commerce and m-commerce

LO 9   Understand customer relationship management

Although the basic nature and purpose of management control does not change, a variety of tools and techniques have been used over the years to help manager's control. As this chapter will show, all these techniques are, in the first instance, tools for planning. They illustrate the fundamental truth that the task of controls is to make plans succeed; naturally, in doing so, controls must reflect plans, and planning must precede control.

THE BUDGET AS A CONTROL DEVICE

A widely used device for managerial control is the budget.* Indeed, it has sometimes been assumed that budgeting is *the* device for accomplishing control. However, many nonbudgetary devices are also essential.

The Concept of Budgeting[1]

Budgeting is the formulation of plans for a given future period in numerical terms. As such, budgets are statements of anticipated results, either in financial terms—as in revenue and expense as well as capital budgets—or in nonfinancial terms—as in budgets of direct-labor-hours, materials, physical sales volume, or units of production. It has sometimes been said, for example, that financial budgets represent the "dollarizing" of plans.

Budgeting The formulation of plans for a given future period in numerical terms.

In New Ventures Cash Is King

While well-established businesses closely budget, track, and report numerous financial measures of their business operations, entrepreneurs that lead new ventures are most focused on their cash flow. This is because in a new venture, cash is usually limited and the planning of cash outlays and receipts is essential to the venture's survival. Issues such as collection of customer receipts, negotiation of extended payment terms to suppliers, and establishing lines of credit with lenders can make or break a new enterprise. Controlling the flows of cash in financing, operations, and investment is always on the entrepreneur's mind as she plots her company's strategy for growth in the short and long term.

We asked a leading Silicon Valley venture capitalist, Elton Sherwin of Ridgewood Capital, how he controls the firms in his portfolio. Mr. Sherwin indicated he uses the budget to control the companies in his portfolio. Specifically, he asks three questions: "1. Have they raised enough money? 2. Are they spending the right amount of money? 3. Are they spending money on the right things?"

ENTREPRENEURIAL PERSPECTIVE

---

* Primarily because of the negative implications of budgeting in the past, the more positive phrase *profit planning* is sometimes used, and the budget is then known as the *profit plan.*

Dangers in Budgeting

Budgets are used for planning and control. Unfortunately, some budgetary control programs are so complete and detailed that they become cumbersome, meaningless, and unduly expensive. In addition, budgetary control may be used for the wrong reasons.

How often have you heard managers say "This is a good idea, but it's not in my budget"? Budgets often control the wrong things. They measure inputs but ignore outputs such as product quality and customer satisfaction. These items are difficult to measure, yet they may be the key to success or failure of the business. Managers may make unwise decisions to meet the budget, especially if incentive pay is given for staying within the budget. They may not invest in research and development, make capital investment for productivity, or invest in activities that will result eventually in greater market share because these investments do not show immediate results. Some of these items should be included in the long-range plan rather than in the one-year budget. Real savings may come from more efficient machines, new products, or other creative ideas, not from adhering to the budget.

Zero-Base Budgeting

Zero-base budgeting Dividing enterprise programs into packages composed of goals, activities, and needed resources and calculating the costs for each package from base zero.

One type of budgeting is **zero-base budgeting**. The idea behind this technique is to divide enterprise programs into "packages" composed of goals, activities, and needed resources and then to calculate the costs for each package from the ground up. By starting the budget of each package from base zero, budgeters calculate costs afresh for each budget period; thus, they avoid the common tendency in budgeting of looking only at changes from a previous period.

This technique has generally been applied to so-called support areas, rather than to actual production areas, on the assumption that there is room for discretion in expenditures for most programs in such areas as marketing, research and development, personnel, planning, and finance. The various programs thought to be desirable are costed and reviewed in terms of their benefits to the enterprise and are then ranked in accordance with those benefits and selected on the basis of which package will yield the benefit desired.

The principal advantage of this technique is of course the fact that it forces managers to plan each program package afresh. As managers do so, they review established programs and their costs in their entirety, along with newer programs and their costs.

TRADITIONAL NONBUDGETARY CONTROL DEVICES

There are of course many traditional control devices not connected with budgets, although some may be related to, and used with, budgetary controls. Among the more important of them are the use of statistical data of many aspects of the operation, special reports and analyses of specific areas, the operational audit and independent appraisal by a staff of internal or external auditors, and personal observation such as managing by walking around.

TIME–EVENT NETWORK ANALYSES

Another planning and control technique is a time–event network analysis called the program evaluation and review technique (PERT). Before the development of PERT, there were other techniques designed to assess how the parts of a program fit together during the passage of time and events.

Gantt Charts

The first of these techniques was the chart system developed by Henry L. Gantt early in the 20th century that culminated in the bar chart bearing his name (see Figure 19.1). Although simple in concept, this chart, showing time relationships between the "events" of a production program, has been regarded as revolutionary in management. What Gantt recognized was that total program goals should be regarded as a series of interrelated supporting plans (or events) that people can comprehend and follow. The most important developments of control reflect this simple principle as well as basic principles of control, such as picking out the more critical elements of a plan to watch carefully.

Gantt chart A bar chart that shows the time relationships between the "events" of a production program.

Milestone Budgeting

As a result of the development of further techniques from the principles of the Gantt chart, and with better appreciation of the network nature of programs, "milepost" or "milestone" budgeting and PERT were devised, contributing much to better planning and control of many projects and operations. Milepost or milestone budgeting breaks a project down into controllable pieces and then carefully follows them. Even relatively simple projects contain a network of supporting plans or projects. In this approach to control, milestones are defined as identifiable segments. When accomplishment of a given segment occurs, costs or other results can be determined.

INNOVATIVE PERSPECTIVE

Planning and Control in Engineering

The best way to plan and control an engineering project is to break it down into a number of events, such as completion of preliminary drawings, an experimental model, a package design, a packaged prototype, and a production design. Or a project might be broken down vertically into subprojects—for example, the design of a circuit, a motor, a driving mechanism, a sensing device, a signal feedback device, and similar components—that can be completed individually, in a time sequence so that components are ready when needed. Milestone budgeting allows a manager to see a complex program as a series of simpler parts and thus to maintain some control through knowing whether a program is succeeding or failing.

FIGURE 19.1 Transition from a Gantt chart to PERT

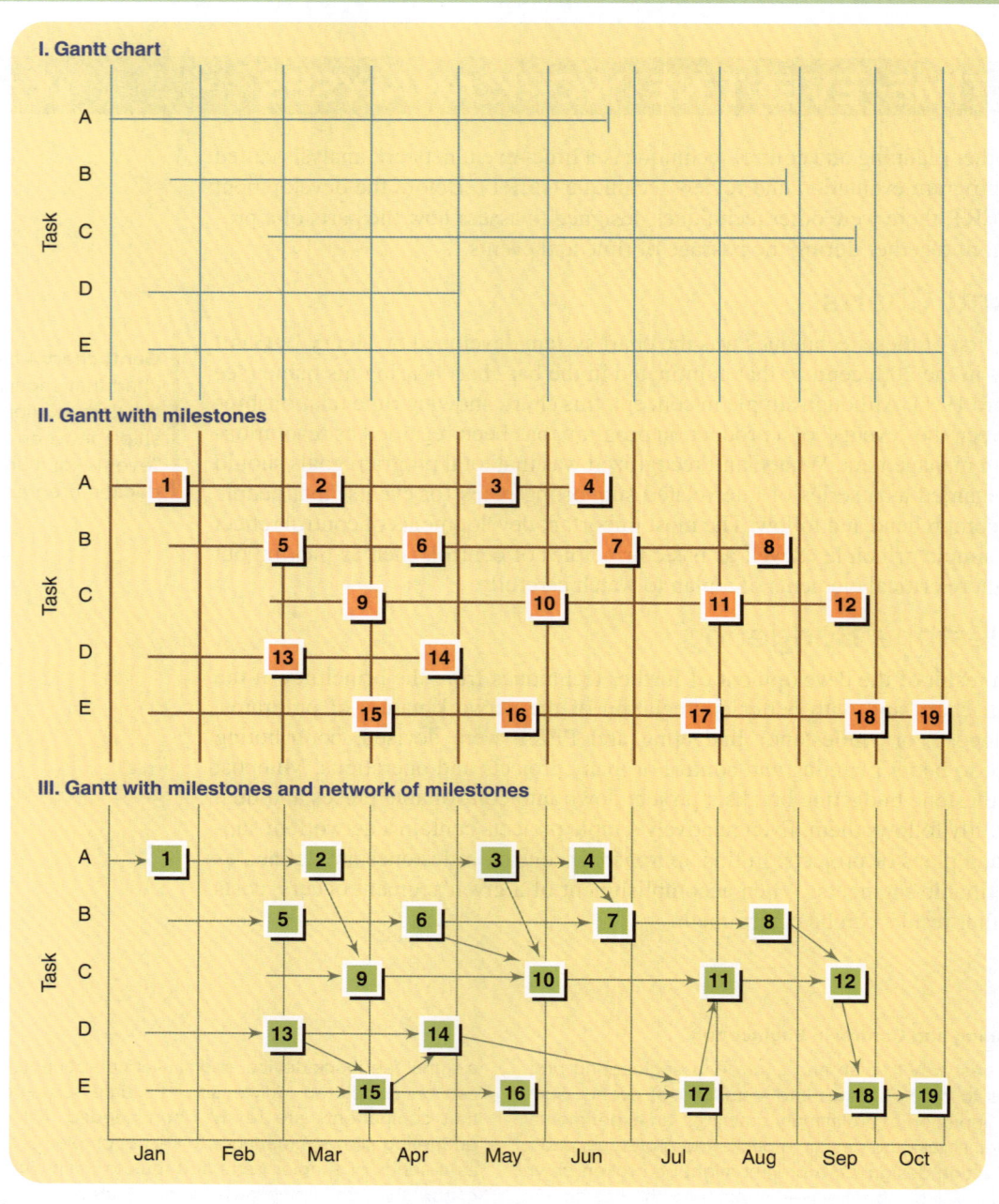

I. Gantt chart

II. Gantt with milestones

III. Gantt with milestones and network of milestones

The Gantt chart in I shows the scheduled time of accomplishing a task, such as procurement (Task A) and the related schedules of doing other tasks, such as manufacture of parts (Task B). When each of these tasks is broken down into milestones, such as the preparation of purchase specifications (Task A-1), and when network relationships between the milestones of each task to those of other tasks are worked out, the result provides the basic elements of a PERT chart.

Program Evaluation and Review Technique (PERT)*

Developed by the Special Projects Office of the U.S. Navy, PERT was first formally applied to the planning and control of the Polaris Weapon System in 1958 and worked well in expediting the completion of that program. For a number of years, it was so enthusiastically received by the armed services that it became virtually a required tool for major contractors and subcontractors in the armament and space industry. Although PERT is no longer much heard of in defense and space contracts, its fundamentals are still essential tools of planning and control. Moreover, in a host of nongovernmental applications, including construction, engineering, and tooling projects, and even such simple tasks as the scheduling of activities to produce monthly financial reports, PERT or its companion network technique, the critical path method, may be used.

Major features of PERT

PERT is a time–event network analysis system in which the various events in a program or project are identified, with a planned time established for each. These events are placed in a network showing the relationships of each event to the other events. In a sense, PERT is a variation of milestone budgeting (see Figure 19.1).

Figure 19.2 shows a PERT flowchart for the major assembly of an airplane. This example illustrates the basic nature of PERT. Each circle represents an *event*—a supporting plan whose completion can be measured at a given time. The circles are numbered in the order in which the events occur. Each arrow represents an *activity*—the time-consuming element of a program, the effort that must be made between events. *Activity time*, represented by the numbers beside the arrows, is the time required to accomplish an event.

In this example, only a single time is shown for each activity, but in the original PERT program there were three *time estimates*: "optimistic" time, an estimate of the time required if everything goes exceptionally well; "most likely" time, an estimate based on the time the project engineer really believes is necessary for the job; and "pessimistic" time, a time estimate based on the assumption that some logically conceivable bad luck, other than a major disaster, will be encountered. These estimates are often included in PERT because it is very difficult, in many engineering and development projects, to estimate time accurately. When several estimates are made, they are usually averaged, with special weight given to the most likely estimate; a single estimate is then used for calculations.

The next step is to compute the *critical path*, which is the sequence of events that takes the longest time and that has zero (or the least) slack time. In Figure 19.2, the critical path comprises events 1–3–4–8–9–13. Over this

> **PERT** A time–event network analysis system in which the various events in a program or project are identified, with a planned time established for each.

---

* The technique was also separately developed as the critical path method by engineers at the Du Pont Company at virtually the same time. Only PERT is discussed here because the critical path method, although different in some respects, utilizes the same principles.

FIGURE 19.2 PERT flowchart

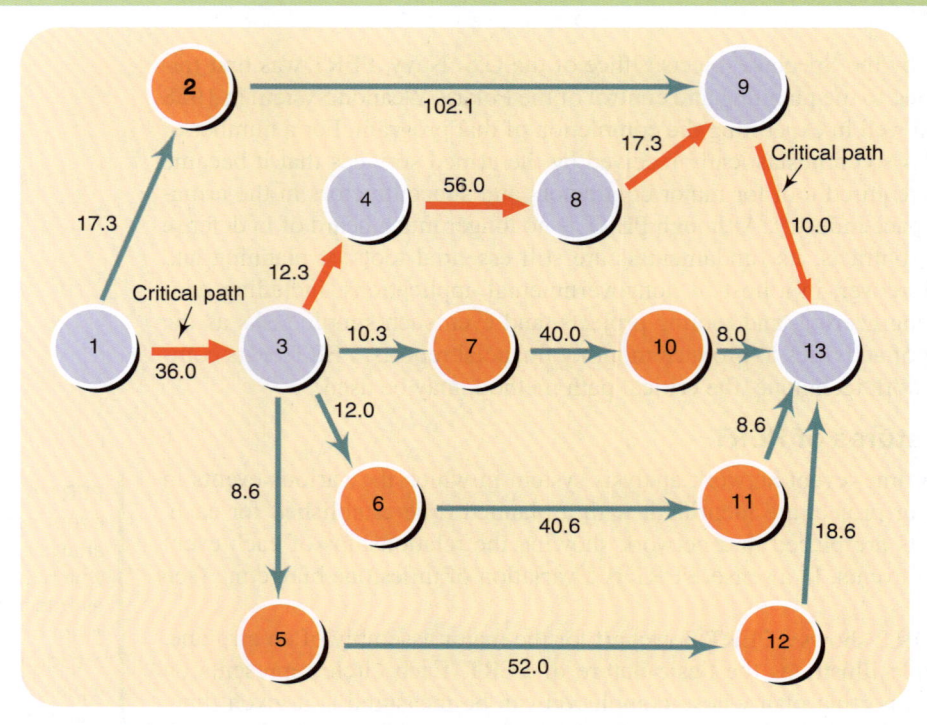

Events (major milestones of progress) in the major assembly of an airplane (shown with time in weeks): (1) order program go-ahead; (2) initiate engine procurement; (3) complete plans and specifications; (4) complete fuselage drawings; (5) submit GFAE* requirements; (6) award tail assembly subcontract; (7) award wings subcontract; (8) complete manufacture of fuselage; (9) complete assembly of fuselage engine; (10) receive wings from subcontractors; (11) receive tail assembly from subcontractors; (12) receive GFAE; (13) complete aircraft.

*GFAE: government-furnished airplane equipment.

Critical path
The sequence of events that takes the longest time and that has zero (or the least) slack time.

path, the activity time for this sequence of events is 131.6 weeks; if promised delivery is in 135 weeks, even this critical path will have been completed 3.4 weeks ahead of time. Some of the other paths are almost as long as the critical path. For example, the path 1–2–9–13 is 129.4 weeks. This is not unusual in PERT charts, and it is customary to identify several crucial paths in order of importance. Although the critical path has a way of changing as key events are delayed in other parts of the program, identifying it at the start makes possible close monitoring of this particular sequence of events to ensure that the whole program is on schedule.

Typical PERT analyses involve hundreds or thousands of events. Even though smaller PERT analyses can be done manually, estimates indicate that when more than 200 to 300 events are involved it is virtually impossible to handle the calculations without a computer.

Strengths and Weaknesses of PERT

There are five important advantages of PERT. First, it forces managers to plan because it is impossible to make a time–event analysis without planning and seeing how the pieces fit together. Second, it forces planning all the way down the line because each subordinate manager must plan the event for which he or she is responsible. Third, it concentrates attention on critical elements that may need correction. Fourth, it makes possible a kind of forward-looking control; a delay will affect succeeding events and possibly the whole project, unless the manager can make up the time by shortening the time allocated to some action in the future. Fifth, the network system with its subsystems enables managers to aim reports and pressure for action at the right spot and level in the organization structure at the right time.

PERT also has certain limitations. Because of the importance of activity time to its operation, the technique is not useful when a program is nebulous and no reasonable "guesstimates" of schedule can be made. Even in this case, however, insurance can be "bought" by such practices as putting two or more groups of people to work on an event when costs permit. A major disadvantage of PERT is its emphasis on time only, not on costs. While this focus is suitable for programs in which time is of the essence or in which, as so often is the case, time and costs have a close, direct relationship, the tool is more useful when considerations other than time are introduced into the analysis. (There is, however, another program called PERT/cost that does consider costs.)

THE BALANCED SCORECARD

The Balanced Scorecard is a management tool that helps ensure the alignment between a company's strategic objectives and its operational activities. Therefore, the Balanced Scorecard approach is complementary to strategic planning tools that focus on developing high-level objectives. Specifically, the Balanced Scorecard helps organizations develop a comprehensive view of their business and operational measures of success that, if attained, will help the firm achieve its strategic goals and desired financial performance. These measures and views are both qualitative and quantitative. They are from an internal and external perspective that provide *balance* of the firm's performance and strategic and management measurements.

While the Balanced Scorecard approach has been developed and modified over the last twenty years,[2] it essentially directs organizations to set targets for and measure performance in organizational functions that are believed to lead to eventual success in high-level objectives. For example, managers are advised to set operational targets for and measure aspects of financial performance, customer perception, internal processes, and organizational learning and innovation. Again, these targets should be set in line with the top-level objectives of the organization. The notion is that if the operational targets are attained, then the top-level objectives will also be met.

For example, if a top-level strategy is for the firm to be perceived as a leading edge technology firm that delights it customers with innovative products and consistently posts increasing earnings, then the company may set targets in each area of its balanced scorecard as indicated in Table 19.1.

TABLE 19.1 An example of the balanced scorecard approach for operationalizing strategic objectives: Be perceived as leading-edge technology firm that delights it customers with innovative products and consistently posts increasing earnings

Perspective/Target	Interim Target	Medium Term Target
Financial Performance	Identification and contract with lower cost/higher quality suppliers	5% lower unit cost than competition with 10% fewer defects
Customer Perception	Decrease defects to 10% below industry average	Increase customer positive recommendations by 25%
Internal Processes	Decrease required managerial approvals for customer refunds by one level	Increase number of positive employee contacts with customers by 10%
Organizational Learning	Provide for creativity training for all employees	Increase new product introductions by 10%

As illustrated in Table 19.1, the balanced scorecard approach ties specific and measurable targets (e.g., lower product defects by 10%) of operational managers to the firm's higher level strategic objective (e.g., delighting its customers). The primary goal of the balanced scorecard approach is to provide attainable targets for front-line managers that, if properly set and met, lead to the attainment of higher level organizational aims.

As the concept has been developed, the scorecard approach has focused on the attainment of two of the perspectives, organizational learning and innovation and efficient internal processes, that if achieved lead to better customer perception, and improved financial results.[3] This approach is also the focus of the development of strategy maps that allow managers to identify the links between specific strategic objectives and measurable targets within each perspective.

Since its introduction, the balanced scorecard approach to increasing company effectiveness has been applied to many organizational types. Government agencies, community organizations, not-for-profit enterprises, and high-technology firms have used the basic premises in varying ways.[4] While debate continues on the proper application and effectiveness of the balanced scorecard approach to strategy implementation, it has withstood the test of time thus far and continues to be a tool that managers can apply in enhancing their organization's performance.

INFORMATION TECHNOLOGY[5]

The developments in information technology greatly facilitate organizational control at a relatively low cost. The systems model of management (Chapter 1) shows that communication is needed for carrying out managerial functions and for linking the organization with its external environment. Communication and the management information system (MIS) are the linkage that makes managing possible.

At the outset, one has to realize the distinction between data and information. *Data* are the raw facts that may not be very useful until they become *information*, that is, after they are processed and become meaningful and understandable by the receiver (see also the communication model in Chapter 17). While this applies to interpersonal communication, it is also true for information technology.

Information technology encompasses a variety of technologies, including various kinds of hardware (e.g., computers, printers), software (e.g., operating systems, word or data processing), and computing and communication technologies (e.g., telecommunication, database management). In fact, new technologies are rapidly developing, such as 4G, the fourth generation of wireless technology, expanding and enhancing the capabilities of information technology. Even before 4G is widely implemented, the fifth-generation (5G) technology is being developed.[6]

Information technology has promoted the development of MIS. The definition of the term **management information system** varies. It is defined here as a formal system of gathering, integrating, comparing, analyzing, and dispersing information internal and external to the enterprise in a timely, effective, and efficient manner to support managers in performing their jobs. MIS has to be tailored to specific needs and may include routine information, such as monthly reports; information that points out exceptions, especially at critical points; and information necessary to predict the future.

Electronic equipment permits fast and economical processing of huge amounts of data. The computer can, with proper programming, process data toward logical conclusions, classify them, and make them readily available for use. As noted above, data do not become information until they are processed into a usable form that informs.

Management information system A formal system of gathering, processing, and dispersing information internal and external to the enterprise in a timely, effective, and efficient manner to support managers in their jobs.

GLOBAL PERSPECTIVE

Will China Assume the Role of India in IT Outsourcing?[7]

Much has been written about outsourcing of software projects to India. Indeed, India has some 200,000 IT engineers working on the architecture level. The proficiency of the English language and the high educational level are other strengths of that country. Yet, India is concerned about competitive services offered by Chinese companies. At this point, China is at a competitive disadvantage. A fragmented IT industry structure is not conducive for developing IT outsourcing capabilities. Perhaps most important, foreign companies are concerned about intellectual property protection. Despite these handicaps, China is working hard to have a role in IT outsourcing.

Microsoft's joint venture with the Shanghai Municipal Government completes some work for Microsoft web-based support. To overcome the weakness in English proficiency, employees receive training in improving their language skills. In addition, every week a thirty-minute "English corner" is held. During that time only English may be spoken. Also top universities require that a large percentage of their course offerings are conducted in English.

Thus, while at the moment, India is a leader in IT outsourcing because of the favorable conditions, the country can expect formidable competition from China.

Expansion of Basic Data

The focus of attention on management information, coupled with its improved processing, has led to the reduction of long-known limitations. Managers have recognized for years that traditional accounting information, aimed at the calculation of profits, has been of limited value for control. Yet, in many companies, this has been virtually the only regularly collected and analyzed type of data. Managers need all kinds of nonaccounting information about the external environment, such as social, economic, political, and technical developments. In addition, they need nonaccounting information on internal operations. The information should be qualitative as well as quantitative.

While not much progress has been made in meeting these requirements, the computer, plus operations research, has led to an enormous expansion of available managerial information. One sees this especially in relation to data on marketing, competition, production and distribution, product costs, technological change and development, labor productivity, and goal accomplishment. When readers of *The Economist* were asked what kind of technology would influence economic activity, the vast majority listed information technology.[8]

Information Indigestion and Intelligence Services

Managers who have experienced the impact of better and faster data processing are justly concerned about the danger of "information indigestion". With their appetite for figures whetted, the data originators and processors are turning out material at an almost frightening rate. Managers are complaining that they are being buried under printouts, reports, projections, and forecasts that they do not have time to read or cannot understand or which do not fill their particular needs.

One attempt at solving the problem of information overload is the establishment of intelligence services and the development of a new profession of intelligence experts. The service is provided by specialists who know (or find out) what information managers need and who know how to digest and interpret such information for managerial use. Some companies have established organizational units under such names as "administrative services" or "management analyses and services" for making information understandable and useful.

Managing by the Numbers[9]

Since early days of the development of managerial thought, attempts have been made to numberize managing. Frederick Taylor, the father or scientific management, aimed at improving productivity and efficiency (Chapter 1 in this book). Similarly, operations management focused on the activities necessary for producing goods and services (Chapter 20). Various tools were used to quantify activities and tasks. Edward Deming, the quality guru, used statistical tools to improve quality (Chapter 1). More recently, the Six Sigma tool (see GE's Jack Welch in Chapter 13) focused on quality and customer satisfaction. Recently, attempts are also made to model workers in large organizations such as IBM by using concepts such as "numerati". The idea is to build mathematical models of people in a large organization.

Modeling organization people may be illustrated by a project using numerati concepts in a worldwide organization such as IBM. Thus, the job may be described in numerical terms, and so would be the skills needed. People may be drawn from different organizational units located around the world. The budget would also be stated in numbers. To find the suitable people, numerical profiles can be searched in a huge database. For this complex project, concepts such as described in the book *The Numerati*, authored by Stephen Baker, may be employed. The attempt is to quantify human variables through the uses of very large databases by combining factors to achieve productivity and efficiency. These databases may consist of employees' e-mails, cell phone conversations, electronic calendars, and computer messages. These bits of data may also identify informal networks.

But this approach must be accompanied by words of caution: People may resist being treated as numbers. They may feel that their privacy has been violated and they want to be treated as dignified human beings, not as commodities. The approach may recall the negative aspects of industrial engineering and companies may be perceived as the BIG BROTHER.

As pointed out in the discussion of the management theory jungle (Chapter 1), numerical approaches to management such as the mathematical or "management science approach" or the reengineering or total quality approaches made great contributions to the development of management thought, but still many human variables cannot be quantified. The authors of this book, as well as most management textbook authors, recognize that the best approach is to organize management knowledge according to the managerial functions of planning, organizing, staffing, leading, and controlling, the framework of this book.

> **GLOBAL PERSPECTIVE**
>
> **UPS: From Time Management to Information Technology (IT)[10]**
>
> In the delivery business, time is critical for United Parcel Service Inc. (UPS) and FedEx Corporation, two fierce competitors. In the 1980s, UPS was known for its low-tech, but labor-intensive trucking operations with a focus on intensive time-management studies. But by 2006, the emphasis is on IT, partly driven by FedEx that was known for high-speed, overnight service. To improve speed, UPS customers can prepare their own labels even before the package is picked up by going to the UPS's web site or using software provided by the company. By using the satellite global positioning system, the company can quite accurately estimate the delivery time. In the future, UPS may even be able to schedule delivery by appointment.

The Twitter Phenomena[11]

One of the recent technology phenomena is Twitter where people broadcast short messages, containing not more that 140 characters. It is a free social networking service with an author who has followers. The messages can be to the public or they can be restricted to friends. The program opens with a question: "What are you doing?" which, however, many people do not answer. Nevertheless, it is an opening to connect.

Twitter started in 2006 during a brainstorming session and is growing rapidly since then. Tweets are used not only between friends, but also by politicians, news reporters (e.g., CBS in the United States), protestors, and people who just want to communicate their ideas. The candidates in the 2008 U.S. presidential election used Twitter. In 2008, during the Mumbai attack, eyewitnesses tweeted vital information such as the location of hospitals. When the US Airways airplane ditched in the Hudson River in New York, news was sent before news reporters arrived. During the 2009 Iranian election, protestors effectively use twitter communication.

Twitter raised a lot of money from venture capital firms. However, the long-term profitability and the business model are not clear at this time. While the Internet may be the next big thing, new technologies are evolving and could threaten the future of Twitter as well as other technology companies.

OPPORTUNITIES AND CHALLENGES CREATED BY INFORMATION TECHNOLOGY

Preventing the unauthorized use of information is just one of many challenges created by information technology. Other challenges as well as opportunities brought by information technology include leveraging the data created to better serve customers and bring innovation.

Innovation Through Analytics

> **Analytics** is a rising field in which sophisticated statistical algorithms are used to analyze the mountain of data available in order to help organizations improve their customer service and operate more efficiently.

The wide application of the Internet by organizations to collect and manage data has created a sea of information, much of which has not been effectively analyzed or leveraged. **Analytics** is a rising field in which sophisticated statistical algorithms are used to analyze the mountains of data available in order to help organizations improve their customer service and operate more efficiently. In a recent *Harvard Business Review* article, Thomas Davenport argues that some organizations are competing on analytics.[12] Davenport identified 11 organizations that he classified as full-bore analytics competitors as analytics was key to their overall enterprise strategy. Firms such as Amazon, Marriott, and UPS leverage a company wide focus on the collection, analysis, and application of customer and operational information to improve how they do business in terms of better customer service to drive additional revenues or to cut operations costs out of their business model. He argues for executive support for this enterprise approach in order to build a company culture that accepts and leverages analytics to improve their business processes.

The findings from the application of analytics to organizational data also may lead to innovation in how the customer experience is improved through more customized products and services. While the innovation process may begin with observing customer behavior, the rigorous analysis of customer data will help to confirm optimal strategies to enhance the customer experience with better crafted products and services and pricing that increase customer retention and profitable revenue growth.

Speech Recognition Devices

One way to encourage the use of computers is through speech recognition devices. The aim is to put data into the computer by speaking in a normal manner, rather than by using the keyboard. Several companies are working on such devices. One program called Dragon Naturally Speaking by Nuance is continuously improved with each new edition. Simple speech recognition has been in limited use for some time. Merely expanding the vocabulary through a larger memory is not enough. Imagine the program sophistication needed to distinguish between similar sounds (in the English vocabulary) such as "then" and "than" or "to" and "too" and "two". Despite the complex problems, some people think that the efforts made in this area will result in products that may revolutionize office operations.

After a slow start, speech recognition is increasingly used at call centers of telephone companies, airlines, and financial service firms.[13] The cost-effectiveness of this technology is one of the major factors for its increasing use. Computers have become less expensive, and broadband access to the Internet and wireless Ethernet have become more common. Still, the greatest impact of speech recognition may be in the car. Perhaps the most important impediment to this development is, at least in the United States, the disagreement about a common industry standard.

Telecommuting

The widespread use of computers and the ease of linking them through telephone lines (or even wireless devices) to a company's mainframe computer have led to **telecommuting**. This means that a person can work at a computer terminal at home instead of commuting to work. Some of the advantages claimed include greater flexibility in scheduling work, the avoidance of traffic congestion, and a reduced need for office space.

> **Telecommuting**
> Working at a computer terminal at home instead of commuting to work.

The futurist Alvin Toffler envisioned an "electronic cottage" with computer terminals installed at home. But John Naisbitt, in his book *Megatrends*, is skeptical of the idea and suggests that, after telecommuting for some time, workers will miss the office gossip and the human interaction with colleagues.[14] Some companies that have contracted work to telecommuters have been criticized for not providing the benefits usually given to office workers. At Pacific Bell, however, participants in the voluntary program are considered full-time employees. Moreover, some employees go to the office at least once a week to check their mail and to mingle with coworkers.

With the worsening traffic congestion, especially in metropolitan areas, one may see a greater use of telecommuting. But it is doubtful that it will replace the office as we know it today.

Computer Networks

The widespread use of stand-alone computers often results in duplication of efforts. The database in the mainframe or the minicomputer, for example, may not be accessible from the desktop computer. Therefore, computer networks have been developed that link workstations with each other, with larger computers, and with peripheral equipment. The interconnection allows users at several workstations to communicate with each other as well as to access other computers. Moreover, workstations can be connected to costly hardware that may be underutilized by a single user. For example, laser printers or tape backup units for saving data files can be shared.

There are many other applications of computer networks, such as e-mail and the collection, dissemination, and exchange of data, information, and knowledge. Although computer networking is still in its infancy, new technological developments are rapidly changing the system of information handling.

INNOVATIVE PERSPECTIVE

Cisco's Approach to "Convergence"[15]

Technology undergoes rapid changes as illustrated by convergence, which means integrating computers, entertainment systems, and the Internet. Many players are in that market ranging from Apple, to Hewlett-Packard to Microsoft, to Sony, and to Cisco. Cisco's competitive strengths are in networking gear with, for example, the Linksys product. To focus on the customer, Cisco introduced the Linksys Wireless Home Audio multi-room system. Other Cisco brands include large-screen TV setup boxes by Scientific Atlanta and Flip by Pure Digital producing very simple video cameras. By combining Cisco's strengths in networking, the company hopes to take advantage of the current networking trend.

INNOVATIVE PERSPECTIVE

Apple's iPhone a Truly Global Product and the New iPhone 5 Introduction[16]

It is very unusual that customers would stand in line to purchase a newly introduced product. But they did when Apple introduced the 3G iPhone, the phone that was technological ahead of its time when it was introduced on July 11, 2008, in America as well as in many other countries. Clearly, it was not the traditional cell phone, but had some features of a minicomputer. Why, then, were people spending hours waiting to obtain the iPhone? What are some of the features that made this phone so special? Here are some features: It can synchronize with the names, phone numbers, addresses, e-mail addresses, and other information in the contact list. Moreover, it can connect with calendars photos, podcasts, movies, and even TV shows. One of the distinguishing features is that others can develop applications that can be accessed for free or they can be purchased from the iTunes store. One of the feature popular with companies is to set up "push accounts", that is when new data is entered, such as e-mail, it is communicated directly to the computer and the iPhone wirelessly. This information can be obtained through the cellular or Wi-Fi connection.

The 3G iPhone is a great improvement over the older iPhone that was introduced about a year earlier. But the new phone is much faster. At the same time, the price has been greatly reduced. Thus, the price reduction and the fast speed, besides the other features, was attracting customers and made them stand in line.

This is truly a global phone. One part was developed in a garage in India, it was designed by Apple computers in the Silicon Valley near San Francisco, and it is produced in China. Partly through this cooperation, the new iPhone could be offered at $199 for the 8Gig—that is, half the price of the previous, much slower phone. But people object that the only carriers in the United States were AT&T and Verizon. In other countries, the iPhone was also limited to a designated carrier or few carriers; for example in Germany it is T-Mobile.

Another feature is the global positioning system (GPS) which works around the world used for finding direction. One can also do multitasking on the phone.

With the camera, one can take pictures and e-mail them to a person on the contacts list. One also has access to the Apple Store where one can purchase music and video. A rather unique feature is the App Store in which developers from all over the world can offer their application programs for the iPhone which allows game playing, obtaining news and sports stories. These features and the international keyboards layouts make the iPhone a truly global product.

While the 3G Phone was an important innovation, technology rapidly changes. In 2011, the 4S iPhone was introduced with the dual-core A5 chip, the 8MP camera, and the Siri feature which allow using voice command, was introduced. The iOS 5 is the most advanced operating system for mobile devices. Again, enthusiasts were standing in line at the Apple stores to purchase the newest iPhone.

In September 2012, the iPhone 5 was introduced. Compared to its preceding iPhone 4S, the new iPhone 5 has many new features such as:

- A new A6 chip compared to the older A5 chip.
- It is taller with a larger display (now 4 inch. diagonally) which is better for viewing many videos.
- It is thinner and lighter.
- It also has additional wireless connections.
- The Face Time camera has been improved.
- Battery life is also better.
- The new reversible connector is smaller, but has been criticized.
- The Google Maps have been replaced with Apple Maps which has new features, but also lacks some Google features, such as "street view". Apple, however, intends to improve its maps features.

Despite increasing competition, the iPhone 5 remains to be the market leader with the 2012 introduction of the iPhone 5 in Australia, Canada, France, Germany, China, Japan, Singapore, the United Kingdom, and, of course, in the United States. Soon, iPhone 5, a truly global produce will soon be available in other countries.

Other Types of Networks

Besides the Internet, there are other types of networks. The **intranet** is a network that applies computer and Internet technologies to an organization or selected groups within the organization. Similarly, the **extranet** also uses computer and Internet technologies, but it connects selected users inside as well as outside the organization. For example, a purchasing agent may be linked to certain vendors for conducting selling and buying transactions.

Groupware

Networks facilitate the management process and other business activities. A group of people on a network can collaborate over long distances at the same time using **groupware**. This software allows a document to be shown to several users on their monitors and for them to comment or make changes to the document. Thus, people who may be located in different parts of the world can collaborate on the same task simultaneously.

> **Groupware** Software that enables a group of people on a network to collaborate over long distances at the same time.

Freeware: The Search for a Business Model[17]

There is not general agreement on the freeware term. It usually pertains to a fully functional software with no cost. However, restrictions may be imposed on the user such as that it is only for personal use and not for commercial purposes. Note that freeware is different from shareware, which generally requires the use to pay after an initial period or to upgrade to extra functionality.

Today, much information that previously cost money can now be obtained free. For example, Wikipedia is a web based free encyclopedia base on the collaboration of contributors. Many web sites replace agents or companies. Trading web sites replaced travel agents, Turbo Tax, the accounting software, replaced accountants, and the search engines replaced travel agents. There are also other free web sites. For example, on the iPhone or iPod Touch one can listen to music for free on Pandora, on Hulu one can see movies for free, and Skype allows free phoning. YouTube is a video sharing web site that is used by individuals and organizations. For example, in 2009 the Vatican entered the new technology world with its own web site on YouTube (http://de.youtube.com/vatican?hl=en). The program is available in several languages. So what is the business model for those companies who provide free access to their offerings?

The traditional model was as follows: First it started with an idea, then money was raised to bring the idea to the market, if successful, additional money was obtained to expand the business, and finally a big company bought the entrepreneurial product of service. However, during the financial global meltdown in 2008, it became difficult to raise money and companies are searching for new business models. The popular Facebook has many customers, but it is also ineffective in raising advertising money. The widely used YouTube is also struggling. One may also be wondering how Microsoft can compete in markets where word processors and spreadsheets are available for free. Microsoft created a web version of is business software and made it available for free to small and young enterprises that are less than three years old and have revenues of less than $1 million. The hope is that as the firms grow, they will buy and use Microsoft's programs.

While users of software benefit from the freebees, companies are struggling to find a profitable business model.

Information Security[18]

With the growing use of information technology, the concern for security also increases. Not only businesses but also individuals are vulnerable to computer break-ins or interception or alteration of electronic transmissions. A hacker (someone who breaks into a computer) may alter or even destroy bank or other records. Protection of computers can be afforded through encryption, whereby a secret code is used to scramble the message so that it is not readable. The use of a firewall also provides some protection. Firewalls come as software programs (e.g., Norton Personal Firewall or Zone Alarm Pro) or as hardware such as the Ethernet router. A great variety of antivirus programs protect against computer viruses or worms, which may cause extensive damage to computers and networks. Of additional concern are the people who work with information systems in organizations. They need to be responsible, be trained, and be held accountable for their behavior with severe penalties attached for breaching security. Individuals and companies also should protect data by regularly making backup copies and storing them in a secure place, perhaps outside their place of work.

THE DIGITAL ECONOMY, E-COMMERCE, AND M-COMMERCE

Alan Greenspan, chairman of the U.S. Federal Reserve Board, one of the most influential persons in the world of finance, stated in 1999: "The newest innovations, which we label information technology, have begun to alter the manner in which we do business and create value, often in ways not readily foreseeable even five years ago." **E-commerce**—business transactions on the web—is changing the way we do business.

The Emerging Digital Economy[19]

Information technology affects most aspects of business and personal life. While computer power is growing rapidly, its price is dropping dramatically. The Ford Taurus car of today has more computing power than the million-dollar mainframe computer in the Apollo space program. Information technology raises productivity not only in the production and distribution of goods but also in services. Productivity improvement, in turn, results in higher living standards. This new technology impact is global, increasing competition and innovation. The ability to easily process vast amounts of data in research and development has shortened the development time of new products, speeding up their introduction to the market.[20]

One of the major impacts of the Internet is on the way business is conducted. Relationships with suppliers and customers are changing dramatically. Telecommunication and information technology have contributed greatly to the longest peacetime economic expansion in the United States. The investment in those technologies finally paid out. Today, we have e-everything: e-mail, e-commerce, e-business, e-cash (use of smart cards and digital cash), e-travel, e-finance, e-loan, e-music, e-books, e-stamps, and many more e-activities.

The economic gains of e-commerce come from the lower costs of online companies (when compared to brick-and-mortar firms with physical stores), reduction in distribution costs, and the elimination of intermediaries. Buyers benefit from being able to compare prices and select the best choice from the comfort of their home or office. How can the brick-and-mortar businesses with their higher costs compete with e-businesses? Stores like Kmart and Wal-Mart now also transact their business through the web, becoming "clicks and mortar" or "clicks and bricks" companies. This means you can make purchases with a click of the mouse or by physically visiting their stores.

The Internet facilitates four kinds of transactions, as shown in Figure 19.3. These transactions are:

FIGURE 19.3 Matrix for e-commerce

	Consumer	Business
Consumer	**C2C** eBay (auction)	**C2B** Priceline ("you name the price" travel offers)
Business	**B2C** Amazon (books, etc.) Travelocity (travel)	**B2B** Ford, General Motors, DailmerChrysler (manufacturers to suppliers)

Adapted from "E-Commerce Survey," *The Economist*, February 26, 2000, Insert p. 11.

1. *Business to consumer (B2C)*. Ordering books or other items from Amazon.com or buying a computer from Dell online are examples of B2C transactions. The Safeway grocery store delivers web-ordered groceries to customers' home.
2. *Consumer to business (C2B)*. An example of C2B transaction is the bidding for airline tickets by would-be flyers through Priceline.com.
3. *Consumer to consumer (C2C)*. The eBay auction web site offers C2C transactions, through which individuals can sell items.
4. *Business to business (B2B)*. B2B transactions are probably going to have the greatest impact on the economy. For example, the two largest car manufacturers, General Motors (GM) and Ford, plan to transfer all purchasing to the web within the next few years. GM claims that its website will be the world's largest virtual marketplace. So what could this mean to the consumer in the future? Ford and GM may build cars to order for delivery in just a few days, just like you order today customized computers from Dell.[21] It is possible that GM and Ford will become virtual companies with expertise in car design and brand marketing.

Covisint, the new joint venture between Ford, GM, DaimlerChrysler, and Renault/Nissan, could become the exchange where suppliers trade with each other.[22] There is concern that this may lead to monopolistic practices, which may prompt the U.S. Justice Department to investigate.

In the airline business, another battle takes shape. The five largest U.S. airlines—Continental, Delta, Northwest, United, and American Airlines—have a common web site called Orbitz.com. This site collides with the traditional travel agents as well as with online travel agents such as Travelocity and Expedia (a Microsoft company) by trying to undercut their prices.[23]

www.covisint.com

www.orbitz.com

Three-quarters of all e-commerce is conducted in the United States, from which 90 percent of all commercial web sites originated.[24] However, the country with the most Internet hosts per inhabitant is Finland; the United States ranks second. Among the world's most admired companies identified by *Fortune* magazine, many are in the information technology business.[25] Here are some familiar names: Microsoft, Dell, Cisco Systems, Intel, Nokia, and Lucent Technologies. However, in 2002, some of the so-called dot-com companies fell out of favor with investors. Outside the information technology industry, many firms use sophisticated technologies to gain a competitive advantage, including Wal-Mart, General Electric, and Ford.

www.nokia.com
www.lucent.com

INNOVATION PERSPECTIVE

The Digital Impact on GE[26]

Many big companies now operate not only in the industrial sector but also in the information business. GE, General Electric, is one of them. Jeff Immelt, CEO and Chairman of GE, described the company's transition from the industrial sector to the information age responding to the digitization. This is the future of GE and many companies.

The jet engine, for example, has hundreds of sensors that transmit continuously data about the environment, the heat of the engine, fuel consumption, and so on. The digitization of the business requires many managerial decision such as hiring the right people who have the knowledge and skills for adapting to the changes in the digital world. Consequently, GE hired data scientists who have to be integrated with the GE culture. Changing the organization culture is a difficult process realizing that the company at one time had 70 percent of its operations *inside* the United States but now has 70 percent of its operations *outside* the United States.

M-Commerce and Wireless Communications

While e-commerce is changing the way business is conducted, wireless communications and m-commerce (mobile commerce) are emerging to take it further. Many companies are trying to exploit opportunities in wireless communications. Wireless applications may include business transactions, provision of financial and travel information, community sites for chatting or sending e-postcards, banking, auctions, marketing, advertising, and many other usages.

The developments in e-business, e-commerce, and m-commerce provide great opportunities for enterprises. Managers need to observe the trends and develop strategies to take advantage of the new technologies.

Customer Relationship Management (CRM)[27]

CRM means promoting the interactions between the customer and the organization by collecting, analyzing, and using the information to better serve the client.

Customers are the reason for an organization's existence. Therefore, to be successful, enterprises need to focus on the needs of their customers. Customer relationship management (CRM) addresses this need. Companies are also faced with the need for a system that reduces costs and coordinates sales and marketing and service efforts to provide a positive experience for their customers (e.g., such as handling complaints). It is through the CRM system that data are collected on customers in a centralized database.

There is no agreed upon definition of customer relationship management. In broad terms CRM means promoting the interactions between the customer and the organization by collecting, analyzing, and using the information to better serve the client. CRM is not new, but it has gone through various overlapping stages. The beginning of CRM probably can be traced to Siebel Systems Inc. in 1993. In the 1990s, CRM approaches were accompanied by a number of failures. At stage 1, the emphasis was on marketing processes; stage 2 focused on customer relationships; stage 3 utilized the Internet for reevaluating the processes, redesigning systems, and self-service. It is in stage 4 that more attention is given to the specific needs of the customers.

Professor Raab and his colleagues view CRM as being based on three pillars: technology, organization, and personnel which are the foundation of customer orientation, customer satisfaction, customer retention, and customer profitability.[28] Another way of looking at the process of CRM is that an effective use of its pillars of personnel, technology and organization lead to customer orientation, product quality, customer satisfaction, customer retention, customer value and eventually to company success.

CRM is used by many organizations. At Marriott, for example, it is used to boost sales, manage the Marriott Rewards program, and for the Broadsystem that expands the company's marketing program. The travel industry has extensively used programs for managing the relationships with its customers. For example, CRM has been employed by companies such as Southwest Airlines, JetBlue, Best Western, British Airways, Delta, American Airlines, Alaska Airlines, Walt Disney, Travelocity, and Expedia.

There are also concerns and limitation of CRM. For one, large investments are required for building and maintaining the system. Hardware and software are required and so is the costly training of the system's users. Customers are also concerned about their privacy and that the collected information about them could be misused.

Clearly, CRM is not a cure-all for solving all the problems in the relationships between an organization and it customers. However, certain steps can help to make the system succeed. Careful planning is certainly necessary. Also, since the installation of the systems requires organizational changes, people need to be prepared for the cultural adjustment. In many cases it might not be wise to begin with a costly comprehensive system. Instead, a company may start with a pilot program and incrementally enlarge the system. At any rate, to remain competitive or better to achieve a competitive edge companies may utilize CRM for systematically staying in contact with their customers who are, the reason for the organization's success.

SUMMARY

A variety of tools and techniques have been used to help manager's control. These techniques are generally, in the first instance, tools for planning, and they illustrate the fact that controls must reflect plans. Some of these tools have long been used by managers; others are refinements. One of the older control devices is the budget. Budgeting is the formulation of plans for a given future period in numerical terms. There are also dangers in budgeting. Budgeting is made much more precise by zero-base budgeting, in which programs are divided into "packages". The costs for each package are calculated from a base of zero. In order to make budgetary control effective in practice, managers must always realize that budgets are tools and are not intended to replace managing. Among the traditional nonbudgetary control devices are statistical data and their analyses, special reports and analyses, the operational audit, and personal observation.

One of the techniques of planning and control is the time–event network analysis. The program evaluation and review technique (PERT) is a refinement of the original Gantt chart, which was designed to show, in bar-chart form, the various tasks that must be done, and when, in order to accomplish a program. PERT is also a refinement of milestone budgeting, in which the tasks that have to be done are broken down into identifiable and controllable pieces called milestones. When milestones are connected to form a network and the time required to complete each milestone is identified, the result is a PERT/time–event network. Using the sequences of events and the times required for them, one can determine the critical path, which is the sequence that takes the longest time and has zero (or the least) slack time.

The management information system is a formal system of gathering, integrating, comparing, analyzing, and dispersing information, internal and external, to the enterprise in a timely, effective, and efficient manner to support managers in their work.

Computers (mainframes, minicomputers, and microcomputers) are now extensively used. Their impact on managers at various organizational levels differs. Information technology provides many challenges. Some managers still resist using computers, but speech recognition devices will encourage computer use. Computers have also contributed to telecommuting, allowing people to work from home at a computer that is linked to a company's mainframe computer. Increasingly, computer networks are installed to link workstations with each other, with larger computers, and with peripheral equipment.

The Internet revolution brings exciting new opportunities for business and personal life. It is changing how business is conducted. The relationships with suppliers and customers are changing dramatically. The four kinds of electronic business transactions are shown in Figure 19.3. There is now a trend toward wireless communications and m-commerce, especially in Japan and Europe. Customer relationship management (CRM) aims at serving the needs of its clients.

KEY IDEAS AND CONCEPTS FOR REVIEW

Budgeting
Types of budgets
Budgeting problems
Zero-base budgeting
Nonbudgetary control devices
Gantt chart
Milestone budgeting
Program evaluation and review technique (PERT), critical path
Information technology
Management information system
Types of computers
Impact of computers on managers
Application of microcomputers
Speech recognition devices
Telecommuting

Computer networks
Internet
Groupware
Information security
E-commerce: B2C, C2B, C2C, B2B
M-commerce and wireless communications
Customer relationship management

FOR DISCUSSION

1. The techniques of control appear to be as much techniques of planning as they are of control. In what ways is this true? Why would you expect it to be so?
2. If you were going to institute a program of special control reports and analyses for a top manager, how would you go about it?
3. PERT is a management invention that takes basic principles and knowledge and, through design to get a desired result, comes up with a useful technique of planning and control. Analyze PERT with this in mind.
4. Give examples of how information technology has affected you.
5. Why do you think computers impact on managers at various organizational levels differently?
6. How will e-commerce affect you in the future on buying or selling of goods and services?
7. How do you feel about your personal data being stored in the customer relationship management system of the organization with which you are doing business?

EXERCISES/ACTION STEPS

1. Prepare a budget for your studies at the university. What are the advantages in preparing a budget? What are some problems?
2. Select an organization that you know and show how it uses computers or conducts e-commerce.
3. Select a firm in which you have an interest in working for and conduct a general balanced score card analysis from publicly available information. Given your analysis do you believe the organization is on the road to continued success? What operational activities in organizational learning, internal processes, customer perception, and financial measures might you suggest that the organization pursue in order to obtain its strategic objective?
4. Identify two enterprise software applications that may help organizations better control their costs and operations. Be able to describe them to class and give examples of their use.

INNOVATION CASE

Amazon.com—One of the Most Innovative Companies Under the Leadership of Entrepreneur Jeff Bezos.[29]

Amazon.com under the leadership of Jeff Bezos, an extraordinary entrepreneur, is one of the most innovative companies. The company started as an electronic bookseller, but now includes selling many products delivered around the world. The company with some 209 million customers is taking away business from established companies such as JC Penney, Best Buy, and Circuit City. Amazon's way of selling, however, is very different from those companies (although they also have some e-business activities).

Amazon's strength is speedy delivery through a network of local fulfilment centers with warehouses where products are stored. There are more than 89 fulfillment centers globally. Amazon invested heavily in warehouses in order to be closer to the customers. It usually takes 2.5 hours from the time an order is placed to the time it is processed. The inventory system uses some robotic features, but still relies extensively on people who use handheld guns for code reading. The recent acquisition of a robotic company may result in wider use of automation.

For the customer, ordering is easy through the 1-click feature. Also customers can Subscribe and Save, which allows for scheduled replenishment of commonly used items. What is considered a bargain is the Amazon Prime feature that can be obtained for $79 a year (increased to $99 for new customers).[1] At any rate, Amazon Prime provides for two-day free shipping of many items. It also allows for free Streaming Video programs and more than 500,000 free books in the Kindle's Owners' Lending Library which include more than 100 books on the New York Times best-seller list. In all, if one takes full advantage of Amazon Prime, it is a bargain. Bezos is willing to lose some money on shipping and services in exchange for customer loyalty.

The company is also experimenting with Amazon Fresh which is a same-day delivery service of groceries. This experiment started in Seattle in Washington State, where Amazon's headquarters are located, but is spreading to other cities as well. After an assessment of Amazon Fresh, the future of this innovation will be evaluated for further implementation.

In December 2013 during the popular 60 Minutes Television program, Jeff Bezos introduced the idea of Amazon Prime Air which could become a possible delivery service of the future. Drones would be used to delivery of small packages. However, this 30-minutes delivery service for the future needs the approval of the Federal Aviation Administration.[30]

Amazon.com is certainly one of the most exciting companies and more innovations can be expected in the future.

Questions:

1. Using the Internet, find out the status of the Amazon Prime Air development.
2. Using the Internet, search for recent developments at Amazon.com.
3. Using the Internet, identify the failures of Amazon's ventures. Why were some of the undertakings not successful?
4. Discuss the advantages and disadvantages of taking risks. What is your inclination for taking risks?

ENDNOTES

1. See also Robin Cooper and W. Bruce Chew, "Control Tomorrow's Costs through Today's Design," *Harvard Business Review*, January–February 1996, pp. 88–97; "Budget Types and Uses," http://able.harvard.edu/fbud, accessed June 25, 2002.
2. The development of the first balanced scorecard (or corporate scorecard) is credited to Art Schneiderman in 1987. Robert Kaplan and David Norton developed the concept further and published the seminal book, *The Balanced Scorecard*, in 1996. Kaplan, Norton, and others continue to advance the concept and its application to this date.
3. Robert Kaplan and David Norton, *Strategy Maps: Converting Intangible Assets into Tangible Outcomes* (Boston: Harvard Business School Press, 2004).
4. See for example, Robert Kaplan and David Norton, "Keeping Score on Community Investment," *Leader to Leader*, 2004, 33; and G. S. Sureshchandar and R. Leisten, "Holistic Scorecard: Strategic Performance Measurement and Management in the Software Industry," *Measuring Business Excellence*, 2005, 9.
5. See also Peter F. Drucker, "The Information Executives Truly Need," *Harvard Business Review*, January–February 1995, pp. 54–63; Peter F. Drucker, "The Next Society," *The Economist*, November 3, 2001, Insert pp. 3–20.
6. Brian Nadel, "Waiting for the Wireless Revolution," *PC Magazine*, May 21, 2002, pp. 84–86.
7. Li Yuan, "Chinese Companies Vie for a Role in U.S. IT Outsourcing," *The Wall Street Journal*, April 5, 2005.
8. "The Same—Only More So?" *The Economist*, December 8, 2001, Insert p. 12.
9. "Management by the Numbers" with book excerpts by Stephen Baker, *Business Week*, September 8, 2008, pp. 32–38; see the cover story "Math Will Rock Your World,: *Business Week*, January 23, 2006; "Math Will Rock Your World," http://www.businessweek.com/magazine/content/06_04/b3968001.htm, accessed August 19, 2011; "The Numerati," http://thenumerati.net/index.cfm?postID=61, accessed August 19, 2011.
10. Corey Dade, "Moving Ahead – How UPS Went from Low-Tech to IT Power – and Where It's Headed Next," The Wall Street Journal, July 24, 2006.
11. Robert D. Hof, "Betting on the Real-Time Web," Business Week, August 17, 2009. "Twitter," https://twitter.com/, accessed August 2, 2012.
12. Thomas Davenport, "Competing on Analytics," Harvard Business Review, January 2006.
13. "Just Talk to Me," The Economist, December 8, 2001, Insert pp. 13–15.
14. John Naisbitt, Megatrends (New York: Warner Books, 1982), chap. 1.
15. Stephen H. Wildstrom, "Meet Cisco, the Consumer Company," Business Week, May 4, 2009, pp. 73–74.
16. Walter Mossberg, "Newer, Faster, Cheaper iPhone 3G," The Wall Street Journal, July 8, 2008; "Lab Tests," Consumer Reports, October 2008, p. 31; see also the Apple website at http://www.apple.com/iphone, accessed September 22, 2012; and "Apple" at http://www.apple.com/iphone/features, accessed November 15, 2011; iPhone-4s-Review, http://www.engadget.com/2011/10/14/iphone-4s-review, accessed September 22, 2012; "iPhone 5 Launches in 9 Countries." http://betanews.com/2012/09/21/iphone-5-launches-in-9-countries/, accessed September 22, 2012; Apple Store, http://store.apple.com/us/browse/home/shop_iphone/family/iphone/compare, accessed September 22, 2012.
17. Chris Anderson, "The Economics of Giving It Away," The Wall Street Journal, January 31, 2009.
18. Robert Luhn and Scott Spanbauer, "Protect Your PC," PC World, July 2002, pp. 92–106; "Cyberspace Invaders," Consumer Reports, June 2002, pp. 16–20; see also "Security," http://www.pcmag.com/category2/0,2806,4829,00.asp, accessed August 19, 2011 and "Security," http://www.pcworld.com/topics/security.html, accessed August 19, 2011; see also The Cyber Solutions Handbook, boozallen.com, accessed October 30, 2015.
19. See also Simon Moore, "Disaster's Future – The Prospect for Corporate Crisis," accessed August 19, 2011. "Management and Communication," in Fred H. Maidment, ed. Annual Editions - Management (New York: McGraw-Hill 2009), pp. 106–113.
20. "Elementary, My Dear Watson," The Economist, September 23, 2000, Insert pp. 7–9.
21. Andy Serwer, "Dell Does Domination," Fortune, January 21, 2002, pp. 71–75.
22. "A Market for Monopoly?" The Economist, June 17, 2000, pp. 59–60.
23. Tyler Maroney, "An Air Battle Comes to the Web," Fortune, June 26, 2000, pp. 315–318.
24. "First America, Then the World," The Economist, February 26, 2000, Insert pp. 49–53.
25. Nicholas Stein, "The World's Most Admired Companies," Fortune, October 2, 2000, pp. 183–196.
26. GE's Jeff Immelt on Digitizing in the Industrial Space, Interview by Rik Kirkland, McKinsey, October 2015, http://www.mckinsey.com/insights/organization/ges_jeff_immelt_on_digitizing_in_the_industrial_space, accessed December 14, 2015.
27. Fraya Wagner-Marsh, "Customer Relationship Management," in Marilyn Helms, ed. *Encyclopedia of Management*, 5th ed. (Detroit: Gale, 2006), pp. 150–152; "Coffee, Tea, or Mortgage? Banks Are Cozying Up To Customers While Using High-Tech Tools To Identify Prospects," *Business Week,* April 3, 2006, p. 48; "Marriott Uses CRM Application to Boost Sales," http://www.informationweek.com/news/showArticle.jhtml?articleID=6506964, accessed November 17, 2011; "Merging Business Cultures to Support Common Goals," http://www.google.com/search?q=Merging+Business+Cultures+to+Support+Common+Goals&rls=com.microsoft-:en-us:IE-SearchBox&ie=UTF-8&oe=UTF-8&sourceid=ie7&rlz=1I7RNWE; http://www.cio.com/article/31068/Merging_Business_Cultures_to_Support_Common_Goals, accessed November 17, 2011; "Marriott Hands CRM to Broadsystem," http://www.brandrepublic.com/News/854476/Marriott-hands-CRM-duties-Broadsystem/, accessed January 11, 2016; "Battleground CRM: How are Leading Travel Companies Using CRM to Unlock the Full Revenue Potentials of their Customers?" http://www.hotel-online.com/News/PR2006_4th/Nov06_EyeForTravel.html, accessed January 11, 2016.
28. Gerhard Raab, Riad A. Ajami, Vidyaranya B. Gargeya, and G. Jason Goddard, *Customer Relationship Management – A Global Perspective* (Burlington, VT: Gower Publishing Company, 2008), Chapter 1.
29. J.J. McCorvey, "The Race Has Just Begun," FastCompany, September 2013, pp. 66–76; Amazon Prime, http://www.amazon.com/gp/help/customer/display.html?nodeId=13819211, accessed February 27, 2014; Kindle Owner's Lending Library, http://www.amazon.com/gp/feature.html?docId=1000739811, accessed February 27, 2014; "Amazon.com Inc.," *New York Times*, February 27, 20014, http://topics.nytimes.com/top/news/business/companies/amazon_inc/index.html, accessed February 27, 2014.
30. See also Gur Kimchi and Daniel Cuchmueller, "For Proving That the Sky is Not the Limit," FastCompany, June 2014, p. 67.

CHAPTER 20

Productivity, Operations Management, and Total Quality Management

Learning Objectives

After studying this chapter, you should be able to:

LO 1 Identify the nature of productivity issues and suggest ways to improve effectiveness and efficiency

LO 2 Describe production and operations management as an applied case of managerial planning and control

LO 3 Understand the operations management system

LO 4 Discuss the tools and techniques for improving productivity

LO 5 Recognize the importance of quality, the nature of a variety of techniques for improving quality, and lean manufacturing

LO 6 Distinguish between supply chain management and value chain management, although the terms are sometimes used interchangeably

In a real sense, this whole book is about the improvement of productivity. But this important topic will receive special attention in this chapter, with an emphasis on the micro level of production and operations management.*

PRODUCTIVITY PROBLEMS AND MEASUREMENT

Undoubtedly, productivity is one of the major concerns of managers in the 21st century. This is a concern in many parts of the world. Even Japan, which is admired for productivity improvement, is now concerned about remaining competitive in the world market.

Productivity Problems

Productivity implies measurement, which in turn is an essential step in the control process. Although there is general agreement about the need for improving productivity, there is little consensus about the fundamental causes of the problem and what to do about them. The blame has been assigned to various factors. Some people place it on the greater proportion of less-skilled workers with respect to the total labor force, but others disagree. There are those who see the cutback in research and the emphasis on immediate results as the main culprit. Another reason given for the productivity dilemma is the growing affluence of people, which makes them less ambitious. Still others cite the breakdown in family structure, workers' attitudes, and government policies and regulations. Increasingly, attention shifts to management as the cause of the problem—as well as the solution, which is the focus of this book.

Measurement of Productivity of Knowledge Workers

As defined in Chapter 1, **productivity** is the output–input ratio within a time period with due consideration for quality. This definition can be applied to the productivity of organizations, managers, staff personnel, and other workers. Measurement of skill work is relatively easy, but it becomes more difficult for knowledge work. The difference between the two kinds of work is the relative use of knowledge and skills. Thus, a person on the production line would be considered a skill worker, while the assistant to the manager with planning as

Productivity The output–input ratio within a time period with due consideration for quality.

---

* Additional topics in production and operations management are discussed in other parts of the book. See, for example, Chapter 6 for various aspects of decision making, Chapter 11 for job design, and Chapter 19 for management information systems and different kinds of control techniques.

his or her main function would be a knowledge worker. Managers, engineers, and programmers are knowledge workers because the relative amount of their work does not consist of utilizing skills, as would be the case for bricklayers, mechanics, and butchers. But the job title cannot be the sole guide for making distinctions. The owner of a gas station may schedule the day's tasks, determine priorities, and direct subordinates, but he or she may also change brakes, adjust the carburetor, or realign the front wheels on a car.

It is clear that, in general, the productivity of the knowledge worker is more difficult to measure than that of the skill worker. (Note also that worker productivity measurement is somewhat artificial because it often ignores the cost of capital.) One difficulty in measuring the productivity of knowledge workers is that some outputs are really activities that help achieve end results. Thus, the engineer contributes indirectly to the final product. Another difficulty is that knowledge workers often assist other organizational units. The advertising manager's efforts should improve sales, but it is hard to say for sure what the exact contribution is. Still another difficulty is that the quality of knowledge workers' outputs is often hard to measure. The effects of a strategic decision, for example, may not be evident for several years, and even then the success or failure of the new strategic direction may depend on many external forces beyond the control of the manager.

It is evident that productivity improvement is achieved by the good management practices advocated throughout this book. But the discussion will now turn to the specific area of production and operations management, where measurement is relatively easy and which consequently has been the focus of productivity improvement programs in the past.

PRODUCTION AND OPERATIONS MANAGEMENT: MANUFACTURING AND SERVICE

Production management deals with activities necessary to manufacture products.

Operations management deals with activities necessary to produce and deliver a service as well as a physical product.

One of the major areas in any kind of enterprise, whether business, government, or others, is production and operations management. It is also the area where managing as a scientifically based art got its start. The contributions of such management pioneers as Frederick Taylor, Henry Gantt, and Frank Gilbreth, to mention only a few, indicate that their interest was largely in improving productivity and manufacturing products most efficiently while still recognizing, as they did, the importance of the human factor as an indispensable input.

In the past, **production management** was the term used to refer to those activities necessary to manufacture products. However, in recent years, the area has been generally expanded to include such activities as purchasing, warehousing, transportation, and other operations from the procurement of raw materials through various activities until a product is available to the buyer. The term **operations management** refers to activities necessary to produce and deliver a service as well as a physical product.

There are of course other essential activities undertaken by a typical enterprise. These activities often include research and development, engineering, marketing and sales, accounting, and finance. This chapter deals only with what has come to be called operations management or production management or, often, production and operations management. It should be pointed out that this is not the same thing as operational management theory. Operational management theory is the study of the practice (managing) which that theory or science is designed to underpin.

Service organizations do not produce a physical output but provide some service as an output. For instance, the input of students with limited knowledge, skills, and attitudes becomes enriched and transformed through attending lectures, doing case analyses, participating in exercises, and engaging in other activities that will result in the output of educated students, which is documented by a degree. Other examples of service providers are hospitals, doctors, consultants, airlines, restaurants, musicians, and the great variety of retail stores.

INNOVATIVE PERSPECTIVE

GE's Transformation from Products to Services[1]

General Electric (GE) is known for a variety of products, including medical imaging equipment such as CAT scanners and magnetic resonance imagers. Now it has expanded its business into servicing not only its own sophisticated products but even those of its competitors. GE's then chief executive, Jack Welch, said: "We are in the services business to expand our pie."

GE offers services ranging from health care to utilities. Thus, it provides such services as maintenance of medical systems, maintenance and overhaul of aircraft engines, operation and maintenance of utility power plants, locomotive maintenance, servicing of electronic tracking devices for railroads, and even providing help in running corporate computer networks. The result is that almost 60 percent of GE's profits come from services. Jack Welch would even like it to be 80 percent. The new direction in U.S. industry may be a trend toward services so that products are only one aspect of the business.

www.ge.com

QUALITY MEASUREMENT IN THE INFORMATION AGE[2]

In the past, the concepts of quality were mostly applied to products, such as cars or refrigerators. With the increase in service companies, quality concepts must also be applied in those firms. This means such things as the measurement of expectations, experiences, and emotions. For example, how do customers feel waiting in line in a restaurant or at Disneyland rides, or waiting on the telephone for help?

Quality in the information age takes on new dimensions. Software package quality does not only include reliability but also technical support services, compatibility, upgradability of the software, and the integration of the information infrastructure not only with the company but also with its suppliers and customers. Wal-Mart, for example, gains a competitive edge through supply chain management. Focusing on the quality of the information infrastructure is critical for company success in the new information age.

ENTREPRENEURIAL PERSPECTIVE

Google Brings Quality Measures to the Advertising Industry

For many years organizations of all types have dedicated major investments in branding and sales with traditional media (newspapers, radio, TV) without clearly knowing the impact of their advertising expenditures. For example, how will the advertiser know how many people actually read the advertisement it paid for in a local or national newspaper? The functionality of the Internet (ability to track users' views and clicks on web advertisements) and Google's effective technology of tracking and placing paid advertisements has enabled organizations to know with much greater assurance the effectiveness and productivity of their advertisement expenditures. In the Google system, advertisers can know exactly how many people viewed their advertisement and how many people clicked on an ad and, thus, visited the their website. Additionally, in the Google model, advertisers pay only for the click-throughs and get the views of their ads for free. This service allows organizations to more productively allocate their limited advertising dollars. Further, it allows small firms establish a global reach with effective and inexpensive Internet media.

THE OPERATIONS MANAGEMENT SYSTEM

Operations management has to be seen as a system. Figure 20.1 gives an overview of the operations function. In the operations management model, the *inputs* include needs of customers, information, technology, management and labor, fixed assets, and variable assets that are relevant to the transformation process. Managers and workers use the information and physical factors to produce outputs. Some physical elements, such as land, plant site, buildings, machines, and warehouses, are relatively permanent. Other physical elements, such as materials and supplies, are consumed in the process of producing outputs. The *transformation process* incorporates planning, operating, and controlling the system. There are many tools and techniques available to facilitate the transformation process. The model also reflects a constant concern with *system improvement*. *Outputs* consist of products and services and may even be information, such as that provided by a consulting organization.

The last part of the model shows that operations are influenced by *external factors*, such as safety regulations or fair labor practices. Since the external environment is discussed elsewhere in this book (especially in Chapter 2 and Part 2), it will not be expanded on here; the important point is that operations management must be an open system interacting with its surroundings.

The operations management model (Figure 20.1) serves as a framework for the discussions that follow. There is a close relationship between this model and the one introduced in Chapter 1 (Figure 1.6), since this operations model may be regarded as a subsystem of a total management system. Examples of operations systems with inputs, transformation (sometimes also called process), and outputs are presented in Table 20.1.

FIGURE 20.1 Operations management system

External environment

Inputs:
- Needs of customers
- Information
- Technology
- Management and labor
- Relatively permanent physical factors (land, plant site, buildings, machines, warehouses)
- Variable physical factors (materials, supplies)

Planning:
- Product/service decision
- Product/service design

Systems design

Transformation processes
Organizing staffing leading

Operating the system:
- Organization structure
- Job design
- Staffing the organization, selection, appraisal, training
- Providing leadership
- Purchasing
- Inventory

Tools and techniques:
1. Operations research
2. Linear programming
3. Inventory planning and control
4. Distribution logistics
5. Decision trees
6. Time-event networks
7. Value engineering
8. Work simplification
9. Quality circles
10. CAD/CAM

Controlling Operations control
- Information for control
- Quality control

Outputs:
- Products
- Services
- Information

Systems improvement

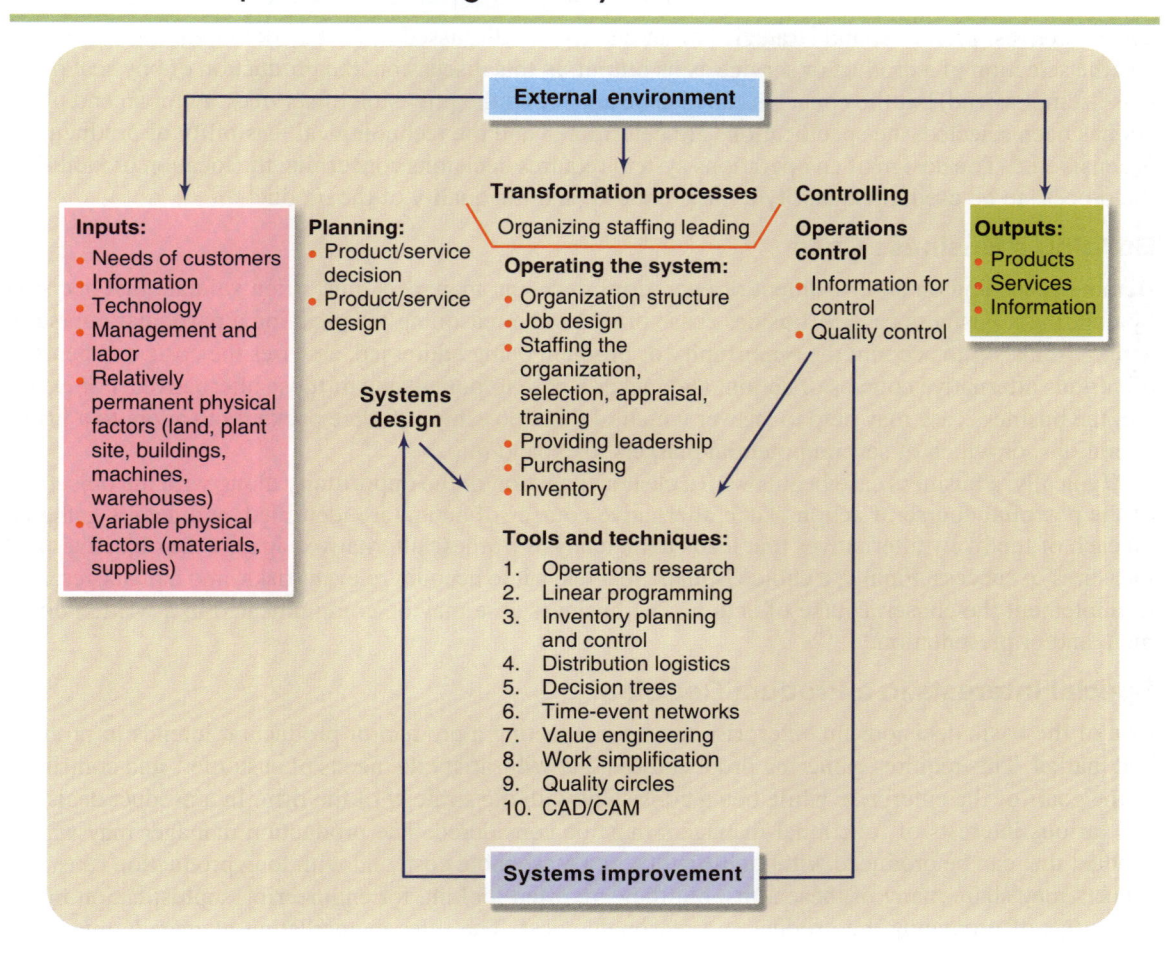

TABLE 20.1 Examples of operations systems

Inputs	Transformation	Outputs
Plant, factory machines, people, materials	Assembling bicycles	Completed bicycles
Students with limited knowledge, skills, and attitudes	Lectures, cases, experiential exercises, term papers	Students with enhanced knowledge, skills, and attitudes
Client problem	Consulting: data collection and analysis, evaluation of alternatives, selection of an alternative, recommendation	Consultant's report recommending course of action

Planning Operations

The objectives, premises, and strategies of an enterprise (discussed in Part 2) determine the search for and the selection of a product or service as its output. In this discussion, the production of physical products is emphasized, but the concepts can also be applied to the provision of services. After an end product has been selected, the specifications are determined and the technological feasibility of producing it is considered. The design of an operations system requires decisions concerning the location of facilities, the process to be used, the quantity to be produced, and the quality of the product.

Building a Business Case

Before proceeding on an investment or operations decision, managers must often validate that decision by building a business case. A business case provides the reasoning for pursuing a particular course of action. It takes into account the opportunity or problem being addressed, assesses the costs and benefits of various alternative courses of action, and makes a case to pursue one of those alternatives. For example, the business case may help to answer which of three possible software packages to adopt to a firm's operations, or which of several potential markets to expand into.

Typically, a business case begins with a clear articulation of the opportunity along with the objectives of the potential course of action. Then alternative courses of action are identified, and data is gathered on each of the likely alternatives that leads to an analysis of these alternatives against the objectives and measures of success. Finally, a choice is made that takes into account relevant risks, and a plan is created to implement the chosen course of action. The business case may be communicated in a written document and/or presentation.[3]

Special Interests in a Product Decision

One of the basic decisions an enterprise makes is selecting a product or products it intends to produce and market. This requires gathering product ideas that will satisfy the needs of customers and contribute to the goals of the enterprise while being consistent with the strategy of the firm. In a product decision, the various interests of functional managers must be considered. The production manager may want a product that can be produced without difficulty, at a reasonable cost, and with long production runs. Engineers may share many of these aims, but they are often looking for engineering sophistication rather than ways of producing the product at a reasonable cost. The sales or marketing manager's interest is likely to be the needs of customers, and his or her aim is to increase the sales of products through ready availability and competitive prices. Moreover, the sales manager may want to offer a broad product line without considering engineering, production, transportation, and warehousing costs and the problems involved. The finance manager's concerns are likely to be costs and profits, high return on investment, and low financial risks. The divergent interests of these functionally oriented managers and professionals influence what products will be produced and marketed, but it is the general manager who has to integrate the various interests and balance revenues with costs, profits with risks, and long-term with short-term growth.

Product and Production Design[4]

The design of a product and its production requires a number of activities. The following steps have often been suggested:

1. Create product ideas by examining consumer needs and screening various alternatives.
2. Select the product on the basis of various considerations, including data from market and economic analyses, and make a general feasibility study.

3. Prepare a preliminary design by evaluating various alternatives, taking into consideration reliability, quality, and maintenance requirements.
4. Reach a final decision by developing, testing, and simulating the processes to see if they work.
5. Decide whether the enterprise's current facilities are adequate or if new or modified facilities are required.
6. Select the process for producing the product, and consider the technology and the methods available.
7. After the product is designed, prepare the layout of the facilities to be used, plan the system of production, and schedule the various tasks that must be done.

Systems Design

In producing a product, several basic kinds of production layouts can be considered. One alternative is to arrange the layout according to the sequence of *production or assembly* of the product. For example, a truck assembly line may be arranged such that first the preassembled front and rear axles are attached to the frame, followed by the installation of the steering, the engine, and the transmission. Then the brake lines and electrical cables are connected, and other parts are assembled and painted. Finally, the truck is road-tested.

A second alternative is to lay out the production system according to the *process* employed. In a hospital, for example, specific steps are likely to be followed: admission of the patient, treatment (which usually involves specific subprocesses), billing for service, and discharge. This may be followed by post-hospitalization treatment.

In a third kind (sometimes called *fixed position* layout), the product stays in one place for assembly. This layout is used for the assembly of extremely large and bulky items, such as printing presses, large strip-mining machines, and ships.

The fourth kind of layout is determined by the nature of the *project*. Building a bridge or tunnel is normally a one-time project designed to fit specific geographic requirements.

In the fifth kind, the layout is designed to facilitate the *sale* of products. In a supermarket, basic food items, such as dairy products, are normally located away from the checkout counters. This causes customers to walk through the long aisles and, it is hoped, select other items on the way to the dairy section.

A sixth basic approach is to design the process so that it facilitates *storage or movement* of products. Storage space is costly, and an effective and efficient design can keep storage costs low. Also, to reach an item, it should not be necessary to move many other items.

Operating the System

After a product has been selected and the system for producing it has been designed and built, the next major step is to operate the system. This requires setting up an organization structure, staffing the positions, and training people. Managers are needed who can provide the supervision and leadership to carry out activities necessary to produce desired products or provide services. Other activities such as purchasing and maintaining the inventory are also required in operating the system. The aim is to obtain the best productivity ratio within a time period with due consideration for quality.

GLOBAL PERSPECTIVE

Volkswagen's High Operating Costs—Should VW Refocus Its Strategy?[5]

Volkswagen, VW, once known for low prices and good quality, faced a strategic shakeup in 2005 when it was loosing money. Factory wages, among the highest in the world, helped to make VW uncompetitive. The VW manufacturing wage of 34 Euros (about US$41) compared unfavorably with the 25.49 Euros in the United States as reported by the German Automotive Industry Association. At the same time, Germany had over 11 percent unemployment rate, the highest in the post-World War II period. In addition, there were alleged bribery charges against top officials who may have paid labor leaders for cooperating in labor contract discussions. VW plants in Europe worked only at 81 percent of capacity, much worse than its competitors Toyota and Renault that operated at over 90 percent capacity. With an aging model line, poor financial performance, and alleged bribery charges, the CEO Bern Pischetsrieder hired the U.S.-educated Wolfgang Bernhard who worked briefly with DaimlerChrysler, the consulting firm of McKinsey, and Mercedes.

Mr. Bernhard's task was to engineer a turnaround strategy which included cost-reduction, quality improvement, focusing on value offered to the mass market, and reducing the emphasis on competing in the high-end quality brands such as Mercedes. To accomplish these aims, Bernhard initiated a program that linked bonuses to quality improvement. Moreover, engineers were instructed to simplify the complexity of products.

Volkswagen started with a low-cost, good quality car image, then attempted to move into the high-end class, and now is moving closer to the high value market. Operation realities may require a reevaluation of the strategy.

More recent issues with its failure to accurately report emissions on some of its vehicles in many markets raises questions on whether VW had proper controls and oversight in place to ensure its operations were managed in an appropriate manner.

www.vw.com

Controlling Operations with Emphasis on Information Systems

Controlling operations, as in any other case of managerial control, requires setting performance criteria, measuring performance against them, and taking actions to correct undesirable deviations. Thus, one can control production, product quality and reliability levels, inventory levels, and work-force performance. A number of tools and techniques have been developed to do this. Because their application extends beyond operations or production, they have been discussed earlier. Some, however, are important to operations; examined here is the role of information systems in operations control.

Information systems, which have been available for several years, integrate information on virtually an instantaneous basis, thereby reducing considerably the delays that usually impede effective control. With the development of computer hardware and software, it is now possible for virtually any measurable data to be reported as events occur. Systems are available for quickly and systematically collecting data bearing on total operation, for keeping these data readily available, and for reporting without delay the status of any of a large number of projects at any instant. They are thus primarily information systems designed to provide effective planning and control.

The growing field of business analytics has focused on using the growing amount of data made available by online systems to provide real-time information to allow managers to better manage supply chains and make key business decisions to help enterprises run more effectively and efficiently.

How an Information System Facilitates Operations

Applied widely now to purchasing, storage, manufacturing, and shipping, information systems may operate through dispatch stations and input centers located throughout a plant. At the dispatch centers, events are recorded as they occur, and the information is dispatched immediately to a computer. For example, when a worker finishes an assigned task on the assembly of a product, the work-order time card is put into a transactor, which electrically transmits to a computer the information that item X has passed through a certain process, has accumulated y hours of labor, and may or may not be on schedule, as well as other pertinent data. The input centers are equipped to originate information needed for a production plan automatically from programmed instructions, purchase orders, shop orders, and other authorizations. These data are fed into a computer and compared against plans, which are used as standards against which actual operations can be compared.

In addition to providing fast entry, comparison, and retrieval of information, such an integrated operations control system furnishes needed information for planning programs in such areas as purchasing, production, and inventory control. Moreover, it permits almost instantaneous comparison of results with plans, pinpointing where they differ and providing a regular (daily or more often, if needed) system of reports on deviations from plans, such as items that are behind schedule or costs that are running above budget.

Other planning, control, and information systems have been developed to reflect quickly the interaction between production and distribution operations and such key financial measures as cost, profit, and cash flow. Companies with real-time computer models can give operating managers virtually instant analysis of such what-if questions as the effects of reducing or raising output, the impact of a decline in demand, and the sensitivity of the system to labor-cost increases, price changes, and new equipment additions. To be sure, system models, simulating actual operations and their impact on financial factors, are primarily planning tools; but so are most control techniques. By making possible exceptionally quick responses to the many what-if questions of operating managers, system models can greatly reduce the time elapsed in correcting for deviations from plans and can materially improve control.

These and other systems that use the technology of fast computation clearly promise to hasten the day when planning of all the areas of production can be more precise and controlling more effective. The drawback is not cost; rather, it is the failure of managers to spend time and mental effort conceptualizing the system and its relationships or to see that someone else in the organization does so. Nevertheless, as pointed out in Chapter 18, fast information availability can never provide true real-time control of the time delay in any feedback system. Only a feedforward approach can overcome these delays.

TOOLS AND TECHNIQUES FOR IMPROVING PRODUCTIVITY

There are many tools and techniques available for improving manufacturing and service operations. They include inventory planning and control, the just-in-time inventory system, outsourcing, operations research, value engineering, work simplification, quality circles, total quality management, lean manufacturing, computer-aided design, and computer-aided manufacturing.

Inventory Planning and Control

In the history of operations research, perhaps more attention has been directed to inventory control than to any other practical area of operations. The essential systems relationships can be seen as a little "black box", as depicted in Figure 20.2.

In mathematical form, these conceptual relationships are expressed by the equation

$$Q_e = \sqrt{\frac{2DS}{H}}$$

where Q_e = economic order quantity
D = demand per year
S = setup costs
H = inventory-holding (carrying) cost per item per year

FIGURE 20.2 Inventory control model

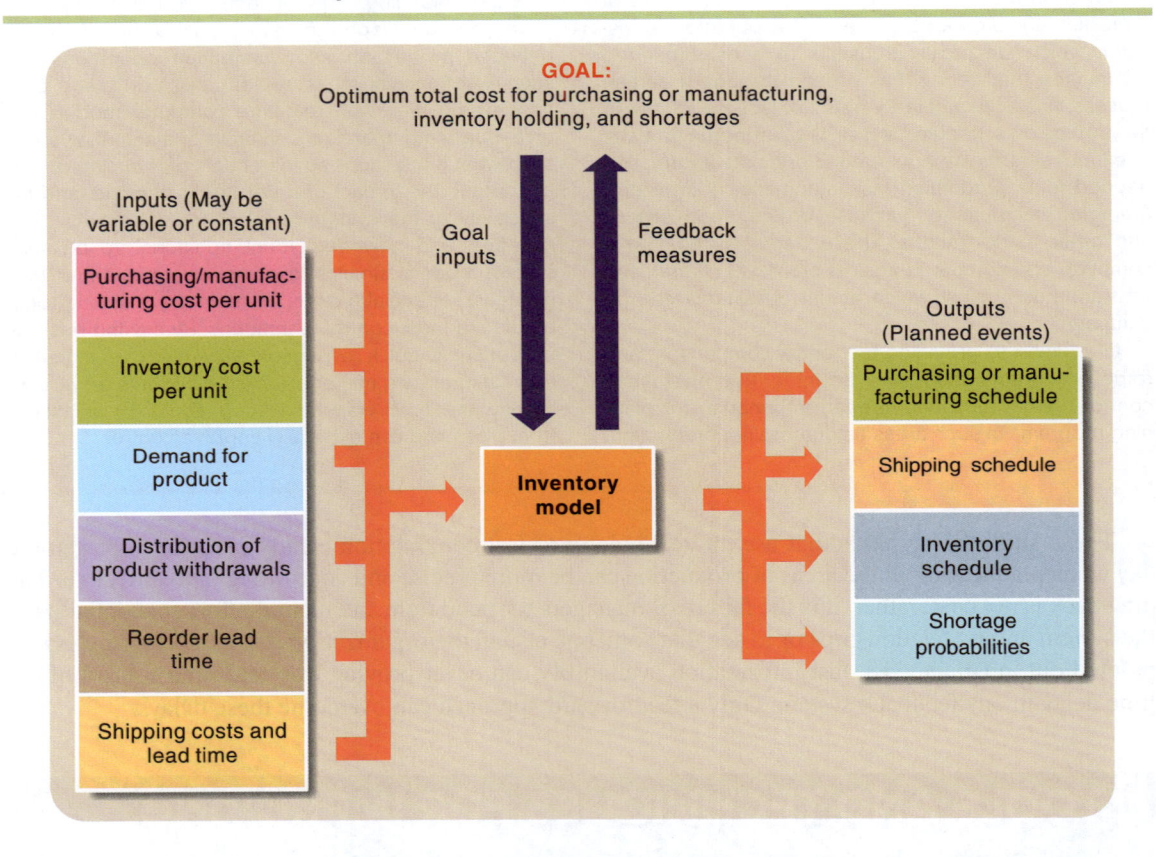

GOAL: Optimum total cost for purchasing or manufacturing, inventory holding, and shortages

Inputs (May be variable or constant)
- Purchasing/manufacturing cost per unit
- Inventory cost per unit
- Demand for product
- Distribution of product withdrawals
- Reorder lead time
- Shipping costs and lead time

Goal inputs → Inventory model ← Feedback measures

Outputs (Planned events)
- Purchasing or manufacturing schedule
- Shipping schedule
- Inventory schedule
- Shortage probabilities

The model in Figure 20.2 illustrates several things. It forces consideration of the goals desired and of the need for placing values on outputs and inputs. It also furnishes a manager with the basis for plans and with standards by which to measure performance. However, with all its advantages, this is a subsystem and does not incorporate other subsystems, such as production planning, distribution planning, and sales planning.

The economic order quantity (EOQ) approach to determining inventory levels has been used by firms for many years. It works reasonably well for finding order quantities when demand is predictable and fairly constant throughout the year (i.e., there are no seasonal patterns). However, for determining the inventory levels of parts and materials used for some production processes, it does not work well. For example, poor quality of parts may increase the demand for these production inputs. Thus, demand is likely to be intermittent, resulting in inventory shortages at sometimes and excesses at other times. Firms determining inventory levels in these manufacturing settings have found that inventory control approaches such as material requirement planning and *kanban* (just-in-time) systems perform better than EOQ.

Just-in-Time Inventory System

One reason for Japan's high manufacturing productivity is the cost reduction it achieves through its just-in-time inventory method. In this system, the supplier delivers the components and parts to the production line only when needed and "just in time" to be assembled. Other names for this or very similar methods are zero inventory and stockless production.

For this method to work, a number of requirements must be fulfilled: First, the quality of the parts must be very high; a defective part could hold up the assembly line. Second, there must be dependable relationships and smooth cooperation with suppliers. Third, the suppliers ideally should be located near the company, with dependable transportation available.

Just-in-time inventory system The supplier delivers the components and parts to the production line only when needed and "just in time" to be assembled.

Outsourcing[6]

One recent trend in the United States and Europe is outsourcing. This means that production and operations are contracted to outside vendors that have expertise in specific areas. The aim may be to reduce costs by saving on personnel benefits, to reduce personnel, or to be able to reassign employees to other tasks that are more important. Thus, outsourcing is an important tool for expanding a company and for maintaining a competitive position. It enables a firm to focus on its core competencies and let outside companies do what they can do best. For example, Nike, Inc., the large supplier of athletic shoes, uses outsourcing for all of its shoe production, keeping only the production of the sophisticated Nike Air system.[7] It also outsources advertising. By focusing on what it can do best, Nike has accomplished an extraordinary growth rate.

Other reasons for outsourcing include gaining access to the best sources available worldwide, sharing of risks between the firm and its suppliers, allocating capital to key success factors, outsourcing functions that are difficult to manage, or lacking the capability to carry out certain tasks.

Outsourcing may also serve as a strategic weapon. General Motors produces almost two-thirds of its parts in-house compared to Chrysler, which "insources" only about one-third of its parts. This gives Chrysler a competitive advantage because General Motors' in-house labor costs are substantially higher than suppliers'. Kodak found it more effective to outsource the day-to-day operation of its fleet of 10,000 vehicles. Similarly, Procter & Gamble benefited from outsourcing its fleet operation, thus lowering its costs and improving the productivity of its sales force. Another function that may be outsourced is property management. Johnson Controls, for example, provides operation and maintenance services of buildings. The Presbyterian Medical Center in Philadelphia selected a single source for managing various tasks, including its food service, security, environmental services, central processing, transportation, maintenance, and engineering functions. Even Apple Computer has outsourced its system and network engineering as well as its telecommunication and help-desk services to a Canadian company. Outsourcing parts of the retailers' information system helped Britain's Woolworth's department store to reduce costs and gain skills.

Outsourcing The contracting of production and operations to outside vendors that have expertise in specific areas.

www.nike.com

It has been suggested that, before deciding on outsourcing, a business-practice reengineering* study should be conducted. The findings of this analysis may indicate which tasks are best suited for being continued within the company and which should be contracted out.

INNOVATIVE PERSPECTIVE

GE's Contribution to India's Outsourcing Boom[8]

In 1989, few companies realized the outsourcing potential of India. When Jack Welch, then CEO of GE, visited India, he was told of India's need for developing high-tech sector. But it was after 1991, when the Indian government began reducing tariff barriers and export controls that India's economy started taking off. Mr. Welch's emphasis of cost-cutting made India's companies aware of their potential competitive strengths. GE's confidence in India's advantage encouraged other investments. GE itself opened the Technology Center in Bangalore providing thousands of employees to work on many projects, including developing new refrigerators, jet engines, and many software projects. GE and other companies greatly contributed to India's economic growth of about 7 percent in 2005.

India's competitive strength becomes clear when comparing its labor rates with that in the United States. For example, software programmers with two- to four-year experience earn approximately $10,000 annually in India while a U.S. counterpart makes some $62,000. Similarly, workers at India's call centers earn some $3,000 a year while as similar job in the United States pays $27,000. While today, many companies have located their service centers to India, only few people realize GE's contribution to India's outsourcing boom.

www.ge.com

Some Disadvantages of Outsourcing.[9]

While many companies are engaged in the outsourcing craze, others rethink their strategy. NCR, the maker of ATM machines notes that the more complex machines want custom-designed machines with customers directly involved in the design process. Making design changes in foreign-produced products delayed delivery. Moreover, NCR's engineers had to travel around the world to make such changes. Therefore, some of machines are now made again in America. But NCR did not give up outsourcing completely. ATMs are still produced in countries such as China, Hungary, and India. Plants in Latin America, Asia, and Europe are still operating for those regions.

Operations research The application of scientific methods to the study of alternatives in a problem situation, with a view to obtaining a quantitative basis for arriving at a best solution.

Operations Research

There are almost as many definitions of operations research as there are writers on the subject. For the purposes of this discussion, the most acceptable definition is that operations research is the application of scientific methods to the study of alternatives in a problem situation, with a view to obtaining a quantitative basis for arriving at a best solution. Thus, the emphasis is on scientific method, on the use of quantitative data, on goals, and on the determination of the best means of reaching the goals. In other words, operations research might be called "quantitative common sense."

---

* See the discussion of reengineering in Chapter 7.

Value Engineering

A product can be improved and its costs lowered through value engineering, which consists of analyzing the operations of the product or service, estimating the value of each operation, and attempting to improve that operation by trying to keep costs low at each step or part. The following specific steps are suggested:

1. Divide the product into parts and operations.
2. Identify the costs for each part and operation.
3. Identify the relative value of the contribution of each part to the final unit or product.
4. Find a new approach for those items that appear to have a high cost and low value.

> **Value engineering** The process of analyzing the operations of the product or service, estimating the value of each operation, and attempting to improve that operation by trying to keep costs low at each step or part.

Work Simplification

Work methods can also be improved through work simplification, which is the process of obtaining the participation of workers in simplifying their work. Training sessions are conducted to teach concepts and principles of techniques such as time and motion studies, workflow analyses, and the layout of the work situation.

> **Work simplification** The process of obtaining workers' participation in simplifying their work.

Quality Circles

A quality control circle, or simply quality circle (QC), is a group of people from the same organizational area who meet regularly to solve problems they experience at work. Members are trained in solving problems, in applying statistical quality control, and in working in groups. Usually a facilitator works with each group, which normally consists of 6 to 12 members. The QCs may meet four hours a month. Although QC members may receive recognition, they usually do not receive monetary rewards.

> **Quality circle** A group of people from the same organizational area who meet regularly to solve problems they experience at work.

GLOBAL PERSPECTIVE

Quality Circles in Japan

For some time now, Japanese products have been well received. To a great extent, this has been due to the quality of the products, but this has not always been the case. In fact, in the 1950s and 1960s, many products made in Japan had the image of poor quality.

In order to compete in the world market, Japanese firms had to improve the quality of their products. The campaign to improve quality was initiated by regulatory action taken by the Japanese government. Shortly after World War II, the Japanese, realizing that their economic success depended on increasing exports, encouraged their government to set up a system of regulations mandating that all exporters submit to a government agency a sample of each product to be exported and that they meet demanding requirements for quality before receiving a permit to export.

The legislative drive for quality was supported by various management techniques encouraging or requiring product quality. One of the interesting techniques is QC, now in widespread use in Japan. At first, the focus was on the analysis of quality problems, but now other problems are also dealt with, such as cost reduction, workshop facilities improvement, safety, employee morale, pollution control, and employee education.

QCs evolved from suggestion programs. In both approaches, workers participate in solving work-related problems. Although in suggestion programs the problems are usually quite specific, those dealt with by QCs are often more complex and require the involvement of several team members. The team consists primarily of rank-and-file workers and sometimes supervisors too. So-called efficiency experts are usually excluded from the team.

It is interesting to note that while the concept of quality control originated in the United States, the Japanese appear to have perfected it. More recently, American firms have "rediscovered" the importance of quality, as shown by advertisements for Chrysler and Ford automobiles. At any rate, there is no reason to doubt that QCs can be used by companies in the United States and other countries, which are now faced with a competitive situation in a world market that demands quality products.

INNOVATIVE PERSPECTIVE

Managing Quality for Success

Managing for quality requires leadership and hard work, and a continuous effort to achieve quality has paid off in many companies. BMW's chief executive attributes the company's success to tailoring the cars to the needs and desires of individual car buyers, which in turn is made possible by German craftsmanship. Procter & Gamble uses quality management concepts to prevent pollution. Motorola's aim is to provide total customer satisfaction by bringing quality to the six-sigma level, which means to have not more than 3.4 defects per million components. Quality management also works in the service industry. At Nissan's Infiniti dealerships, people are trained to treat customers as honored guests. Quality is even used in the public sector. The Internal Revenue Service in Utah and state governments in Arkansas, Minnesota, and Oregon are trying to implement quality concepts in their operations. The approaches to improving quality and customer satisfaction vary—and so do the theories on which quality efforts are based. Some of the approaches advocated by quality proponents seem conflicting, creating a kind of a jungle.

Total Quality Management[10]

Total quality management
Long-term commitment to continuous quality improvement, throughout the organization and with the active participation of all members at all levels, to meet and exceed customer expectations.

One popular approach to improving quality is called total quality management (TQM). However, this term has various meanings. In general, TQM involves the organization's long-term commitment to the continuous improvement of quality, throughout the organization and with the active participation of all members at all levels, to meet and exceed customer expectations. This top-management-driven philosophy is considered a way of organizational life. In a sense, TQM is simply effective management.

Although the specific programs may vary, they usually require a careful analysis of customer needs, an assessment of the degree to which these needs are currently met, and a plan to fill the possible gap between the current and the desired situation. The success of this quality improvement approach often needs the cooperation of suppliers. Furthermore, to make the TQM program effective, top managers must be involved. They must provide a vision, reinforce values emphasizing quality, set quality goals, and deploy resources for the quality program. It is obvious that TQM demands a free flow of information—vertically, horizontally, and diagonally.

Training and development is very important for developing skills and for learning how to use tools and techniques such as statistical quality control. This continual effort for improving quality requires an environment that can be called a learning organization (see Chapter 13). Any quality improvement effort needs not only the support but also the involvement of management, from the top to the bottom, as well as nonmanagerial employees. People need to be empowered to initiate and implement the necessary changes. In the modern, interlocking organization, teamwork often becomes a prerequisite for an effective and efficient operation.

The quality improvement efforts need to be continuously monitored through ongoing data collection, evaluation, feedback, and improvement programs. TQM is not a one-time effort; instead, it is a continual, long-term endeavor that needs to be recognized, reinforced, and rewarded.

When done effectively, TQM should result in greater customer satisfaction, fewer defects and less waste, increased total productivity, reduced costs and improved profitability, and an environment in which quality has high priority.

A concern for quality should not be restricted to business. Principles of quality improvement also apply to government. The mayor of Madison, Wisconsin, demonstrated how quality programs can be implemented in city government. The first test came in the motor equipment division. After the initial success, a formal quality program was started citywide. What is surprising is that resistance to the program came not from unions or from the city council but from middle-level bureaucrats, who saw their power being eroded by the reduction in departmental barriers and by greater teamwork.

Quality management is of global concern. Therefore, the topics of the contributions by quality gurus, the Malcolm Baldrige National Quality Award, ISO 9000, and the European model for total quality management were discussed in Chapter 3 on global management.

Lean Manufacturing[11]

A study at the Massachusetts Institute of Technology that compared American, Japanese, and European car manufacturers showed that the Japanese gained a competitive advantage from the use of fewer workers, a shorter development time, lower inventories, fewer suppliers, less production space, and less investment to produce more models. The Japanese also had much shorter delivery time and were more productive than Americans and Europeans.

Some of the differences between traditional mass production and lean production managerial practices are listed in Table 20.2.

TABLE 20.2 Mass production versus lean production managerial practices

Mass production	Lean production
• Sporadic and inconsistent improvements	• Continuous improvements (*kaizen*) with strategic breakthroughs
• Satisfied with "good enough"	• Aiming at zero defects
• High inventory acceptable	• Just-in-time inventory system
• "Me" management with emphasis on individual performance	• "We", or team, management
• Attitude that workers are the cause of poor quality	• Responsibility for problems rests on everyone, especially management

It should be pointed out that, since the study was conducted, U.S. and European automobile manufacturers have adopted many of the lean production concepts and have become more productive. Lean thinking has even spread to nonautomotive companies. Wal-Mart, a U.S. retail store, installed a just-in-time delivery system that works by letting suppliers connect to its computerized ordering system. Thus, suppliers can anticipate demands for their products. Pratt & Whitney, a U.S. aerospace firm, rearranged its work flow and thereby reduced its stock level by 70 percent and its unit costs by 20 percent.

http://www.pw.utc.com

Computer-aided Techniques

Product design and manufacturing have been changing greatly in recent years, largely because of the application of computer technology. Computer-aided design (CAD) and computer-aided manufacturing (CAM) are part of the cornerstones of the factory of the future.

CAD/CAM help engineers design products much more quickly than they could with the traditional paper-and-pencil approach. This will become increasingly important, since product life cycles are getting shorter. Capturing the market quickly is crucial in the very competitive environment. Moreover, firms can respond more rapidly to the requests of customers with specific requirements. The ultimate aim of many companies is computer-integrated manufacturing.

GLOBAL PERSPECTIVE

Merging the Production Systems of Daimler and Chrysler: A Mission Possible?[12]

An important aim of merging Daimler with Chrysler was to obtain synergy, with resulting cost savings. However, it took quite some time to integrate the production systems, with Chrysler building more than three million cars a year primarily using mass production compared with Mercedes's one million cars designed for upscale customers. Chrysler emphasized the "push" approach, building cars for immediate delivery; whereas Mercedes practiced the "pull" system, building cars after orders are received, resulting in lower inventory costs but also in waiting lists ranging from four months to up to two years for certain models. The integration of the two companies took some time before the American and German engineers began trusting each other and sharing important information.

After a period of adjustment, however, the joint efforts are bearing fruit. Here are examples of how synergies have been achieved. Chrysler engineers took the Mercedes E-Class apart, studied it carefully, and adopted useful concepts. A similar process was employed by German engineers studying Chrysler's 300M model. The renowned NAG automatic gearbox, which is installed in most Mercedes cars, will be used in the next generation of Jeep Grand Cherokees and so may be a modified diesel engine. Chrysler is learning from Mercedes and vice versa. The new DaimlerChrysler is betting that the new collaboration will be the key to success in the very competitive market.

The great expectations of the DaimlerChrysler merger did not materialize, as shown by the divorce in 2007.[13]

www.daimlerchrysler.com

SUPPLY CHAIN AND VALUE CHAIN MANAGEMENT[14]

The terms "supply chain" and "value chain management" are sometimes used interchangeably. However, *Industry Week* points out that **supply chain management** focuses on the sequence of getting raw materials and subassemblies through the manufacturing process in an economical manner. **Value chain management**, on the other hand, has a broader meaning and involves analyzing every step in the process, ranging from the handling of raw materials to servicing end users, providing them with the greatest value at the lowest cost. Therefore, some suggest that supply chain management focuses more on the internal process with an emphasis on efficient flow of resources, such as materials, while value chain management has similar aims with an additional concern for the external environment, such as the customer.

Professor Michael Porter popularized the **value chain process model**, which includes the primary activities of inbound logistics, operations, outbound logistics, marketing/sales, and service. The process is supported by the enterprise infrastructure, the management of human resources, technology, and procurement. Porter's model illustrates that value chain analysis has a broader orientation than supply chain management.

The goal of value chain management is to create a seamless chain of activities from the supplier, through the manufacturer, to the customer to meet and exceed his or her expectations. The process requires that all managerial functions of planning, organizing, staffing, leading, and controlling be carried out effectively and efficiently in a collaborative manner. In addition, technology is used to facilitate the entire process. The previous chapter on the various aspects of information technology discussed how this can be done. Value chain management may require a thorough analysis of the organizational process using reengineering concepts, which were discussed in Chapter 7. Still another way of improving the value chain (especially for manufacturing) is to study and apply the operations management model shown in Figure 20.1.

Integration of the Value Chain with the Managerial Actions

Table 20.3 provides an example of a value chain for a hypothetical computer manufacturer and shows how managers may enhance their effectiveness through applying the systems approach to management by applying effective planning, organizing, leading, staffing, and controlling at each stage of the value chain. The effective execution of the systems approach should lead to lower input costs, less waste, better branding and pricing power, a better customer experience, and ultimately greater sales and profitability.

As seen in the preceding figure, a systems approach to management (deliberate attention to the key management functions of planning, leading, organizing, staffing and controlling) can enhance the efficiency and effectiveness of the individual components of a firm's value chain and help lead to organizational success.

> **Supply chain management** focuses on the sequence of getting raw materials and subassemblies through the manufacturing process economically.
>
> **Value chain management** involves analyzing every step in the process, ranging from the handling of raw materials to servicing end users, providing them with the greatest value at the lowest cost.
>
> The **value chain process** model includes the primary activities of inbound logistics, operations, outbound logistics, marketing/sales, and service, with the process supported by the enterprise infrastructure, human resource management, technology, and procurement.

TABLE 20.3 Sample value chain activities and managerial actions for a computer manufacturer[15]

Manufacturing and Sales Value Chain	Procurement and Inbound Logistics	Operations	Outbound Logistics	Marketing and Sales	Services
Value chain activities	Identify suppliers (integrated circuits, flat panel screens, etc.) and order and receive components	Incorporate supplier and internally developed components into manufacturing process	Schedule shipment of final products to distribution partners and company stores	Develop marketing message, choose media, and set sales force targets	Manage follow-up service to distribution partners and final customers
Systems Approach to managerial actions to enhance effectiveness and efficiency of value chain activities	*Plan* for—select premier suppliers after evaluating alternatives *Organize* formal contract obligations including just-in-time delivery and extended payment terms *Staff* experienced management with appropriate skill set *Lead* clear negotiation of price and terms with suppliers *Control* supplier input quality and budget cost allowance	*Plan* (design-in) supplier components into new product generations *Organize* production targets with input from empowered production managers *Staff* locally and internationally with clear job design descriptions *Lead* and motivate plant managers *Control* and benchmark quality to meet brand image	*Plan* allocation to distribution partners with respect to policy and sales forecasts *Organize* shipment dates relative to geographical and product forecasts *Staff* properly trained delivery personnel *Lead* delivery managers by communicating expectations in preventing loss *Control* accurate and on-time delivery with real-time information	*Plan* strategic marketing message and focused media campaign *Organize* advertising buys across reinforcing media outlets *Staff* well-developed sales personnel and implement continuous evaluation criteria *Lead* and motivate sales force with targeted incentives *Control* sales quotas to meet plan forecasts	*Plan* end-to-end customer services *Organize* decentralized service providers at critical touch points with positive organizational culture *Staff* thoughtful customer service representative (CSR) positions and provide continuous feedback *Lead* and inspire CSRs to provide better than expected service *Control* service quality through customer feedback
Enhancements made to value chain activities from systematic managerial actions	Increase input quality Decrease input costs Minimize shipping and storage time	Shorten product development time Decrease unit costs Enhance brand	Prevent excess production Lower shipment costs Ensure timely supplies	Enhance brand Increase sales Expand margins	Improve customer experience Enhance brand Increase profitability

As seen in the preceding table, a systems approach to management (deliberate attention to the key management functions of planning, leading, organizing, staffing, and controlling) can enhance the efficiency and effectiveness of the individual components of a firm's value chain and help lead to organizational success.

As we pointed out in this book, management is one of the most important human activities. We introduced the systems approach to managing in which key managerial activities are grouped into the managerial functions of planning, organizing, staffing, leading, and controlling. These functions are essential for any organization. However, the application of the key managerial activities and the time spent for each function varies for each organizational level and the kind of enterprise—those aiming for profit and those not-for-profit. Management is an art that uses the underlying sciences. The goal of all managers is the same: to create a surplus that benefits not only people and the organization, but also the nation and the society.

SUMMARY

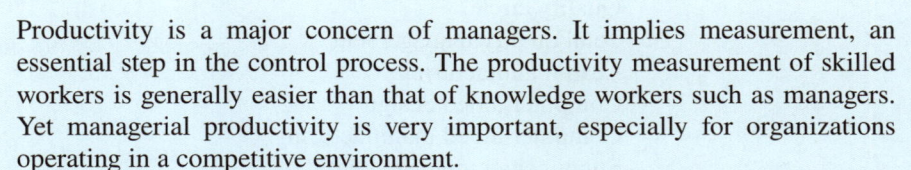

Productivity is a major concern of managers. It implies measurement, an essential step in the control process. The productivity measurement of skilled workers is generally easier than that of knowledge workers such as managers. Yet managerial productivity is very important, especially for organizations operating in a competitive environment.

Production management refers to those activities necessary to manufacture products; it may also include purchasing, warehousing, transportation, and other operations. Operations management has a similar meaning, referring to activities necessary to produce and deliver a service as well as a physical product. Quality measurement in the information age requires including factors other than reliability, such as the information infrastructure and the services of software suppliers.

The operations management system model includes inputs, the transformation process, outputs, and the feedback system. Selecting a product or service to produce requires consideration of customer needs, organizational goals, and the various interests of the functional managers of the enterprise. Planning and designing a product and its production involves several activities. Companies can choose from at least six kinds of production layouts catering for different production or operation needs. In order to operate the system, the managerial functions of organizing, staffing, and leading must be carried out effectively. Controlling operations requires an information system often supported by computers.

A variety of tools and techniques are available for making operations more productive, including inventory planning and control, the just-in-time inventory system, outsourcing, operations research, value engineering, work simplification, quality circles, total quality management, lean manufacturing, and a variety of computer-aided approaches. The concepts of supply chain management and value chain management are similar. However, the latter is more comprehensive and emphasizes the end user of the product or service.

KEY IDEAS AND CONCEPTS FOR REVIEW

Productivity problems and measurement
Production management
Operations management
Quality in the information age
Operations management system
Steps in product and production design
Production layouts
Inventory planning and control
Just-in-time inventory system
Outsourcing
Operations research
Value engineering
Work simplification
Quality circle
Total quality management
Lean manufacturing
Computer-aided design
Computer-aided manufacturing
Supply chain management
Value chain management
Value chain process model
Value chain management and the managerial functions

FOR DISCUSSION

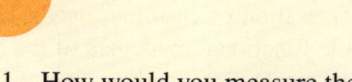

1. How would you measure the productivity of managers and other knowledge workers? Explain in detail.
2. Why is the field of production and operations management good to use as a case example of planning and control techniques? Why do you think this area was favored for analysis and productivity improvement by the pioneers in the field of management?
3. Distinguish between the planning and control techniques that are usually found only in production and operations management and those that are found useful in all areas of management. Why is there a distinction?
4. Explain the nature of and reasons for each step usually found in the development of a production and operations management program.

5. There are many typical layouts used in the design of a production program. Which one is ordinarily used for the manufacture of automobiles? Why?
6. Real-time information can be widely used in the area of production, but this does not solve the problem of control. Why?
7. What tools generally found in operations research have been widely used in production and operations management? Do they have anything in common? If so, what is it?
8. Why do you believe that quality control circles have been used so much in Japan?

EXERCISES/ ACTION STEPS

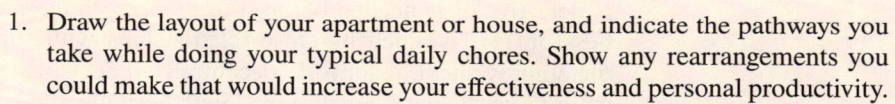

1. Draw the layout of your apartment or house, and indicate the pathways you take while doing your typical daily chores. Show any rearrangements you could make that would increase your effectiveness and personal productivity.
2. Interview several managers in a local company and ask how they measure the quality of their operations.
3. Identify two business analytics software products and be able to describe or demonstrate them to the class.

INTERNET RESEARCH

1. Toyota was the first to adopt the just-in-time (JIT) system. Dell applied the virtual network to JIT. Search the Internet for the term "just in time". Find out how JIT is used by enterprises.
2. Search the Internet for the term "total quality management". How is the approach used by organizations? Present your findings to the class.

GLOBAL CAR INDUSTRY CASE

Toyota's Global Production Strategy[16]

Toyota Motor Corporation is one of the largest car makers in the world. Although headquartered in Toyota City, about 150 miles west of Tokyo, it has production or assembly facilities in many parts of the world. The company is known for its effective and efficient approach to production management, its quality products, and its outstanding labor relations.

The Toyota production system (TPS) integrates craft with mass production, and it is now emulated by its competitors. The system aims at producing high-quality cars at low costs, accomplished in part by having parts delivered to the production line "just in time" to avoid the high inventory costs of the traditional assembly operation. It is sometimes called "just-in-case" inventory system, referring to the practice of storing additional parts just in case a part is defective or is needed because of unforeseen circumstances. The effectiveness of TPS is aided by close relationships with suppliers and by continuous improvement, teamwork, decentralized decision making, and a motivated work force. Vehicles are designed with customers in mind, who can order cars according to their needs. Even after the car is delivered, customers are kept happy by good customer service.

Toyota uses several ways to improve production. Workers are trained in several kinds of skills so that they can operate several machines. Electrical signs, show daily production figures and problems on the assembly line. They also can indicate whether overtime may be necessary. Quality is achieved through the zero defects system. Workers are trained to trace any error to its source. If a production problem occurs on the assembly line, workers pull a cord to draw attention to the problem and request assistance, or to stop the line altogether.

The company developed a unique relationship with its suppliers, who deliver parts daily (often several times a day) to the production line. Suppliers are often responsible for a whole system, such as the brakes, seats, or the electrical system. To make the supplier relationship effective, Toyota people have to be very familiar with the operation of the supplier, often by having representatives at the supplier's site for assistance. Toyota also provides loans or makes equity investment in the operations of its suppliers. The result is long-term cooperative relationships.

One of Toyota's successful strategies was the introduction of the luxury Lexus model. Partly in response to U.S. pressure to limit Japanese car sales in the United States, Toyota focused on high-value luxury cars using BMW and Mercedes as benchmarks. Lexus was also aimed at customers of American luxury cars such as Cadillac and Lincoln. In developing the Lexus, Toyota purchased cars made by Mercedes, BMW, and Jaguar and tested them thoroughly. Then it developed 11 performance goals to improve on the results of those tests. In order to be price-competitive, Toyota invested in automation to reduce labor costs. Great attention was given to high quality standards. The development time was relatively short for the Lexus. However, some critics suggested that it was a luxury model based on the Toyota Camry platform. The initial low price for the luxury car was subsequently hiked several times.

The success of the Japanese operation has been extended overseas. One such example is New United Motor Manufacturing, Inc. (NUMMI) in Fremont near San Francisco. In 1984, Toyota and General Motors (GM) agreed on a 50–50 joint venture. Up to that time, this GM plant was one of the least productive. After the joint venture, it became one of the best GM plants. Critical to the success of the joint venture was good labor–management relations based on trust and respect for each other's point of view. The new arrangement called for the elimination of multiple job categories, extensive use of teams, the use of quality circles, indoctrination, and training. Many of the employees were sent to Japan for additional training. The plant was also changed through rearrangement of the assembly line, replacement of old equipment, employment of the just-in-time inventory system, and enabling workers to stop the assembly line should a problem arises. The relationship with suppliers was also changed from adversarial to cooperative.

Another Toyota plant was opened in Georgetown, Kentucky, in 1988. Great efforts were made in selecting employees, involving tests and simulations to assess not only technical skills but also personal and leadership abilities. Emphasis was also placed on teamwork at the plant. The company's expansion in the U.S. market was not restricted to vehicle production. The Calty Design Center in California developed the Celica model and the Previa minivan especially designed for U.S. consumers. Design and research were done at the technical center in Torrance, California.

Toyota also has many other overseas operations. In Europe too, there were restrictions on Japanese car imports, especially in France and Italy. To overcome these restrictions, Toyota built a plant in Britain, which is a member of the European Union. In 2001, Toyota and the French Peugeot Citroen announced plans to invest 1.3 billion euros to build a plant for producing a small, entry-level car by 2005. Of the 300,000 cars to be produced annually, 100,000 will be sold as Toyotas and 200,000 as Peugeots or Citroens. Profitability will be the challenge for the joint venture because of the slim profit margins for small cars. Cost reduction will be critical for its success. Toyota's contribution to the planned venture is the experience of producing five million cars annually. Peugeot Citroen has the advantage of having a strong brand image in the region as well as a good understanding of the local market. Moreover, the French company has expertise in making supermini cars. But sometimes it is not possible to engage in a joint venture or to set up a company-owned plant. This is the case in some Asian countries, especially in South Korea. Consequently, Toyota acquired minority interests in Korean companies.

Questions:

1. Why has Toyota been successful?
2. What are the strategies for gaining entrance into foreign countries?
3. What should Toyota do to be successful in Asian countries that restrict imports?

PART 6 CLOSING

Global Controlling and Challenges and Entrepreneurial Controlling

In this closing section, we first discuss the impact of the forces in the external environment on the managerial functions of planning, organizing, staffing, leading, and controlling. In other words, the future of management is projected. Second, the entrepreneurial focus is on managing for rapid growth and liquidity events. Finally, the global car industry case asks: "What features do you want in a car?"

GLOBAL FOCUS: THE FUTURE OF MANAGEMENT

No one can predict the future with certainty. Yet there are trends in the environment that may influence the practice of the managerial functions of planning, organizing, staffing, leading, and controlling.

The external environment may be categorized as technological,[18] economic, political and legal, and social, ethical, and ecological, as shown in the future of global management matrix in Figure C6.1. The figure highlights selected key trends in the external environment and the projected impact on key tasks grouped according to the managerial functions. We will discuss selected aspects with the focus on the changes in the technological environment.

We live in a knowledge society in which information technology impacts on most aspects of our lives. Even people in developing countries now have access to the Internet at relatively low costs. The whole world is interconnected. Information technology facilitates intranet (for communication within the organization) as well as extranet (for communicating with others outside the enterprise) communications. This connectivity makes e-business and m-business (business conducted using mobile communications) possible, which in turn impacts on all managerial functions.

For example, information technology aids scenario and contingency *planning* (Part 2 in this book). In strategic planning, many alternatives can be developed and evaluated rapidly because of computing power and the wealth of information available and readily accessible. In fact, there is so much

FIGURE C6.1 The future of global management matrix

Environment / Managerial function	Technological	Economic	Political/legal	Social/Ethical/Ecological
	• Widespread use of IT • Emergence of knowledge society • Easy access to information at low costs • Widespread and global e-commerce	• Economic blocs such as EU and NAFTA reduce internal regional barriers but create external ones • U.S. labor unions' stance shifts from free trade to protectionism to protect jobs • Borderless society • Development of pension plans that represent stakeholders' interests	• Expansion of EU via admittance of new members, mainly from Eastern Europe • Increased protectionism because of declined employment in manufacturing and services (due to, e.g., outsourcing to India)	• Emergence of knowledge workers • People healthier and living longer • Shifts in demographics: low birth rates and increased life expectancies result in "graying" population in developed countries • Greater affluence in developing countries, but also wider wealth disparity • Global "greening" concerns
Planning e.g., setting objectives, strategic planning, decision making	• IT aids scenario planning • Wealth of information helps decision making (but possible information overload) • Consumer access to product and service information allows comparisons with implications for marketing strategies, thus focus on customer needs and service required • Cross-national alliances, joint ventures, cooperative agreements (e.g., between industry and universities), and mergers facilitated, thus global strategies required	• Globalization of strategic management • Scanning for opportunities and threats globally, not only at home • Increased global competition • Borderless society provides threats and opportunities	• Greater wealth in Eastern European countries provides opportunities for developed countries • More powerful EU can become threat to USA • Strategies needed for coping with nontariff barriers	• Opportunity for targeting products at the youth in developing countries • More marketing focus on older population • Strategies must consider ecological impact of products and services (e.g., recycling)
Organizing e.g., organization structure, authority relationships, decentralization	• Organizations become change agents • New organizational forms (e.g., outsourcing, online operation) • Outsourcing requires disintegration of organization structure and restructuring • Knowledge work promotes non-hierarchical structures • Knowledge workers may become shareholders	• Emergence of transnational companies • Forming of cross-national alliances and mergers requires restructuring	• Need for establishing structures that resolve conflict of interest between countries within power blocs and for developing policies to compete in other regional blocs	• Great potential for upward mobility in society and organizations, partly because of impact of knowledge society • Older people as part-timers or consultants with advisory authority

Continued

	- From organization structures based on products and services to alliances based on strategic considerations - Manufacturers join to form purchasing cooperatives (as General Motors, Ford, and DaimlerChrysler have done) - Suppliers run and controlled by manufacturers, who direct and advise		
Staffing e.g., appraisal, change management, management development	- Specialized technical knowledge needed - Greater mobility of knowledge workers in changing jobs - Information enhances knowledge workers' upward mobility - Specialized knowledge workers as consultants or contractors in temporary or part-time employment - Outsourcing of human resource management to specialist firms at home and abroad - Use of older, semi-retired professionals as consultants - Continual training and retraining to keep abreast of new technologies - Development of new measurements for evaluating and rewarding knowledge workers	- Possible growth of labor unions in various countries - Multicultural work force - Need for culturally sensitive personnel with understanding of international macroeconomics	- Political–legal implications posed by multicultural work force - September 11, 2001, attacks on USA make it more difficult to obtain student and work visas, thus hampering staffing of critical positions - Developed countries need immigrant workers, yet immigration may be limited	- Knowledge workers, as key human resources, require good formal education and continual reeducation - Raised retirement age requires organizations to integrate older with younger workers - Need to integrate immigrants into workforce - Greater role of women at workplace
Leading e.g., motivation, leadership, communication, teamwork	- Information availability gives power to knowledge workers and consumers - Knowledge workers demand higher-order needs satisfaction (recognition, self-actualization, responsibility, participation) - Electronic communication technology aids teamwork - Lower communication costs	- Need for political leadership to balance interests of countries within regional blocs - Ways to integrate developed with developing countries required - Greater affluence requires new ways to motivate workers	- Potential communication barriers arising from use of different languages - Increased use of English in global business, political, and social interactions	- Top management has to balance interests of various stakeholders (investors, employees, governments, community, etc.) - More women in leadership positions - Top managers more engaged in ecological policies - Challenge in integrating older with younger workers

Continued

Controlling e.g., control techniques, production, IT, productivity	• Ease of control, but possibly overcontrol • IT facilitates detection and correction of deviations from plans • IT facilitates productivity measurement at low costs • Internet enables worldwide selling • Internet facilitates shift from autonomous ownership to partnerships (e.g., purchasing cooperatives) • Use of Internet more for outside scanning, not only for internal operation	• Controls for transnational companies needed (e.g., tax policy) • Reaching customers globally through Internet • Potential for higher productivity	• Controls for firms within enlarged EU required	• Growing awareness of environmental controls (e.g., measurement of performance against key environmental drivers, use of environmental accounting)

EU: European Union; IT: information technology; NAFTA: North American Free Trade Agreement.

Sources: Peter Drucker, "The Next Society," *The Economist*, November 3, 2001, Insert pp. 3-20; Asia-Pacific Decision Sciences Institute "Decision Making at the Speed of Light: What Is Amiss?" Conference, Bangkok, July 24-27, 2002; Richard N. Cooper and Richard Layard (eds.), *What the Future Holds: Insights from Social Science* (Cambridge, MA: MIT Press, 2002); J. Scott Armstrong (ed.) *Principles of Forecasting: A Handbook for Researchers and Practitioners* (Boston, MA: Kluwer, 2001); John T. Landry, "A Future Perfect: The Essentials of Globalization," *Harvard Business Review*, May 2000, p. 192; Karl Albrecht, *Corporate Radar: Tracking the Forces That Are Shaping Your Business* (New York: AMACOM, 2000).

information that it leads to information overload, as discussed earlier. The ease of communication facilitates the global trend of mergers, such as the cross-national merger of the German Daimler-Benz and the American Chrysler. Similarly, technological developments promote new *organizational* forms (Part 3), such as outsourcing of production and services to contractors and suppliers. Knowledge work and the accessibility of common databases to various levels in the organization promote nonhierarchical structures. Information technology also influences the managerial function of *staffing* (Part 4). The demand for knowledge workers rises, thereby enhancing not only their upward mobility in the organizational hierarchy but also their mobility between organizations, which in turn promote frequent organizational changes. In addition, specialized knowledge workers may become consultants or contractors in short-term or part-time employment in organizations. Human resource activities may also be outsourced to companies specializing in this area. The rapid changes in information technology demand continual training to keep up, and the appraisal and compensation of knowledge workers may require new and creative approaches.

Developments in information technology also impact on the various aspects of *leading* (Part 5). Specifically, power relationships shift in favor of knowledge workers as well as customers.

Teamwork is facilitated by electronic communication technology, such as e-mail, intranets, the Internet, and wireless means. Motivating well-educated knowledge workers may need to be by providing recognition, opportunities for participation, and self-actualization. In general, communication costs can be reduced through the application of the new technologies.

Finally, the managerial function of *controlling* (Part 6) is greatly helped by information technology. Deviations from standards can be detected instantly, and consequently corrective actions can be taken earlier. Similarly, productivity can be measured at low costs, thus encouraging its improvement. The Internet makes worldwide buying and selling possible through electronic transactions, and it allows carmakers General Motors, Ford, and DaimlerChrysler to engage in purchasing cooperatives. The Internet also easily links the enterprise with its external environment.

ENTREPRENEURIAL FOCUS: MANAGING FOR RAPID GROWTH AND LIQUIDITY EVENTS

California's Silicon Valley is famous for its world-class companies which started very small but grew very fast. Companies such as Cisco and Google, though still young, have quickly grown into global enterprises that serve many millions of people around the world. How is such rapid growth achieved? How can entrepreneurial managers lead their firms to this level of success? Clearly, many successful entrepreneurs work closely with the venture capital community and benefit from the strategic financing and advising that venture capitalists can provide. Entrepreneurs also rely on the Silicon Valley eco-system of venture law and accounting firms to support their growth systematically.

Successful entrepreneurial managers of high growth firms set challenging yet achievable milestones in the form of revenue growth, market share, brand awareness, and profitability. These milestones are often set in consultation with the venture capitalists that fund the entrepreneurs' firms, and so, the financing provided is typically tied to achieving these objectives. But, what is the process employed in setting these milestones? An understanding of the venture capital process is necessary to guide a discussion on entrepreneurial management techniques to pursue rapid growth.[19]

Venture capital firms raise capital from institutional investors and pool this money into funds that are invested into private companies for a share of ownership in those private firms. These investments are initially illiquid (meaning they cannot easily be sold). The goal of the venture capital firm is to resell their ownership stake in the firms they finance at a much higher value after several years and then return the increase in value to its fund's investors. The venture capital revenue model is based on two primary components. They earn a small percentage (about 1.5 to 2%) of the funds under their management and they earn a percentage (about 20%) of the gain in the value of the portfolio funds they invest. This gain is determined by the difference in initial and subsequent equity financing that venture capitalists allocate to a particular company and the eventual value of that equity stake as determined by amount the company is eventually sold for (either through a merger or acquisition or through an initial public offering).[20]

To meet their objectives, venture capitalists advise the companies that receive their financing on how to best grow the firm so that it may increase in value and become a more liquid investment by becoming a publicly held firm through an initial public offering or by being acquired by a publicly held company. The life of a venture fund is about eight to ten years, so the firms that receive venture funding are expected to go from a small private enterprise to a public holding within about seven years. Thus, by accepting venture capital funding, the entrepreneur is essentially committing to an effort to achieve rapid growth.

The importance of achieving liquidity of venture backed firms for the venture capital firms that fund them is noted by Igor Sill of Hambrecht Geneva Ventures who offered the following insight in commenting on the state of the high growth venture environment in Silicon Valley in late 2006. "My confidence level in today's strength of the venture capital industry is predicated on some of our industry's basic economic fundamentals, essentially portfolio liquidity opportunities in the public markets. This coming week's IPO calendar lists 13 IPO filings, and we're up to 7 filings already for next week, according to available SEC reports. That represents about a three times increase in IPO filings from the same time a year ago (October 2005). The underlying reason for such a strong outpouring of IPO filers is the strength and momentum of the NASDAQ Composite Index, which serves as the barometer for the IPO market. For those venture funds that have funded, developed and supported the growth of companies now achieving profitability and global momentum, the timing is optimal for realizing liquidity. I anticipate the IPO window will remain attractive well into 2007." Similarly, Mike Carusi of Advanced Technology Ventures agrees, noting, "My firm has enjoyed several strong exits as of late and continues to see strong early stage deal flow. This bodes well for the industry overall—good (not great) exit environment with strong company formation activity." Also, Deepak Kamra of Canaan Partners finds, "Prospects for liquidity options are better in the US, and overseas opportunities appear attractive."[21]

Achieving rapid growth often involves making trade-offs. Profitability is sometimes sacrificed for achieving higher revenue targets or market share. Remember, the goal is to increase the value of the firm quickly, so that the venture backers of the firm can eventually translate their equity holding in the firm back into cash at a multiple of 5–10 times their initial investment to distribute to their fund's investors. Therefore, an aggressive growth strategy is often pursued by venture-backed firms. This aggressive growth strategy is operationalized by setting and achieving a series of milestones over the early years of a firm's life. For example, objectives of product development, initial sales, and growth in sales by region are often delineated in a business plan and these objectives or milestones are then tied to rounds of financing by the venture capital firms that fund the company. Subsequent rounds of financing and/or the valuation of that financing are often tied to achieving these milestones so the entrepreneur has a significant incentive to meet these growth targets.[22] An illustration of a simple time line for rapid growth targets that are tied to financing is provided in Figure C6.2.

FIGURE C6.2 Illustration of milestones and financing to achieve rapid growth and liquidity

Time Horizon	Month 1	Month 18	Month 27	Month 42	Month 60	Month 72
Objective	Incorporate Company, Raise Initial Financing, Select core Management Team	Complete Product Development and Test Market	Begin Sales	Grow sales regionally, target $10 million	Grow sales nationally target $25 million	Ramp sales nationally to $50 million and have IPO or be acquired
Financing	Seed Financing $500k–$1 million	Series A $2 million–$5 million	Series B $5 million–$10 million	Series C $10 million–$20 million	Series D or Mezzanine $20 + million	Initial Public Offering $100 + million

As noted in Figure C6.2, each series of financing is tied to certain objectives of firm performance (e.g., successful product development, growth in sales, profitability). These milestone targets are set by the entrepreneurial leaders of the firm in consultation with the venture backers and board of directors. The time horizon for growth for venture backed firms is bounded somewhat by the life of the VC fund (ten years or less), so it is reasonable to expect that the venture capitalists who fund the firm want to see growth in revenues that is rapid enough to make the firm a potential IPO candidate or acquisition target within seven to eight years from the first investment of the venture firm.[23]

The value of the firm is a function of both its absolute earnings and revenue, and the rate of growth of these earnings and revenue. As earnings can sometimes be managed, revenues and their rate of growth are often used as a yardstick to determine the value of a new private firm. Therefore, entrepreneurial managers may be encouraged to seek revenue growth at the expense of profits and rely on the financing of their venture backers to cover operational losses.

In managing their firms for rapid growth, entrepreneurs must be cognizant of the industry environment in which they operate. Specifically, while the firm must be managed to grow quickly and be successful as a stand-alone entity, the entrepreneur and her financial backers should be keenly aware of other firms that may find this high growth firm a potential acquisition target. Therefore, an analysis of how one's firm may be complementary to other larger more established firms in the industry should be undertaken. Again, the company cannot count on a merger or acquisition, but should be aware of this possibility while managing for growth on its own. This is particularly the case, when the liquidity potential of an initial public offering is unlikely due to larger market forces (e.g., declining NASDAQ). In this case, the entrepreneur may take an even more aggressive stance in seeking potential acquirers.

Recall that most firms do not seek or win venture capital, and in those cases, the need for rapid growth and a search for liquidity is much less urgent. Still, venture backing and guidance often allows firms to grow from idea stage to global players in a relatively short time period so this option should be considered by entrepreneurs who wish to share they vision on a large scale.[24]

Methods of rapid growth are also multidimensional. Growth can be pursued as organic (from the firm's own internally generate sales) or nonorganic (through the acquisition of other firms). Perhaps surprisingly, even new companies can pursue acquisitions of other firms if the deal can be structured correctly. Acquisitions can be made for multiple reasons. For example, an acquisition target could have a needed technology, or the acquisition could be made to incorporate the acquired firm's sales and reduce competition in the industry. This growth-by-acquisition strategy was well demonstrated by Cisco in the 1990s, but it can also be employed by new ventures as well.[25] These acquisitions may be made through cash or stock purchases or some combination—thereby generating rapid sales with a stroke of a pen.

The entrepreneur must be wary of some of the dangers of rapid growth. For example, the firm may grow beyond its core competency and lose focus on what it does best. It may also lose sight of how to best serve its existing customer—possibly alienating them and losing strength in its core business. Dilution of equity or an excessive debt load is also possible if growth is not managed well.[26] Still, if the entrepreneur is passionate about her business—managing for rapid growth allows her to share her creativity much more broadly around the world.

GLOBAL CAR INDUSTRY CASE

What Future Car Do You Want?[27]

Cars are changing continuously. Customers want safer, more fuel-efficient cars, and cars that "think" for the driver. To some extent, the futuristic car is already here—but many new features evolve rather quickly. Demand for gas-electric hybrids from Toyota and Honda is great as gas prices have soured. Hybrids from Toyota (Prius), Lexus (RX 40), Honda (Civic and Accord models), and Ford's SUV (Escape) are now more often seen on U.S. highways. Company's such as DaimlerChrysler and other carmakers investing in hydrogen-fuel research. But it appears that this technology is still far away to be used in large numbers on passenger cars. The higher cost is only one factor in slowing the use of hydrogen-powered cars; safety and the need for a network of fuel stations are other considerations.

But the most dramatic advances can be expected in the use of electronic devices such as "active steering" using computer controlled small electric motors in the BMW, cruise controls that can identify when the driver gets too close to another vehicle. Increasingly. Now, many vehicles are equipped with satellite radios.

The traditional haggling over price at dealerships is also changing. Consumers now can find information not only about the technical details of cars, but also price information on the Internet.

Increasingly, the traditional combustion engine using gasoline or diesel fuel is replaced by the new technologies resulting in Hybrid, Hybrid-electric, electric or even hydrogen or alternative fuels. As previously discussed in the closing Part, almost all car manufacturers are working on the new technologies. Toyota is best known for its Prius hybrid cars. Tesla Motors produces the over $100,000 Roadster, but recently introduced the Model 2, a family sedan. The Chinese BYD company has a joint venture with Mercedes.

One of the limiting factor in the acceptance of the electric cars is the infrastructure. But countries such as Israel, Denmark, Australian, and American states such as Hawaii and California are assisting in the development of the infrastructure. In some way, the future is already here.

Questions:

1. What features would you be looking for in a new car?
2. List and prioritize the features important to you.
3. How important is safety, fuel economy, reliability, looks, entertainment, and others? Give the reason for your choices.
4. Are you concerned about the carbon footprint of your next car? Are you considering an hybrid or electric car?

ENDNOTES

1. Tim Smart, "Jack Welch's Encore," *Business Week*, October 28, 1996, pp. 155–160.
2. Richard B. Chase and Nicholas J. Aquilano, *Production and Operations Management: A Life Cycle Approach*, 8th ed. (Homewood, IL: Irwin, 1997); C. K. Prahalad and M. S. Krishnan, "The New Meaning of Quality in the Information Age," *Harvard Business Review*, September–October 1999, pp. 109–118.
3. Discussion of developing a business case is based on several sources including Harvard Business Press' "Developing a Business Case." 2011.
4. See also Erwin Danneels, "BPS: The Dynamics of Product Innovation and Firm Competences," *Academy of Management Proceedings*, 2000.
5. Stephen Power, "VW Woes Go Beyond Scandal," *The Wall Street Journal*, July 8, 2005.
6. Stephanie Overy, Outsourcing Definition and Solutions, http://www.cio.com/article/40380/Outsourcing_Definition_and_Solutions, accessed January 12, 2016.
7. Henry Mintzberg and James Brian Quinn, *The Strategy Process*, 3rd ed. (Upper Saddle River, NJ: Prentice Hall, 1996), p. 64.
8. "In India's Outsourcing Boom, GE Played a Starring Role," *The Wall Street Journal*, March 23, 2005.
9. Pete Engardio, "The Reset Economy – Why NCR said, 'Let's Go Back Home'," *Business Week*, August 24 and 31, 2009, p. 19; see also Maria Bartiromo interviewing Paul Laudicina of A.T. Kearney, "Rethinking Outsourcing," *Business Week*, August 24 and 31, 2009, pp. 15–17.
10. For a discussion of the integration of leadership and TQM, see Sheila M. Puffer and Daniel J. McCarthy, "A Framework for Leadership in a TQM Context," *Journal of Quality Management*, 1996, 1 (1): 109–130. See also the relationship between quality and performance by Barbara B. Flynn, "The Relationship between Quality and Other Dimensions of Competitive Performance: Tradeoff or Compatibility?" *Academy of Management Proceedings*, 2000. Note also Praveen Gupta, *Six Sigma Business Scorecard* (New York: McGraw-Hill, 2004); the book review is by Nicholas Mathys in *The Academy of Management Review*, May 2005, pp. 163–164.
11. See James P. Womack, Daniel T. Jones, and Daniel Roos, *The Machine that Changed the World* (New York: Harper-Perennial, 1990); "Lean and Its Limits," *The Economist*, September 14, 1996, p. 65.; see also Daniel Friel, "Transferring a Lean Production Concept from Germany to the United States: The Impact of Labor Laws and Training Systems," *The Academy of Management Executive*, May 2005, pp. 50–58.
12. Micheline Maynard, "Amid the Turmoil, a Rare Success at DaimlerChrysler," *Fortune*, January 22, 2001, pp. 112C–P. See also DaimlerChrysler, www.daimlerchrysler.com, accessed June 29, 2002.
13. Joseph Szczesny, "Daimler-Chrysler Divorce Final with Name Change," *Edmunds Auto Observer*, October 05, 2007.
14. Michael E. Porter, *Competitive Advantage: Creating and Sustaining Superior Performance* (New York: Free Press, 1985), especially chap. 2. See also *Industry Week* The Value Chain, www.iwvaluechain.com, accessed August 19, 2011; SAP's supply chain web site, www.sap.com/solutions, accessed December 31, 2008; and Stanford Global Supply Chain Management Forum, www.stanford.edu/group/scforum, accessed August 19, 2011. The value chain model provides little guidance for knowledge-based firms; see the discussion of the value shop approach by Jaana Woiceshyn and Loren Falkenberg, *The Academy of Management Perspectives*, May 2008, pp. 85–99. See also Digitizing the Value Chain, McKinsey Quarterly, March 2015 John Nanry, Subu Narayanan, and Louis Rassey, http://www.mckinsey.com/insights/manufacturing/digitizing_the_value_chain, accessed November 20, 2015.
15. The Value Chain Concept was introduced by Professor Michael Porter in 1985 in *Competitive Advantage*, The Free Press: New York, Chapter 2.
16. Robyn Meredith, *The Elephant and the Dragon* (New York: W. E. Norton & Company, 2008), Chapter 5.
17. Womack, Jones, and Roos, *The Machine that Changed the World*; Jana F. Kuzmicki, "Toyota Motor Corporation in 1994," in Irene Chow, Neil Holbert, Lane Kelley, and Julie Yu, eds. *Business Strategy: An Asia-Pacific Focus* (Singapore: Prentice Hall, 1997), pp. 124–161; "Toyota and PSA Team up to Tackle Toughest Segment," *Automotive News*, July 16, 2001; Kermit Whitfield, "The Current State of Quality at Honda and Toyota," *Automotive Design and Production*, August 2001. Information was also gathered during several visits to the NUMMI plant. See also Chester Dawson, "Taking on BMW," *Business Week*, July 30, 2001; "Toyota Bets on Speed," *Far Eastern Economic Review*,

July 26, 2001; see also www.toyota.com, accessed August 19, 2011.
18. See for example the Technology Quarterly in *The Economist*, December 2, 2006, beginning after page 52.
19. Please see Joseph Bartlett's *Fundamental of Venture Capital* (Madison Books, 1999) for a discussion on the mechanics of the venture capital industry.
20. Please also see John Nesheim's *High Tech Start Up* (New York: Free Press, 2000) for a discussion on the process of firm growth from idea to public enterprise.
21. *USF Silicon Valley Venture Capitalist Confidence Index* 2006, Q3 Report, p. 3, http://www.usfca.edu/sobam/nvc/pub/svvcindex.html
22. Please also see Richard Dorf and Thomas Byers, *Technology Ventures: From Idea to Enterprise* (New York: McGraw Hill, 2005), for a discussion on the setting of growth milestones in a technology firm.
23. According to the National Venture Capital Association, in calendar year 2005, there were 346 mergers and acquisitions and 56 IPOs of venture-backed firms.
24. Please also see Guy Kawasaki's "The Art of the Start" Portfolio (2004) for a discussion on the fundamental purpose of creating organizations.
25. Please see Ed Paulson's, *Inside Cisco: The Real Story of Sustained M&A Growth* (New York: Wiley, 2001), for a discussion of a growth strategy fueled by acquisitions.
26. Jeffry A. Timmons and Stephen Spinelli, *New Venture Creation: Entrepreneurship for the 21st Century*, 7th ed. (New York: McGraw-Hill Irwin 2007).
27. Joseph B. White, "The Car of the Future, " *The Wall Street Journal*, July 25, 2005; see also "Foresight 20/20," Economist Intelligence Unit by *The Economist*, pp. 24–29.

APPENDIX A

Summary of Major Principles or Guides for the Managerial Functions of Planning, Organizing, Staffing, Leading, and Controlling

Although a complete set of empirically proven, interrelated principles has not been discovered and codified, experience and observation of managing indicate certain fundamental managerial principles or guides. They not only provide managers with a conceptual scheme but also indicate to scholars areas for research. To be sure, the key abstractions need to be applied with due consideration for the situation-and this is an art. In this appendix, the principles, which perhaps would be more appropriately called guides to management, are organized (as this book is) according to the managerial functions of planning, organizing, staffing, leading, and controlling. Each principle is given a number with a letter that represents the type of managerial function.

MAJOR PRINCIPLES OR GUIDES FOR PLANNING

The most essential guiding principles for planning are the following.

The Purpose and Nature of Planning

The purpose and nature of planning may be summarized by reference to the following principles.

- P1. *Principle of contribution to objective.* The purpose of every plan and all supporting plans is to promote the accomplishment of enterprise objectives.
- P2. *Principle of objectives.* If objectives are to be meaningful to people, they must be clear, attainable, and verifiable.
- P3. *Principle of primacy of planning.* Planning logically precedes all other managerial functions.
- P4. *Principle of efficiency of plans.* The efficiency of a plan is measured by the amount it contributes to purpose and objectives offset by the costs required to formulate and operate it and by unsought consequences.

The Structure of Plans

Two major principles dealing with the structure of plans can go far in tying plans together, making supporting plans contribute to major plans and ensuring that plans in one department harmonize with those in another.

- P5. *Principle of planning premises.* The more thoroughly individuals charged with planning understand and agree to utilize consistent planning premises, the more coordinated enterprise planning will be.
- P6. *Principle of the strategy and policy framework.* The more strategies and policies are clearly understood and implemented in practice, the more consistent and effective will be the framework of enterprise plans.

The Process of Planning

Within the process of planning, there are four principles that help in the development of a practical science of planning.

- P7. *Principle of the limiting factor.* In choosing among alternatives, the more accurately individuals recognize and allow for factors that are limiting or critical to the attainment of the desired goal, the more easily and accurately can they select the most favorable alternative.
- P8. *The commitment principle.* Logical planning should cover a period of time in the future necessary to foresee as well as possible, through a series of actions, the fulfillment of commitments involved in a decision made today.
- P9. *Principle of flexibility.* Building flexibility into plans will lessen the danger of losses incurred through unexpected events, but the cost of flexibility should be weighed against its advantages.
- P10. *Principle of navigational change.* The more that planning decisions commit individuals to a future path, the more important it is to check on events and expectations periodically and redraw plans as necessary to maintain a course toward a desired goal.

The commitment principle and the principles of flexibility and navigational change are aimed at a contingency approach to planning. Although it makes sense to forecast and draw plans far enough into the future to be reasonably sure of meeting commitments, often it is impossible to do so, or the future is so uncertain that it is too risky to fulfill those commitments.

The principle of flexibility deals with the ability to change plans necessitated by unexpected events. The principle of navigational change, on the other hand, implies reviewing plans from time to time and redrawing them if this is required by changed events and expectations. Unless plans have built-in flexibility, navigational change may be difficult or costly.

MAJOR PRINCIPLES OR GUIDES FOR ORGANIZING

Although the science of organizing has not yet developed to the point where its principles are infallible laws, there is considerable agreement among management scholars and practitioners about a number of them. These principles are truths (or are believed to be truths) of general applicability, although their application is not precise enough to give them the exactness of the laws of pure science. They are more in the nature of essential criteria for effective organizing. The most essential guiding principles of organizing are summarized below.

The Purpose of Organizing

The purpose of organizing is to aid in making objectives meaningful and to contribute to organizational efficiency.

- O1. *Principle of unity of objectives*. An organization structure is effective if it enables individuals to contribute to enterprise objectives.
- O2. *Principle of organizational efficiency*. An organization is efficient if it is structured to aid the accomplishment of enterprise objectives with a minimum of unsought consequences or costs.

The Reason for Organizing

The basic reason for the organization structure is the limitation of the span of management. If there were no such limitation, an enterprise might have only one manager and no organization structure.

- O3. *Principle of the span of management*. In each managerial position, there is a limit to the number of persons an individual can effectively manage, but the exact number will depend on the impact of underlying variables.

The Structure of Organization: Authority

Authority is the cement of the organization structure, the thread that makes it possible, the means by which groups of activities can be placed under a manager and coordination of organizational units can be promoted. It is the tool by which a manager is able to exercise discretion and to create an environment for individual performance. Some of the most useful principles of organizing are related to authority.

- O4. *Scalar principle*. The clearer the line of authority from the ultimate management position in an enterprise to every subordinate position, the clearer will be the responsibility for decision making and the more effective will be organizational communication.

O5. *Principle of delegation by results expected.* Authority delegated to all individual managers should be adequate to ensure their ability to accomplish expected results.
O6. *Principle of absoluteness of responsibility.* The responsibility of subordinates to their superiors for performance is absolute, and superiors cannot escape responsibility for the organizational activities of their subordinates.
O7. *Principle of parity of authority and responsibility.* The responsibility for actions should not be greater than that implied by the authority delegated, nor should it be less.
O8. *Principle of unity of command.* The more complete an individual's reporting relationships to a single superior, the smaller the problem of conflicting instructions and the greater the feeling of personal responsibility for results.
O9. *Authority-level principle.* Maintenance of intended delegation requires that decision within the authority of individual managers should be made by them and not be referred upward in the organization structure.

The Structure of Organization: Departmentalized Activities

Organization involves the design of a departmental framework. Although there are several principles in this area, one is of major importance.

O10. *Principle of functional definition.* The more a position or a department has a clear definition of the results expected, activities to be undertaken, and organizational authority delegated, as well as an understanding of authority and informational relationships with other positions, the more adequately the individual responsible can contribute toward accomplishing enterprise objectives.

The Process of Organizing

The various principles of authority delegation and of departmentation are fundamental truths about the process of organizing. They deal with phases of the two primary aspects of organizing: authority and activity groupings. There are other principles that deal with the process of organizing. It is through their application that managers gain a sense of proportion or a measure of the total organizing process.

O11. *Principle of balance.* In every structure, there is a need for balance. The application of principles or techniques must be balanced to ensure overall effectiveness of the structure in meeting enterprise objectives.
O12. *Principle of flexibility.* The more that provisions are made for building flexibility into an organization structure, the more adequately an organization structure can fulfill its purpose.
O13. *Principle of leadership facilitation.* The more an organization structure and its delegation of authority enable managers to design and maintain an environment for performance, the more they will help the leadership abilities of those managers.

The principle of balance is common to all areas of science and to all functions of the manager. The inefficiencies of broad spans of management must be balanced against the inefficiencies of long lines of communication. The losses from multiple command must be balanced against the gains from expertness and uniformity in delegating functional authority to staff and service departments. The savings of functional specialization in departmentalizing must be balanced against the advantages of establishing profit-responsible, semi-independent product or territorial departments. It is apparent, once again, that the application of management theory depends on the specific situation.

The principle of flexibility demands that devices and techniques for anticipating and reading to change be built into every structure. Every enterprise moves toward its goal in a changing environment, both internal and external. The enterprise that develops inflexibilities, whether these are resistance to change, overcomplicated procedures, or too-firm departmental lines, is risking the inability to meet the challenges of economic, technological, biological, political and social changes.

Since managership depends to a great extent on the quality of leadership of those in managerial positions, it follows from the principle of leadership facilitation that the organization structure should do its part in creating a situation in which a manager can most effectively lead. In this sense, organizing is a technique of promoting leadership. If the authority allocation and the structural arrangements create a situation in which heads of departments tend to be looked upon as leaders and in which their task of leadership is aided, organization structuring has accomplished an essential task.

MAJOR PRINCIPLES OR GUIDES FOR STAFFING

There are no universally accepted staffing principles. Nevertheless, those listed below are useful as guidelines for understanding the staffing function.

The Purpose of Staffing

The purpose of staffing is summarized by the following principles.

S1. *Principle of the objective of staffing*. The objective of managerial staffing is to ensure that organizational roles are filled by qualified personnel who are able and willing to occupy them.

S2. *Principle of staffing*. The clearer the definition of organizational roles and their human resource requirements, and the better the techniques of manager appraisal and training employed, the higher the managerial quality.

The first principle stresses the importance of the desire and ability to undertake the responsibilities of management. There is considerable evidence of failure to achieve results when these qualities are lacking. The second principle rests on an important body of knowledge concerning management practices. Organizations that have no established job definitions, no effective appraisals, and no system for training and development will have to rely on coincidence or outside sources to fill positions with able managers. On the other hand, enterprises applying the systems approach to staffing and human resource management will utilize the potentials of people in the enterprise more effectively and efficiently.

The Process of Staffing

The following principles indicate the means for effective staffing.

S3. *Principle of job definition*. The more precisely the results expected of managers are identified, the more the dimensions of their positions can be defined.

S4. *Principle of managerial appraisal*. The more clearly verifiable objectives and required managerial activities are identified, the more precise can be the appraisal of managers against these criteria.

S5. *Principle of open competition*. The more an enterprise is committed to the assurance of quality management, the more it will encourage open competition among all candidates for management positions.

The first principle is similar to the principle of functional definition in organizing. Since organizational roles are occupied by people with different needs, these roles must have many dimensions that induce managers to perform, such as pay, status, power, discretion, and job satisfaction.

The second principle suggests that performance should be measured both against verifiable objectives—as in an appraisal approach based on management by objectives—and against standards of performance as managers. The appraisal of managers as managers considers how well the key managerial activities within the functions of planning, organizing, staffing, leading, and controlling are carried out.

Violation of the open competition principle has led many firms to appoint managers with inadequate abilities. Although social pressures strongly favor promotion from within the enterprise, these forces should be resisted whenever better candidates can be brought in from the outside. At the same time, the application of this principle obligates an organization to appraise its people accurately and to provide them with opportunities for development.

S6. *Principle of management training and development.* The more management training and development is integrated with the management process and enterprise objectives, the more effective the development programs and activities will be.

S7. *Principle of training objectives.* The more precisely the training objectives are stated; the more likely are the chances of achieving them.

S8. *Principle of continuous development.* The more an enterprise is committed to managerial excellence, the more it requires that managers practice continuous self-development.

The first of these three principles suggests that, in the systems approach, training and development efforts are related to the managerial functions, the aims of the enterprise, and the professional needs of managers.

The analysis of training needs is the basis for determining training objectives that give direction to development and facilitate the measurement of the effectiveness of training efforts. The second principle brings into focus the contribution that training makes to the purpose of the enterprise and the development of individuals.

The third principle reminds us that in a fast-changing and competitive environment, managers cannot stop learning. Instead, they have to update their managerial knowledge continually, reevaluate their approaches to managing, and improve their managerial skills and performance to achieve results.

MAJOR PRINCIPLES OR GUIDES FOR LEADING

The managerial function of leading can be summarized by several principles or guides.

L1. *Principle of harmony of objectives.* The more managers can harmonize the personal goals of individuals with the goals of the enterprise, the more effective and efficient the enterprise will be.

L2. *Principle of motivation.* Since motivation is not a simple matter of cause and effect, the more managers carefully assess a reward structure, look upon it from a situational and contingency point of view, and integrate it into the entire system of managing, the more effective a motivational program will be.

L3. *Principle of leadership.* Since people tend to follow those who, in their view, offer them a means of satisfying their personal goals, the more managers understand what motivates their subordinates and how these motivators operate, and the more they reflect this understanding in carrying out their managerial actions, the more effective they are likely to be as leaders.

For organizational communication to be effective, managers should take note of the following principles.

> L4. *Principle of communication clarity.* Communication tends to be clear when it is expressed in a language and transmitted in a way that can be understood by the receiver.
>
> L5. *Principle of communication integrity.* The greater the integrity and consistency of written, oral, or nonverbal messages, as well as of the moral behavior of the sender, the greater the acceptance of the message by the receiver.
>
> L6. *Principle of supplemental use of informal organization.* Communication tends to be more effective when managers utilize the informal organization to supplement the communication channels of the formal organization.

The sender has the responsibility to formulate the message so that it is understandable to the receiver. This responsibility pertains primarily to written and oral communication and points to the necessity for planning the message, stating the underlying assumptions, and applying the generally accepted rules for effective writing and speaking.

Informal organization is a phenomenon managers must accept. Information, true or not, flows quickly through the informal organization. Consequently, managers should take advantage of this device to correct misinformation and to provide information that cannot be effectively sent or appropriately received through the formal communication system.

MAJOR PRINCIPLES OR GUIDES FOR CONTROLLING

From the discussions in the chapters on management control, there have emerged certain essentials, or basic truths. These, which are referred to as "principles", are designed to highlight aspects of control that are regarded as especially important. In view of the fact that control, even though representing a system itself, is a subsystem of the larger area of management, certain of these principles are understandably similar to those identified in the discussions of the other managerial functions.

The Purpose and Nature of Control

The purpose and nature of control may be summarized by the following principles.

> C1. *Principle of the purpose of control.* The task of control is to ensure the success of plans by detecting deviations from plans and furnishing a basis for taking action to correct potential or actual undesired deviations.
>
> C2. *Principle of future-directed controls.* Because of time lags in the total system of control. the more a control system is based on feedforward rather than simple feedback of information, the more managers have the opportunity to perceive undesirable deviations from plans before they occur and to take action in time to prevent them.

These two principles emphasize that the purpose of control in any system of managerial action is ensuring that objectives are achieved through detecting deviations and taking action designed to correct or prevent them. Control, like planning, should ideally be forward-looking. This principle is often disregarded in practice, largely because the state of the art in managing has not regularly provided for systems of feedforward control. Managers have generally been dependent on historical data, which may be adequate for collecting taxes and determining stockholders' earnings but are not good enough for the most effective control. If means of looking forward are lacking, reference to history, on the questionable assumption that "what is past is prologue", is better than not looking at all. But time lags in the system of management control make it imperative that greater efforts be undertaken to make future-directed control a reality.

C3. *Principle of control responsibility.* The primary responsibility for the exercise of control rests in the manager charged with the performance of the particular plans involved.

C4. *Principle of efficiency of controls.* Control techniques and approaches are efficient if they detect and illuminate the nature and causes of deviations from plans with a minimum of costs or other unsought consequences.

C5. *Principle of preventive control.* The higher the quality of managers in a managerial system, the less will be the need for direct controls.

To maximize the efficiency of controls, the above three principles should be observed. First, since delegation of authority, assignment of tasks, and responsibility for certain objectives rest in individual managers, it follows that control over this work should be exercised by each of these managers. An individual manager's responsibility cannot be waived or rescinded without changing the organization structure.

The second point to note is that control techniques have a way of becoming costly, complex, and burdensome. Managers may become so engrossed in control that they spend more than it is worth to detect a deviation. Detailed budget controls that hamstring a subordinate, complex mathematical controls that thwart innovation, and cumbersome purchasing controls that delay deliveries and cost more than the item purchased are examples of inefficient controls.

Lastly, most controls are based in large part on the fact that human beings make mistakes and often do not react to problems promptly and adequately. The more qualified managers are, the more they will perceive deviations from plans and take timely action to prevent them.

The Structure of Control

The principles that follow are aimed at pointing out how control systems and techniques can be designed to improve the quality of managerial control.

C6. *Principle of reflection of plans.* The more that plans are clear, complete, and integrated, and the more that controls are designed to reflect such plans, the more effectively controls will serve the needs of managers.

C7. *Principle of organizational suitability.* The more that an organization structure is clear, complete, and integrated, and the more that controls are designed to reflect the place in the organization structure where responsibility for action lies, the more controls will facilitate correction of deviations from plans.

C8. *Principle of individuality of controls.* The more that control techniques and information are understandable to individual managers who must utilize them, the more they will actually be used and the more they will result in effective control.

First of all, it is not possible for a system of controls to be devised without plans, since the task of control is to ensure that plans work out as intended. There can be no doubt that the more clear, complete, and integrated these plans are, and the more that control techniques are designed to follow the progress of these plans, the more effective the controls will be.

Secondly, plans are implemented by people. Deviations from plans must be the responsibility primarily of managers who are entrusted with the task of executing planning programs. Since it is the function of an organization structure to define a system of roles, it follows that controls must be designed to affect the role in which responsibility for performance of a plan lies.

Although some control techniques and information can be utilized in the same form by various kinds of enterprises and managers, as a general rule controls should be tailored to meet the individual needs of managers. Some of this individuality is related to position in the organization structure, as noted in the second principle. Another aspect of individuality is the tailoring of controls to the kind and level of managers' understanding. Company presidents as well as supervisors have thrown up their hands in dismay (often for quite different reasons) at the unintelligible nature and inappropriate form of control information. Control information that a manager cannot or will not use has little practical value.

The Process of Control

Control, often being so much a matter of technique, rests heavily on the art of managing, on know-how in given instances. However, there are certain principles that experience has shown have wide applicability.

C9. *Principle of standards*. Effective control requires objective, accurate, and suitable standards.
C10. *Principle of critical point control*. Effective control requires special attention to those factors critical to evaluating performance against plans.
C11. *The exception principle*. The more that managers concentrate control efforts on significant exceptions from planned performance, the more efficient will be the results of their control.

There should be a simple, specific, and verifiable way to measure whether a planning program is being accomplished. Control is accomplished through people. Even the best manager cannot help being influenced by personal factors, and actual performance is sometimes camouflaged by a dull or a sparkling personality or by a subordinate's ability to "sell" a deficient performance. Good standards of performance, objectively applied-as required by the principle of standards—will more likely be accepted by subordinates as fair and reasonable.

It would ordinarily be wasteful and unnecessary for managers to follow every detail of plan execution. What they must know is that plans are being implemented. Therefore, they concentrate their attention on salient factors of performance—the critical points—that will indicate any important deviations from plans. Perhaps all managers can ask themselves what things in their operations will best show them whether the plans for which they are responsible are being accomplished.

The exception principle holds that managers should concern themselves with significant deviations—the especially good or the especially bad situations. It is often confused with the principle of critical point control, and the two do have some kinship. However, critical point control has to do with recognizing the points to be watched, while the exception principle is concerned with watching the size of deviations at these points.

C12. *Principle of flexibility of controls*. If controls are to remain effective despite failure or unforeseen changes of plans, flexibility is required in their design.
C13. *Principle of action*. Control is justified only if indicated or actual deviations from plans are corrected through appropriate planning, organizing, staffing, and leading.

According to the flexibility principle, controls must not be so inflexibly tied in with a plan as to be useless if the entire plan fails or is suddenly changed. Note that this principle applies to failure of plans, not failure of people operating under plans.

There are instances in practice in which this simple truth is forgotten: control is a wasteful use of managerial and staff time unless it is followed by action, as the principle of action stresses. If deviations are found in actual or projected performance, action is indicated, in the form of either redrawing plans or making additional plans to get back on course. The situation may call for reorganization. It may require replacing subordinates or training them to do the task required. Or it may indicate that the fault is a lack of direction and leadership in getting a subordinate to understand the plans or in motivating him or her to accomplish them. In any case, action is implied.

APPENDIX B

Management Excellence Survey

INTRODUCTION

Broadly speaking, the objectives of management education are (1) to increase managerial knowledge, (2) to improve skills in the analysis of cases and in conducting research, (3) to examine one's attitudes and their impact on managing, and (4) to transfer knowledge, skills, and attitudes to the workplace. In short, then, management education aims to make managers and students of management more effective in their performance.

An appropriate way to understand the needs of an organization is to conduct a survey of its managers to find out the areas that require improvement. The survey in this appendix serves this purpose.

The findings can then be used in developing strategies to strengthen the organization and to overcome its weaknesses. The survey can also be used by students and managers for conducting research that will help the understanding of the concepts, theories, and principles discussed in this book. For example, areas that are found to be weak can be improved by reading the appropriate parts in the book.

The authors and the publisher give herewith permission to duplicate the survey that follows for research studies. Appropriate reference to the copyright holders, however, is required.

MANAGEMENT EXCELLENCE SURVEY

Excellent organizations base their management and organization development on a careful analysis of managerial and organizational needs. This survey is designed to identify those needs.

An Overview of the Survey

This comprehensive survey identifies critical success factors grouped according to the managerial functions of planning, organizing, staffing, leading, and controlling. The questions deal with these functions. They pertain to an *organizational division or unit;* they do not refer to, for example, the total worldwide organization.

Your answers are valuable to tailoring management and organization development programs to the needs of individuals and of the organization. Therefore, you are also asked to assess the importance of the need for management development by giving in the second column ("development needs") of the questionnaire a numerical value to the questions.

The Rating System

Column 1. In rating each question, use the following marks (for each rating, use only one of two numbers given, such as 4.0 or 4.5 for *very good,* not other decimals):

- NA = Not applicable to our organization
- ? = Do not know accurately enough for rating
- 5.0 = *Excellent:* a standard of performance which could not be improved upon under any circumstances or conditions known to the rater
- 4.0 or 4.5 = *Very good:* a standard of performance which leaves little to be desired
- 3.0 or 3.5 = *Good:* a standard of performance above the average and meeting all normal requirements
- 2.0 or 2.5 = *Satisfactory:* a standard of performance regarded as average
- 1.0 or 1.5 = *Below standard:* a standard of performance which is below the normal requirements but one that may be regarded as marginally or temporarily acceptable
- 0.0 = *Inadequate:* a standard of performance regarded as unacceptable

Column 2. In the column "development needs", rate how important it is to improve the specific managerial activity for the organization. Use the following scale:

| Need no further development | 1 | 2 | 3 | 4 | 5 | An extreme amount of development needed. |

Select a number between 1 and 5 that represents your judgment. If you marked a question with "NA" or "?" in the first column ("performance rating"), put the same letter in the second column.

In averaging 'ratings for these two columns, *average only the questions rated;* exclude the not-applicable questions ("NA") and those on which you have inadequate information to rate ("?").

Column 3. Comments are optional. You may use the space given to list your ideas for group discussion.

© Copyright by Heinz Weihrich and Harold Koontz, 1995, 1998, 2000, 2002.
This survey is for use in conjunction with the book *Management: A Global Perspective*, 12th edition, by Heinz Weihrich, Mark Cannice and Harold Koontz, published by Tata McGraw-Hill India, 2008. Additional information on a topic can be found by consulting the index in this book.

Excellence in Planning

Planning	Performance Rating	Development needs	Comments
1. Do managers set departmental goals (both short- and long-term) in verifiable terms?			
2. To what extent are organizational goals understood?			
3. How well are people assisted in establishing verifiable and consistent goals for their operations?			
4. To what extent are consistent and approved planning premises (e.g., forecasts) communicated?			
5. To what extent do people understand the role of company policies in decision making?			
6. Do managers encourage innovation?			
7. Do superiors help subordinates get the information they need to assist them in their planning?			
8. Do managers seek out alternatives before making decisions?			
9. In choosing from among alternatives, do managers focus on those factors that are critical to a problem?			
10. Do managers check plans periodically to see if they are still consistent with current expectations?			
11. Do managers consider the need for flexibility (as well as the costs) in arriving at a planning decision?			
12. In developing and implementing plans, do managers consider the long-range implications of their short-range decisions?			
13. When making recommendations, do subordinates submit analyses of alternatives (with advantages and disadvantages)?			
Total number of "NA" and "?"			
Total number of questions on which ratings are made			
Total score of questions given ratings			
Average of ratings in Excellence in Planning			

Comments and overall evaluation of the function of planning (use back of the page):

APPENDIX B Management Excellence Survey

Excellence in Organizing

Organizing	Performance rating	Development needs	Comments
1. Does the organization structure reflect major result areas?			
2. Do managers delegate authority to subordinates in accordance with the results expected of them?			
3. Do managers make delegation clear?			
4. Do managers use position guides, or position descriptions?			
5. Do managers clarify responsibilities for expected contributions to goals and programs?			
6. Do managers maintain adequate control when delegating authority to subordinates?			
7. Do managers understand that they share responsibility when delegating authority (responsibility) to subordinates?			
8. Do managers make sure that their subordinate managers properly delegate authority to their subordinates?			
9. Do managers maintain unity of command whenever possible and use dual command only when the advantages clearly offset the disadvantages?			
10. Do managers utilize staff advice appropriately?			
11. Do managers make clear to subordinates the nature of line and staff relationships?			
12. Do managers limit and make clear functional authority?			
13. Do managers use service departments in an effective and efficient manner?			
14. Is the enterprise free from excessive organizational levels?			
15. Do managers distinguish between lines of authority and lines of information?			
Total number of "NA" and "?"			
Total number of questions on which ratings are made			
Total score of questions given ratings			
Average of ratings in Excellence in Organizing			

Comments and overall evaluation of the function of organizing:

Excellence In Staffing			
Staffing	Performance rating	Development needs	Comments
1. Do managers take full responsibility for the staffing of the department (although using assistance from the personnel department)?			
2. Does the company make it clear that every position in the department is open to the best-qualified individual, either inside or outside the company?			
3. Do managers make certain that subordinates are given opportunity for training for better positions?			
4. Do managers utilize appropriate methods for training and developing subordinates?			
5. Do managers effectively practice coaching of subordinates?			
6. Do managers appraise subordinates objectively and regularly on the basis of performance against preselected goals?			
7. Do superiors appraise managers objectively and regularly on their ability to plan, organize, staff, lead, and control?			
8. Do managers use appraisal as a means of helping subordinates to improve their performance?			
9. Do managers select, or recommend promotion of subordinates, on the basis of objective appraisal of their performance?			
10. Does the organization provide adequate and motivating compensation and conditions of work?			
11. Do managers evaluate and develop the whole organizational unit (e.g., through organization development)?			
Total number of "NA" and "?"			
Total number of questions on which ratings are made			
Total score of questions given ratings			
Average of ratings in Excellence in Staffing			

Comments and overall evaluation of the function of staffing (use back of the page):

APPENDIX B Management Excellence Survey

Excellence in Leading			
Leading	Performance rating	Development needs	Comments
1. Do managers understand what motivates subordinates and attempt to create an environment in which people are productive?			
2. Do managers lead subordinates to recognize that their self-interest is in harmony with (although not necessarily the same as) the company's or department's goals?			
3. Do managers issue clear instructions that are fully understandable to subordinates?			
4. Do managers use effective and efficient communication techniques?			
5. Do managers engage in an appropriate amount of face-to-face contact?			
6. Do managers create an environment where people are encouraged to suggest innovations in product, process, marketing, or other areas?			
7. Are managers receptive to innovative ideas and suggestions, whether from superiors, persons on the same organizational level, subordinates, or customers?			
8. Are subordinates (managers and nonmanagers) free to suggest changes in objectives, policies, programs, or decisions?			
9. Can superiors be easily reached by subordinates to discuss their problems and obtain guidance?			
10. Do superiors help orient subordinates to the company's programs, objectives, and organizational environment?			
11. Do managers exercise participative leadership and, when necessary, authoritative direction?			
12. In general, are managers effective as leaders (possessing the capacity and will to rally men and women to a common purpose)?			
13. Do managers use committees or group meetings only when they are superior to individual decisions?			
14. Do managers make sure that committee or group meetings are preceded by proper agenda, information gathering, analyses, and concrete proposals?			
Total number of "NA" and "?"			
Total number of questions on which ratings are made			
Total score of questions given ratings			
Average of ratings in Excellence in Leading			

Comments and overall evaluation of the function of leading:

Excellence in Controlling

Controlling	Performance rating	Development needs	Comments
1. How effectively do managers tailor control techniques and standards to reflect plans?			
2. Do managers use control techniques, where possible, to anticipate deviations from plans (called preventive control)?			
3. Do control techniques and information promptly report deviations from plans?			
4. Do managers develop and rely upon objective or verifiable control information?			
5. Do controls point up exceptions at critical points?			
6. Are control techniques and information designed to show exactly where in the organization deviations occur?			
7. Are control techniques and information understandable to those who must take action?			
8. Do managers take prompt action when unplanned variations in performance occur?			
9. Do managers keep abreast of and utilize new techniques of planning and control?			
10. Do managers help subordinates (through the use of verifiable objectives) exercise self-control and self-direction?			
11. Do managers keep their superiors informed of significant problems in the operations, their causes, and steps being taken to correct them?			
Total number of "NA" and "?"			
Total number of questions on which ratings are made			
Total score of questions given ratings			
Average of ratings in Excellence in Controlling			

Comments and overall evaluation of the function of controlling (use back of the page):

APPENDIX B Management Excellence Survey

Summary of the Management Excellence Survey

Please copy the scores shown at the end of each function onto this page.

Performance rating

Total number of questions	Number of NA" and "?"	Number of questions answered	Total score	Average rating
13 Planning				
15 Organizing				
11 Staffing				
14 Leading				
11 Controlling				
64 **Total**				

Development needs

Total number of questions	Number of "NA" and "?"	Number of questions answered	Total score	Average rating
13 Planning				
15 Organizing				
11 Staffing				
14 Leading				
11 Controlling				
64 **Total**				

Summary evaluation:

Subject Index

Achievement needs, 372–373, 420
Achievement-oriented leadership, 399
Action plans, 132, 317
Affiliation, or acceptance, needs, 363–376
Alliances (of companies), 66, 136, 139–140
Alliances (of countries), 72–73
Alternatives:
  determination of, 116
  development of, 155
  evaluation of, 153, 155
  identification of, 153
  planning &, 125, 152
  selection from, 152, 158
Amazon.Com, 241–242
Appraisal:
  approaches to, 302–307
  criteria, 301–302
  kinds of, 303–307
  of performance as manager, 302, 307–309, 315
  team approach to, 309–310
  against verifiable objectives, 302–307, 305–307
Apprenticeship system, 347
Aptitude tests, 291
Assessment centers, 291–292
"Assistant to" positions, 3229
Audits, 475, 489
Authority, 231
  committees &, 413
  consolidation of, 412–413
  delegation of, 235–237
  functional, 233
  leadership &, 363

  power vs., 231
  relationships, 248
  responsibility &, 16, 232
  sharing of, 412
  splintered, 412
  teams &, 284
  see also Centralization; Decentralization; Recentralization
Autocratic leaders, 389–390

B2B transactions, 503
B2C transactions, 503
Behavior modification (motivation approach), 371
Benchmarking, 341, 467
Best practices, 341, 345
Biological needs, 366
Board of directors, 120, 410, 412
Body language *see* Nonverbal communication
Boundaryless organizations, 224
"Bounded" rationality, 154
Brainstorming, 164
Bribery, 55–56
Budgets and budgeting:
  control &, 478, 487–489
  planning &, 113
  zero-base, 488
Business portfolio matrix, 131, 138, 142–143

C2B transactions, 503
C2C transactions, 503
Capital standards, 466

Career strategy, 313, 362
Case approach to management, 19
Centralization, 163, 233–235, 238
Change:
   communication &, 427, 439
   country differences in managing, 75
   management of, 56–57, 336–338
   resistance to, 338
   techniques for initiating, 337
Charismatic leadership approach, 389, 401
China, People's Republic of:
   controlling in, 534
   economic development of, 96–100
   guanxi in, 55
   leading in, 401
   TOWS Matrix for, 99
   WTO membership of, 97–98
Claimants, 24
Clan control, 476
Coaching, 329–330
Code of ethics, 52, 59
Collective responsibility, 80
Commitment principle, 315
Committees:
   conflict in, 419
   definition of, 409
   disadvantages of, 413
   formal/informal, 410
   functions of, 409–410
   misuse of, 413
   reasons for using, 412
   successful operation of, 413–415
   temporary/permanent, 410
Committees and junior boards, 329
Communication:
   barriers and breakdowns in, 429, 436–440
      channels and methods of, 428, 431, 436
   in committees and groups, 413–415, 418
   cultural differences in, 429, 437–438
   definition of, 427
   effective, 440, 444
   electronic media in, 446
   flow of, 431–434, 433–434
   "noise" in, 429, 435
   in organizations, 23, 195, 286, 430–436
   process of, 428–430
   purpose of, 427
   see also Grapevine; Oral communication; Written communication
Companies, excellent and most admired, 9–10, 66
Comparative economic advantage, law of, 236
Competitive advantage, 86, 139
Computer-aided design (CAD), 526
Computer-aided manufacturing (CAM), 526
Computers:
   communication using, 444
   information handling using, 496
   networks, 499–500
   resistance to use of, 497–502
   see also Information technology
Conference programs, 330
Conflict and conflict management, 68, 249, 339, 409
Consistency testing, 137, 316–317
Contingency approach to management, 19
Contingency approaches to leadership, 395–400
Contingency planning, 137, 317
Control/controlling:
   budgets &, 113, 487
   bureaucratic, 476
   clan, 476
   corrective action &, 478
   definition of, 28–29, 463
   delegation &, 237
   feedback &, 468
   feedforward &, 470–473
   financial, 473
   flexibility of, 478
   in international companies, 66, 464
   nonbudgetary devices for, 488–489
   objectivity of, 477
   of operations, 516
   organization culture &, 254–255, 478
   of overall performance, 473
   planning &, 109, 463, 467
   process of, 463–464
   productivity &, 511–512
   based on profit and loss, 474
   real-time information &, 469
   requirements for effective, 476–478
   through return on investment, 475

techniques for, 493
time-event network analysis &, 489
Control points, 465–467
Cooperative social systems approach to management, 20
Coordination function of managers, 29
Core competency, 221
Corporate culture *see* Organization culture
Corporate governance, 50, 410
Cost-benefit! cost-effectiveness analysis, 157
Cost leadership strategy, 145
Cost standards, 466
Country and cultural differences:
  in behavior, 75–76
  in communication, 429, 436
  in management styles, 184, 450–451
  in reward systems, 311
  see also Control/controlling; Leading; Organizing; Planning; Staffing
Creative process, 163–164
Creativity, 163
Critical path method, 491
Critical point control, 465–467
Crosswise communication, 433–434
Customer group departmentation, 217

Decentralization, 163, 234, 237, 266
Decision making:
  alternatives &, 156
    centralization/decentralization of, 234, 254
  consensus, 79
  cost-effectiveness analysis &, 157
  definition of, 152–153
  experience &, 157–159
  experimentation &, 159
  by groups/committees, 413, 417
  limiting factor &, 155
  marginal analysis &, 157
    programmed and nonprogrammed decisions, 160–161
    quantitative and qualitative factors in, 156, 159
  rational, 153
  research and analysis &, 158, 159
  under uncertainty, certainty, and risk, 161–162
Decision theory approach to management, 19
Delegation, 232–233, 235–237

Delphi technique, 147
Deming Award, 87
Democratic leaders, 389
Department, definition of, 193
Departmentation:
  choosing the pattern of, 225–226
  in international operations, 224
  mixing types of, 225–226
  patterns of, 212–213
Diagonal communication, 431
Differentiation strategy, 145
Digital economy, 502–504
Dignity, concept of, 360–361
Dissatisfiers, 366–367
Diversification strategy, 136
Downsizing, effects of, 201
Downward communication, 432
Dual-career couples, career strategy for, 319

E-commerce/e-business, 10, 327, 502, 504
E-training/e-Iearning, 333
Ecological environment, 39, 535
Economic blocs, 72–74
Economic environment, 535
Economic order quantity approach, 520
Effectiveness, 12
Efficiency, 12
Electronic media in communication, 444–445
Empirical approach to management, 19
Empowerment, 232–233
Enterprise profile, 132
Entrepreneurship, 197
Environment *see* External environment; Internal environment
Environmental accounting, 42
Equal employment opportunity, 277
Equity theory, 369–370
ERG theory (of Alderfer), 366
Esprit de corps, 14, 16
Esteem needs, 365
Ethical environment, 39, 57–58
Ethics, 50
  code of, 52, 57
  differing standards of, 55–56
  goals &, 125
  institutionalizing, 52–53

raising standards of, 53
theories of, 51–56
Ethics committees, 52–53
Ethnocentric orientation, 69
Europe:
   business education in, 350
   challenges for managers in, 349–350
   management styles of managers in, 77
Exception principle, 477
Expectancy theory of motivation, 367–369
External environment, 23–25, 39
   career planning &, 316
   communication &, 26, 427, 430
   leadership style &, 393
   operations management &, 514
   staffing &, 271, 276–278, 282
   trends in, 534
   see also TOWS Matrix
Extranet, 500

Feedback:
   in communication, 429, 442
   control, 137, 467–468
   feedforward vs., 470
Feedforward control, 470–473
Fiedler's contingency theory of leadership, 396–398
Field force theory, 337
Focus groups, 417
Focused strategy, 147
Forecasting, 115, 146–147
Formal organization, 192
France:
   government planning and managerial elite in, 76
Free-rein leaders, 389
Functional authority, 233
Functional departmentation, 213

Gantt charts, 489
Geocentric orientation, 69
Geographical departmentation, 223
Germany:
   apprenticeship system of, 347–348
      competitive advantages/disadvantages of, 86, 170

   managerial style and codetermination in, 77
   TOWS Matrix for, 170–171
   training and development in, 347–350
Global corporations, 69–70
Globalization trend, 10
Goal setting theory of motivation, 370–371
Grapevine, 253–254, 418, 432–433
"Great man" theory, 388, 395
Grid organization *see* Matrix organization
Group behavior approach to management, 20
Groups:
   characteristics of, 415–416
   conflict in, 419
   conformity pressure in, 416
   definition of, 415
   functions and advantages of, 417–418
   stages in ~he formation of, 409
   see also Committees; Focus groups; Teams
Groupware, 501

Hawthorne studies and Hawthorne effect, 16
Hierarchy of needs theory (of Maslow), 364–367
Horizontal communication, 431, 433
Human factors in managing, 245, 359–361
Human resource accounting, 272

Industry analysis, 132, 145
Informal organization, 193, 253–254
Information:
   control &, 469
   filtering, 195, 432, 440
   flow, 431
   overload, 439–440
   real-time, 469
   security, 501–502
Information systems for controlling, 496, 518–519
Information technology:
   digital economy &, 502
   impact on organizations, 10
   opportunities and challenges created by, 497–502, 534–535
   use for managing, 534
   see also Computers
Innovation, 163–166, 199
Inputs, 24, 514

Insourcing, 521
Instant messaging, 445
Instrumental leadership, 399
Intangible standards, 466
Intelligence tests, 291
Internal environment:
 career planning &, 315
 leadership style &, 393
 staffing &, 271, 273, 281–282
 strategic planning &, 135–136
 see also TOWS Matrix
International business:
 communication barriers in, 437–438
  controlling in, 465
  vs. domestic business, managing of, 65–66
  forms of, 67
  nature and purpose of, 66–68
  organization structures for, 222–223
  staffing in, 278
Internet, 10–11, 445
 digital economy &, 502–504
Interpersonal behavior approach to management, 20
Interviews (for selection), 290–291
Intranet, 500
Intrapreneurship, 197
Inventory planning and control, 471, 472, 519–520
ISO 9000, 89–90
ISO 14001, 42
Italy:
 management style of, 76

Japan:
 business culture of, 451
 car industry of, 181–183
 competitive advantage of, 78–80
 decision making in, 80
 gift giving and business meetings in, 452
 just-in-time inventory system in, 521
 leading in, 450
 lifelong employment in, 79–80
 quality circles in, 523–524
 quality management gurus &, 86–87
 Theory Z &, 80
 worker satisfaction in, 79–80

Job design, 284–285
Job enlargement, 377
Job enrichment, 377–378
Job requirements, 283
Job rotation, 328–329
Joint ventures, 66, 136, 138
Junior boards, 329
Just-in-time inventory system, 521
Justice, theory of, 52

Kaizen, 87
Key result areas, 119
Knowledge workers, 336, 511–512, 538
Korea, *see* South Korea

Leader behavior, 399
Leadership:
 behavior and styles, 389–395
 charismatic approach to, 389
 definition of, 385–386
 effectiveness, 396–398
 ingredients of, 386–388
 managership vs., 384
 principle of, 387–388
 task-oriented vs. relationship-oriented style of, 399–400
 trait approaches to, 388–389
 transactional and transformational, 400–401
Leadership continuum concept, 393
Leading:
 country and cultural differences in, 450–452
 definition of, 28, 359
 organization culture &, 254–257
Lean manufacturing, 525–526
Learning organization, 341–342
Legal environment, 39
Licensing agreements, 66
Lifelong employment *see* Japan
Limited rationality, 154
Limiting factor, 155
Line authority, 233
Line committees, 410
Line-staff relationships, 233
 making staff work effective, 247–249
Liquidation strategy, 136, 138
Listening, 439, 442–443
Low-cost strategy, 145

Subject Index

M-commerce/m-business, 10, 327, 504
Malcolm Baldrige National Quality Award, 88–91
Management:
   art and science of, 13
   definition of, 5
Management analysis, approaches to, 18
Management by objectives, 125
   appraisal &, 302
   motivation &, 370–371
Management by walking (wandering) around, 483
Management contracts, 67
Management information systems, 495
Management inventory, 273
Management process approach, 19, 22–23
Management science approach, 497
Management science approach, 19
Management styles, country differences in, 75–83
   France, 76
   Germany, 77
   Japan, 78–80
   South Korea, 77–78
   Western countries, 77
Management thought, evolution of, 14–17
Manager development:
   definition of, 325
   internal and external training, 330–335
   on-the-job training, 328–330
   process of, 325–328
   see also Training
Managerial functions, 7, 27–29
   manager appraisal by, 307–309
   organization culture &, 254
   organizational levels &, 7
Managerial grid, 391–393
Managerial roles approach, 21–23
Managers:
   creativity &, 166
   goals of, 8
   information needs of, 431
   personal characteristics desired of, 286–287
   requirements for European, 349–350
   skills needed in, 7–8, 286
   sources of, 287

Managership vs. leadership, 385–386
Managing:
   human factors in, 359–361
   rewards of, 311
   stress in, 312–313
Marginal analysis, 157
Marketing strategies, 143–144
Mathematical approach to management, 19
Matrix organization, 220
Mercosur, 73
Mergers, TOWS Matrix for, 139–140
Milestone budgeting, 489
Mission, 110, 118, 134
Modern operational management theory, 14
Motivation:
   definition of, 361–362
   human factors &, 359
   leadership &, 385
   participation &, 375–376, 413
   self-motivation, 362
   systems and contingency approach to, 378
   techniques of, 373–376
   theories of. 362–364
Motivation-hygiene theory (of Herzberg), 366–367
Multinational corporations, 69–70
   advantages and challenges for, 69–70
   orientations of, 69
   see also International business
Multiple management, 329

Needs theory of motivation (of McClelland), 372–373
"Noise" (in communication), 429, 435
Nonbudgetary control devices, 487
Nonprogrammed decisions, 160
Nonverbal communication, 435
Norms, 409, 416

Objectives (goals):
   appraising managers against verifiable, 302–307
   career strategy &, 313–319
   definition of, 111, 118
   departmentation &, 115, 226
   guidelines for setting, 122–123

hierarchy of, 118–120
motivation through setting of, 370–371
multiplicity of, 120–121
setting of, 120
as standards, 465–467
verifiable, 118, 121–122, 125
see also Management by objectives
Ombudspersons, 433
Online education, 332
Open competition (in recruitment), 280
Operational approach to management, 21
Operations:
  control of, 518–519
  planning of, 519
Operations management, 512
  system, 514–515
Operations research, 522
Oral communication, 434–435, 443
Organization:
  definition of, 191
  formal, 192
  informal, 192–193, 254
Organization charts, 213, 249–252
Organization culture:
  of companies, 254
  controlling &, 478
  definition of, 255–256
  leadership &, 256
  managerial practices &, 254
  spiritual, 61
Organization development, 325, 340
Organization manuals, 253
Organization structure *see* Departmentation; Organizing
Organizational change *see* Change
Organizational hierarchy:
  decision making &, 161–163
  managerial functions &, 7
  managerial skills &, 7–8
  objectives &, 118–120
Organizational levels *see* Organizational hierarchy; Span of management
Organizing:
  controlling &, 476–478
  definition of, 27–28
  ensuring understanding of, 252–254
  future trends in, 535–536
  for the global environment, 222–223
  inflexibility in, 246–247
  nature and purpose of, 191
  planning to avoid mistakes in, 245–246
  span of management in, 193–196
  structure and process of, 202–203
Orientation of new employees, 293–294
Outputs, 26–27, 514
Outsourcing, 521–522

Participation as motivator, 375–376
Participative leaders/leadership, 389, 399
Path-goal theory of leadership, 399–400
Performance, rewards for, 311–312, 374
Performance appraisal *see* Appraisal
Personality tests, 291
PERT (program evaluation and review technique), 489, 491–493
Peter Principle, 288–289
Physical standards, 465–466
Physiological needs, 364, 366
Placement (in organizational positions), 273, 282, 288
Planned progression, 328
Planning:
  avoiding mistakes in organizing by, 245–246
  controlling &, 109, 463, 476
  definition of, 27, 109
  of operations, 516–517
  organization culture &, 255
  premises, 109, 146
  steps in, 113–118
  strategic, 132–137
Plans, types of, 110–113
Plural executive, 410
Pluralistic society, 40
Policies, 111–112, 131
Political environment, 39, 535
Polycentric orientation, 69
Porter and Lawler motivation model, 368, 369
Portfolio matrix *see* Business portfolio matrix
  position descriptions, 252
Position requirements, 283–285
Positive reinforcement (motivation approach), 371
Power:

bases of, 231
leadership &, 386
of position and leadership style, 396
responsibility &, 232, 233
Premising, 115, 145–147
Procedures, 112
Product decision, 516
Product departmentation, 217–219
Product design, 516–517
Product strategies, 143
Production design, 516–517
Production layouts, 517
Production management, 512–513
Productivity:
  benchmarking & measures of, 467
  definition of, 12
  information technology &, 501–502
  job enrichment &, 378
  of knowledge workers, measurement of, 511–512
  quality of working life &, 376
  tools and techniques for improving, 519–526
Proficiency tests, 291
Profit and loss control, 474
Profit plans, 113
Program standards, 466
Programmed decisions, 160
Programs (as plans), 113
Promotion, 273, 275, 279, 296
Purposes (in planning), 110–111

Quality:
  awards, 87–91
  management approaches, 75
  measurement in the information age, 513
  service, survey on, 262
Quality control circles, 523–524
Quality of working life (QWL) program, 376

Real-time information and control, 469
Recentralization, 238
Recruitment, 271–272, 275, 280, 287
Reengineering, 20, 137
Regiocentric orientation, 69
Reinforcement theory (of Skinner), 371–372
Responsibility:
  authority &, 16
  empowerment &, 232
  social, 43–50
  for staffing, 281
Return on investment as control, 474
Revenue standards, 466
Rewards:
  extrinsic and intrinsic, 368
  of managing, 311–313
  motivation &, 368, 374
  for performance, 311–312
Rights, ethical theory based on, 50–51
Rules, 113

Satisficing, 154
Satisfiers, 367
Scalar principle, 233
Scientific management approach, 13–15
Security, or safety, needs, 364
Selection, 288
  definition of, 281
  process, 290
  systems approach to, 281–282
Self-actualization needs, 365–366
Self-managing teams, 418
Service quality, survey on, 262
Service strategies, 143
Simulation and experiential exercises, 332–333
Situational approach to management, 19
Situational approaches to leadership, 395–400
Six Sigma approach, 345
Skills:
  needed in managers, 286–287
  organizational hierarchy &, 7–8
Social actions, business involvement in, 46–49
Social environment, 39, 44–45, 521
Social responsibility, 44–45
Social responsiveness, 44–45
Sociotechnical systems approach to management, 20, 338
South Korea:
  car industry of, 259–260
  management style of, 77–78
Span of management, 195
Specialization strategy, 135
Speech recognition devices, 498

Splintered authority, 412–413
Staff *see* Line-staff relationships
Staff committees, 410
Staffing:
   definition of, 28, 271
   future trends in, 536
   in international operations, 66, 278
   organization culture &, 255
   situational factors affecting, 276–281
   systems approach to, 272–276
   see also Selection
Standards (for control), 463
   types of critical point, 465–467
Stock less production, 521
Strategic alliances (of companies), 66, 136, 139–140
Strategic business units (SBU), 221–222
Strategic control, 467
Strategic intent, 134
Strategies:
   alternative, 135–136
   cost leadership, 145
   definition of, 111
   differentiation, 145
   evaluation and choice of, 136
   focused, 145
   formulation of, 132–137
   generic competitive, 144–145
   hierarchy of, 144
   industry analysis for formulation of, 144–145
   kinds of, 143–144
   nature and purpose of, 131–132
   TOWS Matrix &, 138–141
Streams of technology, 221
Stress in managing, 312–313
Stuttgarter Educational Model, 348–349
Subsidiaries, 66
Supply chain management, 527–529
Supportive leadership, 399
SWOT analysis, 138
Synergy, 111
Systems approach to:
   management, 23–27
   management by objectives, 125
   motivation, 378
   selection, 281
   staffing, 272–276

Tactics, 132
Teams:
   building of, 418
   definition of, 418
   requirements for successful, 341
   types of, 418
   see also Groups
Technological environment, 39, 534
Telecommunication, 444
Telecommuting, 499
Teleconferencing, 444–445
Television instruction, 332
Temporary promotions, 329
Territorial departmentation, 193, 225–226
Tests for selecting managers, 291
Theory X and Theory Y, 362–363
Theory Z, 80
Time-event network analysis, 489–493
Total quality management (TQM), 90–91, 524–525
TOWS Matrix, 99, 138–140, 170–186
TOWS Merger Matrix, 139–140
Trade blocs. *see* Economic blocs
Training:
   evaluation and relevance of, 335–336
   German/European model for, 347
   internal and external, 330, 347–348
   needs, 326, 348, 533
   on-the-job, 347
Transactional vs, transformational leadership, 400–401
Transnational corporations, 70–71
Two-factor theory of motivation, 366

United States:
   corporate governance and scandals in, 50, 410
   fair employment laws of, 277
   most admired companies of, 9–10
Unity of command, 16, 233
University management programs, 333
Upward communication, 434
Utilitarian theory, 55

Value chain management, 527
Value engineering, 523
Values, 254–257
Virtual classrooms, 333

Virtual management, 419
Virtual organizations, 223–224
Virtual teams, 419
Vocational Academy (Germany), 348–349
Vocational training schools, 348–349
Vroom's expectancy theory, 367–368

Whistle-blowing, 54
Wireless communication technology, 504

Women:
  equal employment opportunity for, 277
  leadership style of, 389–395
Work simplification, 523
Written communication, 434, 443

Zero-base budgeting, 488
Zero inventory, 521